6e

ESSENTIALS OF
STRATEGIC MANAGEMENT

The Quest for Competitive Advantage

John E. Gamble
Texas A&M University–Corpus Christi

Margaret A. Peteraf
Dartmouth College

Arthur A. Thompson, Jr.
The University of Alabama

Mc
Graw
Hill
Education

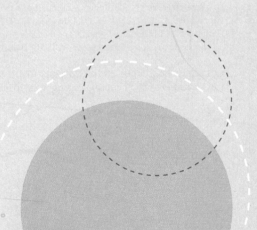

ESSENTIALS OF STRATEGIC MANAGEMENT: THE QUEST FOR COMPETITIVE ADVANTAGE, SIXTH EDITION

Published by McGraw-Hill Education, 2 Penn Plaza, New York, NY 10121. Copyright © 2019 by McGraw-Hill Education. All rights reserved. Printed in the United States of America. Previous editions © 2017, 2015, and 2013. No part of this publication may be reproduced or distributed in any form or by any means, or stored in a database or retrieval system, without the prior written consent of McGraw-Hill Education, including, but not limited to, in any network or other electronic storage or transmission, or broadcast for distance learning.

Some ancillaries, including electronic and print components, may not be available to customers outside the United States.

This book is printed on acid-free paper.

1 2 3 4 5 6 7 8 9 0 LWI 21 20 19 18

ISBN 978-1-259-92763-8 (bound edition)
MHID 1-259-92763-6 (bound edition)
ISBN 978-1-260-13956-3 (loose-leaf edition)
MHID 1-260-13956-5 (loose-leaf edition)

Portfolio Director: *Michael Ablassmeir*
Lead Product Developer: *Kelly Delso*
Product Developer: *Anne Ehrenworth*
Executive Marketing Manager: *Debbie Clare*
Content Project Managers: *Harvey Yep (Core), Keri Johnson (Assessment)*
Buyer: *Laura Fuller*
Design: *Matt Diamond*
Content Licensing Specialists: *DeAnna Dausener (Image and Text)*
Compositor: *SPi Global*
Cover Image: *©view stock/getty images*
Printer: *LSC Communications*

All credits appearing on page or at the end of the book are considered to be an extension of the copyright page.

Library of Congress Cataloging-in-Publication Data

Names: Gamble, John (John E.) author. | Thompson, Arthur A., 1940- author. |
    Peteraf, Margaret Ann, author.
Title: Essentials of strategic management: the quest for competitive advantage/
    John E. Gamble, Texas A&M University-Corpus Christi, Margaret A. Peteraf,
    Dartmouth College, Arthur A. Thompson, Jr., The University of Alabama.
Description: Sixth Edition. | Dubuque : McGraw-Hill Education, 2019. |
    Revised edition of the authors' Essentials of strategic management, [2017]
Identifiers: LCCN 2017059878 | ISBN 9781259927638 (paperback)
Subjects: LCSH: Strategic planning. | Business planning. | Competition. |
    Strategic planning–Case studies. | BISAC: BUSINESS & ECONOMICS /
    Management.
Classification: LCC HD30.28 .G353 2018 | DDC 658.4/012–dc23
LC record available at https://lccn.loc.gov/2017059878

ABOUT THE AUTHORS

John E. Gamble is a Professor of Management and Dean of the College of Business at Texas A&M University–Corpus Christi. His teaching and research has focused on strategic management at the undergraduate and graduate levels. He has conducted courses in strategic management in Germany since 2001, which have been sponsored by the University of Applied Sciences in Worms.

John E. Gamble
©Richard's Photography LLC

Dr. Gamble's research has been published in various scholarly journals, and he is the author or co-author of more than 75 case studies published in an assortment of strategic management and strategic marketing texts. He has done consulting on industry and market analysis for clients in a diverse mix of industries.

Professor Gamble received his PhD, Master of Arts, and Bachelor of Science degrees from the University of Alabama and was a faculty member in the Mitchell College of Business at the University of South Alabama before his appointment to the faculty at Texas A&M University–Corpus Christi.

Margaret A. Peteraf is the Leon E. Williams Professor of Management at the Tuck School of Business at Dartmouth College. She is an internationally recognized scholar of strategic management, with a long list of publications in top management journals. She has earned myriad honors and prizes for her contributions, including the 1999 Strategic Management Society Best Paper Award recognizing the deep influence of her work on the field of strategic management. Professor Peteraf is on the Board of Directors of the Strategic Management Society and has been elected as a Fellow of the Society. She served previously as a member of the Academy of Management's Board of Governors and as Chair of the Business Policy and Strategy Division of the Academy. She has also served in various editorial roles and is presently on nine editorial boards, including the *Strategic Management Journal,* the *Academy of Management Review,* and *Organization Science.* She has taught in Executive Education programs around the world and has won teaching awards at the MBA and Executive level.

Margaret A. Peteraf
©Heather Gere

Professor Peteraf earned her PhD, MA, and MPhil at Yale University and held previous faculty appointments at Northwestern University's Kellogg Graduate School of Management and at the University of Minnesota's Carlson School of Management.

Arthur A. Thompson, Jr.

Arthur A. Thompson, Jr. earned his BS and PhD degrees in economics from The University of Tennessee, spent three years on the economics faculty at Virginia Tech, and served on the faculty of The University of Alabama's College of Commerce and Business Administration for 25 years. In 1974 and again in 1982, Dr. Thompson spent semester-long sabbaticals as a visiting scholar at the Harvard Business School.

His areas of specialization are business strategy, competition and market analysis, and the economics of business enterprises. In addition to publishing over 30 articles in some 25 different professional and trade publications, he has authored or co-authored five textbooks and six computer-based simulation exercises that are used in colleges and universities worldwide.

Dr. Thompson spends much of his off-campus time giving presentations, putting on management development programs, working with companies, and helping operate a business simulation enterprise in which he is a major partner.

Dr. Thompson and his wife of 57 years have two daughters, two grandchildren, and a Yorkshire terrier.

BRIEF CONTENTS

PREFACE

The standout features of this sixth edition of *Essentials of Strategic Management* are its concisely written and robust coverage of strategic management concepts and its compelling collection of cases. The text presents a conceptually strong treatment of strategic management principles and analytic approaches that features straight-to-the-point discussions, timely examples, and a writing style that captures the interest of students. While this edition retains the 10-chapter structure of the prior edition, every chapter has been reexamined, refined, and refreshed. New content has been added to keep the material in line with the latest developments in the theory and practice of strategic management. Also, scores of new examples have been added, along with fresh Concepts & Connections illustrations, to make the content come alive and to provide students with a ringside view of strategy in action. The fundamental character of the sixth edition of *Essentials of Strategic Management* is very much in step with the best academic thinking and contemporary management practice. The chapter content continues to be solidly mainstream and balanced, mirroring *both* the penetrating insight of academic thought and the pragmatism of real-world strategic management.

Complementing the text presentation is a truly appealing lineup of 12 diverse, timely, and thoughtfully crafted cases. All of the cases are tightly linked to the content of the 10 chapters, thus pushing students to apply the concepts and analytical tools they have read about. Seven of the cases were written by the coauthors to illustrate specific tools of analysis or distinct strategic management theories. Cases not written by the coauthors were included because of their exceptional pedagogical value and linkage to strategic management concepts presented in the text. We are confident you will be impressed with how well each of the 12 cases in the collection will work in the classroom and the amount of student interest they will spark.

For some years now, growing numbers of strategy instructors at business schools worldwide have been transitioning from a purely text-cases course structure to a more robust and energizing text-cases-simulation course structure. Incorporating a competition-based strategy simulation has the strong appeal of providing class members with *an immediate and engaging opportunity to apply the concepts and analytical tools covered in the chapters in a head-to-head competition with companies run by other class members.* Two widely used and pedagogically effective online strategy simulations, *The Business Strategy Game* and *GLO-BUS,* are optional companions for this text. Both simulations, like the cases, are closely linked to the content of each chapter in the text. The Exercises for Simulation Participants, found at the end of each chapter, provide clear guidance to class members in applying the concepts and analytical tools covered in the chapters to the issues and decisions that they have to wrestle with in managing their simulation company.

Through our experiences as business school faculty members, we also fully understand the assessment demands on faculty teaching strategic management and business policy courses. In many institutions, capstone courses have emerged as the logical home for assessing student achievement of program learning objectives. The sixth edition includes Assurance of Learning Exercises at the end of each chapter that link to the specific Learning Objectives appearing at the beginning of each chapter and highlighted throughout the text. *An important instructional feature of this edition is the linkage of selected chapter-end Assurance of Learning Exercises and cases to the publisher's Connect® web-based assignment and assessment platform.* Your students will be able to use the online *Connect* supplement to (1) complete two of the Assurance of Learning Exercises appearing at the end of each of the 10 chapters, (2) complete chapter-end quizzes, and (3) complete case tutorials based upon the suggested assignment questions for all 12 cases in this edition. With the exception of some of the chapter-end Assurance of Learning exercises, all of the *Connect* exercises are automatically graded, thereby enabling you to easily assess the learning that has occurred.

In addition, both of the companion strategy simulations have a built-in Learning Assurance Report that quantifies how well each member of your class performed on nine skills/learning measures *versus tens of thousands of other students worldwide* who completed the simulation in the past 12 months. We believe the chapter-end Assurance of Learning Exercises, the all-new online and automatically graded *Connect* exercises, and the Learning Assurance Report generated at the conclusion of *The Business Strategy Game* and *GLO-BUS* simulations provide you with easy-to-use, empirical measures of student learning in your course. All can be used in conjunction with other instructor-developed or school-developed scoring rubrics and assessment tools to comprehensively evaluate course or program learning outcomes.

Taken together, the various components of the sixth edition package and the supporting set of Instructor Resources provide you with enormous course design flexibility and a powerful kit of teaching/learning tools. We've done our very best to ensure that the elements comprising this edition will work well for you in the classroom, help you economize on the time needed to be well prepared for each class, and cause students to conclude that your course is one of the very best they have ever taken—from the standpoint of both enjoyment and learning.

Differentiation from Other Texts

Five noteworthy traits strongly differentiate this text and the accompanying instructional package from others in the field:

1. *Our integrated coverage of the two most popular perspectives on strategic management positioning theory and resource-based theory is unsurpassed by any other leading strategy text.* Principles and concepts from both the positioning perspective and the resource-based perspective are prominently and comprehensively integrated into our coverage of crafting both single-business and multibusiness strategies. By highlighting the relationship between a firm's resources and capabilities to the activities it conducts along its value chain, we show explicitly how these two perspectives relate to one another. Moreover, in Chapters 3 through 8, it is emphasized repeatedly that a company's strategy must be matched not only to its external market circumstances but also to its internal resources and competitive capabilities.

2. *Our coverage of business ethics, core values, social responsibility, and environmental sustainability is unsurpassed by any other leading strategy text.* Chapter 9, "Ethics, Corporate Social Responsibility, Environmental Sustainability, and Strategy," is embellished with fresh content so that it can better fulfill the important functions of (1) alerting students to the role and importance of ethical and socially responsible decision making and (2) addressing the accreditation requirements that business ethics be visibly and thoroughly embedded in the core curriculum. Moreover, discussions of the roles of values and ethics are integrated into portions of other chapters to further reinforce why and how considerations relating to ethics, values, social responsibility, and sustainability should figure prominently into the managerial task of crafting and executing company strategies.

3. *The caliber of the case collection in the sixth edition is truly unrivaled* from the standpoints of student appeal, teachability, and suitability for drilling students in the use of the concepts and analytical treatments in Chapters 1 through 10. The 12 cases included in this edition are the very latest, the best, and the most on-target that we could find. The ample information about the cases in the Instructor's Manual makes it effortless to select a set of cases each term that will capture the interest of students from start to finish.

4. *The publisher's Connect assignment and assessment platform is tightly linked to the text chapters and case lineup.* The *Connect* package for the sixth edition allows professors to assign autograded quizzes and select chapter-end Assurance of Learning Exercises to assess class members' understanding of chapter concepts. In addition, our texts have pioneered the extension of the *Connect* platform to case analysis. The autograded case exercises for each of the 12 cases in this edition are robust and extensive and will better enable students to make meaningful contributions to class discussions. The autograded *Connect* case exercises may also be used as graded assignments in the course.

5. The two cutting-edge and widely used strategy simulations—*The Business Strategy Game* and *GLO-BUS*—that are optional companions to the sixth edition give you unmatched capability to employ a text-case-simulation model of course delivery.

Organization, Content, and Features of the Sixth Edition Text Chapters

The following rundown summarizes the noteworthy features and topical emphasis in this new edition:

- Chapter 1 serves as an introduction to the topic of strategy, focusing on the managerial actions that will determine why a company matters in the marketplace. We introduce students to the primary approaches to building competitive advantage and the key elements of business-level strategy. Following Henry Mintzberg's pioneering research, we also stress why a company's strategy is partly planned and partly reactive and why this strategy tends to evolve. The chapter also discusses why it is important for a company to have a *viable business model* that outlines the company's customer value proposition and its profit formula. This brief chapter is the perfect accompaniment to your opening-day lecture on what the course is all about and why it matters.

- Chapter 2 delves more deeply into the managerial process of actually crafting and executing a strategy. It makes a great assignment for the second day of class and provides a smooth transition into the heart of the course. The focal point of the chapter is the five-stage managerial process of crafting and executing strategy: (1) forming a strategic vision of where the company is headed and why, (2) developing strategic as well as financial objectives with which to measure the company's progress, (3) crafting a strategy to achieve these targets and move the company toward its market destination, (4) implementing and executing the strategy, and (5) evaluating a company's situation and performance to identify corrective adjustments that are needed. Students are introduced to such core concepts as strategic visions, mission statements and core values, the balanced scorecard, and business-level versus corporate-level strategies. There's a robust discussion of why *all managers are on a company's strategy-making, strategy-executing team* and why a company's strategic plan is a collection of strategies devised by different managers at different levels in the organizational hierarchy. The chapter winds up with a section on how to exercise good corporate governance and examines the conditions that led to recent high-profile corporate governance failures.

- Chapter 3 sets forth the now-familiar analytical tools and concepts of industry and competitive analysis and demonstrates the importance of tailoring strategy to fit the circumstances of a company's industry and competitive environment. The standout feature of this chapter is a presentation of Michael Porter's "five forces model of competition" *that has long been the clearest, most straightforward discussion of any text in the field.* Chapter revisions include an improved discussion of the macro-environment, focusing on the use of the PESTEL analysis framework for assessing the *p*olitical, *e*conomic, *s*ocial, *t*echnological, *e*nvironmental, and *l*egal factors in a company's macro-environment. New to this edition is a discussion of Michael Porter's Framework for Competitor Analysis used for assessing a rival's likely strategic moves.

- Chapter 4 presents the resource-based view of the firm, showing why resource and capability analysis is such a powerful tool for sizing up a company's competitive assets. It offers a simple framework for identifying a company's resources and capabilities and explains how the VRIN framework can be used to determine whether they can provide the company with a sustainable competitive advantage over its competitors. Other topics covered in this chapter include dynamic capabilities, SWOT analysis, value chain analysis, benchmarking, and competitive strength assessments, thus enabling a solid appraisal of a company's relative cost position and customer value proposition vis-à-vis its rivals.

- Chapter 5 deals with the basic approaches used to compete successfully and gain a competitive advantage over market rivals. This discussion is framed around the five generic competitive strategies—low-cost leadership, differentiation, best-cost provider, focused differentiation, and focused low-cost. It describes when each of these approaches works best and what pitfalls to avoid. It explains the role of *cost drivers* and *uniqueness drivers* in reducing a company's costs and enhancing its differentiation, respectively.

- Chapter 6 deals with the *strategy options* available to complement a company's competitive approach and maximize the power of its overall strategy. These include a variety of offensive or defensive competitive moves, and their timing, such as blue ocean strategy and first-mover advantages and disadvantages. It also includes choices concerning the breadth of a company's activities (or its scope of operations along an industry's entire value chain), ranging from horizontal mergers and acquisitions, to vertical integration, outsourcing, and strategic alliances. This material serves to segue into that covered in the next two chapters on international and diversification strategies.

- Chapter 7 explores the full range of strategy options for competing in international markets: export strategies, licensing, franchising, establishing a subsidiary in a foreign market, and using strategic alliances and joint ventures to build competitive strength in foreign markets. There is also a discussion of how to best tailor a company's international strategy to cross-country differences in market conditions and buyer preferences; how to use international operations to improve overall competitiveness; the choice between multidomestic, global, and transnational strategies; and the unique characteristics of competing in emerging markets.

- Chapter 8 introduces the topic of corporate-level strategy—a topic of concern for multibusiness companies pursuing diversification. This chapter begins by explaining why successful diversification strategies must create shareholder value and lays out the three essential tests that a strategy must pass to achieve this goal (*the industry attractiveness, cost of entry, and better-off tests*). Corporate strategy topics covered in the chapter include methods of entering new businesses, related diversification, unrelated diversification, combined related and unrelated diversification approaches, and strategic options for improving the overall performance of an already diversified company. The chapter's analytical spotlight is trained on the techniques and procedures for assessing a diversified company's business portfolio—the relative attractiveness of the various businesses the company has diversified into, the company's competitive strength in each of its business lines, and the *strategic fit* and *resource fit* among a diversified company's different businesses. The chapter concludes with a brief survey of a company's four main post-diversification strategy alternatives: (1) sticking closely with the existing business lineup, (2) broadening the diversification base, (3) divesting some businesses and retrenching to a narrower diversification base, and (4) restructuring the makeup of the company's business lineup.

- Although the topic of ethics and values comes up at various points in this textbook, Chapter 9 brings more direct attention to such issues and may be used as a standalone assignment in either the early, middle, or late part of a course. It concerns the themes of ethical standards in business, approaches to ensuring consistent ethical standards for companies with international operations, corporate social responsibility, and environmental sustainability. The contents of this chapter are sure to give students some things to ponder, rouse lively discussion, and help to make students more ethically aware and conscious of *why all companies should conduct their business in a socially responsible and sustainable manner.*

- Chapter 10 is anchored around a pragmatic, compelling conceptual framework: (1) building dynamic capabilities, core competencies, resources, and structure necessary for proficient strategy execution; (2) allocating ample resources to strategy-critical activities; (3) ensuring that policies and procedures facilitate rather than impede strategy execution; (4) pushing for continuous improvement in how value chain activities are performed; (5) installing information and operating systems that enable company personnel to better carry out essential activities; (6) tying rewards and incentives directly to the achievement of performance targets and good strategy execution; (7) shaping the work environment and corporate culture to fit the strategy; and (8) exerting the internal leadership needed to drive execution forward. The recurring theme throughout the chapter is that implementing and executing strategy entails figuring out the specific actions, behaviors, and conditions that are needed for a smooth strategy-supportive operation—the goal here is to ensure that students understand that the strategy implementing/strategy executing phase is a make-it-happen-right kind of managerial exercise that leads to operating excellence and good performance.

In this latest edition, we have put our utmost effort into ensuring that the 10 chapters are consistent with the latest and best thinking of academics and practitioners in the field of strategic management and hit the bull's-eye in topical coverage for senior- and MBA-level strategy courses. The ultimate test of the text, of course, is the positive pedagogical impact it has in the classroom. If this edition sets a more effective stage for your lectures and does a better job of helping you persuade students that the discipline of strategy merits their rapt attention, then it will have fulfilled its purpose.

The Case Collection

The 12-case lineup in this edition is flush with interesting companies and valuable lessons for students in the art and science of crafting and executing strategy. There is a good blend of cases from a length perspective—about one-third are under 10 pages yet offer plenty for students to chew on; about a third are medium-length cases; and the remaining one-third are detail-rich cases that call for sweeping analysis.

At least 11 of the 12 cases involve companies, products, people, or activities that students will have heard of, know about from personal experience, or can easily identify with. The lineup includes at least four cases that will provide students with insight into the special demands of competing in industry environments where technological developments are an everyday event, product life cycles are short, and competitive maneuvering among rivals comes fast and furious. All of the cases involve situations where the role of company resources and competitive capabilities in the strategy formulation, strategy execution scheme is emphasized. Scattered throughout the lineup are seven cases concerning non-U.S. companies, globally competitive industries, and/or cross-cultural situations; these cases, in conjunction with the globalized content of the text chapters, provide abundant material for linking the study of strategic management tightly to the ongoing globalization of the world economy. You will also find five cases dealing with the strategic problems of family-owned or relatively small entrepreneurial businesses and 10 cases involving public companies and situations where students can do further research on the Internet. A number of the cases have accompanying videotape segments.

The Two Strategy Simulation Supplements: *The Business Strategy Game* and *GLO-BUS*

The Business Strategy Game and *GLO-BUS: Developing Winning Competitive Strategies*—two competition-based strategy simulations that are delivered online and that feature automated processing and grading of performance—are being marketed by the publisher as companion supplements for use with the sixth edition (and other texts in the field). In both *The Business Strategy Game (BSG)* and *GLO-BUS,* class members are divided into teams of one to five persons and assigned to run a company that competes head-to-head against companies run by other class members. In *BSG,* the teams run an athletic footwear company; in *GLO-BUS,* teams run a company that produces wearable action cameras and camera-equipped copter drones used for commercial purposes. In both simulations, companies compete in a global market arena, selling their products in four geographic regions—Europe-Africa, North America, Asia-Pacific, and Latin America. Each management team is called upon to craft a strategy for their company and make decisions relating to plant operations, workforce compensation, pricing and marketing, social responsibility/citizenship, and finance.

Company co-managers are held accountable for their decision making. Each company's performance is scored on the basis of earnings per share, return-on-equity investment, stock price, credit rating, and image rating. Rankings of company performance, along with a wealth of industry and company statistics, are available to company co-managers after each decision round to use in making strategy adjustments and operating decisions for the next competitive round. You can be certain that the market environment, strategic issues, and operating challenges that company co-managers must contend with are *very tightly linked* to what your class members will be reading about in the text chapters.

We suggest that you schedule 1 or 2 practice rounds and anywhere from 4 to 10 regular (scored) decision rounds (more rounds are better than fewer rounds). Each decision round represents a year of company operations and will entail roughly two hours of time for company co-managers to complete. In traditional 13-week, semester-long courses, there is merit in scheduling one decision round per week. In courses that run 5 to 10 weeks, it is wise to schedule two decision rounds per week for the last several weeks of the term (sample course schedules are provided for courses of varying length and varying numbers of class meetings).

When the instructor-specified deadline for a decision round arrives, the simulation server automatically accesses the saved decision entries of each company, determines the competitiveness and buyer appeal of each company's product offering relative to the other companies being run by students in your class, and then awards sales and market shares to the competing companies, geographic region by geographic region. The unit sales volumes awarded to each company *are totally governed by:*

- How its prices compare against the prices of rival brands.
- How its product quality compares against the quality of rival brands.
- How its product line breadth and selection compare.
- How its advertising effort compares.
- And so on, for a total of 11 competitive factors that determine unit sales and market shares.

The competitiveness and overall buyer appeal of each company's product offering *in comparison to the product offerings of rival companies* is all-decisive—this algorithmic feature is what makes *BSG* and *GLO-BUS* "competition-based" strategy simulations. Once each company's sales and market shares are awarded based on the competitiveness and buyer appeal of its respective overall product offering vis-à-vis those of rival companies, the various company and industry reports detailing the outcomes of the decision round are then generated. Company co-managers can access the results of the decision round 15 to 20 minutes after the decision deadline.

The Compelling Case for Incorporating Use of a Strategy Simulation

There are *three exceptionally important benefits* associated with using a competition-based simulation in strategy courses taken by seniors and MBA students:

- *A three-pronged text-case-simulation course model delivers significantly more teaching and learning power than the traditional text-case model.* Using *both* cases and a strategy simulation to drill students in thinking strategically and applying what they read in the text chapters is a stronger, more effective means of helping them connect theory with practice and develop better business judgment. What cases do that a simulation cannot is give class members broad exposure to a variety of companies and industry situations and insight into the kinds of strategy-related problems managers face. But what a competition-based strategy simulation does far better than case analysis is thrust class members squarely into *an active, hands-on managerial role* where they are totally responsible for assessing market conditions, determining how to respond to the actions of competitors, forging a long-term direction and strategy for their company, and making all kinds of operating decisions. Because they are held fully accountable for their decisions and their company's performance, *co-managers are strongly motivated* to dig deeply into company operations, probe for ways to be more cost-efficient and competitive, and ferret out strategic moves and decisions calculated to boost company performance. *Consequently, incorporating both case assignments and a strategy simulation to develop the skills of class members in thinking strategically and applying the concepts and tools of strategic analysis turns out to be more pedagogically powerful than relying solely on case assignments: there is stronger retention of the lessons learned and better achievement of course learning objectives.* To provide you with quantitative evidence of the learning that occurs with using *The Business Strategy Game* or *GLO-BUS*, there is a built-in Learning Assurance Report showing how well each class member performs on nine skills/learning measures versus tens of thousands of students worldwide who have completed the simulation in the past 12 months.

- *The competitive nature of a strategy simulation arouses positive energy and steps up the whole tempo of the course by a notch or two.* Nothing sparks class excitement quicker or better than the concerted efforts on the part of class members during each decision round to achieve a high industry ranking and avoid the perilous consequences of being outcompeted by other class members. Students really enjoy taking on the role of a manager, running their own company, crafting strategies, making all kinds of operating decisions, trying to outcompete rival companies, and getting immediate feedback on the resulting company performance. Co-managers become *emotionally invested* in running their company and figuring out what strategic moves to make to boost their company's performance. All this stimulates learning and causes students to see the practical relevance of the subject matter and the benefits of taking your course.

- *Use of a fully automated online simulation reduces the time instructors spend on course preparation, course administration, and grading.* Since the simulation exercise involves a 20- to 30-hour workload for student-teams (roughly 2 hours per decision round times 10 to 12 rounds, plus optional assignments), simulation adopters often compensate by trimming the number of assigned cases from, say, 10 to 12 to perhaps 4 to 6. This significantly reduces the time instructors spend reading cases, studying teaching notes, and otherwise getting ready to lead class discussion of a case or grade oral team presentations. Course preparation time is further cut because you can use several class days to have students meet in the computer lab to work on upcoming decision rounds or a three-year strategic plan (in lieu of lecturing on a chapter or covering an additional assigned case). Not only does use of a simulation permit assigning fewer cases, but it also permits you to eliminate at least one assignment that entails considerable grading on your part. Grading one less written case or essay exam or other written assignment saves enormous time. With *BSG* and *GLO-BUS,* grading is effortless and takes only minutes; once you enter percentage weights for each assignment in your online grade book, a suggested overall grade is calculated for you. You'll be pleasantly surprised—and quite pleased—at how little time it takes to gear up for and to administer *The Business Strategy Game* or *GLO-BUS.*

In sum, incorporating use of a strategy simulation turns out to be *a win-win proposition for both students and instructors.* Moreover, a very convincing argument can be made that a competition-based strategy simulation is *the single most effective teaching/learning tool that instructors can employ to teach the discipline of business and competitive strategy, to make learning more enjoyable, and to promote better achievement of course learning objectives.*

Administration and Operating Features of the Two Simulations

The Internet delivery and user-friendly designs of both *BSG* and *GLO-BUS* make them incredibly easy to administer, even for first-time users. And the menus and controls are so similar that you can readily switch between the two simulations or use one in your undergraduate class and the other in a graduate class. If you have not yet used either of the two simulations, you may find the following of particular interest:

- Setting up the simulation for your course is done online and takes about 10 to 15 minutes. Once setup is completed, no other administrative actions are required beyond that of moving participants to a different team (should the need arise) and monitoring the progress of the simulation (to whatever extent desired).

- Participant's Guides are delivered electronically to class members at the website— students can read it on their monitors or print out a copy, as they prefer.

- There are two- to four-minute Video Tutorials scattered throughout the software (including each decision screen and each page of each report) that provide on-demand guidance to class members who may be uncertain about how to proceed.

- Complementing the Video Tutorials are detailed and clearly written Help sections explaining "all there is to know" about (a) each decision entry and the relevant cause-effect relationships, (b) the information on each page of the Industry Reports, and (c) the numbers presented in the Company Reports. *The Video Tutorials and the Help screens allow company co-managers to figure things out for themselves, thereby curbing the need for students to ask the instructor "how things work."*

- Team members running the same company who are logged-in simultaneously on different computers at different locations can click a button to enter Collaboration Mode, enabling them to work collaboratively from the same screen in viewing reports and making decision entries, and click a second button to enter Audio Mode, letting them talk to one another.

  - When in "Collaboration Mode," each team member sees the same screen at the same time as all other team members who are logged in and have joined Collaboration Mode. If one team member chooses to view a particular decision screen, that same screen appears on the monitors for all team members in Collaboration Mode.

  - Team members each control their own color-coded mouse pointer (with their first-name appearing in a color-coded box linked to their mouse pointer) and can make a decision entry or move the mouse to point to particular on-screen items.

  - A decision entry change made by one team member is seen by all, in real time, and all team members can immediately view the on-screen calculations that result from the new decision entry.

  - If one team member wishes to view a report page and clicks on the menu link to the desired report, that same report page will immediately appear for the other team members engaged in collaboration.

  - Use of Audio Mode capability requires that team members work from a computer with a built-in microphone (if they want to be heard by their team members) and speakers (so they may hear their teammates) or else have a headset with a microphone that they can plug into their desktop or laptop. A headset is recommended for best results, but most laptops now are equipped with a built-in microphone and speakers that will support use of our new voice chat feature.

  - Real-time VoIP audio chat capability among team members who have entered both the Audio Mode and the Collaboration Mode is a tremendous boost in functionality that enables team members to go online simultaneously on computers at different locations and conveniently and effectively collaborate in running their simulation company.

  - In addition, instructors have the capability to join the online session of any company and speak with team members, thus circumventing the need for team members to arrange for and attend a meeting in the instructor's office. Using the standard menu for administering a particular industry, instructors can connect with the company desirous of assistance. Instructors who wish not only to talk but also enter Collaboration (highly recommended because all attendees are then viewing the same screen) have a red-colored mouse pointer linked to a red box labeled Instructor.

Without a doubt, the Collaboration and Voice-Chat capabilities are hugely valuable for students enrolled in online and distance-learning courses where meeting face-to-face is impractical or time-consuming. Likewise, the instructors of online and distance-learning courses will appreciate having the capability to join the online meetings of particular company teams when their advice or assistance is requested.

- Both simulations are quite suitable for use in distance-learning or online courses (and are currently being used in such courses on numerous campuses).

- Participants and instructors are notified via e-mail when the results are ready (usually about 15 to 20 minutes after the decision round deadline specified by the instructor/game administrator).

- Following each decision round, participants are provided with a complete set of reports—a six-page Industry Report, a one-page Competitive Intelligence report for each geographic region that includes strategic group maps and bulleted lists of competitive strengths and weaknesses, and a set of Company Reports (income statement, balance sheet, cash flow statement, and assorted production, marketing, and cost statistics).

- Two "open-book" multiple-choice tests of 20 questions are built into each simulation. The quizzes, which you can require or not as you see fit, are taken online and automatically graded, with scores reported instantaneously to participants and automatically recorded in the instructor's electronic grade book. Students are automatically provided with three sample questions for each test.

- Both simulations contain a three-year strategic plan option that you can assign. Scores on the plan are automatically recorded in the instructor's online grade book.

- At the end of the simulation, you can have students complete online peer evaluations (again, the scores are automatically recorded in your online grade book).

- Both simulations have a Company Presentation feature that enables each team of company co-managers to easily prepare PowerPoint slides for use in describing their strategy and summarizing their company's performance in a presentation to either the class, the instructor, or an "outside" board of directors.

- *A Learning Assurance Report provides you with hard data concerning how well your students performed vis-à-vis students playing the simulation worldwide over the past 12 months.* The report is based on nine measures of student proficiency, business know-how, and decision-making skill and can also be used in evaluating the extent to which your school's academic curriculum produces the desired degree of student learning insofar as accreditation standards are concerned.

For more details on either simulation, please consult Section 2 of the Instructor's Manual accompanying this text or register as an instructor at the simulation websites (www.bsg-online.com and www.globus.com) to access even more comprehensive information. You should also consider signing up for one of the webinars that the simulation authors conduct several times each month (sometimes several times weekly) to demonstrate how the software works, walk you through the various features and menu options, and answer any questions. You have an open invitation to call the senior author of this text at (205) 722-9145 to arrange a personal demonstration or talk about how one of the simulations might work in one of your courses. We think you'll be quite impressed with the cutting-edge capabilities that have been programmed into *The Business Strategy Game* and *GLO-BUS,* the simplicity with which both simulations can be administered, and their exceptionally tight connection to the text chapters, core concepts, and standard analytical tools.

Resources and Support Materials for the Sixth Edition for Students

Key Points Summaries

At the end of each chapter is a synopsis of the core concepts, analytical tools, and other key points discussed in the chapter. These chapter-end synopses, along with the core concept definitions and margin notes scattered throughout each chapter, help students focus on basic strategy principles, digest the messages of each chapter, and prepare for tests.

Two Sets of Chapter-End Exercises

Each chapter concludes with two sets of exercises. The Assurance of Learning Exercises can be used as the basis for class discussion, oral presentation assignments, short written reports, and substitutes for case assignments. The Exercises for Simulation Participants are designed expressly for use by adopters who have incorporated use of a simulation and wish to go a step further in tightly and explicitly connecting the chapter content to the simulation company their students are running. The questions in both sets of exercises (along with those Concepts & Connections illustrations that qualify as "mini cases") can be used to round out the rest of a 75-minute class period, should your lecture on a chapter only last for 50 minutes.

The *Connect* Web-Based Assignment and Assessment Platform

The *Essentials of Strategic Management* sixth edition takes full advantage of the publisher's innovative *Connect* assignment and assessment platform. The *Connect* package for this edition includes several robust and valuable features that simplify the task of assigning and grading three types of exercises for students:

- There are autograded chapter tests consisting of 20 multiple-choice questions that students can take to measure their grasp of the material presented in each of the 10 chapters.

- *Connect Management* includes interactive versions of two Assurance of Learning Exercises for each chapter that drill students in the use and application of the concepts and tools of strategic analysis. There is both an autograded and open-ended short-answer interactive exercise for each of the 10 chapters.

- The *Connect Management* platform also includes fully autograded interactive application exercises for each of the 12 cases in this edition. The exercises require students to work through tutorials based upon the analysis set forth in the assignment questions for the case; these exercises have multiple components such as resource and capability analysis, financial ratio analysis, identification of a company's strategy, or analysis of the five competitive forces. The content of these case exercises is tailored to match the circumstances presented in each case, calling upon students to do whatever strategic thinking and strategic analysis is called for to arrive at pragmatic, analysis-based action recommendations for improving company performance. The entire exercise is autograded, allowing instructors to focus on grading only the students' strategic recommendations.

All of the *Connect* exercises are automatically graded (with the exception of a few exercise components that entail student entry of essay answers), thereby simplifying the task of evaluating each class member's performance and monitoring the learning outcomes. The progress-tracking function built into the *Connect* system enables you to

- View scored work immediately and track individual or group performance with assignment and grade reports.
- Access an instant view of student or class performance relative to learning objectives.
- Collect data and generate reports required by many accreditation organizations, such as AACSB International.

For Instructors

Connect Management

Connect's Instructor Resources includes an Instructor's Manual and other support materials. Your McGraw-Hill representative can arrange delivery of instructor support materials in a format-ready Standard Cartridge for Blackboard, WebCT, and other web-based educational platforms.

Instructor's Manual

The accompanying IM contains:

- A section on suggestions for organizing and structuring your course.
- Sample syllabi and course outlines.
- A set of lecture notes on each chapter.
- Answers to the chapter-end Assurance of Learning Exercises.
- A comprehensive case teaching note for each of the 12 cases. These teaching notes are filled with suggestions for using the case effectively, have very thorough, analysis-based answers to the suggested assignment questions for the case, and contain an epilogue detailing any important developments since the case was written.

A Comprehensive Test Bank and TestGen Software

There is a 600+-question test bank, consisting of both multiple-choice questions and short-answer/essay questions. All of the test bank questions are also accessible via **TestGen**.

TestGen is a complete, state-of-the-art test generator and editing application software that allows instructors to quickly and easily select test items from McGraw Hill's TestGen testcontent and to organize, edit, and customize the questions and answers to rapidly generate paper tests. Questions can include stylized text, symbols, graphics, and equations that are inserted directly into questions using built-in mathematical templates. TestGen's random generator provides the option to display different text or calculated number values each time questions are used. With both quick-and-simple test creation and flexible and robust editing tools, TestGen is a test generator system for today's educators.

Test Bank and EZ Test Online

There is a test bank containing over 700 multiple-choice questions and short-answer/essay questions. It has been tagged with AACSB and Bloom's Taxonomy criteria. All of the test bank questions are accessible within Connect. All of the test bank questions are also accessible within a computerized test bank powered by McGraw-Hill's flexible electronic testing program, EZ Test Online (www.eztestonline.com). Using EZ Test Online allows you to create paper or online tests and quizzes. With EZ Test Online, instructors can select questions from multiple McGraw-Hill test banks or author their own and then either print the test for paper distribution or give it online.

PowerPoint Slides

To facilitate delivery preparation of your lectures and to serve as chapter outlines, you'll have access to approximately 350 colorful and professional-looking slides displaying core concepts, analytical procedures, key points, and all the figures in the text chapters.

The Business Strategy Game and *GLO-BUS* Online Simulations

Using one of the two companion simulations is a powerful and constructive way of emotionally connecting students to the subject matter of the course. We know of no more effective way to arouse the competitive energy of students and prepare them for the challenges of real-world business decision making than to have them match strategic wits with classmates in running a company in head-to-head competition for global market leadership.

ACKNOWLEDGMENTS

We heartily acknowledge the contributions of the case researchers whose case-writing efforts appear herein and the companies whose cooperation made the cases possible. To each one goes a very special thank-you. We cannot overstate the importance of timely, carefully researched cases in contributing to a substantive study of strategic management issues and practices. From a research standpoint, strategy-related cases are invaluable in exposing the generic kinds of strategic issues that companies face in forming hypotheses about strategic behavior and in drawing experienced-based generalizations about the practice of strategic management. From an instructional standpoint, strategy cases give students essential practice in diagnosing and evaluating the strategic situations of companies and organizations, in applying the concepts and tools of strategic analysis, in weighing strategic options and crafting strategies, and in tackling the challenges of successful strategy execution. Without a continuing stream of fresh, well-researched, and well-conceived cases, the discipline of strategic management would lose its close ties to the very institutions whose strategic actions and behavior it is aimed at explaining. There's no question, therefore, that first-class case research constitutes a valuable scholarly contribution to the theory and practice of strategic management.

A great number of colleagues and students at various universities, business acquaintances, and people at McGraw-Hill provided inspiration, encouragement, and counsel during the course of this project. Like all text authors in the strategy field, we are intellectually indebted to the many academics whose research and writing have blazed new trails and advanced the discipline of strategic management.

We also express our thanks to Todd M. Alessandri, Michael Anderson, Gerald D. Baumgardner, Edith C. Busija, Gerald E. Calvasina, Sam D. Cappel, Richard Churchman, John W. Collis, Connie Daniel, Christine DeLaTorre, Vickie Cox Edmondson, Diane D. Galbraith, Naomi A. Gardberg, Sanjay Goel, Les Jankovich, Jonatan Jelen, William Jiang, Bonnie Johnson, Roy Johnson, John J. Lawrence, Robert E. Ledman, Mark Lehrer, Fred Maidment, Frank Markham, Renata Mayrhofer, Simon Medcalfe, Elouise Mintz, Michael Monahan, Gerry Nkombo Muuka, Cori J. Myers, Jeryl L. Nelson, David Olson, John Perry, L. Jeff Seaton, Charles F. Seifert, Eugene S. Simko, Karen J. Smith, Susan Steiner, Troy V. Sullivan, Elisabeth J. Teal, Lori Tisher, Vincent Weaver, Jim Whitlock, and Beth Woodard. These reviewers provided valuable guidance in steering our efforts to improve earlier editions.

As always, we value your recommendations and thoughts about the book. Your comments regarding coverage and contents will be taken to heart, and we always are grateful for the time you take to call our attention to printing errors, deficiencies, and other shortcomings. Please e-mail us at john.gamble@tamucc.edu, or athompso@cba.ua.edu, or margaret.a.peteraf@tuck.dartmouth.edu.

John E. Gamble
Margaret A. Peteraf
Arthur A. Thompson

TABLE OF CONTENTS

Chapter 4   Evaluating a Company's Resources, Capabilities, and Competitiveness   64

Section C: Crafting a Strategy

Chapter 5   The Five Generic Competitive Strategies   88

Chapter 6   Strengthening a Company's Competitive Position: Strategic Moves, Timing, and Scope of Operations   111

PART TWO   CASES IN CRAFTING AND EXECUTING STRATEGY   233

Cases

 **connect®**

McGraw-Hill Connect® is a highly reliable, easy-to-use homework and learning management solution that utilizes learning science and award-winning adaptive tools to improve student results.

Homework and Adaptive Learning

- Connect's assignments help students contextualize what they've learned through application, so they can better understand the material and think critically.
- Connect will create a personalized study path customized to individual student needs through SmartBook®.
- SmartBook helps students study more efficiently by delivering an interactive reading experience through adaptive highlighting and review.

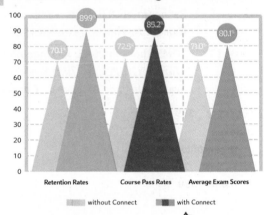

Connect's Impact on Retention Rates, Pass Rates, and Average Exam Scores

Retention Rates: 70.1%, 89.9%
Course Pass Rates: 72.5%, 85.2%
Average Exam Scores: 71.0%, 80.1%

without Connect   with Connect

Using **Connect** improves retention rates by **19.8** percentage points, passing rates by **12.7** percentage points, and exam scores by **9.1** percentage points.

Over **7 billion questions** have been answered, making McGraw-Hill Education products more intelligent, reliable, and precise.

73% of instructors who use Connect require it; instructor satisfaction increases by 28% when Connect is required.

Quality Content and Learning Resources

- Connect content is authored by the world's best subject matter experts, and is available to your class through a simple and intuitive interface.
- The Connect eBook makes it easy for students to access their reading material on smartphones and tablets. They can study on the go and don't need internet access to use the eBook as a reference, with full functionality.
- Multimedia content such as videos, simulations, and games drive student engagement and critical thinking skills.

Robust Analytics and Reporting

©Hero Images/Getty Images

- Connect Insight® generates easy-to-read reports on individual students, the class as a whole, and on specific assignments.

- The Connect Insight dashboard delivers data on performance, study behavior, and effort. Instructors can quickly identify students who struggle and focus on material that the class has yet to master.

- Connect automatically grades assignments and quizzes, providing easy-to-read reports on individual and class performance.

Impact on Final Course Grade Distribution

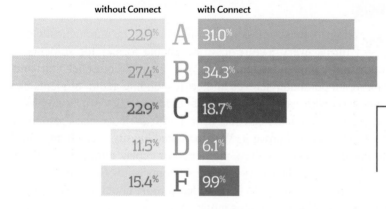

without Connect		with Connect
22.9%	A	31.0%
27.4%	B	34.3%
22.9%	C	18.7%
11.5%	D	6.1%
15.4%	F	9.9%

More students earn **As** and **Bs** when they use **Connect**.

Trusted Service and Support

- Connect integrates with your LMS to provide single sign-on and automatic syncing of grades. Integration with Blackboard®, D2L®, and Canvas also provides automatic syncing of the course calendar and assignment-level linking.

- Connect offers comprehensive service, support, and training throughout every phase of your implementation.

- If you're looking for some guidance on how to use Connect, or want to learn tips and tricks from super users, you can find tutorials as you work. Our Digital Faculty Consultants and Student Ambassadors offer insight into how to achieve the results you want with Connect.

www.mheducation.com/connect

COURSE DESIGN AND DELIVERY

CREATE

Instructors can now tailor their teaching resources to match the way they teach! With McGraw-Hill Create, www.mcgrawhillcreate.com, instructors can easily rearrange chapters, combine material from other content sources, and quickly upload and integrate their own content, such as course syllabi or teaching notes. Find the right content in Create by searching through thousands of leading McGraw-Hill textbooks. Arrange the material to fit your teaching style. Order a Create book and receive a complimentary print review copy in three to five business days or a complimentary electronic review copy via e-mail within one hour. Go to www.mcgrawhillcreate.com today and register.

TEGRITY CAMPUS

Tegrity makes class time available 24/7 by automatically capturing every lecture in a searchable format for students to review when they study and complete assignments. With a simple one-click start-and-stop process, you capture all computer screens and corresponding audio. Students can replay any part of any class with easy-to-use browser-based viewing on a PC or Mac. Educators know that the more students can see, hear, and experience class resources, the better they learn. In fact, studies prove it. With patented Tegrity "search anything" technology, students instantly recall key class moments for replay online or on iPods and mobile devices. Instructors can help turn all their students' study time into learning moments immediately supported by their lecture. To learn more about Tegrity, watch a two-minute Flash demo at http://tegritycampus.mhhe.com.

BLACKBOARD® PARTNERSHIP

McGraw-Hill Education and Blackboard have teamed up to simplify your life. Now you and your students can access Connect and Create right from within your Blackboard course—all with one single sign-on. The grade books are seamless, so when a student completes an integrated Connect assignment, the grade for that assignment automatically (and instantly) feeds your Blackboard grade center. Learn more at www.domorenow.com.

McGRAW-HILL CAMPUS™

Campus McGraw-Hill Campus is a new one-stop teaching and learning experience available to users of any learning management system. This institutional service allows faculty and students to enjoy single sign-on (SSO) access to all McGraw-Hill Higher Education materials, including the award-winning McGraw-Hill Connect platform, from directly within the institution's website. With McGraw-Hill Campus, faculty receive instant access to teaching materials (e.g., eTextbooks, test banks, PowerPoint slides, animations, learning objectives, etc.), allowing them to browse, search, and use any instructor ancillary content in our vast library at no additional cost to instructor or students. In addition, students enjoy SSO access to a variety of free content (e.g., quizzes, flash cards, narrated presentations, etc.) and subscription-based products (e.g., McGraw-Hill Connect). With McGraw-Hill Campus enabled, faculty and students will never need to create another account to access McGraw-Hill products and services. Learn more at www.mhcampus.com.

ESSENTIALS OF
STRATEGIC
MANAGEMENT

Strategy, Business Models, and Competitive Advantage

chapter 10

LEARNING OBJECTIVES

After reading this chapter, you should be able to:

LO1-1   Understand what is meant by a company's strategy.

LO1-2   Explain why a company needs a creative, distinctive strategy that sets it apart from rivals.

LO1-3   Explain why it is important for a company to have a viable business model that outlines the company's customer value proposition and its profit formula.

LO1-4   Identify the five most dependable strategic approaches for setting a company apart from rivals and winning a sustainable competitive advantage.

LO1-5   Understand that a company's strategy tends to evolve over time because of changing circumstances and ongoing management efforts to improve the company's strategy.

LO1-6   Identify the three tests of a winning strategy.

According to *The Economist,* a leading publication on business, economics, and international affairs, "In business, strategy is king. Leadership and hard work are all very well and luck is mighty useful, but it is strategy that makes or breaks a firm."[1] Luck and circumstance can explain why some companies are blessed with initial, short-lived success. But only a well-crafted, well-executed, constantly evolving strategy can explain why an elite set of companies somehow manages to rise to the top and stay there, year after year, pleasing their customers, shareholders, and other stakeholders alike in the process. Companies such as Apple, Samsung, Disney, Emirates Airlines, Microsoft, Alphabet (formerly Google), Berkshire Hathaway, General Electric, and Southwest Airlines come to mind.

In this opening chapter, we define the concept of *strategy* and describe its many facets. We explain what is meant by a competitive advantage, discuss the relationship between a company's strategy and its business model, and introduce you to the kinds of competitive strategies that can give a company an advantage over rivals in attracting customers and earning above-average profits. We look at what sets a winning strategy apart from others and why the caliber of a company's strategy determines whether the company will enjoy a competitive advantage over other firms. By the end of this chapter, you will have a clear idea of why the tasks of crafting and executing strategy are core management functions and why excellent execution of an excellent strategy is the most reliable recipe for turning a company into a standout performer over the long term.

 LO1-1   Understand what is meant by a company's strategy.

CORE CONCEPT

A company's **strategy** is the set of actions that its managers take to outperform the company's competitors and achieve superior profitability.

A company's **strategy** is the set of actions that its managers take to outperform the company's competitors and achieve superior profitability. The objective of a well-crafted strategy is not merely temporary competitive success and profits in the short run, but rather the sort of lasting success that can support growth and secure the company's future over the long term. Achieving this entails making a managerial commitment to a coherent array of well-considered choices about how to compete.[2] These include choices about:

- *How* to create products or services that attract and please customers.
- *How* to position the company in the industry.
- *How* to develop and deploy resources to build valuable competitive capabilities.
- *How* each functional piece of the business (R&D, supply chain activities, production, sales and marketing, distribution, finance, and human resources) will be operated.
- *How* to achieve the company's performance targets.

In most industries, companies have considerable freedom in choosing the *hows* of strategy. Thus some rivals strive to create superior value for customers by achieving lower costs than rivals, while others pursue product superiority or personalized customer service or the development of capabilities that rivals cannot match. Some competitors position themselves in only one part of the industry's chain of production/distribution activities, while others are partially or fully integrated, with operations ranging from components production to manufacturing and assembly to wholesale distribution or retailing. Some competitors deliberately confine their operations to local or regional markets; others opt to compete nationally, internationally (several countries), or globally. Some companies decide to operate in only one industry, while others diversify broadly or narrowly, into related or unrelated industries.

The Importance of a Distinctive Strategy and Competitive Approach

LO1-2   Explain why a company needs a creative, distinctive strategy that sets it apart from rivals.

For a company to matter in the minds of customers, its strategy needs a distinctive element that sets it apart from rivals and produces a competitive edge. A strategy must tightly fit a company's own particular situation, but there is no shortage of opportunity to fashion a strategy that is discernibly different from the strategies of rivals. In fact, competitive success requires a company's managers to make strategic choices about the key building blocks of its strategy that differ from the choices made by competitors—not 100 percent different but at least different in several important respects. A strategy stands a chance of succeeding only when it is predicated on actions, business approaches, and competitive moves aimed at appealing to buyers *in ways that set a company apart from rivals.* Simply trying to mimic the strategies of the industry's successful companies never works. Rather, every company's strategy needs to have some distinctive element that draws in customers and produces a competitive edge. Strategy, at its essence, is about competing differently—doing what rival firms *don't* do or, better yet, what rival firms *can't* do.[3]

> Mimicking the strategies of successful industry rivals—with either copycat product offerings or efforts to stake out the same market position—rarely works. A creative, distinctive strategy that sets a company apart from rivals and yields a competitive advantage is a company's most reliable ticket for earning above-average profits.

The Relationship Between a Company's Strategy and Business Model

LO1-3   Explain why it is important for a company to have a viable business model that outlines the company's customer value proposition and its profit formula.

Closely related to the concept of strategy is the concept of a company's **business model.** While the company's strategy sets forth an approach to offering superior value, a company's business model is management's blueprint for delivering a valuable product or service to customers in a manner that will yield an attractive profit.[4] The two elements of a company's business model are (1) its *customer value proposition* and (2) its *profit formula.* The customer value proposition is

CORE CONCEPT

A company's **business model** sets forth how its strategy and operating approaches will create value for customers, while at the same time generating ample revenues to cover costs and realizing a profit. The two elements of a company's business model are its (1) customer value proposition and (2) its profit formula.

established by the company's overall strategy and lays out the company's approach to satisfying buyer wants and needs at a price customers will consider a good value. The greater the value provided and the lower the price, the more attractive the value proposition is to customers. The profit formula describes the company's approach to determining a cost structure that will allow for acceptable profits given the pricing tied to its customer value proposition. The lower the costs given the customer value proposition, the greater the ability of the business model to be a moneymaker. The nitty-gritty issue surrounding a company's business model is whether it can execute its customer value proposition profitably. Just because company managers have crafted a strategy for competing and running the business does not automatically mean the strategy will lead to profitability—it may or it may not.[5]

Cable television providers utilize a business model, keyed to delivering news and entertainment that viewers will find valuable, to secure sufficient revenues from subscriptions and advertising to cover operating expenses and allow for profits. Aircraft engine manufacturer Rolls-Royce employs a "power-by-the-hour" business model that charges airlines leasing fees for engine use, maintenance, and repairs based upon actual hours flown. The company retains ownership of the engines and is able to minimize engine maintenance costs through the use of sophisticated sensors that optimize maintenance and repair schedules. Gillette's business model in razor blades involves achieving economies of scale in the production of its shaving products, selling razors at an attractively low price, and then making money on repeat purchases of razor blades. Concepts & Connections 1.1 discusses three contrasting business models in radio broadcasting.

Strategy and the Quest for Competitive Advantage

 LO1-4 Identify the five most dependable strategic approaches for setting a company apart from rivals and winning a sustainable competitive advantage.

The heart and soul of any strategy is the actions and moves in the marketplace that managers are taking to gain a competitive edge over rivals.[6] Five of the most frequently used and dependable strategic approaches to setting a company apart from rivals and winning a sustainable competitive advantage are:

1. *A low-cost provider strategy*—achieving a cost-based advantage over rivals. Walmart and Southwest Airlines have earned strong market positions because of the low-cost advantages they have achieved over their rivals. Low-cost provider strategies can produce a durable competitive edge when rivals find it hard to match the low-cost leader's approach to driving costs out of the business.

2. *A broad differentiation strategy*—seeking to differentiate the company's product or service from rivals' in ways that will appeal to a broad spectrum of buyers. Successful adopters of broad differentiation strategies include Johnson & Johnson in baby products (product reliability) and Apple (innovative products). Differentiation strategies can be powerful so long as a company is sufficiently innovative to thwart rivals' attempts to copy or closely imitate its product offering.

Concepts&Connections 1.1

PANDORA, SIRIUS XM, AND OVER-THE-AIR BROADCAST RADIO: THREE CONTRASTING BUSINESS MODELS

	Pandora	Sirius XM	Over-the-Air Radio Broadcasters
Customer value proposition	• Through free-of-charge Internet radio service, allowed PC, tablet computer, and smartphone users to create up to 100 personalized music and comedy stations • Utilized algorithms to generate playlists based on users' predicted music preferences • Offered programming interrupted by brief, occasional ads; eliminated advertising for Pandora One subscribers	• For a monthly subscription fee, provided satellite-based music, news, sports, national and regional weather, traffic reports in limited areas, and talk radio programming • Also offered subscribers streaming Internet channels and the ability to create personalized, commercial-free stations for online and mobile listening • Offered programming interrupted only by brief, occasional ads	• Provided free-of-charge music, national and local news, local traffic reports, national and local weather, and talk radio programming • Included frequent programming interruption for ads
Profit Formula	Revenue generation: Display, audio, and video ads targeted to different audiences and sold to local and national buyers; subscription revenues generated from an advertising-free option called Pandora One	Revenue generation: Monthly subscription fees, sales of satellite radio equipment, and advertising revenues	Revenue generation: Advertising sales to national and local businesses
	Cost structure: Fixed costs associated with developing software for computers, tablets, and smartphones	Cost structure: Fixed costs associated with operating a satellite-based music delivery service and streaming Internet service	Cost structure: Fixed costs associated with terrestrial broadcasting operations
	Fixed and variable costs related to operating data centers to support streaming network content royalties, marketing, and support activities	Fixed and variable costs related to programming and content royalties, marketing, and support activities	Fixed and variable costs related to local news reporting, advertising sales operations, network affiliate fees, programming and content royalties, commercial production activities, and support activities
	Profit margin: Profitability dependent on generating sufficient advertising revenues and subscription revenues to cover costs and provide attractive profits	Profit margin: Profitability dependent on attracting a sufficiently large number of subscribers to cover costs and provide attractive profits	Profit margin: Profitability dependent on generating sufficient advertising revenues to cover costs and provide attractive profits

Sources: Company documents, 10-Ks, and information posted on their websites.

3. *A focused low-cost strategy*—concentrating on a narrow buyer segment (or market niche) and outcompeting rivals by having lower costs than rivals and thus being able to serve niche members at a lower price. Private-label manufacturers of food, health and beauty products, and nutritional supplements use their low-cost advantage to offer supermarket buyers lower prices than those demanded by producers of branded products.

4. *A focused differentiation strategy*—concentrating on a narrow buyer segment (or market niche) and outcompeting rivals by offering niche members customized attributes that meet their tastes and requirements better than rivals' products. Louis Vuitton and Rolex have sustained their advantage in the luxury goods industry through a focus on affluent consumers demanding luxury and prestige.

5. *A best-cost provider strategy*—giving customers more value for the money by satisfying buyers' expectations on key quality/features/performance/service attributes, while beating their price expectations. This approach is a hybrid strategy that blends elements of low-cost provider and differentiation strategies; the aim is to have the lowest (best) costs and prices among sellers offering products with comparable differentiating attributes. Target's best-cost advantage allows it to give discount store shoppers more value for the money by offering an attractive product lineup and an appealing shopping ambience at low prices.

In Concepts & Connections 1.2, it is evident that Starbucks has gained a competitive advantage over rivals through its efforts to offer the highest quality coffee-based beverages, create an emotional attachment with customers, expand its global presence, expand the product line, and ensure consistency in store operations. A creative, distinctive strategy such as that used by Starbucks is a company's most reliable ticket for developing a sustainable competitive advantage and earning above-average profits. A **sustainable competitive advantage** allows a company to attract sufficiently large numbers of buyers who have a lasting preference for its products or services over those offered by rivals, despite the efforts of competitors to offset that appeal and overcome the company's advantage. The bigger and more durable the competitive advantage, the better a company's prospects for winning in the marketplace and earning superior long-term profits relative to rivals.

> **CORE CONCEPT**
>
> A company achieves **sustainable competitive advantage** when an attractively large number of buyers develop a durable preference for its products or services over the offerings of competitors, despite the efforts of competitors to overcome or erode its advantage.

The Importance of Capabilities in Building and Sustaining Competitive Advantage

Winning a *sustainable* competitive edge over rivals with any of the previous five strategies generally hinges as much on building competitively valuable capabilities that rivals cannot readily match as it does on having a distinctive product offering. Clever rivals can nearly always copy the attributes of a popular product or service, but it is

Concepts & Connections 1.2

STARBUCKS' STRATEGY IN THE SPECIALTY COFFEE MARKET

Since its founding in 1985 as a modest nine-store operation in Seattle, Washington, Starbucks had become the premier roaster and retailer of specialty coffees in the world, with nearly 25,000 store locations in 70 countries as of April 2016 and annual sales that exceed $21 billion in fiscal 2016. The key elements of Starbucks' strategy in specialty coffees included:

- **Train "baristas" to serve a wide variety of specialty coffee drinks that allow customers to satisfy their individual preferences in a customized way.** Starbucks essentially brought specialty coffees, such as cappuccinos, lattes, and macchiatos, to the mass market in the United States, encouraging customers to personalize their coffee drinking habits. Requests for such items as a "Smoked Butterscotch Latte with Soy Milk" could be served up quickly with consistent quality.

- **Emphasis on store ambience and elevating the customer experience at Starbucks stores.** Starbucks management viewed each store as a billboard for the company and as a contributor to building the company's brand and image. Each detail was scrutinized to enhance the mood and ambiance of the store to make sure everything signaled "best-of-class" and reflected the personality of the community and the neighborhood. The thesis was "everything mattered." The company went to great lengths to make sure the store fixtures, the merchandise displays, the colors, the artwork, the banners, the music, and the aromas all blended to create a consistent, inviting, stimulating environment that evoked the romance of coffee, that signaled the company's passion for coffee, and that rewarded customers with ceremony, stories, and surprise.

- **Purchase and roast only top-quality coffee beans.** The company purchased only the highest quality arabica beans and carefully roasted coffee to exacting standards of quality and flavor. Starbucks did not use chemicals or artificial flavors when preparing its roasted coffees.

- **Commitment to corporate responsibility.** Starbucks was protective of the environment and contributed positively to the communities where Starbucks stores were located. In addition, Starbucks promoted fair trade practices and paid above-market prices for coffee beans to provide its growers/suppliers with sufficient funding to sustain their operations and provide for their families.

- **Expansion of the number of Starbucks stores domestically and internationally.** Starbucks operated stores in high-traffic, high-visibility locations in the United States and abroad. The company's ability to vary store size and format made it possible to locate stores in settings such as downtown and suburban shopping areas, office buildings, and university campuses. Starbucks added 321 new company-owned locations in the United States and another 155 company-owned stores internationally in fiscal 2016. Starbucks also added 330 licensed store locations in the United States and 1,236 licensed stores internationally in 2016. The company planned to open 12,000 new stores globally by fiscal 2021, with 3,400 new units being opened in the United States.

- **Broaden and periodically refresh in-store product offerings.** Noncoffee products offered by Starbucks included teas, fresh pastries and other food items, and coffee mugs and coffee accessories. The company's new Mercato stores would extend food offerings to include grab-and-go salads and sandwiches and novel health-conscious items such as gluten-free smoked Canadian bacon breakfast sandwiches and Sous Vide Egg Bites.

- **Fully exploit the growing power of the Starbucks name and brand image with out-of-store sales.** Starbucks consumer packaged goods division included domestic and international sales of Frappuccino, coffee ice creams, and Starbucks coffees.

Sources: Company documents, 10-Ks, and information posted on Starbucks' website.

substantially more difficult for rivals to match the know-how and specialized capabilities a company has developed and perfected over a long period. FedEx, for example, has superior capabilities in next-day delivery of small packages. And Hyundai has become the world's fastest-growing automaker as a result of its advanced manufacturing processes and unparalleled quality control system. The capabilities of both of these companies have proven difficult for competitors to imitate or best and have allowed each to build and sustain competitive advantage.

Why a Company's Strategy Evolves over Time

LO1-5 Understand that a company's strategy tends to evolve over time because of changing circumstances and ongoing management efforts to improve the company's strategy.

The appeal of a strategy that yields a sustainable competitive advantage is that it offers the potential for an enduring edge over rivals. However, managers of every company must be willing and ready to modify the strategy in response to the unexpected moves of competitors, shifting buyer needs and preferences, emerging market opportunities, new ideas for improving the strategy, and mounting evidence that the strategy is not working well. Most of the time, a company's strategy evolves incrementally as management fine-tunes various pieces of the strategy and adjusts the strategy to respond to unfolding events. However, on occasion, major strategy shifts are called for, such as when the strategy is clearly failing or when industry conditions change in dramatic ways.

Regardless of whether a company's strategy changes gradually or swiftly, the important point is that the task of crafting strategy is not a one-time event but is always a work in progress.[7] The evolving nature of a company's strategy means the typical company strategy is a blend of (1) *proactive* moves to improve the company's financial performance and secure a competitive edge and (2) *adaptive* reactions to unanticipated developments and fresh market conditions—see Figure 1.1.[8] The biggest portion of a company's current strategy flows from ongoing actions that have proven themselves in the marketplace and newly launched initiatives aimed at building a larger lead over rivals and further boosting financial performance. This part of management's action plan for running the company is its proactive, **deliberate strategy.**

> Changing circumstances and ongoing management efforts to improve the strategy cause a company's strategy to evolve over time—a condition that makes the task of crafting a strategy a work in progress, not a one-time event.

At times, certain components of a company's deliberate strategy will fail in the marketplace and become **abandoned strategy elements.** Also, managers must always be willing to supplement or modify planned, deliberate strategy elements with as-needed

FIGURE 1.1 **A Company's Strategy Is a Blend of Planned Initiatives and Unplanned Reactive Adjustments**

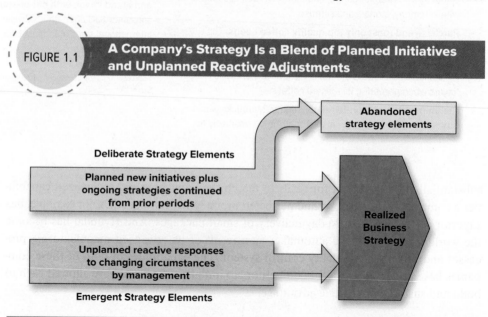

reactions to unanticipated developments. Inevitably, there will be occasions when market and competitive conditions take unexpected turns that call for some kind of strategic reaction. Novel strategic moves on the part of rival firms, unexpected shifts in customer preferences, fast-changing technological developments, and new market opportunities call for unplanned, reactive adjustments that form the company's **emergent strategy.** As shown in Figure 1.1, a company's **realized strategy** tends to be a *combination* of deliberate planned elements and unplanned, emergent elements.

> **CORE CONCEPT**
>
> A company's **realized strategy** is a combination *deliberate planned elements* and *unplanned emergent elements*. Some components of a company's deliberate strategy will fail in the marketplace and become *abandoned strategy elements.*

The Three Tests of a Winning Strategy

> **LO1-6**   Identify the three tests of a winning strategy.

Three questions can be used to distinguish a winning strategy from a so-so or flawed strategy:

1. *How well does the strategy fit the company's situation?* To qualify as a winner, a strategy has to be well matched to the company's external and internal situations. The strategy must fit competitive conditions in the industry and other aspects of the enterprise's external environment. At the same

> A winning strategy must fit the company's external and internal situation, build sustainable competitive advantage, and improve company performance.

time, it should be tailored to the company's collection of competitively important resources and capabilities. It's unwise to build a strategy upon the company's weaknesses or pursue a strategic approach that requires resources that are deficient in the company. Unless a strategy exhibits a tight fit with both the external and internal aspects of a company's overall situation, it is unlikely to produce respectable, first-rate business results.

2. *Is the strategy helping the company achieve a sustainable competitive advantage?* Strategies that fail to achieve a durable competitive advantage over rivals are unlikely to produce superior performance for more than a brief period of time. Winning strategies enable a company to achieve a competitive advantage over key rivals that is long lasting. The bigger and more durable the competitive edge that the strategy helps build, the more powerful it is.

3. *Is the strategy producing good company performance?* The mark of a winning strategy is strong company performance. Two kinds of performance improvements tell the most about the caliber of a company's strategy: (1) gains in profitability and financial strength and (2) advances in the company's competitive strength and market standing.

Strategies that come up short on one or more of these tests are plainly less appealing than strategies passing all three tests with flying colors. Managers should use the same questions when evaluating either proposed or existing strategies. New initiatives that don't seem to match the company's internal and external situation should be scrapped before they come to fruition, while existing strategies must be scrutinized on a regular basis to ensure they have a good fit, offer a competitive advantage, and have contributed to above-average performance or performance improvements.

Why Crafting and Executing Strategy Are Important Tasks

High-achieving enterprises are nearly always the product of astute, creative, and proactive strategy making. Companies don't get to the top of the industry rankings or stay there with illogical strategies, copycat strategies, or timid attempts to try to do better. Among all the things managers do, nothing affects a company's ultimate success or failure more fundamentally than how well its management team charts the company's direction, develops competitively effective strategic moves and business approaches, and pursues what needs to be done internally to produce good day-in, day-out strategy execution and operating excellence. Indeed, *good strategy and good strategy execution are the most telling signs of good management.* The rationale for using the twin standards of good strategy making and good strategy execution to determine whether a company is well managed is therefore compelling: *The better conceived a company's strategy and the more competently it is executed, the more likely that the company will be a standout performer in the marketplace.* In stark contrast, a company that lacks clear-cut direction, has a flawed strategy, or cannot execute its strategy competently is a company whose financial performance is probably suffering, whose business is at long-term risk, and whose management is sorely lacking.

> How well a company performs is directly attributable to the caliber of its strategy and the proficiency with which the strategy is executed.

The Road Ahead

Throughout the chapters to come and the accompanying case collection, the spotlight is trained on the foremost question in running a business enterprise: *What must managers do, and do well, to make a company a winner in the marketplace?* The answer that emerges is that doing a good job of managing inherently requires good strategic thinking and good management of the strategy-making, strategy-executing process.

The mission of this book is to provide a solid overview of what every business student and aspiring manager needs to know about crafting and executing strategy. We will explore what good strategic thinking entails, describe the core concepts and tools of strategic analysis, and examine the ins and outs of crafting and executing strategy. The accompanying cases will help build your skills in both diagnosing how well the strategy-making, strategy-executing task is being performed and prescribing actions for how the strategy in question or its execution can be improved. The strategic management course that you are enrolled in may also include a strategy simulation exercise where you will run a company in head-to-head competition with companies run by your classmates. Your mastery of the strategic management concepts presented in the following chapters will put you in a strong position to craft a winning strategy for your company and figure out how to execute it in a cost-effective and profitable manner. As you progress through the chapters of the text and the activities assigned during the term, we hope to convince you that first-rate capabilities in crafting and executing strategy are essential to good management.

KEY POINTS

1. A company's strategy is the set of actions that its managers take to outperform the company's competitors and achieve superior profitability.

2. Closely related to the concept of strategy is the concept of a company's business model. A company's business model is management's blueprint for delivering customer value in a manner that will generate revenues sufficient to cover costs and yield an attractive profit. The two elements of a company's business model are its (1) customer value proposition and (2) its profit formula.

3. The central thrust of a company's strategy is undertaking moves to build and strengthen the company's long-term competitive position and financial performance by competing differently from rivals and gaining a sustainable competitive advantage over them.

4. A company's strategy typically evolves over time, arising from a blend of (1) proactive and deliberate actions on the part of company managers and (2) adaptive emergent responses to unanticipated developments and fresh market conditions.

5. A winning strategy fits the circumstances of a company's external and internal situations, builds competitive advantage, and boosts company performance.

ASSURANCE OF LEARNING EXERCISES

1. Based on your experiences as a coffee consumer, does Starbucks' strategy as described in Concepts & Connections 1.2 seem to set it apart from rivals? Does the strategy seem to be keyed to a cost-based advantage, differentiating features, serving the unique needs of a niche, or some combination of these? What is there about Starbucks' strategy that can lead to sustainable competitive advantage?

    connect
    LO1-1, LO1-2, LO1-4

2. Go to investor.siriusxm.com and check whether SiriusXM's recent financial reports indicate that its business model is working. Are its subscription fees increasing or declining? Is its revenue stream from advertising and equipment sales growing or declining? Does its cost structure allow for acceptable profit margins?

    connect
    LO1-3

    LO1-5, LO1-6

3. Elements of eBay's strategy have evolved in meaningful ways since the company's founding in 1995. After reviewing the company's history at www.ebayinc.com/our-company/our-history/ and all of the links at the company's investor relations site (investors.ebayinc.com/), prepare a one- to two-page report that discusses how its strategy has evolved. Your report should also assess how well eBay's strategy passes the three tests of a winning strategy.

EXERCISES FOR SIMULATION PARTICIPANTS

After you have read the Participant's Guide or Player's Manual for the strategy simulation exercise that you will participate in this academic term, you and your co-managers should come up with brief one- or two-paragraph answers to the questions that follow *before* entering your first set of decisions. While your answers to the first of the four questions can be developed from your reading of the manual, the remaining questions will require a collaborative discussion among the members of your company's management team about how you intend to manage the company you have been assigned to run.

1. What is our company's current situation? A substantive answer to this question should cover the following issues: **LO1-6**

    • Does your company appear to be in sound financial condition?

    • What problems does your company have that need to be addressed?

LO1-2, LO1-4   2.   Why will our company matter to customers? A complete answer to this question should say something about each of the following:

- How will you create customer value?

- What will be distinctive about the company's products or services?

- How will capabilities and resources be deployed to deliver customer value?

LO1-3   3.   What are the primary elements of your company's business model?

- Describe your customer value proposition.

- Discuss the profit formula tied to your business model.

- What level of revenues is required for your company's business model to become a moneymaker?

LO1-4, LO1-5, LO1-6   4.   How will you build and sustain competitive advantage?

- Which of the basic strategic and competitive approaches discussed in this chapter do you think makes the most sense to pursue?

- What kind of competitive advantage over rivals will you try to achieve?

- How do you envision that your strategy might evolve as you react to the competitive moves of rival firms?

- Does your strategy have the ability to pass the three tests of a winning strategy? Explain.

 ENDNOTES

1. B. R., "Strategy," *The Economist,* October 19, 2012, www.economist.com/blogs/schumpeter/2012/10/z-business-quotations-1 (accessed January 4, 2014).

2. Jan Rivkin, "An Alternative Approach to Making Strategic Choices," Harvard Business School case 9-702-433, 2001.

3. Michael E. Porter, "What Is Strategy?" *Harvard Business Review* 74, no. 6 (November–December 1996).

4. Mark W. Johnson, Clayton M. Christensen, and Henning Kagermann, "Reinventing Your Business Model," *Harvard Business Review* 86, no. 12

(December 2008); and Joan Magretta, "Why Business Models Matter," *Harvard Business Review* 80, no. 5 (May 2002).

5. W. Chan Kim and Renée Mauborgne, "How Strategy Shapes Structure," *Harvard Business Review* 87, no. 9 (September 2009).

6. Porter, "What Is Strategy?"

7. Cynthia A. Montgomery, "Putting Leadership Back into Strategy," *Harvard Business Review* 86, no. 1 (January 2008).

8. Henry Mintzberg and Joseph Lampel, "Reflecting on the Strategy Process,"

Sloan Management Review 40, no. 3 (Spring 1999); Henry Mintzberg and J. A. Waters, "Of Strategies, Deliberate and Emergent," *Strategic Management Journal* 6 (1985); Costas Markides, "Strategy as Balance: From 'Either-Or' to 'And,'" *Business Strategy Review* 12, no. 3 (September 2001); Henry Mintzberg, Bruce Ahlstrand, and Joseph Lampel, *Strategy Safari: A Guided Tour Through the Wilds of Strategic Management* (New York: Free Press, 1998); C. K. Prahalad and Gary Hamel, "The Core Competence of the Corporation," *Harvard Business Review* 70, no. 3 (May–June 1990).

Strategy Formulation, Execution, and Governance

After reading this chapter, you should be able to:

LO2-1 Understand why it is critical for company managers to have a clear strategic vision of where a company needs to head and why.

LO2-2 Explain the importance of setting both strategic and financial objectives.

LO2-3 Explain why the strategic initiatives taken at various organizational levels must be tightly coordinated to achieve companywide performance targets.

LO2-4 Recognize what a company must do to achieve operating excellence and to execute its strategy proficiently.

LO2-5 Identify the role and responsibility of a company's board of directors in overseeing the strategic management process.

Crafting and executing strategy are the heart and soul of managing a business enterprise. But exactly what is involved in developing a strategy and executing it proficiently? What are the various components of the strategy formulation, strategy execution process, and to what extent are company personnel—aside from senior management—involved in the process? This chapter presents an overview of the ins and outs of crafting and executing company strategies. Special attention will be given to management's direction-setting responsibilities—charting a strategic course, setting performance targets, and choosing a strategy capable of producing the desired outcomes. We will also explain why strategy formulation is a task for a company's entire management team and discuss which kinds of strategic decisions tend to be made at which levels of management. The chapter concludes with a look at the roles and responsibilities of a company's board of directors and how good corporate governance protects shareholder interests and promotes good management.

The Strategy Formulation, Strategy Execution Process

The managerial process of crafting and executing a company's strategy is an ongoing, continuous process consisting of five integrated stages:

1. *Developing a strategic vision* that charts the company's long-term direction, a *mission statement* that describes the company's business, and a set of *core values* to guide the pursuit of the strategic vision and mission.

2. *Setting objectives* for measuring the company's performance and tracking its progress in moving in the intended long-term direction.

3. *Crafting a strategy* for advancing the company along the path to management's envisioned future and achieving its performance objectives.

4. *Implementing and executing the chosen strategy* efficiently and effectively.

5. *Evaluating and analyzing the external environment and the company's internal situation and performance* to identify corrective adjustments that are needed in the company's long-term direction, objectives, strategy, or approach to strategy execution.

Figure 2.1 displays this five-stage process. The model illustrates the need for management to evaluate a number of external and internal factors in deciding upon a strategic direction, appropriate objectives, and approaches to crafting and executing strategy (see Table 2.1). Management's decisions that are made in the strategic management process must be shaped by the prevailing economic conditions and competitive environment and the company's own internal resources and competitive capabilities. These strategy-shaping conditions will be the focus of Chapters 3 and 4.

The model shown in Figure 2.1 also illustrates the need for management to evaluate the company's performance on an ongoing basis. Any indication that the company is failing to achieve its objectives calls for corrective adjustments in one of the first four stages of the process. The company's implementation efforts might have fallen short, and new tactics must be devised to fully exploit the potential of the company's strategy. If management determines that the company's execution efforts are sufficient, it should challenge the assumptions underlying the company's business strategy and alter the strategy to better fit competitive conditions and the company's internal capabilities. If

FIGURE 2.1   **The Strategy Formulation, Strategy Execution Process**

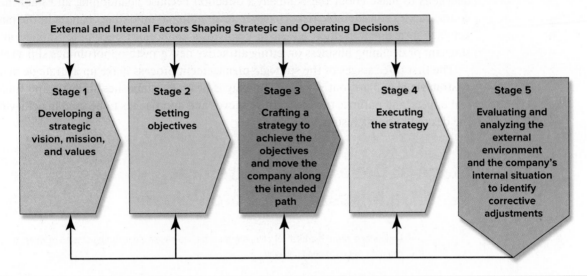

the company's strategic approach to competition is rated as sound, then perhaps management set overly ambitious targets for the company's performance.

The evaluation stage of the strategic management process shown in Figure 2.1 also allows for a change in the company's vision, but this should be necessary only when it

TABLE 2.1

Factors Shaping Decisions in the Strategy Formulation, Strategy Execution Process

External Considerations

- Does sticking with the company's present strategic course present attractive opportunities for growth and profitability?
- What kind of competitive forces are industry members facing, and are they acting to enhance or weaken the company's prospects for growth and profitability?
- What factors are driving industry change, and what impact on the company's prospects will they have?
- How are industry rivals positioned, and what strategic moves are they likely to make next?
- What are the key factors of future competitive success, and does the industry offer good prospects for attractive profits for companies possessing those capabilities?

Internal Considerations

- Does the company have an appealing customer value proposition?
- What are the company's competitively important resources and capabilities, and are they potent enough to produce a sustainable competitive advantage?
- Does the company have sufficient business and competitive strength to seize market opportunities and nullify external threats?
- Are the company's costs competitive with those of key rivals?
- Is the company competitively stronger or weaker than key rivals?

becomes evident to management that the industry has changed in a significant way that renders the vision obsolete. Such occasions can be referred to as **strategic inflection points.** When a company reaches a strategic inflection point, management has tough decisions to make about the company's direction because abandoning an established course carries considerable risk. However, responding to unfolding changes in the marketplace in a timely fashion lessens a company's chances of becoming trapped in a stagnant or declining business or letting attractive new growth opportunities slip away.

The first three stages of the strategic management process make up a strategic plan. A **strategic plan** maps out where a company is headed, establishes strategic and financial targets, and outlines the competitive moves and approaches to be used in achieving the desired business results.[1]

Stage 1: Developing a Strategic Vision, a Mission, and Core Values

 LO2-1   Understand why it is critical for company managers to have a clear strategic vision of where a company needs to head and why.

At the outset of the strategy formulation, strategy execution process, a company's senior managers must wrestle with the issue of what directional path the company should take and whether its market positioning and future performance prospects could be improved by changing the company's product offerings and/or the markets in which it participates and/or the customers it caters to and/or the technologies it employs. Top management's views about the company's direction and future product-customer-market-technology focus constitute a **strategic vision** for the company. A clearly articulated strategic vision communicates management's aspirations to stakeholders about "where we are going" and helps steer the energies of company personnel in a common direction. For instance, the vision of Google's co-founders Larry Page and Sergey Brin "to organize the world's information and make it universally accessible and useful" captured the imagination of Google employees, served as the basis for crafting the company's strategic actions, and aided internal efforts to mobilize and direct the company's resources.

> **CORE CONCEPT**
>
> A **strategic vision** describes "where we are going"—the course and direction management has charted and the company's future product-customer-market-technology focus.

Well-conceived visions are *distinctive* and *specific* to a particular organization; they avoid generic, feel-good statements such as "We will become a global leader and the first choice of customers in every market we choose to serve"—which could apply to any of hundreds of organizations.[2] And they are not the product of a committee charged with coming up with an innocuous but well-meaning one-sentence vision that wins consensus approval from various stakeholders. Nicely worded vision statements with no specifics about the company's product-market-customer-technology focus fall well short of what it takes for a vision to measure up.

For a strategic vision to function as a valuable managerial tool, it must provide understanding of what management wants its business to look like and provide managers with a reference point in making strategic decisions. It must say something definitive about how the company's leaders intend to position the company beyond where it is today. Table 2.2 lists some characteristics of effective vision statements.

A surprising number of the vision statements found on company websites and in annual reports are vague and unrevealing, saying very little about the company's future product-market-customer-technology focus. Some could apply to most any company in any industry. Many read like a public relations statement—lofty words that someone came up with because it is fashionable for companies to have an official vision statement.[3] Table 2.3 provides a list of the most common shortcomings in company vision statements. Like any tool, vision statements can be used properly or improperly, either clearly conveying a company's strategic course or not. Concepts & Connections 2.1 provides a critique of the strategic visions of several prominent companies.

TABLE 2.2

Characteristics of Effectively Worded Vision Statements

Graphic—Paints a picture of the kind of company that management is trying to create and the market position(s) the company is striving to stake out

Directional—Is forward-looking; describes the strategic course that management has charted and the kinds of product-market-customer-technology changes that will help the company prepare for the future

Focused—Is specific enough to provide managers with guidance in making decisions and allocating resources

Flexible—Is not so focused that it makes it difficult for management to adjust to changing circumstances in markets, customer preferences, or technology

Feasible—Is within the realm of what the company can reasonably expect to achieve

Desirable—Indicates why the directional path makes good business sense

Easy to communicate—Is explainable in 5 to 10 minutes and, ideally, can be reduced to a simple, memorable "slogan" (like Henry Ford's famous vision of "a car in every garage")

Source: Based partly on John P. Kotter, *Leading Change* (Boston: Harvard Business School Press, 1996), p. 72.

TABLE 2.3

Common Shortcomings in Company Vision Statements

Vague or incomplete—Short on specifics about where the company is headed or what the company is doing to prepare for the future

Not forward-looking—Does not indicate whether or how management intends to alter the company's current product-market-customer-technology focus

Too broad—So all-inclusive that the company could head in most any direction, pursue most any opportunity, or enter most any business

Bland or uninspiring—Lacks the power to motivate company personnel or inspire shareholder confidence about the company's direction

Not distinctive—Provides no unique company identity; could apply to companies in any of several industries (including rivals operating in the same market arena)

Too reliant on superlatives—Does not say anything specific about the company's strategic course beyond the pursuit of such distinctions as being a recognized leader, a global or worldwide leader, or the first choice of customers

Sources: Based on information in Hugh Davidson, *The Committed Enterprise* (Oxford: Butterworth Heinemann, 2002), chapter 2; and Michel Robert, *Strategy Pure and Simple II* (New York: McGraw-Hill, 1998), chapters 2, 3, and 6.

Concepts & Connections 2.1

EXAMPLES OF STRATEGIC VISIONS—HOW WELL DO THEY MEASURE UP?

Vision Statement	Effective Elements	Shortcomings
Whole Foods Whole Foods Market is a dynamic leader in the quality food business. We are a mission-driven company that aims to set the standards of excellence for food retailers. We are building a business in which high standards permeate all aspects of our company. Quality is a state of mind at Whole Foods Market. Our motto—Whole Foods, Whole People, Whole Planet—emphasizes that our vision reaches far beyond just being a food retailer. Our success in fulfilling our vision is measured by customer satisfaction, team member happiness and excellence, return on capital investment, improvement in the state of the environment and local and larger community support. Our ability to instill a clear sense of interdependence among our various stakeholders (the people who are interested and benefit from the success of our company) is contingent upon our efforts to communicate more often, more openly, and more compassionately. Better communication equals better understanding and more trust.	• Forward-looking • Graphic • Focused • Desirable	• Long • Not memorable
Keurig Become the world's leading personal beverage systems company.	• Focused • Flexible • Desirable	• Vague • Not graphic • Not forward-looking
Caterpillar Our vision is a world in which all people's basic needs—such as shelter, clean water, sanitation, food and reliable power—are fulfilled in an environmentally sustainable way and a company that improves the quality of the environment and the communities where we live and work.	• Graphic • Desirable	• Too broad • Too reliant on superlatives • Not distinctive
Nike NIKE, Inc., fosters a culture of invention. We create products, services and experiences for today's athlete* while solving problems for the next generation. *If you have a body, you are an athlete.	• Forward-looking • Flexible	• Vague • Not focused • Too reliant on superlatives

Sources: Company documents and websites.

The Importance of Communicating the Strategic Vision

A strategic vision has little value to the organization unless it's effectively communicated down the line to lower-level managers and employees. It would be difficult for a vision statement to provide direction to decision makers and energize employees toward achieving long-term strategic intent unless they know of the vision and observe management's commitment to that vision. Communicating the vision to organization members nearly always means putting "where we are going and why" in writing, distributing the statement organization-wide, and having executives personally explain the vision and its rationale to as many people as feasible. Ideally, executives should present their vision for the company in a manner that reaches out and grabs people's attention. An engaging and convincing strategic vision has enormous motivational value—for the same reason that a stonemason is inspired by building a great cathedral for the ages. Therefore, an executive's ability to paint a convincing and inspiring picture of a company's journey to a future destination is an important element of effective strategic leadership.[4]

Expressing the Essence of the Vision in a Slogan   The task of effectively conveying the vision to company personnel is assisted when management can capture the vision of where to head in a catchy or easily remembered slogan. A number of organizations have summed up their vision in a brief phrase. Disney's overarching vision for its five business groups—theme parks, movie studios, television channels, consumer products, and interactive media entertainment—is to "create happiness by providing the finest in entertainment for people of all ages, everywhere." The Mayo Clinic's vision is to provide "The best care to every patient every day," while Greenpeace's envisioned future is "To halt environmental abuse and promote environmental solutions."

> An effectively communicated vision is a valuable management tool for enlisting the commitment of company personnel to engage in actions that move the company in the intended direction.

Creating a short slogan to illuminate an organization's direction and then using it repeatedly as a reminder of "where we are headed and why" helps rally organization members to hurdle whatever obstacles lie in the company's path and maintain their focus.

Why a Sound, Well-Communicated Strategic Vision Matters   A well-thought-out, forcefully communicated strategic vision pays off in several respects: (1) it crystallizes senior executives' own views about the firm's long-term direction; (2) it reduces the risk of rudderless decision making by management at all levels; (3) it is a tool for winning the support of employees to help make the vision a reality; (4) it provides a beacon for lower-level managers in forming departmental missions; and (5) it helps an organization prepare for the future.

Developing a Company Mission Statement

The defining characteristic of a well-conceived **strategic vision** is what it says about the company's *future strategic course—"where we are headed and what our future product-customer-market-technology focus will be."* In contrast, a **mission statement** describes the enterprise's *present* business scope and purpose—"who we are, what we do, and why we are here." It is purely descriptive. Ideally, a company mission statement (1) identifies the company's products and/or services, (2) specifies the buyer needs that the company seeks to satisfy and the customer groups or markets that it serves, and (3) gives the company its own identity. Consider, for example, the mission statement of Singapore Airlines, which is consistently rated among the world's best airlines in terms of passenger safety and comfort:

> The distinction between a **strategic vision** and a **mission statement** is fairly clear-cut: A strategic vision portrays a company's *future business scope* ("where we are going"), whereas a company's mission statement typically describes its *present business and purpose* ("who we are, what we do, and why we are here").

CORE CONCEPT

A well-conceived **mission statement** conveys a company's purpose in language specific enough to give the company its own identity.

> Singapore Airlines is a global company dedicated to providing air transportation services of the highest quality and to maximizing returns for the benefit of its shareholders and employees.

Note that Singapore Airlines' mission statement does a good job of conveying "who we are, what we do, and why we are here," but it provides no sense of "where we are headed."

An example of a well-stated mission statement with ample specifics about what the organization does is that of St. Jude Children's Research Hospital: "to advance cures, and means of prevention, for pediatric catastrophic diseases through research and treatment. Consistent with the vision of our founder Danny Thomas, no child is denied treatment based on race, religion or a family's ability to pay." Twitter's mission statement, while short, still captures the essence of what the company is about: "to give everyone the power to create and share ideas and information instantly, without barriers." An example of a not-so-revealing mission statement is that of Microsoft. "To empower every person and every organization on the planet to achieve more" says nothing about its products or business and does not give the company its own identity. A mission statement that provides scant indication of "who we are and what we do" has no apparent value.

Occasionally, companies state that their mission is to simply earn a profit. This is misguided. Profit is more correctly an *objective* and a *result* of what a company does. Moreover, earning a profit is the obvious intent of every commercial enterprise. Such companies as BMW, Netflix, Shell Oil, Procter & Gamble, and Citigroup are each striving to earn a profit for shareholders, but the fundamentals of their businesses are substantially different when it comes to "who we are and what we do." It is management's answer to "make a profit doing what and for whom?" that reveals the substance of a company's true mission and business purpose.

Linking the Strategic Vision and Mission with Company Values

Many companies have developed a statement of **values** (sometimes called *core values*) to guide the actions and behavior of company personnel in conducting the company's business and pursuing its strategic vision and mission. These values are the designated beliefs and desired ways of doing things at the company and frequently relate to such things as fair treatment, honor and integrity, ethical behavior, innovativeness, teamwork, a passion for excellence, social responsibility, and community citizenship.

CORE CONCEPT

A company's **values** are the beliefs, traits, and behavioral norms that company personnel are expected to display in conducting the company's business and pursuing its strategic vision and mission.

Most companies normally have four to eight core values. At Samsung, five core values are linked to its philosophy of devoting its talent and technology to create superior products and services that contribute to a better global society: (1) giving people opportunities to reach their full potential, (2) developing the best products and services on the market, (3) embracing change, (4) operating in an ethical way, and (5) dedication to social and environmental responsibility. L. L. Bean's two core values are encompassed in a quote from founder Leon Leonwood Bean—"Sell good merchandise at a reasonable profit, treat your customers like human beings, and they will always come back for more."

Do companies practice what they preach when it comes to their professed values? Sometimes no, sometimes yes—it runs the gamut. At one extreme are companies with window-dressing values; the professed values are given lip service by top executives but have little discernible impact on either how company personnel behave or how the company operates. At the other extreme are companies whose executives are committed to grounding company operations on sound values and principled ways of doing

Concepts & Connections 2.2

PATAGONIA, INC.: A VALUES-DRIVEN COMPANY

PATAGONIA'S MISSION STATEMENT

Build the best product, cause no unnecessary harm, use business to inspire, and implement solutions to the environmental crisis.

PATAGONIA'S CORE VALUES

Quality: Pursuit of ever-greater quality in everything we do.

Integrity: Relationships built on integrity and respect.

Environmentalism: Serve as a catalyst for personal and corporate action.

Not Bound by Convention: Our success—and much of the fun—lies in developing innovative ways to do things.

Patagonia, Inc., is an American outdoor clothing and gear company that clearly "walks the talk" with respect to its mission and values. While its mission is relatively vague about the types of products Patagonia offers, it clearly states the foundational "how" and "why" of the company. The four core values individually reinforce the mission in distinct ways, charting a defined path for employees to follow. At the same time, each value is reliant on the others for maximum effect. The values' combined impact on internal operations and

public perception has made Patagonia a strong leader in the outdoor gear world.

While many companies espouse the pursuit of **quality** as part of their strategy, at Patagonia quality must come through honorable practices or not at all. Routinely, the company opts for more expensive materials and labor to maintain internal consistency with the mission. Patagonia learned early on that it could not make good products in bad factories, so it holds its manufacturers accountable through a variety of auditing partnerships and alliances. In this way, the company maintains relationships built on **integrity** and respect. In addition to keeping faith with those who make its products, Patagonia relentlessly pursues integrity in sourcing production inputs. Central to its **environmental** mission and core values, it targets for use sustainable and recyclable materials, ethically procured. Demonstrating leadership in environmentalism, Patagonia established foundations to support ecological causes, even **defying convention** by giving one percent of profits to conservation causes. These are but a few examples of the ways in which Patagonia's core values fortify each other and support the mission.

For Patagonia, quality would not be possible without integrity, unflinching environmentalism, and the company's unconventional approach. Since its founding in 1973 by rock climber Yvon Chouinard, Patagonia has remained remarkably consistent to the spirit of these values. This has endeared the company to legions of loyal customers while leading other businesses in protecting the environment. More than an apparel and gear company, Patagonia inspires everyone it touches to do their best for the planet and each other, in line with its mission and core values.

©George Frey/Getty Images

Note: Developed with Nicholas J. Ziemba.

Sources: Patagonia, Inc., "Corporate Social Responsibility," *The Footprint Chronicles,* 2007, and "Becoming a Responsible Company," www.patagonia.com/us/patagonia.go?assetid=2329 (accessed February 28, 2014).

business. Executives at these companies deliberately seek to ingrain the designated core values into the corporate culture—the core values thus become an integral part of the company's DNA and what makes it tick. At such values-driven companies, executives "walk the talk" and company personnel are held accountable for displaying the stated values. Concepts & Connections 2.2 describes how core values drive the company's mission at Patagonia, a widely known and quite successful outdoor clothing and gear company.

Stage 2: Setting Objectives

 LO2-2 Explain the importance of setting both strategic and financial objectives.

The managerial purpose of setting **objectives** is to convert the strategic vision into specific performance targets. Objectives reflect management's aspirations for company performance in light of the industry's prevailing economic and competitive conditions and the company's internal capabilities. Well-stated objectives are *quantifiable,* or *measurable,* and contain a *deadline for achievement.* Concrete, measurable objectives are managerially valuable for three reasons: (1) They focus organizational attention and align actions throughout the organization, (2) they serve as yardsticks for tracking a company's performance and progress, and (3) they motivate employees to expend greater effort and perform at a high level.

The Imperative of Setting Stretch Objectives

The experiences of countless companies teach that one of the best ways to promote outstanding company performance is for managers to deliberately set performance targets high enough to stretch an organization to perform at its full potential. Challenging company personnel to go all out and deliver "stretch" gains in performance pushes an enterprise to be more inventive and to exhibit more urgency in improving its financial performance and business position. Stretch objectives spur exceptional performance and help build a firewall against contentment with modest gains in organizational performance.

A company exhibits *strategic intent* when it relentlessly pursues an ambitious strategic objective, concentrating the full force of its resources and competitive actions on achieving that objective. Both Google (now Alphabet) and Amazon have had the strategic intent of developing drones, Amazon's for delivery and Google's for both delivery and high-speed Internet delivery from the skies. Elon Musk, CEO of both Tesla Motors and SpaceX, is well-known for his ambitious stretch goals and strategic intent. In 2016, he said that his commercial flight program, SpaceX, should be ready to send people to Mars in 10 years.

What Kinds of Objectives to Set

Two very distinct types of performance yardsticks are required: those relating to financial performance and those relating to strategic performance. **Financial objectives** communicate management's targets for financial performance. Common financial objectives relate to revenue growth, profitability, and return on investment. **Strategic objectives** are related to a company's

CORE CONCEPT

Objectives are an organization's performance targets—the results management wants to achieve.

Stretch objectives set performance targets high enough to stretch an organization to perform at its full potential and deliver the best possible results.

A company exhibits **strategic intent** when it relentlessly pursues an ambitious strategic objective, concentrating the full force of its resources and competitive actions on achieving that objective.

marketing standing and competitive vitality. The importance of attaining financial objectives is intuitive. Without adequate profitability and financial strength, a company's long-term health and ultimate survival is jeopardized. Furthermore, subpar earnings and a weak balance sheet alarm shareholders and creditors and put the jobs of senior executives at risk. However, good financial performance, by itself, is not enough.

A company's financial objectives are really *lagging indicators* that reflect the results of past decisions and organizational activities.[5] The results of past decisions and organizational activities are not reliable indicators of a company's future prospects. Companies that have been poor financial performers are sometimes able to turn things around, and good financial performers on occasion fall upon hard times. Hence, the best and most reliable predictors of a company's success in the marketplace and future financial performance are strategic objectives. Strategic outcomes are *leading indicators* of a company's future financial performance and business prospects. The accomplishment of strategic objectives signals the company is well positioned to sustain or improve its performance. For instance, if a company is achieving ambitious strategic objectives, then there's reason to expect that its *future* financial performance will be better than its current or past performance. If a company begins to lose competitive strength and fails to achieve important strategic objectives, then its ability to maintain its present profitability is highly suspect.

Consequently, utilizing a performance measurement system that strikes a *balance* between financial objectives and strategic objectives is optimal.[6] Just tracking a company's financial performance overlooks the fact that what ultimately enables a company to deliver better financial results is the achievement of strategic objectives that improve its competitiveness and market strength. Representative examples of financial and strategic objectives that companies often include in a **balanced scorecard** approach to measuring their performance are displayed in Table 2.4.[7]

In 2015, nearly 50 percent of global companies used a balanced scorecard approach to measuring strategic and financial performance.[8] Examples of organizations that have adopted a balanced scorecard approach to setting objectives and measuring performance include Siemens AG, Wells Fargo Bank, Ann Taylor Stores, Ford Motor Company, Hilton Hotels, and over 30 colleges and universities.[9] Concepts & Connections 2.3 provides selected strategic and financial objectives of three prominent companies.

> **CORE CONCEPT**
>
> **Financial objectives** relate to the financial performance targets management has established for the organization to achieve.
>
> **Strategic objectives** relate to target outcomes that indicate a company is strengthening its market standing, competitive vitality, and future business prospects.

> **CORE CONCEPT**
>
> The **balanced scorecard** is a widely used method for combining the use of both strategic and financial objectives, tracking their achievement, and giving management a more complete and balanced view of how well an organization is performing.

Short-Term and Long-Term Objectives A company's set of financial and strategic objectives should include both near-term and long-term performance targets. Short-term objectives focus attention on delivering performance improvements in the current period, whereas long-term targets force the organization to consider

Concepts & Connections 2.3

EXAMPLES OF COMPANY OBJECTIVES

UPS

Increase percentage of business-to-consumer package deliveries from 46 percent of domestic deliveries in 2014 to 51 percent of domestic deliveries in 2019; increase intraregional export shipments from 66 percent of exported packages in 2014 to 70 percent of exported packages in 2019; lower U.S. domestic average cost per package by 40 basis points between 2014 and 2019; increase total revenue from $58.2 billion in 2014 to $74.3–$81.6 billion in 2019; increase total operating profit from $4.95 billion in 2014 to $7.62–$9.12 billion by 2019; increase capital expenditures from 4 percent of revenues in 2014 to 5 percent of revenues in 2019.

FIAT CHRYSLER AUTOMOBILES

Localize production of Jeep vehicles in all geographic regions by 2018; revive Alfa Romeo distinctive brand with new models; increase platform sharing between Chrysler and Fiat brands; increase total vehicle sales in the U.S. and NAFTA region from 19.9 million in 2014 to 21.1 million in 2018; increase total vehicle sales in Asia Pacific and China from 27.6 million in 2014 to 33.4 million in 2018; increase total vehicle sales in Europe, Middle East and Africa from 21.4 million in 2014 to 24.2 million in 2018; increase adjusted EBIT from €3.2 billion in 2013 to €8.7 billion–€9.8 billion in 2018; increase adjusted net profit from €0.7 billion in 2013 to €4.7 billion–€5.5 billion in 2018.

YUM! BRANDS (KFC, PIZZA HUT, TACO BELL)

Decrease unit ownership by 70 percent from 2016 to achieve 98 percent franchise ownership by 2018; reduce annual capital expenditures from $973 million in 2015 to $100 million by 2019; achieve 70 percent increase in EPS from $2.20 in 2015 to $3.75 in 2019; add 1,000 new Taco Bell units in the United States by 2020; increase Taco Bell revenues from $7 billion in 2012 to $14 billion in 2022; achieve #2 ranking in quick service chicken in Western Europe, the United Kingdom, and Australia; expand the number of Pizza Hut locations in China by 300 percent by 2020; expand digital ordering options in all quick service concepts; increase the number of restaurant locations in India from 705 in 2013 to 2,000 by 2020.

Source: Information posted on company websites.

TABLE 2.4

The Balanced Scorecard Approach to Performance Measurement

Financial Objectives

- An x percent increase in annual revenues
- Annual increases in earnings per share of x percent
- An x percent return on capital employed (ROCE) or shareholder investment (ROE)
- Bond and credit ratings of x
- Internal cash flows of x to fund new capital investment

Strategic Objectives

- Win an x percent market share
- Achieve customer satisfaction rates of x percent
- Achieve a customer retention rate of x percent
- Acquire x number of new customers
- Introduce x number of new products in the next three years
- Reduce product development times to x months
- Increase percentage of sales coming from new products to x percent
- Improve information systems capabilities to give frontline managers defect information in x minutes
- Improve teamwork by increasing the number of projects involving more than one business unit to x

how actions currently under way will affect the company later. Specifically, long-term objectives stand as a barrier to an undue focus on short-term results by nearsighted management. When trade-offs have to be made between achieving long-run and short-run objectives, long-run objectives should take precedence (unless the achievement of one or more short-run performance targets has unique importance).

The Need for Objectives at All Organizational Levels Objective setting should not stop with the establishment of companywide performance targets. Company objectives need to be broken into performance targets for each of the organization's separate businesses, product lines, functional departments, and individual work units. Employees within various functional areas and operating levels will be guided much better by narrow objectives relating directly to their departmental activities than broad organizational-level goals. Objective setting is thus a top-down process that must extend to the lowest organizational levels. And it means that each organizational unit must take care to set performance targets that support—rather than conflict with or negate—the achievement of companywide strategic and financial objectives.

Stage 3: Crafting a Strategy

LO2-3 Explain why the strategic initiatives taken at various organizational levels must be tightly coordinated to achieve companywide performance targets.

As indicated earlier, the task of stitching a strategy together entails addressing a series of *hows: how* to attract and please customers, *how* to compete against rivals, *how* to position the company in the marketplace and capitalize on attractive opportunities to grow the business, *how* best to respond to changing economic and market conditions, *how* to manage each functional piece of the business, and *how* to achieve the company's performance targets. It also means choosing among the various strategic alternatives and proactively searching for opportunities to do new things or to do existing things in new or better ways.[10]

In choosing among opportunities and addressing the *hows* of strategy, strategists must embrace the risks of uncertainty and the discomfort that naturally accompanies such risks. Bold strategies involve making difficult choices and placing bets on the future. Good strategic planning is not about eliminating risks, but increasing the odds of success. In sorting through the possibilities of what the company should and should not do, managers may conclude some opportunities are unrealistic or not sufficiently attractive to pursue. However, innovative strategy making that results in a powerful customer value proposition or pushes the company into new markets will likely require the development of new resources and capabilities and force the company outside its comfort zone.[11]

Strategy Formulation Involves Managers at All Organizational Levels

In some enterprises, the CEO or owner functions as strategic visionary and chief architect of the strategy, personally deciding what the key elements of the company's strategy will be, although the CEO may seek the advice of key subordinates in fashioning

In most companies, crafting strategy is a *collaborative team effort* that includes managers in various positions and at various organizational levels. Crafting strategy is rarely something only high-level executives do.

an overall strategy and deciding on important strategic moves. However, it is a mistake to view strategy making as a *top* management function—the exclusive province of owner-entrepreneurs, CEOs, high-ranking executives, and board members. The more a company's operations cut across different products, industries, and geographical areas, the more that headquarters executives have little option but to delegate considerable strategy-making authority to down-the-line managers. On-the-scene managers who oversee specific operating units are likely to have a more detailed command of the strategic issues and choices for the particular operating unit under their supervision—knowing the prevailing market and competitive conditions, customer requirements and expectations, and all the other relevant aspects affecting the several strategic options available.

A Company's Strategy-Making Hierarchy

The larger and more diverse the operations of an enterprise, the more points of strategic initiative it will have and the more managers at different organizational levels will have a relevant strategy-making role. In diversified companies, where multiple and sometimes strikingly different businesses have to be managed, crafting a full-fledged strategy involves four distinct types of strategic actions and initiatives, each undertaken at different levels of the organization and partially or wholly crafted by managers at different organizational levels, as shown in Figure 2.2. A company's overall strategy is therefore *a collection of strategic initiatives and actions* devised by managers up and down the whole organizational hierarchy. Ideally, the pieces of a company's strategy up and down the strategy hierarchy should be cohesive and mutually reinforcing, fitting together like a jigsaw puzzle.

As shown in Figure 2.2, **corporate strategy** is orchestrated by the CEO and other senior executives and establishes an overall game plan for managing a *set of businesses* in a diversified, multibusiness company. Corporate strategy addresses the questions of how to capture cross-business synergies, what businesses to hold or divest, which new markets to enter, and how to best enter new markets—by acquisition, by creation of a strategic alliance, or through internal development. Corporate strategy and business diversification are the subject of Chapter 8, where they are discussed in detail.

Business strategy is primarily concerned with building competitive advantage in a single business unit of a diversified company or strengthening the market position of a nondiversified single business company. Business strategy is also the responsibility of the CEO and other senior executives, but key business-unit heads may also be influential, especially in strategic decisions affecting the businesses they lead. *In single-business companies, the corporate and business levels of the strategy-making hierarchy merge into a single level—business strategy—*because the strategy for the entire enterprise involves only one distinct business. So, a single-business company has three levels of strategy: business strategy, functional-area strategies, and operating strategies.

Corporate strategy establishes an overall game plan for managing a *set of businesses* in a diversified, multibusiness company.

Business strategy is primarily concerned with strengthening the company's market position and building competitive advantage in a single-business company or a single business unit of a diversified multibusiness corporation.

Functional-area strategies concern the actions related to particular functions or processes within a business.

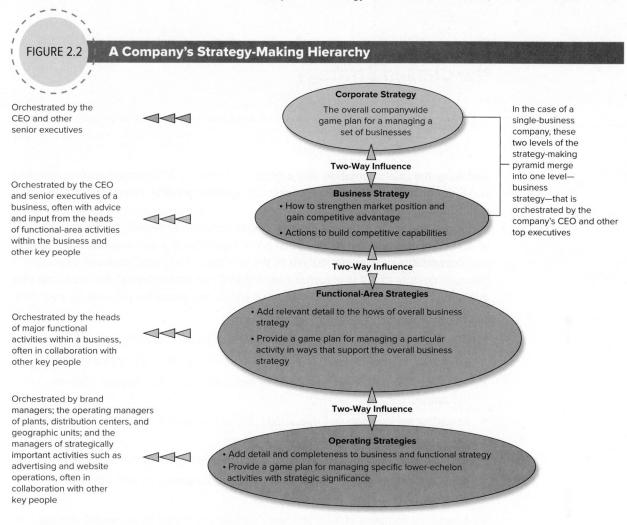

FIGURE 2.2 **A Company's Strategy-Making Hierarchy**

Orchestrated by the CEO and other senior executives

Orchestrated by the CEO and senior executives of a business, often with advice and input from the heads of functional-area activities within the business and other key people

Orchestrated by the heads of major functional activities within a business, often in collaboration with other key people

Orchestrated by brand managers; the operating managers of plants, distribution centers, and geographic units; and the managers of strategically important activities such as advertising and website operations, often in collaboration with other key people

Corporate Strategy
The overall companywide game plan for a managing a set of businesses

Two-Way Influence

Business Strategy
• How to strengthen market position and gain competitive advantage
• Actions to build competitive capabilities

Two-Way Influence

Functional-Area Strategies
• Add relevant detail to the hows of overall business strategy
• Provide a game plan for managing a particular activity in ways that support the overall business strategy

Two-Way Influence

Operating Strategies
• Add detail and completeness to business and functional strategy
• Provide a game plan for managing specific lower-echelon activities with strategic significance

In the case of a single-business company, these two levels of the strategy-making pyramid merge into one level— business strategy—that is orchestrated by the company's CEO and other top executives

A company's product development strategy, for example, represents the managerial game plan for creating new products that are in tune with what buyers are looking for. Lead responsibility for functional strategies within a business is normally delegated to the heads of the respective functions, with the general manager of the business having final approval over functional strategies. For the overall business strategy to have maximum impact, a company's marketing strategy, production strategy, finance strategy, customer service strategy, product development strategy, and human resources strategy should be compatible and mutually reinforcing rather than each serving its own narrower purpose.

Operating strategies concern the relatively narrow strategic initiatives and approaches for managing key operating units (plants, distribution centers, geographic units) and specific operating activities such as materials purchasing or Internet sales. Operating strategies are limited in scope but add further detail to functional-area strategies and the overall business strategy. Lead responsibility for operating strategies is usually delegated to frontline managers, subject to review and approval by higher-ranking managers.

Stage 4: Implementing and Executing the Chosen Strategy

 LO2-4 Recognize what a company must do to achieve operating excellence and to execute its strategy proficiently.

Managing the implementation and execution of strategy is easily the most demanding and time-consuming part of the strategic management process. Good strategy execution entails that managers pay careful attention to how key internal business processes are performed and see to it that employees' efforts are directed toward the accomplishment of desired operational outcomes. The task of implementing and executing the strategy also necessitates an ongoing analysis of the efficiency and effectiveness of a company's internal activities and a managerial awareness of new technological developments that might improve business processes. In most situations, managing the strategy execution process includes the following principal aspects:

- Staffing the organization to provide needed skills and expertise.
- Allocating ample resources to activities critical to good strategy execution.
- Ensuring that policies and procedures facilitate rather than impede effective execution.
- Installing information and operating systems that enable company personnel to perform essential activities.
- Pushing for continuous improvement in how value chain activities are performed.
- Tying rewards and incentives directly to the achievement of performance objectives.
- Creating a company culture and work climate conducive to successful strategy execution.
- Exerting the internal leadership needed to propel implementation forward.

Stage 5: Evaluating Performance and Initiating Corrective Adjustments

The fifth stage of the strategy management process—evaluating and analyzing the external environment and the company's internal situation and performance to identify needed corrective adjustments—is the trigger point for deciding whether to continue or change the company's vision, objectives, strategy, and/or strategy execution methods. So long as the company's direction and strategy seem well matched to industry and competitive conditions and performance targets are being met, company executives may well decide to stay the course. Simply fine-tuning the strategic plan and continuing with efforts to improve strategy execution are sufficient.

But whenever a company encounters disruptive changes in its environment, questions need to be raised about the appropriateness of its direction and strategy.

A company's vision, objectives, strategy, and approach to strategy execution are never final; managing strategy is an ongoing process, not an every-now-and-then task.

If a company experiences a downturn in its market position or persistent shortfalls in performance, then company managers are obligated to ferret out the causes—do they relate to poor strategy, poor strategy execution, or both?—and take timely corrective action. A company's direction, objectives, and strategy have to be revisited any time external or internal conditions warrant.

Also, it is not unusual for a company to find that one or more aspects of its strategy implementation and execution are not going as well as intended. Proficient strategy execution is always the product of much organizational learning. It is achieved unevenly—coming quickly in some areas and proving nettlesome in others. Successful strategy execution entails vigilantly searching for ways to improve and then making corrective adjustments whenever and wherever it is useful to do so.

Corporate Governance: The Role of the Board of Directors in the Strategy Formulation, Strategy Execution Process

Although senior managers have *lead responsibility* for crafting and executing a company's strategy, it is the duty of the board of directors to exercise strong oversight and see that the five tasks of strategic management are done in a manner that benefits shareholders (in the case of investor-owned enterprises) or stakeholders (in the case of not-for-profit organizations). In watching over management's strategy formulation, strategy execution actions, a company's board of directors has four important corporate governance obligations to fulfill:

LO2-5 Identify the role and responsibility of a company's board of directors in overseeing the strategic management process.

1. *Oversee the company's financial accounting and financial reporting practices.* While top management, particularly the company's CEO and CFO (chief financial officer), is primarily responsible for seeing that the company's financial statements accurately report the results of the company's operations, board members have a fiduciary duty to protect shareholders by exercising oversight of the company's financial practices. In addition, corporate boards must ensure that generally acceptable accounting principles (GAAP) are properly used in preparing the company's financial statements and determine whether proper financial controls are in place to prevent fraud and misuse of funds. Virtually all boards of directors monitor the financial reporting activities by appointing an audit committee, always composed entirely of *outside directors* (*inside directors* hold management positions in the company and either directly or indirectly report to the CEO). The members of the audit committee have lead responsibility for overseeing the decisions of the company's financial officers and consulting with both internal and external auditors to ensure that financial reports are accurate and adequate financial controls are in place.

2. *Diligently critique and oversee the company's direction, strategy, and business approaches.* Even though board members have a legal obligation to warrant the

accuracy of the company's financial reports, directors must set aside time to guide management in choosing a strategic direction and to make independent judgments about the validity and wisdom of management's proposed strategic actions. Many boards have found that meeting agendas become consumed by compliance matters and little time is left to discuss matters of strategic importance. The board of directors and management at Philips Electronics hold annual two- to three-day retreats devoted to evaluating the company's long-term direction and various strategic proposals. The company's exit from the semiconductor business and its increased focus on medical technology and home health care resulted from management–board discussions during such retreats.[12]

3. *Evaluate the caliber of senior executives' strategy formulation and strategy execution skills.* The board is always responsible for determining whether the current CEO is doing a good job of strategic leadership and whether senior management is actively creating a pool of potential successors to the CEO and other top executives.[13] Evaluation of senior executives' strategy formulation and strategy execution skills is enhanced when outside directors go into the field to personally evaluate how well the strategy is being executed. Independent board members at GE visit operating executives at each major business unit once per year to assess the company's talent pool and stay abreast of emerging strategic and operating issues affecting the company's divisions. Home Depot board members visit a store once per quarter to determine the health of the company's operations.[14]

4. *Institute a compensation plan for top executives that rewards them for actions and results that serve shareholder interests.* A basic principle of corporate governance is that the owners of a corporation delegate operating authority and managerial control to top management in return for compensation. In their role as an *agent* of shareholders, top executives have a clear and unequivocal duty to make decisions and operate the company in accord with shareholder interests (but this does not mean disregarding the interests of other stakeholders, particularly those of employees, with whom they also have an agency relationship). Most boards of directors have a compensation committee, composed entirely of directors from outside the company, to develop a salary and incentive compensation plan that rewards senior executives for boosting the company's *long-term performance* and growing the economic value of the enterprise on behalf of shareholders; the compensation committee's recommendations are presented to the full board for approval.

But during the past 10 to 15 years, many boards of directors have done a poor job of ensuring that executive salary increases, bonuses, and stock option awards are tied tightly to performance measures that are truly in the long-term interests of shareholders. Rather, compensation packages at many companies have rewarded executives for *short-term performance* improvements—most notably, achieving quarterly and annual earnings targets and boosting the stock price by specified percentages. This has had the perverse effect of causing company managers to become preoccupied with actions to improve a company's near-term performance, even if excessively risky and damaging to long-term company performance. As a consequence, the need to overhaul and reform executive compensation has become a hot topic in both public circles and corporate boardrooms. Concepts & Connections 2.4 discusses how weak governance at Volkswagen contributed to the 2015 emissions cheating scandal, which cost the company billions of dollars and the trust of its stakeholders.

Concepts & Connections 2.4

CORPORATE GOVERNANCE FAILURES AT VOLKSWAGEN

In 2015, Volkswagen admitted to installing "defeat devices" on at least 11 million vehicles with diesel engines. These devices enabled the cars to pass emission tests, even though the engines actually emitted pollutants up to 40 times above what is allowed in the United States. Current estimates are that it will cost the company at least €7 billion to cover the cost of repairs and lawsuits. Although management must have been involved in approving the use of cheating devices, the Volkswagen supervisory board has been unwilling to accept any responsibility. Some board members even questioned whether it was the board's responsibility to be aware of such problems, stating "matters of technical expertise were not for us" and "the scandal had nothing, not one iota, to do with the advisory board." Yet governing boards do have a responsibility to be well informed, to provide oversight, and to become involved in key decisions and actions. So what caused this corporate governance failure? Why is this the third time in the past 20 years that Volkswagen has been embroiled in scandal?

The key feature of Volkswagen's board that appears to have led to these issues is a lack of independent directors. However, before explaining this in more detail it is important to understand the German governance model. German corporations operate two-tier governance structures, with a management board and a separate supervisory board that does not contain any current executives. In addition, German law requires large companies to have at least 50 percent supervisory board representation from workers. This structure is meant to provide more oversight by independent board members and greater involvement by a wider set of stakeholders.

In Volkswagen's case, these objectives have been effectively circumvented. Although Volkswagen's supervisory board does not include any current management, the chairmanship appears to be a revolving door of former senior executives. Ferdinand Piëch, the chair during the scandal, was CEO for nine years prior to becoming chair in 2002. Martin Winterkorn, the recently ousted CEO, was expected to become supervisory board chair prior to the scandal. The company continues to elevate management to the supervisory board even though they have presided over past scandals. Hans Dieter Poetsch, the newly appointed chair, was part of the management team that did not inform the supervisory board of the EPA investigation for two weeks.

VW also has a unique ownership structure where a single family, Porsche, controls more than 50 percent of voting shares. Piëch, a family member and chair until 2015, forced out CEOs and installed unqualified family members on the board, such as his former nanny and current wife. He also pushed out independent-minded board members, such as Gerhard Cromme, author of Germany's corporate governance code. The company has lost numerous independent directors over the past 10 years, leaving it with only one non-shareholder, non-labor representative. Although Piëch has now been removed, it is unclear that Volkswagen's board has solved the underlying problem. Shareholders have seen billions of dollars wiped away and the Volkswagen brand tarnished. As long as the board continues to lack independent directors, change will likely be slow.

Note: Developed with Jacob M. Crandall.

Sources: "Piëch under Fire," *The Economist,* December 8, 2005; Chris Bryant and Richard Milne, "Boardroom Politics at Heart of VW Scandal," *Financial Times,* October 4, 2015; Andreas Cremer and Jan Schwartz, "Volkswagen Mired in Crisis as Board Members Criticize Piech," Reuters, April 24, 2015; Richard Milne, "Volkswagen: System Failure," *Financial Times,* November 4, 2015.

R&P: ©AR Pictures/Shutterstock

Every corporation should have a strong, independent board of directors that (1) is well informed about the company's performance, (2) guides and judges the CEO and other top executives, (3) has the courage to curb management actions it believes are inappropriate or unduly risky, (4) certifies to shareholders that the CEO is doing what the board expects, (5) provides insight and advice to management, and (6) is intensely involved in debating the pros and cons of key decisions and actions.[15] Boards of directors that lack the backbone to challenge a strong-willed or "imperial" CEO or that rubber-stamp most anything the CEO recommends without probing inquiry and debate abandon their duty to represent and protect shareholder interests.

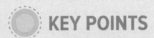

KEY POINTS

The strategic management process consists of five interrelated and integrated stages:

1. Developing a *strategic vision* of the company's future, a *mission statement* that defines the company's current purpose, and a set of *core values* to guide the pursuit of the vision and mission. This stage of strategy making provides direction for the company, motivates and inspires company personnel, aligns and guides actions throughout the organization, and communicates to stakeholders management's aspirations for the company's future.

2. *Setting objectives* and using the targeted results as yardsticks for measuring the company's performance. Objectives need to spell out *how much* of *what kind* of performance *by when*. A *balanced scorecard* approach for measuring company performance entails setting both *financial objectives and strategic objectives. Stretch objectives* spur exceptional performance and help build a firewall against complacency and mediocre performance. A company exhibits *strategic intent* when it relentlessly pursues an ambitious strategic objective, concentrating the full force of its resources and competitive actions on achieving that objective.

3. *Crafting a strategy to achieve the objectives* and move the company along the strategic course that management has charted. The total strategy that emerges is really a collection of strategic actions and business approaches initiated partly by senior company executives, partly by the heads of major business divisions, partly by functional-area managers, and partly by operating managers on the front lines. A single business enterprise has three levels of strategy—business strategy for the company as a whole, functional-area strategies for each main area within the business, and operating strategies undertaken by lower-echelon managers. In diversified, multibusiness companies, the strategy-making task involves four distinct types or levels of strategy: corporate strategy for the company as a whole, business strategy (one for each business the company has diversified into), functional-area strategies within each business, and operating strategies. Typically, the strategy-making task is more top-down than bottom-up, with higher-level strategies serving as the guide for developing lower-level strategies.

4. *Implementing and executing the chosen strategy efficiently and effectively.* Managing the implementation and execution of strategy is an operations-oriented, make-things-happen activity aimed at shaping the performance of core business activities in a strategy supportive manner. Management's handling of the strategy implementation process can be considered successful if things go smoothly enough that the company meets or beats its strategic and financial performance targets and shows good progress in achieving management's strategic vision.

5. *Evaluating and analyzing the external environment and the company's internal situation and performance to identify corrective adjustments* in vision, objectives, strategy, or execution. This stage of the strategy management process is the trigger point for deciding whether to

continue or change the company's vision, objectives, strategy, and/or strategy execution methods.

The sum of a company's strategic vision, objectives, and strategy constitutes a *strategic plan.* Boards of directors have a duty to shareholders to play a vigilant role in overseeing management's handling of a company's strategy formulation, strategy execution process. A company's board is obligated to (1) ensure that the company issues accurate financial reports and has adequate financial controls, (2) critically appraise and ultimately approve strategic action plans, (3) evaluate the strategic leadership skills of the CEO, and (4) institute a compensation plan for top executives that rewards them for actions and results that serve stakeholder interests, most especially those of shareholders.

ASSURANCE OF LEARNING EXERCISES

1. Using the information in Tables 2.2 and 2.3, critique the adequacy and merit of the following vision statements, listing effective elements and shortcomings. Rank the vision statements from best to worst once you complete your evaluation.

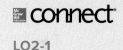

LO2-1

VISION STATEMENT	Effective Elements	Shortcomings

American Express

We work hard every day to make American Express the world's most respected service brand.

Hilton Hotels Corporation

Our vision is to be the first choice of the world's travelers. Hilton intends to build on the rich heritage and strength of our brands by:

- Consistently delighting our customers
- Investing in our team members
- Delivering innovative products and services
- Continuously improving performance
- Increasing shareholder value
- Creating a culture of pride
- Strengthening the loyalty of our constituents

MasterCard

A world beyond cash.

BASF

We are "The Chemical Company" successfully operating in all major markets.

- Our customers view BASF as their partner of choice.
- Our innovative products, intelligent solutions and services make us the most competent worldwide supplier in the chemical industry.
- We generate a high return on assets.
- We strive for sustainable development.
- We welcome change as an opportunity.
- We, the employees of BASF, together ensure our success.

Source: Company websites and annual reports.

2. Go to the company investor relations websites for Starbucks (investor.starbucks.com), Pfizer (www.pfizer.com/investors), and Salesforce (investor.salesforce.com) to find examples of strategic and financial objectives. List four objectives for each company, and indicate which of these are strategic and which are financial.

LO2-2

3. Boeing has been recognized by *Forbes* and other business publications as one of the world's best managed companies. The company discusses how its people and

LO2-3

organizational units bring to bear the "best of Boeing" to its customers in 150 countries at www.boeing.com/company. Prepare a one- to two-page report that explains how the company has become a leader in commercial aviation through tight coordination of strategic initiatives at various organizational levels and functional areas.

LO2-4   4.   Go to the investor relations website for Walmart Stores, Inc., (http://investors.walmartstores.com) and review past presentations it has made during various investor conferences by clicking on the Events option in the navigation bar. Prepare a one- to two-page report that outlines what Walmart has said to investors about its approach to strategy execution. Specifically, what has management discussed concerning staffing, resource allocation, policies and procedures, information and operating systems, continuous improvement, rewards and incentives, corporate culture, and internal leadership at the company?

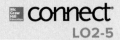
LO2-5   5.   Based on the information provided in Concepts & Connections 2.4, describe the ways in which Volkswagen did not fulfill the requirements of effective corporate governance. In what ways did the board of directors sidestep its obligations to protect shareholder interests? How could Volkswagen better select its board of directors to avoid mistakes such as the emissions scandal in 2015?

EXERCISES FOR SIMULATION PARTICIPANTS

LO2-1   1.   Meet with your co-managers and prepare a strategic vision statement for your company. It should be at least one sentence long and no longer than a brief paragraph. When you are finished, check to see if your vision statement meets the conditions for an effectively worded strategic vision set forth in Table 2.2 and avoids the shortcomings set forth in Table 2.3. If not, then revise it accordingly. What would be a good slogan that captures the essence of your strategic vision and that could be used to help communicate the vision to company personnel, shareholders, and other stakeholders?

LO2-2   2.   What are your company's financial objectives? What are your company's strategic objectives?

LO2-3   3.   What are the three or four key elements of your company's strategy?

ENDNOTES

1. Gordon Shaw, Robert Brown, and Philip Bromiley, "Strategic Stories: How 3M Is Rewriting Business Planning," *Harvard Business Review* 76, no. 3 (May–June 1998); David J. Collins and Michael G. Rukstad, "Can You Say What Your Strategy Is?" *Harvard Business Review* 86, no. 4 (April 2008).

2. Hugh Davidson, *The Committed Enterprise: How to Make Vision and Values Work* (Oxford: Butterworth Heinemann, 2002); W. Chan Kim and Renée Mauborgne, "Charting Your Company's Future," *Harvard Business Review* 80, no. 6 (June 2002); James C. Collins and Jerry I. Porras, "Building Your Company's Vision," *Harvard Business Review* 74, no. 5 (September–October 1996);

Jim Collins and Jerry Porras, *Built to Last: Successful Habits of Visionary Companies* (New York: HarperCollins, 1994); Michel Robert, *Strategy Pure and Simple II: How Winning Companies Dominate Their Competitors* (New York: McGraw-Hill, 1998).

3. Hugh Davidson, *The Committed Enterprise* (Oxford: Butterworth Heinemann, 2002).

4. Ibid.

5. Robert S. Kaplan and David P. Norton, *The Strategy-Focused Organization* (Boston: Harvard Business School Press, 2001).

6. Ibid. Also, see Robert S. Kaplan and David P. Norton, *The Balanced

Scorecard: Translating Strategy into Action (Boston: Harvard Business School Press, 1996); Kevin B. Hendricks, Larry Menor, and Christine Wiedman, "The Balanced Scorecard: To Adopt or Not to Adopt," *Ivey Business Journal* 69, no. 2 (November–December 2004); Sandy Richardson, "The Key Elements of Balanced Scorecard Success," *Ivey Business Journal* 69, no. 2 (November–December 2004).

7. Kaplan and Norton, *The Balanced Scorecard: Translating Strategy into Action,* pp. 25–29. Kaplan and Norton classify strategic objectives under the categories of customer-related, business processes, and learning and growth. In practice, companies using the balanced scorecard

may choose categories of strategic objectives that best reflect the organization's value-creating activities and processes.

8. Information posted on the website of Bain and Company, www.bain.com (accessed May 27, 2011).

9. Information posted on the website of Balanced Scorecard Institute (accessed May 27, 2011).

10. Henry Mintzberg, Bruce Ahlstrand, and Joseph Lampel, *Strategy Safari: A Guided Tour Through the Wilds of Strategic Management* (New York: Free Press, 1998); Bruce Barringer and Allen C. Bluedorn, "The Relationship Between Corporate Entrepreneurship and Strategic Management," *Strategic Management Journal* 20 (1999); Jeffrey G. Covin and Morgan P. Miles, "Corporate Entrepreneurship and the Pursuit of Competitive Advantage," *Entrepreneurship: Theory and Practice* 23, no. 3 (Spring 1999); David A. Garvin and Lynne C. Levesque, "Meeting the Challenge of Corporate Entrepreneurship," *Harvard Business Review* 84, no. 10 (October 2006).

11. Roger L. Martin, "The Big Lie of Strategic Planning," *Harvard Business Review* 92, no. 1/2 (January–February 2014), pp. 78–84.

12. Jay W. Lorsch and Robert C. Clark, "Leading from the Boardroom," *Harvard Business Review* 86, no. 4 (April 2008).

13. Ibid., p. 110.

14. Stephen P. Kaufman, "Evaluating the CEO," *Harvard Business Review* 86, no. 10 (October 2008).

15. David A. Nadler, "Building Better Boards," *Harvard Business Review* 82, no. 5 (May 2004); Cynthia A. Montgomery and Rhonda Kaufman, "The Board's Missing Link," *Harvard Business Review* 81, no. 3 (March 2003); John Carver, "What Continues to Be Wrong with Corporate Governance and How to Fix It," *Ivey Business Journal* 68, no. 1 (September/October 2003); Gordon Donaldson, "A New Tool for Boards: The Strategic Audit," *Harvard Business Review* 73, no. 4 (July–August 1995).

chapter

3

Evaluating a Company's External Environment

LEARNING OBJECTIVES

After reading this chapter, you should be able to:

LO3-1   Identify factors in a company's broad macro-environment that may have strategic significance.

LO3-2   Recognize the factors that cause competition in an industry to be fierce, more or less normal, or relatively weak.

LO3-3   Map the market positions of key groups of industry rivals.

LO3-4   Determine whether an industry's outlook presents a company with sufficiently attractive opportunities for growth and profitability.

In Chapter 2, we learned that the strategy formulation, strategy execution process begins with an appraisal of the company's present situation. The company's situation includes two facets: (1) its external environment—most notably, the competitive conditions in the industry in which the company operates; and (2) its internal environment—particularly the company's resources and organizational capabilities.

Charting a company's long-term direction, conceiving its customer value proposition, setting objectives, or crafting a strategy without first gaining an understanding of the company's external and internal environments hamstrings attempts to build competitive advantage and boost company performance. Indeed, the first test of a winning strategy inquires, *"How well does the strategy fit the company's situation?"*

This chapter presents the concepts and analytical tools for zeroing in on a single-business company's external environment. Attention centers on the competitive arena in which the company operates, the drivers of market change, the market positions of rival companies, and the factors that determine competitive success. Chapter 4 explores the methods of evaluating a company's internal circumstances and competitiveness.

Assessing the Company's Industry and Competitive Environment

Thinking strategically about a company's industry and competitive environment entails using some well-validated concepts and analytical tools to get clear answers to seven questions:

1. Do macro-environmental factors and industry characteristics offer sellers opportunities for growth and attractive profits?
2. What kinds of competitive forces are industry members facing, and how strong is each force?
3. What forces are driving industry change, and what impact will these changes have on competitive intensity and industry profitability?
4. What market positions do industry rivals occupy—who is strongly positioned and who is not?
5. What strategic moves are rivals likely to make next?
6. What are the key factors of competitive success?
7. Does the industry outlook offer good prospects for profitability?

Analysis-based answers to these questions are prerequisites for a strategy offering good fit with the external situation. The remainder of this chapter is devoted to describing the methods of obtaining solid answers to these seven questions.

Question 1: What Are the Strategically Relevant Components of the Macro-Environment?

LO3-1 Identify factors in a company's broad macro-environment that may have strategic significance.

A company's external environment includes the immediate industry and competitive environment and broader macro-environmental factors such as general economic conditions, societal values and cultural norms, political factors, the legal and regulatory environment, ecological considerations, and technological factors. These two levels of a company's external environment—the broad outer ring macro-environment and immediate inner ring industry and competitive environment—are illustrated in Figure 3.1. Strictly speaking, the **macro-environment** encompasses all of the *relevant factors* making up the broad environmental context in which a company operates; by *relevant,* we mean the factors are important enough that they should shape management's decisions regarding the company's long-term direction, objectives, strategy, and business model. The relevance of macro-environmental factors can be evaluated using **PESTEL analysis,** an acronym for the six principal components of the macro-environment: political factors, economic conditions in the firm's general environment, sociocultural forces, technological factors, environmental forces, and legal/regulatory factors. Table 3.1 provides a description of each of the six PESTEL components of the macro-environment.

The impact of outer ring macro-environmental factors on a company's choice of strategy can be big or small. But even if the factors of the macro-environment change slowly or are likely to have a low impact on the company's business situation, they still merit a watchful eye. Changes in sociocultural forces and technological factors have begun to have strategy-shaping effects on companies competing in industries ranging from news and entertainment to taxi services. As company managers scan the external environment, they must be alert for potentially important outer ring developments,

FIGURE 3.1 **The Components of a Company's External Environment**

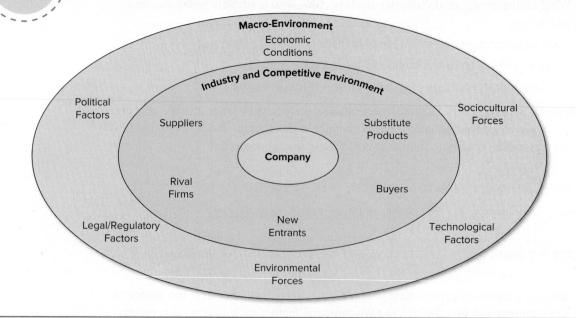

TABLE 3.1

The Six Components of the Macro-Environment Included in a PESTEL Analysis

Component	Description
Political factors	These factors include political policies and processes, including the extent to which a government intervenes in the economy. They include such matters as tax policy, fiscal policy, tariffs, the political climate, and the strength of institutions such as the federal banking system. Some political factors, such as bailouts, are industry-specific. Others, such as energy policy, affect certain types of industries (energy producers and heavy users of energy) more than others.
Economic conditions	Economic conditions include the general economic climate and specific factors such as interest rates, exchange rates, the inflation rate, the unemployment rate, the rate of economic growth, trade deficits or surpluses, savings rates, and per capita domestic product. Economic factors also include conditions in the markets for stocks and bonds, which can affect consumer confidence and discretionary income. Some industries, such as construction, are particularly vulnerable to economic downturns but are positively affected by factors such as low interest rates. Others, such as discount retailing, may benefit when general economic conditions weaken, as consumers become more price-conscious. Economic characteristics of the industry such as market size and growth rate are also important to evaluate when assessing an industry's prospects for growth and attractive profits.
Sociocultural forces	Sociocultural forces include the societal values, attitudes, cultural factors, and lifestyles that impact businesses, as well as demographic factors such as the population size, growth rate, and age distribution. Sociocultural forces vary by locale and change over time. An example is the trend toward healthier lifestyles, which can shift spending toward exercise equipment and health clubs and away from alcohol and snack foods. Population demographics can have large implications for industries such as health care, where costs and service needs vary with demographic factors such as age and income distribution.
Technological factors	Technological factors include the pace of technological change and technical developments that have the potential for wide-ranging effects on society, such as genetic engineering and nanotechnology. They include institutions involved in creating knowledge and controlling the use of technology, such as R&D consortia, university-sponsored technology incubators, patent and copyright laws, and government control over the Internet. Technological change can encourage the birth of new industries, such as those based on nanotechnology, and disrupt others, such as the recording industry.
Environmental forces	These include ecological and environmental forces such as weather, climate, climate change, and associated factors such as water shortages. These factors can directly impact industries such as insurance, farming, energy production, and tourism. They may have an indirect but substantial effect on other industries such as transportation and utilities.
Legal and regulatory factors	These factors include the regulations and laws with which companies must comply such as consumer laws, labor laws, antitrust laws, and occupational health and safety regulations. Some factors, such as banking deregulation, are industry-specific. Others, such as minimum wage legislation, affect certain types of industries (low-wage, labor-intensive industries) more than others.

assess their impact and influence, and adapt the company's direction and strategy as needed.

However, the factors and forces in a company's external environment that have the *biggest* strategy-shaping impact typically pertain to the company's immediate inner ring industry and competitive environment—the competitive pressures brought about by the actions of rival firms, the competitive effects of buyer behavior, supplier-related competitive considerations, the impact of new entrants to the industry, and availability of acceptable or superior substitutes for a company's products or services. The inner ring industry and competitive environment is fully explored in Question 2 of this chapter using Porter's Five Forces Model of Competition.

Question 2: How Strong Are the Industry's Competitive Forces?

LO3-2 Recognize the factors that cause competition in an industry to be fierce, more or less normal, or relatively weak.

After an understanding of the industry's general economic characteristics is gained, industry and competitive analysis should focus on the competitive dynamics of the industry. The nature and subtleties of competitive forces are never the same from one industry to another and must be wholly understood to accurately assess the company's current situation. Far and away the most powerful and widely used tool for assessing the strength of the industry's competitive forces is the *five forces model of competition.*[1] This model, as depicted in Figure 3.2, holds that competitive forces affecting industry attractiveness go beyond rivalry among competing sellers and

FIGURE 3.2   **The Five Forces Model of Competition**

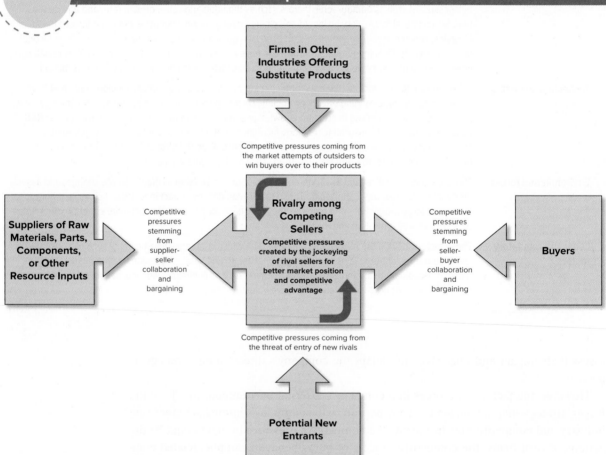

Sources: Based on Michael E. Porter, "How Competitive Forces Shape Strategy," *Harvard Business Review* 57, no. 2 (March–April 1979), pp. 137–45; and Michael E. Porter, "The Five Competitive Forces That Shape Strategy," *Harvard Business Review* 86, no. 1 (January 2008), pp. 80–86.

include pressures stemming from four coexisting sources. The five competitive forces affecting industry attractiveness are listed.

1. Competitive pressures stemming from *buyer* bargaining power.

2. Competitive pressures coming from companies in other industries to win buyers over to *substitute products.*

3. Competitive pressures stemming from *supplier* bargaining power.

4. Competitive pressures associated with the threat of *new entrants* into the market.

5. Competitive pressures associated with *rivalry among competing sellers* to attract customers. This is usually the strongest of the five competitive forces.

The Competitive Force of Buyer Bargaining Power

Whether seller-buyer relationships represent a minor or significant competitive force depends on (1) whether some or many buyers have sufficient bargaining leverage to obtain price concessions and other favorable terms, and (2) the extent to which buyers are price sensitive. Buyers with strong bargaining power can limit industry profitability by demanding price concessions, better payment terms, or additional features and services that increase industry members' costs. Buyer price sensitivity limits the profit potential of industry members by restricting the ability of sellers to raise prices without losing volume or unit sales.

The leverage that buyers have in negotiating favorable terms of the sale can range from weak to strong. Individual consumers, for example, rarely have much bargaining power in negotiating price concessions or other favorable terms with sellers. The primary exceptions involve situations in which price haggling is customary, such as the purchase of new and used motor vehicles, homes, and other big-ticket items such as jewelry and pleasure boats. For most consumer goods and services, individual buyers have no bargaining leverage—their option is to pay the seller's posted price, delay their purchase until prices and terms improve, or take their business elsewhere.

In contrast, large retail chains such as Walmart, Best Buy, Staples, and Lowe's typically have considerable negotiating leverage in purchasing products from manufacturers because retailers usually stock just two or three competing brands of a product and rarely carry all competing brands. In addition, the strong bargaining power of major supermarket chains such as Kroger, Publix, and Albertsons allows them to demand promotional allowances and lump-sum payments (called slotting fees) from food products manufacturers in return for stocking certain brands or putting them in the best shelf locations. Motor vehicle manufacturers have strong bargaining power in negotiating to buy original equipment tires from Goodyear, Michelin, Bridgestone, Continental, and Pirelli not only because they buy in large quantities but also because tire makers have judged original equipment tires to be important contributors to brand awareness and brand loyalty.

Even if buyers do not purchase in large quantities or offer a seller important market exposure or prestige, they gain a degree of bargaining leverage in the following circumstances:

• *If buyers' costs of switching to competing brands or substitutes are relatively low.* When the products of rival sellers are virtually identical, it is relatively easy for buyers to switch from seller to seller at little or no cost. The potential for buyers to easily switch from one seller to another encourages sellers to make concessions to win or retain a buyer's business.

- *If the number of buyers is small or if a customer is particularly important to a seller.* The smaller the number of buyers, the less easy it is for sellers to find alternative buyers when a customer is lost to a competitor. The prospect of losing a customer who is not easily replaced often makes a seller more willing to grant concessions of one kind or another.

- *If buyer demand is weak.* Weak or declining demand creates a "buyers' market"; conversely, strong or rapidly growing demand creates a "sellers' market" and shifts bargaining power to sellers.

- *If buyers are well informed about sellers' products, prices, and costs.* The more information buyers have, the better bargaining position they are in. The mushrooming availability of product information on the Internet (and is readily available on smartphones) has given added bargaining power to consumers.

- *If buyers pose a credible threat of integrating backward into the business of sellers.* Anheuser-Busch InBev has integrated backward into metal can manufacturing to gain bargaining power in obtaining the balance of its can requirements from otherwise powerful metal can manufacturers.

Figure 3.3 summarizes factors causing buyer bargaining power to be strong or weak. It is important to recognize that *not all buyers of an industry's product have equal degrees of bargaining power with sellers,* and some may be less sensitive than others to price, quality, or service differences. For example, apparel manufacturers confront significant bargaining power when selling to big retailers such as Macy's, T. J. Maxx, or Kohl's, but they can command much better prices selling to small owner-managed apparel boutiques.

FIGURE 3.3 **Factors Affecting the Strength of Buyer Bargaining Power**

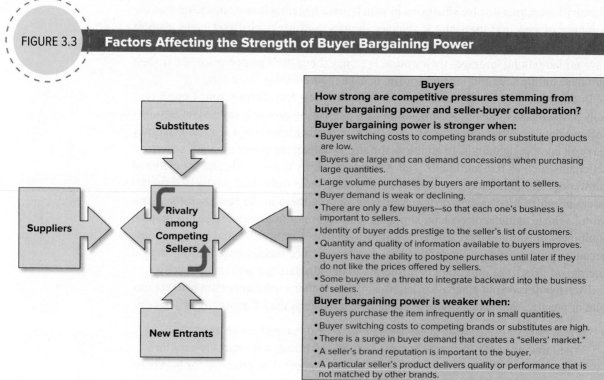

Buyers
How strong are competitive pressures stemming from buyer bargaining power and seller-buyer collaboration?

Buyer bargaining power is stronger when:
- Buyer switching costs to competing brands or substitute products are low.
- Buyers are large and can demand concessions when purchasing large quantities.
- Large volume purchases by buyers are important to sellers.
- Buyer demand is weak or declining.
- There are only a few buyers—so that each one's business is important to sellers.
- Identity of buyer adds prestige to the seller's list of customers.
- Quantity and quality of information available to buyers improves.
- Buyers have the ability to postpone purchases until later if they do not like the prices offered by sellers.
- Some buyers are a threat to integrate backward into the business of sellers.

Buyer bargaining power is weaker when:
- Buyers purchase the item infrequently or in small quantities.
- Buyer switching costs to competing brands or substitutes are high.
- There is a surge in buyer demand that creates a "sellers' market."
- A seller's brand reputation is important to the buyer.
- A particular seller's product delivers quality or performance that is not matched by other brands.

Substitutes

Suppliers

Rivalry among Competing Sellers

New Entrants

The Competitive Force of Substitute Products

Companies in one industry are vulnerable to competitive pressure from the actions of companies in another industry whenever buyers view the products of the two industries as good substitutes. For instance, the producers of sugar experience competitive pressures from the sales and marketing efforts of the makers of Splenda, Truvia, and Sweet'N Low. Similarly, cable television networks and providers are finding it more difficult to maintain their relevance to subscribers who find greater value in streaming devices and services.

Just how strong the competitive pressures are from the sellers of substitute products depends on three factors:

1. *Whether substitutes are readily available and attractively priced.* The presence of readily available and attractively priced substitutes creates competitive pressure by placing a ceiling on the prices industry members can charge. When substitutes are cheaper than an industry's product, industry members come under heavy competitive pressure to reduce their prices and find ways to absorb the price cuts with cost reductions.

2. *Whether buyers view the substitutes as comparable or better in terms of quality, performance, and other relevant attributes.* Customers are prone to compare performance and other attributes as well as price. For example, consumers have found smartphones to be a superior substitute to digital cameras because of constant availability of smartphones and superior ease of use in managing images.

3. *Whether the costs that buyers incur in switching to the substitutes are high or low.* High switching costs deter switching to substitutes, whereas low switching costs make it easier for the sellers of attractive substitutes to lure buyers to their products. Typical switching costs include the inconvenience of switching to a substitute, the costs of additional equipment, the psychological costs of severing old supplier relationships, and employee retraining costs.

Figure 3.4 summarizes the conditions that determine whether the competitive pressures from substitute products are strong, moderate, or weak. As a rule, the lower the price of substitutes, the higher their quality and performance, and the lower the user's switching costs, the more intense the competitive pressures posed by substitute products.

The Competitive Force of Supplier Bargaining Power

Whether the suppliers of industry members represent a weak or strong competitive force depends on the degree to which suppliers have sufficient *bargaining power* to influence the terms and conditions of supply in their favor. Suppliers with strong bargaining power can erode industry profitability by charging industry members higher prices, passing costs on to them, and limiting their opportunities to find better deals. For instance, Microsoft and Intel, both of which supply PC makers with essential components, have been known to use their dominant market status not only to charge PC makers premium prices but also to leverage PC makers in other ways. The bargaining power possessed by Microsoft and Intel when negotiating with customers is so great that both companies have faced antitrust charges on numerous occasions. Before a legal agreement ending the practice, Microsoft pressured PC makers to load only Microsoft

FIGURE 3.4   **Factors Affecting Competition from Substitute Products**

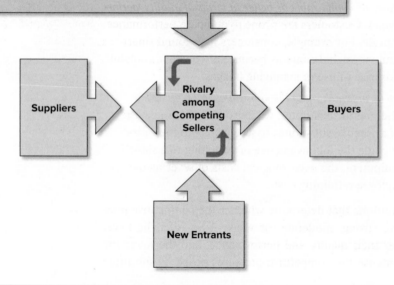

Firms in Other Industries Offering Substitute Products

How strong are competitive pressures coming from substitute products from outside the industry?

Competitive pressures from substitutes are stronger when:
- Good substitutes are readily available or new ones are emerging.
- Substitutes are attractively priced.
- Substitutes have comparable or better performance features.
- End users have low costs in switching to substitutes.
- End users grow more comfortable with using substitutes.

Competitive pressures from substitutes are weaker when:
- Good substitutes are not readily available or don't exist.
- Substitutes are higher priced relative to the performance they deliver.
- End users have high costs in switching to substitutes.

Signs That Competition from Substitutes Is Strong
- Sales of substitutes are growing faster than sales of the industry being analyzed (an indication that the sellers of substitutes are drawing customers away from the industry in question).
- Producers of substitutes are moving to add new capacity.
- Profits of the producers of substitutes are on the rise.

Suppliers   **Rivalry among Competing Sellers**   Buyers

New Entrants

products on the PCs they shipped. Intel has also defended against antitrust charges resulting from its bargaining strength but continues to give PC makers that use the biggest percentages of Intel chips in their PC models top priority in filling orders for newly introduced Intel chips. Being on Intel's list of preferred customers helps a PC maker get an early allocation of Intel's latest chips and thus allows a PC maker to get new models to market ahead of rivals.

The factors that determine whether any of the industry suppliers are in a position to exert substantial bargaining power or leverage are fairly clear-cut:

- *If the item being supplied is a commodity that is readily available from many suppliers.* Suppliers have little or no bargaining power or leverage whenever industry members have the ability to source from any of several alternative and eager suppliers.

- *The ability of industry members to switch their purchases from one supplier to another or to switch to attractive substitutes.* High switching costs increase supplier bargaining power, whereas low switching costs and the ready availability of good substitute inputs weaken supplier bargaining power.

- *If certain inputs are in short supply.* Suppliers of items in short supply have some degree of pricing power.

- *If certain suppliers provide a differentiated input that enhances the performance, quality, or image of the industry's product.* The greater the ability of a particular input to enhance a product's performance, quality, or image, the more bargaining leverage its suppliers are likely to possess.

- *Whether certain suppliers provide equipment or services that deliver cost savings to industry members in conducting their operations.* Suppliers who provide cost-saving equipment or services are likely to possess some degree of bargaining leverage.

- *The fraction of the costs of the industry's product accounted for by the cost of a particular input.* The bigger the cost of a specific part or component, the more opportunity for competition in the marketplace to be affected by the actions of suppliers to raise or lower their prices.

- *If industry members are major customers of suppliers.* As a rule, suppliers have less bargaining leverage when their sales to members of this one industry constitute a big percentage of their total sales. In such cases, the well-being of suppliers is closely tied to the well-being of their major customers.

- *Whether it makes good economic sense for industry members to vertically integrate backward.* The make-or-buy decision generally boils down to whether suppliers are able to supply a particular component at a lower cost than industry members could achieve if they were to integrate backward.

Figure 3.5 summarizes the conditions that tend to make supplier bargaining power strong or weak.

The Competitive Force of Potential New Entrants

New entrants into an industry place additional competitive pressure on existing firms since they are likely to compete fiercely to establish market share and will add to the industry's production capacity. But even the *threat* of new entry can be an important competitive force. This is because credible *threat* of entry often prompts industry members to lower their prices and initiate defensive actions in an attempt to deter new entrants. Just how serious the threat of entry is in a particular market depends on two classes of factors: (1) *the expected reaction of incumbent firms to new entry* and (2) *barriers to entry.* The threat of entry is low in industries where incumbent firms are likely to retaliate against new entrants with sharp price discounting and other moves designed to make entry unprofitable. The threat of entry is also low when entry barriers are high.

The most widely encountered barriers that entry candidates must hurdle include:[2]

- *The presence of sizable economies of scale in production or other areas of operation.* When incumbent companies enjoy cost advantages associated with large-scale operations, outsiders must either enter on a large scale (a costly and perhaps risky move) or accept a cost disadvantage and consequently lower profitability.

FIGURE 3.5   **Factors Affecting the Strength of Supplier Bargaining Power**

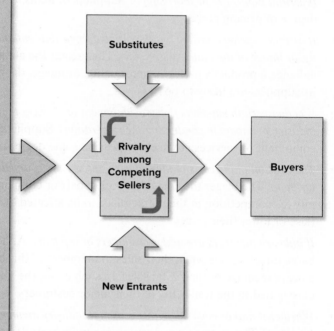

Suppliers of Resource Inputs

How strong are the competitive pressures stemming from supplier bargaining power and seller-supplier collaboration?

Supplier bargaining power is stronger when:

- Industry members incur high costs in switching their purchases to alternative suppliers.
- Needed inputs are in short supply (which gives suppliers more leverage in setting prices).
- A supplier has a differentiated input that enhances the quality, performance, or image of sellers' products or is a valuable or critical part of sellers' production processes.
- There are only a few suppliers of a particular input.

Supplier bargaining power is weaker when:

- The item being supplied is a "commodity" that is readily available from many suppliers at the going market price.
- Seller switching costs to alternative suppliers are low.
- Good substitute inputs exist or new ones emerge.
- There is a surge in the availability of supplies (thus greatly weakening supplier pricing power).
- Industry members account for a big fraction of suppliers' total sales and continued high-volume purchases are important to the well-being of suppliers.
- Industry members are a threat to integrate backward into the business of suppliers and to self-manufacture their own requirements.

- *Cost and resource disadvantages not related to scale of operation.* Aside from enjoying economies of scale, industry incumbents can have cost advantages that stem from the possession of proprietary technology, partnerships with the best and cheapest suppliers, low fixed costs (because they have older facilities that have been mostly depreciated), and experience/learning-curve effects. Manufacturing unit costs for microprocessors tend to decline about 20 percent each time *cumulative* production volume doubles. With a 20 percent experience-curve effect, if the first 1 million chips cost $100 each, once production volume reaches 2 million, the unit cost would fall to $80 (80 percent of $100), and by a production volume of 4 million, the unit cost would be $64 (80 percent of $80).[3] The bigger the learning- or experience-curve effect, the bigger the cost advantage of the company with the largest *cumulative* production volume.

- *Strong brand preferences and high degrees of customer loyalty.* The stronger the attachment of buyers to established brands, the harder it is for a newcomer to break into the marketplace.

- *High capital requirements.* The larger the total dollar investment needed to enter the market successfully, the more limited the pool of potential entrants. The most obvious capital requirements for new entrants relate to manufacturing facilities and equipment, introductory advertising and sales promotion campaigns, working capital to finance inventories and customer credit, and sufficient cash to cover start-up costs.

- *The difficulties of building a network of distributors-retailers and securing adequate space on retailers' shelves.* A potential entrant can face numerous distribution channel challenges. Wholesale distributors may be reluctant to take on a product that lacks buyer recognition. Retailers have to be recruited and convinced to give a new brand ample display space and an adequate trial period. Potential entrants sometimes have to "buy" their way into wholesale or retail channels by cutting their prices to provide dealers and distributors with higher markups and profit margins or by giving them big advertising and promotional allowances.

- *Patents and other forms of intellectual property protection.* In a number of industries, entry is prevented due to the existence of intellectual property protection laws that remain in place for a given number of years. Often, companies have a "wall of patents" in place to prevent other companies from entering with a "me too" strategy that replicates a key piece of technology.

- *Strong "network effects" in customer demand.* In industries where buyers are more attracted to a product when there are many other users of the product, there are said to be "network effects." Video game systems are an example, since many users prefer multiplayer games and sharing games. When incumbents have a large existing base of users, new entrants with otherwise comparable products face a serious disadvantage in attracting buyers.

- *Restrictive regulatory policies.* Government agencies can limit or even bar entry by requiring licenses and permits. Regulated industries such as cable TV, telecommunications, electric and gas utilities, and radio and television broadcasting entail government-controlled entry.

- *Tariffs and international trade restrictions.* National governments commonly use tariffs and trade restrictions (antidumping rules, local content requirements, local ownership requirements, quotas, etc.) to raise entry barriers for foreign firms and protect domestic producers from outside competition.

- *The ability and willingness of industry incumbents to launch vigorous initiatives to block a newcomer's successful entry.* Even if a potential entrant has or can acquire the needed competencies and resources to attempt entry, it must still worry about the reaction of existing firms.[4] Sometimes, there's little that incumbents can do to throw obstacles in an entrant's path. But there are times when incumbents use price cuts, increase advertising, introduce product improvements, and launch legal attacks to prevent the entrant from building a clientele. Taxicab companies across the world are aggressively lobbying local governments to impose regulations that would bar ride-sharing services such as Uber or Lyft.

Figure 3.6 summarizes conditions making the threat of entry strong or weak.

The Competitive Force of Rivalry Among Competing Sellers

The strongest of the five competitive forces is nearly always the rivalry among competing sellers of a product or service. In effect, *a market is a competitive battlefield* where there's no end to the campaign for buyer patronage. Rival sellers are prone to employ whatever weapons they have in their business arsenal to improve their market positions, strengthen their market position with buyers, and earn good profits. The strategy formulation challenge is to craft a competitive strategy that, at the very least, allows a company to hold its own against rivals and that, ideally, *produces a competitive edge*

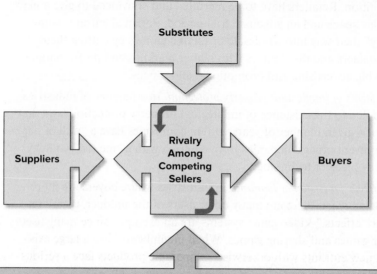

FIGURE 3.6   Factors Affecting the Threat of Entry

Substitutes

Suppliers → Rivalry Among Competing Sellers ← Buyers

Potential New Entrants

How strong are the competitive pressures associated with the entry threat from new rivals?

Entry threats are stronger when:

- The pool of entry candidates is large and some have resources that would make them formidable market contenders.
- Entry barriers are low or can be readily hurdled by the likely entry candidates.
- Existing industry members are looking to expand their market reach by entering product segments or geographic areas where they currently do not have a presence.
- Newcomers can expect to earn attractive profits.
- Buyer demand is growing rapidly.
- Industry members are unable (or unwilling) to strongly contest the entry of newcomers.

Entry threats are weaker when:

- The pool of entry candidates is small.
- Entry barriers are high.
- Existing competitors are struggling to earn good profits.
- The industry's outlook is risky or uncertain.
- Buyer demand is growing slowly or is stagnant.
- Industry members will strongly contest the efforts of new entrants to gain a market foothold.

over rivals. But competitive contests are ongoing and dynamic. When one firm makes a strategic move that produces good results, its rivals typically respond with offensive or defensive countermoves of their own. This pattern of action and reaction produces a continually evolving competitive landscape in which the market battle ebbs and flows and produces winners and losers. But the current market leaders have no guarantees of continued leadership. In every industry, the ongoing jockeying of rivals leads to one or more companies gaining or losing momentum in the marketplace according to whether their latest strategic maneuvers succeed or fail.[5]

Figure 3.7 shows a sampling of competitive weapons that firms can deploy in battling rivals and indicates the factors that influence the intensity of their rivalry. Some factors that influence the tempo of rivalry among industry competitors include:

- *Rivalry is stronger in industries when the number of competitors increases and they become more equal in size and capability.* Competitive rivalry in the quick-service restaurant industry is particularly strong where there are numerous relatively equal-sized hamburger, deli sandwich, chicken, and taco chains. For the most part,

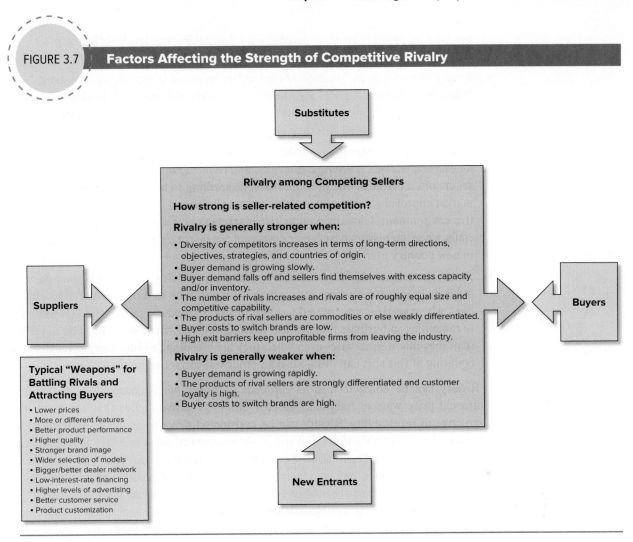

FIGURE 3.7   Factors Affecting the Strength of Competitive Rivalry

McDonald's, Burger King, Taco Bell, Arby's, Chick-fil-A, and other national fast-food chains have comparable capabilities and are required to compete aggressively to hold their own in the industry.

- *Rivalry is usually stronger when demand is growing slowly or declining.* Rapidly expanding buyer demand produces enough new business for all industry members to grow. But in markets where growth is sluggish or where buyer demand drops off unexpectedly, it is not uncommon for competitive rivalry to intensify significantly as rivals battle for market share and volume gains.

- *Rivalry increases as it becomes less costly for buyers to switch brands.* The less costly it is for buyers to switch their purchases from one seller to another, the easier it is for sellers to steal customers away from rivals. Switching costs include not only monetary costs but also the time, inconvenience, and psychological costs involved in switching brands. For example, retailers may not switch to the brands of rival manufacturers because they are hesitant to sever long-standing supplier relationships or incur the additional expense of retraining employees, accessing technical support, or testing the quality and reliability of the new brand.

- *Rivalry increases when sellers find themselves with excess capacity and/or inventory.* Excess supply conditions create a "buyers' market," putting added competitive pressure on industry rivals to scramble for profitable sales levels (often by price discounting).

- *Rivalry increases as the products of rival sellers become less strongly differentiated.* When the offerings of rivals are identical or weakly differentiated, buyers have less reason to be brand loyal—a condition that makes it easier for rivals to persuade buyers to switch to their offering.

- *Rivalry becomes more intense as the diversity of competitors increases in terms of long-term directions, objectives, strategies, and countries of origin.* A diverse group of sellers often contains one or more mavericks willing to try novel or rule-breaking market approaches, thus generating a more volatile and less predictable competitive environment. Globally competitive markets are often more rivalrous, especially when aggressors have lower costs and are intent on gaining a strong foothold in new country markets.

- *Rivalry is stronger when high exit barriers keep unprofitable firms from leaving the industry.* In industries where the assets cannot easily be sold or transferred to other uses, where workers are entitled to job protection, or where owners are committed to remaining in business for personal reasons, failing firms tend to hold on longer than they might otherwise—even when they are bleeding red ink. Deep price discounting of this sort can destabilize an otherwise attractive industry.

Rivalry can be characterized as *cutthroat* or *brutal* when competitors engage in protracted price wars or habitually employ other aggressive tactics that are mutually destructive to profitability. Rivalry can be considered *fierce* to *strong* when the battle for market share is so vigorous that the profit margins of most industry members are squeezed to bare-bones levels. Rivalry can be characterized as *moderate* or *normal* when the maneuvering among industry members, while lively and healthy, still allows most industry members to earn acceptable profits. Rivalry is *weak* when most companies in the industry are relatively well satisfied with their sales growth and market share and rarely undertake offensives to steal customers away from one another.

The Collective Strengths of the Five Competitive Forces and Industry Profitability

Scrutinizing each of the five competitive forces one by one provides a powerful diagnosis of what competition is like in a given market. Once the strategist has gained an understanding of the competitive pressures associated with each of the five forces, the next step is to evaluate the collective strength of the five forces and determine if companies in this industry should reasonably expect to earn decent profits.

As a rule, the stronger the collective impact of the five competitive forces, the lower the combined profitability of industry participants. The most extreme case of a "competitively unattractive" industry is when all five forces are producing strong competitive pressures: Rivalry among sellers is vigorous, low entry barriers allow new rivals to gain a market foothold, competition from substitutes is intense, and both suppliers and customers are able to exercise considerable bargaining leverage. Fierce to strong competitive pressures coming from all five directions nearly always drive industry profitability to unacceptably low levels, frequently producing losses for many industry members and forcing some out of business. But an industry can be competitively unattractive without all five competitive forces being strong. Fierce competitive pressures from just one of the five forces, such as brutal price competition among rival sellers, may suffice to destroy the conditions for good profitability.

> The stronger the forces of competition, the harder it becomes for industry members to earn attractive profits.

In contrast, when the collective impact of the five competitive forces is moderate to weak, an industry is competitively attractive in the sense that industry members can reasonably expect to earn good profits and a nice return on investment. The ideal competitive environment for earning superior profits is one in which both suppliers and customers are in weak bargaining positions, there are no good substitutes, high barriers block further entry, and rivalry among present sellers generates only moderate competitive pressures. Weak competition is the best of all possible worlds for companies with mediocre strategies and second-rate implementation because even they can expect a decent profit.

Question 3: What Are the Industry's Driving Forces of Change, and What Impact Will They Have?

The intensity of competitive forces and the level of industry attractiveness are almost always fluid and subject to change. It is essential for strategy makers to understand the current competitive dynamics of the industry, but it is equally important for strategy makers to consider how the industry is changing and the effect of industry changes that are under way. Any strategies devised by management will play out in a dynamic industry environment, so it's imperative that such plans consider what the industry environment might look like during the near term.

The Concept of Industry Driving Forces

Industry and competitive conditions change because forces are enticing or pressuring certain industry participants (competitors, customers, suppliers) to alter their actions in important ways. The most powerful of the change agents are called **driving forces** because they have the biggest influences in reshaping the industry landscape and altering competitive conditions. Some driving forces originate in the outer ring of the company's macro-environment (see Figure 3.1), but most originate in the company's more immediate industry and competitive environment.

> **CORE CONCEPT**
>
> **Driving forces** are the major underlying causes of change in industry and competitive conditions.

Driving forces analysis has three steps: (1) identifying what the driving forces are, (2) assessing whether the drivers of change are, individually or collectively, acting to make the industry more or less attractive, and (3) determining what strategy changes are needed to prepare for the impact of the driving forces.

Identifying an Industry's Driving Forces

Many developments can affect an industry powerfully enough to qualify as driving forces, but most drivers of industry and competitive change fall into one of the following categories:

- *Changes in an industry's long-term growth rate.* Shifts in industry growth have the potential to affect the balance between industry supply and buyer demand, entry and exit, and the character and strength of competition. An upsurge in buyer demand triggers a race among established firms and newcomers to capture the new sales opportunities. A slowdown in the growth of demand nearly always brings an increase in rivalry and increased efforts by some firms to maintain their high rates of growth by taking sales and market share away from rivals.

- *Increasing globalization.* Competition begins to shift from primarily a regional or national focus to an international or global focus when industry members begin seeking customers in foreign markets or when production activities begin to migrate to countries where costs are lowest. The forces of globalization are sometimes such a strong driver that companies find it highly advantageous, if not necessary, to spread their operating reach into more and more country markets. Globalization is very much a driver of industry change in such industries as energy, mobile phones, steel, social media, and pharmaceuticals.

- *Changes in who buys the product and how they use it.* Shifts in buyer demographics and the ways products are used can alter competition by affecting how customers perceive value, how customers make purchasing decisions, and where customers purchase the product. The burgeoning popularity of streaming video has affected broadband providers, wireless phone carriers, and television broadcasters, and created opportunities for such new entertainment businesses as Hulu and Netflix.

- *Product innovation.* An ongoing stream of product innovations tends to alter the pattern of competition in an industry by attracting more first-time buyers, rejuvenating industry growth, and/or creating wider or narrower product differentiation among rival sellers. Philips Lighting Hue bulbs allow homeowners to use a smartphone app to remotely turn lights on and off, blink if an intruder is detected, and create a wide range of white and color ambiances.

- *Technological change and manufacturing process innovation.* Advances in technology can cause disruptive change in an industry by lowering costs, introducing new substitutes, or opening new industry frontiers. For instance, revolutionary change in autonomous system technology has put Google, Tesla, Apple, and every major automobile manufacturer into a race to develop viable self-driving vehicles.

- *Marketing innovation.* When firms are successful in introducing *new ways* to market their products, they can spark a burst of buyer interest, widen industry demand, increase product differentiation, and lower unit costs—any or all of which can alter the competitive positions of rival firms and force strategy revisions.

- *Entry or exit of major firms.* The entry of one or more foreign companies into a geographic market once dominated by domestic firms nearly always shakes up competitive conditions. Likewise, when an established domestic firm from another industry attempts entry either by acquisition or by launching its own start-up venture, it usually pushes competition in new directions.

- *Diffusion of technical know-how across more companies and more countries.* As knowledge about how to perform a particular activity or execute a particular manufacturing technology spreads, the competitive advantage held by firms originally possessing this know-how erodes. Knowledge diffusion can occur through scientific journals, trade publications, on-site plant tours, word of mouth among suppliers and customers, employee migration, and Internet sources.

- *Changes in cost and efficiency.* Widening or shrinking differences in the costs among key competitors tend to dramatically alter the state of competition.

Declining costs to produce tablet computers have enabled price cuts and spurred tablet sales by making them more affordable to users.

- *Growing buyer preferences for differentiated products instead of a commodity product (or for a more standardized product instead of strongly differentiated products).* When a shift from standardized to differentiated products occurs, rivals must adopt strategies to outdifferentiate one another. However, buyers sometimes decide that a standardized, budget-priced product suits their requirements as well as a premium-priced product with lots of snappy features and personalized services.

- *Regulatory influences and government policy changes.* Government regulatory actions can often force significant changes in industry practices and strategic approaches. New rules and regulations pertaining to government-sponsored health insurance programs are driving changes in the health care industry. In international markets, host governments can drive competitive changes by opening their domestic markets to foreign participation or closing them.

- *Changing societal concerns, attitudes, and lifestyles.* Emerging social issues and changing attitudes and lifestyles can be powerful instigators of industry change. Consumer concerns about the use of chemical additives and the nutritional content of food products have forced food producers to revamp food-processing techniques, redirect R&D efforts into the use of healthier ingredients, and compete in developing nutritious, good-tasting products.

While many forces of change may be at work in a given industry, *no more than three or four* are likely to be true driving forces powerful enough to qualify as the *major determinants* of why and how the industry is changing. Thus, company strategists must resist the temptation to label every change they see as a driving force. Table 3.2 lists the most common driving forces.

Assessing the Impact of the Industry Driving Forces

The second step in driving forces analysis is to determine whether the prevailing driving forces are acting to make the industry environment more or less attractive. Getting a handle on the

TABLE 3.2

Common Driving Forces

1. Changes in the long-term industry growth rate
2. Increasing globalization
3. Emerging new Internet capabilities and applications
4. Changes in who buys the product and how they use it
5. Product innovation
6. Technological change and manufacturing process innovation
7. Marketing innovation
8. Entry or exit of major firms
9. Diffusion of technical know-how across more companies and more countries
10. Changes in cost and efficiency
11. Growing buyer preferences for differentiated products instead of a standardized commodity product (or for a more standardized product instead of strongly differentiated products)
12. Regulatory influences and government policy changes
13. Changing societal concerns, attitudes, and lifestyles

An important part of driving forces analysis is to determine whether the individual or collective impact of the driving forces will be to increase or decrease market demand, make competition more or less intense, and lead to higher or lower industry profitability.

collective impact of the driving forces usually requires looking at the likely effects of each force separately, because the driving forces may not all be pushing change in the same direction. For example, two driving forces may be acting to spur demand for the industry's product, while one driving force may be working to curtail demand. Whether the net effect on industry demand is up or down hinges on which driving forces are the more powerful.

Determining Strategy Changes Needed to Prepare for the Impact of Driving Forces

The third step of driving forces analysis—where the real payoff for strategy making comes—is for managers to draw some conclusions about what strategy adjustments will be needed to deal with the impact of the driving forces. Without understanding the forces driving industry change and the impacts these forces will have on the industry environment over the next one to three years, managers are ill prepared to craft a strategy tightly matched to emerging conditions. Similarly, if managers are uncertain about the implications of one or more driving forces, or if their views are off-base, it will be

The real payoff of driving forces analysis is to help managers understand what strategy changes are needed to prepare for the impacts of the driving forces.

difficult for them to craft a strategy that is responsive to the consequences of driving forces. So driving forces analysis is not something to take lightly; it has practical value and is basic to the task of thinking strategically about where the industry is headed and how to prepare for the changes ahead.

Question 4: How Are Industry Rivals Positioned?

LO3-3   Map the market positions of key groups of industry rivals.

The nature of competitive strategy inherently positions companies competing in an industry into strategic groups with diverse price/quality ranges, different distribution channels, varying product features, and different geographic coverages. The best technique for revealing the market positions of industry competitors is **strategic group mapping.** This analytical tool is useful for comparing the market positions of industry competitors or for grouping industry combatants into like positions.

CORE CONCEPT

Strategic group mapping is a technique for displaying the different market or competitive positions that rival firms occupy in the industry.

Using Strategic Group Maps to Assess the Positioning of Key Competitors

A **strategic group** consists of those industry members with similar competitive approaches and positions in the market. Companies in the same strategic group can resemble one another in any of several ways: they may have comparable product-line breadth, sell in the same price/quality range, emphasize the same distribution channels, use essentially the same product attributes to appeal to similar types of buyers, depend on identical technological approaches, or offer buyers similar services and technical assistance.[6] An industry with a commodity-like product may contain only one strategic group whereby all sellers pursue essentially identical strategies and have comparable market positions. But even with commodity products, there is likely some attempt at differentiation occurring in the form of varying delivery times, financing terms, or lev-

CORE CONCEPT

A **strategic group** is a cluster of industry rivals that have similar competitive approaches and market positions.

els of customer service. Most industries offer a host of competitive approaches that allow companies to find unique industry positioning and avoid fierce competition in a crowded strategic group. Evaluating strategy options entails examining what strategic groups exist, identifying which companies exist within each group, and determining if a competitive "white space" exists where industry competitors are able to create and capture altogether new demand.

The procedure for constructing a *strategic group map* is straightforward:

- Identify the competitive characteristics that delineate strategic approaches used in the industry. Typical variables used in creating strategic group maps are the price/ quality range (high, medium, low), geographic coverage (local, regional, national, global), degree of vertical integration (none, partial, full), product-line breadth (wide, narrow), choice of distribution channels (retail, wholesale, Internet, multiple channels), and degree of service offered (no-frills, limited, full).

- Plot firms on a two-variable map based upon their strategic approaches.

- Assign firms occupying the same map location to a common strategic group.

- Draw circles around each strategic group, making the circles proportional to the size of the group's share of total industry sales revenues.

This produces a two-dimensional diagram like the one for the U.S. casual dining industry in Concepts & Connections 3.1.

Several guidelines need to be observed in creating strategic group maps. First, the two variables selected as axes for the map should *not* be highly correlated; if they are, the circles on the map will fall along a diagonal and strategy makers will learn nothing more about the relative positions of competitors than they would by considering just one of the variables. For instance, if companies with broad product lines use multiple distribution channels, while companies with narrow lines use a single distribution channel, then looking at product line-breadth reveals just as much about industry positioning as looking at the two competitive variables. Second, the variables chosen as axes for the map should reflect key approaches to offering value to customers and expose big differences in how rivals position themselves in the marketplace. Third, the variables used as axes do not have to be either quantitative or continuous; rather, they can be discrete variables or defined in terms of distinct classes and combinations. Fourth, drawing the sizes of the circles on the map proportional to the combined sales of the firms in each strategic group allows the map to reflect the relative sizes of each strategic group. Fifth, if more than two good competitive variables can be used as axes for the map, multiple maps can be drawn to give different exposures to the competitive positioning in the industry. Because there is not necessarily one best map for portraying how competing firms are positioned in the market, it is advisable to experiment with different pairs of competitive variables.

Concepts & Connections 3.1

COMPARATIVE MARKET POSITIONS OF SELECTED COMPANIES IN THE CASUAL DINING INDUSTRY: A STRATEGIC GROUP MAP EXAMPLE

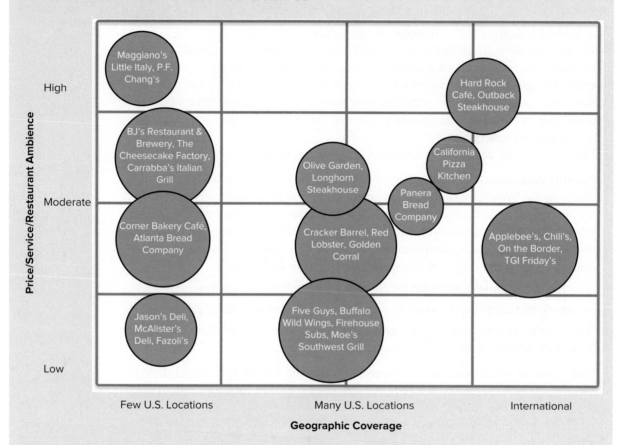

Note: Circles are drawn roughly proportional to the sizes of the chains, based on revenues.

The Value of Strategic Group Maps

Strategic group maps are revealing in several respects. The *most important* has to do with identifying which rivals are similarly positioned and are thus close rivals and which are distant rivals. Generally, *the closer strategic groups are to each other on the map, the stronger the cross-group competitive rivalry tends to be.* Although firms in the same strategic group are the closest rivals, the next closest rivals are in the immediately adjacent groups.[7] Often, firms in strategic groups that are far apart on the map hardly compete. For instance, Walmart's clientele, merchandise selection, and pricing points are much too different to justify calling Walmart a close competitor of Neiman Marcus or Saks Fifth Avenue in

> Some strategic groups are more favorably positioned than others because they confront weaker competitive forces and/or because they are more favorably impacted by industry driving forces.

retailing. For the same reason, Timex is not a meaningful competitive rival of Rolex, and Kia is not a close competitor of Porsche or BMW.

The second thing to be gleaned from strategic group mapping is that *not all positions on the map are equally attractive.* Two reasons account for why some positions can be more attractive than others:

1. *Industry driving forces may favor some strategic groups and hurt others.* Driving forces in an industry may be acting to grow the demand for the products of firms in some strategic groups and shrink the demand for the products of firms in other strategic groups—as is the case in the news industry where Internet news services and cable news networks are gaining ground at the expense of newspapers and network television. The industry driving forces of emerging Internet capabilities and applications, changes in who buys the product and how they use it, and changing societal concerns, attitudes, and lifestyles are making it increasingly difficult for traditional media to increase audiences and attract new advertisers.

2. *Competitive pressures may cause the profit potential of different strategic groups to vary.* The profit prospects of firms in different strategic groups can vary from good to poor because of differing degrees of competitive rivalry within strategic groups, differing degrees of exposure to competition from substitute products outside the industry, and differing degrees of supplier or customer bargaining power from group to group. For instance, the competitive battle between Walmart and Target is more intense (with consequently smaller profit margins) than the rivalry among Tory Burch, Carolina Herrera, Dolce & Gabbana, and other high-end fashion retailers.

Thus, part of strategic group analysis always entails drawing conclusions about where on the map is the "best" place to be and why. Which companies or strategic groups are in the best positions to prosper, and which might be expected to struggle? And equally important, how might firms in poorly positioned strategic groups reposition themselves to improve their prospects for good financial performance?

Question 5: What Strategic Moves Are Rivals Likely to Make Next?

Unless a company pays attention to the strategies and situations of competitors and has some inkling of what moves they will be making, it ends up flying blind into competitive battle. As in sports, scouting the business opposition is an essential part of game plan development. Having good information about the strategic direction and likely moves of key competitors allows a company to prepare defensive countermoves, to craft its own strategic moves with some confidence about what market maneuvers to expect from rivals in response, and to exploit any openings that arise from competitors' missteps. The question is where to look for such information, since rivals rarely reveal their strategic intentions openly. If information is not directly available, what are the best indicators?

Michael Porter's **Framework for Competitor Analysis** points to four indicators of a rival's likely strategic moves. These include a rival's *current strategy, objectives, capabilities,* and *assumptions* about itself and the industry. A strategic profile of a rival that provides good clues to its behavioral proclivities can be constructed by characterizing the rival along these four dimensions.

Current Strategy To succeed in predicting a competitor's next moves, company strategists need to have a good understanding of each rival's current strategy. Questions to consider include: How is the competitor positioned in the market? What is the basis for its competitive advantage? What kinds of investments in infrastructure, technology, or other resources is it making?

Objectives An appraisal of a rival's objectives should include not only its financial objectives but strategic objectives as well. What is even more important is to consider the extent to which the rival is meeting these objectives and if its management is under pressure to improve. Rivals with good financial performance are likely to continue their present strategy with only minor fine-tuning. Poorly performing rivals are virtually certain to make fresh strategic moves.

Capabilities A rival's strategic moves and countermoves are both enabled and constrained by the set of capabilities it has at hand. Thus a rival's capabilities (and efforts to acquire new capabilities) serve as a strong signal of future strategic actions.

> Studying competitors' past behavior and preferences provides a valuable assist in anticipating what moves rivals are likely to make next and outmaneuvering them in the marketplace.

Assumptions How a rival's top managers think about their strategic situation can have a big impact on how they behave. Managers of casual dining chains convinced that sociocultural forces and economic conditions will drive industry growth may turn to franchising to vastly expand a chain's footprint and number of units. Assessing a rival's assumptions entails considering their assumptions about itself as well as the industry it participates in.

Information regarding these four analytical components can often be gleaned from company press releases, information posted on the company's website (especially investor presentations), and such public documents as annual reports and 10-K filings. Many companies also have a competitive intelligence unit that sifts through the available information to construct up-to-date strategic profiles of rivals.

Doing the necessary detective work can be time-consuming, but scouting competitors well enough to anticipate their next moves allows managers to prepare effective countermoves and to take rivals' probable actions into account in crafting their own strategic offensives.

Question 6: What Are the Industry Key Success Factors?

An industry's **key success factors (KSFs)** are those competitive factors that most affect industry members' ability to prosper in the marketplace. Key success factors may include particular strategy elements, product attributes, resources, competitive capabilities, or intangible assets. KSFs by their very nature are so important to future competitive success that *all firms* in the industry must pay close attention to them or risk an eventual exit from the industry.

In the ready-to-wear apparel industry, the KSFs are appealing designs and color combinations, low-cost

> **CORE CONCEPT**
>
> **Key success factors** are the strategy elements, product attributes, competitive capabilities, or intangible assets with the greatest impact on future success in the marketplace.

manufacturing, a strong network of retailers or company-owned stores, distribution capabilities that allow stores to keep the best-selling items in stock, and advertisements that effectively convey the brand's image. These attributes and capabilities apply to all brands of apparel ranging from private-label brands sold by discounters to premium-priced ready-to-wear brands sold by upscale department stores. Table 3.3 lists the most common types of industry key success factors.

TABLE 3.3

Common Types of Industry Key Success Factors

Technology-related KSFs	• Expertise in a particular technology or in scientific research (important in pharmaceuticals, Internet applications, mobile communications, and most high-tech industries) • Proven ability to improve production processes (important in industries where advancing technology opens the way for higher manufacturing efficiency and lower production costs)
Manufacturing-related KSFs	• Ability to achieve scale economies and/or capture experience curve effects (important to achieving low production costs) • Quality control know-how (important in industries where customers insist on product reliability) • High utilization of fixed assets (important in capital-intensive/high-fixed-cost industries) • Access to attractive supplies of skilled labor • High labor productivity (important for items with high labor content) • Low-cost product design and engineering (reduces manufacturing costs) • Ability to manufacture or assemble products that are customized to buyer specifications
Distribution-related KSFs	• A strong network of wholesale distributors/dealers • Strong direct sales capabilities via the Internet and/or having company-owned retail outlets • Ability to secure favorable display space on retailer shelves
Marketing-related KSFs	• Breadth of product line and product selection • A well-known and well-respected brand name • Fast, accurate technical assistance • Courteous, personalized customer service • Accurate filling of buyer orders (few back orders or mistakes) • Customer guarantees and warranties (important in mail-order and online retailing, big-ticket purchases, and new-product introductions) • Clever advertising
Skills- and capability-related KSFs	• A talented workforce (superior talent is important in professional services such as accounting and investment banking) • National or global distribution capabilities • Product innovation capabilities (important in industries where rivals are racing to be first to market with new product attributes or performance features) • Design expertise (important in fashion and apparel industries) • Short delivery time capability • Supply chain management capabilities • Strong e-commerce capabilities—a user-friendly website and/or skills in using Internet technology applications to streamline internal operations
Other types of KSFs	• Overall low costs (not just in manufacturing) to be able to meet low-price expectations of customers • Convenient locations (important in many retailing businesses) • Ability to provide fast, convenient, after-the-sale repairs and service • A strong balance sheet and access to financial capital (important in newly emerging industries with high degrees of business risk and in capital-intensive industries) • Patent protection

An industry's key success factors can usually be deduced through identifying the industry's dominant characteristics, assessing the five competitive forces, considering the impacts of the driving forces, comparing the market positions of industry members, and forecasting the likely next moves of key rivals. In addition, the answers to three questions help identify an industry's key success factors. Those questions are:

1. On what basis do buyers of the industry's product choose between the competing brands of sellers? That is, what product attributes are crucial?

2. Given the nature of the competitive forces prevailing in the marketplace, what resources and competitive capabilities does a company need to have to be competitively successful?

3. What shortcomings are almost certain to put a company at a significant competitive disadvantage?

Only rarely are there more than five or six key factors for future competitive success. Managers should therefore resist the temptation to label a factor that has only minor importance a KSF. To compile a list of every factor that matters even a little bit defeats the purpose of concentrating management attention on the factors truly critical to long-term competitive success.

Question 7: Does the Industry Offer Good Prospects for Attractive Profits?

 LO3-4 Determine whether an industry's outlook presents a company with sufficiently attractive opportunities for growth and profitability.

The final step in evaluating the industry and competitive environment is boiling down the results of the analyses performed in Questions 1 through 6 to determine if the industry offers a company strong prospects for attractive profits.

The important factors on which to base such a conclusion include:

- The industry's growth potential.
- Whether powerful competitive forces are squeezing industry profitability to subpar levels and whether competition appears destined to grow stronger or weaker.
- Whether industry profitability will be favorably or unfavorably affected by the prevailing driving forces.
- The company's competitive position in the industry vis-à-vis rivals. (Well-entrenched leaders or strongly positioned contenders have a much better chance of earning attractive margins than those fighting a steep uphill battle.)
- How competently the company performs industry key success factors.

It is a mistake to think of a particular industry as being equally attractive or unattractive to all industry participants and all potential entrants. Conclusions have to be drawn from the perspective of a particular company. Industries attractive to insiders may be unattractive to outsiders. Industry environments unattractive to weak competitors may be attractive to strong competitors. A favorably positioned company may

survey a business environment and see a host of opportunities that weak competitors cannot capture.

When a company decides an industry is fundamentally attractive, a strong case can be made that it should
invest aggressively to capture the opportunities it sees.
When a strong competitor concludes an industry is
relatively unattractive, it may elect to simply protect its
present position, investing cautiously, if at all, and begin
looking for opportunities in other industries. A competitively weak company in an unattractive industry may see its best option as finding a buyer, perhaps a rival, to acquire
its business.

> The degree to which an industry is attractive or
> unattractive is not the same for all industry partici-
> pants and potential new entrants. The attractive-
> ness of an industry depends on the degree of fit
> between a company's competitive capabilities
> and industry key success factors.

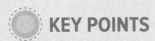 KEY POINTS

Thinking strategically about a company's external situation involves probing for answers to seven
questions:

1. *What are the strategically relevant components of the macro-environment?* Industries differ as
   to how they are affected by conditions in the broad macro-environment. PESTEL analysis
   of the political, economic, sociocultural, technological, environmental/ecological, and
   legal/regulatory factors provides a framework for approaching this issue systematically.

2. *What kinds of competitive forces are industry members facing, and how strong is each force?*
   The strength of competition is a composite of five forces: (1) competitive pressures stemming from buyer bargaining power and seller-buyer collaboration, (2) competitive pressures associated with the sellers of substitutes, (3) competitive pressures stemming from
   supplier bargaining power and supplier-seller collaboration, (4) competitive pressures
   associated with the threat of new entrants into the market, and (5) competitive pressures
   stemming from the competitive jockeying among industry rivals.

3. *What forces are driving changes in the industry, and what impact will these changes have on
   competitive intensity and industry profitability?* Industry and competitive conditions change
   because forces are in motion that create incentives or pressures for change. The first phase
   is to identify the forces that are driving industry change. The second phase of driving
   forces analysis is to determine whether the driving forces, taken together, are acting to
   make the industry environment more or less attractive.

4. *What market positions do industry rivals occupy—who is strongly positioned and who is not?*
   Strategic group mapping is a valuable tool for understanding the similarities and differences inherent in the market positions of rival companies. Rivals in the same or nearby
   strategic groups are close competitors, whereas companies in distant strategic groups usually pose little or no immediate threat. Some strategic groups are more favorable than others. The profit potential of different strategic groups may not be the same because industry
   driving forces and competitive forces likely have varying effects on the industry's distinct
   strategic groups.

5. *What strategic moves are rivals likely to make next?* Scouting competitors well enough to
   anticipate their actions can help a company prepare effective countermoves and allows
   managers to take rivals' probable actions into account in designing their own company's
   best course of action. Using a Framework for Competitor Analysis that considers rivals'

current strategy, objectives, resources and capabilities, and assumptions can be helpful in this regard.

6. *What are the key factors for competitive success?* An industry's key success factors (KSFs) are the particular product attributes, competitive capabilities, and intangible assets that spell the difference between being a strong competitor and a weak competitor—and sometimes between profit and loss. KSFs by their very nature are so important to competitive success that *all firms* in the industry must pay close attention to them or risk being driven out of the industry.

7. *Does the outlook for the industry present the company with sufficiently attractive prospects for profitability?* Conclusions regarding industry attractiveness are a major driver of company strategy. When a company decides an industry is fundamentally attractive and presents good opportunities, a strong case can be made that it should invest aggressively to capture the opportunities it sees. When a strong competitor concludes an industry is relatively unattractive and lacking in opportunity, it may elect to simply protect its present position, investing cautiously, if at all, and looking for opportunities in other industries. A competitively weak company in an unattractive industry may see its best option as finding a buyer, perhaps a rival, to acquire its business. On occasion, an industry that is unattractive overall is still very attractive to a favorably situated company with the skills and resources to take business away from weaker rivals.

ASSURANCE OF LEARNING EXERCISES

connect

LO3-2

1. Prepare a brief analysis of the organic food industry using the information provided by the Organic Trade Association. Based upon information provided in the *Organic Report* magazine, draw a five-forces diagram for the organic food industry and briefly discuss the nature and strength of each of the five competitive forces.

connect

LO3-3

2. Based on the strategic group map in Concepts & Connections 3.1, which casual dining chains are Applebee's closest competitors? With which strategic group does California Pizza Kitchen compete the least, according to this map? Why do you think no casual dining chains are positioned in the area above the Olive Garden's group?

LO3-1, LO3-4

3. The National Restaurant Association publishes an annual industry fact book that can be found at www.restaurant.org. Based on information in the latest report, does it appear that macro-environmental factors and the economic characteristics of the industry will present industry participants with attractive opportunities for growth and profitability? Explain.

EXERCISES FOR SIMULATION PARTICIPANTS

LO3-1, LO3-2, LO3-3, LO3-4

1. Which of the five competitive forces is creating the strongest competitive pressures for your company?

2. What are the "weapons of competition" that rival companies in your industry can use to gain sales and market share? See Figure 3.7 to help you identify the various competitive factors.

3. What are the factors affecting the intensity of rivalry in the industry in which your company is competing? Use Figure 3.7 and the accompanying discussion to help you in pinpointing the specific factors most affecting competitive intensity. Would you characterize the rivalry and jockeying for better market position, increased sales, and market share among the companies in your industry as fierce, very strong, strong, moderate, or relatively weak? Why?

4.   Are there any driving forces in the industry in which your company is competing? What impact will these driving forces have? Will they cause competition to be more or less intense? Will they act to boost or squeeze profit margins? List at least two actions your company should consider taking to combat any negative impacts of the driving forces.

5.   Draw a strategic group map showing the market positions of the companies in your industry. Which companies do you believe are in the most attractive position on the map? Which companies are the most weakly positioned? Which companies do you believe are likely to try to move to a different position on the strategic group map?

6.   What do you see as the key factors for being a successful competitor in your industry? List at least three.

7.   Does your overall assessment of the industry suggest that industry rivals have sufficiently attractive opportunities for growth and profitability? Explain.

⦾ ENDNOTES

1. Michael E. Porter, *Competitive Strategy: Techniques for Analyzing Industries and Competitors* (New York: Free Press, 1980), chapter 1; Michael E. Porter, "The Five Competitive Forces That Shape Strategy," *Harvard Business Review* 86, no. 1 (January 2008).

2. J. S. Bain, *Barriers to New Competition* (Cambridge, MA: Harvard University Press, 1956); F. M. Scherer, *Industrial Market Structure and Economic Performance* (Chicago: Rand McNally & Co., 1971).

3. Pankaj Ghemawat, "Building Strategy on the Experience Curve," *Harvard Business Review* 64, no. 2 (March–April 1985).

4. Michael E. Porter, "How Competitive Forces Shape Strategy," *Harvard Business Review* 57, no. 2 (March–April 1979).

5. Pamela J. Derfus, Patrick G. Maggitti, Curtis M. Grimm, and Ken G. Smith, "The Red Queen Effect: Competitive Actions and Firm Performance," *Academy of Management Journal* 51, no. 1 (February 2008).

6. Mary Ellen Gordon and George R. Milne, "Selecting the Dimensions That Define Strategic Groups: A Novel Market-Driven Approach," *Journal of Managerial Issues* 11, no. 2 (Summer 1999).

7. Avi Fiegenbaum and Howard Thomas, "Strategic Groups as Reference Groups: Theory, Modeling and Empirical Examination of Industry and Competitive Strategy," *Strategic Management Journal* 16 (1995); S. Ade Olusoga, Michael P. Mokwa, and Charles H. Noble, "Strategic Groups, Mobility Barriers, and Competitive Advantage," *Journal of Business Research* 33 (1995).

4

Evaluating a Company's Resources, Capabilities, and Competitiveness

LEARNING OBJECTIVES

After reading this chapter, you should be able to:

LO4-1 Assess how well a company's strategy is working.

LO4-2 Understand why a company's resources and capabilities are centrally important in giving the company a competitive edge over rivals.

LO4-3 Grasp how a company's value chain activities can affect the company's cost structure and customer value proposition.

LO4-4 Evaluate a company's competitive strength relative to key rivals.

LO4-5 Understand how a comprehensive evaluation of a company's external and internal situations can assist managers in making critical decisions about their next strategic moves.

Chapter 3 described how to use the tools of industry and competitive analysis to assess a company's external environment and lay the groundwork for matching a company's strategy to its external situation. This chapter discusses the techniques of evaluating a company's internal situation, including its collection of resources and capabilities, its cost structure and customer value proposition, and its competitive strength versus that of its rivals. The analytical spotlight will be trained on five questions:

1. How well is the company's strategy working?
2. What are the company's competitively important resources and capabilities?
3. Are the company's cost structure and customer value proposition competitive?
4. Is the company competitively stronger or weaker than key rivals?
5. What strategic issues and problems merit front-burner managerial attention?

   The answers to these five questions complete management's understanding of the company's overall situation and position the company for a good strategy-situation fit required by the "The Three Tests of a Winning Strategy" (see Chapter 1).

Question 1: How Well Is the Company's Strategy Working?

LO4-1   Assess how well a company's strategy is working.

The two best indicators of how well a company's strategy is working are (1) whether the company is recording gains in financial strength and profitability, and (2) whether the company's competitive strength and market standing are improving. Persistent short-falls in meeting company financial performance targets and weak performance relative to rivals are reliable warning signs that the company suffers from poor strategy making, less-than-competent strategy execution, or both. Other indicators of how well a company's strategy is working include:

*   Trends in the company's sales and earnings growth.
*   Trends in the company's stock price.
*   The company's overall financial strength.
*   The company's customer retention rate.
*   The rate at which new customers are acquired.
*   Changes in the company's image and reputation with customers.
*   Evidence of improvement in internal processes such as defect rate, order fulfill-ment, delivery times, days of inventory, and employee productivity.

   The stronger a company's current overall performance, the less likely the need for radical changes in strategy. The weaker a company's financial performance and market standing, the more its current strategy must be questioned. (A compilation of financial ratios most commonly used to evaluate a company's financial performance and balance sheet strength is presented in the Appendix.)

Question 2: What Are the Company's Competitively Important Resources and Capabilities?

LO4-2 Understand why a company's resources and capabilities are centrally important in giving the company a competitive edge over rivals.

As discussed in Chapter 1, a company's business model and strategy must be well matched to its collection of resources and capabilities. An attempt to create and deliver customer value in a manner that depends on resources or capabilities that are deficient and cannot be readily acquired or developed is unwise and positions the company for failure. A company's competitive approach requires a tight fit with a company's internal situation and is strengthened when it exploits resources that are competitively valuable, rare, hard to copy, and not easily trumped by rivals' substitute resources. In addition, long-term competitive advantage requires the ongoing development and expansion of resources and capabilities to pursue emerging market opportunities and defend against future threats to its market standing and profitability.[1]

Sizing up the company's collection of resources and capabilities and determining whether they can provide the foundation for competitive success can be achieved through **resource and capability analysis.** This is a two-step process: (1) identify the company's resources and capabilities, and (2) examine them more closely to ascertain which are the most competitively important and whether they can support a sustainable competitive advantage over rival firms.[2] This second step involves applying the *four tests of a resource's competitive power.*

Identifying Competitively Important Resources and Capabilities

A company's **resources** are competitive assets that are owned or controlled by the company and may either be *tangible resources* such as plants, distribution centers, manufacturing equipment, patents, information systems, and capital reserves or creditworthiness, or *intangible assets* such as a well-known brand or a results-oriented organizational culture. Table 4.1 lists the common types of tangible and intangible resources that a company may possess.

A **capability** is the capacity of a firm to competently perform some internal activity. A capability may also be referred to as a **competence.** Capabilities or competences also vary in form, quality, and competitive importance, with some being more competitively valuable than others. *Organizational capabilities are developed and enabled through the deployment of a company's resources or some combination of its resources.*[3] Some capabilities rely heavily on a company's intangible resources such as human assets and intellectual capital. For example, Nestlé's brand management capabilities for its 2,000+ food, beverage, and pet care brands draw upon the knowledge of the company's brand managers, the expertise of its marketing department, and the company's relationships with retailers in nearly 200 countries. W. L. Gore's product innovation capabilities in its fabrics,

> **CORE CONCEPT**
>
> A **resource** is a competitive asset that is owned or controlled by a company; a **capability** is the capacity of a company to competently perform some internal activity. Capabilities are developed and enabled through the deployment of a company's resources.

TABLE 4.1

Common Types of Tangible and Intangible Resources

Tangible Resources

- *Physical resources*—state-of-the-art manufacturing plants and equipment, efficient distribution facilities, attractive real estate locations, or ownership of valuable natural resource deposits
- *Financial resources*—cash and cash equivalents, marketable securities, and other financial assets such as a company's credit rating and borrowing capacity
- *Technological assets*—patents, copyrights, superior production technology, and technologies that enable activities
- *Organizational resources*—information and communication systems (servers, workstations, etc.), proven quality control systems, and a strong network of distributors or retail dealers

Intangible Resources

- *Human assets and intellectual capital*—an experienced and capable workforce, talented employees in key areas, collective learning embedded in the organization, or proven managerial know-how
- *Brand, image, and reputational assets*—brand names, trademarks, product or company image, buyer loyalty, and reputation for quality, superior service
- *Relationships*—alliances or joint ventures that provide access to technologies, specialized know-how, or geographic markets, and trust established with various partners
- *Company culture*—the norms of behavior, business principles, and ingrained beliefs within the company

medical, and industrial products businesses result from the personal initiative, creative talents, and technological expertise of its associates and the company's culture that encourages accountability and creative thinking.

Determining the Competitive Power of a Company's Resources and Capabilities

What is most telling about a company's aggregation of resources and capabilities is how powerful they are in the marketplace. The competitive power of a resource or capability is measured by how many of four tests for sustainable competitive advantage it can pass.[4]

The tests are often referred to as the **VRIN tests for sustainable competitive advantage**—an acronym for *valuable, rare, inimitable,* and *nonsubstitutable.* The first two tests determine whether the resource or capability may contribute to a competitive advantage. The last two determine the degree to which the competitive advantage potential can be sustained.

1. *Is the resource or capability competitively **valuable**?*
    All companies possess a collection of resources and capabilities—some have the potential to contribute to a competitive advantage, while others may not. Google failed in converting its technological resources and software innovation capabilities into success for Google Wallet, which incurred losses of more than $300 million before being abandoned in 2016. While these resources and capabilities have made Google the world's number-one search engine, they proved to be less valuable in the mobile payments industry.

CORE CONCEPT

The **VRIN tests for sustainable competitive advantage** ask if a resource or capability is *valuable, rare, inimitable,* and *nonsubstitutable*.

2. *Is the resource or capability **rare**—is it something rivals lack?* Resources and capabilities that are common among firms and widely available cannot be a source of competitive advantage. All makers of branded cookies and sweet snacks have valuable marketing capabilities and brands. Therefore, these skills are not rare or unique in the industry. However, the brand strength of Oreo is uncommon and has provided Kraft Foods with greater market share as well as the opportunity to benefit from brand extensions such as Golden Oreo cookies, Oreo Thins, and Mini Oreo cookies.

3. *Is the resource or capability **inimitable** or hard to copy?* The more difficult and more expensive it is to imitate a company's resource or capability, the more likely that it can also provide a *sustainable* competitive advantage. Resources tend to be difficult to copy when they are unique (a fantastic real estate location, patent protection), when they must be built over time (a brand name, a strategy-supportive organizational culture), and when they carry big capital requirements (a cost-effective plant to manufacture cutting-edge microprocessors). Imitation by rivals is most challenging when capabilities reflect a high level of *social complexity* (for example, a stellar team-oriented culture or unique trust-based relationships with employees, suppliers, or customers) and *causal ambiguity,* a term that signifies the hard-to-disentangle nature of complex processes such as the web of intricate activities enabling a new drug discovery.

4. *Is the resource or capability **nonsubstitutable** or is it vulnerable to the threat of substitution from different types of resources and capabilities?* Resources that are competitively valuable, rare, and costly to imitate may lose much of their ability to offer competitive advantage if rivals possess equivalent substitute resources. For example, manufacturers relying on automation to gain a cost-based advantage in production activities may find their technology-based advantage nullified by rivals' use of low-wage offshore manufacturing. Resources can contribute to a competitive advantage only when resource substitutes do not exist.

> **CORE CONCEPT**
>
> **Social complexity** and **causal ambiguity** are two factors that inhibit the ability of rivals to imitate a firm's most valuable resources and capabilities. Causal ambiguity makes it very hard to figure out how a complex resource contributes to competitive advantage and therefore exactly what to imitate.

Very few firms have resources and capabilities that can pass all four tests, but those that do enjoy a sustainable competitive advantage with far greater profit potential. Costco is a notable example, with strong employee incentive programs and capabilities in supply chain management that have surpassed those of its warehouse club competitors for over 35 years. Lincoln Electric Company, less well known but no less notable in its achievements, has been the world leader in welding products for over 100 years as a result of its unique piecework incentive system for compensating production workers and the unsurpassed worker productivity and product quality that this system has fostered.[5]

If management determines that the company does not possess a resource that independently passes all four test with high marks, it may have a bundle of resources that can pass the tests. Although PetSmart's supply chain and marketing capabilities are matched well by rival Petco, the company has and continues to outperform competitors through its customer service capabilities (including animal grooming, veterinary, and day care services). Nike's bundle of styling expertise, marketing research skills, professional endorsements, brand name, and managerial know-how has allowed it to remain number one in the athletic footwear and apparel industry for more than 20 years.

The Importance of Dynamic Capabilities in Sustaining Competitive Advantage

Resources and capabilities must be continually strengthened and nurtured to sustain their competitive power and, at times, may need to be broadened and deepened to allow the company to position itself to pursue emerging market opportunities.[6] Organizational resources and capabilities that grow stale can impair competitiveness unless they are refreshed, modified, or even phased out and replaced in response to ongoing market changes and shifts in company strategy. In addition, disruptive environmental change may destroy the value of key strategic assets, turning *static* resources and capabilities "from diamonds to rust."[7]

> **CORE CONCEPT**
>
> Companies that lack a standalone resource that is competitively powerful may nonetheless develop a competitive advantage through **resource bundles** that enable the superior performance of important cross-functional capabilities.

Management's organization-building challenge has two elements: (1) attending to ongoing recalibration of existing capabilities and resources, and (2) casting a watchful eye for opportunities to develop totally new capabilities for delivering better customer value and/or outcompeting rivals. Companies that know the importance of recalibrating and upgrading resources and capabilities make it a routine management function to build new resource configurations and capabilities. Such a managerial approach allows a company to prepare for market changes and pursue emerging opportunities. This ability to build and integrate new competitive assets becomes a capability in itself—a **dynamic capability.** A dynamic capability is the ability to modify, deepen, or reconfigure the company's existing resources and capabilities in response to its changing environment or market opportunities.[8]

> **CORE CONCEPT**
>
> A **dynamic capability** is the ability to modify, deepen, or reconfigure the company's existing resources and capabilities in response to its changing environment or market opportunities.

Management at Toyota has aggressively upgraded the company's capabilities in fuel-efficient hybrid engine technology and constantly fine-tuned the famed Toyota Production System to enhance the company's already proficient capabilities in manufacturing top-quality vehicles at relatively low costs. Likewise, management at BMW developed new organizational capabilities in hybrid engine design that allowed the company to launch its highly touted i3 and i8 plug-in hybrids. Resources and capabilities can also be built and augmented through alliances and acquisitions.[9] Bristol-Myers Squibb's famed "string of pearls" acquisition strategy has enabled it to replace degraded resources such as expiring patents with new patents and newly acquired capabilities in drug discovery for new disease domains.

> A company requires a dynamically evolving portfolio of resources and capabilities in order to sustain its competitiveness and position itself to pursue future market opportunities.

Is the Company Able to Seize Market Opportunities and Nullify External Threats?

An essential element in evaluating a company's overall situation entails examining the company's resources and competitive capabilities in terms of the degree to which they enable it to pursue its best market opportunities and defend against the external

CORE CONCEPT

SWOT analysis is a simple but powerful tool for sizing up a company's internal strengths and competitive deficiencies, its market opportunities, and the external threats to its future well-being.

threats to its future well-being. The simplest and most easily applied tool for conducting this examination is widely known as **SWOT analysis**, so named because it zeros in on a company's internal Strengths and Weaknesses, market Opportunities, and external Threats. *A company's internal strengths should always serve as the basis of its strategy—placing heavy reliance on a company's best competitive assets is the soundest route to attracting customers and competing successfully against rivals.*[10]

As a rule, strategies that place heavy demands on areas where the company is weakest or has unproven competencies should be avoided. Plainly, managers must look toward correcting competitive weaknesses that make the company vulnerable, hold down profitability, or disqualify it from pursuing an attractive opportunity. Furthermore, a company's strategy should be aimed squarely at capturing those market opportunities that are most attractive and suited to the company's collection of capabilities. How much attention to devote to defending against external threats to the company's future performance hinges on how vulnerable the company is, whether defensive moves can be taken to lessen their impact, and whether the costs of undertaking such moves represent the best use

Basing a company's strategy on its strengths resulting from most competitively valuable resources and capabilities gives the company its best chance for market success.

of company resources. A first-rate SWOT analysis provides the basis for crafting a strategy that capitalizes on the company's strengths, aims squarely at capturing the company's best opportunities, and defends against the threats to its well-being. Table 4.2 lists the kinds of factors to consider in compiling a company's resource strengths and weaknesses.

Simply listing a company's strengths, weaknesses, opportunities, and threats is not enough; the payoff from SWOT analysis comes from the conclusions about a company's situation and the implications for strategy improvement that flow from the four lists.

The Value of a SWOT Analysis A SWOT analysis involves more than making four lists. The most important parts of SWOT analysis are:

1. Drawing conclusions from the SWOT listings about the company's overall situation.

2. Translating these conclusions into strategic actions to better match the company's strategy to its strengths and market opportunities, correcting problematic weaknesses, and defending against worrisome external threats.

Question 3: Are the Company's Cost Structure and Customer Value Proposition Competitive?

LO4-3 Grasp how a company's value chain activities can affect the company's cost structure and customer value proposition.

Company managers are often stunned when a competitor cuts its prices to "unbelievably low" levels or when a new market entrant comes on strong with a great new product offered at a surprisingly low price. Such competitors may not, however, be buying market positions with prices that are below costs. They may simply have substantially

TABLE 4.2

Factors to Consider When Identifying a Company's Strengths, Weaknesses, Opportunities, and Threats

Potential Internal Strengths and Competitive Capabilities
- Core competencies in _____
- A strong financial condition; ample financial resources to grow the business
- Strong brand-name image/company reputation
- Economies of scale and/or learning and experience curve advantages over rivals
- Proprietary technology/superior technological skills/important patents
- Cost advantages over rivals
- Product innovation capabilities
- Proven capabilities in improving production processes
- Good supply chain management capabilities
- Good customer service capabilities
- Better product quality relative to rivals
- Wide geographic coverage and/or strong global distribution capability
- Alliances/joint ventures with other firms that provide access to valuable technology, competencies, and/or attractive geographic markets

Potential Internal Weaknesses and Competitive Deficiencies
- No clear strategic direction
- No well-developed or proven core competencies
- A weak balance sheet; burdened with too much debt
- Higher overall unit costs relative to key competitors
- A product/service with features and attributes that are inferior to those of rivals
- Too narrow a product line relative to rivals
- Weak brand image or reputation
- Weaker dealer network than key rivals
- Behind on product quality, R&D, and/or technological know-how
- Lack of management depth
- Short on financial resources to grow the business and pursue promising initiatives

Potential Market Opportunities
- Serving additional customer groups or market segments
- Expanding into new geographic markets
- Expanding the company's product line to meet a broader range of customer needs
- Utilizing existing company skills or technological know-how to enter new product lines or new businesses
- Falling trade barriers in attractive foreign markets
- Acquiring rival firms or companies with attractive technological expertise or capabilities

Potential External Threats to a Company's Future Prospects
- Increasing intensity of competition among industry rivals—may squeeze profit margins
- Slowdowns in market growth
- Likely entry of potent new competitors
- Growing bargaining power of customers or suppliers
- A shift in buyer needs and tastes away from the industry's product
- Adverse demographic changes that threaten to curtail demand for the industry's product
- Vulnerability to unfavorable industry driving forces
- Restrictive trade policies on the part of foreign governments
- Costly new regulatory requirements

lower costs and therefore are able to offer prices that result in more appealing customer value propositions. One of the most telling signs of whether a company's business position is strong or precarious is whether its cost structure and customer value proposition are competitive with those of industry rivals.

Cost comparisons are especially critical in industries where price competition is typically the ruling market force. But even in industries where products are differentiated, rival companies have to keep their costs in line with rivals offering value propositions based upon a similar mix of differentiating features. But a company must also remain competitive in terms of its customer value proposition. Patagonia's value proposition, for example, remains attractive to customers who value quality, wide selection, and corporate environmental responsibility over cheaper outerwear alternatives. Target's customer value proposition has withstood the Walmart low-price juggernaut by attention to product design, image, and attractive store layouts in addition to efficiency. The key for managers is to keep close track of how *cost-effectively* the company can deliver value to customers relative to its competitors. *If the company can deliver the same amount of value with lower expenditures (or more value at a similar cost), it will maintain a competitive edge.* Two analytical tools are particularly useful in determining whether a company's value proposition and costs are competitive: value chain analysis and benchmarking.

> Competitive advantage hinges on how cost-effectively a company can execute its customer value proposition.

Company Value Chains

Every company's business consists of a collection of activities undertaken in the course of designing, producing, marketing, delivering, and supporting its product or service. All of the various activities that a company performs internally combine to form a **value chain,** so called because the underlying intent of a company's activities is to do things that ultimately *create value for buyers.*

> **CORE CONCEPT**
>
> A company's **value chain** identifies the primary activities that create customer value and related support activities.

As shown in Figure 4.1, a company's value chain consists of two broad categories of activities that drive costs and create customer value: the *primary activities* that are foremost in creating value for customers and the requisite *support activities* that facilitate and enhance the performance of the primary activities.[11] For example, the primary activities and cost drivers for a department store retailer such as Nordstrom include merchandise selection and buying, store layout and product display, advertising, and customer service; its support activities that affect customer value and costs include hiring and training, store maintenance, plus the usual assortment of administrative activities. The primary value chain activities and costs of a hotel operator like Marriott International are mainly comprised of reservations and hotel operations (check-in and check-out, maintenance and housekeeping, dining and room service, and conventions and meetings); principal support activities that drive costs and impact customer value include accounting, hiring and training hotel staff, and general administration. Supply chain management is a crucial activity for Boeing and Amazon.com but is not a value chain component at LinkedIn or DirectTV. Sales and marketing are dominant activities at Ford Motor Company and J. Crew but have minor roles at oil and gas drilling and exploration companies and pipeline companies. With its focus on value-creating activities, the value chain is an

FIGURE 4.1 **A Representative Company Value Chain**

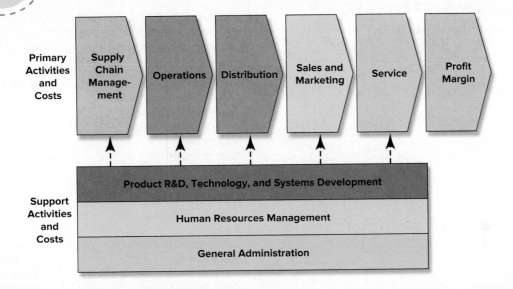

PRIMARY ACTIVITIES

- **Supply Chain Management**—Activities, costs, and assets associated with purchasing fuel, energy, raw materials, parts and components, merchandise, and consumable items from vendors; receiving, storing, and disseminating inputs from suppliers; inspection; and inventory management.

- **Operations**—Activities, costs, and assets associated with converting inputs into final product form (production, assembly, packaging, equipment maintenance, facilities, operations, quality assurance, environmental protection).

- **Distribution**—Activities, costs, and assets dealing with physically distributing the product to buyers (finished goods warehousing, order processing, order picking and packing, shipping, delivery vehicle operations, establishing and maintaining a network of dealers and distributors).

- **Sales and Marketing**—Activities, costs, and assets related to sales force efforts, advertising and promotion, market research and planning, and dealer/distributor support.

- **Service**—Activities, costs, and assets associated with providing assistance to buyers, such as installation, spare parts delivery, maintenance and repair, technical assistance, buyer inquiries, and complaints.

SUPPORT ACTIVITIES

- **Product R&D, Technology, and Systems Development**—Activities, costs, and assets relating to product R&D, process R&D, process design improvement, equipment design, computer software development, telecommunications systems, computer-assisted design and engineering, database capabilities, and development of computerized support systems.

- **Human Resources Management**—Activities, costs, and assets associated with the recruitment, hiring, training, development, and compensation of all types of personnel; labor relations activities; and development of knowledge-based skills and core competencies.

- **General Administration**—Activities, costs, and assets relating to general management, accounting and finance, legal and regulatory affairs, safety and security, management information systems, forming strategic alliances and collaborating with strategic partners, and other "overhead" functions.

Source: Based on the discussion in Michael E. Porter, *Competitive Advantage* (New York: Free Press, 1985), pp. 37–43.

Concepts&Connections 4.1

THE VALUE CHAIN FOR BOLL & BRANCH

R&P: ©Bohbeh/Shutterstock

A KING-SIZE SET OF SHEETS FROM BOLL & BRANCH IS MADE FROM 6 METERS OF FABRIC, REQUIRING 11 KILOGRAMS OF RAW COTTON.

Raw Cotton	$ 28.16
Spinning/Weaving/Dyeing	12.00
Cutting/Sewing/Finishing	9.50
Material Transportation	3.00
Factory Fee	15.80
Cost of Goods	**$ 68.46**
Inspection Fees	5.48
Ocean Freight/Insurance	4.55
Import Duties	8.22
Warehouse/Packing	8.50
Packaging	15.15
Customer Shipping	14.00
Promotions/Donations*	30.00
Total Cost	**$154.38**
Boll & Brand Markup	About 60%
Boll & Brand Retail Price	**$250.00**
Gross Margin**	**$ 95.62**

*A $5 donation for every set of sheets sold is paid to an anti–human-trafficking organization.

**Gross margin covers overhead, advertising costs, and profit.

Source: Adapted from Christina Brinkley, "What Goes into the Price of Luxury Sheets?" *The Wall Street Journal*, March 29, 2014, www.wsj .com/articles/SB10001424052702303725404579461953672838672 (accessed February 16, 2016).

ideal tool for examining how a company delivers on its customer value proposition. It permits a deep look at the company's cost structure and ability to offer low prices. It reveals the emphasis that a company places on activities that enhance differentiation and support higher prices, such as service and marketing.

The value chain also includes a profit margin component; profits are necessary to compensate the company's owners/shareholders and investors, who bear risks and provide capital. Tracking the profit margin along with the value-creating activities is critical because unless an enterprise succeeds in delivering customer value profitably (with a sufficient return on invested capital), it cannot survive for long. Attention to a company's profit formula in addition to its customer value proposition is the essence of a sound business model, as described in Chapter 1. Concepts & Connections 4.1 shows representative costs for various activities performed by Boll & Branch, a maker of luxury linens and bedding sold directly to consumers online.

Benchmarking: A Tool for Assessing Whether a Company's Value Chain Activities Are Competitive

Benchmarking entails comparing how different companies perform various value chain activities—how materials are purchased, how inventories are managed, how products are assembled, how customer orders are filled and shipped, and how maintenance is performed—and then making cross-company comparisons of the costs and effectiveness of these activities.[12] The objectives of benchmarking are to identify the best practices in performing an activity and to emulate those best practices when they are possessed by others.

A **best practice** is a method of performing an activity or business process that consistently delivers superior results compared to other approaches.[13] To qualify as a legitimate best practice, the method must have been employed by at least one enterprise and shown to be consistently more effective in lowering costs, improving quality or performance, shortening time requirements, enhancing safety, or achieving some other highly positive operating outcome. Best practices thus identify a path to operating excellence with respect to value chain activities.

> **CORE CONCEPT**
>
> **Benchmarking** is a potent tool for learning which companies are best at performing particular activities and then using their techniques (or "best practices") to improve the cost and effectiveness of a company's own internal activities.

> **CORE CONCEPT**
>
> A **best practice** is a method of performing an activity that consistently delivers superior results compared to other approaches.

Xerox led the way in the use of benchmarking to become more cost-competitive by deciding not to restrict its benchmarking efforts to its office equipment rivals, but by comparing itself to *any company* regarded as "world class" in performing activities relevant to Xerox's business. Other companies quickly picked up on Xerox's approach. Toyota managers got their idea for just-in-time inventory deliveries by studying how U.S. supermarkets replenished their shelves. Southwest Airlines reduced the turnaround time of its aircraft at each scheduled stop by studying pit crews on the auto-racing circuit. More than 80 percent of Fortune 500 companies reportedly use benchmarking for comparing themselves against rivals on cost and other competitively important measures.

The tough part of benchmarking is not whether to do it, but rather how to gain access to information about other companies' practices and costs. Sometimes benchmarking can be accomplished by collecting information from published reports, trade groups, and industry research firms and by talking to knowledgeable industry analysts, customers, and suppliers. Sometimes field trips to the facilities of competing or noncompeting companies can be arranged to observe how things are done, compare practices and processes, and perhaps exchange data on productivity and other cost components. However, such companies, even if they agree to host facilities tours and answer questions, are unlikely to share competitively sensitive cost information. Furthermore, comparing two companies' costs may not involve comparing apples to apples if the two companies employ different cost accounting principles to calculate the costs of particular activities.

However, a fairly reliable source of benchmarking information has emerged. The explosive interest of companies in benchmarking costs and identifying best practices has prompted consulting organizations (e.g., Accenture, A. T. Kearney, Benchnet—The Benchmarking Exchange, and Best Practices, LLC) and several councils and associations (e.g., the Qualserve Benchmarking Clearinghouse and the Strategic Planning Institute's Council on Benchmarking) to gather benchmarking data, distribute information about best practices, and provide comparative cost data without identifying the names of particular companies. Having an independent group gather the information and report it in a manner that disguises the names of individual companies avoids the disclosure of competitively sensitive data and lessens the potential for unethical behavior on the part of company personnel in gathering their own data about competitors.

The Value Chain System for an Entire Industry

A company's value chain is embedded in a larger system of activities that includes the value chains of its suppliers and the value chains of whatever distribution channel allies it utilizes in getting its product or service to end users. The value chains of forward channel partners are relevant because (1) the costs and margins of a company's distributors and retail dealers are part of the price the consumer ultimately pays, and (2) the activities that distribution allies perform affect the company's customer value proposition. For these reasons, companies normally work closely with their suppliers and forward channel allies to perform value chain activities in mutually beneficial ways. For instance, motor vehicle manufacturers work closely with their forward channel allies (local automobile dealers) to ensure that owners are satisfied with dealers' repair and maintenance services.[14] Also, many automotive parts suppliers have built plants near the auto assembly plants they supply to facilitate just-in-time deliveries, reduce warehousing and shipping costs, and promote close collaboration on parts design and production scheduling. Irrigation equipment companies, suppliers of grape-harvesting and winemaking equipment, and firms making barrels, wine bottles, caps, corks, and labels all have facilities in the California wine country to be close to the nearly 700 winemakers they supply.[15] The lesson here is that a company's value chain activities are often closely linked to the value chains of its suppliers and the forward allies.

> A company's customer value proposition and cost competitiveness depend not only on internally performed activities (its own company value chain), but also on the value chain activities of its suppliers and forward channel allies.

As a consequence, *accurately assessing the competitiveness of a company's cost structure and customer value proposition requires that company managers understand an industry's entire value chain system for delivering a product or service to customers, not just the company's own value chain.* A typical industry value chain that incorporates the value-creating activities, costs, and margins of suppliers and forward channel allies, if any, is shown in Figure 4.2. However, industry value chains vary significantly by industry. For example, the primary value chain activities in the pulp and paper industry (timber farming, logging, pulp mills, and papermaking) differ from those for the home appliance industry (parts and components manufacture, assembly, wholesale distribution, retail sales) and yet again from the cloud computing industry (IT hardware infrastructure, systems software infrastructure, application development, and application hosting, management, and security services).

Strategic Options for Remedying a Cost or Value Disadvantage

The results of value chain analysis and benchmarking may disclose cost or value disadvantages relative to key rivals. These competitive disadvantages are likely to lower a company's relative profit margin or weaken its customer value proposition. In such instances, actions to improve a company's value chain are called for to boost profitability or to allow for the addition of new features that drive customer value. There are three main areas in a company's overall value chain where important differences between firms in costs and value can occur: a company's own internal activities, the

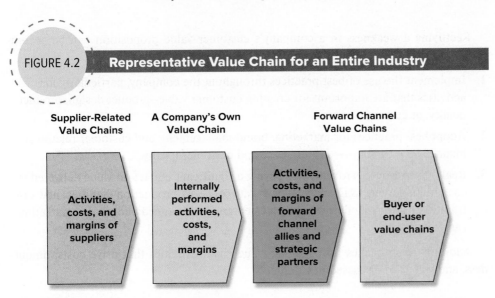

FIGURE 4.2

Representative Value Chain for an Entire Industry

Source: Based in part on the single-industry value chain displayed in Michael E. Porter, *Competitive Advantage* (New York: Free Press, 1985), p. 35.

suppliers' part of the industry value chain, and the forward channel portion of the industry chain.

Improving Internally Performed Value Chain Activities   Managers can pursue any of several strategic approaches to reduce the costs of internally performed value chain activities and improve a company's cost competitiveness.

1. *Implement the use of best practices* throughout the company, particularly for high-cost activities.

2. *Try to eliminate some cost-producing activities* by revamping the value chain. Many retailers have found that donating returned items to charitable organizations and taking the appropriate tax deduction results in a smaller loss than incurring the costs of the value chain activities involved in reverse logistics.

3. *Relocate high-cost activities* (such as manufacturing) to geographic areas such as China, Latin America, or Eastern Europe where they can be performed more cheaply.

4. *Outsource certain internally performed activities* to vendors or contractors if they can perform them more cheaply than can be done in-house.

5. *Invest in productivity-enhancing, cost-saving technological improvements* (robotics, flexible manufacturing techniques, state-of-the-art electronic networking).

6. *Find ways to detour around the activities or items where costs are high.* Computer chip makers regularly design around the patents held by others to avoid paying royalties; automakers have substituted lower-cost plastic for metal at many exterior body locations.

7. *Redesign the product* and/or some of its components to facilitate speedier and more economical manufacture or assembly.

8. *Try to make up the internal cost disadvantage* by reducing costs in the supplier or forward channel portions of the industry value chain—usually a last resort.

Rectifying a weakness in a company's customer value proposition can be accomplished by applying one or more of the following approaches:

1. Implement the use of best practices throughout the company, particularly for activities that are important for creating customer value—product design, product quality, or customer service.

2. Adopt best practices for marketing, brand management, and customer relationship management to improve brand image and customer loyalty.

3. Reallocate resources to activities having a significant impact on value delivered to customers—larger R&D budgets, new state-of-the-art production facilities, new distribution centers, modernized service centers, or enhanced budgets for marketing campaigns.

Additional approaches to managing value chain activities that drive costs, uniqueness, and value are discussed in Chapter 5.

Improving Supplier-Related Value Chain Activities Supplier-related cost disadvantages can be attacked by pressuring suppliers for lower prices, switching to lower-priced substitute inputs, and collaborating closely with suppliers to identify mutual cost-saving opportunities.[16] For example, just-in-time deliveries from suppliers can lower a company's inventory and internal logistics costs, eliminate capital expenditures for additional warehouse space, and improve cash flow and financial ratios by reducing accounts payable. In a few instances, companies may find that it is cheaper to integrate backward into the business of high-cost suppliers and make the item in-house instead of buying it from outsiders.

Similarly, a company can enhance its customer value proposition through its supplier relationships. Some approaches include selecting and retaining suppliers that meet higher-quality standards, providing quality-based incentives to suppliers, and integrating suppliers into the design process. When fewer defects exist in components provided by suppliers, this not only improves product quality and reliability, but it can also lower costs because there is less disruption to production processes and lower warranty expenses.

Improving Value Chain Activities of Forward Channel Allies There are three main ways to combat a cost disadvantage in the forward portion of the industry value chain: (1) Pressure dealers-distributors and other forward channel allies to reduce their costs and markups; (2) work closely with forward channel allies to identify win-win opportunities to reduce costs—for example, Walmart and Target require suppliers to meet a two-day shipping arrival window, which not only improves distribution center operating efficiency but also reduces costly unloading wait times for the shipper; and (3) change to a more economical distribution strategy or perhaps integrate forward into company-owned retail outlets.

A company can improve its customer value proposition through the activities of forward channel partners by the use of (1) cooperative advertising and promotions with forward channel allies; (2) training programs for dealers, distributors, or retailers to improve the purchasing experience or customer service; and (3) creating and enforcing operating standards for resellers or franchisees to ensure consistent store operations. Papa John's International, for example, is consistently rated highly by customers for its pizza quality, convenient ordering systems, and responsive customer service across its 5,100 company-owned and franchised units. The company's marketing campaigns and extensive employee training and development programs enhance its value proposition and the unit sales and operating profit for its franchisees in all 50 states and 45 countries.

How Value Chain Activities Relate to Resources and Capabilities

A close relationship exists between the value-creating activities that a company performs and its resources and capabilities. When companies engage in a value-creating activity, they do so by drawing on specific company resources and capabilities that underlie and enable the activity. For example, brand-building activities that enhance a company's customer value proposition can depend on human resources, such as experienced brand managers, as well as organizational capabilities related to developing and executing effective marketing campaigns. Distribution activities that lower costs may derive from organizational capabilities in inventory management and resources such as cutting-edge inventory tracking systems.

Because of the linkage between activities and enabling resources and capabilities, value chain analysis complements resource and capability analysis as another tool for assessing a company's competitive advantage. Resources and capabilities that are *both valuable and rare* provide a company with the *necessary preconditions* for competitive advantage. When these assets are deployed in the form of a value-creating activity, *that potential is realized.* Resource analysis is a valuable tool for assessing the competitive advantage potential of resources and capabilities. But the actual competitive benefit provided by resources and capabilities can only be assessed objectively after they are deployed in the form of activities.

Question 4: What Is the Company's Competitive Strength Relative to Key Rivals?

LO4-4 Evaluate a company's competitive strength relative to key rivals.

An additional component of evaluating a company's situation is developing a comprehensive assessment of the company's overall competitive strength. Making this determination requires answers to two questions:

1. How does the company rank relative to competitors on each of the important factors that determine market success?

2. All things considered, does the company have a net competitive advantage or disadvantage versus major competitors?

Step 1 in doing a competitive strength assessment is to list the industry's key success factors and other telling measures of competitive strength or weakness (6 to 10 measures usually suffice). Step 2 is to assign a weight to each measure of competitive strength based on its perceived importance in shaping competitive success. (The sum of the weights for each measure must add up to 1.0.) Step 3 is to calculate weighted strength ratings by scoring each competitor on each strength measure (using a 1-to-10 rating scale where 1 is very weak and 10 is very strong) and multiplying the assigned rating by the assigned weight. Step 4 is to sum the weighted strength ratings on each factor to get an overall measure of competitive strength for each company being rated. Step 5 is to use the overall strength ratings to draw conclusions about the size and extent of the company's net competitive advantage or disadvantage and to take specific note of areas of strength and weakness. Table 4.3 provides an example of a competitive strength assessment using the hypothetical ABC Company against four rivals. ABC's total score of 5.95 signals a net competitive advantage over Rival 3 (with a score of 2.10) and Rival 4 (with a score of 3.70) but indicates a net competitive disadvantage against Rival 1 (with a score of 7.70) and Rival 2 (with an overall score of 6.85).

Interpreting the Competitive Strength Assessments

Competitive strength assessments provide useful conclusions about a company's competitive situation. The ratings show how a company compares against rivals, factor by factor or capability by capability, thus revealing where it is strongest and weakest. Moreover, the overall competitive strength scores indicate whether the company is at a net competitive advantage or disadvantage against each rival.

> A company's competitive strength scores pinpoint its strengths and weaknesses against rivals and point to offensive and defensive strategies capable of producing first-rate results.

In addition, the strength ratings provide guidelines for designing wise offensive and defensive strategies. For example, consider the ratings and weighted scores in Table 4.3. If ABC Co. wants to go on the offensive to win additional sales and market share, such an offensive probably needs to be aimed directly at winning customers away from Rivals 3 and 4 (which have lower overall strength scores) rather than Rivals 1 and 2 (which have higher overall strength scores). ABC's advantages over Rival 4 tend to be in areas that are moderately important to competitive success in the industry, but ABC outclasses Rival 3 on the two most heavily weighted strength factors—relative cost position and customer service capabilities. Therefore, Rival 3 should be viewed as the primary target of ABC's offensive strategies, with Rival 4 being a secondary target.

A competitively astute company should utilize the strength scores in deciding what strategic moves to make. When a company has important competitive strengths in areas where one or more rivals are weak, it makes sense to consider offensive moves to exploit rivals' competitive weaknesses. When a company has competitive weaknesses in important areas where one or more rivals are strong, it makes sense to consider defensive moves to curtail its vulnerability.

Question 5: What Strategic Issues and Problems Must Be Addressed by Management?

LO4-5 Understand how a comprehensive evaluation of a company's external and internal situations can assist managers in making critical decisions about their next strategic moves.

The final and most important analytical step is to zero in on exactly what strategic issues company managers need to address. This step involves drawing on the results of

TABLE 4.3

Illustration of a Competitive Strength Assessment

Key Success Factor/ Strength Measure	Importance Weight	ABC CO.		RIVAL 1		RIVAL 2		RIVAL 3		RIVAL 4	
		Strength Rating	Score	Strength Rating	Score	Strength Rating	Score	Strength Rating	Score	Strength Rating	Score
Quality/product performance	0.10	8	0.80	5	0.50	10	1.00	1	0.10	6	0.60
Reputation/image	0.10	8	0.80	7	0.70	10	1.00	1	0.10	6	0.60
Manufacturing capability	0.10	2	0.20	10	1.00	4	0.40	5	0.50	1	0.10
Technological skills	0.05	10	0.50	1	0.05	7	0.35	3	0.15	8	0.40
Dealer network/distribution capability	0.05	9	0.45	4	0.20	10	0.50	5	0.25	1	0.05
New product innovation capability	0.05	9	0.45	4	0.20	10	0.50	5	0.25	1	0.05
Financial resources	0.10	5	0.50	10	1.00	7	0.70	3	0.30	1	0.10
Relative cost position	0.30	5	1.50	10	3.00	3	0.90	1	0.30	4	1.20
Customer service capabilities	0.15	5	0.75	7	1.05	10	1.50	1	0.15	4	0.60
Sum of importance weights	1.00										
Weighted overall strength rating			**5.95**		**7.70**		**6.85**		**2.10**		**3.70**

(Rating scale: 1 = very weak; 10 = very strong)

both industry and competitive analysis and the evaluations of the company's internal situation. The task here is to get a clear fix on exactly what industry and competitive challenges confront the company, which of the company's internal weaknesses need fixing, and what specific problems merit front-burner attention by company managers. *Pinpointing the precise things that management needs to worry about sets the agenda for deciding what actions to take next to improve the company's performance and business outlook.*

> Compiling a "worry list" of problems and issues creates an agenda for managerial strategy making.

If the items on management's "worry list" are relatively minor, which suggests the company's strategy is mostly on track and reasonably well matched to the company's overall situation, company managers seldom need to go much beyond fine-tuning the present strategy. If, however, the issues and problems confronting the company are serious and indicate the present strategy is not well suited for the road ahead, the task of crafting a better strategy has got to go to the top of management's action agenda.

KEY POINTS

In analyzing a company's own particular competitive circumstances and its competitive position vis-à-vis key rivals, consider five key questions:

1. *How well is the present strategy working?* This involves evaluating the strategy in terms of the company's financial performance and competitive strength and market standing. The stronger a company's current overall performance, the less likely the need for radical strategy changes. The weaker a company's performance and/or the faster the changes in its external situation (which can be gleaned from industry and competitive analysis), the more its current strategy must be questioned.

2. *Do the company's resources and capabilities have sufficient competitive power to give it a sustainable advantage over competitors?* The answer to this question comes from conducting the four tests of a resource's competitive power—the VRIN tests. If a company has resources and capabilities that are competitively *valuable* and *rare,* the firm will have the potential for a competitive advantage over market rivals. If its resources and capabilities are also hard to copy (*inimitable*) with no good substitutes (*nonsubstitutable*), then the firm may be able to sustain this advantage even in the face of active efforts by rivals to overcome it.

   SWOT analysis can be used to assess if a company's resources and capabilities are sufficient to seize market opportunities and overcome external threats to its future well-being. The two most important parts of SWOT analysis are (1) drawing conclusions about what story the compilation of strengths, weaknesses, opportunities, and threats tells about the company's overall situation, and (2) acting on the conclusions to better match the company's strategy to its internal strengths and market opportunities, to correct the important internal weaknesses, and to defend against external threats. A company's strengths and competitive assets are strategically relevant because they are the most logical and appealing building blocks for strategy; internal weaknesses are important because they may represent vulnerabilities that need correction. External opportunities and threats come into play because a good strategy necessarily aims at capturing a company's most attractive opportunities and at defending against threats to its well-being.

3. *Are the company's cost structure and customer value proposition competitive?* One telling sign of whether a company's situation is strong or precarious is whether its costs are competitive with those of industry rivals. Another sign is how it compares with rivals in terms of its customer value proposition. Value chain analysis and benchmarking are essential tools in determining whether the company is performing particular functions and activities well, whether its costs are in line with competitors, whether it is able to offer an attractive value proposition to customers, and whether particular internal activities and business processes need improvement. Value chain analysis complements resource and capability analysis because of the tight linkage between activities and enabling resources and capabilities.

4. *Is the company competitively stronger or weaker than key rivals?* The key appraisals here involve how the company matches up against key rivals on industry key success factors and other chief determinants of competitive success and whether and why the company has a competitive advantage or disadvantage. Quantitative competitive strength assessments, using the method presented in Table 4.3, indicate where a company is competitively strong and weak and provide insight into the company's ability to defend or enhance its market position. As a rule, a company's competitive strategy should be built around its competitive strengths and should aim at shoring up areas where it is competitively vulnerable. When a company has important competitive strengths in areas where one or more rivals are weak, it makes sense to consider offensive moves to exploit rivals' competitive weaknesses. When a company has important competitive weaknesses in areas where one or more rivals are strong, it makes sense to consider defensive moves to curtail its vulnerability.

5. *What strategic issues and problems merit front-burner managerial attention?* This analytical step zeros in on the strategic issues and problems that stand in the way of the company's success. It involves using the results of both industry and competitive analysis and company situation analysis to identify a "worry list" of issues to be resolved for the company to be financially and competitively successful in the years ahead. Actually deciding upon a strategy and what specific actions to take comes after the list of strategic issues and problems that merit front-burner management attention has been developed.

Good company situation analysis, like good industry and competitive analysis, is a valuable precondition for good strategy making.

 ## ASSURANCE OF LEARNING EXERCISES

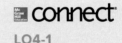

LO4-1

1. Using the financial ratios provided in the Appendix and the following financial statement information for Macy's, Inc., calculate the following ratios for Macy's for both 2015 and 2016.

   1. Gross profit margin
   2. Operating profit margin
   3. Net profit margin
   4. Times interest earned coverage
   5. Return on shareholders' equity
   6. Return on assets
   7. Long-term debt-to-equity ratio
   8. Days of inventory
   9. Inventory turnover ratio
   10. Average collection period

Based on these ratios, did Macy's financial performance improve, weaken, or remain about the same from 2015 to 2016?

Consolidated Statements of Income for Macy's, Inc., 2015–2016 (in millions, except per share amounts)

	2016	2015
Net sales	$25,778	$27,079
Cost of sales	(15,621)	(16,496)
Gross margin	10,157	10,583
Selling, general and administrative expenses	(8,265)	(8,256)
Impairments, store closing and other costs	(479)	(288)
Settlement charges	(98)	—
Operating income	1,315	2,039
Interest expense	(367)	(363)
Premium on early retirement of debt	—	—
Interest income	4	2
Income before income taxes	952	1,678
Federal, state, and local income tax expense	(341)	(608)
Net income	611	1,070
Net loss attributable to noncontrolling interest	8	2
Net income attributable to Macy's, Inc., shareholders	619	1,072
Basic earnings per share attributable to Macy's, Inc., shareholders	$ 2.01	$ 3.26
Diluted earnings per share attributable to Macy's, Inc., shareholders	$ 1.99	$ 3.22

Consolidated Balance Sheets for Macy's, Inc., 2015–2016 (in millions)

	2016	2015
ASSETS		
Current Assets:		
Cash and cash equivalents	$ 1,297	$ 1,109
Receivables	522	558
Merchandise inventories	5,399	5,506
Prepaid expenses and other current assets	408	479
Total Current Assets	7,626	7,652
Property and Equipment – net	7,017	7,616
Goodwill	3,897	3,897
Other Intangible Assets – net	498	514
Other Assets	813	897
Total Assets	$19,851	$20,576
LIABILITIES AND SHAREHOLDERS' EQUITY		
Current Liabilties:		
Short-term debt	$309	$642
Merchandise accounts payable	1,423	1,526
Accounts payable and accrued liabilities	3,563	3,333
Income taxes	352	227
Total Current Liabilities	5,647	5,728
Long-Term Debt	6,562	6,995
Deferred Income Taxes	1,443	1,477
Other Liabilities	1,877	2,123

	2016	2015
Shareholders' Equity:		
Common stock (304.1 and 310.3 shares outstanding)	3	3
Additional paid-in capital	617	621
Accumulated equity	6,088	6,334
Treasury stock	(1,489)	(1,665)
Accumulated other comprehensive loss	(896)	(1,043)
Total Macy's, Inc., Shareholders' Equity	4,323	4,250
Noncontrolling interest	(1)	3
Total Shareholders' Equity	4,322	4,253
Total Liabilities and Shareholders' Equity	$19,851	$20,576

Source: Macy's, Inc., 2016 10-K.

2.   REI operates more than 140 sporting goods and outdoor recreation stores in 36 states. How many of the four tests of the competitive power of a resource does the retail store network pass? Explain your answer.   LO4-2

3.   Review the information in Concepts & Connections 4.1 concerning Boll & Branch's average costs of producing and selling a king-sized sheet set, and compare this with the representative value chain depicted in Figure 4.1. Then answer the following questions: LO4-3

   a.   Which of the company's costs correspond to the primary value chain activities depicted in Figure 4.1?

   b.   Which of the company's costs correspond to the support activities described in Figure 4.1?

   c.   What value chain activities might be important in securing or maintaining Boll & Branch's competitive advantage? Explain your answer.

4.   Using the methodology illustrated in Table 4.3 and your knowledge as an automobile owner, prepare a competitive strength assessment for General Motors and its rivals Ford, Chrysler, Toyota, and Honda. Each of the five automobile manufacturers should be evaluated on the key success factors/strength measures of cost competitiveness, product-line breadth, product quality and reliability, financial resources and profitability, and customer service. What does your competitive strength assessment disclose about the overall competitiveness of each automobile manufacturer? What factors account most for Toyota's competitive success? Does Toyota have competitive weaknesses that were disclosed by your analysis? Explain.   connect   LO4-4

 EXERCISES FOR SIMULATION PARTICIPANTS

1.   Using the formulas in the Appendix and the data in your company's latest financial statements, calculate the following measures of financial performance for your company: LO4-1

   1.   Operating profit margin

   2.   Return on total assets

   3.   Current ratio

   4.   Working capital

   5.   Long-term debt-to-capital ratio

   6.   Price-earnings ratio

LO4-1   2.   Based on your company's latest financial statements and all of the other available data regarding your company's performance that appear in the Industry Report, list the three measures of financial performance on which your company did "best" and the three measures on which your company's financial performance was "worst."

LO4-1   3.   What hard evidence can you cite that indicates your company's strategy is working fairly well (or perhaps not working so well, if your company's performance is lagging that of rival companies)?

LO4-2   4.   What internal strengths and weaknesses does your company have? What external market opportunities for growth and increased profitability exist for your company? What external threats to your company's future well-being and profitability do you and your co-managers see? What does the preceding SWOT analysis indicate about your company's present situation and future prospects—where on the scale from "exceptionally strong" to "alarmingly weak" does the attractiveness of your company's situation rank?

LO4-2   5.   Does your company have any core competencies? If so, what are they?

LO4-3   6.   What are the key elements of your company's value chain? Refer to Figure 4.1 in developing your answer.

LO4-4   7.   Using the methodology illustrated in Table 4.3, do a weighted competitive strength assessment for your company and two other companies that you and your co-managers consider to be very close competitors.

ENDNOTES

1. Birger Wernerfelt, "A Resource-Based View of the Firm," *Strategic Management Journal* 5, no. 5 (September–October 1984); Jay Barney, "Firm Resources and Sustained Competitive Advantage," *Journal of Management* 17, no. 1 (1991); Margaret A. Peteraf, "The Cornerstones of Competitive Advantage: A Resource-Based View," *Strategic Management Journal* 14, no. 3 (March 1993).

2. Birger Wernerfelt, "A Resource-Based View of the Firm," *Strategic Management Journal* 5, no. 5 (September–October 1984), pp. 171–80; Jay Barney, "Firm Resources and Sustained Competitive Advantage," *Journal of Management* 17, no. 1 (1991); and Margaret A. Peteraf, "The Cornerstones of Competitive Advantage: A Resource-Based View," *Strategic Management Journal* 14, no. 3 (March 1993).

3. R. Amit and P. Schoemaker, "Strategic Assets and Organizational Rent," *Strategic Management Journal* 14, no. 1 (1993).

4. David J. Collis and Cynthia A. Montgomery, "Competing on Resources: Strategy in the 1990s," *Harvard Business Review* 73, no. 4 (July–August 1995).

5. Margaret A. Peteraf and Mark E. Bergen, "Scanning Dynamic Competitive Landscapes: A Market-Based and Resource-Based Framework," *Strategic Management Journal* 24 (2003), pp. 1027-42.

6. David J. Teece, Gary Pisano, and Amy Shuen, "Dynamic Capabilities and Strategic Management," *Strategic Management Journal* 18, no. 7 (1997); and Constance E. Helfat and Margaret A. Peteraf, "The Dynamic Resource-Based View: Capability Lifecycles," *Strategic Management Journal* 24, no. 10 (2003).

7. C. Montgomery, "Of Diamonds and Rust: A New Look at Resources" in *Resource-Based and Evolutionary Theories of the Firm,* ed. C. Montgomery (Boston: Kluwer Academic Publishers, 1995), pp. 251-68.

8. D. Teece, G. Pisano, and A. Shuen, "Dynamic Capabilities and Strategic Management," *Strategic Management Journal* 18, no. 7 (1997); K. Eisenhardt and J. Martin, "Dynamic Capabilities: What Are They?" *Strategic Management Journal* 21, nos. 10–11 (2000); M. Zollo and S. Winter, "Deliberate Learning and the Evolution of Dynamic Capabilities,"

Organization Science 13 (2002); and C. Helfat et al., *Dynamic Capabilities: Understanding Strategic Change in Organizations* (Malden, MA: Blackwell, 2007).

9. W. Powell, K. Koput, and L. Smith-Doerr, "Interorganizational Collaboration and the Locus of Innovation," *Administrative Science Quarterly* 41, no. 1 (1996).

10. M. Peteraf, "The Cornerstones of Competitive Advantage: A Resource-Based View," *Strategic Management Journal,* March 1993, pp. 179-91.

11. Michael E. Porter, *Competitive Advantage* (New York: Free Press, 1985).

12. Gregory H. Watson, *Strategic Benchmarking: How to Rate Your Company's Performance Against the World's Best* (New York: John Wiley & Sons, 1993); Robert C. Camp, *Benchmarking: The Search for Industry Best Practices That Lead to Superior Performance* (Milwaukee: ASQC Quality Press, 1989); Christopher E. Bogan and Michael J. English, *Benchmarking for Best Practices: Winning through Innovative Adaptation* (New York: McGraw-Hill, 1994); and Dawn Iacobucci and Christie

Nordhielm, "Creative Benchmarking," *Harvard Business Review* 78, no. 6 (November–December 2000).

13. www.businessdictionary.com/definition/best-practice.html (accessed June 5, 2017).

14. M. Hegert and D. Morris, "Accounting Data for Value Chain Analysis,"

Strategic Management Journal 10 (1989); Robin Cooper and Robert S. Kaplan, "Measure Costs Right: Make the Right Decisions," *Harvard Business Review* 66, no. 5 (September–October 1988); and John K. Shank and Vijay Govindarajan, *Strategic Cost Management* (New York: Free Press, 1993).

15. Michael E. Porter, "Clusters and the New Economics of Competition," *Harvard Business Review* 76, no. 6 (November–December 1998).

16. Reuben E. Stone, "Leading a Supply Chain Turnaround," *Harvard Business Review* 82, no. 10 (October 2004).

5

The Five Generic Competitive Strategies

LEARNING OBJECTIVES

After reading this chapter, you should be able to:

LO5-1   Understand what distinguishes each of the five generic strategies and why some of these strategies work better in certain kinds of industry and competitive conditions than in others.

LO5-2   Explain the major avenues for achieving a competitive advantage based on lower costs.

LO5-3   Explain the major avenues for developing a competitive advantage based on differentiating a company's product or service offering from the offerings of rivals.

LO5-4   Recognize the attributes of a best-cost provider strategy—a hybrid of low-cost provider and differentiation strategies.

A company can employ any of several basic approaches to competing successfully and gaining a competitive advantage, but they all involve giving buyers what they perceive as superior value compared to the offerings of rival sellers. A superior value proposition can be based on offering a good product at a lower price, a superior product that is worth paying more for, or a best-value offering that represents an attractive combination of price, features, quality, service, and other appealing attributes.

This chapter describes the five *generic competitive strategy options* for building competitive advantage and delivering superior value to customers. Which of the five to employ is a company's first and foremost choice in crafting an overall strategy and beginning its quest for competitive advantage.

The Five Generic Competitive Strategies

 LO5-1 Understand what distinguishes each of the five generic strategies and why some of these strategies work better in certain kinds of industry and competitive conditions than in others.

A company's **competitive strategy** *deals exclusively with the specifics of management's game plan for competing successfully*—its specific efforts to please customers, strengthen its market position, counter the maneuvers of rivals, respond to shifting market conditions, and achieve a particular competitive advantage. The chances are remote that any two companies—even companies in the same industry—will employ competitive strategies that are exactly alike. However, when one strips away the details to get at the real substance, the two biggest factors that distinguish one competitive strategy from another boil down to (1) whether a company's market target is broad or narrow, and (2) whether the company is pursuing a competitive advantage linked to lower costs or differentiation. These two factors give rise to the five competitive strategy options shown in Figure 5.1.[1]

> **CORE CONCEPT**
>
> A **competitive strategy** concerns the specifics of management's game plan for competing successfully and securing a competitive advantage over rivals in the marketplace.

1. *A low-cost provider strategy*—striving to achieve lower overall costs than rivals and appealing to a broad spectrum of customers, usually by underpricing rivals

2. *A broad differentiation strategy*—seeking to differentiate the company's product or service from rivals' in ways that will appeal to a broad spectrum of buyers

3. *A focused low-cost strategy*—concentrating on a narrow buyer segment (or market niche) and outcompeting rivals by having lower costs than rivals and thus being able to serve niche members at a lower price

4. *A focused differentiation strategy*—concentrating on a narrow buyer segment (or market niche) and outcompeting rivals by offering niche members customized attributes that meet their tastes and requirements better than rivals' products

5. *A best-cost provider strategy*—giving customers more value for the money by satisfying buyers' expectations on key quality/features/performance/service attributes while beating their price expectations. This option is a *hybrid* strategy that blends elements of low-cost provider and differentiation strategies; the aim is to have the lowest (best) costs and prices among sellers offering products with comparable differentiating attributes.

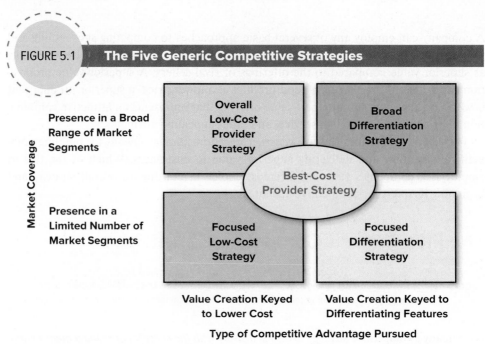

FIGURE 5.1 | **The Five Generic Competitive Strategies**

Source: This is an author-expanded version of a three-strategy classification discussed in Michael E. Porter, *Competitive Strategy* (New York: Free Press, 1980), pp. 35–40.

The remainder of this chapter explores the ins and outs of the five generic competitive strategies and how they differ.

Low-Cost Provider Strategies

LO5-2   Explain the major avenues for achieving a competitive advantage based on lower costs.

Striving to be the industry's overall low-cost provider is a powerful competitive approach in markets with many price-sensitive buyers. A company achieves low-cost leadership when it becomes the industry's lowest-cost provider rather than just being one of perhaps several competitors with low costs. Successful low-cost providers boast meaningfully lower costs than rivals, but not necessarily the absolutely lowest possible cost. In striving for a cost advantage over rivals, managers must include features and services that buyers consider essential. A product offering that is too frills-free can be viewed by consumers as offering little value, regardless of its pricing.

> **CORE CONCEPT**
>
> A **low-cost leader**'s basis for competitive advantage is lower overall costs than competitors'. Success in achieving a low-cost edge over rivals comes from eliminating and/or curbing "nonessential" activities and/or outmanaging rivals in performing essential activities.

A company has two options for translating a low-cost advantage over rivals into attractive profit performance. Option 1 is to use the lower-cost edge to underprice competitors and attract price-sensitive buyers in great enough numbers to increase total profits. Option 2 is to maintain the present price, be content with the present market share, and use the lower-cost edge to earn a higher profit margin on each unit sold, thereby raising the firm's total profits and overall return on investment.

The Two Major Avenues for Achieving Low-Cost Leadership

To achieve a low-cost edge over rivals, a firm's cumulative costs across its overall value chain must be lower than competitors' cumulative costs. There are two major avenues for accomplishing this:[2]

1. Performing essential value chain activities more cost-effectively than rivals.

2. Revamping the firm's overall value chain to eliminate or bypass some cost-producing activities.

Cost-Efficient Management of Value Chain Activities For a company to do a more cost-efficient job of managing its value chain than rivals, managers must launch a concerted, ongoing effort to ferret out cost-saving opportunities in every part of the value chain. No activity can escape cost-saving scrutiny, and all company personnel must be expected to use their talents and ingenuity to come up with innovative and effective ways to keep costs down. Particular attention needs to be paid to **cost drivers**, which are factors that have an especially strong effect on the costs of a company's value chain activities. The number of products in a company's product line, its capacity utilization, the type of components used in the assembly of its products, and the extent of its employee benefits package are all factors affecting the company's overall cost position. Figure 5.2 shows the most important cost drivers. Cost-saving approaches that demonstrate effective management of the cost drivers in a company's value chain include:

*   *Striving to capture all available economies of scale.* Economies of scale stem from an ability to lower unit costs by increasing the scale of operation. For example, Anheuser-Busch InBev was able to capture scale economies with its $5 million SuperBowl ad in 2016 because the cost could be distributed over the millions of cases of Budweiser and Bud Light sold that year.

*   *Taking full advantage of experience and learning-curve effects.* The cost of performing an activity can decline over time as the learning and experience of company personnel build.

*   *Trying to operate facilities at full capacity.* Whether a company is able to operate at or near full capacity has a big impact on unit costs when its value chain contains activities associated with substantial fixed costs. Higher rates of capacity utilization allow depreciation and other fixed costs to be spread over a larger unit volume, thereby lowering fixed costs per unit.

*   *Substituting lower-cost inputs whenever there is little or no sacrifice in product quality or product performance.* If the costs of certain raw materials and parts are "too high," a company can switch to using lower-cost alternatives when they exist.

*   *Employing advanced production technology and process design to improve overall efficiency.* Often production costs can be cut by utilizing design for manufacture (DFM) procedures and computer-assisted design (CAD) techniques that enable more integrated and efficient production methods, investing in highly automated robotic production technology, and shifting to production processes that enable manufacturing multiple versions of a product as cost efficiently as mass producing a single version. A number of companies are ardent users of total quality management systems, business process reengineering, Six Sigma methodology, and other business process management techniques that aim at boosting efficiency and reducing costs.

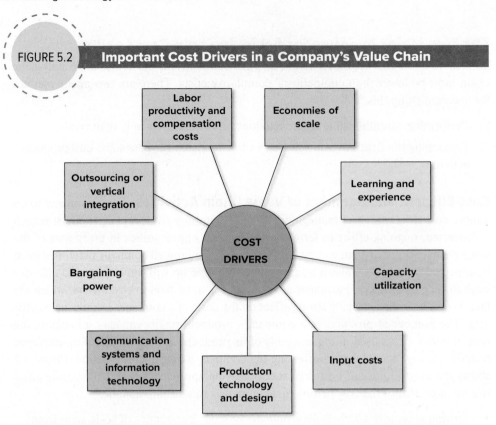

FIGURE 5.2 **Important Cost Drivers in a Company's Value Chain**

Sources: Adapted by the authors from M. Porter, *The Competitive Advantage: Creating and Sustaining Superior Performance* (New York: Free Press, 1985).

- *Using communication systems and information technology to achieve operating efficiencies.* For example, sharing data and production schedules with suppliers, coupled with the use of enterprise resource planning (ERP) and manufacturing execution system (MES) software, can reduce parts inventories, trim production times, and lower labor requirements.

- *Using the company's bargaining power vis-à-vis suppliers to gain concessions.* A company may have sufficient bargaining clout with suppliers to win price discounts on large-volume purchases or realize other cost savings.

- *Being alert to the cost advantages of outsourcing and vertical integration.* Outsourcing the performance of certain value chain activities can be more economical than performing them in-house if outside specialists, by virtue of their expertise and volume, can perform the activities at lower cost.

- *Pursuing ways to boost labor productivity and lower overall compensation costs.* A company can economize on labor costs by using incentive compensation systems that promote high productivity, installing labor-saving equipment, shifting production from geographic areas where pay scales are high to geographic areas where pay scales are low, and avoiding the use of union labor where possible (because costly work rules can stifle productivity and because of union demands for above-market pay scales and costly fringe benefits).

CORE CONCEPT

A **cost driver** is a factor having a strong effect on the cost of a company's value chain activities and cost structure.

Revamping the Value Chain Dramatic cost advantages can often emerge from reengineering the company's value chain in ways that eliminate costly work steps and bypass certain cost-producing value chain activities. Such value chain revamping can include:

- *Selling directly to consumers and cutting out the activities and costs of distributors and dealers.* To circumvent the need for distributors–dealers, a company can (1) create its own direct sales force (which adds the costs of maintaining and supporting a sales force but may be cheaper than utilizing independent distributors and dealers to access buyers), and/or (2) conduct sales operations at the company's website (costs for website operations and shipping may be a substantially cheaper way to make sales to customers than going through distributor–dealer channels). Costs in the wholesale/retail portions of the value chain frequently represent 35 to 50 percent of the price final consumers pay, so establishing a direct sales force or selling online may offer big cost savings.

- *Streamlining operations by eliminating low-value-added or unnecessary work steps and activities.* Southwest Airlines has achieved considerable cost savings by reconfiguring the traditional value chain of commercial airlines to eliminate low-value-added activities and work steps. Southwest does not offer assigned seating, baggage transfer to connecting airlines, or first-class seating and service, thereby eliminating all the cost-producing activities associated with these features. Also, the company's carefully designed point-to-point route system minimizes connections, delays, and total trip time for passengers, allowing about 75 percent of Southwest passengers to fly nonstop to their destinations and at the same time helping reduce Southwest's costs for flight operations.

- *Improving supply chain efficiency to reduce materials handling and shipping costs.* Collaborating with suppliers to streamline the ordering and purchasing process, to reduce inventory carrying costs via just-in-time inventory practices, to economize on shipping and materials handling, and to ferret out other cost-saving opportunities is a much-used approach to cost reduction. A company with a distinctive competence in cost-efficient supply chain management, such as BASF (the world's leading chemical company), can sometimes achieve a sizable cost advantage over less adept rivals.

Concepts & Connections 5.1 describes the path that Amazon.com has followed on the way to becoming not only the largest online retailer (as measured by revenues) but also the lowest-cost provider in the industry.

When a Low-Cost Provider Strategy Works Best
A competitive strategy predicated on low-cost leadership is particularly powerful when:

1. *Price competition among rival sellers is especially vigorous.* Low-cost providers are in the best position to compete offensively on the basis of price and to survive price wars.

2. *The products of rival sellers are essentially identical and are readily available from several sellers.* Commodity-like products and/or ample supplies set the stage for lively price competition; in such markets, it is the less efficient, higher-cost companies that are most vulnerable.

Concepts & Connections 5.1

AMAZON'S PATH TO BECOMING THE LOW-COST PROVIDER IN E-COMMERCE

In 1996, shortly after founding Amazon.com, CEO Jeff Bezos told his employees, *"When you are small, someone else that is bigger can always come along and take away what you have."* Since then, the company has relentlessly pursued growth, aiming to become the global cost leader in "customer-centric E-commerce" across nearly all consumer merchandise lines. Amazon.com now offers over 230 million items for sale in America—approximately 30 times more than Walmart—and its annual sales are greater than the next five largest e-retailers combined.

In scaling up, Amazon has achieved lower costs not only through economies of scale, but also by increasing its bargaining power over its supplies and distribution partners. With thousands of suppliers, Amazon.com is not reliant on any one relationship. Suppliers, however, have few other alternative e-retailers that can match Amazon's reach and popularity. This gives Amazon bargaining power when negotiating revenue sharing and payment schedules. Amazon has even been able to negotiate for space inside suppliers' warehouses, reducing its own inventory costs.

©Simon Dawson/Bloomberg/Getty Images

On the distribution side, Amazon has been developing its own capabilities to reduce reliance on third-party delivery services. Unlike most mega retailers, Amazon's distribution operation was designed to send small orders to residential customers. Amazon.com attained proximity to its customers by building a substantial network of warehousing facilities and processing capability—249 fulfillment and delivery stations globally. This wide footprint decreases the marginal cost of quick delivery, as well as Amazon's reliance on cross-country delivery services. In addition, Amazon has adopted innovative delivery services to further lower costs and extend its reach. In India and the UK, for example, through Easy Ship Amazon's crew picks up orders directly from sellers, eliminating the time and cost of sending goods to a warehouse and the need for more space.

Amazon's size has also enabled it to spread the fixed costs of its massive up-front investment in automation across many units. Amazon.com was a pioneer of algorithms generating customized recommendations for customers. While developing these algorithms was resource-intensive, the costs of employing them are low. The more Amazon uses its automated sales tools to drive revenue, the more the up-front development cost is spread thin across total revenue. As a result, the company has lower capital intensity for each dollar of sales than other large retailers (like Walmart and Target). Other proprietary tools that increase the volume and speed of sales—without increasing variable costs—include Amazon.com's patented One Click Buy feature. All in all, these moves have been helping secure Amazon's position as the low-cost provider in this industry.

Note: Developed with Danielle G. Garver.

Sources: Company websites; seekingalpha.com/article/2247493-amazons-competitive-advantage-quantified; Brad Stone, *The Everything Store* (New York: Back Bay Books, 2013); www.reuters.com/article/us-amazon-com-india-logistics-idUSKCN0T12PL20151112 (accessed February 16, 2016).

3. *There are few ways to achieve product differentiation that have value to buyers.* When the product or service differences between brands do not matter much to buyers, buyers nearly always shop the market for the best price.

4. *Buyers incur low costs in switching their purchases from one seller to another.* Low switching costs give buyers the flexibility to shift purchases to lower-priced sellers having equally good products. A low-cost leader is well positioned to use low price to induce its customers not to switch to rival brands.

5. *The majority of industry sales are made to a few, large-volume buyers.* Low-cost providers are in the best position among sellers in bargaining with high-volume buyers because they are able to beat rivals' pricing to land a high-volume sale while maintaining an acceptable profit margin.

6. *Industry newcomers use introductory low prices to attract buyers and build a customer base.* The low-cost leader can use price cuts of its own to make it harder for a new rival to win customers.

As a rule, the more price-sensitive buyers are, the more appealing a low-cost strategy becomes. A low-cost company's ability to set the industry's price floor and still earn a profit erects protective barriers around its market position.

Pitfalls to Avoid in Pursuing a Low-Cost Provider Strategy

Perhaps the biggest pitfall of a low-cost provider strategy is getting carried away with *overly aggressive price cutting* and ending up with lower, rather than higher, profitability. A low-cost/low-price advantage results in superior profitability only if (1) prices are cut by less than the size of the cost advantage or (2) the added volume is large enough to bring in a bigger total profit despite lower margins per unit sold. Thus, a company with a 5 percent cost advantage cannot cut prices 20 percent, end up with a volume gain of only 10 percent, and still expect to earn higher profits!

A second big pitfall is *relying on an approach to reduce costs that can be easily copied by rivals.* The value of a cost advantage depends on its sustainability. Sustainability, in turn, hinges on whether the company achieves its cost advantage in ways difficult for rivals to replicate or match. If rivals find it relatively easy or inexpensive to imitate the leader's low-cost methods, then the leader's advantage will be too short-lived to yield a valuable edge in the marketplace.

A third pitfall is becoming *too fixated on cost reduction.* Low costs cannot be pursued so zealously that a firm's offering ends up being too features-poor to gain the interest of buyers. Furthermore, a company driving hard to push its costs down has to guard against misreading or ignoring increased buyer preferences for added features or declining buyer price sensitivity. Even if these mistakes are avoided, a low-cost competitive approach still carries risk. Cost-saving technological breakthroughs or process improvements by rival firms can nullify a low-cost leader's hard-won position.

Broad Differentiation Strategies

Differentiation strategies are attractive whenever buyers' needs and preferences are too diverse to be fully satisfied by a standardized product or service. A company attempting to succeed through differentiation must study buyers' needs and behavior carefully to learn what buyers think has value and what they are willing to pay for. Then the company must include these desirable features to clearly set itself apart from rivals lacking such product or service attributes.

> **CORE CONCEPT**
>
> The essence of a **broad differentiation strategy** is to offer unique product or service attributes that a wide range of buyers find appealing and worth paying for.

Successful differentiation allows a firm to:

• Command a premium price, and/or

- Increase unit sales (because additional buyers are won over by the differentiating features), and/or
- Gain buyer loyalty to its brand (because some buyers are strongly attracted to the differentiating features and bond with the company and its products).

Differentiation enhances profitability whenever the extra price the product commands outweighs the added costs of achieving the differentiation. Company differentiation strategies fail when buyers do not value the brand's uniqueness and/or when a company's approach to differentiation is easily copied or matched by its rivals.

Approaches to Differentiation

 LO5-3   Explain the major avenues for developing a competitive advantage based on differentiating a company's product or service offering from the offerings of rivals.

Companies can pursue differentiation from many angles: a unique taste (Red Bull, Doritos), multiple features (Microsoft Office, Apple iPhone), wide selection and one-stop shopping (Home Depot, Amazon.com), superior service (Ritz-Carlton, Nordstrom), spare parts availability (Caterpillar guarantees 48-hour spare parts delivery to any customer anywhere in the world or else the part is furnished free), engineering design and performance (Mercedes-Benz, BMW), luxury and prestige (Rolex, Gucci, Chanel), product reliability (Whirlpool and Bosch in large home appliances), quality manufacturing (Michelin in tires, Toyota and Honda in automobiles), technological leadership (3M Corporation in bonding and coating products), a full range of services (Charles Schwab in stock brokerage), and a complete line of products (Campbell soups, Frito-Lay snack foods).

The most appealing approaches to differentiation are those that are hard or expensive for rivals to duplicate. Resourceful competitors can, in time, clone almost any product or feature or attribute. If Toyota introduces lane departure warning or adaptive cruise control features, so can Ford and Honda. Socially complex intangible attributes, such as company reputation, long-standing relationships with buyers, and image are much harder to imitate.

Differentiation that creates switching costs that lock in buyers also provides a route to sustainable advantage. For example, if a buyer makes a substantial investment in mastering usage of a product, that buyer is less likely to switch to a competitor's system. This has kept many users from switching away from Microsoft Office products, despite the efforts of rivals to develop and market superior performing software applications. As a rule, differentiation yields a longer-lasting and more profitable competitive edge when it is based on product innovation, technical superiority, product quality and reliability, comprehensive customer service, and unique competitive capabilities. Such differentiating attributes tend to be tough for rivals to copy or offset profitably, and buyers widely perceive them as having value.

> Easy-to-copy differentiating features cannot produce sustainable competitive advantage; differentiation based on hard-to-copy competencies and capabilities tends to be more sustainable.

Managing the Value Chain in Ways That Enhance Differentiation

Success in employing a differentiation strategy results from management's ability to offer superior customer value through the addition of product/service attributes and features that differentiate a company's offering from the offerings of rivals. Differentiation opportunities can exist in activities all along an industry's value chain and particularly in activities and factors that meaningfully impact customer value. Such activities are referred to as **uniqueness drivers**—analogous to cost drivers—but have a high impact on differentiation rather than on a company's overall cost position. Figure 5.3 lists important uniqueness drivers found in a company's value chain. Ways that managers can enhance differentiation through the systematic management of uniqueness drivers include the following:

- *Seeking out high-quality inputs.* Input quality can ultimately spill over to affect the performance or quality of the company's end product. Starbucks, for example, gets high ratings on its coffees partly because of its very strict specifications for coffee beans purchased from suppliers.

- *Striving for innovation and technological advances.* Successful innovation is the route to more frequent first-on-the-market victories and is a powerful differentiator. If the innovation proves hard to replicate, through patent protection or other means, it can provide a company with a first-mover advantage that is sustainable.

- *Creating superior product features, design, and performance.* The physical and functional features of a product have a big influence on differentiation. Styling and appearance are big differentiating factors in the apparel and motor vehicle

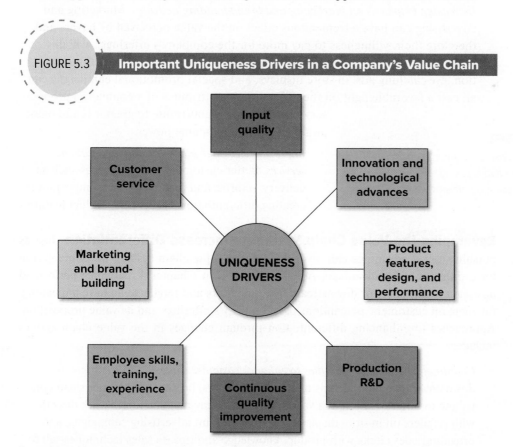

FIGURE 5.3   **Important Uniqueness Drivers in a Company's Value Chain**

Source: Adapted from M. Porter, *The Competitive Advantage: Creating and Sustaining Superior Performance* (New York: Free Press, 1985).

industries. Graphics resolution and processing speed matter in video game consoles. Most companies employing broad differentiation strategies make a point of incorporating innovative and novel features in their product/service offering, especially those that improve performance.

- *Investing in production-related R&D activities.* Engaging in production R&D may permit custom-order manufacture at an efficient cost, provide wider product variety and selection, or improve product quality. Many manufacturers have developed flexible manufacturing systems that allow different models and product versions to be made on the same assembly line. Being able to provide buyers with made-to-order products can be a potent differentiating capability.

- *Pursuing continuous quality improvement.* Quality control processes reduce product defects, prevent premature product failure, extend product life, make it economical to offer longer warranty coverage, improve economy of use, result in more end-user convenience, enhance product appearance, or improve customer service.

- *Emphasizing human resource management activities that improve the skills, expertise, and knowledge of company personnel.* A company with high-caliber intellectual capital often has the capacity to generate the kinds of ideas that drive product innovation, technological advances, better product design and product performance, improved production techniques, and higher product quality.

- *Increasing emphasis on marketing and brand-building activities.* Marketing and advertising can have a tremendous effect on the value perceived by buyers and therefore their willingness to pay more for the company's offerings. A highly skilled and competent sales force, effectively communicated product information, eye-catching ads, in-store displays, and special promotional campaigns can all cast a favorable light on the differentiating attributes of a company's product/service offering and contribute to greater brand-name awareness and brand-name power.

> **CORE CONCEPT**
>
> A **uniqueness driver** is a value chain activity or factor that can have a strong effect on customer value and creating differentiation.

- *Improving customer service or adding additional services.* Better customer service, in areas such as delivery, returns, and repair, can be as important in creating differentiation as superior product features.

Revamping the Value Chain System to Increase Differentiation Just as pursuing a cost advantage can involve the entire value chain system, the same is true for a differentiation advantage. As was discussed in Chapter 4, activities performed upstream by suppliers or downstream by distributors and retailers can have a meaningful effect on customers' perceptions of a company's offerings and its value proposition. Approaches to enhancing differentiation through changes in the value chain system include:

- *Coordinating with channel allies to enhance customer value.* Coordinating with downstream partners such as distributors, dealers, brokers, and retailers can contribute to differentiation in a variety of ways. Many manufacturers work directly with retailers on in-store displays and signage, joint advertising campaigns, and providing sales clerks with product knowledge and tips on sales techniques—all to enhance customer buying experiences. Companies can work with distributors and shippers to ensure fewer "out-of-stock" annoyances, quicker delivery to customers, more-accurate order filling, lower shipping costs, and a variety of shipping choices to customers.

- *Coordinating with suppliers to better address customer needs.* Collaborating with suppliers can also be a powerful route to a more effective differentiation strategy. This is particularly true for companies that engage only in assembly operations, such as Dell in PCs and Ducati in motorcycles. Close coordination with suppliers can also enhance differentiation by speeding up new product development cycles or speeding delivery to end customers. Strong relationships with suppliers can also mean that the company's supply requirements are prioritized when industry supply is insufficient to meet overall demand.

Delivering Superior Value via a Differentiation Strategy

While it is easy enough to grasp that a successful differentiation strategy must offer value in ways unmatched by rivals, a big issue in crafting a differentiation strategy is deciding what is valuable to customers. Typically, value can be delivered to customers in three basic ways.

1. *Include product attributes and user features that lower the buyer's costs.* Commercial buyers value products that can reduce their cost of doing business. For example, making a company's product more economical for a buyer to use can be done by reducing the buyer's raw materials waste (providing cut-to-size components), reducing a buyer's inventory requirements (providing just-in-time deliveries), increasing product reliability to lower a buyer's repair and maintenance costs, and providing free technical support. Similarly, consumers find value in differentiating features that will reduce their expenses. Rising costs for gasoline prices have spurred the efforts of motor vehicle manufacturers worldwide to introduce models with better fuel economy.

2. *Incorporate tangible features that improve product performance.* Commercial buyers and consumers alike value higher levels of performance in many types of products. Product reliability, output, durability, convenience, and ease of use are aspects of product performance that differentiate products offered to buyers. Tablet computer manufacturers are currently in a race to develop next-generation tablets with the functionality and processing power to capture market share from rivals and cannibalize the laptop computer market.

3. *Incorporate intangible features that enhance buyer satisfaction in noneconomic ways.* Toyota's Prius appeals to environmentally conscious motorists who wish to help reduce global carbon dioxide emissions. Bentley, Ralph Lauren, Louis Vuitton, Tiffany, Cartier, and Rolex have differentiation-based competitive advantages linked to buyer desires for status, image, prestige, upscale fashion, superior craftsmanship, and the finer things in life.

> Differentiation can be based on *tangible* or *intangible* features and attributes.

Perceived Value and the Importance of Signaling Value

The price premium commanded by a differentiation strategy reflects *the value actually delivered* to the buyer and *the value perceived* by the buyer. The value of certain differentiating features is rather easy for buyers to detect, but in some instances, buyers may

Concepts & Connections 5.2

HOW BMW'S DIFFERENTIATION STRATEGY ALLOWED IT TO BECOME THE NUMBER-ONE LUXURY CAR BRAND

BMW was little known outside of Europe prior to the mid-1970s, with many Americans assuming that BMW meant "British Motor Works." The company set about building brand recognition through its BMW Motorsport program that quickly gained its automobiles a worldwide reputation as the "Ultimate Driving Machine." BMW's success on the race track and the instant popularity of its 320i introduced in 1977 helped build one of the world's strongest luxury brands by the mid-1980s. The 320i was wildly popular with young professionals, and with each new generation of the 3-series, BMW attracted new young buyers and increased demand for its larger, more expensive models such as the 5-series, 6-series, and 7-series as its repeat buyers moved up in their careers.

BMW's customer value proposition was also keyed to state-of-the-art engineering that resulted in high-performing engines, innovative features, and responsive handling. Through the late 2000s, the average pricing for BMW models was at the upper

end of the industry, which limited its market share and solidified its reputation as an aspirational luxury brand focused on high-income consumers. However, the introduction of the BMW 1-series in 2008 that carried a sticker price of $28,600 vastly expanded the market for BMWs and allowed the company to overtake Lexus as the number-one luxury car brand in the United States that same year.

The company also expanded its product line to include six sedan models, five sports activity vehicle models, seven two-door coupes and convertible models, four hybrid models, the plug-in hybrid i8 sports car, and an all-electric i3. BMW sold approximately 2.36 million cars worldwide in 2016. The base pricing for BMW's product line in 2017 ranged from $33,150 for the 2-series coupe to $143,400 for the i8.

Source: BMW Magazine, Spring/Summer 2015; and www.bmwusa.com.

have trouble assessing what their experience with the product will be. Successful differentiators go to great lengths to make buyers knowledgeable about a product's value and incorporate signals of value such as attractive packaging, extensive ad campaigns, the quality of brochures and sales presentations, the seller's list of customers, the length of time the firm has been in business, and the professionalism, appearance, and personality of the seller's employees. Such signals of value may be as important as actual value (1) when the nature of differentiation is subjective or hard to quantify, (2) when buyers are making a first-time purchase, (3) when repurchase is infrequent, and (4) when buyers are unsophisticated.

Concepts & Connections 5.2 describes key elements of BMW's differentiation strategy that has allowed it to become the world's number-one selling luxury automobile brand.

When a Differentiation Strategy Works Best

Differentiation strategies tend to work best in market circumstances where:

1. *Buyer needs and uses of the product are diverse.* Diverse buyer preferences allow industry rivals to set themselves apart with product attributes that appeal to particular buyers. For instance, the diversity of consumer preferences for menu selection, ambience, pricing, and customer service gives restaurants exceptionally wide latitude in creating differentiated concepts. Other industries offering opportunities for differentiation based upon diverse buyer needs and uses include magazine publishing, automobile manufacturing, footwear, kitchen appliances, and computers.

2. *There are many ways to differentiate the product or service that have value to buyers.* Industries that allow competitors to add features to product attributes are well suited to differentiation strategies. For example, hotel chains can differentiate on such features as location, size of room, range of guest services, in-hotel dining, and the quality and luxuriousness of bedding and furnishings. Similarly, cosmetics producers are able to differentiate based upon prestige and image, formulations that fight the signs of aging, UV light protection, exclusivity of retail locations, the inclusion of antioxidants and natural ingredients, or prohibitions against animal testing.

3. *Few rival firms are following a similar differentiation approach.* The best differentiation approaches involve trying to appeal to buyers on the basis of attributes that rivals are not emphasizing. A differentiator encounters less head-to-head rivalry when it goes its own separate way to create uniqueness and does not try to outdifferentiate rivals on the very same attributes.

4. *Technological change is fast-paced and competition revolves around rapidly evolving product features.* Rapid product innovation and frequent introductions of next-version products heighten buyer interest and provide space for companies to pursue distinct differentiating paths. In smartphones, wearable devices, and commercial and hobby drones, competitors are locked into an ongoing battle to set themselves apart by introducing the best next-generation products; companies that fail to come up with new and improved products and distinctive performance features quickly lose out in the marketplace.

Pitfalls to Avoid in Pursuing a Differentiation Strategy

Differentiation strategies can fail for any of several reasons. *A differentiation strategy keyed to product or service attributes that are easily and quickly copied is always suspect.* Rapid imitation means that no rival achieves meaningful differentiation, because whatever new feature one firm introduces that strikes the fancy of buyers is almost immediately added by rivals. This is why a firm must search out sources of uniqueness that are time-consuming or burdensome for rivals to match if it hopes to use differentiation to win a sustainable competitive edge over rivals.

Differentiation strategies can also falter when buyers see little value in the unique attributes of a company's product. Thus, even if a company sets the attributes of its brand apart from its rivals' brands, its strategy can fail because of trying to differentiate on the basis of something that does not deliver adequate value to buyers. Any time many potential buyers look at a company's differentiated product offering and conclude "so what," the company's differentiation strategy is in deep trouble; buyers will likely decide the product is not worth the extra price, and sales will be disappointingly low.

Overspending on efforts to differentiate is a strategy flaw that can erode profitability. Company efforts to achieve differentiation nearly always raise costs. The trick to profitable differentiation is either to keep the costs of achieving differentiation below the price premium the differentiating attributes can command in the marketplace or to offset thinner profit margins by selling enough additional units to increase total profits. If a company goes overboard in pursuing costly differentiation, it could be saddled with unacceptably thin profit margins or even losses. The need to contain differentiation costs is why many companies add little touches of differentiation that add to buyer satisfaction but are inexpensive to institute.

Other common pitfalls and mistakes in crafting a differentiation strategy include:

- *Failing to open up meaningful gaps in quality or service or performance features vis-à-vis the products of rivals.* Trivial differences between rivals' product offerings may not be visible or important to buyers. In markets where differentiators achieve only weak differentiation, customer loyalty is weak, the costs of brand switching are low, and competitors end up chasing the same buyers with much the same product offerings.

- *Over-differentiating so that product quality or service levels exceed buyers' needs.* A dazzling array of features and options not only drives up product price but also runs the risk that many buyers will conclude that a less deluxe and lower-priced brand is a better value since they have little occasion to use the deluxe attributes.

- *Trying to charge too high a price premium.* Even if buyers view certain extras or deluxe features as "nice to have," they may still conclude that the added benefit or luxury is not worth the price differential over that of lesser differentiated products.

A low-cost provider strategy can always defeat a differentiation strategy when buyers are satisfied with a basic product and do not think "extra" attributes are worth a higher price.

Focused (or Market Niche) Strategies

What sets focused strategies apart from low-cost leadership or broad differentiation strategies is a concentration on a narrow piece of the total market. The targeted segment, or niche, can be defined by geographic uniqueness or by special product attributes that appeal only to niche members. The advantages of focusing a company's entire competitive effort on a single market niche are considerable, especially for smaller and medium-sized companies that may lack the breadth and depth of resources to tackle going after a national customer base with a "something for everyone" lineup of models, styles, and product selection.

Community Coffee, the largest family-owned specialty coffee retailer in the United States, has a geographic focus on the state of Louisiana and communities across the Gulf of Mexico. Community holds only a small share of the national coffee market but has recorded sales in excess of $100 million and has won a strong following in the 20-state region where its coffee is distributed. Examples of firms that concentrate on a well-defined market niche keyed to a particular product or buyer segment include Zipcar (hourly and daily car rental in urban areas), Airbnb and HomeAway (by owner lodging rental), Fox News Channel and HGTV (cable TV), Blue Nile (online jewelry), Tesla Motors (electric cars), and CGA, Inc. (a specialist in providing insurance to cover the cost of lucrative hole-in-one prizes at golf tournaments). Microbreweries, local bakeries, bed-and-breakfast inns, and retail boutiques have also scaled their operations to serve narrow or local customer segments.

A Focused Low-Cost Strategy

A focused strategy based on low cost aims at securing a competitive advantage by serving buyers in the target market niche at a lower cost and a lower price than rival competitors. This strategy has considerable attraction when a firm can lower costs significantly by limiting its customer base to a well-defined buyer segment. The avenues to achieving a cost advantage over rivals also serving the target market niche are the same as for low-cost leadership—outmanage rivals in keeping the costs to a bare minimum and searching for innovative ways to bypass or reduce nonessential activities. The only real difference between a low-cost provider strategy and a focused low-cost strategy is the size of the buyer group to which a company is appealing.

Focused low-cost strategies are fairly common. Producers of private-label goods are able to achieve low costs in product development, marketing, distribution, and advertising by concentrating on making generic items similar to name-brand merchandise and selling directly to retail chains wanting a low-priced store brand. The Perrigo Company has become a leading manufacturer of over-the-counter health care products with 2016 sales of more than $5.3 billion by focusing on producing private-label brands for retailers such as Walmart, CVS, Walgreens, Rite Aid, and Safeway. Even though Perrigo does not make branded products, a focused low-cost strategy is appropriate for the makers of branded products as well. Budget motel chains, like Motel 6, Sleep Inn, and Super 8, cater to price-conscious travelers who just want to pay for a clean, no-frills place to spend the night.

A Focused Differentiation Strategy

Focused differentiation strategies are keyed to offering carefully designed products or services to appeal to the unique preferences and needs of a narrow, well-defined group of buyers (as opposed to a broad differentiation strategy aimed at many buyer groups and market segments). Companies such as Four Seasons Hotels and Resorts in lodging, Molton Brown in bath, body, and beauty products, and Louis Vuitton in leather goods employ successful differentiation-based focused strategies targeted at buyers seeking products and services with world-class attributes. Indeed, most markets contain a buyer segment willing to pay a price premium for the very finest items available, thus opening the strategic window for some competitors to pursue differentiation-based focused strategies aimed at the very top of the market pyramid.

Another successful focused differentiator is "fashion food retailer" Trader Joe's, a 464-store, 41-state chain that is a combination gourmet deli and food warehouse. Customers shop Trader Joe's as much for entertainment as for conventional grocery items; the store stocks out-of-the-ordinary culinary treats such as raspberry salsa, salmon burgers, and jasmine fried rice, as well as the standard goods normally found in supermarkets. What sets Trader Joe's apart is not just its unique combination of food novelties and competitively priced grocery items but also its capability to turn an otherwise mundane grocery excursion into a whimsical treasure hunt that is just plain fun. Concepts & Connections 5.3 describes how Canada Goose has become a popular winter apparel brand with revenues of nearly $300 million in 2016 through its focused differentiation strategy.

When a Focused Low-Cost or Focused Differentiation Strategy Is Viable

A focused strategy aimed at securing a competitive edge based on either low cost or differentiation becomes increasingly attractive as more of the following conditions are met:

- The target market niche is big enough to be profitable and offers good growth potential.

Concepts & Connections 5.3

CANADA GOOSE'S FOCUSED DIFFERENTIATION STRATEGY

Open up a winter edition of *People* and you will probably see photos of a celebrity sporting a Canada Goose parka. Recognizable by a distinctive red, white, and blue arm patch, the brand's parkas have been spotted on movie stars like Emma Stone and Bradley Cooper, on New York City streets, and on the cover of *Sports Illustrated.* Lately, Canada Goose has become extremely successful thanks to a focused differentiation strategy that enables it to thrive within its niche in the $1.2 trillion fashion industry. By targeting upscale buyers and providing a uniquely functional and stylish jacket, Canada Goose can charge nearly $1,000 per jacket and never need to put its products on sale.

While Canada Goose was founded in 1957, its recent transition to a focused differentiation strategy allowed it to rise to the top of the luxury parka market. In 2001, CEO Dani Reiss took control of the company and made two key decisions. First, he cut private-label and non-outerwear production in order to focus on the branded outerwear portion of Canada Goose's

business. Second, Reiss decided to remain in Canada despite many North American competitors moving production to Asia to increase profit margins. Fortunately for him, these two strategy decisions have led directly to the company's current success. While other luxury brands, like Moncler, are priced similarly, no competitor's products fulfill the promise of handling harsh winter weather quite like a Canada Goose "Made in Canada" parka. The Canadian heritage, use of down sourced from rural Canada, real coyote fur (humanely trapped), and promise to provide warmth in minus 25°F temperatures have let Canada Goose break away from the pack when it comes to selling parkas. The company's distinctly Canadian product has made it a hit among buyers, which is reflected in the willingness to pay a steep premium for extremely high-quality and warm winter outerwear.

Since Canada Goose's shift to a focused differentiation strategy, the company has seen a boom in revenue and appeal across the globe. Prior to Reiss' strategic decisions in 2001, Canada Goose had annual revenue of about $3 million. By 2016, the company's revenues had grown at an annual rate of 35 percent to reach nearly $300 million with sales in 50 countries. The strength of the company's strategy allowed it to raise $255 million through a successful IPO in 2017.

©Noam Galai/WireImage/Getty Images

Note: Developed with Arthur J. Santry.

Sources: Matthew Zeitlin, "Here are 7 Things We Learned About Canada Goose from Its IPO Filing, *BuzzFeed News,* February 16, 2017, www.cnbc.com; Drake Bennett, "How Canada Goose Parkas Migrated South," *Bloomberg Businessweek,* March 13, 2015, www.bloomberg.com; Hollie Shaw, "Canada Goose's Made-in-Canada Marketing Strategy Translates into Success," *Financial Post,* May 18, 2012, www.financialpost.com; "The Economic Impact of the Fashion Industry," *The Economist,* June 13, 2015, www.maloney.house.gov; and company website (accessed February 21, 2016).

- Industry leaders have chosen not to compete in the niche—focusers can avoid battling head-to-head against the industry's biggest and strongest competitors.

- It is costly or difficult for multisegment competitors to meet the specialized needs of niche buyers and at the same time satisfy the expectations of mainstream customers.

- The industry has many different niches and segments, thereby allowing a focuser to pick a niche suited to its resource strengths and capabilities.

- Few, if any, rivals are attempting to specialize in the same target segment.

The Risks of a Focused Low-Cost or Focused Differentiation Strategy

Focusing carries several risks. The *first major risk* is the chance that competitors will find effective ways to match the focused firm's capabilities in serving the target niche. In the lodging business, large chains such as Marriott and Hilton have launched multibrand strategies that allow them to compete effectively in several lodging segments simultaneously. Hilton has flagship hotels with a full complement of services and amenities that allow it to attract travelers and vacationers going to major resorts; it has Waldorf Astoria, Conrad Hotels & Resorts, Hilton Hotels & Resorts, and DoubleTree hotels that provide deluxe comfort and service to business and leisure travelers; it has Homewood Suites, Embassy Suites, and Home2 Suites designed as a "home away from home" for travelers staying five or more nights; and it has nearly 700 Hilton Garden Inn and 2,100 Hampton by Hilton locations that cater to travelers looking for quality lodging at an "affordable" price. Tru by Hilton is the company's newly introduced brand focused on value-conscious travelers seeking basic accommodations. Hilton has also added Curio Collection, Tapestry Collection, and Canopy by Hilton hotels that offer stylish, distinctive decors and personalized services that appeal to young professionals seeking distinctive lodging alternatives. Multibrand strategies are attractive to large companies such as Hilton precisely because they enable a company to enter a market niche and siphon business away from companies that employ a focus strategy.

A *second risk* of employing a focus strategy is the potential for the preferences and needs of niche members to shift over time toward the product attributes desired by the majority of buyers. An erosion of the differences across buyer segments lowers entry barriers into a focuser's market niche and provides an open invitation for rivals in adjacent segments to begin competing for the focuser's customers. A *third risk* is that the segment may become so attractive it is soon inundated with competitors, intensifying rivalry and splintering segment profits.

Best-Cost Provider Strategies

LO5-4   Recognize the attributes of a best-cost provider strategy—a hybrid of low-cost provider and differentiation strategies.

As Figure 5.1 indicates, **best-cost provider strategies** are a *hybrid* of low-cost provider and differentiation strategies that aim at satisfying buyer expectations on key quality/features/performance/service attributes and beating customer expectations on price. Companies pursuing best-cost strategies aim squarely at the sometimes great mass of value-conscious buyers looking for a good-to-very-good product or service at an economical price. The essence of a best-cost provider strategy is giving customers *more value for the money* by satisfying buyer desires for appealing features/performance/quality/service and charging a lower price for these attributes compared to that of rivals with similar-caliber product offerings.[3]

To profitably employ a best-cost provider strategy, a company *must have the capability to incorporate attractive*

CORE CONCEPT

Best-cost provider strategies are a *hybrid* of low-cost provider and differentiation strategies that aim at satisfying buyer expectations on key quality/features/performance/service attributes and beating customer expectations on price.

or upscale attributes at a lower cost than rivals. This capability is contingent on (1) a superior value chain configuration that eliminates or minimizes activities that do not add value, (2) unmatched efficiency in managing essential value chain activities, and (3) core competencies that allow differentiating attributes to be incorporated at a low cost. When a company can incorporate appealing features, good-to-excellent product performance or quality, or more satisfying customer service into its product offering *at a lower cost than that of rivals,* then it enjoys "best-cost" status—it is the low-cost provider of a product or service with *upscale attributes.* A best-cost provider can use its low-cost advantage to underprice rivals whose products or services have similar upscale attributes and still earn attractive profits.

Concepts & Connections 5.4 describes how American Giant has applied the principles of a best-cost provider strategy in producing and marketing its hoodie sweatshirts.

When a Best-Cost Provider Strategy Works Best

A best-cost provider strategy works best in markets where product differentiation is the norm and attractively large numbers of value-conscious buyers can be induced to purchase midrange products rather than the basic products of low-cost producers or the expensive products of top-of-the-line differentiators. A best-cost provider usually needs to position itself near the middle of the market with either a medium-quality product at a below-average price or a high-quality product at an average or slightly higher-than-average price. Best-cost provider strategies also work well in recessionary times when great masses of buyers become value-conscious and are attracted to economically priced products and services with especially appealing attributes.

The Danger of an Unsound Best-Cost Provider Strategy

A company's biggest vulnerability in employing a best-cost provider strategy is not having the requisite core competencies and efficiencies in managing value chain activities to support the addition of differentiating features without significantly increasing costs. A company with a modest degree of differentiation and no real cost advantage will most likely find itself squeezed between the firms using low-cost strategies and those using differentiation strategies. Low-cost providers may be able to siphon customers away with the appeal of a lower price (despite having marginally less appealing product attributes). High-end differentiators may be able to steal customers away with the appeal of appreciably better product attributes (even though their products carry a somewhat higher price tag). Thus, a successful best-cost provider must offer buyers *significantly* better product attributes to justify a price above what low-cost leaders are charging. Likewise, it has to achieve significantly lower costs in providing upscale features so that it can outcompete high-end differentiators on the basis of a *significantly* lower price.

Successful Competitive Strategies Are Resource Based

For a company's competitive strategy to succeed in delivering good performance and the intended competitive edge over rivals, it has to be well matched to a company's internal situation and underpinned by an appropriate set of resources, know-how, and competitive capabilities. To succeed in employing a low-cost provider strategy, a

Concepts & Connections 5.4

AMERICAN GIANT'S BEST-COST PROVIDER STRATEGY

Bayard Winthrop, founder and owner of American Giant, set out to make a hoodie like the soft, ultra-thick Navy sweatshirts his dad used to wear in the 1950s. But he also had two other aims: He wanted it to have a more updated look with a tailored fit, and he wanted it produced cost-effectively so that it could be sold at a great price. To accomplish these aims, he designed the sweatshirt with the help of a former industrial engineer from Apple and an internationally renowned pattern maker, rethinking every aspect of sweatshirt design and production along the way. The result was a hoodie differentiated from others on the basis of extreme attention to fabric, fit, construction, and durability. The hoodie is made from heavy-duty cotton that is run through a machine that carefully picks loops of thread out of the fabric to create a thick, combed, ring-spun fleece fabric that feels three times thicker than most sweatshirts. A small amount of spandex paneling along the shoulders and sides creates the fitted look and maintains the shape, keeping the sweatshirt from looking slouchy or sloppy. It has double stitching with strong thread on critical seams to avoid deterioration and boost durability. The

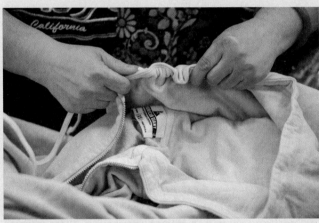

©David Paul Morris/Bloomberg/Getty Images

zippers and draw cord are customized to match the sweatshirt's color—an uncommon practice in the business.

American Giant sources yarn from Parkdale, South Carolina, and turns it into cloth at the nearby Carolina Cotton Works. This reduces transport costs, creates a more dependable, durable product that American Giant can easily quality-check, and shortens product turnaround to about a month, lowering inventory costs. This process also enables the company to use a genuine "Made in the USA" label, a perceived quality driver.

American Giant disrupts the traditional, expensive distribution models by having no stores or resellers. Instead, it sells directly to customers from its website, with free two-day shipping and returns. Much of the company's growth comes from word of mouth and a strong public relations effort that promotes the brand in magazines, newspapers, and key business-oriented television programs. American Giant has a robust refer-a-friend program that offers a discount to friends of, and a credit to, current owners. Articles in popular media proclaiming its product "the greatest hoodie ever made" have made demand for its sweatshirts skyrocket.

At $79 for the original men's hoodie, American Giant is not cheap but offers customers value in terms of both price and quality. The price is higher than what one would pay at The Gap or American Apparel and comparable to Levi's, J.Crew, or Banana Republic. But its quality is more on par with high-priced designer brands, while its price is far more affordable.

Note: Developed with Sarah Boole.

Sources: www.nytimes.com/2013/09/20/business/us-textile-factories-return.html?emc=eta1&_r=0; www.american-giant.com ; www.slate.com/articles/technology/technology/2012/12/american_giant_hoodie_this_is_the_greatest_sweatshirt_known_to_man.html; www.businessinsider.com/this-hoodie-is-so-insanely-popular-you-have-to-wait-months-to-get-it-2013-12.

company has to have the resources and capabilities to keep its costs below those of its competitors; this means having the expertise to cost-effectively manage value chain activities better than rivals and/or the innovative capability to bypass certain value chain activities being performed by rivals. To succeed in strongly differentiating its product in ways that are appealing to buyers, a company must have the resources and capabilities (such as better technology, strong skills in product innovation, expertise in customer service) to incorporate unique attributes into its product offering

A company's competitive strategy should be well matched to its internal situation and predicated on leveraging its collection of competitively valuable resources and competencies.

that a broad range of buyers will find appealing and worth paying for. Strategies focusing on a narrow segment of the market require the capability to do an outstanding job of satisfying the needs and expectations of niche buyers. Success in employing a strategy keyed to a best-value offering requires the resources and capabilities to incorporate upscale product or service attributes at a lower cost than that of rivals.

KEY POINTS

1. Early in the process of crafting a strategy, company managers have to decide which of the five basic competitive strategies to employ: overall low-cost, broad differentiation, focused low-cost, focused differentiation, or best-cost provider.

2. In employing a low-cost provider strategy, a company must do a better job than rivals of cost-effectively managing internal activities, and/or it must find innovative ways to eliminate or bypass cost-producing activities. Particular attention should be paid to cost drivers, which are factors having a strong effect on the cost of a company's value chain activities and cost structure. Low-cost provider strategies work particularly well when price competition is strong and the products of rival sellers are very weakly differentiated. Other conditions favoring a low-cost provider strategy are when supplies are readily available from eager sellers, when there are not many ways to differentiate that have value to buyers, when the majority of industry sales are made to a few large buyers, when buyer switching costs are low, and when industry newcomers are likely to use a low introductory price to build market share.

3. Broad differentiation strategies seek to produce a competitive edge by incorporating attributes and features that set a company's product/service offering apart from rivals in ways that buyers consider valuable and worth paying for. Such features and attributes are best integrated through the systematic management of uniqueness—value chain activities or factors that can have a strong effect on customer value and creating differentiation. Successful differentiation allows a firm to (1) command a premium price for its product, (2) increase unit sales (because additional buyers are won over by the differentiating features), and/or (3) gain buyer loyalty to its brand (because some buyers are strongly attracted to the differentiating features and bond with the company and its products). Differentiation strategies work best in markets with diverse buyer preferences where there are big windows of opportunity to strongly differentiate a company's product offering from those of rival brands, in situations where few other rivals are pursuing a similar differentiation approach, and in circumstances where technological change is fast-paced and competition centers on rapidly evolving product features. A differentiation strategy is doomed when competitors are able to quickly copy most or all of the appealing product attributes a company comes up with, when a company's differentiation efforts meet with a ho-hum or so-what market reception, or when a company erodes profitability by overspending on efforts to differentiate its product offering.

4. A focused strategy delivers competitive advantage either by achieving lower costs than rivals' in serving buyers comprising the target market niche or by offering niche buyers an appealingly differentiated product or service that meets their needs better than rival brands. A focused strategy becomes increasingly attractive when the target market niche is big enough to be profitable and offers good growth potential, when it is costly or difficult

for multisegment competitors to put capabilities in place to meet the specialized needs of the target market niche and at the same time satisfy the expectations of their mainstream customers, when there are one or more niches that present a good match with a focuser's resource strengths and capabilities, and when few other rivals are attempting to specialize in the same target segment.

5. Best-cost provider strategies stake out a middle ground between pursuing a low-cost advantage and a differentiation-based advantage and between appealing to the broad market as a whole and a narrow market niche. The aim is to create competitive advantage by giving buyers more value for the money—satisfying buyer expectations on key quality/features/performance/service attributes while beating customer expectations on price. To profitably employ a best-cost provider strategy, a company *must have the capability to incorporate attractive or upscale attributes at a lower cost than that of rivals.* This capability is contingent on (1) a superior value chain configuration, (2) unmatched efficiency in managing essential value chain activities, and (3) resource strengths and core competencies that allow differentiating attributes to be incorporated at a low cost. A best-cost provider strategy works best in markets where opportunities to differentiate exist and where many buyers are sensitive to price and value.

6. Deciding which generic strategy to employ is perhaps the most important strategic commitment a company makes—it tends to drive the rest of the strategic actions a company decides to undertake, and it sets the whole tone for the pursuit of a competitive advantage over rivals.

ASSURANCE OF LEARNING EXERCISES

1. Best Buy is the largest consumer electronics retailer in the United States with fiscal 2017 sales of nearly $40 billion. The company competes aggressively on price with rivals such as Costco Wholesale, Sam's Club, Walmart, and Target but is also known by consumers for its first-rate customer service. Best Buy customers have commented that the retailer's sales staff is exceptionally knowledgeable about products and can direct them to the exact location of difficult-to-find items. Best Buy customers also appreciate that demonstration models of PC monitors, digital media players, and other electronics are fully powered and ready for in-store use. Best Buy's Geek Squad tech support and installation services are additional customer service features valued by many customers.

   How would you characterize Best Buy's competitive strategy? Should it be classified as a low-cost provider strategy? A differentiation strategy? A best-cost strategy? Explain your answer.

   LO5-1, LO5-2, LO5-3, LO5-4

2. Concepts & Connections 5.1 discusses Amazon's low-cost position in the electronic commerce industry. Based on information provided in the capsule, explain how Amazon has built its low-cost advantage in the industry and why a low-cost provider strategy is well suited to the industry.

   LO5-2

3. USAA is a Fortune 500 insurance and financial services company with 2016 annual revenues exceeding $27 billion. The company was founded in 1922 by 25 Army officers who decided to insure each other's vehicles and continues to limit its membership to active-duty and retired military members, officer candidates, and adult children and spouses of military-affiliated USAA members. The company has received countless awards, including being listed among *Fortune*'s World's Most Admired Companies in 2014 through 2016 and 100 Best Companies to Work For in 2010 through 2016. USAA was also ranked as the number-one Bank, Credit Card and Insurance Company by Forrester Research from 2013 to 2016. You can read more about the company's history and strategy at www.usaa.com.

   LO5-1, LO5-2, LO5-3, LO5-4

How would you characterize USAA's competitive strategy? Should it be classified as a low-cost provider strategy? A differentiation strategy? A best-cost strategy? Also, has the company chosen to focus on a narrow piece of the market, or does it appear to pursue a broad market approach? Explain your answer.

LO5-3

4. Explore Kendra Scott's website at www.kendrascott.com and see if you can identify at least three ways in which the company seeks to differentiate itself from rival jewelry firms. Is there reason to believe that Kendra Scott's differentiation strategy has been successful in producing a competitive advantage? Why or why not?

EXERCISES FOR SIMULATION PARTICIPANTS

LO5-1, LO5-2, LO5-3, LO5-4

1. Which one of the five generic competitive strategies best characterizes your company's strategic approach to competing successfully?

2. Which rival companies appear to be employing a low-cost provider strategy?

3. Which rival companies appear to be employing a broad differentiation strategy?

4. Which rival companies appear to be employing a best-cost provider strategy?

5. Which rival companies appear to be employing some type of focus strategy?

6. What is your company's action plan to achieve a sustainable competitive advantage over rival companies? List at least three (preferably, more than three) specific kinds of decision entries on specific decision screens that your company has made or intends to make to win this kind of competitive edge over rivals.

ENDNOTES

1. Michael E. Porter, *Competitive Strategy: Techniques for Analyzing Industries and Competitors* (New York: Free Press, 1980), chapter 2; and Michael E. Porter, "What Is Strategy?" *Harvard Business Review* 74, no. 6 (November–December 1996).

2. Michael E. Porter, *Competitive Advantage* (New York: Free Press, 1985).

3. Peter J. Williamson and Ming Zeng, "Value-for-Money Strategies for Recessionary Times," *Harvard Business Review* 87, no. 3 (March 2009).

Strengthening a Company's Competitive Position: Strategic Moves, Timing, and Scope of Operations

LEARNING OBJECTIVES

After reading this chapter, you should be able to:

LO6-1   Understand whether and when to pursue offensive or defensive strategic moves to improve a company's market position.

LO6-2   Recognize when being a first mover or a fast follower or a late mover can lead to competitive advantage.

LO6-3   Understand the strategic benefits and risks of expanding a company's horizontal scope through mergers and acquisitions.

LO6-4   Understand the advantages and disadvantages of extending a company's scope of operations via vertical integration.

LO6-5   Understand the conditions that favor farming out certain value chain activities to outside parties.

LO6-6   Understand how strategic alliances and collaborative partnerships can bolster a company's collection of resources and capabilities.

Once a company has settled on which of the five generic competitive strategies to employ, attention turns to what *other strategic actions* it can take to complement its competitive approach and maximize the power of its overall strategy. Several decisions regarding the company's operating scope and how to best strengthen its market standing must be made:

- Whether and when to go on the offensive and initiate aggressive strategic moves to improve the company's market position
- Whether and when to employ defensive strategies to protect the company's market position
- When to undertake strategic moves based upon whether it is advantageous to be a first mover or a fast follower or a late mover
- Whether to integrate backward or forward into more stages of the industry value chain
- Which value chain activities, if any, should be outsourced
- Whether to enter into strategic alliances or partnership arrangements with other enterprises
- Whether to bolster the company's market position by merging with or acquiring another company in the same industry

This chapter presents the pros and cons of each of these measures that round out a company's overall strategy.

Launching Strategic Offensives to Improve a Company's Market Position

LO6-1 Understand whether and when to pursue offensive or defensive strategic moves to improve a company's market position.

No matter which of the five generic competitive strategies a company employs, there are times when a company *should be aggressive and go on the offensive.* Strategic offensives are called for when a company spots opportunities to gain profitable market share at the expense of rivals or when a company has no choice but to try to whittle away at a strong rival's competitive advantage. Companies such as Samsung, Amazon, Autonation, and Google play hardball, aggressively pursuing competitive advantage and trying to reap the benefits a competitive edge offers—a leading market share, excellent profit margins, and rapid growth.[1]

Choosing the Basis for Competitive Attack

Generally, strategic offensives should be grounded in a company's competitive assets and strong points and should be aimed at exploiting competitor weaknesses.[2] Ignoring the need to tie a strategic offensive to a company's competitive strengths is like going to war with a popgun—the prospects for success are dim. For instance, it is foolish for a company with relatively high costs to employ a price-cutting

> The best offensives use a company's most competitively potent resources to attack rivals in those competitive areas where they are weakest.

offensive. Likewise, it is ill advised to pursue a product innovation offensive without having proven expertise in R&D, new product development, and speeding new or improved products to market.

The principal offensive strategy options include:

1. *Offering an equally good or better product at a lower price.* Lower prices can produce market share gains if competitors offering similarly performing products do not respond with price cuts of their own. Price-cutting offensives are best initiated by companies that have *first achieved a cost advantage.*[3]

2. *Leapfrogging competitors by being the first to market with next-generation technology or products.* Eero got its whole home Wi-Fi system to market nearly one year before Linksys and Netgear developed competing systems, helping it build a sizable market share and develop a reputation for cutting-edge innovation in Wi-Fi systems.

3. *Pursuing continuous product innovation to draw sales and market share away from less innovative rivals.* Ongoing introductions of new or improved products can put rivals under tremendous competitive pressure, especially when rivals' new product development capabilities are weak.

4. *Pursuing disruptive product innovations to create new markets.* While this strategy can be riskier and more costly than a strategy of continuous innovation, it can be a game changer if successful. Disruptive innovation involves perfecting new products or services that offer an altogether new and better value proposition. Examples include Netflix, Venmo, Twitter, and Amazon's Kindle.

5. *Adopting and improving on the good ideas of other companies (rivals or otherwise).* The idea of warehouse-type home improvement centers did not originate with Home Depot co-founders Arthur Blank and Bernie Marcus; they got the "big box" concept from their former employer, Handy Dan Home Improvement. But they were quick to improve on Handy Dan's business model and strategy and take Home Depot to a higher plateau in terms of product-line breadth and customer service.

6. *Using hit-and-run or guerrilla warfare tactics to grab sales and market share from complacent or distracted rivals.* Options for "guerrilla offensives" include occasional lowballing on price (to win a big order or steal a key account from a rival) or surprising key rivals with sporadic but intense bursts of promotional activity (offering a 20 percent discount for one week to draw customers away from rival brands).[4] Guerrilla offensives are particularly well suited to small challengers who have neither the resources nor the market visibility to mount a full-fledged attack on industry leaders.

7. *Launching a preemptive strike to capture a rare opportunity or secure an industry's limited resources.*[5] What makes a move preemptive is its one-of-a-kind nature—whoever strikes first stands to acquire competitive assets that rivals cannot readily match. Examples of preemptive moves include (1) securing the best distributors in a particular geographic region or country; (2) moving to obtain the most favorable site at a new interchange or intersection, in a new shopping mall, and so on; and (3) tying up the most reliable, high-quality suppliers via exclusive partnerships, long-term contracts, or even acquisition. To be successful, a preemptive move doesn't have to totally block rivals from following or copying; it merely needs to give a firm a prime position that is not easily circumvented.

Choosing Which Rivals to Attack

Offensive-minded firms need to analyze which of their rivals to challenge as well as how to mount that challenge. The best targets for offensive attacks are:

- *Market leaders that are vulnerable.* Offensive attacks make good sense when a company that leads in terms of size and market share is not a true leader in terms of serving the market well. Signs of leader vulnerability include unhappy buyers, an inferior product line, a weak competitive strategy with regard to low-cost leadership or differentiation, a preoccupation with diversification into other industries, and mediocre or declining profitability.

- *Runner-up firms with weaknesses in areas where the challenger is strong.* Runner-up firms are an especially attractive target when a challenger's resource strengths and competitive capabilities are well suited to exploiting their weaknesses.

- *Struggling enterprises that are on the verge of going under.* Challenging a hard-pressed rival in ways that further sap its financial strength and competitive position can hasten its exit from the market.

- *Small local and regional firms with limited capabilities.* Because small firms typically have limited expertise and resources, a challenger with broader capabilities is well positioned to raid their biggest and best customers.

Blue Ocean Strategy—A Special Kind of Offensive

A **blue ocean strategy** seeks to gain a dramatic and durable competitive advantage *by abandoning efforts to beat out competitors in existing markets and, instead, inventing a new industry or distinctive market segment that renders existing competitors largely irrelevant and allows a company to create and capture altogether new demand.*[6] This strategy views the business universe as consisting of two distinct types of market space. One is where industry boundaries are defined and accepted, the competitive rules of the game are well understood by all industry members, and companies try to outperform rivals by capturing a bigger share of existing demand; in such markets, lively competition constrains a company's prospects for rapid growth and superior profitability since rivals move quickly to either imitate or counter the successes of competitors. The second type of market space is a "blue ocean" where the industry does not really exist yet, is untainted by competition, and offers wide-open opportunity for profitable and rapid growth if a company can come up with a product offering and strategy that allows it to create new demand rather than fight over existing demand. A terrific example of such wide-open or blue ocean market space is the online auction industry that eBay created and now dominates.

Other examples of companies that have achieved competitive advantages by creating blue ocean market spaces include Drybar in hair blowouts, FedEx in overnight package delivery, Uber in ride-sharing services, and Cirque du Soleil in live entertainment. Cirque du Soleil "reinvented the circus" by creating a distinctively different market space for its performances (Las Vegas nightclubs and theater-type settings) and pulling in a whole new group of customers—adults and corporate clients—who were willing to pay several times more than the price of a conventional circus ticket to have an "entertainment experience" featuring sophisticated clowns and star-quality acrobatic acts in a comfortable atmosphere.

CORE CONCEPT

Blue ocean strategies offer growth in revenues and profits by discovering or inventing new industry segments that create altogether new demand.

Concepts & Connections 6.1

BONOBOS' BLUE OCEAN STRATEGY IN THE U.S. MEN'S FASHION RETAIL INDUSTRY

It was not too long ago that young, athletic men struggled to find clothing that adequately fit their athletic frames. It was this issue that led two male Stanford MBA students to create Bonobos, a men's clothing brand that initially focused on selling well-fitting men's pants via the Internet, in 2007. At the time this concept occupied relatively blue waters as most other clothing brands and retailers in reasonable price ranges had largely focused on innovating in women's clothing, as opposed to men's. In the years since, Bonobos has expanded its product portfolio to include a full line of men's clothing, while growing its revenue from $4 million in 2009 to over $100 million in 2016.

This success has not gone unnoticed by both established players as well as other entrepreneurs. Numerous startups have jumped on the custom men's clothing bandwagon ranging from the low-cost Combatant Gentlemen, to the many bespoke suit tailors that exist in major cities around the United States. In addition, more mainstream clothing retailers have also identified this

new type of male customer, with the CEO of Men's Wearhouse, Doug Ewert, stating that he views custom clothing as a "big growth opportunity." That company recently acquired Joseph Abboud to focus more on millennial customers, and plans to begin offering more types of customized clothing in the future.

In response, Bonobos has focused on a new area of development to move to bluer waters in the brick-and-mortar space. The company's innovation is the Guideshop—a store where you can't actually buy anything to take home. Instead, the Guideshop allows men to have a personalized shopping experience, where they can try on clothing in any size or color, and then have it delivered the next day to their home or office. This model was based on the insight that most men want an efficient shopping experience, with someone to help them identify the right product and proper fit, so that they could order with ease in the future. As Bonobos CEO Andy Dunn stated more simply, the idea was to provide a different experience from existing retail, which had become "a job about keeping clothes folded [rather] than delivering service." Since opening its first Guideshop in 2011, the company has now expanded to 20 Guideshops nationwide and plans to continue this growth moving forward. This strategy has been fueling the company's success, but how long Bonobos has before retail clothing copycats turn these blue waters red remains to be seen.

R&P: ©Spencer Platt/Getty Images

Note: Developed with Jacob M. Crandall.

Sources: Richard Feloni, "After 8 Years and $128 Million Raised, the Clock Is Ticking for Men's Retailer Bonobos," BusinessInsider.com, October 6, 2015; Vikram Alexei Kansara, "Andy Dunn of Bonobos on Building the Armani of the E-commerce Era," Businessoffashion.com, July 19, 2013; Hadley Malcolm, "Men's Wearhouse Wants to Suit Up Millennials," *USA Today*, June 8, 2015.

Blue ocean strategies provide a company with a great opportunity in the short run. But they do not guarantee a company's long-term success, which depends more on whether a company can protect the market position it opened up. Concepts & Connections 6.1 discusses how Bonobos used a blue ocean strategy to open a new competitive space in men's apparel retailing.

Using Defensive Strategies to Protect a Company's Market Position and Competitive Advantage

In a competitive market, all firms are subject to offensive challenges from rivals. The purposes of defensive strategies are to lower the risk of being attacked, weaken the

> Good defensive strategies can help protect competitive advantage but rarely are the basis for creating it.

impact of any attack that occurs, and influence challengers to aim their efforts at other rivals. While defensive strategies usually do not enhance a firm's competitive advantage, they can definitely help fortify its competitive position. Defensive strategies can take either of two forms: actions to block challengers and actions signaling the likelihood of strong retaliation.

Blocking the Avenues Open to Challengers

The most frequently employed approach to defending a company's present position involves actions to restrict a competitive attack by a challenger. A number of obstacles can be put in the path of would-be challengers.[7] A defender can introduce new features, add new models, or broaden its product line to close vacant niches to opportunity-seeking challengers. It can thwart the efforts of rivals to attack with a lower price by maintaining economy-priced options of its own. It can try to discourage buyers from trying competitors' brands by making early announcements about upcoming new products or planned price changes. Finally, a defender can grant volume discounts or better financing terms to dealers and distributors to discourage them from experimenting with other suppliers.

Signaling Challengers That Retaliation Is Likely

The goal of signaling challengers that strong retaliation is likely in the event of an attack is either to dissuade challengers from attacking or to divert them to less threatening options. Either goal can be achieved by letting challengers know the battle will cost more than it is worth. Would-be challengers can be signaled by:

- Publicly announcing management's commitment to maintain the firm's present market share.
- Publicly committing the company to a policy of matching competitors' terms or prices.
- Maintaining a war chest of cash and marketable securities.
- Making an occasional strong counterresponse to the moves of weak competitors to enhance the firm's image as a tough defender.

Timing a Company's Offensive and Defensive Strategic Moves

 LO6-2 Recognize when being a first mover or a fast follower or a late mover can lead to competitive advantage.

When to make a strategic move is often as crucial as *what* move to make. Timing is especially important when **first-mover advantages or disadvantages** exist. Under certain conditions, being first to initiate a strategic move can have a high payoff in the form of a competitive advantage that later movers cannot dislodge. Moving first is no guarantee of success, however, since first movers also face some significant disadvantages.

Indeed, there are circumstances in which it is more advantageous to be a fast follower or even a late mover. Because the timing of strategic moves can be consequential, it is important for company strategists to be aware of the nature of first-mover advantages and disadvantages and the conditions favoring each type of move.[8]

Sometimes, though, markets are slow to accept the innovative product offering of a first mover, in which case a fast follower with substantial resources and marketing muscle can overtake a first mover. CNN had enjoyed a powerful first-mover advantage in cable news for more than 20 years, until it was surpassed by Fox News as the number-one cable news network. Fox has used innovative programming and intriguing hosts to expand its demographic appeal to retain its number-one ranking since 2002. Sometimes furious technological change or product innovation makes a first mover vulnerable to quickly appearing next-generation technology or products. For instance, former market leaders in mobile phones Nokia and BlackBerry have been victimized by far more innovative iPhone and Android models. Hence, there are no guarantees that a first mover will win sustainable competitive advantage.[9]

There are five conditions in which first-mover advantages are most likely to arise:

1. *When pioneering helps build a firm's reputation and creates strong brand loyalty.* Customer loyalty to an early mover's brand can create a tie that binds, limiting the success of later entrants' attempts to poach from the early mover's customer base and steal market share.

2. *When a first mover's customers will thereafter face significant switching costs.* Switching costs can protect first movers when consumers make large investments in learning how to use a specific company's product or in purchasing complementary products that are also brand-specific.

3. *When property rights protections thwart rapid imitation of the initial move.* In certain types of industries, property rights protections in the form of patents, copyrights, and trademarks prevent the ready imitation of an early mover's initial moves. First-mover advantages in pharmaceuticals, for example, are heavily dependent on patent protections, and patent races in this industry are common.

4. *When an early lead enables the first mover to move down the learning curve ahead of rivals.* When there is a steep learning curve and when learning can be kept proprietary, a first-mover advantage can be preserved over long periods of time. Intel's advantage in microprocessors has been attributed to such an effect.

5. *When a first mover can set the technical standard for the industry.* In many technology-based industries, the market will converge around a single technical standard. By establishing the industry standard, a first mover can gain a powerful advantage that, like experience-based advantages, builds over time. The keys to developing such an advantage is to enter early on the basis of strong fast-cycle product development capabilities, gain the support of key customers and suppliers, employ penetration pricing, and make allies of the producers of complementary products.

Concepts & Connections 6.2 describes how Uber has achieved a first-mover advantage in ride-sharing services.

Concepts&Connections 6.2

UBER'S FIRST-MOVER ADVANTAGE IN MOBILE RIDE-HAILING SERVICES

In February 2008, Travis Kalanick and Garrett Camp stood on a Paris street struggling to hail a cab when an idea hit them: get a ride by using an app on your smartphone. The result of this brainstorm was the ride-sharing company Uber. The company's mobile app pairs individuals looking for a car with the nearest available driver. Within minutes of summoning a car with Uber, a rider can be on her way. The Uber app takes care of everything: giving the driver directions, charging the ride to the customer's credit card, and tipping the driver. There is no need to carry cash or scan streets for an open cab. Uber has been extremely successful with customers looking for an on-demand cab and individuals looking to make money driving. After its founding in March 2009, Uber became one of the fastest-growing companies in history, faster than Facebook or Twitter, and dominated the on-demand transportation market, leaving competitors like Lyft, Taxify, and Sidecar in the dust.

Uber's rapid rise had much to do with the advantages of being the first mover in the on-demand transportation market.

Upon introducing its car service to new cities, Uber aggressively established itself, offering monetary bonuses for drivers who signed up and providing free first rides to encourage new customers to download the Uber app. When competitors entered a city after Uber, they found that the market was largely saturated; many potential customers and drivers were already using Uber. Once the app was downloaded, Uber customers had little reason to try a new ride-sharing service. With more drivers working for them, Uber could provide customers with shorter wait times, on average. Similarly, with more customers using Uber's app, drivers had little incentive to work for a competitor since Uber could provide steadier work.

In 2017, Uber served over 600 cities worldwide, which was more than three times the number of cities where Lyft was available. The company expanded its product offering, with low-cost UberX and UberPool, to capture new customer segments before competitors could; both times, Lyft launched similar services later but had already missed out on most of the market. With rapid growth and a large customer base, Uber booked rides totaling more than $20 billion and recorded revenue of $6.5 billion in 2016. However, Uber recorded losses of $2.8 billion in 2016 and its future success depends on whether Uber can improve its cost structure while continuing to stay a step ahead of its competition.

Note: Developed with Arthur J. Santry.

Sources: D. MacMillan and T. Demos, "Uber Valued at More Than $50 Billion," *Wall Street Journal* Online, July 15, 2015, www.wsj.com; Edmund Ingham, "Start-ups Take Note," *Forbes,* December 5, 2014, www.forbes.com; Heather Kelly, "Lyft Battles Uber for Drivers with New Perks," CNN, October 8, 2015, www.cnn.com; "Uber: Driving Hard," *The Economist,* June 13, 2015, www.economist.com; company website (accessed November 30, 2015).

R&P: ©Simon Dawson/Bloomberg/Getty Images

The Potential for Late-Mover Advantages or First-Mover Disadvantages

There are instances when there are actually *advantages* to being an adept follower rather than a first mover. Late-mover advantages (or *first-mover disadvantages*) arise in four instances:

- When pioneering leadership is more costly than followership and only negligible experience or learning-curve benefits accrue to the leader—a condition that allows a follower to end up with lower costs than the first mover.

- When the products of an innovator are somewhat primitive and do not live up to buyer expectations, thus allowing a clever follower to win disenchanted buyers away from the leader with better-performing products.

- When potential buyers are skeptical about the benefits of a new technology or product being pioneered by a first mover.
- When rapid market evolution (due to fast-paced changes in either technology or buyer needs and expectations) gives fast followers and maybe even cautious late movers the opening to leapfrog a first mover's products with more attractive next-version products.

Deciding Whether to Be an Early Mover or Late Mover

In weighing the pros and cons of being a first mover versus a fast follower versus a slow mover, it matters whether the race to market leadership in a particular industry is a marathon or a sprint. In marathons, a slow mover is not unduly penalized—first-mover advantages can be fleeting, and there's ample time for fast followers and sometimes even late movers to catch up.[10] Thus the speed at which the pioneering innovation is likely to catch on matters considerably as companies struggle with whether to pursue a particular emerging market opportunity aggressively or cautiously. For instance, it took 5.5 years for worldwide mobile phone use to grow from 10 million to 100 million worldwide and close to 10 years for the number of at-home broadband subscribers to grow to 100 million worldwide. The lesson here is that there is a market-penetration curve for every emerging opportunity; typically, the curve has an inflection point at which all the pieces of the business model fall into place, buyer demand explodes, and the market takes off. The inflection point can come early on a fast-rising curve (as with the use of e-mail) or farther on up a slow-rising curve (such as the use of broadband). Any company that seeks competitive advantage by being a first mover thus needs to ask some hard questions:

- Does market takeoff depend on the development of complementary products or services that currently are not available?
- Is new infrastructure required before buyer demand can surge?
- Will buyers need to learn new skills or adopt new behaviors? Will buyers encounter high switching costs?
- Are there influential competitors in a position to delay or derail the efforts of a first mover?

When the answers to any of these questions are yes, then a company must be careful not to pour too many resources into getting ahead of the market opportunity—the race is likely going to be more of a 10-year marathon than a 2-year sprint.

Strengthening a Company's Market Position via Its Scope of Operations

LO6-3 Understand the strategic benefits and risks of expanding a company's horizontal scope through mergers and acquisitions.

Apart from considerations of offensive and defensive competitive moves and their timing, another set of managerial decisions can affect the strength of a company's market position. These decisions concern the **scope of the firm**—the breadth of a company's activities and the extent of its market reach. For example, Ralph Lauren Corporation designs, markets, and distributes fashionable apparel and other merchandise to more than 13,000 major department stores and specialty retailers around the world, plus it also operates over 200 Ralph Lauren retail stores, 270-plus factory stores, and 10 e-commerce sites. Scope decisions also concern which segments of the market to serve—decisions that can include geographic market segments as well as product and service segments. Almost 40 percent of Ralph Lauren's sales are made outside the United States, and its product line includes apparel, fragrances, home furnishings, eyewear, watches and jewelry, and handbags and other leather goods. The company has also expanded its brand lineup through the acquisitions of Chaps menswear and casual retailer Club Monaco.

Four dimensions of firm scope have the capacity to strengthen a company's position in a given market: the breadth of its product and service offerings, the range of activities the firm performs internally, the extent of its geographic market presence, and its mix of businesses. In this chapter, we discuss horizontal and vertical scope decisions in relation to its breadth of offerings and range of internally performed activities. A company's **horizontal scope**, which is the range of product and service segments that it serves, can be expanded through new-business development or mergers and acquisitions of other companies in the marketplace. The company's **vertical scope** is the extent to which it engages in the various activities that make up the industry's entire value chain system—from raw-material or component production all the way to retailing and after-sales service. Expanding a company's vertical scope by means of vertical integration can also affect the strength of a company's market position.

Additional dimensions of a firm's scope are discussed in Chapter 7, which focuses on the company's geographic scope and expansion into foreign markets, and Chapter 8, which takes up the topic of business diversification and corporate strategy.

Horizontal Merger and Acquisition Strategies

Mergers and acquisitions are much-used strategic options to strengthen a company's market position. A *merger* is the combining of two or more companies into a single corporate entity, with the newly created company often taking on a new name. An *acquisition* is a combination in which one company, the acquirer, purchases and absorbs the operations of another, the acquired. The difference between a merger and an acquisition relates more to the details of ownership, management control, and financial arrangements than to strategy and competitive advantage. The resources and competitive capabilities of the newly created enterprise end up much the same whether the combination is the result of an acquisition or merger.

Horizontal mergers and acquisitions, which involve combining the operations of companies within the same product or service market, allow companies to rapidly increase scale and horizontal scope. For example, the merger of AMR Corporation (parent of American Airlines) with US Airways has increased the airlines' scale of operations and their reach geographically to create the world's largest airline.

> Combining the operations of two companies, via merger or acquisition, is an attractive strategic option for achieving operating economies, strengthening the resulting company's competencies and competitiveness, and opening avenues of new market opportunity.

Merger and acquisition strategies typically set sights on achieving any of five objectives:[11]

1. *Extending the company's business into new product categories.* Many times a company has gaps in its product line that need to be filled. Acquisition can be a quicker and more potent way to broaden a company's product line than going through the exercise of introducing a company's own new product to fill the gap. Coca-Cola's strategy to expand beyond carbonated soft drinks has been supported by acquisitions of of producers of fruit juices, soy-based beverages, and bottled water.

2. *Creating a more cost-efficient operation out of the combined companies.* When a company acquires another company in the same industry, there's usually enough overlap in operations that certain inefficient plants can be closed or distribution and sales activities can be partly combined and downsized. The combined companies may also be able to reduce supply chain costs through buying in greater volume from common suppliers. Likewise, it is usually feasible to squeeze out cost savings in administrative activities, again by combining and downsizing such activities as finance and accounting, information technology, human resources, and so on.

3. *Expanding a company's geographic coverage.* One of the best and quickest ways to expand a company's geographic coverage is to acquire rivals with operations in the desired locations. Food products companies such as Nestlé, Kraft, Unilever, and Procter & Gamble have made acquisitions an integral part of their strategies to expand internationally.

4. *Gaining quick access to new technologies or complementary resources and capabilities.* Making acquisitions to bolster a company's technological know-how or to expand its skills and capabilities allows a company to bypass a time-consuming and expensive internal effort to build desirable new resources and capabilities. From 2000 through June 2017, Cisco Systems purchased 140 companies to give it more technological reach and product breadth, thereby enhancing its standing as the world's largest provider of hardware, software, and services for building and operating Internet networks.

5. *Leading the convergence of industries whose boundaries are being blurred by changing technologies and new market opportunities.* Such acquisitions are the result of a company's management betting that two or more distinct industries are converging into one and deciding to establish a strong position in the consolidating markets by bringing together the resources and products of several different companies. News Corporation has prepared for the convergence of media services with the purchase of satellite TV companies to complement its media holdings in TV broadcasting (the Fox network and TV stations in various countries), cable TV (Fox News, Fox Sports, and FX), filmed entertainment (20th Century Fox and Fox Studios), newspapers, magazines, and book publishing.

Why Mergers and Acquisitions Sometimes Fail to Produce Anticipated Results

Despite many successes, mergers and acquisitions do not always produce the hoped-for outcomes.[12] Cost savings may prove smaller than expected. Gains in competitive capabilities may take substantially longer to realize or, worse, may never materialize. Efforts to mesh the corporate cultures can stall due to formidable resistance from organization members. Key employees at the acquired company can quickly become disenchanted and leave; the morale of company personnel who remain can drop to disturbingly low levels because they disagree with newly instituted changes. Differences in management styles and operating procedures can prove hard to resolve. In addition, the managers appointed to oversee the integration of a newly acquired company can make mistakes in deciding which activities to leave alone and which activities to meld into their own operations and systems.

A number of mergers/acquisitions have been notably unsuccessful. Google's $12.5 billion acquisition of struggling smartphone manufacturer Motorola Mobility in 2012 turned out to be minimally beneficial in helping to "supercharge Google's Android ecosystem" (Google's stated reason for making the acquisition). Google invested over $1.3 billion to rejuvenate Motorola's smartphone lineup but failed to boost sales and incurred substantial operating losses, Google sold Motorola Mobility to China-based PC maker Lenovo for $2.9 billion in 2014. The jury is still out on whether Lenovo's acquisition of Motorola will prove to be a moneymaker.

Vertical Integration Strategies

LO6-4 Understand the advantages and disadvantages of extending a company's scope of operations via vertical integration.

Vertical integration extends a firm's competitive and operating scope within the same industry. It involves expanding the firm's range of value chain activities backward into sources of supply and/or forward toward end users. Thus, if a manufacturer invests in facilities to produce certain component parts that it formerly purchased from outside suppliers or if it opens its own chain of retail stores to market its products to consumers, it is engaging in vertical integration. For example, paint manufacturer Sherwin-Williams remains in the paint business even though it has integrated forward into retailing by operating more than 4,000 retail stores that market its paint products directly to consumers.

CORE CONCEPT

A **vertically integrated** firm is one that performs value chain activities along more than one stage of an industry's overall value chain.

A firm can pursue vertical integration by starting its own operations in other stages of the vertical activity chain, by acquiring a company already performing the activities it wants to bring in-house, or by means of a strategic alliance or joint venture. Vertical integration strategies can aim at *full integration* (participating in all stages of the vertical chain) or *partial integration* (building positions in selected stages of the vertical chain). Companies may choose to pursue *tapered integration,* a strategy that involves both outsourcing and performing the activity internally. Oil companies' practice of supplying their refineries with both crude oil produced from their own wells and crude oil supplied by third-party operators and well owners is an example of tapered backward integration. Coach, Inc., the maker of Coach handbags and accessories, engages in tapered forward

integration since it operates full-price and factory outlet stores but also sells its products through third-party
department store outlets.

The Advantages of a Vertical Integration Strategy

*The two best reasons for investing company resources in
vertical integration are to strengthen the firm's competitive
position and/or to boost its profitability.*[13] Vertical integration has no real payoff unless it produces sufficient cost
savings to justify the extra investment, adds materially to a company's technological and
competitive strengths, and/or helps differentiate the company's product offering.

Integrating Backward to Achieve Greater Competitiveness It is harder
than one might think to generate cost savings or boost profitability by integrating backward into activities such as parts and components manufacture. For backward integration to be a viable and profitable strategy, a company must be able to (1) achieve the
same scale economies as outside suppliers and (2) match or beat suppliers' production
efficiency with no decline in quality. Neither outcome is easily achieved. To begin with, a
company's in-house requirements are often too small to reach the optimum size for low-
cost operation; for instance, if it takes a minimum production volume of 1 million units
to achieve scale economies and a company's in-house requirements are just 250,000 units,
then it falls way short of being able to match the costs of outside suppliers (who may readily find buyers for 1 million or more units).

But that said, there are still occasions when a company can improve its cost position
and competitiveness by performing a broader range of value chain activities in-house rather
than having these activities performed by outside suppliers. The best potential for being
able to reduce costs via a backward integration strategy exists in situations where suppliers
have very large profit margins, where the item being supplied is a major cost component,
and where the requisite technological skills are easily mastered or acquired. Backward vertical integration can produce a differentiation-based competitive advantage when performing activities internally contributes to a better-quality product/service offering, improves the
caliber of customer service, or in other ways enhances the performance of a final product.
Other potential advantages of backward integration include sparing a company the uncertainty of being dependent on suppliers for crucial components or support services and
lessening a company's vulnerability to powerful suppliers inclined to raise prices at every
opportunity. Spanish clothing maker Inditex has backward integrated into fabric making, as
well as garment design and manufacture, for its successful Zara chain of clothing stores. By
tightly controlling the design and production processes, it can quickly respond to changes in
fashion trends to keep its stores stocked with the hottest new items and lines.

Integrating Forward to Enhance Competitiveness Vertical integration into
forward stages of the industry value chain allows manufacturers to gain better access
to end users, improve market visibility, and include the end user's purchasing experience as a differentiating feature. For example, Harley-Davidson's company-owned retail
stores bolster the company's image and appeal through personalized selling, attractive
displays, and riding classes that create new motorcycle riders and build brand loyalty.
Insurance companies and brokerages such as Allstate and Edward Jones have the ability

to make consumers' interactions with local agents and office personnel a differentiating feature by focusing on building relationships.

Most consumer goods companies have opted to integrate forward into retailing by selling direct to consumers via their websites. Bypassing regular wholesale/retail channels in favor of direct sales and Internet retailing can have appeal if it lowers distribution costs, produces a relative cost advantage over certain rivals, offers higher margins, or results in lower selling prices to end users. In addition, sellers are compelled to include the Internet as a retail channel when a sufficiently large number of buyers in an industry prefer to make purchases online. However, a company that is vigorously pursuing online sales to consumers at the same time that it is also heavily promoting sales to consumers through its network of wholesalers and retailers *is competing directly against its distribution allies.* Such actions constitute *channel conflict* and create a tricky route to negotiate. A company that is actively trying to grow online sales to consumers is signaling *a weak strategic commitment to its dealers* and *a willingness to cannibalize dealers' sales and growth potential.* The likely result is angry dealers and loss of dealer goodwill. Quite possibly, a company may stand to lose more sales by offending its dealers than it gains from its own online sales effort. Consequently, in industries where the strong support and goodwill of dealer networks are essential, companies may conclude that it is important to avoid channel conflict and that *their website should be designed to partner with dealers rather than compete with them.*

The Disadvantages of a Vertical Integration Strategy

Vertical integration has some substantial drawbacks beyond the potential for channel conflict.[14] The most serious drawbacks to vertical integration include:

- Vertical integration *increases a firm's capital investment* in the industry.
- Integrating into more industry value chain segments *increases business risk* if industry growth and profitability sour.
- Vertically integrated companies are often *slow to embrace technological advances* or more-efficient production methods when they are saddled with older technology or facilities.
- Integrating backward potentially results in less flexibility in accommodating shifting buyer preferences when a new product design does not include parts and components that the company makes in-house.
- Vertical integration poses all kinds of *capacity matching problems.* In motor vehicle manufacturing, for example, the most efficient scale of operation for making axles is different from the most economic volume for radiators and different yet again for both engines and transmissions. Consequently, integrating across several production stages in ways that achieve the lowest feasible costs can be a monumental challenge.
- Integration forward or backward often requires the *development of new skills and business capabilities.* Parts and components manufacturing, assembly operations, wholesale distribution and retailing, and direct sales via the Internet are different businesses with different key success factors.

A vertical integration strategy has appeal *only if* it significantly strengthens a firm's competitive position and/or boosts its profitability.

Kaiser Permanente, the largest managed care organization in the Untied States, has made vertical integration a central part of its strategy, as described in Concepts & Connections 6.3.

Concepts&Connections 6.3

KAISER PERMANENTE'S VERTICAL INTEGRATION STRATEGY

Kaiser Permanente's unique business model features a vertical integration strategy that enables it to deliver higher-quality care to patients at a lower cost. Kaiser Permanente is the largest vertically integrated health care delivery system in the United States, with $64.6 billion in revenues and $3.1 billion in net income in 2016. It functions as a health insurance company with over 11 million members and a provider of health care services with 38 hospitals, 673 medical offices, and more than 21,000 physicians. As a result of its vertical integration, Kaiser Permanente is better able to efficiently match demand for services by health plan members to capacity of its delivery infrastructure, including physicians and hospitals. Moreover, its prepaid financial model helps to incentivize the appropriate delivery of health care services.

Unlike Kaiser Permanente, the majority of physicians and hospitals in the United States provide care on a fee-for-service revenue model or per-procedure basis. Consequently, most physicians and hospitals earn higher revenues by providing more services, which limits investments in preventive care. In contrast, Kaiser Permanente providers are incentivized to focus on health promotion, disease prevention, and chronic disease management. Kaiser Permanente pays primary care physicians more than local averages to attract top talent, and surgeons are salaried rather than paid by procedure to encourage the optimal level of care. Physicians from multiple specialties work collaboratively to coordinate care and treat the overall health of patients rather than individual health issues.

One result of this strategy is enhanced efficiency, enabling Kaiser Permanente to provide health insurance that is, on average, 10 percent cheaper than that of its competitors. Further, the care provided is of higher quality based on national standards of care. For the sixth year in a row, Kaiser Permanente health plans received the highest overall quality-of-care rating of any health plan in California, which accounts for 7 million of its 11 million members. Kaiser Permanente is also consistently praised for member satisfaction. Four of Kaiser's health plan regions, accounting for 90 percent of its membership, were ranked highest in member satisfaction by J. D. Power and Associates. The success of Kaiser Permanente's vertical integration strategy is the primary reason why many health care organizations are seeking to replicate its model as they transition from a fee-for-service revenue model to an accountable care model.

Note: Developed with Christopher C. Sukenik.

Sources: "Kaiser Foundation Health Plan Report and Hospitals Annual Financial Results for 2016," PRNewswire, February 13, 2017, www.prnewswire.com; Kaiser Permanente website and 2012 annual report; and J. O'Donnell, "Kaiser Permanente CEO on Saving Lives, Money," *USA Today,* October 23, 2012.

R&P: ©Bryan Chan/Los Angeles Times/Getty Images

Outsourcing Strategies: Narrowing the Scope of Operations

LO6-5   Understand the conditions that favor farming out certain value chain activities to outside parties.

Outsourcing forgoes attempts to perform certain value chain activities internally and instead farms them out to outside specialists and strategic allies. Outsourcing makes strategic sense whenever:

- *An activity can be performed better or more cheaply by outside specialists.* A company should generally *not* perform any value chain activity internally that can be performed more efficiently or effectively by outsiders. The chief exception is when a particular activity is strategically crucial and internal control over that activity is deemed essential.

- *The activity is not crucial to the firm's ability to achieve sustainable competitive advantage and will not hollow out its capabilities, core competencies, or technical know-how.* Outsourcing of support activities such as maintenance services, data processing and data storage, fringe benefit management, and website operations has become common. Colgate-Palmolive, for instance, has been able to reduce its information technology operational costs by more than 10 percent per year through an outsourcing agreement with IBM.

- *It improves organizational flexibility and speeds time to market.* Outsourcing gives a company the flexibility to switch suppliers in the event that its present supplier falls behind competing suppliers. Also, to the extent that its suppliers can speedily get next-generation parts and components into production, a company can get its own next-generation product offerings into the marketplace quicker.

- *It reduces the company's risk exposure to changing technology and/or buyer preferences.* When a company outsources certain parts, components, and services, its suppliers must bear the burden of incorporating state-of-the-art technologies and/or undertaking redesigns and upgrades to accommodate a company's plans to introduce next-generation products.

- *It allows a company to concentrate on its core business, leverage its key resources and core competencies, and do even better what it already does best.* A company is better able to build and develop its own competitively valuable competencies and capabilities when it concentrates its full resources and energies on performing those activities. Apple outsources production of its iPod, iPhone, and iPad models to Chinese contract manufacturer Foxconn. Hewlett-Packard and others have sold some of their manufacturing plants to outsiders and contracted to repurchase the output from the new owners.

The Big Risk of an Outsourcing Strategy The biggest danger of outsourcing is that a company will farm out the wrong types of activities and thereby hollow out its own capabilities.[15] In such cases, a company loses touch with the very activities and expertise that over the long run determine its success. But most companies are alert to this danger and take actions to protect against being held hostage by outside suppliers. Cisco Systems guards against loss of control and protects its manufacturing expertise by designing the production methods that its contract manufacturers must use. Cisco keeps the source code for its designs proprietary, thereby controlling the initiation of all improvements and safeguarding its innovations from imitation. Further, Cisco uses the Internet to monitor the factory operations of contract manufacturers around the clock and can know immediately when problems arise and decide whether to get involved.

Strategic Alliances and Partnerships

LO6-6   Understand how strategic alliances and collaborative partnerships can bolster a company's collection of resources and capabilities.

Companies in all types of industries have elected to form strategic alliances and partnerships to complement their accumulation of resources and capabilities and strengthen their competitiveness in domestic and international markets. A **strategic alliance** is a formal agreement between two or more separate companies in which there is strategically relevant collaboration of some sort, joint contribution of resources, shared risk, shared control, and mutual dependence. Collaborative relationships between partners may entail a contractual agreement, but they commonly stop short of formal ownership ties between the partners (although there are a few strategic alliances where one or more allies have minority ownership in certain of the other alliance members). Collaborative arrangements involving shared ownership are called joint ventures. A **joint venture** is a partnership involving the establishment of an independent corporate entity that is jointly owned and controlled by two or more companies. Since joint ventures involve setting up a mutually owned business, they tend to be more durable but also riskier than other arrangements.

> **CORE CONCEPT**
>
> A **strategic alliance** is a formal agreement between two or more companies to work cooperatively toward some common objective.

The most common reasons companies enter into strategic alliances are to expedite the development of promising new technologies or products, to overcome deficits in their own technical and manufacturing expertise, to bring together the personnel and expertise needed to create desirable new skill sets and capabilities, to improve supply chain efficiency, to gain economies of scale in production and/or marketing, and to acquire or improve market access through joint marketing agreements.[16] Arabian Chemical Insulation Company (ACIC) is a joint venture established in 1976 between Dow Chemical Company and E.A. Juffali & Brothers to manufacture and sell polystyrene insulation products throughout the Middle East. ACIC continued to be one of the leading producers of insulation in the Middle East in 2017 and was Dow Chemical's longest running joint venture in the region. Volkswagen established a joint venture with China-based Anhui Jianghuai Automobile Company in 2017 to develop and produce electric and plug-in hybrid vehicles for sale in China. The two partners expected the joint venture would sell 400,000 vehicles by 2020 and 1.5 million electric cars by 2025.

Because of the varied benefits of strategic alliances, many large corporations have become involved in 30 to 50 alliances, and a number have formed hundreds of alliances. Roche, a leader in pharmaceuticals and diagnostics, has formed R&D alliances with over 160 companies to boost its prospects for developing new cures for various diseases. In 2016, more than one-third of its pharmaceutical sales came from partnered products. Companies that have formed a host of alliances need to manage their alliances like a portfolio—terminating those that no longer serve a useful purpose or that have produced meager results, forming promising new alliances, and restructuring existing alliances to correct performance problems and/or redirect the collaborative effort.

> **CORE CONCEPT**
>
> A **joint venture** is a type of strategic alliance that involves the establishment of an independent corporate entity that is jointly owned and controlled by the two partners.

Failed Strategic Alliances and Cooperative Partnerships

Most alliances with an objective of technology sharing or providing market access turn out to be temporary, fulfilling their purpose after a few years because the benefits of mutual learning have occurred. Although long-term alliances sometimes prove mutually beneficial, most partners do not hesitate to terminate the alliance and go it alone when the payoffs run out. Alliances are more likely to be long lasting when (1) they involve collaboration with partners that do not compete directly, (2) a trusting relationship has been established, and (3) both parties conclude that continued collaboration is in their mutual interest, perhaps because new opportunities for learning are emerging.

A surprisingly large number of alliances never live up to expectations, with estimates that as many as 60 to 70 percent of alliances fail each year. The high "divorce rate" among strategic allies has several causes, the most common of which are:[17]

- Diverging objectives and priorities.
- An inability to work well together.
- Changing conditions that make the purpose of the alliance obsolete.
- The emergence of more attractive technological paths.
- Marketplace rivalry between one or more allies.

Experience indicates that *alliances stand a reasonable chance of helping a company reduce competitive disadvantage, but very rarely have they proved a strategic option for gaining a durable competitive edge over rivals.*

The Strategic Dangers of Relying on Alliances for Essential Resources and Capabilities

The Achilles' heel of alliances and cooperative strategies is becoming dependent on other companies for *essential* expertise and capabilities. To be a market leader (and perhaps even a serious market contender), a company must ultimately develop its own resources and capabilities in areas where internal strategic control is pivotal to protecting its competitiveness and building competitive advantage. Moreover, some alliances hold only limited potential because the partner guards its most valuable skills and expertise; in such instances, acquiring or merging with a company possessing the desired know-how and resources is a better solution.

KEY POINTS

Once a company has selected which of the five basic competitive strategies to employ in its quest for competitive advantage, then it must decide whether and how to supplement its choice of a basic competitive strategy approach.

1. Companies have a number of offensive strategy options for improving their market positions and trying to secure a competitive advantage: (1) attacking competitors' weaknesses, (2) offering an equal or better product at a lower price, (3) pursuing sustained product innovation, (4) leapfrogging competitors by being first to adopt next-generation technologies or the first to introduce next-generation products, (5) adopting and improving on the good ideas of other companies, (6) deliberately attacking those market segments where key rivals

make big profits, (7) going after less contested or unoccupied market territory, (8) using hit-and-run tactics to steal sales away from unsuspecting rivals, and (9) launching preemptive strikes. A blue ocean offensive strategy seeks to gain a dramatic and durable competitive advantage by abandoning efforts to beat out competitors in existing markets and, instead, inventing a new industry or distinctive market segment that renders existing competitors largely irrelevant and allows a company to create and capture altogether new demand.

2. Defensive strategies to protect a company's position usually take the form of making moves that put obstacles in the path of would-be challengers and fortify the company's present position while undertaking actions to dissuade rivals from even trying to attack (by signaling that the resulting battle will be more costly to the challenger than it is worth).

3. The timing of strategic moves also has relevance in the quest for competitive advantage. Company managers are obligated to carefully consider the advantages or disadvantages that attach to being a first mover versus a fast follower versus a wait-and-see late mover.

4. Decisions concerning the scope of a company's operations can also affect the strength of a company's market position. The scope of the firm refers to the range of its activities, the breadth of its product and service offerings, the extent of its geographic market presence, and its mix of businesses. Companies can expand their scope horizontally (more broadly within their focal market) or vertically (up or down the industry value chain system that starts with raw-materials production and ends with sales and service to the end consumer). Horizontal mergers and acquisitions (combinations of market rivals) provide a means for a company to expand its horizontal scope. Vertical integration expands a firm's vertical scope.

5. Horizontal mergers and acquisitions can be an attractive strategic option for strengthening a firm's competitiveness. When the operations of two companies are combined via merger or acquisition, the new company's competitiveness can be enhanced in any of several ways—lower costs; stronger technological skills; more or better competitive capabilities; a more attractive lineup of products and services; wider geographic coverage; and/or greater financial resources with which to invest in R&D, add capacity, or expand into new areas.

6. Vertically integrating forward or backward makes strategic sense only if it strengthens a company's position via either cost reduction or creation of a differentiation-based advantage. Otherwise, the drawbacks of vertical integration (increased investment, greater business risk, increased vulnerability to technological changes, and less flexibility in making product changes) are likely to outweigh any advantages.

7. Outsourcing pieces of the value chain formerly performed in-house can enhance a company's competitiveness whenever (1) an activity can be performed better or more cheaply by outside specialists; (2) the activity is not crucial to the firm's ability to achieve sustainable competitive advantage and will not hollow out its core competencies, capabilities, or technical know-how; (3) it improves a company's ability to innovate; and/or (4) it allows a company to concentrate on its core business and do what it does best.

8. Many companies are using strategic alliances and collaborative partnerships to help them in the race to build a global market presence or be a leader in the industries of the future. Strategic alliances are an attractive, flexible, and often cost-effective means by which companies can gain access to missing technology, expertise, and business capabilities.

⊙ ASSURANCE OF LEARNING EXERCISES

1. Live Nation operates music venues, provides management services to music artists, and promotes more than 26,000 live music events annually. The company acquired House of Blues, merged with Ticketmaster, and has also acquired concert and festival promoters

LO6-1, LO6-2, LO6-3

in the United States, Australia, and Great Britain. How has the company used horizontal mergers and acquisitions to strengthen its competitive position? Are these moves primarily offensive or defensive? Has either Live Nation or Ticketmaster achieved any type of advantage based on the timing of its strategic moves?

LO6-4

2.   Kaiser Permanente, a standout among managed health care systems, has become a model for how to deliver good health care cost-effectively. Concepts & Connections 6.3 describes how Kaiser Permanente has made vertical integration a central part of its strategy. What value chain segments has Kaiser Permanente chosen to enter and perform internally? How has vertical integration aided the company in building competitive advantage? Has vertical integration strengthened its market position? Explain why or why not.

LO6-5

3.   Perform an Internet search to identify at least two companies in different industries that have entered into outsourcing agreements with firms with specialized services. In addition, describe what value chain activities the companies have chosen to outsource. Do any of these outsourcing agreements seem likely to threaten any of the companies' competitive capabilities?

LO6-6

4.   Using your university library's business research resources, find two examples of how companies have relied on strategic alliances or joint ventures to substitute for horizontal or vertical integration.

EXERCISES FOR SIMULATION PARTICIPANTS

LO6-1, LO6-2

1.   Has your company relied more on offensive or defensive strategies to achieve your rank in the industry? What options for being a first mover does your company have? Do any of these first-mover options hold competitive advantage potential?

LO6-3

2.   Does your company have the option to merge with or acquire other companies? If so, which rival companies would you like to acquire or merge with?

LO6-4

3.   Is your company vertically integrated? Explain.

LO6-5

4.   Is your company able to engage in outsourcing? If so, what do you see as the pros and cons of outsourcing?

ENDNOTES

1.   George Stalk, Jr., and Rob Lachenauer, "Hardball: Five Killer Strategies for Trouncing the Competition," *Harvard Business Review* 82, no. 4 (April 2004); Richard D'Aveni, "The Empire Strikes Back: Counterrevolutionary Strategies for Industry Leaders," *Harvard Business Review* 80, no. 11 (November 2002); and David J. Bryce and Jeffrey H. Dyer, "Strategies to Crack Well-Guarded Markets," *Harvard Business Review* 85, no. 5 (May 2007).

2.   David B. Yoffie and Mary Kwak, "Mastering Balance: How to Meet and Beat a Stronger Opponent," *California Management Review* 44, no. 2 (Winter 2002).

3.   Ian C. MacMillan, Alexander B. van Putten, and Rita Gunther McGrath, "Global Gamesmanship," *Harvard Business Review* 81, no. 5 (May 2003); and Askay R. Rao, Mark E. Bergen, and Scott Davis, "How to Fight a Price War," *Harvard Business Review* 78, no. 2 (March–April 2000).

4.   Ming-Jer Chen and Donald C. Hambrick, "Speed, Stealth, and Selective Attack: How Small Firms Differ from Large Firms in Competitive Behavior," *Academy of Management Journal* 38, no. 2 (April 1995); Ian MacMillan, "How Business Strategists Can Use Guerrilla Warfare Tactics," *Journal of Business Strategy* 1, no. 2 (Fall 1980); William E. Rothschild, "Surprise and the Competitive Advantage," *Journal of Business Strategy* 4, no. 3 (Winter 1984); Kathryn R. Harrigan, *Strategic Flexibility* (Lexington, MA: Lexington Books, 1985); and

Liam Fahey, "Guerrilla Strategy: The Hit-and-Run Attack," in *The Strategic Management Planning Reader*, ed. Liam Fahey (Englewood Cliffs, NJ: Prentice Hall, 1989).

5.   Ian MacMillan, "Preemptive Strategies," *Journal of Business Strategy* 14, no. 2 (Fall 1983).

6.   W. Chan Kim and Renée Mauborgne, "Blue Ocean Strategy," *Harvard Business Review* 82, no. 10 (October 2004).

7.   Michael E. Porter, *Competitive Advantage* (New York: Free Press, 1985).

8.   Jeffrey G. Covin, Dennis P. Slevin, and Michael B. Heeley, "Pioneers and Followers: Competitive Tactics, Environment, and Growth," *Journal of Business Venturing* 15, no. 2 (March 1999); and

Christopher A. Bartlett and Sumantra Ghoshal, "Going Global: Lessons from Late-Movers," *Harvard Business Review* 78, no. 2 (March–April 2000).

9. Fernando Suarez and Gianvito Lanzolla, "The Half-Truth of First-Mover Advantage," *Harvard Business Review* 83 no. 4 (April 2005).

10. Costas Markides and Paul A. Geroski, "Racing to Be 2nd: Conquering the Industries of the Future," *Business Strategy Review* 15, no. 4 (Winter 2004).

11. Joseph L. Bower, "Not All M&As Are Alike—and That Matters," *Harvard Business Review* 79, no. 3 (March 2001); and O. Chatain and P. Zemsky, "The Horizontal Scope of the Firm: Organizational Tradeoffs vs. Buyer–Supplier Relationships," *Management Science* 53, no. 4 (April 2007), pp. 550–65.

12. Jeffrey H. Dyer, Prashant Kale, and Harbir Singh, "When to Ally and When to Acquire," *Harvard Business Review* 82, no. 4 (July–August 2004), pp. 109–10.

13. Kathryn R. Harrigan, "Matching Vertical Integration Strategies to Competitive Conditions," *Strategic Management Journal* 7, no. 6 (November–December 1986); and John Stuckey and David White, "When and When Not to Vertically Integrate," *Sloan Management Review,* Spring 1993.

14. Thomas Osegowitsch and Anoop Madhok, "Vertical Integration Is Dead, or Is It?" *Business Horizons* 46, no. 2 (March–April 2003).

15. Jérôme Barthélemy, "The Seven Deadly Sins of Outsourcing," *Academy of Management Executive* 17, no. 2 (May 2003); Gary P. Pisano and Willy C. Shih, "Restoring American Competitiveness," *Harvard Business Review* 87, no. 7/8 (July–August 2009); and Ronan McIvor, "What Is the Right Outsourcing Strategy for Your Process?" *European Management Journal* 26, no. 1 (February 2008).

16. Michael E. Porter, *The Competitive Advantage of Nations* (New York: Free Press, 1990); K. M. Eisenhardt and C. B. Schoonhoven, "Resource-Based View of Strategic Alliance Formation: Strategic and Social Effects in Entrepreneurial Firms," *Organization Science* 7, no. 2 (March–April 1996); Nancy J. Kaplan and Jonathan Hurd, "Realizing the Promise of Partnerships," *Journal of Business Strategy* 23, no. 3 (May–June 2002); Salvatore Parise and Lisa Sasson, "Leveraging Knowledge Management across Strategic Alliances," *Ivey Business Journal* 66, no. 4 (March–April 2002); and David Ernst and James Bamford, "Your Alliances Are Too Stable," *Harvard Business Review* 83, no. 6 (June 2005).

17. Yves L. Doz and Gary Hamel, *Alliance Advantage: The Art of Creating Value Through Partnering* (Boston: Harvard Business School Press, 1998).

7 Strategies for Competing in International Markets

LEARNING OBJECTIVES

After reading this chapter, you should be able to:

LO7-1   Identify the primary reasons companies choose to compete in international markets.

LO7-2   Understand why and how differing market conditions across countries influence a company's strategy choices in international markets.

LO7-3   Identify the five general modes of entry into foreign markets.

LO7-4   Identify the three main options for tailoring a company's international strategy to cross-country differences in market conditions and buyer preferences.

LO7-5   Explain how multinational companies are able to use international operations to improve overall competitiveness.

LO7-6   Understand the unique characteristics of competing in developing-country markets.

Any company that aspires to industry leadership in the 21st century must think in terms of global, not domestic, market leadership. The world economy is globalizing at an accelerating pace as countries previously closed to foreign companies open their markets, as countries with previously planned economies embrace market or mixed economies, as information technology shrinks the importance of geographic distance, and as ambitious, growth-minded companies race to build stronger competitive positions in the markets of more and more countries. The forces of globalization are changing the competitive landscape in many industries, offering companies attractive new opportunities but at the same time introducing new competitive threats. Companies in industries where these forces are greatest are under considerable pressure to develop strategies for competing successfully in international markets.

This chapter focuses on strategy options for expanding beyond domestic boundaries and competing in the markets of either a few or many countries. We will discuss the factors that shape the choice of strategy in international markets and the specific market circumstances that support the adoption of multidomestic, transnational, and global strategies. The chapter also includes sections on strategy options for entering foreign markets; how international operations may be used to improve overall competitiveness; and the special circumstances of competing in such emerging markets as China, India, Brazil, Russia, and Eastern Europe.

Why Companies Expand into International Markets

LO7-1	Identify the primary reasons companies choose to compete in international markets.

A company may opt to expand outside its domestic market for any of five major reasons:

1. *To gain access to new customers.* Expanding into foreign markets offers potential for increased revenues, profits, and long-term growth, and becomes an especially attractive option when a company's home markets are mature. Honda has done this with its classic 50-cc motorcycle, the Honda Cub, which is still selling well in developing markets, more than 50 years after it was introduced in Japan.

2. *To achieve lower costs through economies of scale, experience, and increased purchasing power.* Many companies are driven to sell in more than one country because domestic sales volume alone is not large enough to capture fully economies of scale in product development, manufacturing, or marketing. Similarly, firms expand internationally to increase the rate at which they accumulate experience and move down the learning curve. International expansion can also lower a company's input costs through greater pooled purchasing power. The relatively small size of country markets in Europe and limited domestic volume explains why companies like Michelin, BMW, and Nestlé long ago began selling their products all across Europe and then moved into markets in North America and Latin America.

3. *To gain access to low-cost inputs of production.* Companies in industries based on natural resources (e.g., oil and gas, minerals, rubber, and lumber) often find it necessary to operate in the international arena since raw-material supplies are located in different parts of the world and can be accessed more cost-effectively

at the source. Other companies enter foreign markets to access low-cost human resources; this is particularly true of industries in which labor costs make up a high proportion of total production costs.

4. *To further exploit its core competencies.* A company may be able to extend a market-leading position in its domestic market into a position of regional or global market leadership by leveraging its core competencies further. H&M is capitalizing on its considerable expertise in online retailing to expand its reach internationally. By bringing its easy-to-use and mobile-friendly online shopping to 23 different countries, the company hopes to pave the way for setting up physical stores in these countries. Companies can often leverage their resources internationally by replicating a successful business model, using it as a basic blueprint for international operations, as Starbucks and McDonald's have done.

5. *To gain access to resources and capabilities located in foreign markets.* An increasingly important motive for entering foreign markets is to acquire resources and capabilities that cannot be accessed as readily in a company's home market. Companies often enter into cross-border alliances, make acquisitions abroad, or establish operations in foreign countries to access local resources such as distribution networks, low-cost labor, natural resources, or specialized technical knowledge.[1]

In addition, companies that are the suppliers of other companies often expand internationally when their major customers do so, to meet their customers' needs abroad and retain their position as a key supply chain partner. For example, when motor vehicle companies have opened new plants in foreign locations, big automotive parts suppliers have frequently opened new facilities nearby to permit timely delivery of their parts and components to the plant.

Factors That Shape Strategy Choices in International Markets

LO7-2   Understand why and how differing market conditions across countries influence a company's strategy choices in international markets.

Four important factors shape a company's strategic approach to competing in foreign markets: (1) the degree to which there are important cross-country differences in demographic, cultural, and market conditions; (2) whether opportunities exist to gain a location-based advantage based on wage rates, worker productivity, inflation rates, energy costs, tax rates, and other factors that impact cost structure; (3) the risks of adverse shifts in currency exchange rates; and (4) the extent to which governmental policies affect the local business climate.

Cross-Country Differences in Demographic, Cultural, and Market Conditions

Buyer tastes for a particular product or service sometimes differ substantially from country to country. For example, ice cream flavors such as eel, shark fin, and dried shrimp appeal to Japanese customers, whereas fruit-based flavors have more appeal in the United States and Europe. In France, top-loading washing machines are very popular with consumers, whereas in most other European countries, consumers prefer front-loading machines. Consequently, companies operating in a global marketplace must wrestle with *whether and how much to customize their offerings in each different country market to match the tastes and preferences of local buyers or whether to pursue a strategy of offering a mostly standardized product worldwide.* While making products that are closely matched to local tastes makes them more appealing to local buyers, customizing a company's products country by country may raise production and distribution costs. Greater standardization of a global company's product offering, on the other hand, can lead to scale economies and learning curve effects, thus contributing to the achievement of a low-cost advantage. *The tension between the market pressures to localize a company's product offerings country by country and the competitive pressures to lower costs is one of the big strategic issues that participants in foreign markets have to resolve.*

Understandably, differing population sizes, income levels, and other demographic factors give rise to considerable differences in market size and growth rates from country to country. In emerging markets such as India, China, Brazil, and Malaysia, market growth potential is far higher for such products as mobile phones, steel, credit cards, and electric energy than in the more mature economies of Britain, Canada, and Japan. The potential for market growth in automobiles is explosive in China, where 2016 sales of new vehicles amounted to 24.4 million, surpassing U.S. sales of 15.6 million and making China the world's largest market for the seventh year in a row.[2] Owing to widely differing population demographics and income levels, there is a far bigger market for luxury automobiles in the United States and Germany than in Argentina, India, Mexico, and Thailand. Cultural influences can also affect consumer demand for a product. For instance, in China, many parents are reluctant to purchase PCs even when they can afford them because of concerns that their children will be distracted from their schoolwork by surfing the web, playing PC-based video games, and downloading and listening to pop music.

Market growth can be limited by the lack of infrastructure or established distribution and retail networks in emerging markets. India has well-developed national channels for distribution of goods to the nation's 3 million retailers, whereas in China distribution is primarily local. Also, the competitive rivalry in some country marketplaces is only moderate, whereas others are characterized by strong or fierce competition. The managerial challenge at companies with international or global operations is how best to tailor a company's strategy to take all these cross-country differences into account.

Opportunities for Location-Based Cost Advantages

Differences from country to country in wage rates, worker productivity, energy costs, environmental regulations, tax rates, inflation rates, and the like are often so big that *a company's operating costs and profitability are significantly impacted by where its production, distribution, and customer service activities are located.* Wage rates, in particular, vary enormously from country to country. For example, in 2015, hourly compensation for manufacturing workers averaged about $1.59 in India, $4.12 in China, $5.90 in Mexico, $9.51 in Taiwan, $8.25 in Hungary, $7.97 in Brazil, $11.08 in Portugal, $22.68 in South Korea, $23.60 in Japan, $30.94 in Canada, $37.71 in the United States, $42.42 in Germany, and $49.67 in Norway.[3] Not surprisingly, China has emerged as the manufacturing capital of the world—virtually all of the world's major manufacturing companies now have facilities in China. This in turn has driven up manufacturing wages in China by more than double the average hourly compensation cost of $1.98 in 2010.

For other types of value chain activities, input quality or availability are more important considerations. Tiffany entered the mining industry in Canada to access diamonds that could be certified as "conflict free" and not associated with either the funding of African wars or unethical mining conditions. Many U.S. companies locate call centers in countries such as India and Ireland, where English is spoken and the workforce is well educated. Other companies locate R&D activities in countries where there are prestigious research institutions and well-trained scientists and engineers. Likewise, concerns about short delivery times and low shipping costs make some countries better locations than others for establishing distribution centers.

Industry Cluster Knowledge Sharing Opportunities

There are advantages available to companies operating in a location containing a cluster of related industries, including others within the same value chain system (e.g., suppliers of components and equipment, distributors) and the makers of complementary products or those that are technologically related. The sports car makers Ferrari and Maserati, for example, are located in an area of Italy known as the "engine technological district," which includes other firms involved in racing, such as Ducati Motorcycles, along with hundreds of small suppliers. The advantage to firms that develop as part of a related-industry cluster comes from the close collaboration with key suppliers and the greater knowledge sharing throughout the cluster, resulting in greater efficiency and innovativeness.

The Risks of Adverse Exchange Rate Shifts

When companies produce and market their products and services in many different countries, they are subject to the impacts of sometimes favorable and sometimes unfavorable changes in currency exchange rates. The rates of exchange between different currencies can vary by as much as 20 to 40 percent annually, with the changes occurring sometimes gradually and sometimes swiftly. Sizable shifts in exchange rates, which tend to be hard to predict because of the variety of factors involved and the uncertainties surrounding when and by how much these factors will change, *shuffle the global cards of which countries represent the low-cost manufacturing location* and *which rivals have the upper hand in the marketplace.*

To illustrate the competitive risks associated with fluctuating exchange rates, consider the case of a U.S. company that has located manufacturing facilities in Brazil (where the currency is reals—pronounced *ray-alls*) and that exports most of its Brazilian-made goods to markets in the European Union (where the currency is euros). To keep the numbers simple, assume the exchange rate is 4 Brazilian reals for 1 euro and that the product being made in Brazil has a manufacturing cost of 4 Brazilian reals (or 1 euro). Now suppose that for some reason the exchange rate shifts from 4 reals per euro to 5 reals per euro (meaning the real has declined in value and the euro is stronger). Making the product in Brazil is now more cost-competitive because a Brazilian good costing 4 reals to produce has fallen to only 0.8 euro at the new exchange rate (4 reals divided by 5 reals per euro = 0.8 euro). On the other hand, should the value of the Brazilian real grow stronger in relation to the euro—resulting in an exchange rate of 3 reals to 1 euro—the same Brazilian-made good formerly costing 4 reals to produce now has a cost of 1.33 euros (4 reals divided by 3 reals per euro = 1.33). This increase in the value of the real has eroded the cost advantage of the Brazilian manufacturing facility for goods shipped to Europe and affects the ability of the U.S. company to underprice European producers of similar goods. Thus, *the lesson of fluctuating exchange rates is that companies that export goods to foreign countries always gain in competitiveness when the currency of the country in which the goods are manufactured is weak. Exporters are disadvantaged when the currency of the country where goods are being manufactured grows stronger.*

The Impact of Government Policies on the Business Climate in Host Countries

National governments enact all kinds of measures affecting business conditions and the operation of foreign companies in their markets. It matters whether these measures create a favorable or unfavorable business climate. Governments of countries eager to spur economic growth, create more jobs, and raise living standards for their citizens usually make a special effort to create a business climate that outsiders will view favorably. They may provide such incentives as reduced taxes, low-cost loans, and site-development assistance to companies agreeing to construct or expand production and distribution facilities in the host country.

On the other hand, governments sometimes enact policies that, from a business perspective, make locating facilities within a country's borders less attractive. For example, the nature of a company's operations may make it particularly costly to achieve compliance with environmental regulations in certain countries. Some governments, wishing to discourage foreign imports, may enact deliberately burdensome customs procedures and requirements or impose tariffs or quotas on imported goods. Host-country governments may also specify that products contain a certain percentage of locally produced parts and components, require prior approval of capital spending projects, limit withdrawal of funds from the country, and require local ownership stakes in foreign-company operations in the host country. Such governmental actions make a country's business climate unattractive and in some cases may be sufficiently onerous as to discourage a company from locating facilities in that country or selling its products there.

A country's business climate is also a function of the political and economic risks associated with operating within its borders. **Political risks** have to do with the instability of weak governments, the likelihood of new onerous legislation or regulations on foreign-owned businesses, or the potential for future elections to produce government leaders hostile to foreign-owned businesses. In a growing number of emerging markets, governments are pursuing state capitalism in industries deemed to be of national importance. Financial

> **CORE CONCEPT**
>
> **Political risks** stem from instability or weakness in national governments and hostility to foreign business; **economic risks** stem from the stability of a country's monetary system, economic and regulatory policies, and the lack of property rights protections.

services, information technology, telecommunications, and food sectors have become politicized in some emerging markets and are tightly controlled by government. In 2017, for example, Venezuela nationalized a General Motors plant in Valencia employing nearly 2,700 workers. China has established very low price ceilings on as many as 500 prescription drugs, which helps boost the profitability of its state-owned hospitals but makes it challenging for global pharmaceutical companies to do business in China.

Economic risks have to do with the threat of piracy and lack of protection for the company's intellectual property and the stability of a country's economy—whether inflation rates might skyrocket or whether uncontrolled deficit spending on the part of government could lead to a breakdown of the country's monetary system and prolonged economic distress.

Strategy Options for Entering Foreign Markets

LO7-3   Identify the five general modes of entry into foreign markets.

A company choosing to expand outside its domestic market may elect one of the following five general modes of entry into a foreign market:

1. Maintain a national (one-country) production base and export goods to foreign markets.
2. License foreign firms to produce and distribute the company's products abroad.
3. Employ a franchising strategy.
4. Establish a subsidiary in a foreign market via acquisition or internal development.
5. Rely on strategic alliances or joint ventures with foreign partners to enter new country markets.

This section of the chapter discusses the five general options in more detail.

Export Strategies

Using domestic plants as a production base for exporting goods to foreign markets is an excellent initial strategy for pursuing international sales. It is a conservative way to test the international waters. The amount of capital needed to begin exporting is often quite minimal, and existing production capacity may be sufficient to make goods for export. With an export-based entry strategy, a manufacturer can limit its involvement in foreign markets by contracting with foreign wholesalers experienced in importing to handle the entire distribution and marketing function in their countries or regions of the world. If it is more advantageous to maintain control over these functions, however, a manufacturer can establish its own distribution and sales organizations in some or all of the target foreign markets. Either way, a home-based production and export strategy helps the firm minimize its direct investments in foreign countries.

An export strategy is vulnerable when (1) manufacturing costs in the home country are substantially higher than in foreign countries where rivals have plants, (2) the costs of shipping the product to distant foreign markets are relatively high, or (3) adverse shifts occur in currency exchange rates. Unless an exporter can both keep its production and shipping costs competitive with rivals and successfully hedge against unfavorable changes in currency exchange rates, its success will be limited.

Licensing Strategies

Licensing as an entry strategy makes sense when a firm with valuable technical know-how or a unique patented product has neither the internal organizational capability nor the resources to enter foreign markets. Licensing also has the advantage of avoiding the risks of committing resources to country markets that are unfamiliar, politically volatile, economically unstable, or otherwise risky. By licensing the technology or the production rights to foreign-based firms, the firm does not have to bear the costs and risks of entering foreign markets on its own, yet it is able to generate income from royalties. The big disadvantage of licensing is the risk of providing valuable technological know-how to foreign companies and thereby losing some degree of control over its use. Also, monitoring licensees and safeguarding the company's proprietary know-how can prove quite difficult in some circumstances. But if the royalty potential is considerable and the companies to which the licenses are being granted are both trustworthy and reputable, then licensing can be a very attractive option. Many software and pharmaceutical companies use licensing strategies.

Franchising Strategies

While licensing works well for manufacturers and owners of proprietary technology, franchising is often better suited to the global expansion efforts of service and retailing enterprises. McDonald's, Yum! Brands (the parent of Pizza Hut, KFC, and Taco Bell), the UPS Store, 7-Eleven, and Hilton Hotels have all used franchising to build a presence in international markets. Franchising has much the same advantages as licensing. The franchisee bears most of the costs and risks of establishing foreign locations, so a franchisor has to expend only the resources to recruit, train, support, and monitor franchisees. The big problem a franchisor faces is maintaining quality control. In many cases, foreign franchisees do not always exhibit strong commitment to consistency and standardization, especially when the local culture does not stress the same kinds of quality concerns. Another problem that can arise is whether to allow foreign franchisees to modify the franchisor's product offering to better satisfy the tastes and expectations of local buyers. Should McDonald's allow its franchised units in Japan to modify Big Macs slightly to suit Japanese tastes? Should the franchised KFC units in China be permitted to substitute spices that appeal to Chinese consumers? Or should the same menu offerings be rigorously and unvaryingly required of all franchisees worldwide?

Foreign Subsidiary Strategies

While exporting, licensing, and franchising rely upon the resources and capabilities of allies in international markets to deliver goods or services to buyers, companies pursuing international expansion may elect to take responsibility for the performance of all essential value chain activities in foreign markets. Companies that prefer direct control over all aspects of operating in a foreign market can establish a wholly owned subsidiary, either by acquiring a foreign company or by establishing operations from the ground up via internal development.

Acquisition is the quicker of the two options, and it may be the least risky and cost-efficient means of hurdling such entry barriers as gaining access to local distribution channels, building supplier relationships, and establishing working relationships with key government officials and other constituencies. Buying an ongoing operation allows the acquirer to move directly to the tasks of transferring resources and personnel to the newly acquired business, integrating and redirecting the activities of the acquired business into its own operation, putting its own strategy into place, and accelerating efforts to build a strong market position.[4]

The big issue an acquisition-minded firm must consider is whether to pay a premium price for a successful local company or to buy a struggling competitor at a bargain price. If the buying firm has little knowledge of the local market but ample capital, it is often better off purchasing a capable, strongly positioned firm—unless the acquisition price is prohibitive. However, when the acquirer sees promising ways to transform a weak firm into a strong one and has the resources and managerial know-how to do it, a struggling company can be the better long-term investment.

Entering a new foreign country via internal development and building a foreign subsidiary from scratch makes sense when a company already operates in a number of countries, has experience in getting new subsidiaries up and running and overseeing their operations, and has a sufficiently large pool of resources and competencies to rapidly equip a new subsidiary with the personnel and capabilities it needs to compete successfully and profitably. Four other conditions make an internal startup strategy appealing:

- When creating an internal startup is cheaper than making an acquisition
- When adding new production capacity will not adversely impact the supply–demand balance in the local market
- When a startup subsidiary has the ability to gain good distribution access (perhaps because of the company's recognized brand name)
- When a startup subsidiary will have the size, cost structure, and resources to compete head-to-head against local rivals

Alliance and Joint Venture Strategies

Strategic alliances, joint ventures, and other cooperative agreements with foreign companies are a favorite and potentially fruitful means for entering a foreign market or strengthening a firm's competitiveness in world markets.[5] Historically, export-minded firms in industrialized nations sought alliances with firms in less-developed countries to import and market their products locally; such arrangements were often necessary to win approval for entry from the host country's government. Both Japanese and American companies are actively forming alliances with European companies to strengthen their ability to compete in the 28-nation European Union (and the five countries that are candidates to become EU members) and to capitalize on the opening of Eastern European markets. Many U.S. and European companies are allying with Asian companies in their efforts to enter markets in China, India, Malaysia, Thailand, and other Asian countries. Many foreign companies, of course, are particularly interested in strategic partnerships that will strengthen their ability to gain a foothold in the U.S. market.

However, cooperative arrangements between domestic and foreign companies have strategic appeal for reasons besides gaining better access to attractive country markets.[6] A second big appeal of cross-border alliances is to capture economies of scale in production and/or marketing. By joining forces in producing components, assembling models, and marketing their products, companies can realize cost savings not achievable with their own small volumes. A third motivation for entering into a cross-border alliance is to fill gaps in technical expertise and/or knowledge of local markets (buying habits and product preferences of consumers, local customs, and so on). A fourth motivation for cross-border alliances is to share distribution facilities and dealer networks, and to mutually strengthen each partner's access to buyers.

A fifth benefit is that cross-border allies can direct their competitive energies more toward mutual rivals and less toward one another; teaming up may help them close the gap on leading companies. A sixth driver of cross-border alliances comes into

Concepts&Connections 7.1

WALGREENS BOOTS ALLIANCE, INC.: ENTERING FOREIGN MARKETS VIA ALLIANCE FOLLOWED BY MERGER

Walgreens pharmacy began in 1901 as a single store on the South Side of Chicago, and grew to become the largest chain of pharmacy retailers in America. Walgreens was an early pioneer of the "self-service" pharmacy and found success by moving quickly to build a vast domestic network of stores after World War II. This growth-focused strategy served Walgreens well until the beginning of the 21st century, by which time it had nearly saturated the U.S. market. By 2014, 75 percent of Americans lived within five miles of a Walgreens. The company was also facing threats to its core business model. Walgreens relies heavily on pharmacy sales, which generally are paid for by someone other than the patient—usually the government or an insurance company. As the government and insurers started to make a more sustained effort to cut costs, Walgreens's core profit center was at risk. To mitigate these threats, Walgreens looked to enter foreign markets.

Walgreens found an ideal international partner in Alliance Boots. Based in the United Kingdom, Alliance Boots had a global footprint with 3,300 stores across 10 countries. A partnership

R&P: ©Oli Scarff/Getty Images

with Alliance Boots had several strategic advantages, allowing Walgreens to gain swift entry into foreign markets as well as complementary assets and expertise. First, it gave Walgreens access to new markets beyond the saturated United States for its retail pharmacies. Second, it provided Walgreens with a new revenue stream in wholesale drugs. Alliance Boots held a vast European distribution network for wholesale drug sales; Walgreens could leverage that network and expertise to build a similar model in the United States. Finally, a merger with Alliance Boots would strengthen Walgreens's existing business by increasing the company's market position and therefore bargaining power with drug companies. In light of these advantages, Walgreens moved quickly to partner with and later acquire Alliance Boots and merged both companies in 2014 to become Walgreens Boots Alliance. Walgreens Boots Alliance, Inc., is now one of the world's largest drug purchasers, able to negotiate from a strong position with drug companies and other suppliers to realize economies of scale in its current businesses.

The market has thus far responded favorably to the merger. Walgreens Boots Alliance's stock has more than doubled in value since the first news of the partnership in 2012. However, the company is still struggling to integrate and faces new risks such as currency fluctuation in its new combined position. Yet as the pharmaceutical industry continues to consolidate, Walgreens is in an undoubtedly stronger position to continue to grow in the future thanks to its strategic international acquisition.

Note: Developed with Katherine Coster.

Sources: Company 10-K Form, 2015, investor.walgreensbootsalliance.com/secfiling.cfm?filingID=1140361-15-38791&CIK=1618921; L. Capron and W. Mitchell, "When to Change a Winning Strategy," *Harvard Business Review,* July 25, 2012, hbr.org/2012/07/when-to-change-a-winning-strat; T. Martin and R. Dezember, "Walgreens Spends $6.7 Billion on Alliance Boots Stake," *The Wall Street Journal,* June 20, 2012.

play when companies wanting to enter a new foreign market conclude that alliances with local companies are an effective way to establish working relationships with key officials in the host-country government.[7] And, finally, alliances can be a particularly useful way for companies across the world to gain agreement on important technical standards—they have been used to arrive at standards for assorted PC devices, Internet-related technologies, high-definition televisions, and mobile phones.

What makes cross-border alliances an attractive strategic means of gaining the aforementioned types of benefits (as compared to acquiring or merging with foreign-based companies) is that entering into alliances and strategic partnerships allows a company to preserve its independence and avoid using perhaps scarce financial resources to fund acquisitions. Furthermore, an alliance offers the flexibility to readily disengage once its purpose has been served or if the benefits prove elusive, whereas an acquisition is a more permanent sort of arrangement.[8] Concepts & Connections 7.1 discusses how Walgreens has expanded internationally through an alliance followed by merger with U.K.-based Alliance Boots.

The Risks of Strategic Alliances with Foreign Partners   Alliances and joint ventures with foreign partners have their pitfalls, however. Cross-border allies typically have to overcome language and cultural barriers and figure out how to deal with diverse (or perhaps conflicting) operating practices. The communication, trust-building, and coordination costs are high in terms of management time.[9] It is not unusual for partners to discover they have conflicting objectives and strategies, deep differences of opinion about how to proceed, or important differences in corporate values and ethical standards. Tensions build, working relationships cool, and the hoped-for benefits never materialize. The recipe for successful alliances requires many meetings of many people working in good faith over a period of time to iron out what is to be shared, what is to remain proprietary, and how the cooperative arrangements will work.[10]

Even if the alliance becomes a win-win proposition for both parties, there is the danger of becoming overly dependent on foreign partners for essential expertise and competitive capabilities. If a company is aiming for global market leadership and needs to develop capabilities of its own, then at some juncture cross-border merger or acquisition may have to be substituted for cross-border alliances and joint ventures. One of the lessons about cross-border alliances is that they are more effective in helping a company establish a beachhead of new opportunity in world markets than they are in enabling a company to achieve and sustain global market leadership.

International Strategy: The Three Principal Options

 LO7-4   Identify the three main options for tailoring a company's international strategy to cross-country differences in market conditions and buyer preferences.

Broadly speaking, a company's **international strategy** is simply its strategy for competing in two or more countries simultaneously. Typically, a company will start to compete internationally by entering just one or perhaps a select few foreign markets, selling its products or services in countries where there is a ready market for them. But as it expands further internationally, it will have to confront head-on the conflicting pressures of local responsiveness versus efficiency gains from standardizing its product offering globally. As discussed earlier in the chapter, deciding upon the degree to vary its competitive approach to fit the specific market conditions and buyer preferences in each host country is perhaps the foremost strategic issue that must be addressed when operating in two or

CORE CONCEPT

A company's **international strategy** is its strategy for competing in two or more countries simultaneously.

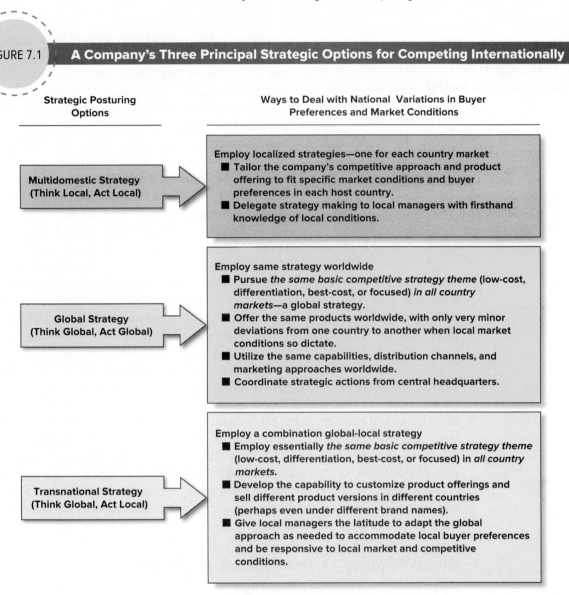

FIGURE 7.1 **A Company's Three Principal Strategic Options for Competing Internationally**

Strategic Posturing Options

Ways to Deal with National Variations in Buyer Preferences and Market Conditions

Multidomestic Strategy (Think Local, Act Local)

Employ localized strategies—one for each country market
- Tailor the company's competitive approach and product offering to fit specific market conditions and buyer preferences in each host country.
- Delegate strategy making to local managers with firsthand knowledge of local conditions.

Global Strategy (Think Global, Act Global)

Employ same strategy worldwide
- Pursue *the same basic competitive strategy theme* (low-cost, differentiation, best-cost, or focused) *in all country markets*—a global strategy.
- Offer the same products worldwide, with only very minor deviations from one country to another when local market conditions so dictate.
- Utilize the same capabilities, distribution channels, and marketing approaches worldwide.
- Coordinate strategic actions from central headquarters.

Transnational Strategy (Think Global, Act Local)

Employ a combination global-local strategy
- Employ essentially *the same basic competitive strategy theme* (low-cost, differentiation, best-cost, or focused) in *all country markets*.
- Develop the capability to customize product offerings and sell different product versions in different countries (perhaps even under different brand names).
- Give local managers the latitude to adapt the global approach as needed to accommodate local buyer preferences and be responsive to local market and competitive conditions.

more foreign markets.[11] Figure 7.1 shows a company's three strategic approaches for competing internationally and resolving this issue.

Multidomestic Strategy—A Think Local, Act Local Approach to Strategy Making

A **multidomestic strategy** or **think local, act local** approach to strategy making is essential when there are significant country-to-country differences in customer preferences and buying habits, when there are significant cross-country differences in distribution channels and marketing methods, when host governments enact regulations requiring that products sold locally meet strict manufacturing specifications or performance standards, and when the trade restrictions of host governments are so diverse and complicated that they preclude a uniform, coordinated worldwide market approach. With localized strategies, a company often has different product versions for different countries and sometimes sells the products under different brand names. Government requirements for gasoline additives that help reduce carbon monoxide, smog, and other emissions are almost never the same from country to country. BP utilizes localized strategies in its gasoline and service station business segment because of these cross-country formulation differences and because of customer familiarity with local brand names. For example, the company markets gasoline in the United States under its BP and Arco brands, but markets gasoline in Germany, Belgium, Poland, Hungary, and the Czech Republic under the Aral brand. Companies in the food products industry often vary the ingredients in their products and sell the localized versions under local brand names to cater to country-specific tastes and eating preferences. The strength of employing a set of localized or multidomestic strategies is that the company's actions and business approaches are deliberately crafted to appeal to the tastes and expectations of buyers in each country and to stake out the most attractive market positions vis-à-vis local competitors.[12]

However, think local, act local strategies have two big drawbacks: (1) They hinder transfer of a company's competencies and resources across country boundaries because the strategies in different host countries can be grounded in varying competencies and capabilities; and (2) they do not promote building a single, unified competitive advantage, especially one based on low cost. Companies employing highly localized or multidomestic strategies face big hurdles in achieving low-cost leadership *unless* they find ways to customize their products and *still* be in a position to capture scale economies and learning-curve effects. Toyota's unique mass customization production capability has been key to its ability to effectively adapt product offerings to local buyer tastes, while maintaining low-cost leadership.

Global Strategy—A Think Global, Act Global Approach to Strategy Making

While multidomestic strategies are best suited for industries where a fairly high degree of local responsiveness is important, global strategies are best suited for globally standardized industries. A **global strategy** is one in which the company's approach is predominantly the same in all countries: it sells the same products under the same brand names everywhere, utilizes much the same distribution channels in all countries, and competes on the basis of the same capabilities and marketing approaches worldwide. Although the company's strategy or product offering may be adapted in very minor ways to accommodate specific situations in a few host countries, the company's fundamental competitive approach (low-cost, differentiation, or focused) remains very much intact worldwide, and local managers stick close to the global strategy. A **think global, act global** strategic theme prompts company managers to integrate and coordinate the company's strategic moves worldwide and to expand into most, if not all, nations where there is significant buyer demand. It puts considerable strategic emphasis on building a *global* brand name and aggressively pursuing opportunities to transfer ideas, new products, and capabilities from one country to another.

Ford's global design strategy is a move toward a think global, act global strategy by the company and involves the development and production of standardized models with country-specific modifications limited primarily to what is required to meet local country emission and safety standards. The 2010 Ford Fiesta and 2011 Ford Focus were the company's first global design models to be marketed in Europe, North America, Asia, and Australia. In 2014, Ford added the Edge utility vehicle as a global model that would be sold in more than 60 countries. Whenever country-to-country differences are small enough to be accommodated within the framework of a global strategy, a global strategy is preferable to localized strategies because a company can more readily unify its operations and focus on establishing a brand image and reputation that is uniform from country to country. Moreover, with a global strategy, a company is better able to focus its full resources on securing a sustainable low-cost or differentiation-based competitive advantage over both domestic rivals and global rivals.

Transnational Strategy—A Think Global, Act Local Approach to Strategy Making

A **transnational strategy** is a **think global, act local** approach to developing strategy that accommodates cross-country variations in buyer tastes, local customs, and market conditions while also striving for the benefits of standardization. This middle-ground approach entails utilizing the same basic competitive theme (low-cost, differentiation, or focused) in each country but allows local managers the latitude to (1) incorporate whatever country-specific variations in product attributes are needed to best satisfy local buyers and (2) make whatever adjustments in production, distribution, and marketing are needed to respond to local market conditions and compete successfully against local rivals. Both McDonald's and KFC have discovered ways to customize their menu offerings in various countries without compromising costs, product quality, and operating effectiveness. Otis Elevator found that a transnational strategy delivers better results than a global strategy when competing in countries such as China where local needs are highly differentiated. By switching from its customary single-brand approach to a multi-brand strategy aimed at serving different segments of the market, Otis was able to double its market share in China and increased its revenues sixfold over a nine-year period.[13]

> **CORE CONCEPT**
>
> A **transnational strategy** is a **think global, act local** approach to strategy making that involves employing essentially the same strategic theme (low-cost, differentiation, focused, best-cost) in all country markets, while allowing some country-to-country customization to fit local market conditions.

Concepts & Connections 7.2 explains how Four Seasons Hotels has been able to compete successfully on the basis of a transnational strategy.

As a rule, most companies that operate multinationally endeavor to employ as global a strategy as customer needs and market conditions permit. Electronic Arts has two

Concepts&Connections 7.2

FOUR SEASONS HOTELS: LOCAL CHARACTER, GLOBAL SERVICE

Four Seasons Hotels is a Toronto, Canada—based manager of luxury hotel properties. With nearly 100 properties located in many of the world's most popular tourist destinations and business centers, Four Seasons commands a following of many of the world's most discerning travelers. In contrast to its key competitor, Ritz-Carlton, which strives to create one uniform experience globally, Four Seasons Hotels has gained market share by deftly combining local architectural and cultural experiences with globally consistent luxury service.

When moving into a new market, Four Seasons always seeks out a local capital partner. The understanding of local custom and business relationships this financier brings is critical to the process of developing a new Four Seasons hotel. Four Seasons also insists on hiring a local architect and design consultant for each property, as opposed to using architects or designers it has worked with in other locations. While this can be a challenge, particularly in emerging markets, Four Seasons has found it is worth it in the long run to have a truly local team.

The specific layout and programming of each hotel are also unique. For instance, when Four Seasons opened its hotel in Mumbai, India, it prioritized space for large banquet halls to target the Indian wedding market. In India, weddings often draw guests numbering in the thousands. When moving into the Middle East, Four Seasons designed its hotels with separate prayer rooms for men and women. In Bali, where destination weddings are common, the hotel employs a "weather shaman" who, for some guests, provides reassurance that the weather will cooperate for their special day. In all cases, the objective is to provide a truly local experience.

When staffing its hotels, Four Seasons seeks to strike a fine balance between employing locals who have an innate understanding of the local culture alongside expatriate staff or "culture carriers" who understand the DNA of Four Seasons. It also uses global systems to track customer preferences and employs globally consistent service standards. Four Seasons claims that its guests experience the same high level of service globally but that no two experiences are the same.

While it is much more expensive and time-consuming to design unique architectural and programming experiences, doing so is a strategic trade-off Four Seasons has made to achieve the local experience demanded by its high-level clientele. Likewise, it has recognized that maintaining globally consistent operation processes and service standards is important too. Four Seasons has struck the right balance between thinking globally and acting locally—the marker of a truly transnational strategy. As a result, the company has been rewarded with an international reputation for superior service and a leading market share in the luxury hospitality segment.

Note: Developed with Brian R. McKenzie.

Sources: Four Seasons annual report and corporate website; and interview with Scott Woroch, Executive Vice President of Development, Four Seasons Hotels, February 22, 2014.

©Kay Maeritz/LOOK-foto/Getty Images

major design studios—one in Vancouver, British Columbia, and one in Los Angeles—and smaller design studios in San Francisco, Orlando, London, and Tokyo. This dispersion of design studios helps EA to design games that are specific to different cultures: for example, the London studio took the lead in designing the popular FIFA Soccer game to suit European tastes and to replicate the stadiums, signage, and team rosters; the U.S. studio took the lead in designing games involving NFL football, NBA basketball, and NASCAR racing.

Using International Operations to Improve Overall Competitiveness

LO7-5 Explain how multinational companies are able to use international operations to improve overall competitiveness.

A firm can gain competitive advantage by expanding outside its domestic market in two important ways. One, it can use location to lower costs or help achieve greater product differentiation. And two, it can use cross-border coordination in ways that a domestic-only competitor cannot.

Using Location to Build Competitive Advantage

To use location to build competitive advantage, a company must consider two issues: (1) whether to concentrate each internal process in a few countries or to disperse performance of each process to many nations, and (2) in which countries to locate particular activities.

When to Concentrate Internal Processes in a Few Locations Companies tend to concentrate their activities in a limited number of locations in the following circumstances:

- *When the costs of manufacturing or other activities are significantly lower in some geographic locations than in others.* For example, much of the world's athletic footwear is manufactured in Asia (China and Korea) because of low labor costs; much of the production of circuit boards for PCs is located in Taiwan because of both low costs and the high-caliber technical skills of the Taiwanese labor force.

- *When there are significant scale economies.* The presence of significant economies of scale in components production or final assembly means a company can gain major cost savings from operating a few superefficient plants as opposed to a host of small plants scattered across the world. Makers of digital cameras and LED TVs located in Japan, South Korea, and Taiwan have used their scale economies to establish a low-cost advantage.

- *When there is a steep learning curve associated with performing an activity.* In some industries, learning-curve effects in parts manufacture or assembly are so great that a company establishes one or two large plants from which it serves the world market. The key to riding down the learning curve is to concentrate production in a few locations to increase the accumulated volume at a plant (and thus the experience of the plant's workforce) as rapidly as possible.

- *When certain locations have superior resources, allow better coordination of related activities, or offer other valuable advantages.* A research unit or a sophisticated production facility may be situated in a particular nation because of its pool of technically trained personnel. Samsung became a leader in memory chip technology by establishing a major R&D facility in Silicon Valley and transferring the know-how it gained back to headquarters and its plants in South Korea.

Companies that compete multinationally can pursue competitive advantage in world markets by locating their value chain activities in whichever nations prove most advantageous.

When to Disperse Internal Processes Across Many Locations   There are several instances when dispersing a process is more advantageous than concentrating it in a single location. Buyer-related activities, such as distribution to dealers, sales and advertising, and after-sale service, usually must take place close to buyers. This makes it necessary to physically locate the capability to perform such activities in every country market where a global firm has major customers. For example, large public accounting firms have numerous international offices to service the foreign operations of their multinational corporate clients. Dispersing activities to many locations is also competitively important when high transportation costs, diseconomies of large size, and trade barriers make it too expensive to operate from a central location. In addition, it is strategically advantageous to disperse activities to hedge against the risks of fluctuating exchange rates and adverse political developments.

Using Cross-Border Coordination to Build Competitive Advantage

Multinational and global competitors are able to coordinate activities across different countries to build competitive advantage.[14] If a firm learns how to assemble its product more efficiently at, say, its Brazilian plant, the accumulated expertise and knowledge can be shared with assembly plants in other world locations. Also, knowledge gained in marketing a company's product in Great Britain, for instance, can readily be exchanged with company personnel in New Zealand or Australia. Other examples of cross-border coordination include shifting production from a plant in one country to a plant in another to take advantage of exchange rate fluctuations and to respond to changing wage rates, energy costs, or changes in tariffs and quotas.

Efficiencies can also be achieved by shifting workloads from where they are unusually heavy to locations where personnel are underutilized. Whirlpool's efforts to link its product R&D and manufacturing operations in North America, Latin America, Europe, and Asia allowed it to accelerate the discovery of innovative appliance features, coordinate the introduction of these features in the appliance products marketed in different countries, and create a cost-efficient worldwide supply chain. Whirlpool's conscious efforts to integrate and coordinate its various operations around the world have helped it achieve operational excellence and speed product innovations to market.

Strategies for Competing in the Markets of Developing Countries

| LO7-6 | Understand the unique characteristics of competing in developing-country markets. |

Companies racing for global leadership have to consider competing in developing-economy markets such as China, India, Brazil, Indonesia, Thailand, Poland, Russia, and Mexico—countries where the business risks are considerable but where the opportunities for growth are huge, especially as their economies develop and living standards climb toward levels in the industrialized world.[15] For example, in 2017 China was the world's second-largest economy (behind the United States) based upon purchasing power, and its population of 1.4 billion people made it the world's largest market for many commodities and types of consumer goods. China's growth in demand for consumer goods has made it the fifth-largest market for luxury goods, with sales greater than those in developed markets such as Germany, Spain, and the United Kingdom.[16] Thus, no company pursuing global market leadership can afford to ignore the strategic importance of establishing competitive market positions in China, India, other parts of the Asian-Pacific region, Latin America, and Eastern Europe.

Tailoring products to fit conditions in an emerging country market such as China, however, often involves more than making minor product changes and becoming more familiar with local cultures. McDonald's has had to offer vegetable burgers in parts of Asia and to rethink its prices, which are often high by local standards and affordable only by the well-to-do. Kellogg has struggled to introduce its cereals successfully because consumers in many less-developed countries do not eat cereal for breakfast—changing habits is difficult and expensive. Single-serving packages of detergents, shampoos, pickles, cough syrup, and cooking oils are very popular in India because they allow buyers to conserve cash by purchasing only what they need immediately. Thus, many companies find that trying to employ a strategy akin to that used in the markets of developed countries is hazardous.[17] Experimenting with some, perhaps many, local twists is usually necessary to find a strategy combination that works.

Strategy Options for Competing in Developing-Country Markets

Several strategy options for tailoring a company's strategy to fit the sometimes unusual or challenging circumstances presented in developing-country markets include:

- *Prepare to compete on the basis of low price.* Consumers in emerging markets are often highly focused on price, which can give low-cost local competitors the edge unless a company can find ways to attract buyers with bargain prices as well as better products. For example, when Unilever entered the market for laundry detergents in India, it developed a low-cost detergent (named Wheel) that was not harsh to the skin, constructed new superefficient production facilities, distributed the product to local merchants by handcarts, and crafted an economical marketing campaign that included painted signs on buildings and demonstrations near stores. The new brand quickly captured $100 million in sales and was the top detergent brand in India in 2014 based on dollar sales. Unilever later replicated the strategy with low-price shampoos and deodorants in India and in South America with a detergent brand named Ala.

- *Modify aspects of the company's business model or strategy to accommodate local circumstances (but not so much that the company loses the advantage of global scale and global branding).* For instance, Honeywell had sold industrial products and services for more than 100 years outside the United States and Europe using a foreign subsidiary model that focused international activities on sales only. When Honeywell entered China, it discovered that industrial customers in that country considered how many key jobs foreign companies created in China in addition to the quality and price of the product or service when making purchasing decisions. Honeywell added about 150 engineers, strategists, and marketers in China to demonstrate its commitment to bolstering the Chinese economy. Honeywell replicated its "East for East" strategy when it entered the market for industrial products and services in India. Within 10 years of Honeywell establishing operations in China and three years of expanding into India, the two emerging markets accounted for 30 percent of the firm's worldwide growth.

- *Try to change the local market to better match the way the company does business elsewhere.* A multinational company often has enough market clout to drive major changes in the way a local country market operates. When Japan's Suzuki entered India, it triggered a quality revolution among Indian auto parts manufacturers. Local parts and components suppliers teamed up with Suzuki's vendors in Japan and worked with Japanese experts to produce higher-quality products. Over the next two decades, Indian companies became very proficient in making top-notch parts and components for vehicles, won more prizes for quality than companies in any country other than Japan, and broke into the global market as suppliers to many automakers in Asia and other parts of the world. Mahindra and Mahindra, one of India's premier automobile manufacturers, has been recognized by a number of organizations for its product quality. Among its most noteworthy awards was its number-one ranking by J. D. Power Asia Pacific for new-vehicle overall quality.

- *Stay away from those emerging markets where it is impractical or uneconomical to modify the company's business model to accommodate local circumstances.* Home Depot expanded successfully into Mexico but has avoided entry into other emerging countries because its value proposition of good quality, low prices, and attentive customer service relies on (1) good highways and logistical systems to minimize store inventory costs, (2) employee stock ownership to help motivate store personnel to provide good customer service, and (3) high labor costs for housing construction and home repairs to encourage homeowners to engage in do-it-yourself projects. Relying on these factors in the U.S. and Canadian markets has worked spectacularly for Home Depot, but Home Depot has found that it cannot count on these factors in China, from which it withdrew in 2012.

> Profitability in emerging markets rarely comes quickly or easily. New entrants have to adapt their business models and strategies to local conditions and be patient in earning a profit.

Company experiences in entering developing markets such as China, India, Russia, and Brazil indicate that profitability seldom comes quickly or easily. Building a market for the company's products can often turn into a long-term process that involves reeducation of consumers, sizable investments in advertising and promotion to alter tastes and buying habits, and upgrades of the local infrastructure (the supplier base, transportation systems, distribution channels, labor markets, and capital markets). In such cases, a company must be patient, work within the system to improve the infrastructure, and lay the foundation for generating sizable revenues and profits once conditions are ripe for market takeoff.

KEY POINTS

1. Competing in international markets allows multinational companies to (1) gain access to new customers, (2) achieve lower costs and enhance the firm's competitiveness by more easily capturing scale economies or learning-curve effects, (3) leverage core competencies refined domestically in additional country markets, (4) gain access to resources and capabilities located in foreign markets, and (5) spread business risk across a wider market base.

2. Companies electing to expand into international markets must consider cross-country differences in buyer tastes, market sizes, and growth potential; location-based cost drivers; adverse exchange rates; and host-government policies when evaluating strategy options.

3. Options for entering foreign markets include maintaining a national (one-country) production base and exporting goods to foreign markets, licensing foreign firms to use the company's technology or produce and distribute the company's products, employing a franchising strategy, establishing a foreign subsidiary, and using strategic alliances or other collaborative partnerships.

4. In posturing to compete in foreign markets, a company has three basic options: (1) a multidomestic or think local, act local approach to crafting a strategy, (2) a global or think global, act global approach to crafting a strategy, and (3) a transnational strategy or combination think global, act local approach. A "think local, act local" or multicountry strategy is appropriate for industries or companies that must vary their product offerings and competitive approaches from country to country to accommodate differing buyer preferences and market conditions. A "think global, act global" approach (or global strategy) works best in markets that support employing the same basic competitive approach (low-cost, differentiation, focused) in all country markets and marketing essentially the same products under the same brand names in all countries where the company operates. A "think global, act local" approach can be used when it is feasible for a company to employ essentially the same basic competitive strategy in all markets but still customize its product offering and some aspect of its operations to fit local market circumstances.

5. There are two general ways in which a firm can gain competitive advantage (or offset domestic disadvantages) in global markets. One way involves locating various value chain activities among nations in a manner that lowers costs or achieves greater product differentiation. A second way draws on a multinational or global competitor's ability to deepen or broaden its resources and capabilities and to coordinate its dispersed activities in ways that a domestic-only competitor cannot.

6. Companies racing for global leadership have to consider competing in emerging markets such as China, India, Brazil, Indonesia, and Mexico—countries where the business risks are considerable but the opportunities for growth are huge. To succeed in these markets, companies often have to (1) compete on the basis of low price, (2) be prepared to modify aspects of the company's business model or strategy to accommodate local circumstances (but not so much that the company loses the advantage of global scale and global branding), and/or (3) try to change the local market to better match the way the company does business elsewhere. Profitability is unlikely to come quickly or easily in emerging markets, typically because of the investments needed to alter buying habits and tastes and/or the need for infrastructure upgrades. And there may be times when a company should simply stay away from certain emerging markets until conditions for entry are better suited to its business model and strategy.

ASSURANCE OF LEARNING EXERCISES

1. L'Oréal markets 34 brands of cosmetics, fragrances, and hair care products in 130 countries. The company's international strategy involves manufacturing these products in 42 plants located around the world. L'Oréal's international strategy is discussed in its operations section of the company's website (http://www.loreal.com/careers/who-you-can-be/operations) and in its press releases, annual reports, and presentations. Why has the company chosen to pursue a foreign subsidiary strategy? Are there strategic advantages to global sourcing and production in the cosmetics, fragrances, and hair care products industry relative to an export strategy?

LO7-1, LO7-3

LO7-1, LO7-3

2. Alliances, joint ventures, and mergers with foreign companies are widely used as a means of entering foreign markets. Such arrangements have many purposes, including learning about unfamiliar environments, and the opportunity to access the complementary resources and capabilities of a foreign partner. Concepts & Connections 7.1 provides an example of how Walgreens used a strategy of entering foreign markets via alliance, followed by a merger with the same entity. What was this entry strategy designed to achieve, and why would this make sense for a company like Walgreens?

LO7-2, LO7-3

3. Assume you are in charge of developing the strategy for a multinational company selling products in some 50 countries around the world. One of the issues you face is whether to employ a multidomestic, transnational, or global strategy.

   a. If your company's product is mobile phones, do you think it would make better strategic sense to employ a multidomestic strategy, a transnational strategy, or a global strategy? Why?

   b. If your company's product is dry soup mixes and canned soups, would a multidomestic strategy seem to be more advisable than a transnational or global strategy? Why or why not?

   c. If your company's product is large home appliances such as washing machines, ranges, ovens, and refrigerators, would it seem to make more sense to pursue a multidomestic strategy or a transnational strategy or a global strategy? Why?

LO7-5, LO7-6

4. Using your university library's business research resources and Internet sources, identify and discuss three key strategies that Volkswagen is using to compete in China.

EXERCISES FOR SIMULATION PARTICIPANTS

The following questions are for simulation participants whose companies operate in an international market arena. If your company competes only in a single country, then skip the questions in this section.

LO7-2

1. To what extent, if any, have you and your co-managers adapted your company's strategy to take shifting exchange rates into account? In other words, have you undertaken any actions to try to minimize the impact of adverse shifts in exchange rates?

LO7-2

2. To what extent, if any, have you and your co-managers adapted your company's strategy to consider geographic differences in import tariffs or import duties?

LO7-4

3. Which one of the following best describes the strategic approach your company is taking to try to compete successfully on an international basis?

   - Multidomestic or think local, act local approach
   - Global or think global, act global approach
   - Transnational or think global, act local approach

   Explain your answer and indicate two or three chief elements of your company's strategy for competing in two or more different geographic regions.

ENDNOTES

1. A. C. Inkpen and A. Dinur, "Knowledge Management Processes and International Joint Ventures," *Organization Science* 9, no. 4 (July–August 1998); P. Dussauge, B. Garrette, and W. Mitchell, "Learning from Competing Partners: Outcomes and Durations of Scale and Link Alliances in Europe, North America and Asia," *Strategic Management Journal* 21, no. 2 (February 2000); C. Dhanaraj, M. A. Lyles, H. K. Steensma, et al., "Managing Tacit and Explicit Knowledge Transfer in IJVS: The Role of Relational Embeddedness and the Impact on Performance," *Journal of*

International Business Studies 35, no. 5 (September 2004); K. W. Glaister and P. J. Buckley, "Strategic Motives for International Alliance Formation," *Journal of Management Studies* 33, no. 3 (May 1996); J. Anand and B. Kogut, "Technological Capabilities of Countries, Firm Rivalry and Foreign Direct Investment," *Journal of International Business Studies* 28, no. 3 (1997); J. Anand and A. Delios, "Absolute and Relative Resources as Determinants of International Acquisitions," *Strategic Management Journal* 23, no. 2 (February 2002); A. Seth, K. Song, and A. Pettit, "Value Creation and Destruction in Cross-Border Acquisitions: An Empirical Analysis of Foreign Acquisitions of U.S. Firms," *Strategic Management Journal* 23, no. 10 (October 2002); and J. Anand, L. Capron, and W. Mitchell, "Using Acquisitions to Access Multinational Diversity: Thinking Beyond the Domestic Versus Cross-Border M&A Comparison," *Industrial & Corporate Change* 14, no. 2 (April 2005).

2. Kelvin Chan, "China Auto Sales Shrink in April As Demand Cools Sharply," AP News Archive, May 11, 2017, http://www.apnewsarchive.com/2017/China-s-auto-sales-shrank-in-April-as-demand-wilted-in-world-s-biggest-car-market/id-2c11cd31d4e34d79be8a72922460d8f6; Bill Vlasic, "Record 2016 for U.S. Auto Industry; Long Road Back May Be at End," *The New York Times,* January 4, 2017, https://www.nytimes.com/2017/01/04/business/2016-record-united-states-auto-sales.html.

3. Actual and estimated rates reported by The Conference Board, "International Comparisons of Hourly Compensation Costs in Manufacturing, 2015," April 12, 2016. (Rates for India and China based upon 2012 and 2013 estimates, respectively.)

4. E. Pablo, "Determinants of Cross-Border M&As in Latin America," *Journal of Business Research* 62, no. 9 (2009); R. Olie, "Shades of Culture and Institutions in International Mergers," *Organization Studies* 15, no. 3 (1994); and K. E. Meyer, M. Wright, and S. Pruthi, "Institutions, Resources, and Entry Strategies in Emerging Economies," *Strategic Management Journal* 30, no. 5 (2009).

5. Joel Bleeke and David Ernst, "The Way to Win in Cross-Border Alliances," *Harvard Business Review* 69, no. 6 (November–December 1991); Gary Hamel, Yves L. Doz, and C. K. Prahalad, "Collaborate with Your Competitors—and Win," *Harvard Business Review* 67, no. 1 (January–February 1989).

6. Yves L. Doz and Gary Hamel, *Alliance Advantage* (Boston: Harvard Business School Press, 1998); Bleeke and Ernst, "The Way to Win in Cross-Border Alliances"; Hamel, Doz, and Prahalad, "Collaborate with Your Competitors—and Win"; and Michael Porter, *The Competitive Advantage of Nations* (New York: Free Press, 1990).

7. H. Kurt Christensen, "Corporate Strategy: Managing a Set of Businesses," in *The Portable MBA in Strategy,* ed. Liam Fahey and Robert M. Randall (New York: John Wiley & Sons, 2001).

8. Jeffrey H. Dyer, Prashant Kale, and Harbir Singh, "When to Ally and When to Acquire," *Harvard Business Review* 82, no. 7/8 (July–August 2004).

9. Rosabeth Moss Kanter, "Collaborative Advantage: The Art of the Alliance," *Harvard Business Review* 72, no. 4 (July–August 1994).

10. Jeremy Main, "Making Global Alliances Work," *Fortune,* December 19, 1990, p. 125.

11. Pankaj Ghemawat, "Managing Differences: The Central Challenge of Global Strategy," *Harvard Business Review* 85, no. 3 (March 2007).

12. C. A. Bartlett and S. Ghoshal, *Managing Across Borders: The Transnational Solution,* 2nd ed. (Boston: Harvard Business School Press, 1998).

13. Lynn S. Paine, "The China Rules," *Harvard Business Review* 88, no. 6 (June 2010), pp. 103–8.

14. C. K. Prahalad and Yves L. Doz, *The Multinational Mission* (New York: Free Press, 1987), pp. 58–60.

15. David J. Arnold and John A. Quelch, "New Strategies in Emerging Markets," *Sloan Management Review* 40, no. 1 (Fall 1998); and C. K. Prahalad, *The Fortune at the Bottom of the Pyramid: Eradicating Poverty Through Profits* (Upper Saddle River, NJ: Wharton, 2005).

16. *Global Powers of Luxury Goods,* Deloitte Touche Tohmatsu Limited, 2017.

17. Tarun Khanna, Krishna G. Palepu, and Jayant Sinha, "Strategies That Fit Emerging Markets," *Harvard Business Review* 83, no. 6 (June 2005); and Arindam K. Bhattacharya and David C. Michael, "How Local Companies Keep Multinationals at Bay," *Harvard Business Review* 86, no. 3 (March 2008).

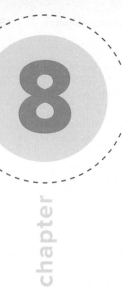

8 Corporate Strategy: Diversification and the Multibusiness Company

LEARNING OBJECTIVES

After reading this chapter, you should be able to:

LO8-1 Understand when and how business diversification can enhance shareholder value.

LO8-2 Explain how related diversification strategies can produce cross-business strategic fit capable of delivering competitive advantage.

LO8-3 Recognize the merits and risks of corporate strategies keyed to unrelated diversification.

LO8-4 Evaluate a company's diversification strategy.

LO8-5 Understand a diversified company's four main corporate strategy options for solidifying its diversification strategy and improving company performance.

This chapter moves up one level in the strategy-making hierarchy, from strategy making in a single-business enterprise to strategy making in a diversified enterprise. Because a diversified company is a collection of individual businesses, the strategy-making task is more complicated. In a one-business company, managers have to come up with a plan for competing successfully in only a single industry environment—the result is what Chapter 2 labeled as *business strategy* (or *business-level strategy*). But in a diversified company, the strategy-making challenge involves assessing multiple industry environments and developing a *set* of business strategies, one for each industry arena in which the diversified company operates. And top executives at a diversified company must still go one step further and devise a companywide or *corporate strategy* for improving the attractiveness and performance of the company's overall business lineup and for making a rational whole out of its diversified collection of individual businesses.

In most diversified companies, corporate-level executives delegate considerable strategy-making authority to the heads of each business, usually giving them the latitude to craft a business strategy suited to their particular industry and competitive circumstances and holding them accountable for producing good results. But the task of crafting a diversified company's overall corporate strategy falls squarely in the lap of top-level executives and involves four distinct facets:

1. *Picking new industries to enter and deciding on the means of entry.* The decision to pursue business diversification requires that management decide what new industries offer the best growth prospects and whether to enter by starting a new business from the ground up, acquiring a company already in the target industry, or forming a joint venture or strategic alliance with another company.

2. *Pursuing opportunities to leverage cross-business value chain relationships into competitive advantage.* Companies that diversify into businesses with strategic fit across the value chains of their business units have a much better chance of gaining a $1 + 1 = 3$ effect than do multibusiness companies lacking strategic fit.

3. *Establishing investment priorities and steering corporate resources into the most attractive business units.* A diversified company's business units are usually not equally attractive, and it is incumbent on corporate management to channel resources into areas where earnings potentials are higher.

4. *Initiating actions to boost the combined performance of the corporation's collection of businesses.* Corporate strategists must craft moves to improve the overall performance of the corporation's business lineup and sustain increases in shareholder value. Strategic options for diversified corporations include *(a)* sticking closely with the existing business lineup and pursuing opportunities presented by these businesses, *(b)* broadening the scope of diversification by entering additional industries, *(c)* retrenching to a narrower scope of diversification by divesting poorly performing businesses, and *(d)* broadly restructuring the business lineup with multiple divestitures and/or acquisitions.

The first portion of this chapter describes the various means a company can use to diversify and explores the pros and cons of related versus unrelated diversification strategies. The second part of the chapter looks at how to evaluate the attractiveness of a diversified company's business lineup, decide whether it has a good diversification strategy, and identify ways to improve its future performance.

When Business Diversification Becomes a Consideration

LO8-1   Understand when and how business diversification can enhance shareholder value.

As long as a single-business company can achieve profitable growth opportunities in its present industry, there is no urgency to pursue diversification. However, a company's opportunities for growth can become limited if the industry becomes competitively unattractive. Consider, for example, what mobile phone companies and marketers of Voice over Internet Protocol (VoIP) have done to the revenues of long-distance providers such as AT&T, British Telecommunications, and NTT in Japan. Thus, *diversifying into new industries always merits strong consideration whenever a single-business company encounters diminishing market opportunities and stagnating sales in its principal business.*[1]

Building Shareholder Value: The Ultimate Justification for Business Diversification

Diversification must do more for a company than simply spread its business risk across various industries. In principle, diversification cannot be considered a success unless it results in *added shareholder value*—value that shareholders cannot capture on their own by spreading their investments across the stocks of companies in different industries.

Business diversification stands little chance of building shareholder value without passing the following three tests:[2]

1. *The industry attractiveness test.* The industry to be entered through diversification must offer an opportunity for profits and return on investment that is equal to or better than that of the company's present business(es).

2. *The cost-of-entry test.* The cost to enter the target industry must not be so high as to erode the potential for good profitability. A catch-22 can prevail here, however. The more attractive an industry's prospects are for growth and good long-term profitability, the more expensive it can be to enter. It's easy for acquisitions of companies in highly attractive industries to fail the cost-of-entry test.

3. *The better-off test.* Diversifying into a new business must offer potential for the company's existing businesses and the new business to perform better together under a single corporate umbrella than they would perform operating as independent, standalone businesses. For example, let's say company A diversifies by purchasing company B in another industry. If A and B's consolidated profits in the years to come prove no greater than what each could have earned on its own, then A's diversification will not provide its shareholders with added value. Company A's shareholders could have achieved the same $1 + 1 = 2$ result by merely purchasing stock in company B. Shareholder value is not created by diversification unless it produces a $1 + 1 = 3$ effect.

Creating added value for shareholders via diversification requires building a multibusiness company in which the whole is greater than the sum of its parts.

Diversification moves that satisfy all three tests have the greatest potential to grow shareholder value over the long term. Diversification moves that can pass only one or two tests are suspect.

Approaches to Diversifying the Business Lineup

The means of entering new industries and lines of business can take any of three forms: acquisition, internal development, or joint ventures with other companies.

Diversification by Acquisition of an Existing Business

Acquisition is a popular means of diversifying into another industry. Not only is it quicker than trying to launch a new operation, but it also offers an effective way to hurdle such entry barriers as acquiring technological know-how, establishing supplier relationships, achieving scale economies, building brand awareness, and securing adequate distribution. Buying an ongoing operation allows the acquirer to move directly to the task of building a strong market position in the target industry, rather than getting bogged down in the fine points of launching a startup.

The big dilemma an acquisition-minded firm faces is whether to pay a premium price for a successful company or to buy a struggling company at a bargain price.[3] If the buying firm has little knowledge of the industry but has ample capital, it is often better off purchasing a capable, strongly positioned firm—unless the price of such an acquisition is prohibitive and flunks the cost-of-entry test. However, when the acquirer sees promising ways to transform a weak firm into a strong one, a struggling company can be the better long-term investment.

Entering a New Line of Business Through Internal Development

Achieving diversification through *internal development* involves starting a new business subsidiary from scratch. Generally, forming a startup subsidiary to enter a new business has appeal only when (1) the parent company already has in-house most or all of the skills and resources needed to compete effectively; (2) there is ample time to launch the business; (3) internal entry has lower costs than entry via acquisition; (4) the targeted industry is populated with many relatively small firms such that the new startup does not have to compete against large, powerful rivals; (5) adding new production capacity will not adversely impact the supply–demand balance in the industry; and (6) incumbent firms are likely to be slow or ineffective in responding to a new entrant's efforts to crack the market.

Using Joint Ventures to Achieve Diversification

A joint venture to enter a new business can be useful in at least two types of situations.[4] First, a joint venture is a good vehicle for pursuing an opportunity that is too complex, uneconomical, or risky for one company to pursue alone. Second, joint ventures make sense when the opportunities in a new industry require a broader range of competencies and know-how than an expansion-minded company can marshal. Many of the opportunities in biotechnology call for the coordinated development of complementary innovations and tackling an intricate web of technical, political, and regulatory factors simultaneously. In such cases, pooling the resources and competencies of two or more companies is a wiser and less risky way to proceed.

However, as discussed in Chapters 6 and 7, partnering with another company—in the form of either a joint venture or a collaborative alliance—has significant drawbacks due to the potential for conflicting objectives, disagreements over how to best operate the venture, culture clashes, and so on. Joint ventures are generally the least durable of the entry options, usually lasting only until the partners decide to go their own ways.

Choosing the Diversification Path: Related Versus Unrelated Businesses

Once a company decides to diversify, its first big corporate strategy decision is whether to diversify into **related businesses**, **unrelated businesses**, or some mix of both (see Figure 8.1). *Businesses are said to be related when their value chains possess competitively valuable cross-business relationships.* These value chain matchups present opportunities for the businesses to perform better under the same corporate umbrella than they could by operating as standalone entities. *Businesses are said to be unrelated when the activities comprising their respective value chains and resource requirements are so dissimilar that no competitively valuable cross-business relationships are present.*

The next two sections explore the ins and outs of related and unrelated diversification.

FIGURE 8.1 **Strategic Themes of Multibusiness Corporation**

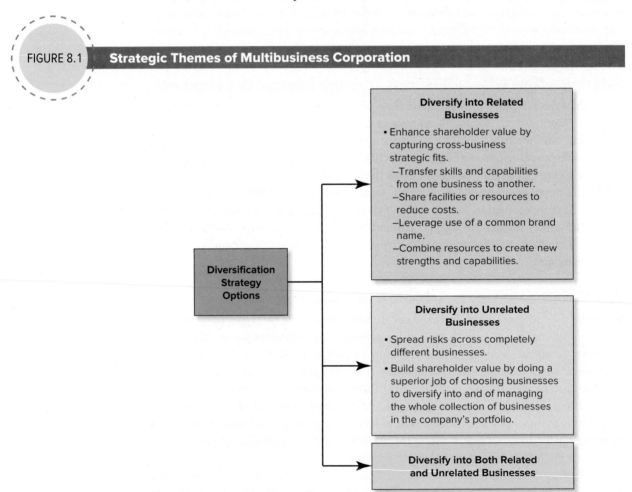

Diversify into Related Businesses

• Enhance shareholder value by capturing cross-business strategic fits.
 –Transfer skills and capabilities from one business to another.
 –Share facilities or resources to reduce costs.
 –Leverage use of a common brand name.
 –Combine resources to create new strengths and capabilities.

Diversification Strategy Options

Diversify into Unrelated Businesses

• Spread risks across completely different businesses.
• Build shareholder value by doing a superior job of choosing businesses to diversify into and of managing the whole collection of businesses in the company's portfolio.

Diversify into Both Related and Unrelated Businesses

Diversifying into Related Businesses

LO8-2 Explain how related diversification strategies can produce cross-business strategic fit capable of delivering competitive advantage.

A related diversification strategy involves building the company around businesses whose value chains possess competitively valuable strategic fit, as shown in Figure 8.2. **Strategic fit** exists whenever one or more activities comprising the value chains of different businesses are sufficiently similar to present opportunities for:[5]

CORE CONCEPT

Strategic fit exists when value chains of different businesses present opportunities for cross-business skills transfer, cost sharing, or brand sharing.

- *Transferring competitively valuable resources, expertise, technological know-how, or other capabilities from one business to another.* Google's technological know-how and innovation capabilities refined in its Internet search business have aided considerably in the development of its Android mobile operating system and Chrome operating system for computers. After acquiring Marvel Comics in 2009 and Lucasfilm in 2012, Walt Disney Company integrated Marvel's iconic characters

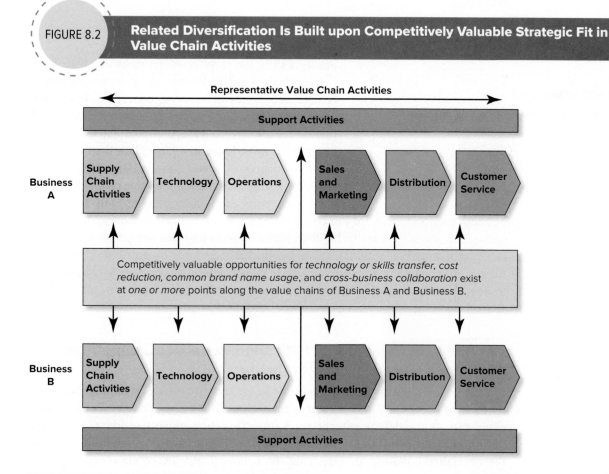

FIGURE 8.2 **Related Diversification Is Built upon Competitively Valuable Strategic Fit in Value Chain Activities**

such as Spider-Man and Iron Man and Lucasfilm's Star Wars and Indiana Jones franchises into other Disney businesses, including its theme parks, retail stores, motion picture division, and video game business.

- *Cost sharing between separate businesses where value chain activities can be combined.* For instance, it is often feasible to manufacture the products of different businesses in a single plant or have a single sales force for the products of different businesses if they are marketed to the same types of customers.

- *Brand sharing between business units that have common customers or that draw upon common core competencies.* For example, Apple's reputation for producing easy-to-operate computers and stylish designs were competitive assets that facilitated the company's diversification into smartphones, tablet computers, and wearable technology.

Cross-business strategic fit can exist anywhere along the value chain: in R&D and technology activities, in supply chain activities, in manufacturing, in sales and marketing, or in distribution activities. Likewise, different businesses can often use the same administrative and customer service infrastructure. For instance, a cable operator that diversifies as a broadband provider can use the same customer data network, the same customer call centers and local offices, the same billing and customer accounting systems, and the same customer service infrastructure to support all its products and services.[6]

Strategic Fit and Economies of Scope

Strategic fit in the value chain activities of a diversified corporation's different businesses opens up opportunities for economies of scope—a concept distinct from *economies of scale*. Economies of *scale* are cost savings that accrue directly from a larger operation; for example, unit costs may be lower in a large plant than in a small plant. **Economies of scope,** however, stem directly from cost-saving strategic fit along the value chains of related businesses. Such economies are open only to a multi-business enterprise and are the result of a related diversification strategy that allows sibling businesses to share technology, perform R&D together, use common manufacturing or distribution facilities, share a common sales force or distributor/dealer network, and/or share the same administrative infrastructure. *The greater the cross-business economies associated with cost-saving strategic fit, the greater the potential for a related diversification strategy to yield a competitive advantage based on lower costs than rivals.*

The Ability of Related Diversification to Deliver Competitive Advantage and Gains in Shareholder Value

Economies of scope and the other strategic-fit benefits provide a dependable basis for earning higher profits and returns than what a diversified company's businesses could earn as standalone enterprises. Converting the competitive advantage potential into greater profitability is what fuels $1 + 1 = 3$ gains in shareholder value—the necessary outcome for satisfying the *better-off test*. There are three things to bear in mind here: (1) Capturing cross-business strategic fit via related diversification builds shareholder value in ways that shareholders cannot replicate by simply owning a diversified portfolio of stocks; (2) the capture of cross-business strategic-fit benefits is possible only through related diversification; and (3) the benefits of cross-business strategic fit are not automatically realized—*the benefits materialize only after management has successfully pursued internal actions to capture them.*[7]

Concepts & Connections 8.1 describes the merger of Kraft Foods Group, Inc., with the H. J. Heinz Holding Corporation, in pursuit of the strategic fit benefits of a related diversification strategy.

Concepts & Connections 8.1

THE KRAFT–HEINZ MERGER: PURSUING THE BENEFITS OF CROSS-BUSINESS STRATEGIC FIT

The $62.6 billion merger between Kraft and Heinz that was finalized in 2015 created the third-largest food and beverage company in North America and the fifth-largest in the world. It was a merger predicated on the idea that the strategic fit between these two companies was such that they could create more value as a combined enterprise than they could as two separate companies. As a combined enterprise, Kraft Heinz would be able to exploit its cross-business value chain activities and resource similarities to more efficiently produce, distribute, and sell profitable processed food products.

Kraft and Heinz products share many of the same raw materials (milk, sugar, salt, wheat, etc.), which allows the new company to leverage its increased bargaining power as a larger business to get better deals with suppliers, using strategic fit in supply chain activities to achieve lower input costs and greater inbound efficiencies. Moreover, because both of these brands specialized in prepackaged foods, there is ample manufacturing-related strategic fit in production processes and packaging technologies that allow the new company to trim and streamline manufacturing operations.

Their distribution-related strategic fit will allow for the complete integration of distribution channels and transportation networks, resulting in greater outbound efficiencies and a reduction in travel time for products moving from factories to stores. The Kraft Heinz Company is currently looking to leverage Heinz's global platform to expand Kraft's products internationally. By utilizing Heinz's already highly developed global distribution network and brand familiarity (key specialized resources), Kraft can more easily expand into the global market of prepackaged and processed food. Because these two brands are sold at similar types of retail stores (supermarket chains, wholesale retailers, and local grocery stores), they are now able to claim even more

©Scott Olson/Getty Images

shelf space with the increased bargaining power of the combined company.

Strategic fit in sales and marketing activities will allow the company to develop coordinated and more effective advertising campaigns. Toward this aim, the Kraft Heinz Company is moving to consolidate its marketing capabilities under one marketing firm. Also, by combining R&D teams, the Kraft Heinz Company could come out with innovative products that may appeal more to the growing number of on-the-go and health-conscious buyers in the market. Many of these potential and predicted synergies for the Kraft Heinz Company have yet to be realized, since merger integration activities always take time.

Note: Developed with Maria Hart.

Sources: www.forbes.com/sites/paulmartyn/2015/03/31/heinz-and-kraft-merger-makes-supply-management-sense/; fortune.com/2015/03/25/kraft-mess-how-heinz-deal-helps/; www.nytimes.com/2015/03/26/business/dealbook/kraft-and-heinz-to-merge.html?_r=2; company websites (accessed December 3, 2015).

Diversifying into Unrelated Businesses

LO8-3 Recognize the merits and risks of corporate strategies keyed to unrelated diversification.

An unrelated diversification strategy discounts the importance of pursuing cross-business strategic fit and, instead, focuses squarely on entering and operating businesses in industries that allow the company as a whole to increase its earnings. Companies that pursue a strategy of unrelated diversification generally exhibit a willingness to diversify into *any industry* where senior managers see opportunity to realize improved financial results. Such companies are frequently labeled *conglomerates* because their business interests range broadly across diverse industries.

Companies that pursue unrelated diversification nearly always enter new businesses by acquiring an established company rather than by internal development. The premise of acquisition-minded corporations is that growth by acquisition can deliver enhanced shareholder value through upward-trending corporate revenues and earnings and a stock price that *on average* rises enough year after year to amply reward and please shareholders. Three types of acquisition candidates are usually of particular interest: (1) businesses that have bright growth prospects but are short on investment capital, (2) undervalued companies that can be acquired at a bargain price, and (3) struggling companies whose operations can be turned around with the aid of the parent company's financial resources and managerial know-how.

Building Shareholder Value Through Unrelated Diversification

Given the absence of cross-business strategic fit with which to capture added competitive advantage, the task of building shareholder value via unrelated diversification ultimately hinges on the ability of the parent company to improve its businesses via other means. To succeed with a corporate strategy keyed to unrelated diversification, corporate executives must:

- Do a superior job of identifying and acquiring new businesses that can produce consistently good earnings and returns on investment.

- Do an excellent job of negotiating favorable acquisition prices.

- Do such a good job *overseeing* and *parenting* the firm's businesses that they perform at a higher level than they would otherwise be able to do through their own efforts alone. The parenting activities of corporate executives can take the form of providing expert problem-solving skills, creative strategy suggestions, and first-rate advice and guidance on how to improve competitiveness and financial performance to the heads of the various business subsidiaries.[8] Royal Little, the founder of Textron, was a major reason that the company became an exemplar of the unrelated diversification strategy while he was CEO. Little's bold moves transformed the company from its origins as a small textile manufacturer into a global powerhouse known for its Bell helicopters, Cessna aircraft, and host of other strong brands in an array of industries.

The Pitfalls of Unrelated Diversification

Unrelated diversification strategies have two important negatives that undercut the pluses: very demanding managerial requirements and limited competitive advantage potential.

Demanding Managerial Requirements   Successfully managing a set of fundamentally different businesses operating in fundamentally different industry and competitive environments is an exceptionally difficult proposition for corporate-level managers. The greater the number of businesses a company is in and the more diverse they are, the more difficult it is for corporate managers to:

1. Stay abreast of what's happening in each industry and each subsidiary.
2. Pick business-unit heads having the requisite combination of managerial skills and know-how to drive gains in performance.
3. Tell the difference between those strategic proposals of business-unit managers that are prudent and those that are risky or unlikely to succeed.
4. Know what to do if a business unit stumbles and its results suddenly head downhill.[9]

As a rule, the more unrelated businesses that a company has diversified into, the more corporate executives are forced to "manage by the numbers"—that is, keep a close track on the financial and operating results of each subsidiary and assume that the heads of the various subsidiaries have most everything under control so long as the latest key financial and operating measures look good. Managing by the numbers works if the heads of the various business units are quite capable and consistently meet their numbers. But problems arise when things start to go awry and corporate management has to get deeply involved in turning around a business it does not know much about.

> Unrelated diversification requires that corporate executives rely on the skills and expertise of business-level managers to build competitive advantage and boost the performance of individual businesses.

Limited Competitive Advantage Potential   The second big negative associated with unrelated diversification is that such a strategy *offers limited potential for competitive advantage beyond what each individual business can generate on its own.* Unlike a related diversification strategy, there is no cross-business strategic fit to draw on for reducing costs; transferring capabilities, skills, and technology; or leveraging use of a powerful brand name and thereby adding to the competitive advantage possessed by individual businesses. *Without the competitive advantage potential of strategic fit, consolidated performance of an unrelated group of businesses is unlikely to be better than the sum of what the individual business units could achieve independently in most instances.*

Misguided Reasons for Pursuing Unrelated Diversification

Competently overseeing a set of widely diverse businesses can turn out to be much harder than it sounds. In practice, comparatively few companies have proved that they have top management capabilities that are up to the task. Far more corporate executives have failed than have been successful at delivering consistently good financial results with an unrelated diversification strategy.[10] Odds are that the result of unrelated diversification will be $1 + 1 = 2$ or less. In addition, management sometimes undertakes a strategy of unrelated diversification for the wrong reasons.

- *Risk reduction.* Managers sometimes pursue unrelated diversification to reduce risk by spreading the company's investments over a set of diverse industries. But this cannot create long-term shareholder value alone since the company's shareholders can more efficiently reduce their exposure to risk by investing in a diversified portfolio of stocks and bonds.

- *Growth.* While unrelated diversification may enable a company to achieve rapid or continuous growth in revenues, only profitable growth can bring about increases in shareholder value and justify a strategy of unrelated diversification.

- *Earnings stabilization.* In a broadly diversified company, there's a chance that market downtrends in some of the company's businesses will be partially offset by cyclical upswings in its other businesses, thus producing somewhat less earnings volatility. In actual practice, however, there's no convincing evidence that the consolidated profits of firms with unrelated diversification strategies are more stable than the profits of firms with related diversification strategies.

- *Managerial motives.* Unrelated diversification can provide benefits to managers such as higher compensation, which tends to increase with firm size and degree of diversification. Diversification for this reason alone is far more likely to reduce shareholder value than to increase it.

Diversifying into Both Related and Unrelated Businesses

There's nothing to preclude a company from diversifying into both related and unrelated businesses. Indeed, the business makeup of diversified companies varies considerably. Some diversified companies are really *dominant-business enterprises*—one major "core" business accounts for 50 to 80 percent of total revenues, and a collection of small related or unrelated businesses accounts for the remainder. Some diversified companies are *narrowly diversified* around a few (two to five) related or unrelated businesses. Others are *broadly diversified* around a wide-ranging collection of related businesses, unrelated businesses, or a mixture of both. And a number of multibusiness enterprises have diversified into *several unrelated groups of related businesses.* There's ample room for companies to customize their diversification strategies to incorporate elements of both related and unrelated diversification.

Evaluating the Strategy of a Diversified Company

 LO8-4   Evaluate a company's diversification strategy.

Strategic analysis of diversified companies builds on the methodology used for single-business companies discussed in Chapters 3 and 4 but utilizes tools that streamline the overall process. The procedure for evaluating the pluses and minuses of a diversified company's strategy and deciding what actions to take to improve the company's performance involves six steps:

1. Assessing the attractiveness of the industries the company has diversified into.

2. Assessing the competitive strength of the company's business units.

3. Evaluating the extent of cross-business strategic fit along the value chains of the company's various business units.

4. Checking whether the firm's resources fit the requirements of its present business lineup.

5. Ranking the performance prospects of the businesses from best to worst and determining a priority for allocating resources.

6. Crafting new strategic moves to improve overall corporate performance.

   The core concepts and analytical techniques underlying each of these steps are discussed further in this section of the chapter.

Step 1: Evaluating Industry Attractiveness

A principal consideration in evaluating the caliber of a diversified company's strategy is the attractiveness of the industries in which it has business operations. The more attractive the industries (both individually and as a group) a diversified company is in, the better its prospects for good long-term performance. A simple and reliable analytical tool for gauging industry attractiveness involves calculating quantitative industry attractiveness scores based upon the following measures:

- *Market size and projected growth rate.* Big industries are more attractive than small industries, and fast-growing industries tend to be more attractive than slow-growing industries, other things being equal.

- *The intensity of competition.* Industries in which competitive pressures are relatively weak are more attractive than industries with strong competitive pressures.

- *Emerging opportunities and threats.* Industries with promising opportunities and minimal threats on the near horizon are more attractive than industries with modest opportunities and imposing threats.

- *The presence of cross-industry strategic fit.* The more the industry's value chain and resource requirements match up well with the value chain activities of other industries in which the company has operations, the more attractive the industry is to a firm pursuing related diversification. However, cross-industry strategic fit may be of no consequence to a company committed to a strategy of unrelated diversification.

- *Resource requirements.* Industries having resource requirements within the company's reach are more attractive than industries where capital and other resource requirements could strain corporate financial resources and organizational capabilities.

- *Seasonal and cyclical factors.* Industries where buyer demand is relatively steady year-round and not unduly vulnerable to economic ups and downs tend to be more attractive than industries with wide seasonal or cyclical swings in buyer demand.

- *Social, political, regulatory, and environmental factors.* Industries with significant problems in such areas as consumer health, safety, or environmental pollution or that are subject to intense regulation are less attractive than industries where such problems are not burning issues.

- *Industry profitability.* Industries with healthy profit margins are generally more attractive than industries where profits have historically been low or unstable.

- *Industry uncertainty and business risk.* Industries with less uncertainty on the horizon and lower overall business risk are more attractive than industries whose prospects for one reason or another are quite uncertain.

   Each attractiveness measure should be assigned a weight reflecting its relative importance in determining an industry's attractiveness; it is weak methodology to assume that the various attractiveness measures are equally important. The intensity of competition in an industry should nearly always carry a high weight (say, 0.20 to 0.30). Strategic-fit considerations should be assigned a high weight in the case of companies with related diversification strategies; but for companies with an unrelated diversification strategy, strategic fit with other industries may be given a low weight or even dropped from the list of attractiveness measures. Seasonal and cyclical factors generally are assigned a low weight (or maybe even eliminated from the analysis) unless a company has diversified into industries strongly characterized by seasonal demand and/or heavy vulnerability to cyclical upswings and downswings. The importance weights must add up to 1.0.

Next, each industry is rated on each of the chosen industry attractiveness measures, using a rating scale of 1 to 10 (where 10 signifies *high* attractiveness and 1 signifies *low* attractiveness). Weighted attractiveness scores are then calculated by multiplying the industry's rating on each measure by the corresponding weight. For example, a rating of 8 times a weight of 0.25 gives a weighted attractiveness score of 2.00. The sum of the weighted scores for all the attractiveness measures provides an overall industry attractiveness score. This procedure is illustrated in Table 8.1.

Calculating Industry Attractiveness Scores Two conditions are necessary for producing valid industry attractiveness scores using this method. One is deciding on appropriate weights for the industry attractiveness measures. This is not always easy because different analysts have different views about which weights are most appropriate. Also, different weightings may be appropriate for different companies—based on their strategies, performance targets, and financial circumstances. For instance, placing a low weight on financial resource requirements may be justifiable for a cash-rich company, whereas a high weight may be more appropriate for a financially strapped company.

TABLE 8.1

Calculating Weighted Industry Attractiveness Scores

Rating scale: 1 = Very unattractive to company; 10 = Very attractive to company

Industry Attractiveness Measure	Importance Weight	Industry A Rating/Score	Industry B Rating/Score	Industry C Rating/Score	Industry D Rating/Score
Market size and projected growth rate	0.10	8/0.80	5/0.50	2/0.20	3/0.30
Intensity of competition	0.25	8/2.00	7/1.75	3/0.75	2/0.50
Emerging opportunities and threats	0.10	2/0.20	9/0.90	4/0.40	5/0.50
Cross-industry strategic fit	0.20	8/1.60	4/0.80	8/1.60	2/0.40
Resource requirements	0.10	9/0.90	7/0.70	5/0.50	5/0.50
Seasonal and cyclical influences	0.05	9/0.45	8/0.40	10/0.50	5/0.25
Societal, political, regulatory, and environmental factors	0.05	10/0.50	7/0.35	7/0.35	3/0.15
Industry profitability	0.10	5/0.50	10/1.00	3/0.30	3/0.30
Industry uncertainty and business risk	0.05	5/0.25	7/0.35	10/0.50	1/0.05
Sum of the assigned weights	1.00				
Overall weighted industry attractiveness scores		**7.20**	**6.75**	**5.10**	**2.95**

The second requirement for creating accurate attractiveness scores is to have sufficient knowledge to rate the industry on each attractiveness measure. It's usually rather easy to locate statistical data needed to compare industries on market size, growth rate, seasonal and cyclical influences, and industry profitability. Cross-industry fit and resource requirements are also fairly easy to judge. But the attractiveness measure that is toughest to rate is that of intensity of competition. It is not always easy to conclude whether competition in one industry is stronger or weaker than in another industry. In the event that the available information is too skimpy to confidently assign a rating value to an industry on a particular attractiveness measure, then it is usually best to use a score of 5, which avoids biasing the overall attractiveness score either up or down.

Despite the hurdles, calculating industry attractiveness scores is a systematic and reasonably reliable method for ranking a diversified company's industries from most to least attractive.

Step 2: Evaluating Business-Unit Competitive Strength

The second step in evaluating a diversified company is to determine how strongly positioned its business units are in their respective industries. Doing an appraisal of each business unit's strength and competitive position in its industry not only reveals its chances for industry success but also provides a basis for ranking the units from competitively strongest to weakest. Quantitative measures of each business unit's competitive strength can be calculated using a procedure similar to that for measuring industry attractiveness. The following factors may be used in quantifying the competitive strengths of a diversified company's business subsidiaries:

- *Relative market share.* A business unit's *relative market share* is defined as the ratio of its market share to the market share held by the largest rival firm in the industry, with market share measured in unit volume, not dollars. For instance, if business A has a market-leading share of 40 percent and its largest rival has 30 percent, A's relative market share is 1.33. If business B has a 15 percent market share and B's largest rival has 30 percent, B's relative market share is 0.5.

- *Costs relative to competitors' costs.* There's reason to expect that business units with higher relative market shares have lower unit costs than competitors with lower relative market shares because of the possibility of scale economies and experience- or learning-curve effects. Another indicator of low cost can be a business unit's supply chain management capabilities.

- *Products or services that satisfy buyer expectations.* A company's competitiveness depends in part on being able to offer buyers appealing features, performance, reliability, and service attributes.

- *Ability to benefit from strategic fit with sibling businesses.* Strategic fit with other businesses within the company enhances a business unit's competitive strength and may provide a competitive edge.

- *Number and caliber of strategic alliances and collaborative partnerships.* Well-functioning alliances and partnerships may be a source of potential competitive advantage and thus add to a business's competitive strength.

- *Brand image and reputation.* A strong brand name is a valuable competitive asset in most industries.

- *Competitively valuable capabilities.* All industries contain a variety of important competitive capabilities related to product innovation, production capabilities, distribution capabilities, or marketing prowess.
- *Profitability relative to competitors.* Above-average returns on investment and large profit margins relative to rivals are usually accurate indicators of competitive advantage.

After settling on a set of competitive strength measures that are well matched to the circumstances of the various business units, weights indicating each measure's importance need to be assigned. As in the assignment of weights to industry attractiveness measures, the importance weights must add up to 1.0. Each business unit is then rated on each of the chosen strength measures, using a rating scale of 1 to 10 (where 10 signifies competitive *strength* and a rating of 1 signifies competitive *weakness*). If the available information is too skimpy to confidently assign a rating value to a business unit on a particular strength measure, then it is usually best to use a score of 5. Weighted strength ratings are calculated by multiplying the business unit's rating on each strength measure by the assigned weight. For example, a strength score of 6 times a weight of 0.15 gives a weighted strength rating of 0.90. The sum of weighted ratings across all the strength measures provides a quantitative measure of a business unit's overall market strength and competitive standing. Table 8.2 provides sample calculations of competitive strength ratings for four businesses.

Using a Nine-Cell Matrix to Evaluate the Strength of a Diversified Company's Business Lineup
The industry attractiveness and business strength scores can be used to portray the strategic positions of each business in a diversified company. Industry attractiveness is plotted on the vertical axis and competitive strength on the horizontal axis. A nine-cell grid emerges from dividing the vertical

TABLE 8.2

Calculating Weighted Competitive Strength Scores for a Diversified Company's Business Units

[Rating scale: 1 = Very weak; 10 = Very strong]

Competitive Strength Measure	Importance/ Weight	Business A in Industry A Rating/Score	Business B in Industry B Rating/Score	Business C in Industry C Rating/Score	Business D in Industry D Rating/Score
Relative market share	0.15	10/1.50	1/0.15	6/0.90	2/0.30
Costs relative to competitors' costs	0.20	7/1.40	2/0.40	5/1.00	3/0.60
Ability to match or beat rivals on key product attributes	0.05	9/0.45	4/0.20	8/0.40	4/0.20
Ability to benefit from strategic fits with sister businesses	0.20	8/1.60	4/0.80	4/0.80	2/0.60
Bargaining leverage with suppliers/ buyers; caliber of alliances	0.05	9/0.45	3/0.15	6/0.30	2/0.10
Brand image and reputation	0.10	9/0.90	2/0.20	7/0.70	5/0.50
Competitively valuable capabilities	0.15	7/1.05	2/0.30	5/0.75	3/0.45
Profitability relative to competitors	0.10	5/0.50	1/0.10	4/0.40	4/0.40
Sum of the assigned weights	1.00				
Overall weighted competitive strength scores		**7.85**	**2.30**	**5.25**	**3.15**

axis into three regions (high, medium, and low attractiveness) and the horizontal axis into three regions (strong, average, and weak competitive strength). As shown in Figure 8.3, high attractiveness is associated with scores of 6.7 or greater on a rating scale of 1 to 10, medium attractiveness with scores of 3.3 to 6.7, and low attractiveness with scores below 3.3. Likewise, high competitive strength is defined as a score greater than 6.7, average strength as scores of 3.3 to 6.7, and low strength as scores below 3.3. *Each business unit is plotted on the nine-cell matrix according to*

FIGURE 8.3   **A Nine-Cell Industry Attractiveness–Competitive Strength Matrix**

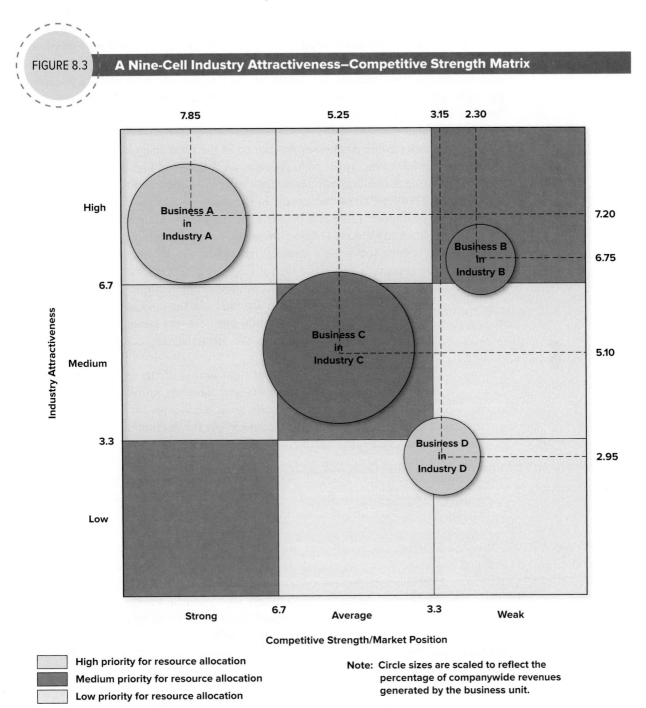

High priority for resource allocation
Medium priority for resource allocation
Low priority for resource allocation

Note: Circle sizes are scaled to reflect the percentage of companywide revenues generated by the business unit.

its overall attractiveness and strength scores, and then shown as a "bubble." The size of each bubble is scaled to what percentage of revenues the business generates relative to total corporate revenues. The bubbles in Figure 8.3 were located on the grid using the four industry attractiveness scores from Table 8.1 and the strength scores for the four business units in Table 8.2.

The locations of the business units on the attractiveness–competitive strength matrix provide valuable guidance in deploying corporate resources. In general, *a diversified company's best prospects for good overall performance involve concentrating corporate resources on business units having the greatest competitive strength and industry attractiveness.* Businesses plotted in the three cells in the upper left portion of the attractiveness–competitive strength matrix have both favorable industry attractiveness and competitive strength and should receive a high investment priority. Business units plotted in these three cells (such as business A in Figure 8.3) are referred to as "grow and build" businesses because of their capability to drive future increases in shareholder value.

Next in priority come businesses positioned in the three diagonal cells stretching from the lower left to the upper right (businesses B and C in Figure 8.3). Such businesses usually merit medium or intermediate priority in the parent's resource allocation ranking. However, some businesses in the medium-priority diagonal cells may have brighter or dimmer prospects than others. For example, a small business in the upper right cell of the matrix (like business B), despite being in a highly attractive industry, may occupy too weak a competitive position in its industry to justify the investment and resources needed to turn it into a strong market contender. If, however, a business in the upper right cell has attractive opportunities for rapid growth and a good potential for winning a much stronger market position over time, management may designate it as a grow and build business—the strategic objective here would be to move the business leftward in the attractiveness–competitive strength matrix over time.

Businesses in the three cells in the lower right corner of the matrix (business D in Figure 8.3) typically are weak performers and have the lowest claim on corporate resources. Such businesses are typically good candidates for being divested or else managed in a manner calculated to squeeze out the maximum cash flows from operations. The cash flows from low-performing/low-potential businesses can then be diverted to financing expansion of business units with greater market opportunities. In exceptional cases where a business located in the three lower right cells is nonetheless fairly profitable or has the potential for good earnings and return on investment, the business merits retention and the allocation of sufficient resources to achieve better performance.

The nine-cell attractiveness–competitive strength matrix provides clear, strong logic for why a diversified company needs to consider both industry attractiveness and business strength in allocating resources and investment capital to its different businesses. A good case can be made for concentrating resources in those businesses that enjoy higher degrees of attractiveness and competitive strength, being very selective in making investments in businesses with intermediate positions on the grid, and withdrawing resources from businesses that are lower in attractiveness and strength unless they offer exceptional profit or cash flow potential.

Step 3: Determining the Competitive Value of Strategic Fit in Multibusiness Companies

The potential for competitively important strategic fit is central to making conclusions about the effectiveness of a company's related diversification strategy. This step can be bypassed for diversified companies whose businesses are all unrelated (because, by design, no cross-business strategic fit is present). Checking the competitive advantage potential of cross-business strategic fit involves evaluating how much benefit a diversified company can gain from value chain matchups that present:

1. Opportunities to combine the performance of certain activities, thereby reducing costs and capturing economies of scope.

2. Opportunities to transfer skills, technology, or intellectual capital from one business to another.

3. Opportunities to share use of a well-respected brand name across multiple product and/or service categories.

> The greater the value of cross-business strategic fit in enhancing a company's performance in the marketplace or the bottom line, the more powerful is its strategy of related diversification.

But more than just strategic-fit identification is needed. The real test is what competitive value can be generated from this fit. To what extent can cost savings be realized? How much competitive value will come from cross-business transfer of skills, technology, or intellectual capital? Will transferring a potent brand name to the products of sibling businesses grow sales significantly? Absent significant strategic fit and dedicated company efforts to capture the benefits, one has to be skeptical about the potential for a diversified company's businesses to perform better together than apart.

Step 4: Evaluating Resource Fit

The businesses in a diversified company's lineup need to exhibit good resource fit. **Resource fit** exists when (1) businesses, individually, strengthen a company's overall mix of resources and capabilities and (2) the parent company has sufficient resources that add customer value to support its entire group of businesses without spreading itself too thin.

> **CORE CONCEPT**
>
> A diversified company exhibits **resource fit** when its businesses add to a company's overall mix of resources and capabilities and when the parent company has sufficient resources to support its entire group of businesses without spreading itself too thin.

Financial Resource Fit   One important dimension of resource fit concerns whether a diversified company can generate the internal cash flows sufficient to fund the capital requirements of its businesses, pay its dividends, meet its debt obligations, and otherwise remain financially healthy. While additional capital can usually be raised in financial markets, it is also important for a diversified firm to have a healthy **internal capital market** that can support the financial requirements of its business lineup. The greater the extent to which a diversified company is able to fund investment in its businesses through internally generated free cash flows rather than from equity issues or borrowing, the more powerful its financial resource fit and the less dependent the firm is on external financial resources.

> **CORE CONCEPT**
>
> A strong **internal capital market** allows a diversified company to add value by shifting capital from business units generating *free cash flow* to those needing additional capital to expand and realize their growth potential.

A *portfolio approach* to ensuring financial fit among the firm's businesses is based on the fact that different businesses have different cash flow and investment characteristics. For example, business units in rapidly growing industries are often **cash hogs**—so labeled because the cash flows they generate from internal operations are not big enough to fund their expansion. To keep pace with rising buyer demand, rapid-growth businesses frequently need sizable annual capital infusions—for new facilities and equipment, technology improvements, and additional working capital to support inventory expansion. Because a cash hog's financial resources must be provided by the corporate parent, corporate managers have to decide whether it makes good financial and strategic sense to keep pouring new money into a cash hog business.

In contrast, business units with leading market positions in mature industries may be **cash cows**—businesses that generate substantial cash surpluses over what is needed to adequately fund their operations. Market leaders in slow-growth industries often generate sizable positive cash flows *over and above what is needed for growth and reinvestment* because the slow-growth nature of their industry often entails relatively modest annual investment requirements. Cash cows, though not always attractive from a growth standpoint, are valuable businesses from a financial resource perspective. The surplus cash flows they generate can be used to pay corporate dividends, finance acquisitions, and provide funds for investing in the company's promising cash hogs. It makes good financial and strategic sense for diversified companies to keep cash cows in healthy condition, fortifying and defending their market position to preserve their cash-generating capability over the long term and thereby have an ongoing source of financial resources to deploy elsewhere.

A diversified company has good financial resource fit when the excess cash generated by its cash cow businesses is sufficient to fund the investment requirements of promising cash hog businesses. Ideally, investing in promising cash hog businesses over time results in growing the hogs into self-supporting *star businesses* that have strong or market-leading competitive positions in attractive, high-growth markets and high levels of profitability. Star businesses are often the cash cows of the future—when the markets of star businesses begin to mature and their growth slows, their competitive strength should produce self-generated cash flows more than sufficient to cover their investment needs. The "success sequence" is thus cash hog to young star (but perhaps still a cash hog) to self-supporting star to cash cow.

If, however, a cash hog has questionable promise (because of either low industry attractiveness or a weak competitive position), then it becomes a logical candidate for divestiture. Aggressively investing in a cash hog with an uncertain future seldom makes sense because it requires the corporate parent to keep pumping more capital into the business with only a dim hope of turning the cash hog into a future star. Such businesses are a financial drain and fail the resource-fit test because they strain the corporate parent's ability to adequately fund its other businesses. Divesting a less-attractive cash hog business is usually the best alternative unless (1) it has highly valuable strategic fit with other business units or (2) the capital infusions needed from the corporate parent are modest relative to the funds available, and (3) there is a decent chance of growing the business into a solid bottom-line contributor.

Aside from cash flow considerations, two other factors to consider in assessing the financial resource fit for businesses in a diversified firm's portfolio are:

- *Do individual businesses adequately contribute to achieving companywide performance targets?* A business exhibits poor financial fit if it soaks up a disproportionate share of the company's financial resources, while making subpar or insignificant contributions to the bottom line. Too many underperforming businesses reduce the company's overall performance and ultimately limit growth in shareholder value.

- *Does the corporation have adequate financial strength to fund its different businesses and maintain a healthy credit rating?* A diversified company's strategy fails the resource fit test when the resource needs of its portfolio unduly stretch the company's financial health and threaten to impair its credit rating. Many of the world's largest banks, including Royal Bank of Scotland, Citigroup, and HSBC, recently found themselves so undercapitalized and financially overextended that they were forced to sell some of their business assets to meet regulatory requirements and restore public confidence in their solvency.

Examining a Diversified Company's Nonfinancial Resource Fit

A diversified company must also ensure that the nonfinancial resource needs of its portfolio of businesses are met by its corporate capabilities. Just as a diversified company must avoid allowing an excessive number of cash-hungry businesses to jeopardize its financial stability, it should also avoid adding to the business lineup in ways that overly stretch such nonfinancial resources as managerial talent, technology and information systems, and marketing support.

- *Does the company have or can it develop the specific resources and competitive capabilities needed to be successful in each of its businesses?*[11] Sometimes the resources a company has accumulated in its core business prove to be a poor match with the competitive capabilities needed to succeed in businesses into which it has diversified. For instance, BTR, a multibusiness company in Great Britain, discovered that the company's resources and managerial skills were quite well suited for parenting industrial manufacturing businesses but not for parenting its distribution businesses (National Tyre Services and Texas-based Summers Group). As a result, BTR decided to divest its distribution businesses and focus exclusively on diversifying around small industrial manufacturing.

> Resource fit extends beyond financial resources to include a good fit between the company's resources and core competencies and the key success factors of each industry it has diversified into.

- *Are the company's resources being stretched too thinly by the resource requirements of one or more of its businesses?* A diversified company has to guard against overtaxing its resources, a condition that can arise when (1) it goes on an acquisition spree and management is called upon to assimilate and oversee many new businesses very quickly or (2) when it lacks sufficient resource depth to do a creditable job of transferring skills and competencies from one of its businesses to another.

Step 5: Ranking Business Units and Setting a Priority for Resource Allocation

Once a diversified company's businesses have been evaluated from the standpoints of industry attractiveness, competitive strength, strategic fit, and resource fit, the next step is to use this information to rank the performance prospects of the businesses from best to worst. Such rankings help top-level executives assign each business a priority for corporate resource support and new capital investment.

The locations of the different businesses in the nine-cell industry attractiveness–competitive strength matrix provide a solid basis for identifying high-opportunity businesses and low-opportunity businesses. Normally, competitively strong businesses in attractive industries have significantly better performance prospects than competitively weak businesses in unattractive industries. Also, normally, the revenue and earnings outlook for businesses in fast-growing businesses is better than for businesses in slow-growing industries. As a rule, *business subsidiaries with the brightest profit and growth prospects, attractive positions in the nine-cell matrix, and solid strategic and resource fit should receive top priority for allocation of corporate resources.* However, in ranking the prospects of the different businesses from best to worst, it is usually wise to also consider each business's past performance as concerns sales growth, profit growth, contribution to company earnings, return on capital invested in the business, and cash flow from operations. While past performance is not always a reliable predictor of future performance, it does signal whether a business already has good to excellent performance or has problems to overcome.

Allocating Financial Resources   Figure 8.4 shows the chief strategic and financial options for allocating a diversified company's financial resources. Divesting businesses with the weakest future prospects and businesses that lack adequate strategic fit and/or resource fit is one of the best ways of generating additional funds for redeployment to businesses with better opportunities and better strategic and resource fit.

FIGURE 8.4   **The Chief Strategic and Financial Options for Allocating a Diversified Company's Financial Resources**

Strategic Options for Allocating Company Financial Resources

- Invest in ways to strengthen or grow existing business
- Make acquisitions to establish positions in new industries or to complement existing businesses
- Fund long-range R&D ventures aimed at opening market opportunities in new or existing businesses

Financial Options for Allocating Company Financial Resources

- Pay off existing long-term or short-term debt
- Increase dividend payments to shareholders
- Repurchase shares of the company's common stock
- Build cash reserves; invest in short-term securities

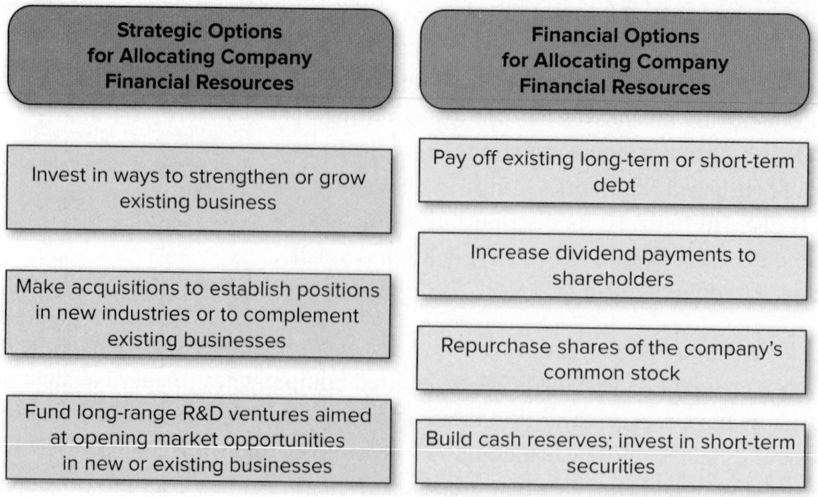

Free cash flows from cash cow businesses also add to the pool of funds that can be usefully redeployed. *Ideally,* a diversified company will have sufficient financial resources to strengthen or grow its existing businesses, make any new acquisitions that are desirable, fund other promising business opportunities, pay off existing debt, and periodically increase dividend payments to shareholders and/or repurchase shares of stock. But, as a practical matter, a company's financial resources are limited. Thus, for top executives to make the best use of the available funds, they must steer resources to those businesses with the best opportunities and performance prospects and allocate little, if any, resources to businesses with marginal or dim prospects—this is why ranking the performance prospects of the various businesses from best to worst is so crucial. Strategic uses of corporate financial resources (see Figure 8.4) should usually take precedence unless there is a compelling reason to strengthen the firm's balance sheet or better reward shareholders.

Step 6: Crafting New Strategic Moves to Improve the Overall Corporate Performance

> **LO8-5**   Understand a diversified company's four main corporate strategy options for solidifying its diversification strategy and improving company performance.

The conclusions flowing from the five preceding analytical steps set the agenda for crafting strategic moves to improve a diversified company's overall performance. The strategic options boil down to four broad categories of actions:

1. Sticking closely with the existing business lineup and pursuing the opportunities these businesses present
2. Broadening the company's business scope by making new acquisitions in new industries
3. Divesting some businesses and retrenching to a narrower base of business operations
4. Restructuring the company's business lineup and putting a whole new face on the company's business makeup

Sticking Closely with the Existing Business Lineup   The option of sticking with the current business lineup makes sense when the company's present businesses offer attractive growth opportunities and can be counted on to generate good earnings and cash flows. As long as the company's set of existing businesses puts it in a good position for the future and these businesses have good strategic and/or resource fit, then rocking the boat with major changes in the company's business mix is usually unnecessary. Corporate executives can concentrate their attention on getting the best performance from each of the businesses, steering corporate resources into those areas of greatest potential and profitability. However, in the event that corporate executives are not entirely satisfied with the opportunities they see in the company's present set of businesses, they can opt for any of the three strategic alternatives listed in the remainder of this section.

Broadening the Diversification Base   Diversified companies sometimes find it desirable to add to the diversification base for any one of the same reasons a single-business company might pursue initial diversification. Sluggish growth in revenues or profits, vulnerability to seasonality or recessionary influences, potential for transferring resources and capabilities to other related businesses, or unfavorable driving forces facing core businesses are all reasons management of a diversified company might choose to broaden diversification. An additional, and often very important, motivating factor for adding new businesses is to complement and strengthen the market position and competitive capabilities of one or more of its present businesses. Procter & Gamble's acquisition of Gillette strengthened and extended P&G's reach into personal care and household products—Gillette's businesses included Oral-B toothbrushes, Gillette razors and razor blades, Duracell batteries, Braun shavers and small appliances (coffeemakers, mixers, hair dryers, and electric toothbrushes), and toiletries (Right Guard, Foamy, Soft & Dry, White Rain, and Dry Idea).

Divesting Some Businesses and Retrenching to a Narrower Diversification Base

A number of diversified firms have had difficulty managing a diverse group of businesses and have elected to get out of some of them. Selling a business outright to another company is far and away the most frequently used option for divesting a business. In 2012, Sara Lee Corporation sold its International Coffee and Tea business to J.M. Smucker and Nike sold its Umbro and Cole Haan brands to focus on the Jordan brand and Converse that are more complementary to the Nike brand. But sometimes a business selected for divestiture has ample resources and capabilities to compete successfully on its own. In such cases, a corporate parent may elect to **spin off** the unwanted business as a financially and managerially independent company, either by selling shares to the public via an initial public offering or by distributing shares in the new company to shareholders of the corporate parent. eBay spun off PayPal in 2015 at a valuation of $45 billion—a value 30 times more than what eBay paid for the company in a 2002 acquisition.

> **CORE CONCEPT**
>
> A **spin-off** is an independent company created when a corporate parent divests a business either by selling shares to the public via an initial public offering or by distributing shares in the new company to shareholders of the corporate parent.

Retrenching to a narrower diversification base is usually undertaken when top management concludes that its diversification strategy has ranged too far afield and that the company can improve long-term performance by concentrating on building stronger positions in a smaller number of core businesses and industries. But there are other important reasons for divesting one or more of a company's present businesses. Sometimes divesting a business has to be considered because market conditions in a once-attractive industry have badly deteriorated. A business can become a prime candidate for divestiture because it lacks adequate strategic or resource fit, because it is a cash hog with questionable long-term potential, or because it is weakly positioned in its industry with little prospect of earning a decent return on investment. Sometimes a company acquires businesses that, down the road, just do not work out as expected, even though management has tried all it can think of to make them profitable. On occasion, a diversification move that seems sensible from a strategic fit standpoint turns out to be a poor cultural fit.[12]

Evidence indicates that pruning businesses and narrowing a firm's diversification base improves corporate performance.[13] Corporate parents often end up selling businesses too late and at too low a price, sacrificing shareholder value.[14] A useful guide to determine whether or when to divest a business subsidiary is to ask, "If we were not in this business today, would we want to get into it now?"[15] When the answer is no or probably not, divestiture should be considered. Another signal that a business should become a divestiture candidate is whether it is worth more to another company than to the present parent; in such cases, shareholders would be well served if the company were to sell the business and collect a premium price from the buyer for whom the business is a valuable fit.[16]

Broadly Restructuring the Business Lineup Through a Mix of Divestitures and New Acquisitions
Corporate restructuring strategies involve divesting some businesses and acquiring others so as to put a new face on the company's business lineup. Performing radical surgery on a company's group of businesses is an appealing corporate strategy when its financial performance is squeezed or eroded by:

CORE CONCEPT

Corporate restructuring involves radically altering the business lineup by divesting businesses that lack strategic fit or are poor performers and acquiring new businesses that offer better promise for enhancing shareholder value.

- A serious mismatch between the company's resources and capabilities and the type of diversification that it has pursued.
- Too many businesses in slow-growth, declining, low-margin, or otherwise unattractive industries.
- Too many competitively weak businesses.
- The emergence of new technologies that threaten the survival of one or more important businesses.
- Ongoing declines in the market shares of one or more major business units that are falling prey to more market-savvy competitors.
- An excessive debt burden with interest costs that eat deeply into profitability.
- Ill-chosen acquisitions that have not lived up to expectations.

Candidates for divestiture in a corporate restructuring effort typically include not only weak or up-and-down performers or those in unattractive industries but also business units that lack strategic fit with the businesses to be retained, businesses that are cash hogs or that lack other types of resource fit, and businesses incompatible with the company's revised diversification strategy (even though they may be profitable or in an attractive industry). As businesses are divested, corporate restructuring generally involves aligning the remaining business units into groups with the best strategic fit and then redeploying the cash flows from the divested business to either pay down debt or make new acquisitions.

Over the past decade, corporate restructuring has become a popular strategy at many diversified companies, especially those that had diversified broadly into many different industries and lines of business. VF Corporation, maker of North Face and other popular "lifestyle" apparel brands, has used a restructuring strategy to provide its shareholders with returns that are more than five times greater than shareholder returns for competing apparel makers. Since its acquisition and turnaround of North Face in 2000, VF has spent nearly $5 billion to acquire 20 additional businesses, including about $2 billion in 2011 for Timberland. New apparel brands acquired by VF Corporation include Rock & Republic jeans, Vans skateboard shoes, Nautica, Reef surf wear, and Lucy athletic wear. By 2016, VF Corporation had become a $12 billion powerhouse—one of the largest and most profitable apparel and footwear companies in the world. It was listed as number 230 on *Fortune*'s 2017 list of the 500 largest U.S. companies.

KEY POINTS

1. The purpose of diversification is to build shareholder value. Diversification builds share-holder value when a diversified group of businesses can perform better under the auspices of a single corporate parent than they would as independent, standalone businesses—the goal is to achieve not just a $1 + 1 = 2$ result but rather to realize important $1 + 1 = 3$ performance benefits. Whether getting into a new business has potential to enhance share-holder value hinges on whether a company's entry into that business can pass the attrac-tiveness test, the cost-of-entry test, and the better-off test.

2. Entry into new businesses can take any of three forms: acquisition, internal development, or joint venture/strategic partnership. Each has its pros and cons, but acquisition usually provides the quickest entry into a new business; internal development takes the longest to produce home-run results; and joint venture/strategic partnership tends to be the least durable.

3. There are two fundamental approaches to diversification: into related businesses and into unrelated businesses. The rationale for *related* diversification is based on cross-business *strategic fit:* Diversify into businesses with strategic fit along their respective value chains, capitalize on strategic-fit relationships to gain competitive advantage, and then use competitive advantage to achieve the desired $1 + 1 = 3$ impact on shareholder value.

4. *Unrelated diversification* strategies surrender the competitive advantage potential of strategic fit. Given the absence of cross-business strategic fit, the task of building shareholder value through a strategy of unrelated diversification hinges on the ability of the parent company to (1) do a superior job of identifying and acquiring new businesses that can produce consistently good earnings and returns on investment; (2) do an excellent job of negotiat-ing favorable acquisition prices; and (3) do such a good job of overseeing and parenting the collection of businesses that they perform at a higher level than they would on their own efforts. The greater the number of businesses a company has diversified into and the more diverse these businesses are, the harder it is for corporate executives to select capable managers to run each business, know when the major strategic proposals of business units are sound, or decide on a wise course of recovery when a business unit stumbles.

5. Evaluating a company's diversification strategy is a six-step process:

    *   Step 1: *Evaluate the long-term attractiveness of the industries into which the firm has diversified.* Determining industry attractiveness involves developing a list of industry attractiveness measures, each of which might have a different importance weight.

    *   Step 2: *Evaluate the relative competitive strength of each of the company's business units.* The purpose of rating each business's competitive strength is to gain clear understand-ing of which businesses are strong contenders in their industries, which are weak con-tenders, and the underlying reasons for their strength or weakness. The conclusions about industry attractiveness can be joined with the conclusions about competitive strength by drawing an industry attractiveness–competitive strength matrix that helps identify the prospects of each business and what priority each business should be given in allocating corporate resources and investment capital.

    *   Step 3: *Check for cross-business strategic fit.* A business is more attractive strategi-cally when it has value chain relationships with sibling business units that offer the potential to (1) realize economies of scope or cost-saving efficiencies; (2) transfer technology, skills, know-how, or other resources and capabilities from one business to another; and/or (3) leverage use of a well-known and trusted brand name. Cross-business strategic fit represents a significant avenue for producing competitive advantage beyond what any one business can achieve on its own.

- Step 4: *Check whether the firm's resources fit the requirements of its present business lineup.* Resource fit exists when (1) businesses, individually, strengthen a company's overall mix of resources and capabilities and (2) a company has sufficient resources to support its entire group of businesses without spreading itself too thin. One important test of financial resource fit involves determining whether a company has ample cash cows and not too many cash hogs.

- Step 5: *Rank the performance prospects of the businesses from best to worst, and determine what the corporate parent's priority should be in allocating resources to its various businesses.* The most important considerations in judging business-unit performance are sales growth, profit growth, contribution to company earnings, cash flow characteristics, and the return on capital invested in the business. Normally, strong business units in attractive industries should head the list for corporate resource support.

- Step 6: *Crafting new strategic moves to improve overall corporate performance.* This step entails using the results of the preceding analysis as the basis for selecting one of four different strategic paths for improving a diversified company's performance: *(a)* Stick closely with the existing business lineup and pursue opportunities presented by these businesses, *(b)* broaden the scope of diversification by entering additional industries, *(c)* retrench to a narrower scope of diversification by divesting poorly performing businesses, and *(d)* broadly restructure the business lineup with multiple divestitures and/or acquisitions.

ASSURANCE OF LEARNING EXERCISES

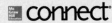

1. See if you can identify the value chain relationships that make the businesses of the following companies related in competitively relevant ways. In particular, you should consider whether there are cross-business opportunities for *(a)* transferring competitively valuable resources, expertise, technological know-how, and other capabilities, *(b)* cost sharing where value chain activities can be combined, and/or *(c)* leveraging use of a well-respected brand name.

LO8-1, LO8-2, LO8-3, LO8-4

Bloomin' Brands

- Outback Steakhouse
- Carrabba's Italian Grill
- Bonefish Grill (market-fresh fine seafood)
- Fleming's Prime Steakhouse & Wine Bar

L'Oréal

- Maybelline, Lancôme, Helena Rubinstein, Kiehl's, Garner, and Shu Uemura cosmetics
- L'Oréal and Soft Sheen/Carson hair care products
- Redken, Matrix, L'Oréal Professional, and Kerastase Paris professional hair care and skin care products
- Ralph Lauren and Giorgio Armani fragrances
- Biotherm skin care products
- La Roche–Posay and Vichy Laboratories dermo-cosmetics

Johnson & Johnson

- Baby products (powder, shampoo, oil, lotion)
- Band-Aids and other first-aid products
- Women's health and personal care products (Stayfree, Carefree, Sure & Natural)

- Neutrogena and Aveeno skin care products
- Nonprescription drugs (Tylenol, Motrin, Pepcid AC, Mylanta, Monistat)
- Prescription drugs
- Prosthetic and other medical devices
- Surgical and hospital products
- Acuvue contact lenses

LO8-1, LO8-2,
LO8-3, LO8-4

2. Peruse the business group listings for Ingersoll Rand shown as follows and listed at its website (company.ingersollrand.com). How would you characterize the company's corporate strategy? Related diversification, unrelated diversification, or a combination related-unrelated diversification strategy? Explain your answer.

Club Car—golf carts and other zero-emissions electric vehicles

Thermo King—transportation temperature control systems for truck, trailer, transit, marine, and rail applications

Ingersoll Rand—compressed air systems, tools and pumps, and fluid handling systems

Trane—heating, ventilating, and air conditioning systems

American Standard—home heating and air conditioning systems

ARO—fluid handling equipment for chemical, manufacturing, energy, pharmaceutical, and mining industries

LO8-1, LO8-2,
LO8-3, LO8-4,
LO8-5

3. ITT is a technology-oriented engineering and manufacturing company with the following business divisions and products:

Industrial Process Division—industrial pumps, valves, and monitoring and control systems; aftermarket services for the chemical, oil and gas, mining, pulp and paper, power, and biopharmaceutical markets

Motion Technologies Division—durable brake pads, shock absorbers, and damping technologies for the automotive and rail markets

Interconnect Solutions—connectors and fittings for the production of automobiles, aircraft, railcars and locomotives, oil field equipment, medical equipment, and industrial equipment

Control Technologies—energy absorption and vibration dampening equipment, transducers and regulators, and motion controls used in the production of robotics, medical equipment, automobiles, subsea equipment, industrial equipment, aircraft, and military vehicles

Based on this listing, would you say that ITT's business lineup reflects a strategy of related diversification, unrelated diversification, or a combination of related and unrelated diversification? What benefits are generated from any strategic fit existing between ITT's businesses? Also, what types of companies should ITT consider acquiring that might improve shareholder value? Justify your answer.

EXERCISES FOR SIMULATION PARTICIPANTS

LO8-1, LO8-2,
LO8-3

1. In the event that your company had the opportunity to diversify into other products or businesses of your choosing, would you opt to pursue related diversification, unrelated diversification, or a combination of both? Explain why.

LO8-1, LO8-2

2. What specific resources and capabilities does your company possess that would make it attractive to diversify into related businesses? Indicate what kinds of strategic-fit benefits could be captured by transferring these resources and competitive capabilities to newly acquired related businesses.

3. If your company opted to pursue a strategy of related diversification, what industries or product categories could your company diversify into that would allow it to achieve economies of scope? Name at least two or three such industries/product categories, and indicate the specific kinds of cost savings that might accrue from entry into each of these businesses/product categories.

   LO8-1, LO8-2

4. If your company opted to pursue a strategy of related diversification, what industries or product categories could your company diversify into that would allow your company to capitalize on using your company's present brand name and corporate image to good advantage in these newly entered businesses or product categories? Name at least two or three such industries or product categories, and indicate *the specific benefits* that might be captured by transferring your company's brand name to each of these other businesses/product categories.

   LO8-1, LO8-2, LO8-3, LO8-4, LO8-5

   Would you prefer to pursue a strategy of related or unrelated diversification? Why?

◉ ENDNOTES

1. Constantinos C. Markides, "To Diversify or Not to Diversify," *Harvard Business Review* 75, no. 6 (November–December 1997).

2. Michael E. Porter, "From Competitive Advantage to Corporate Strategy," *Harvard Business Review* 45, no. 3 (May–June 1987).

3. Michael E. Porter, *Competitive Strategy: Techniques for Analyzing Industries and Competitors* (New York: Free Press, 1980).

4. Yves L. Doz and Gary Hamel, *Alliance Advantage: The Art of Creating Value Through Partnering* (Boston: Harvard Business School Press, 1998).

5. Michael E. Porter, *Competitive Advantage* (New York: Free Press, 1985); and Constantinos C. Markides and Peter J. Williamson, "Corporate Diversification and Organization Structure: A Resource-Based View," *Academy of Management Journal* 39, no. 2 (April 1996).

6. Jeanne M. Liedtka, "Collaboration Across Lines of Business for Competitive Advantage," *Academy of Management Executive* 10, no. 2 (May 1996).

7. Kathleen M. Eisenhardt and D. Charles Galunic, "Coevolving: At Last, a Way to Make Synergies Work," *Harvard Business Review* 78, no. 1 (January–February 2000); and Constantinos C. Markides and Peter J. Williamson, "Related Diversification, Core Competencies and Corporate Performance," *Strategic Management Journal* 15 (Summer 1994).

8. A. Campbell, M. Goold, and M. Alexander, "Corporate Strategy: The Quest for Parenting Advantage," *Harvard Business Review* 73, no. 2 (March–April 1995); and Cynthia A. Montgomery and Birger Wernerfelt, "Diversification, Ricardian Rents, and Tobin-Q," *RAND Journal of Economics* 19, no. 4 (1988).

9. Patricia L. Anslinger and Thomas E. Copeland, "Growth Through Acquisitions: A Fresh Look," *Harvard Business Review* 74, no. 1 (January–February 1996).

10. Lawrence G. Franko, "The Death of Diversification? The Focusing of the World's Industrial Firms, 1980–2000," *Business Horizons* 47, no. 4 (July–August 2004).

11. Andrew Campbell, Michael Gould, and Marcus Alexander, "Corporate Strategy: The Quest for Parenting Advantage," *Harvard Business Review* 73, no. 2 (March–April 1995).

12. Peter F. Drucker, Management: Tasks, Responsibilities, Practices (New York: Harper & Row, 1974). p. 709.

13. Constantinos C. Markides, "Diversification, Restructuring, and Economic Performance," *Strategic Management Journal* 16 (February 1995).

14. Lee Dranikoff, Tim Koller, and Antoon Schneider, "Divestiture: Strategy's Missing Link," *Harvard Business Review* 80, no. 5 (May 2002).

15. Peter F. Drucker, *Management: Tasks, Responsibilities, Practices* (New York: Harper & Row, 1974).

16. David J. Collis and Cynthia A. Montgomery, "Creating Corporate Advantage," *Harvard Business Review* 76, no. 3 (May–June 1998).

9

Ethics, Corporate Social Responsibility, Environmental Sustainability, and Strategy

LEARNING OBJECTIVES

After reading this chapter, you should be able to:

LO9-1   Understand why the standards of ethical behavior in business are no different from ethical standards in general.

LO9-2   Recognize conditions that give rise to unethical business strategies and behavior.

LO9-3   Identify the costs of business ethics failures.

LO9-4   Understand the concepts of corporate social responsibility and environmental sustainability and how companies balance these duties with economic responsibilities to shareholders.

Clearly, a company has a responsibility to make a profit and grow the business, but just as clearly, a company and its personnel also have a duty to obey the law and play by the rules of fair competition. But does a company have a duty to go beyond legal requirements and operate according to the ethical norms of the societies in which it operates? And does it have a duty or obligation to contribute to the betterment of society independent of the needs and preferences of the customers it serves? Should a company display a social conscience and devote a portion of its resources to bettering society? Should its strategic initiatives be screened for possible negative effects on future generations of the world's population?

This chapter focuses on whether a company, in the course of trying to craft and execute a strategy that delivers value to both customers and shareholders, also has a duty to (1) act in an ethical manner, (2) demonstrate socially responsible behavior by being a committed corporate citizen, and (3) adopt business practices that conserve natural resources, protect the interest of future generations, and preserve the well-being of the planet.

What Do We Mean by Business Ethics?

 LO9-1 Understand why the standards of ethical behavior in business are no different from ethical standards in general.

Business ethics is the application of ethical principles and standards to the actions and decisions of business organizations and the conduct of their personnel.[1] Ethical principles in business are not materially different from ethical principles in general because business actions have to be judged in the context of society's standards of right and wrong. There is not a special set of rules that businesspeople decide to apply to their own conduct. If dishonesty is considered unethical and immoral, then dishonest behavior in business—whether it relates to customers, suppliers, employees, or shareholders—qualifies as equally unethical and immoral. If being ethical entails adhering to generally accepted norms about conduct that is right and wrong, then managers must consider such norms when crafting and executing strategy.

> **CORE CONCEPT**
>
> **Business ethics** involves the application of general ethical principles to the actions and decisions of businesses and the conduct of their personnel.

While most company managers are careful to ensure that a company's strategy is within the bounds of what is legal, evidence indicates they are not always so careful to ensure that their strategies are within the bounds of what is considered ethical. In recent years, there have been revelations of ethical misconduct on the part of managers at such organizations as Volkswagen, FIFA, Wells Fargo, several leading investment banking firms, and a host of mortgage lenders. The consequences of crafting strategies that cannot pass the test of moral scrutiny are manifested in sharp drops in stock price that cost shareholders billions of dollars, devastating public relations hits, sizable fines, and criminal indictments and convictions of company executives.

Drivers of Unethical Strategies and Business Behavior

 LO9-2   Recognize conditions that give rise to unethical business strategies and behavior.

Apart from "the business of business is business, not ethics" kind of thinking apparent in recent high-profile business scandals, three other main drivers of unethical business behavior also stand out:[2]

- *Faulty oversight, enabling the unscrupulous pursuit of personal gain and other selfish interests.* People who are obsessed with wealth accumulation, greed, power, status, and other selfish interests often push ethical principles aside in their quest for self-gain. Driven by their ambitions, they exhibit few qualms in skirting the rules or doing whatever is necessary to achieve their goals. A general disregard for business ethics can prompt all kinds of unethical strategic maneuvers and behaviors at companies.

  The U.S. government has been conducting a multiyear investigation of insider trading, the illegal practice of exchanging confidential information to gain an advantage in the stock market. Focusing on the hedge fund industry and nick-named "Operation Perfect Hedge," the investigation has brought to light scores of violations and led to more than more than 70 guilty pleas or convictions by 2015. Among the most prominent of those convicted was Raj Rajaratnam, the former head of Galleon Group, who was sentenced to 11 years in prison and fined $10 million. At SAC Capital, a $14 billion hedge fund, eight hedge fund mangers were convicted of insider trading in what has been called the most lucrative insider trading scheme in U.S. history. The company has agreed to pay $1.8 billion in penalties and has been forced to stop managing money for outside investors.[3]

- *Heavy pressures on company managers to meet or beat performance targets.* When key personnel find themselves scrambling to meet the quarterly and annual sales and profit expectations of investors and financial analysts or to hit other ambitious performance targets, they often feel enormous pressure to *do whatever it takes* to protect their reputation for delivering good results. As the pressure builds, they start stretching the rules further and further, until the limits of ethical conduct are overlooked.[4] Once people cross ethical boundaries to "meet or beat their numbers," the threshold for making more extreme ethical compromises becomes lower. In 2014, the U.S. Securities and Exchange Commission charged Diamond Foods (maker of Pop Secret and Emerald Nuts) with accounting fraud, alleging that the company falsified costs in order to boost earnings and stock prices. The company has agreed to pay $5 million, while its (now ousted) CEO must pay $125,000 to settle a separate charge of negligence and return $4 million in bonuses to the company. The real blow for the company was that its pending acquisition of potato chip giant Pringles fell apart as a result of the scandal, thwarting the company's dreams of becoming the second-largest snack company in the world.[5]

- *A company culture that puts profitability and good business performance ahead of ethical behavior.* When a company's culture spawns an ethically corrupt or amoral work climate, people have a company-approved license to ignore "what's right" and engage in most any behavior or employ most any strategy they think they can get away with. Such cultural norms as "everyone else does it" and "it is OK to bend the rules to get the job done" permeate the work environment. At such companies, ethically immoral or amoral people are certain to play down observance of ethical strategic actions and business conduct. Moreover, cultural pressures to utilize unethical means if circumstances become challenging can prompt otherwise honorable people to behave unethically. Enron's leaders created a culture that pressured company personnel to be innovative and aggressive in figuring out how to grow current earnings—regardless of the methods. Enron's annual "rank and yank" performance evaluation process, in which the lowest-ranking 15 to 20 percent of employees were let go, made it abundantly clear that bottom-line results were what mattered most. The name of the game at Enron became devising clever ways to boost revenues and earnings, even if this sometimes meant operating outside established policies. In fact, outside-the-lines behavior was celebrated if it generated profitable new business.

The Business Case for Ethical Strategies

LO9-3 Identify the costs of business ethics failures.

While it is inarguable that there is a *moral case for an ethical business strategy* that reflects well on the character of the company and its personnel, it is also true that *an ethical strategy is good business and serves the self-interest of shareholders.* Pursuing unethical strategies and tolerating unethical conduct will in time damage a company's reputation and result in a wide-ranging set of other costly consequences. Figure 9.1 shows the wide-ranging

FIGURE 9.1 **The Costs Companies Incur When Ethical Wrongdoing Is Discovered and Punished**

Visible Costs	Internal Administrative Costs	Intangible or Less Visible Costs
• Government fines and penalties • Civil penalties arising from class-action lawsuits and other litigation aimed at punishing the company for its offense and the harm done to others • The costs to shareholders in the form of a lower stock price (and possibly lower dividends)	• Legal and investigative costs incurred by the company • The costs of providing remedial education and ethics training to company personnel • Costs of taking corrective actions • Administration costs associated with ensuring future compliance	• Customer defections • Loss of reputation • Lost employee morale and higher degrees of employee cynicism • Higher employee turnover • Higher recruiting costs and difficulty in attracting employees • Adverse effects on employee productivity • The costs of complying with often harsher government regulation

Source: Adapted from Terry Thomas, John R. Schermerhorn, and John W. Dienhart, "Strategic Leadership of Ethical Behavior," *Academy of Management Executive* 18, no. 2 (May 2004), p. 58.

costs a company can incur when unethical behavior is discovered and it is forced to make amends for its behavior. The more egregious a company's ethical violations, the higher are the costs and the bigger the damage to its reputation (and to the reputations of the company personnel involved). In high-profile instances, the costs of ethical misconduct can easily run into the hundreds of millions and even billions of dollars, especially if they provoke widespread public outrage and many people were harmed.

The fallout of ethical misconduct on the part of a company goes well beyond just the costs of making amends for the misdeeds. Buyers shun companies known for their shady behavior. Companies known to have engaged in unethical conduct have difficulty recruiting and retaining talented employees.[6] Most ethically upstanding people do not want to get entrapped in a compromising situation, nor do they want their personal reputations tarnished by the actions of an unsavory employer. A company's unethical behavior risks considerable damage to shareholders in the form of lost revenues, higher costs, lower profits, lower stock prices, and a diminished business reputation. To a significant degree, therefore, ethical strategies and ethical conduct are *good business*.

> Shareholders suffer major damage when a company's unethical behavior is discovered and punished. Making amends for unethical business conduct is costly, and it takes years to rehabilitate a tarnished company reputation.

Ensuring a Strong Commitment to Business Ethics in Companies with International Operations

Notions of right and wrong, fair and unfair, moral and immoral, ethical and unethical are present in all societies, organizations, and individuals. But there are three schools of thought about the extent to which the ethical standards travel across cultures and whether multinational companies can apply the same set of ethical standards in all of the locations where they operate. Concepts & Connections 9.1 describes how IKEA enforces its ethical principles regarding child labor across its vast international supplier network.

CORE CONCEPT

According to the school of **ethical universalism**, the same standards of what is ethical and what is unethical resonate with peoples of most societies, regardless of local traditions and cultural norms; hence, common ethical standards can be used to judge employee conduct in a variety of country markets and cultural circumstances.

The School of Ethical Universalism

According to the school of **ethical universalism**, some concepts of what is right and what is wrong are *universal* and transcend most all cultures, societies, and religions.[7] For instance, being truthful strikes a chord of what is right in the peoples of all nations. Ethical norms considered universal by many ethicists include honesty, trustworthiness, respecting the rights of others, practicing the Golden Rule, and avoiding unnecessary harm to workers or to the users of the company's product or service.[8] *To the extent there is common moral agreement about right and wrong actions and behaviors across multiple cultures and countries, there exists a set of universal ethical standards to which all societies, companies, and individuals can be held accountable.* The strength of ethical universalism is that it draws upon the collective views of multiple societies and cultures to put some clear boundaries on what constitutes ethical business behavior no matter what country market its personnel are operating in. This means that in those instances in which basic moral standards really do not vary

Concepts Connections 9.1

IKEA'S GLOBAL SUPPLIER STANDARDS: MAINTAINING LOW COSTS WHILE FIGHTING THE ROOT CAUSES OF CHILD LABOR

Known for its stylish, ready-to-assemble home furnishings, IKEA has long relied on an extensive supplier network to manufacture its products and support its rapid global expansion. It has worked hard to develop a successful approach to encourage high ethical standards among its suppliers, including standards concerning the notoriously difficult issue of child labor.

IKEA's initial plan to combat the use of child labor by its suppliers involved (1) contracts that threatened immediate cancellation and (2) random audits by a third-party partner. Despite these safeguards, the company discovered that some of its Indian suppliers were still employing children. IKEA realized that this issue would crop up again and again if it continued to use low-cost suppliers in developing countries—a critical element in its cost-containment strategy.

To address this problem, IKEA developed and introduced its new code for suppliers, IWAY, that addresses social, safety, and environmental issues across its purchasing model. When faced with a supplier slip-up, IKEA works with the company to figure out and tackle the root cause of violations. Using child labor, for example, can signal bigger problems: production inefficiencies that require the lowest-cost labor, lack of alternative options for children such as school or supervised community centers, family health or income challenges that mean children need to become breadwinners, and so on. IKEA takes action to provide technical expertise to improve working conditions and processes, offer financing help at reasonable rates, run training programs onsite, and help develop resources and infrastructure in areas where its suppliers are based. The IKEA Foundation also began focusing on these issues through partnerships with UNICEF and Save the Children aimed at funding long-term community programs that support access to education, health care, and sustainable family incomes. The programs had reached 12 million children by 2016.

IKEA's proactive approach has reduced some of the risks involved in relying on suppliers in developing countries. Through its approach, IKEA has been able to maintain its core strategic principles even when they seem to be at odds: low costs, great design, adherence to its ethical principles, and a commitment to a better world.

Note: Developed with Kiera O'Brien.

Sources: IKEA, "About the Company: This is IKEA," www.ikea.com/ms/en_US/this-is-ikea/people-and-planet/people-and-communities/ (accessed January 24, 2014); and Elaine Cohen, "Banning Child Labor: The Symptom or the Cause?" *CSR Newswire*, www.csrwire.com/blog/posts/547-banning-child-labor-the-symptom-or-the-cause (accessed January 24, 2014).

©Anthony Baggett/123RF

significantly according to local cultural beliefs, traditions, or religious convictions, a multinational company can develop a code of ethics that it applies more or less evenly across its worldwide operations.

The School of Ethical Relativism

Beyond widely accepted ethical norms, many ethical standards likely vary from one country to another because of divergent religious beliefs, social customs, and prevailing political and economic doctrines (whether a country leans more toward a capitalistic market economy or one heavily dominated by socialistic or state-directed capitalism principles). The school of **ethical relativism** holds that when there are national or cross-cultural differences in what is deemed an ethical or unethical business situation, it is appropriate for local moral standards to take precedence over what the ethical standards may be in a company's home market. The thesis is that whatever a culture thinks is right or wrong really is right or wrong for that culture.[9]

A company that adopts the principle of ethical relativism and holds company personnel to local ethical standards necessarily assumes that what prevails as local morality is an adequate guide to ethical behavior. This can be ethically dangerous; it leads to the conclusion that if a country's culture generally accepts bribery or environmental degradation or exposing workers to dangerous conditions, then managers working in that country are free to engage in such activities. Adopting such a position places a company in a perilous position if it is required to defend these activities to its stakeholders in countries with higher ethical expectations. Moreover, from a global markets perspective, ethical relativism results in a maze of conflicting ethical standards for multinational companies. Imagine, for example, that a multinational company in the name of ethical relativism takes the position that it is acceptable for company personnel to pay bribes and kickbacks in countries where such payments are customary but forbids company personnel from making such payments in those countries where bribes and kickbacks are considered unethical or illegal. Having thus adopted conflicting ethical standards for operating in different countries, company managers have little moral basis for enforcing ethical standards companywide. Rather, the clear message to employees would be that the company has no ethical standards or principles of its own, preferring to let its practices be governed by the countries in which it operates.

Integrative Social Contracts Theory

Integrative social contracts theory provides a middle position between the opposing views of universalism and relativism.[10] According to **integrative social contracts theory**, the ethical standards a company should try to uphold are governed both by (1) a limited number of universal ethical principles that are widely recognized as putting legitimate ethical boundaries on actions and behavior in *all* situations and (2) the circumstances of local cultures, traditions, and shared values that further prescribe what constitutes ethically permissible behavior and what does not. This "social contract" by which managers in all situations have a duty to serve provides that *"first-order" universal ethical norms always take precedence over "second-order" local ethical norms in circumstances in which local ethical norms are more permissive.* Integrative social contracts theory offers managers in multinational companies clear guidance in resolving cross-country ethical differences: Those parts of the company's code of ethics that involve universal ethical norms must be enforced worldwide, but within these boundaries, there is room for ethical diversity and opportunity for host-country cultures to exert *some* influence in setting their own moral and ethical standards.

A good example of the application of integrative social contracts theory involves the payment of bribes and kickbacks. Bribes and kickbacks seem to be common in some countries, but does this justify paying them? Just because bribery flourishes in a country does not mean that it is an authentic or legitimate ethical norm. Virtually all of the world's major religions (Buddhism, Christianity, Confucianism, Hinduism, Islam, Judaism, Sikhism, and Taoism) and all moral schools of thought condemn bribery and corruption.[11] Therefore, a multinational company might reasonably conclude that the right ethical standard is one of refusing to condone bribery and kickbacks on the part of company personnel no matter what the second-order local norm is and no matter what the sales consequences are.

Strategy, Corporate Social Responsibility, and Environmental Sustainability

LO9-4   Understand the concepts of corporate social responsibility and environmental sustainability and how companies balance these duties with economic responsibilities to shareholders.

The idea that businesses have an obligation to foster social betterment, a much-debated topic in the past 50 years, took root in the 19th century when progressive companies in the aftermath of the industrial revolution began to provide workers with housing and other amenities. The notion that corporate executives should balance the interests of all stakeholders—shareholders, employees, customers, suppliers, the communities in which they operated, and society at large—began to blossom in the 1960s.

What Do We Mean by Corporate Social Responsibility?

The essence of socially responsible business behavior is that a company should balance strategic actions to benefit shareholders against the *duty* to be a good corporate citizen. The underlying thesis is that company managers should display a *social conscience* in operating the business and specifically consider how management decisions and company actions affect the well-being of employees, local communities, the environment, and society at large.[12] Acting in a socially responsible manner thus encompasses more than just participating in community service projects and donating monies to charities and other worthy social causes. Demonstrating **corporate social responsibility (CSR)** also entails undertaking actions that earn trust and respect from all stakeholders—operating in an honorable and ethical manner, striving to make the company a great place to work, demonstrating genuine respect for the environment, and trying to make a difference in bettering society. Corporate social responsibility programs commonly involve:

> **CORE CONCEPT**
>
> **Corporate social responsibility (CSR)** refers to a company's *duty* to operate in an honorable manner, provide good working conditions for employees, encourage workforce diversity, be a good steward of the environment, and actively work to better the quality of life in the local communities in which it operates and in society at large.

- *Efforts to employ an ethical strategy and observe ethical principles in operating the business.* A sincere commitment to observing ethical principles is a necessary component of a CSR strategy simply because unethical conduct is incompatible with the concept of good corporate citizenship and socially responsible business behavior.

- *Making charitable contributions, supporting community service endeavors, engaging in broader philanthropic initiatives, and reaching out to make a difference in the lives of the disadvantaged.* Some companies fulfill their philanthropic obligations by spreading their efforts over a multitude of charitable and community activities; for instance, Microsoft and Johnson & Johnson support a broad variety of community, art, and social welfare programs. Others prefer to focus their energies more narrowly. McDonald's, for example, concentrates on sponsoring the Ronald McDonald House program (which provides a home away from home for the families of seriously ill children receiving treatment at nearby hospitals). Leading prescription drug maker GlaxoSmithKline and other pharmaceutical companies either donate or heavily discount medicines for distribution in the least-developed nations. Companies frequently reinforce their philanthropic efforts by encouraging employees to support charitable causes and participate in community affairs, often through programs that match employee contributions.

- *Actions to protect the environment and, in particular, to minimize or eliminate any adverse impact on the environment stemming from the company's own business activities.* Corporate social responsibility as it applies to environmental protection entails actively striving to be good stewards of the environment. This means using the best available science and technology to reduce environmentally harmful aspects of its operations *below the levels required by prevailing environmental regulations.* It also means putting time and money into improving the environment in ways that extend past a company's own industry boundaries—such as participating in recycling projects, adopting energy conservation practices, and supporting efforts to clean up local water supplies.

- *Actions to create a work environment that enhances the quality of life for employees.* Numerous companies exert extra effort to enhance the quality of life for their employees, both at work and at home. This can include onsite day care, flexible work schedules, workplace exercise facilities, special leaves to care for sick family members, work-at-home opportunities, career development programs and education opportunities, special safety programs, and the like.

- *Actions to build a workforce that is diverse with respect to gender, race, national origin, and other aspects that different people bring to the workplace.* Most large companies in the United States have established workforce diversity programs, and some go the extra mile to ensure that their workplaces are attractive to ethnic minorities and inclusive of all groups and perspectives.

CORE CONCEPT

A company's **corporate social responsibility strategy** is defined by the specific combination of socially beneficial activities it opts to support with its contributions of time, money, and other resources.

The particular combination of socially responsible endeavors a company elects to pursue defines its **corporate social responsibility strategy**. Concepts & Connections 9.2 describes Warby Parker's approach to corporate social responsibility. But the specific components emphasized in a CSR strategy vary from company to company and are typically linked to a company's core values. General Mills, for example, builds its CSR strategy around the theme of "nourishing lives" to emphasize its commitment to good nutrition as well as philanthropy, community building, and environmental protection.[13] Starbucks's CSR strategy includes four main elements (ethical sourcing, community service, environmental stewardship, and farmer support), all of which have touch points with the way that the company procures its coffee—a key aspect of its product differentiation strategy.[14]

Concepts & Connections 9.2

WARBY PARKER: COMBINING CORPORATE SOCIAL RESPONSIBILITY WITH AFFORDABLE FASHION

©Carolyn Cole/Los Angeles Times/Getty Images

Since its founding in 2010, Warby Parker has succeeded in selling over one million pairs of high-fashion glasses at a discounted price of $95—roughly 80 percent below the average $500 price tag on a comparable pair of eyeglasses from another producer. With more than 50 stores in the United States, the company has built a brand recognized universally as one of the strongest in the world; it consistently posts a net promoter score (a measure of how likely someone would be to recommend the product) of close to 90—higher than companies like Zappos and Apple.

Corporate responsibility is at Warby Parker's core. For each pair of glasses sold, the company provides international nonprofit partners like VisionSpring with a monthly donation of glasses; with Warby Parker's support, these partners provide basic eye exams and teach community members how to manufacture and sell glasses at very low prices to amplify beneficial effects in their communities. By 2017, the company had distributed more than 2 million pairs of glasses to people in 35 countries. The average impact on a recipient of a pair of donated glasses was a 20 percent increase in personal income and a 35 percent increase in productivity.

Efforts to be a responsible company expand beyond Warby Parker's international partnerships. The company voluntarily evaluates itself against benchmarks in the fields of "environment," "workers," "customers," "community," and "governance," demonstrating a nearly unparalleled dedication to outcomes outside of profit. The company is widely seen as an employer of choice and regularly attracts top talent for all roles across the organization. It holds to an extremely high environmental standard, running an entirely carbon neutral operation.

While socially impactful actions matter at Warby Parker, the company is mindful of the critical role of its customers as well. Both founders spent countless hours coordinating partnerships with dedicated suppliers to ensure quality, invested deeply in building a lean manufacturing operation to minimize cost, and sought to build an organization that would keep buyers happy. The net effect is a very economically healthy company—they post around $3,000 in sales per square foot, in line with Tiffany & Co.—with financial stability to pursue responsibilities outside of customer satisfaction.

The strong fundamentals put in place by the firm's founders blend responsibility into its DNA and attach each piece of commercial success to positive outcomes in the world. The company was recently recognized as number one on *Fast Company*'s "Most Innovative Companies" list and continues to build loyal followers—both of its products and its CSR efforts—as it expands.

Note: Developed with Jeremy P. Reich.

Sources: Warby Parker and "B Corp" websites; Max Chafkin, "Warby Parker Sees the Future of Retail," *Fast Company,* February 17, 2015, www.fastcompany.com/3041334/warby-parker-sees-the-future-of-retail (accessed February 22, 2016); Jenni Avins, "Warby Parker Proves Customers Don't Have to Care about Your Social Mission," *Quartz,* December 29, 2014, https://qz.com/318499/warby-parker-proves-customers-dont-have-to-care-about-your-social-mission/ (accessed February 14, 2016); www.warbyparker.com.

Corporate Social Responsibility and the Triple Bottom Line   CSR initiatives undertaken by companies are frequently directed at improving the company's "triple bottom line"—a reference to three types of performance metrics: *economic, social, environmental.* The goal is for a company to succeed simultaneously in all three dimensions.[15] The three dimensions of performance are often referred to in terms of the three pillars of "people, planet, and profit." The term *people* refers to the various social initiatives that make up CSR strategies, such as corporate giving and community involvement. *Planet* refers to a firm's ecological impact and environmental practices. The term *profit* has a broader meaning with respect to the triple bottom line than it does otherwise. It encompasses not only the profit a firm earns for its shareholders but also the economic impact the company has on society more generally. Triple-bottom-line (TBL) reporting is emerging as an increasingly important way for companies to make the results of their CSR strategies apparent to stakeholders.

What Do We Mean by Sustainability and Sustainable Business Practices?

The term *sustainability* is used in a variety of ways. In many firms, it is synonymous with corporate social responsibility; it is seen by some as a term that is gradually replacing CSR in the business lexicon. Indeed, sustainability reporting and TBL reporting are often one and the same. More often, however, the term takes on a more focused meaning, concerned with the relationship of a company to its *environment* and its use of *natural resources,* including land, water, air, minerals, and fossil fuels. Since corporations are the biggest users of finite natural resources, managing and maintaining these resources is critical for the long-term economic interests of corporations.

For some companies, this issue has direct and obvious implications for the continued viability of their business model and strategy. Pacific Gas and Electric has begun measuring the full carbon footprint of its supply chain to become not only "greener" but also a more efficient energy producer.[16] For other companies, the connection is less direct, but all companies are part of a business ecosystem whose economic health depends on the availability of natural resources. In response, most major companies have begun to change *how* they do business, emphasizing the use of **sustainable business practices**, defined as those capable of meeting the needs of the present without compromising the ability to meet the needs of the future.[17] Many have also begun to incorporate a consideration of environmental sustainability into their strategy-making activities.

Environmental sustainability strategies entail deliberate and concerted actions to operate businesses in a manner that protects and maybe even enhances natural resources and ecological support systems, guards against outcomes that will ultimately endanger the planet, and is therefore sustainable for centuries.[18] Sustainability initiatives undertaken by companies are directed at improving the company's triple bottom line—its performance on economic, environment, and social metrics.[19] Unilever, a diversified producer of processed foods, personal care, and home cleaning products, is among the most committed corporations pursuing environmentally sustainable business practices. The company tracks 11 sustainable agricultural indicators in its processed-foods business and has launched a variety of programs to improve the environmental performance of its suppliers. Examples of such programs include special low-rate financing for tomato suppliers choosing to switch to water-conserving irrigation systems and training programs in India

> **CORE CONCEPT**
>
> **Sustainable business practices** are those that meet the needs of the present without compromising the ability to meet the needs of the future.

> **CORE CONCEPT**
>
> **Environmental sustainability** involves deliberate actions to protect the environment, provide for the longevity of natural resources, maintain ecological support systems for future generations, and guard against the ultimate endangerment of the planet.

that have allowed contract cucumber growers to reduce pesticide use by 90 percent, while improving yields by 78 percent.

Unilever has also reengineered many internal processes to improve the company's overall performance on sustainability measures. For example, the company's factories have reduced water usage by 50 percent and manufacturing waste by 14 percent through the implementation of sustainability initiatives. Unilever has also redesigned packaging for many of its products to conserve natural resources and reduce the volume of consumer waste. The company's Suave shampoo bottles in the United States were reshaped to save almost 150 tons of plastic resin per year, which is the equivalent of 15 million fewer empty bottles. As the producer of Lipton Tea, Unilever is the world's largest purchaser of tea leaves; the company has committed to sourcing all of its tea from Rainforest Alliance Certified farms by 2015, due to Unilever's comprehensive triple-bottom-line approach toward sustainable farm management. Because 40 percent of Unilever's sales are made to consumers in developing countries, the company also is committed to addressing societal needs of consumers in those countries. Examples of the company's social performance include free laundries in poor neighborhoods in developing countries, startup assistance for women-owned micro businesses in India, and free drinking water provided to villages in Ghana.

Sometimes cost savings and improved profitability are drivers of corporate sustainability strategies. Nike's sustainability initiatives have reduced energy consumption by 24 percent, emissions by 21 percent, water consumption by 13 percent, waste by 35 percent, and chemical usage by 20 percent between 2010 and 2015. Procter & Gamble's Swiffer cleaning system, one of the company's best-selling products, was developed as a sustainable product; not only does the Swiffer system have an earth-friendly design, but it also outperforms less ecologically friendly alternatives. Although most consumers probably aren't aware that the Swiffer mop reduces demands on municipal water sources, saves electricity that would be needed to heat water, and does not add to the amount of detergent making its way into waterways and waste treatment facilities, they are attracted to purchasing Swiffer mops because they prefer Swiffer's disposable cleaning sheets to filling and refilling a mop bucket and wringing out a wet mop until the floor is clean.

Crafting Corporate Social Responsibility and Sustainability Strategies

While striving to be socially responsible and to engage in environmentally sustainable business practices, there's plenty of room for every company to make its own statement about what charitable contributions to make, what kinds of community service projects to emphasize, what environmental actions to support, how to make the company a good place to work, where and how workforce diversity fits into the picture, and what else it will do to support worthy causes and projects that benefit society. A company may choose to focus its social responsibility strategy on generic social issues, but social responsibility strategies linked to its customer value proposition or key value chain activities may also help build competitive advantage.[20]

Ford's sustainability strategy for reducing carbon emissions has contributed to competitive advantage and produced environmental benefits. Its Ford Fusion hybrid is among the least polluting automobiles on the road and ranks first among hybrid cars in terms of fuel economy and cabin size. The development of hybrid models like the Fusion has helped Ford gain the loyalty of fuel-conscious buyers and given the company a new green image. Green Mountain Coffee Roasters' commitment to protect the welfare of coffee growers and their families (in particular, making sure they receive a fair price) also meets its customers' wants and needs. In its dealings with suppliers at small farmer cooperatives in Peru, Mexico, and Sumatra, Green Mountain pays fair trade prices for coffee beans. Green Mountain also purchases about 29 percent of its coffee directly from farmers so as to cut out intermediaries and see that farmers realize a higher price for their efforts. The consumers of Green Mountain coffee are aware of these efforts and purchase the company's products, in part, to encourage such practices.

> CSR strategies that have the effect of both providing valuable social benefits and fulfilling customer needs in a superior fashion can lead to competitive advantage. Corporate social agendas that address generic social issues may help boost a company's reputation but are unlikely to improve its competitive strength in the marketplace.

The Business Case for Socially Responsible Behavior

The moral case for why businesses should act in a manner that benefits all of the company's stakeholders—not just shareholders—boils down to "It's the right thing to do." In today's social climate, most business leaders can be expected to acknowledge that socially responsible actions are important and that businesses have a duty to be good corporate citizens. But there is a complementary school of thought that business operates on the basis of an implied social contract with the members of society. According to this contract, society grants a business the right to conduct its business affairs and agrees not to unreasonably restrain its pursuit of a fair profit for the goods or services it sells. In return for this "license to operate," a business is obligated to act as a responsible citizen, do its fair share to promote the general welfare, and avoid doing any harm. Such a view clearly puts a moral burden on a company to operate honorably, provide good working conditions to employees, be a good environmental steward, and display good corporate citizenship.

Whatever the moral arguments for socially responsible business behavior and environmentally sustainable business practices, there are definitely good business reasons why companies should devote time and resources to social responsibility initiatives, environmental sustainability, and good corporate citizenship:

- *Such actions can lead to increased buyer patronage.* A strong, visible social responsibility strategy gives a company an edge in differentiating itself from rivals and in appealing to those consumers who prefer to do business with companies that are good corporate citizens. Whole Foods Market, TOMS, Green Mountain Coffee Roasters, and Patagonia have definitely expanded their customer bases because of their visible and well-publicized activities as socially conscious companies.

- *A strong commitment to socially responsible behavior reduces the risk of reputation-damaging incidents.* Companies that place little importance on operating in a socially responsible manner are more prone to scandal and embarrassment. Consumer, environmental, and human rights activist groups are quick to criticize businesses whose behavior they consider to be out of line, and they are adept at getting their message into the media and onto the Internet. For many years, Nike received stinging criticism for not policing sweatshop conditions in the Asian factories that produced Nike footwear, causing Nike co-founder and former CEO Phil Knight to observe, "Nike has become synonymous with slave wages, forced overtime, and arbitrary abuse."[21] Nike began an extensive effort to monitor conditions in the 800 factories of the contract manufacturers that produced Nike shoes. As Knight said,

"Good shoes come from good factories and good factories have good labor relations." Nonetheless, Nike has continually been plagued by complaints from human rights activists that its monitoring procedures are flawed and that it is not doing enough to correct the plight of factory workers.

- *Socially responsible actions and sustainable business practices can lower costs and enhance employee recruiting and workforce retention.* Companies with deservedly good reputations for contributing time and money to the betterment of society are better able to attract and retain employees compared to companies with tarnished reputations. Some employees just feel better about working for a company committed to improving society.[22] This can contribute to lower turnover and better worker productivity. Other direct and indirect economic benefits include lower costs for staff recruitment and training. For example, Starbucks is said to enjoy much lower rates of employee turnover because of its full benefits package for both full-time and part-time employees, management efforts to make Starbucks a great place to work, and the company's socially responsible practices. When a U.S. manufacturer of recycled paper, taking eco-efficiency to heart, discovered how to increase its fiber recovery rate, it saved the equivalent of 20,000 tons of waste paper—a factor that helped the company become the industry's lowest-cost producer. By helping two-thirds of its employees stop smoking and investing in a number of wellness programs for employees, Johnson & Johnson has saved $250 million on its health care costs over a 10-year period.[23]

- *Opportunities for revenue enhancement may also come from CSR and environmental sustainability strategies.* The drive for sustainability and social responsibility can spur innovative efforts that in turn lead to new products and opportunities for revenue enhancement. Electric cars such as the BMW i3 and the Nissan Leaf are one example. In many cases, the revenue opportunities are tied to a company's core products. PepsiCo and Coca-Cola, for example, have expanded into the juice business to offer a healthier alternative to their carbonated beverages. In other cases, revenue enhancement opportunities come from innovative ways to reduce waste and use the by-products of a company's production. Staples has become one of the largest non-utility corporate producers of renewable energy in the United States due to its installation of solar power panels in all of its outlets (and the sale of what it does not consume in renewable energy credit markets).

- *Well-conceived social responsibility strategies work to the advantage of shareholders.* A two-year study of leading companies found that improving environmental compliance and developing environmentally friendly products can enhance earnings per share, profitability, and the likelihood of winning contracts. The stock prices of companies that rate high on social and environmental performance criteria have been found to perform 35 to 45 percent better than the average of the 2,500 companies comprising the Dow Jones Global Index.[24] A review of some 135 studies indicated there is a positive, but small, correlation between good corporate behavior and good financial performance; only 2 percent of the studies showed that dedicating corporate resources to social responsibility harmed the interests of shareholders.[25]

In sum, companies that take social responsibility seriously can improve their business reputations and operational efficiency while also reducing their risk exposure and encouraging loyalty and innovation. Overall, companies that take special pains to protect the environment (beyond what is required by law), are active in community affairs, and are generous supporters of charitable causes and projects that benefit society are more likely to be seen as good investments and as good companies to work for or do business with. Shareholders are likely to view the business case for social responsibility as a strong one, even though they certainly have a right to be concerned about whether the time and money their company spends to carry out its social responsibility strategy outweigh the benefits and reduce the bottom line by an unjustified amount.

KEY POINTS

1. Business ethics concerns the application of ethical principles and standards to the actions and decisions of business organizations and the conduct of their personnel. Ethical principles in business are not materially different from ethical principles in general.

2. The three main drivers of unethical business behavior stand out:
    - Overzealous or obsessive pursuit of personal gain, wealth, and other selfish interests
    - Heavy pressures on company managers to meet or beat earnings targets
    - A company culture that puts profitability and good business performance ahead of ethical behavior

3. Business ethics failures can result in visible costs (fines, penalties, civil penalties arising from lawsuits, stock price declines), the internal administrative or "cleanup" costs, and intangible or less visible costs (customer defections, loss of reputation, higher turnover, harsher government regulations).

4. There are three schools of thought about ethical standards for companies with international operations:
    - According to the *school of ethical universalism,* the same standards of what is ethical and unethical resonate with peoples of most societies, regardless of local traditions and cultural norms; hence, common ethical standards can be used to judge the conduct of personnel at companies operating in a variety of international markets and cultural circumstances.
    - According to the *school of ethical relativism,* different societal cultures and customs have divergent values and standards of right and wrong; thus, what is ethical or unethical must be judged in the light of local customs and social mores and can vary from one culture or nation to another.
    - According to *integrative social contracts theory,* universal ethical principles or norms based on the collective views of multiple cultures and societies combine to form a "social contract" that all individuals in all situations have a duty to observe. Within the boundaries of this social contract, local cultures can specify other impermissible actions; however, universal ethical norms always take precedence over local ethical norms.

5. The term *corporate social responsibility* concerns a company's *duty* to operate in an honorable manner, provide good working conditions for employees, encourage workforce diversity, be a good steward of the environment, and support philanthropic endeavors in local communities in which it operates and in society at large. The particular combination of socially responsible endeavors a company elects to pursue defines its corporate social responsibility (CSR) strategy.

6. The triple bottom line refers to company performance in three realms: economic, social, environmental. Increasingly, companies are reporting their performance with respect to all three performance dimensions.

7. *Sustainability* is a term that is used variously, but most often, it concerns a firm's relationship to the environment and its use of natural resources. Environmentally sustainable

business practices are those capable of meeting the needs of the present without compromising the world's ability to meet future needs. A company's environmental sustainability strategy consists of its deliberate actions to protect the environment, provide for the longevity of natural resources, maintain ecological support systems for future generations, and guard against ultimate endangerment of the planet.

8. There are also solid reasons CSR and environmental sustainability strategies may be good business: they can be conducive to greater buyer patronage, reduce the risk of reputation-damaging incidents, lower costs and enhance employee recruitment and retention, and provide opportunities for revenue enhancement. Well-crafted CSR and environmental sustainability strategies are in the best long-term interest of shareholders for the reasons above and because they can avoid or preempt costly legal or regulatory actions.

ASSURANCE OF LEARNING EXERCISES

1. Dell is widely known as an ethical company and has recently committed itself to becoming a more environmentally sustainable business. After reviewing the Corporate Social Responsibility section of Dell's website (www.dell.com/learn/us/en/uscorp1/cr?~ck=mn), prepare a list of 10 specific policies and programs that help the company bring about social and environmental change while still remaining innovative and profitable.

   LO9-1, LO9-4

2. Prepare a one- to two-page analysis of a recent ethics scandal using your university library's resources. Your report should *(a)* discuss the conditions that gave rise to unethical business strategies and behavior and *(b)* provide an overview of the costs resulting from the company's business ethics failure.

   LO9-2, LO9-3

3. Based on the information provided in Concepts & Connections 9.2, explain how Warby Parker's CSR strategy has contributed to its success in the marketplace. How are the company's various stakeholder groups affected by its commitment to social responsibility? How would you evaluate its triple-bottom-line performance?

   connect
   LO9-4

4. Páramo was a Guardian Sustainable Business Award winner in 2016. The company's fabric technology and use of chemicals is discussed at https://www.theguardian.com/sustainable-business/2016/may/27/outdoor-clothing-paramo-toxic-pfc-greenpeace-fabric-technology. Describe how Páramo's business practices allowed it to become recognized for its bold moves. How do these initiatives help build competitive advantage?

   connect
   LO9-4

EXERCISES FOR SIMULATION PARTICIPANTS

1. Is your company's strategy ethical? Why or why not? Is there anything that your company has done or is now doing that could legitimately be considered as "shady" by your competitors?

   LO9-1

2. In what ways, if any, is your company exercising corporate social responsibility? What are the elements of your company's CSR strategy? What changes to this strategy would you suggest?

   LO9-4

3. If some shareholders complained that you and your co-managers have been spending too little or too much on corporate social responsibility, what would you tell them?

   LO9-3, LO9-4

4. Is your company striving to conduct its business in an environmentally sustainable manner? What specific *additional* actions could your company take that would make an even greater contribution to environmental sustainability?

   LO9-4

5. In what ways is your company's environmental sustainability strategy in the best long-term interest of shareholders? Does it contribute to your company's competitive advantage or profitability?

   LO9-4

ENDNOTES

1. James E. Post, Anne T. Lawrence, and James Weber, *Business and Society: Corporate Strategy, Public Policy, Ethics,* 10th ed. (New York: McGraw-Hill Irwin, 2002).

2. John F. Veiga, Timothy D. Golden, and Kathleen Dechant, "Why Managers Bend Company Rules," *Academy of Management Executive* 18, no. 2 (May 2004).

3. Jason M. Breslow, "Isn't This Illegal," *Frontline,* January 6, 2014, http://www.pbs.org/wgbh/pages/ frontline/business-economy-financial- crisis/to-catch-a-trader/isnt-this- illegal/ (accessed July 13, 2015).

4. Ronald R. Sims and Johannes Brinkmann, "Enron Ethics (Or: Culture Matters More Than Codes)," *Journal of Business Ethics* 45, no. 3 (July 2003).

5. Andrew Ross, "SEC Charges Diamond Foods with Accounting Fraud," *SFGate,* January 13, 2014, http://www.sfgate .com/business/bottomline/article/ SEC-charges-Diamond-Foods-with- accounting-fraud-5129129.php (accessed July 13, 2015).

6. Archie B. Carroll, "The Four Faces of Corporate Citizenship," *Business and Society Review* 100/101 (September 1998).

7. Mark S. Schwartz, "Universal Moral Values for Corporate Codes of Ethics," *Journal of Business Ethics* 59, no. 1 (June 2005).

8. Mark S. Schwartz, "A Code of Ethics for Corporate Codes of Ethics," *Journal of Business Ethics* 41, nos. 1–2 (November– December 2002).

9. T. L. Beauchamp and N. E. Bowie, *Ethical Theory and Business* (Upper Saddle River, NJ: Prentice Hall, 2001).

10. Thomas Donaldson and Thomas W. Dunfee, "Towards a Unified Conception of Business Ethics: Integrative Social Contracts Theory," *Academy of Management Review* 19, no. 2 (April 1994); Thomas Donaldson and Thomas W. Dunfee, *Ties That Bind: A Social Contracts Approach to Business Ethics* (Boston: Harvard Business School Press, 1999); Andrew Spicer, Thomas W. Dunfee, and Wendy J. Bailey, "Does National Context Matter in Ethical Decision Making? An Empirical Test of Integrative Social Contracts Theory,"

Academy of Management Journal 47, no. 4 (August 2004).

11. P. M. Nichols, "Outlawing Transnational Bribery Through the World Trade Organization," *Law and Policy in International Business* 28, no. 2 (1997).

12. Timothy M. Devinney, "Is the Socially Responsible Corporation a Myth? The Good, the Bad, and the Ugly of Corporate Social Responsibility," *Academy of Management Perspectives* 23, no. 2 (May 2009).

13. "General Mills' 2010 Corporate Social Responsibility Report Highlights New and Longstanding Achievements in the Areas of Health, Community, and Environment," CSRwire, April 15, 2010, www.csrwire.com/press_releases/29347- General-Mills-2010-Corporate-Social- Responsibility-report-now-available.html.

14. Arthur A. Thompson and Amit J. Shah, "Starbucks' Strategy and Internal Initiatives to Return to Profitable Growth," *Crafting & Executing Strategy: The Quest for Competitive Advantage,* 18th ed. (New York: McGraw-Hill Irwin, 2012).

15. Gerald I. J. M. Zwetsloot and Marcel N. A. van Marrewijk, "From Quality to Sustainability," *Journal of Business Ethics* 55 (December 2004), pp. 79–82.

16. Tilde Herrera, "PG&E Claims Industry First with Supply Chain Footprint Project," *GreenBiz.com ,* June 30, 2010, www.greenbiz.com/news/2010/06/30/ pge-claims-industry-first-supply-chain- carbon-footprint-project.

17. This definition is based on the Brundt- land Commission's report, which described sustainable development in a like manner: United Nations General Assembly, "Report of the World Commission on Environment and Development: Our Common Future," 1987, www.un-documents.net/wced-ocf.htm, transmitted to the General Assembly as an annex to document A/42/427— "Development and International Co- operation: Environment" (accessed February 15, 2009).

18. Robert Goodland, "The Concept of Environmental Sustainability," *Annual Review of Ecology and Systematics* 26 (1995); J. G. Speth, *The Bridge at the*

End of the World: Capitalism, the Environment, and Crossing from Crisis to Sustainability (New Haven, CT: Yale University Press, 2008).

19. Gerald I. J. M. Zwetsloot and Marcel N. A. van Marrewijk, "From Quality to Sustainability," *Journal of Business Ethics* 55 (December 2004); John B. Elkington, *Cannibals with Forks: The Triple Bottom Line of 21st Century Business* (Oxford: Capstone Publishing, 1997).

20. Michael E. Porter and Mark R. Kramer, "Strategy & Society: The Link Between Competitive Advantage and Corporate Social Responsibility," *Harvard Business Review* 84, no. 12 (December 2006).

21. Tom McCawley, "Racing to Improve Its Reputation: Nike Has Fought to Shed Its Image as an Exploiter of Third-World Labor Yet It Is Still a Target of Activists," *Financial Times,* December 2000.

22. N. Craig Smith, "Corporate Responsibility: Whether and How," *California Management Review* 45, no. 4 (Summer 2003), p. 63; see also "Findings of a Survey on Global Corporate Leadership," World Economic Forum and The Prince of Wales International Business Leaders Forum (2003), p. 14–16.

23. Michael E. Porter and Mark Kramer, "Creating Shared Value," *Harvard Business Review* 89, nos. 1–2 (January–February 2011).

24. James C. Collins and Jerry I. Porras, *Built to Last: Successful Habits of Visionary Companies,* 3rd ed. (London: Harper- Business, 2002).

25. Joshua D. Margolis and Hillary A. Elfenbein, "Doing Well by Doing Good: Don't Count on It," *Harvard Business Review* 86, no. 1 (January 2008); Lee E. Preston and Douglas P. O'Bannon, "The Corporate Social-Financial Performance Relationship," *Business and Society* 36, no. 4 (December 1997); Ronald M. Roman, Sefa Hayibor, and Bradley R. Agle, "The Relationship Between Social and Financial Performance: Repainting a Portrait," *Business and Society* 38, no. 1 (March 1999); Joshua D. Margolis and James P. Walsh, *People and Profits* (Mahwah, NJ: Lawrence Erlbaum, 2001).

Superior Strategy Execution—Another Path to Competitive Advantage

LEARNING OBJECTIVES

After reading this chapter, you should be able to:

LO10-1 Recognize what managers must do to build an organization capable of good strategy execution.

LO10-2 Explain why resource allocation should always be based on strategic priorities.

LO10-3 Understand why policies and procedures should be designed to facilitate good strategy execution.

LO10-4 Understand how process management programs that drive continuous improvement help an organization achieve operating excellence.

LO10-5 Recognize the role of information and operating systems in enabling company personnel to carry out their strategic roles proficiently.

LO10-6 Explain how and why the use of well-designed incentives and rewards can be management's single most powerful tool for promoting operating excellence.

LO10-7 Explain how and why a company's culture can aid the drive for proficient strategy execution.

LO10-8 Recognize what constitutes effective managerial leadership in achieving superior strategy execution.

Once managers have decided on a strategy, the emphasis turns to converting it into actions and good results. Putting the strategy into place and getting the organization to execute it well call for different sets of managerial skills. Whereas crafting strategy is largely a market-driven and resource-driven activity, strategy implementation is an operations-driven activity primarily involving the management of people and business processes. Successful strategy execution depends on management's ability to direct organizational change and do a good job of allocating resources, building and strengthening competitive capabilities, instituting strategy-supportive policies, improving processes and systems, motivating and rewarding people, creating and nurturing a strategy-supportive culture, and consistently meeting or beating performance targets. While an organization's chief executive officer and other senior managers are ultimately responsible for ensuring that the strategy is executed successfully, it is middle and lower-level managers who must see to it that frontline employees and work groups competently perform the strategy-critical activities that allow companywide performance targets to be met. *Hence, strategy execution requires every manager to think through the answer to the question "What does my area have to do to implement its part of the strategic plan, and what should I do to get these things accomplished effectively and efficiently?"*

> **CORE CONCEPT**
>
> Good strategy execution requires a *team effort*. All managers have strategy execution responsibility in their areas of authority, and all employees are active participants in the strategy execution.

The Principal Managerial Components of Strategy Execution

Executing strategy entails figuring out the specific techniques, actions, and behaviors that are needed to get things done and deliver results. The exact items that need to be placed on management's action agenda always have to be customized to fit the particulars of a company's situation. The hot buttons for successfully executing a low-cost provider strategy are different from those in executing a differentiation strategy. Implementing a new strategy for a struggling company in the midst of a financial crisis is different from improving strategy execution in a company where the execution is already pretty good. While there's no definitive managerial recipe for successful strategy execution that cuts across all company situations and all types of strategies, certain managerial bases have to be covered no matter what the circumstances. Eight managerial tasks crop up repeatedly in company efforts to execute strategy (see Figure 10.1).

1. Building an organization with the capabilities, people, and structure needed to execute the strategy successfully
2. Allocating ample resources to strategy-critical activities
3. Ensuring that policies and procedures facilitate rather than impede effective strategy execution
4. Adopting process management programs that drive continuous improvement in how strategy execution activities are performed
5. Installing information and operating systems that enable company personnel to perform essential activities
6. Tying rewards directly to the achievement of performance objectives

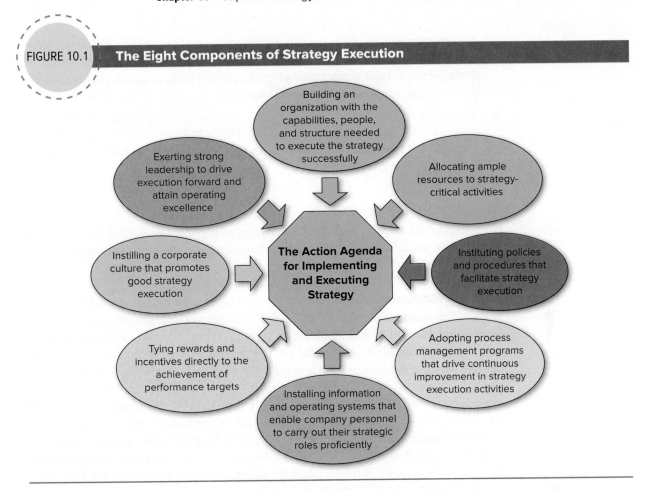

FIGURE 10.1   The Eight Components of Strategy Execution

7. Fostering a corporate culture that promotes good strategy execution

8. Exerting the internal leadership needed to propel implementation forward

How well managers perform these eight tasks has a decisive impact on whether the outcome is a spectacular success, a colossal failure, or something in between. In the remainder of this chapter, we will discuss what is involved in performing the eight key managerial tasks that shape the process of implementing and executing strategy.

Building an Organization Capable of Good Strategy Execution: Three Key Actions

LO10-1   Recognize what managers must do to build an organization capable of good strategy execution.

Proficient strategy execution depends heavily on competent personnel, better-than-adequate competitive capabilities, and an effective internal organization. Building a capable organization is thus always a top priority in strategy execution. Three types of organization building actions are paramount:

1. *Staffing the organization*—putting together a strong management team, and recruiting and retaining employees with the needed experience, technical skills, and intellectual capital

2. *Acquiring, developing, and strengthening strategy-supportive resources and capabilities*—accumulating the required resources, developing proficiencies in performing strategy-critical value chain activities, and updating them to match changing market conditions and customer expectations

3. *Structuring the organization and work effort*—organizing value chain activities and business processes, establishing lines of authority and reporting relationships, and deciding how much decision-making authority to push down to lower-level managers and frontline employees

Staffing the Organization

No company can hope to perform the activities required for successful strategy execution without attracting and retaining talented managers and employees with suitable skills and intellectual capital.

Building Managerial Talent Assembling a capable management team is a cornerstone of the organization-building task.[1] While company circumstances sometimes call for different mixes of backgrounds, experiences, management styles, and know-how, *the most important consideration is to fill key managerial slots with people who are good at figuring out what needs to be done and skilled in "making it happen" and delivering good results.*[2] Without a capable, results-oriented management team, the implementation-execution process ends up being hampered by missed deadlines, misdirected or wasteful efforts, and/or managerial ineptness.[3] Weak executives are serious impediments to getting optimal results because they are unable to differentiate between ideas that have merit and those that are misguided. In contrast, managers with strong strategy-implementing capabilities have a talent for asking tough, incisive questions. They know enough about the details of the business to be able to challenge and ensure the soundness of the approaches of the people around them, and they can discern whether the resources people are asking for make sense strategically. They are good at getting things done through others, typically by making sure they have the right people under them and that these people are put in the right jobs. They consistently follow through on issues and do not let important details slip through the cracks.

Sometimes a company's existing management team is suitable; at other times, it may need to be strengthened or expanded by promoting qualified people from within or by bringing in outsiders. The overriding aim in building a management team should be to assemble a critical mass of talented managers who can function as agents of change and further the cause of first-rate strategy execution. When a first-rate manager enjoys the help and support of other first-rate managers, it's possible to create a managerial whole that is greater than the sum of individual efforts: talented managers who work well together as a team can produce organizational results that are dramatically better than what one- or two-star managers acting individually can achieve.[4]

Recruiting and Retaining a Capable Workforce Assembling a capable management team is not enough. Staffing the organization with the right kinds of people must go much deeper than managerial jobs in order for value chain activities to be performed competently. *The quality of an organization's people is always an essential ingredient of successful strategy execution—knowledgeable, engaged employees are a* *company's best source of creative ideas for the nuts-and-bolts operating improvements that lead to operating excellence.* Companies such as Mercedes-Benz, Google, Boston Consulting Group, and Procter & Gamble make a concerted effort to recruit the best and brightest people they can find and then retain them with excellent compensation packages, opportunities for rapid advancement and professional growth, and challenging and interesting assignments. Having a pool of "A players" with strong skill sets and lots of brainpower is essential to their business. Facebook makes a point of hiring the very brightest and most talented programmers it can find and motivating them with both good monetary incentives and the challenge of working on cutting-edge technology projects. The leading global accounting firms screen candidates not only on the basis of their accounting expertise but also on whether they possess the people skills needed to relate well with clients and colleagues. Southwest Airlines goes to considerable lengths to hire people who can have fun and be fun on the job; it uses special interviewing and screening methods to gauge whether applicants for customer-contact jobs have outgoing personality traits that match its strategy of creating a high-spirited, fun-loving, in-flight atmosphere for passengers. Southwest Airlines is so selective that only about 3 percent of the people who apply are offered jobs.

The tactics listed here are common among companies dedicated to staffing jobs with the best people they can find:

1. Putting forth considerable effort in screening and evaluating job applicants—selecting only those with suitable skill sets, energy, initiative, judgment, aptitudes for learning, and adaptability to the company's culture

2. Investing in training programs that continue throughout employees' careers

3. Providing promising employees with challenging, interesting, and skill-stretching assignments

4. Rotating people through jobs that span functional and geographic boundaries

5. Striving to retain talented, high-performing employees via promotions, salary increases, performance bonuses, stock options and equity ownership, fringe benefit packages, and other perks

6. Coaching average performers to improve their skills and capabilities, while weeding out underperformers and benchwarmers

Acquiring, Developing, and Strengthening Key Resources and Capabilities

High among the organization-building priorities in the strategy execution process is the need to build and strengthen competitively valuable resources and capabilities. As explained in Chapter 1, a company's ability to perform value-creating activities and realize its strategic objectives depends upon its resources and capabilities. In the course of crafting strategy, it is important for managers to identify the resources and capabilities that will enable the firm's strategy to succeed. Good strategy execution requires putting those resources and capabilities into place, refreshing and strengthening them as needed, and then modifying them as market conditions evolve. "Fast fashion" retailer Zara has developed valuable resources and capabilities that allow it to execute its strategy with great proficiency; see Concepts & Connections 10.1.

Concepts & Connections 10.1

ZARA'S STRATEGY EXECUTION CAPABILITIES

Zara, a member of Inditex Group, is a "fast fashion" retailer. As soon as designs are seen in high-end fashion houses such as Prada, Zara's design team sets to work altering the clothing designs so that they can produce high fashion at mass-retailing prices. Zara's strategy is clever but by no means unique. The company's competitive advantage is in strategy execution. Every step of Zara's value chain execution is geared toward putting fashionable clothes in stores quickly, realizing high turnover, and strategically driving traffic.

The first key lever is a quick production process. Zara's design team uses inspiration from high fashion and nearly real-time feedback from stores to create up-to-the-minute pieces. Manufacturing largely occurs in factories close to headquarters in Spain, northern Africa, and Turkey, all areas considered to have a high cost of labor. Placing the factories strategically close allows for more flexibility and greater responsiveness to market needs, thereby outweighing the additional labor costs. The entire production process, from design to arrival at stores, takes only two weeks, while other retailers take six months. While traditional retailers commit up to 80 percent of their lines by the start of the season, Zara commits only 50 to 60 percent, meaning that up to half of the merchandise to hit stores is designed and manufactured during the season. Zara purposefully manufactures in small lot sizes to avoid discounting later on and also to encourage impulse shopping, as a particular item could be gone in a few days. From start to finish, Zara has engineered its production process to maximize turnover and turnaround time, creating a true advantage in this step of strategy execution.

Zara also excels at driving traffic to stores. First, the small lot sizes and frequent shipments (up to twice a week per store) drive customers to visit often and purchase quickly. Zara shoppers average 17 visits per year, versus 4 to 5 for The Gap. On average, items stay in a Zara store only 11 days. Second, Zara spends no money on advertising, but it occupies some of the most expensive retail space in town, always near the high-fashion houses it imitates. Proximity reinforces the high-fashion association, while the busy street drives significant foot traffic.

©jordi2r/123RF

Overall, Zara has managed to create competitive advantage in every level of strategy execution by tightly aligning design, production, advertising, and real estate with the overall strategy of fast fashion: extremely fast and extremely flexible.

Note: Developed with Sara Paccamonti.

Sources: Suzy Hansen, "How Zara Grew into the World's Largest Fashion Retailer," *New York Times,* November 9, 2012, www.nytimes.com/2012/11/11/magazine/how-zara-grew-into-the-worlds-largest-fashion-retailer.html?pagewanted=all (accessed February 5, 2014); and Seth Stevenson, "Polka Dots Are In? Polka Dots It Is!" *Slate,* June 21, 2012, www.slate.com/articles/arts/operations/2012/06/zara_s_fast_fashion_how_the_company_gets_new_styles_to_stores_so_quickly_.html (accessed February 5, 2014).

Three Approaches to Building and Strengthening Capabilities Building core competencies and competitive capabilities is a time-consuming, managerially challenging exercise. But with deliberate effort and continued practice, it is possible for a firm to become proficient at capability building. Indeed, by making capability-building activities a routine part of their strategy execution, some firms are able to develop *dynamic capabilities* that assist them in managing resource and capability change, as discussed in Chapter 4. The most common approaches to capability building include (1) internal development, (2) acquiring capabilities through mergers and acquisitions, and (3) accessing capabilities via collaborative partnerships.[5]

> Building new competencies and capabilities is a multistage process that occurs over a period of months and years. It is not something that is accomplished overnight.

Developing Capabilities Internally Capabilities develop incrementally along an evolutionary path as organizations search for solutions to their problems. The process is complex because capabilities are the product of bundles of skills and know-how. In addition, capabilities tend to require the combined efforts of teams that are often cross-functional in nature, spanning a variety of departments and locations. For instance, the capability of speeding new products to market involves the collaborative efforts of personnel in R&D, engineering and design, purchasing, production, marketing, and distribution.

Because the process is incremental, the first step is to develop the *ability* to do something, however imperfectly or inefficiently. This entails selecting people with the requisite skills and experience, upgrading or expanding individual abilities as needed, and then molding the efforts of individuals into a collaborative effort to create an organizational ability. At this stage, progress can be fitful since it depends on experimentation, active search for alternative solutions, and learning through trial and error.[6] As experience grows and company personnel learn how to perform the activities consistently well and at an acceptable cost, the ability evolves into a tried-and-true competence.

It is generally much easier and less time-consuming to update and remodel a company's existing capabilities as external conditions and company strategy change than it is to create them from scratch. Maintaining capabilities in top form may simply require exercising them continually and fine-tuning them as necessary. Similarly, augmenting a capability may require less effort if it involves the recombination of well-established company capabilities and draws on existing company resources.[7] For example, Williams-Sonoma first developed the capability to expand sales beyond its brick-and-mortar location in 1970, when it launched a catalog that was sent to customers throughout the United States. The company extended its mail-order business with the acquisitions of Hold Everything, a garden products catalog, and Pottery Barn, and entered online retailing in 2000 when it launched e-commerce sites for Pottery Barn and Williams-Sonoma. The ongoing renewal of these capabilities has allowed Williams-Sonoma to generate revenues of nearly $5 billion in 2016 and become the 13th-largest online retailer in the United States.

> A company's capabilities must be continually refreshed and renewed to remain aligned with changing customer expectations, altered competitive conditions, and new strategic initiatives.

Acquiring Capabilities Through Mergers and Acquisitions Sometimes a company can build and refresh its competencies by acquiring another company with attractive resources and capabilities.[8] An acquisition aimed at building a stronger portfolio of resources and capabilities can be every bit as valuable as an acquisition aimed at adding new products or services to the company's lineup of offerings. The advantage of this mode of acquiring new capabilities is primarily one of speed, since developing new capabilities internally can take many years. Capabilities-motivated acquisitions are essential (1) when a market opportunity can slip by faster than a needed capability can be created internally and (2) when industry conditions, technology, or competitors are moving at such a rapid clip that time is of the essence.

At the same time, acquiring capabilities in this way is not without difficulty. Capabilities tend to involve tacit knowledge and complex routines that cannot be transferred readily from one organizational unit to another. This may limit the extent to which the new capability can be utilized by the acquiring organization. For example, since 2005 Facebook has spent more than $23 billion to acquire producers of augmented reality, voice recognition, image filters, language translation, face recognition, and other technologies to add capabilities that might enhance the social media experience. Transferring and integrating these capabilities to other parts of the Facebook organization prove easier said than done, however, as many technology acquisitions fail to yield the hoped-for benefits.

Accessing Capabilities Through Collaborative Partnerships Another method of acquiring capabilities from an external source is to access them via collaborative partnerships with suppliers, competitors, or other companies having the cutting-edge expertise. There are three basic ways to pursue this course of action:

1. *Outsource the function or activity requiring new capabilities to an outside provider.* As discussed in Chapter 6, outsourcing has the advantage of conserving resources so the firm can focus its energies on those activities most central to its strategy. It may be a good choice for firms that are too small and resource-constrained to execute all the parts of their strategy internally.

2. *Collaborate with a firm that has complementary resources and capabilities in a joint venture, strategic alliance, or other type of partnership to achieve a shared strategic objective.* Since the success of the venture will depend on how well the partners work together, potential partners should be selected as much for their management style, culture, and goals as for their resources and capabilities.

3. *Engage in a collaborative partnership for the purpose of learning how the partner performs activities, internalizing its methods and thereby acquiring its capabilities.* This may be a viable method when each partner has something to learn from the other. But in other cases, it involves an abuse of trust and puts the cooperative venture at risk.

Matching Organizational Structure to the Strategy

Building an organization capable of good strategy execution also relies on an organizational structure that lays out lines of authority and reporting relationships in a manner that supports the company's key strategic initiatives. The best approach to settling on an organizational structure is to first consider the key value chain activities that deliver value to the customer. In any business, some activities in the value chain are always more critical than others. For instance, hotel/motel enterprises have to be good at fast check-in/check-out, housekeeping, food service, and creating a pleasant ambience. In specialty chemicals, the strategy-critical activities include R&D, product innovation, getting new products onto the market quickly, effective marketing, and expertise in assisting customers. It is important for management to build its organization structure around proficient performance of these activities, making them the centerpieces or main building blocks on the organization chart.

The rationale for making strategy-critical activities the main building blocks in structuring a business is compelling: If activities crucial to strategic success are to have the resources, decision-making influence, and organizational impact they need, they have to be centerpieces in the organizational scheme. In addition, a new or changed strategy is likely to entail new or different key activities or capabilities and therefore to require a new or different organizational structure.[9] Attempting to carry out a new strategy with an old organizational structure is usually unwise.

Types of Organizational Structures   It is common for companies engaged in a single line of business to utilize a **functional (or departmental) organizational structure** that organizes strategy-critical activities into distinct *functional, product, geographic, process,* or *customer* groups. For instance, a technical instruments manufacturer may be organized around research and development, engineering, supply chain management, assembly, quality control, marketing technical services, and corporate administration. A company with operations scattered across a large geographic area or many countries may organize activities and reporting relationships by geography.

Many diversified companies utilize a **multidivisional (or divisional) organizational structure** consisting of a set of operating divisions organized along market, customer, product, or geographic lines, along with a central corporate headquarters, which monitors divisional activities, allocates resources, and exercises overall control. A multidivisional structure is appropriate for a diversified building materials company that designs, produces, and markets cabinets, plumbing fixtures, windows, and paints and stains. The divisional structure organizes all of the value chain activities involved with making each type of home construction product available to home builders and do-it-yourselfers into a common division and makes each division an independent profit center. Therefore the paint division, plumbing products division, cabinets division, and windows division all operate separately and report to a central corporate headquarters.

Matrix organizational structures is a combination structure in which the organization is organized along two or more dimensions at once (e.g., business, geographic region, value chain function) for the purpose of enhancing cross-unit communication, collaboration, and coordination. In essence, it overlays one type of structure onto another type. Matrix structures are managed through multiple reporting relationships, so a middle manager may report to several bosses. For example, in a matrix structure based on product line, region, and function, a sales manager for plastic containers in Georgia might report to the manager of the plastics division, the head of the southeast sales region, and the head of marketing.

Organizational Structure and Authority in Decision Making   Responsibility for results of decisions made throughout the organization ultimately lies with managers at the top of the organizational structure, but in practice, lower-level managers might possess a great deal of authority in decision making. Companies vary in the degree of authority delegated to managers of each organization unit and how much decision-making latitude is given to individual employees in performing their jobs. The two extremes are to *centralize decision making* at the top (the CEO and a few close lieutenants) or to *decentralize decision making* by giving managers and employees considerable decision-making latitude in their areas of responsibility. The two approaches are based on sharply different underlying principles and beliefs, with each having its pros and cons. *In a highly decentralized organization, decision-making authority is pushed* *down to the lowest organizational level capable of making timely, informed, competent decisions.* The objective is to put adequate decision-making authority in the hands of the people closest to and most familiar with the situation and train them to weigh all the factors and exercise good judgment. Decentralized decision making means that the managers of each organizational unit are delegated lead responsibility for deciding how best to execute strategy.

The case for empowering down-the-line managers and employees to make decisions related to daily operations and executing the strategy is based on the belief that a company that draws on the combined intellectual capital of all its employees can outperform a command-and-control company.[10] Decentralized decision making means, for example, employees may be empowered to do what it takes to please customers and increase sales. At TJX, parent company of T. J. Maxx, Marshalls, and four other fashion and home decor retail store chains, buyers are encouraged to be intelligent risk takers in deciding what items to purchase for TJX stores—there is the story of a buyer for a seasonal product category who cut her own budget to have dollars allocated to other categories where sales were expected to be stronger. Another example of employee empowerment involves an employee at Starbucks who enthusiastically offered free coffee to waiting customers when a store's computerized cash register system went offline.

Pushing decision-making authority deep down into the organization structure and empowering employees presents its own organizing challenge: *how to exercise adequate control over the actions of empowered employees so that the business is not put at risk at the same time that the benefits of empowerment are realized.* Maintaining adequate organizational control over empowered employees is generally accomplished by placing limits on the authority that empowered personnel can exercise, holding people accountable for their decisions, instituting compensation incentives that reward people for doing their jobs in a manner that contributes to good company performance, and creating a corporate culture where there's strong peer pressure on individuals to act responsibly.

In a highly centralized organization structure, top executives retain authority for most strategic and operating decisions and keep a tight rein on business-unit heads, department heads, and the managers of key operating units; comparatively little discretionary authority is granted to frontline supervisors and rank-and-file employees. The command-and-control paradigm of centralized structures is based on the underlying assumptions that frontline personnel have neither the time nor the inclination to direct and properly control the work they are performing and that they lack the knowledge and judgment to make wise decisions about how best to do it.

The big advantage of an authoritarian structure is that it is easy to know who is accountable when things do not go well. But there are some serious disadvantages. Hierarchical command-and-control structures make an organization sluggish in responding to changing conditions because of the time it takes for the review/approval process to run up all the layers of the management bureaucracy. Also, centralized decision making is often impractical—the larger the company and the more scattered its operations, the more that decision-making authority has to be delegated to managers closer to the scene of the action.

Facilitating Collaboration with External Partners and Strategic Allies

Strategic alliances, outsourcing arrangements, joint ventures, and cooperative partnerships can contribute little of value without active management of the relationship. Building organizational bridges with external partners and strategic allies can be accomplished by appointing "relationship managers" with responsibility for fostering the success of strategic partnerships. Relationship managers have many roles and functions: getting the right people together, promoting good rapport, facilitating the flow of information, nurturing interpersonal communication and cooperation, and ensuring effective coordination.[11] Communication and coordination are particularly important since information sharing is required to make the relationship work and to address conflicts, trouble spots, and changing situations.

> **CORE CONCEPT**
>
> A **network structure** is the arrangement linking a number of independent organizations involved in some common undertaking.

> The ultimate goal of decentralized decision making is to put decision-making authority in the hands of those persons or teams closest to and most knowledgeable about the situation.

Communication and coordination are also aided by the adoption of a **network structure** that links independent organizations involved in cooperative arrangements to achieve some common undertaking. A well-managed network structure typically includes one firm in a more central role, with the responsibility of ensuring that the right partners are included and the activities across the network are coordinated. The high-end Italian motorcycle company Ducati operates in this manner, assembling its motorcycles from parts obtained from a hand-picked, integrated network of parts suppliers.

Allocating Resources to Strategy-Critical Activities

LO10-2 Explain why resource allocation should always be based on strategic priorities.

Early in the process of implementing and executing a new or different strategy, top management must determine what funding is needed to execute new strategic initiatives, to bolster value-creating processes, and to strengthen the company's capabilities and competencies. This includes careful screening of requests for more people and new facilities and equipment, approving those that hold promise for making a contribution to strategy execution, and turning down those that do not. Should internal cash flows prove insufficient to fund the planned strategic initiatives, then management must raise additional funds through borrowing or selling additional shares of stock to willing investors.

A company's ability to marshal the resources needed to support new strategic initiatives has a major impact on the strategy execution process. Too little funding slows progress and impedes the efforts of organizational units to execute their pieces of the strategic plan proficiently. Too much funding wastes organizational resources and reduces financial performance. Both outcomes argue for managers to be deeply involved in reviewing budget proposals and directing the proper amounts of resources to strategy-critical organization units.

A change in strategy nearly always calls for budget reallocations and resource shifting. Previously important units having a lesser role in the new strategy may need downsizing. Units that now have a bigger strategic role may need more people, new equipment, additional facilities, and above-average increases in their operating budgets. Strategy implementers have to exercise their power to put enough resources behind new strategic initiatives to make things happen, and they have to make the tough decisions to kill projects and activities that are no longer justified.

Google's strong support of R&D activities helped it to grow to a $527 billion giant in just 18 years. In 2013, however, Google decided to kill its 20 percent time policy, which allowed its staff to work on side projects of their choice one day a week. While this side project program gave rise to many innovations, such as Gmail and AdSense (a big contributor to Google's revenues), it also meant that fewer resources were available to projects that were deemed closer to the core of Google's mission. In the years

> A company's strategic priorities must drive how capital allocations are made and the size of each unit's operating budgets.

since Google killed the 20 percent policy, the company has consistently topped *Fortune, Forbes,* and *Fast Company* magazine's "most innovative companies" list for ideas such as Google Chromebooks and its Waymo self-driving automobile project.

Instituting Strategy-Supportive Policies and Procedures

LO10-3   Understand why policies and procedures should be designed to facilitate good strategy execution.

A company's policies and procedures can either assist or become a barrier to good strategy execution. Anytime a company makes changes to its business strategy, managers are well advised to carefully review existing policies and procedures, and revise or discard those that are out of sync. Well-conceived policies and operating procedures act to facilitate organizational change and good strategy execution in three ways:

> Well-conceived policies and procedures aid strategy execution; out-of-sync ones are barriers to effective implementation.

1. *Policies and procedures help enforce needed consistency in how particular strategy-critical activities are performed.* Standardization and strict conformity are sometimes desirable components of good strategy execution. Eliminating significant differences in the operating practices of different plants, sales regions, or customer service centers helps a company deliver consistent product quality and service to customers.

2. *Policies and procedures support change programs by providing top-down guidance regarding how certain things now need to be done.* Asking people to alter established habits and procedures always upsets the internal order of things. It is normal for pockets of resistance to develop and for people to exhibit some degree of stress and anxiety about how the changes will affect them. Policies are a particularly useful way to counteract tendencies for some people to resist change—most people refrain from violating company policy or going against recommended practices and procedures without first gaining clearance or having strong justification.

3. *Well-conceived policies and procedures promote a work climate that facilitates good strategy execution.* Managers can use the policy-changing process as a powerful lever for changing the corporate culture in ways that produce a stronger fit with the new strategy.

McDonald's policy manual spells out detailed procedures that personnel in each McDonald's unit are expected to observe to ensure consistent quality across its 31,000 units. For example, "Cooks must turn, never flip, hamburgers. If they haven't been purchased, Big Macs must be discarded in 10 minutes after being cooked and French fries in 7 minutes." To get store personnel to dedicate themselves to outstanding customer service, Nordstrom has a policy of promoting only those people whose personnel records contain evidence of "heroic acts" to please customers, especially customers who may have made "unreasonable requests" that require special efforts.

One of the big policy-making issues concerns what activities need to be rigidly prescribed and what activities allow room for independent action on the part of empowered personnel. Few companies need thick policy manuals to prescribe exactly how daily operations are to be conducted. Too much policy can be confusing and erect obstacles to good strategy implementation. There is wisdom in a middle approach: *Prescribe enough policies to place boundaries on employees' actions; then empower them to act within these boundaries in whatever way they think makes sense.* Allowing company personnel to act anywhere between the "white lines" is especially appropriate when individual creativity and initiative are more essential to good strategy execution than standardization and strict conformity.

Striving for Continuous Improvement in Processes and Activities

LO10-4 Understand how process management programs that drive continuous improvement help an organization achieve operating excellence.

Company managers can significantly advance the cause of superior strategy execution by pushing organization units and company personnel to strive for continuous improvement in how value chain activities are performed. In aiming for operating excellence, many companies have come to rely on three potent management tools: business process reengineering, total quality management (TQM) programs, and Six Sigma quality control techniques. *Business process reengineering* involves pulling the pieces of strategy-critical activities out of different departments and unifying their performance in a single department or cross-functional work group.[12] When done properly, business process reengineering can produce dramatic operating benefits. Hallmark reengineered its process for developing new greeting cards, creating teams of mixed-occupation personnel (artists, writers, lithographers, merchandisers, and administrators) to work on a single holiday or greeting card theme. The reengineered process speeded development times for new lines of greeting cards by up to 24 months, was more cost-efficient, and increased customer satisfaction.[13]

Total quality management (TQM) is a philosophy of managing a set of business practices that emphasizes continuous improvement in all phases of operations, 100 percent accuracy in performing tasks, involvement and empowerment of employees at all levels, team-based work design, benchmarking, and total customer satisfaction.[14] While TQM concentrates on the production of quality goods and fully satisfying customer expectations, it achieves its biggest successes when it is extended to employee efforts in *all departments*—human resources, billing, R&D, engineering, accounting and records, and information systems. It involves reforming the corporate culture and shifting to a total quality/continuous improvement business philosophy that permeates every facet of the organization.[15] TQM doctrine preaches that there is no such thing as "good enough" and that everyone has a responsibility to participate in continuous improvement. TQM is thus a race without a finish. Success comes from making little steps forward each day, a process that the Japanese call *kaizen.*

Six Sigma quality control consists of a disciplined, statistics-based system aimed at producing not more than 3.4 defects per million iterations for any business process—from manufacturing to customer transactions.[16] The Six Sigma process of define, measure, analyze, improve, and control (DMAIC, pronounced *dee-may-ic*) is an improvement system for existing processes falling below specification. The Six Sigma DMADV (define, measure, analyze, design, and verify) methodology is used to develop *new* processes or products at Six Sigma quality levels.[17] DMADV is sometimes referred to as Design for Six Sigma (DFSS). The statistical thinking underlying Six Sigma is based on the following three principles: all work is a process, all processes have variability, and all processes create data that explain variability.[18]

Since the programs were first introduced, thousands of companies and nonprofit organizations around the world have used Six Sigma to promote operating excellence. In the first five years of its adoption, Six Sigma at Bank of America helped the bank reap about $2 billion in revenue gains and cost savings. General Electric (GE), one of the most successful companies implementing Six Sigma training and pursuing Six Sigma perfection across the company's entire operations, estimated benefits of some $10 billion during the first five years of implementation—its Lighting division, for example, cut invoice defects and disputes by 98 percent. Concepts & Connections 10.2 describes Charleston Area Medical Center's use of Six Sigma as a health care provider coping with the challenges facing the industry. The hospital implemented a program requiring doctors to type the prescription into a computer, which slashed the number of errors dramatically.

While Six Sigma programs often improve the efficiency of many operating activities and processes, evidence shows that Six Sigma programs can stifle innovation. The essence of Six Sigma is to reduce variability in processes, but creative processes, by nature, include quite a bit of variability. In many instances, breakthrough innovations occur only after thousands of ideas have been abandoned and promising ideas have gone through multiple iterations and extensive prototyping. Alphabet Executive Chairman of the Board Eric Schmidt has commented that the innovation process is "anti–Six Sigma" and applying Six Sigma principles to those performing creative work at Google would choke off innovation at the company.[19]

A blended approach to Six Sigma implementation that is gaining in popularity pursues incremental improvements in operating efficiency, while R&D and other processes that allow the company to develop new ways of offering value to customers are given more free rein. Managers of these *ambidextrous organizations* are adept at employing continuous improvement in operating processes but allowing R&D to operate under a set of rules that allows for the development of breakthrough innovations. Ciba Vision, a global leader in contact lenses, dramatically reduced operating expenses through the use of continuous improvement programs, while simultaneously and harmoniously developing new series of contact lens products that grew its revenues by 300 percent over a 10-year period.[20]

Concepts & Connections 10.2

CHARLESTON AREA MEDICAL CENTER'S SIX SIGMA PROGRAM

Established in 1972, Charleston Area Medical Center (CAMC) is West Virginia's largest health care provider in terms of beds, admissions, and revenues. In 2000, CAMC implemented a Six Sigma program to examine quality problems and standardize care processes. Performance improvement was important to CAMC's management for a variety of strategic reasons, including competitive positioning and cost control.

The United States has been evolving toward a pay-for-performance structure, which rewards hospitals for providing quality care. CAMC has utilized its Six Sigma program to take advantage of these changes in the health care environment. For example, to improve its performance in acute myocardial infarction (AMI), CAMC applied a Six Sigma DMAIC (define-measure-analyze-improve-control)

©ERproductions Ltd/Blend Images LLC

approach. Nursing staff members were educated on AMI care processes, performance targets were posted in nursing units, and adherence to the eight Hospital Quality Alliance (HQA) indicators of quality care for AMI patients was tracked. As a result of the program, CAMC improved its compliance with HQA-recommended treatment for AMI from 50 to 95 percent. Harvard researchers identified CAMC as one of the top-performing hospitals reporting comparable data.

Controlling cost has also been an important aspect of CAMC's performance improvement initiatives due to local regulations. West Virginia is one of two states where medical services rates are set by state regulators. This forces CAMC to limit expenditures because the hospital cannot raise prices. CAMC first applied Six Sigma in an effort to control costs by managing the supply chain more effectively. The effort created a one-time $150,000 savings by working with vendors to remove outdated inventory. As a result of continuous improvement, a 2015 report stated that CAMC had achieved supply chain management savings of $12 million in the past four years.

Since CAMC introduced Six Sigma, over 100 quality improvement projects have been initiated. A key to CAMC's success has been instilling a continuous improvement mindset into the organization's culture. Dale Wood, chief quality officer at CAMC, stated: "If you have people at the top who completely support and want these changes to occur, you can still fall flat on your face. . . . You need a group of networkers who can carry change across an organization." Due to CAMC's performance improvement culture, the hospital ranks high nationally in ratings for quality of care and patient safety, as reported on the Centers for Medicare and Medicaid Services (CMS) website.

Note: Developed with Robin A. Daley.

Sources: CAMC website; Martha Hostetter, "Case Study: Improving Performance at Charleston Area Medical Center," *The Commonwealth Fund*, November–December 2007, www.commonwealthfund .org/publications/newsletters/quality-matters/2007/november-december/case-study-improving-performance-at-charleston-area-medical-center (accessed January 2016); J. C. Simmons, "Using Six Sigma to Make a Difference in Health Care Quality," *The Quality Letter,* April 2002.

The Difference Between Business Process Reengineering and Continuous Improvement Programs

Business process reengineering and continuous improvement efforts such as TQM and Six Sigma both aim at improved efficiency, better product quality, and greater customer satisfaction. The essential difference between business process reengineering and continuous improvement programs is that reengineering aims at *quantum gains* on the order of 30 to 50 percent or more, whereas total quality programs stress *incremental progress*—striving for inch-by-inch gains again and again in a never-ending stream.

The two approaches to improved performance of value chain activities and operating excellence are not mutually exclusive; it makes sense to use them in tandem. Reengineering can be used first to produce a good basic design that yields quick, dramatic improvements in performing a business process. Total quality programs can then be used as a follow-up to deliver continuing improvements.

> The purpose of using benchmarking, best practices, business process reengineering, TQM, Six Sigma, or other operational improvement programs is to improve the performance of strategy-critical activities and promote superior strategy execution.

Installing Information and Operating Systems

LO10-5   Recognize the role of information and operating systems in enabling company personnel to carry out their strategic roles proficiently.

Company strategies and value-creating internal processes cannot be executed well without a number of internal operating systems. FedEx has internal communication systems that allow it to coordinate its more than 49,000 vehicles in handling a daily average of 11 million shipments to 220 countries. Its leading-edge flight operations systems allow a single controller to direct as many as 200 of FedEx's 650 aircraft simultaneously, overriding their flight plans should weather problems or other special circumstances arise. In addition, FedEx has created e-business tools for customers that allow them to track packages online, create address books, review shipping history, generate custom reports, simplify customer billing, reduce internal warehousing and inventory management costs, purchase goods and services from suppliers, and respond to quickly changing customer demands. All of FedEx's systems support the company's strategy of providing businesses and individuals with a broad array of package delivery services and enhancing its competitiveness against United Parcel Service, DHL, and the U.S. Postal Service.

Siemens Healthcare, one of the largest suppliers to the health care industry, uses a cloud-based business activity monitoring (BAM) system to continuously monitor and improve the company's processes across more than 190 countries. Customer satisfaction is one of Siemens's most important business objectives, so the reliability of its order management and services is crucial. Caesars Entertainment uses a sophisticated customer relationship database that records detailed information about its customers' gambling habits. When a member of the Caesars' Total Rewards program calls to make a reservation, the representative can review previous spending, including average bet size, to offer an upgrade or complimentary stay at Caesars Palace or one of the company's other properties. At Uber, there are systems for locating vehicles near a customer and real-time demand monitoring to price fares during high-demand periods.

> Having state-of-the-art operating systems, information systems, and real-time data is integral to competent strategy execution and operating excellence.

Information systems need to cover five broad areas: (1) customer data, (2) operations data, (3) employee data, (4) supplier/partner/collaborative ally data, and (5) financial performance data. All key strategic performance indicators must be tracked and reported in real time whenever possible. Real-time information systems permit company managers to stay on top of implementation initiatives and daily operations and to intervene if things seem to be drifting off course. Tracking key performance indicators, gathering information from operating personnel, quickly identifying and diagnosing problems, and taking corrective actions are all integral pieces of the process of managing strategy execution and overseeing operations.

Using Rewards and Incentives to Promote Better Strategy Execution

 LO10-6   Explain how and why the use of well-designed incentives and rewards can be management's single most powerful tool for promoting operating excellence.

To create a strategy-supportive system of rewards and incentives, a company must emphasize rewarding people for accomplishing results related to creating value for customers, not for just dutifully performing assigned tasks. Focusing jobholders' attention and energy on what to *achieve* as opposed to what to *do* makes the work environment results-oriented. It is flawed management to tie incentives and rewards to satisfactory performance of duties and activities instead of desired business outcomes and company achievements.[21] In any job, performing assigned tasks is not equivalent to achieving intended outcomes. Diligently showing up for work and attending to job assignment does not, by itself, guarantee results. As any student knows, the fact that an instructor teaches and students go to class doesn't necessarily mean that the students are learning.

> A properly designed reward structure is management's most powerful tool for gaining employee commitment to superior strategy execution and excellent operating results.

Motivation and Reward Systems

It is important for both organization units and individuals to be properly aligned with strategic priorities and enthusiastically committed to executing strategy. *To get employees' sustained, energetic commitment, management has to be resourceful in designing and using motivational incentives—both monetary and nonmonetary.* The more a manager understands what motivates subordinates and is able to use appropriate motivational incentives, the greater will be employees' commitment to good day-in, day-out strategy execution and achievement of performance targets.

Guidelines for Designing Monetary Incentive Systems

Guidelines for creating incentive compensation systems that link employee behavior to organizational objectives include:

1. *Make the performance payoff a major, not a minor, piece of the total compensation package.* The payoff for high-performing individuals and teams must be meaningfully greater than the payoff for average performers, and the payoff for average performers meaningfully bigger than for below-average performers.

2. *Have incentives that extend to all managers and all workers, not just top management.* Lower-level managers and employees are just as likely as senior executives to be motivated by the possibility of lucrative rewards.

3. *Administer the reward system with scrupulous objectivity and fairness.* If performance standards are set unrealistically high or if individual/group performance evaluations are not accurate and well documented, dissatisfaction with the system will overcome any positive benefits.

4. *Tie incentives to performance outcomes directly linked to good strategy execution and financial performance.* Incentives should never be paid just because people are thought to be "doing a good job" or because they "work hard." An argument can be presented that exceptions should be made in giving rewards to people who have come up short because of circumstances beyond their control. The problem with making exceptions for unknowable, uncontrollable, or unforeseeable circumstances is that once good excuses start to creep into justifying rewards for subpar results, the door is open for all kinds of reasons actual performance has failed to match targeted performance.

5. *Make sure the performance targets that each individual or team is expected to achieve involve outcomes that the individual or team can personally affect.* The role of incentives is to enhance individual commitment and channel behavior in beneficial directions.

6. *Keep the time between achieving the target performance outcome and the payment of the reward as short as possible.* Weekly or monthly payments for good performance work much better than annual payments for employees in most job categories. Annual bonus payouts work best for higher-level managers and for situations in which target outcome relates to overall company profitability or stock price performance.

Once the incentives are designed, they have to be communicated and explained. Everybody needs to understand how their incentive compensation is calculated and how individual/group performance targets contribute to organizational performance targets.

Nonmonetary Rewards

Financial incentives generally head the list of motivating tools for trying to gain whole-hearted employee commitment to good strategy execution and operating excellence. But most successful companies also make extensive use of nonmonetary incentives. Some of the most important nonmonetary approaches used to enhance motivation are listed here:[22]

- *Provide attractive perks and fringe benefits.* The various options include full coverage of health insurance premiums; college tuition reimbursement; paid vacation time; onsite child care; onsite fitness centers; telecommuting; and compressed workweeks (four 10-hour days instead of five 8-hour days).

- *Adopt promotion-from-within policies.* This practice helps bind workers to their employers and employers to their workers, plus it is an incentive for good performance.

- *Act on suggestions from employees.* Research indicates that the moves of many companies to push decision making down the line and empower employees increase employee motivation and satisfaction, as well as boost productivity.

- *Create a work atmosphere in which there is genuine sincerity, caring, and mutual respect among workers and between management and employees.* A "family" work environment in which people are on a first-name basis and there is strong camara-derie promotes teamwork and cross-unit collaboration.

- *Share information with employees about financial performance, strategy, operational measures, market conditions, and competitors' actions.* Broad disclosure and prompt communication send the message that managers trust their workers.

- *Have attractive office spaces and facilities.* A workplace environment with appealing features and amenities usually has decidedly positive effects on employee morale and productivity.

Concepts & Connections 10.3 presents specific examples of the motivational tactics employed by several prominent companies that have appeared on *Fortune*'s list of the "100 Best Companies to Work For" in America.

Instilling a Corporate Culture That Promotes Good Strategy Execution

LO10-7   Explain how and why a company's culture can aid the drive for proficient strategy execution.

Every company has its own unique culture. The character of a company's culture or work climate defines "how we do things around here," its approach to people man-agement, and the "chemistry" that permeates its work environment. The meshing of shared core values, beliefs, ingrained behaviors and attitudes, and business principles constitutes a company's **corporate culture**. A company's culture is important because it influences the organization's actions and approaches to conducting business—in a very real sense, the culture is the company's organizational DNA.[23]

> **CORE CONCEPT**
>
> **Corporate culture** is a company's internal work climate and is shaped by its core values, beliefs, and business principles. A company's culture is important because it influences its traditions, work practices, and style of operating

The psyche of corporate cultures varies widely. For instance, the bedrock of Walmart's culture is dedica-tion to customer satisfaction, zealous pursuit of low costs and frugal operating practices, a strong work ethic, ritualistic Saturday-morning headquarters meet-ings to exchange ideas and review problems, and company executives' commitment to visiting stores, listening to customers, and soliciting suggestions from employees. At Nordstrom, the corporate culture is centered on delivering exceptional service to customers, where the company's motto is "Respond to unreasonable cus-tomer requests," and each out-of-the-ordinary request is seen as an opportunity for a "heroic" act by an employee that can further the company's reputation for unparalleled customer service. Nordstrom makes a point of promoting employees noted for their heroic acts and dedication to outstanding service. The company motivates its sales-people with a commission-based compensation system that enables Nordstrom's best salespeople to earn more than double what other department stores pay. Concepts & Connections 10.4 describes the corporate culture at Epic Systems, a provider of soft-ware used in the health care industry.

Concepts & Connections 10.3

HOW THE BEST COMPANIES TO WORK FOR MOTIVATE AND REWARD EMPLOYEES

Companies design a variety of motivational and reward practices to create a work environment that energizes employees and promotes better strategy execution. Other benefits of a successful recognition system include high job satisfaction, high retention rates, and increased output. Here's a sampling of what some of the best companies to work for in America are doing to motivate their employees:

- Software developer SAS prioritizes work-life balance and mental health for its workforce of 7,200. The onsite Work-Life Center helps employees with such personal matters as planning for their kids' college or evaluating eldercare options. The center also includes an on-site gym, indoor swimming pool, walking and biking trails, massage therapists, and a nail salon. With such an environment, it should come as no surprise that 95 percent of employees report looking forward to heading to the office every day.

- Salesforce.com Inc., a global cloud-computing company based in San Francisco, has been listed by *Forbes* magazine as the most innovative company in America. More than quadrupling its workforce from 5,000 to 22,000 between 2011 and 2017, Salesforce.com incentivizes new hires to work cooperatively with existing teams. The company's recognition programs include rewards for achievement both in the office and in the larger community. In addition, the company provides employees with seven paid days off to volunteer and $5,000 in matching grants for philanthropic causes supported by employees.

- Publix is the largest employee-owned company in the United States and Florida-based grocer with 2016 annual sales of $32.4 billion. The company's stock ownership program extends to part-time workers with the goal of giving

©Corey Lowenstein/Raleigh News & Observer/MCT/Tribune News Service/Getty Images

employees a "great opportunity to retire worry-free." Publix also offers job sharing, health insurance for part-time employees, onsite child care, and college tuition reimbursement.

- Hilcorp, an oil and gas exploration company, made headlines in 2011 for its shocking generosity. After reaching its five-year goal to double in size, the company gave every employee a $50,000 dream car voucher (or $35,000 in cash). Employees are encouraged to "work like you own the company" and are eligible for annual bonuses averaging 36 percent in 2016. Also in 2016, Hilcorp awarded every employee a $100,000 bonus after the company achieved its ambitious Dream 2015 five-year financial objectives.

Source: "100 Best Companies to Work For, 2017," *Fortune,* http://fortune.com/best-companies/ (accessed July 13, 2017).

High-Performance Cultures

Some companies have so-called "high-performance" cultures in which the standout cultural traits are a "can-do" spirit, pride in doing things right, no-excuses accountability, and a pervasive results-oriented work climate in which people go the extra mile to meet or beat stretch objectives. In high-performance cultures, there is a strong sense of involvement on the part of company personnel and emphasis on individual initiative and creativity. Performance expectations are clearly stated for the company as a whole, for each organizational unit, and for each individual. Issues and problems are promptly addressed—there's a razor-sharp focus on what needs to be done. A high-performance culture in which there's constructive pressure to achieve good results is a valuable contributor to good strategy execution and operating excellence. Results-oriented cultures are permeated with a spirit of achievement and have a good track record in meeting or beating performance targets.[24]

Concepts & Connections 10.4

STRONG GUIDING PRINCIPLES DRIVE THE HIGH-PERFORMANCE CULTURE AT EPIC

Epic Systems Corporation creates software to support record keeping for mid- to large-sized health care organizations, such as hospitals and managed care organizations. Founded in 1979 by CEO Judith Faulkner, the company claims that its software is "quick to implement, easy to use, and highly interoperable through industry standards." Widely recognized for superior products and high levels of customer satisfaction, Epic won the Best Overall Software Suite award for the sixth consecutive year—a ranking determined by health care professionals and compiled by KLAS, a provider of company performance reviews. Part of this success has been attributed to Epic's strong corporate culture—one based on the slogan "Do good, have fun, make money." By remaining true to its 10 commandments and principles, its homegrown version of core values, Epic has nurtured a work climate where employees are on the same page and all have an overarching standard to guide their actions.

©ERproductions Ltd/Blend Images LLC

Epic's 10 Commandments:

1. Do not go public.

2. Do not be acquired.

3. Software must work.

4. Expectations = reality.

5. Keep commitments.

6. Focus on competency. Do not tolerate mediocrity.

7. Have standards. Be fair to all.

8. Have courage. What you put up with is what you stand for.

9. Teach philosophy and culture.

10. Be frugal. Do not take on debt for operations.

Epic's Principles:

1. Make our products a joy to use.

2. Have fun with customers.

3. Design in collaboration with users.

4. Make it easy for users to do the right thing.

5. Improve the patient's health and health care experience.

6. Generalize to benefit more.

7. Follow processes. Find root causes. Fix processes.

8. Dissent when you disagree; once decided, support.

9. Do what is difficult for us if it makes things easier for our users.

10. Escalate problems at the start, not when all hell breaks loose.

Epic fosters this high-performance culture from the get-go. It targets top-tier universities to hire entry-level talent, focusing on skills rather than personality. A rigorous training and orientation program indoctrinates each new employee. In 2002, Faulkner claimed that someone coming straight from college could become an "Epic person" in three years, whereas it takes six years for someone coming from another company. This culture positively affects Epic's strategy execution because employees are focused on the most important actions, there is peer pressure to contribute to Epic's success, and employees are genuinely excited to be involved. Epic's faith in its ability to acculturate new team members and stick true to its core values has allowed it to sustain its status as a premier provider of health care IT systems.

Note: Developed with Margo Cox.

Sources: Company website; communications with an Epic insider; "Epic Takes Back 'Best in KLAS' title," *Healthcare IT News,* January 29, 2015, www.healthcareitnews.com/news/epic-takes-back-best-klas; "Epic Systems' Headquarters Reflect Its Creativity, Growth," *Boston Globe,* July 28, 2015, www.bostonglobe.com/business/2015/07/28/epic-systems-success-like-its-headquarters-blend-creativity-and-diligence/LpdQ5m0DDS4UViiCVooRUJ/story.html (accessed December 5, 2015).

The challenge in creating a high-performance culture is to inspire high loyalty and dedication on the part of employees such that they are energized to put forth their very best efforts to do things right. Managers have to take pains to reinforce constructive behavior, reward top performers, and purge habits and behaviors that stand in the way of good results. They must work at knowing the strengths and weaknesses of their subordinates so as to better match talent with task. In sum, there has to be an overall disciplined, performance-focused approach to managing the organization.

Adaptive Cultures

In direct contrast to change-resistant cultures, **adaptive cultures** are very supportive of managers and employees at all ranks who propose or help initiate useful change. The hallmark of adaptive cultures is a willingness on the part of organizational members to accept change and take on the challenge of introducing and executing new strategies. Company personnel share a feeling of confidence that the organization can deal with whatever threats and opportunities arise; they are receptive to risk taking, innovation, and changing strategies and practices. Internal entrepreneurship on the part of individuals and groups is encouraged and rewarded. Senior executives seek out, support, and promote individuals who exercise initiative, spot opportunities for improvement, and display the skills to take advantage of them. As in high-performance cultures, the company exhibits a proactive approach to identifying issues, evaluating the implications and options, and quickly moving ahead with workable solutions.

> As a company's strategy evolves, an adaptive culture is a definite ally in the strategy execution process.

Technology companies, software companies, and Internet-based companies are good illustrations of organizations with adaptive cultures. Such companies thrive on change—driving it, leading it, and capitalizing on it (but sometimes also succumbing to change when they make the wrong move or are swamped by better technologies or the superior business models of rivals). Companies such as Amazon, Groupon, Apple, Adobe, Google, and Intel cultivate the capability to act and react rapidly. They are avid practitioners of entrepreneurship and innovation, with a demonstrated willingness to take bold risks to create new products, new businesses, and new industries. To create and nurture a culture that can adapt rapidly to changing or shifting business conditions, they staff their organizations with people who are proactive, who rise to the challenge of change, and who have an aptitude for adapting.

In fast-changing business environments, a corporate culture that is receptive to altering organizational practices and behaviors is a virtual necessity. However, adaptive cultures work to the advantage of all companies, not just those in rapid-change environments. Every company operates in a market and business climate that is changing to one degree or another. *As a company's strategy evolves, an adaptive culture is a definite ally in the strategy implementation, strategy execution process as compared to cultures that have to be coaxed and cajoled to change.*

Unhealthy Corporate Cultures

The distinctive characteristic of an unhealthy corporate culture is the presence of counterproductive cultural traits that adversely impact the work climate and company performance.[25] Five particularly unhealthy cultural traits are a heavily politicized internal environment, hostility to change, an insular "not invented here" mindset, a disregard for high ethical standards, and the presence of incompatible, clashing subcultures.

Politicized Cultures A politicized internal environment is unhealthy because political infighting consumes a great deal of organizational energy and often results in the company's strategic agenda taking a backseat to political maneuvering. In companies in which internal politics pervades the work climate, empire-building managers pursue their own agendas, and the positions they take on issues are usually aimed at protecting or expanding their turf. The support or opposition of politically influential executives and/or coalitions among departments with vested interests in a particular outcome typically weighs heavily in deciding what actions the company takes. All this maneuvering detracts from efforts to execute strategy with real proficiency and frustrates company personnel who are less political and more inclined to do what is in the company's best interests.

Change-Resistant Cultures Change-resistant cultures encourage a number of undesirable or unhealthy behaviors—avoiding risks, hesitation in pursuing emerging opportunities, and widespread aversion to continuous improvement in performing value chain activities. Change-resistant companies have little appetite for being first movers or fast followers, believing that being in the forefront of change is too risky and that acting too quickly increases vulnerability to costly mistakes. They are more inclined to adopt a wait-and-see posture, learn from the missteps of early movers, and then move forward cautiously with initiatives that are deemed safe. Hostility to change is most often found in companies with multilayered management bureaucracies that have enjoyed considerable market success in years past and that are wedded to the "We have done it this way for years" syndrome.

General Motors, IBM, Sears, and Eastman Kodak are classic examples of companies whose change-resistant bureaucracies have damaged their market standings and financial performance; clinging to what made them successful, they were reluctant to alter operating practices and modify their business approaches when signals of market change first sounded. As strategies of gradual change won out over bold innovation, all four lost market share to rivals that quickly moved to institute changes more in tune with evolving market conditions and buyer preferences. While IBM and GM have made strides in building a culture needed for market success, Sears and Kodak are still struggling to recoup lost ground.

Insular, Inwardly Focused Cultures Sometimes a company reigns as an industry leader or enjoys great market success for so long that its personnel start to believe they have all the answers or can develop them on their own. Such confidence breeds arrogance—company personnel discount the merits of what outsiders are doing and what can be learned by studying best-in-class performers. Benchmarking and a search for the best practices of outsiders are seen as offering little payoff. The big risk of a must-be-invented-here mindset and insular cultural thinking is that the company can underestimate the competencies and accomplishments of rival companies and overestimate its own progress—with a resulting loss of competitive advantage over time.

Unethical and Greed-Driven Cultures Companies that have little regard for ethical standards or that are run by executives driven by greed and ego gratification are scandals waiting to happen. Executives exude the negatives of arrogance, ego, greed, and an "ends-justify-the-means" mentality in pursuing overambitious revenue and profitability targets.[26] Senior managers wink at unethical behavior and may cross the line to unethical (and sometimes criminal) behavior themselves. They are prone to adopt accounting principles that make financial performance look better than it really is. Legions of companies have fallen prey to unethical behavior and greed, most notably Enron, Countrywide Financial, World Savings Bank, JPMorgan Chase, and BP with executives being indicted and/or convicted of criminal behavior.

Incompatible Subcultures   It is not unusual for companies to have multiple subcultures with values, beliefs, and ingrained behaviors and attitudes varying to some extent by department, geographic location, division, or business unit. These subcultures within a company don't pose a problem as long as the subcultures don't conflict with the overarching corporate work climate and are supportive of the strategy execution effort. Multiple subcultures become unhealthy when they are incompatible with each other or the overall corporate culture. The existence of conflicting business philosophies and values eventually leads to inconsistent strategy execution. Incompatible subcultures arise most commonly because of important cultural differences between a company's culture and those of a recently acquired company or because of a merger between companies with cultural differences. Cultural due diligence is often as important as financial due diligence in deciding whether to go forward on an acquisition or merger. On a number of occasions, companies have decided to pass on acquiring particular companies because of culture conflicts they believed would be hard to resolve.

Changing a Problem Culture

Changing a company culture that impedes proficient strategy execution is among the toughest management tasks. It is natural for company personnel to cling to familiar practices and to be wary, if not hostile, to new approaches toward how things are to be done. Consequently, it takes concerted management action over a period of time to root out certain unwanted behaviors and replace an out-of-sync culture with more effective ways of doing things. *The single most visible factor that distinguishes successful culture-change efforts from failed attempts is competent leadership at the top.* Great power is needed to force major cultural change and overcome the unremitting resistance of entrenched cultures—and great power is possessed only by the most senior executives, especially the CEO. However, while top management must lead the culture-change effort, instilling new cultural behaviors is a job for the whole management team. Middle managers and frontline supervisors play a key role in implementing the new work practices and operating approaches, helping win rank-and-file acceptance of and support for the changes, and instilling the desired behavioral norms.

As shown in Figure 10.2, the first step in fixing a problem culture is for top management to identify those facets of the present culture that pose obstacles to executing new strategic initiatives. Second, managers have to clearly define the desired new behaviors and features of the culture they want to create. Third, managers have to convince company personnel why the present culture poses problems and why and how new behaviors and operating approaches will improve company performance. Finally, all the talk about remodeling the present culture has to be followed swiftly by visible, forceful actions on the part of management to promote the desired new behaviors and work practices.

Making a Compelling Case for a Culture Change   The place for management to begin a major remodeling of the corporate culture is by selling company personnel on the need for new-style behaviors and work practices. This means making a compelling

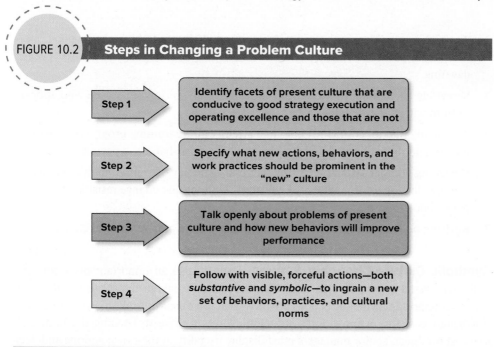

FIGURE 10.2   **Steps in Changing a Problem Culture**

Step 1 → Identify facets of present culture that are conducive to good strategy execution and operating excellence and those that are not

Step 2 → Specify what new actions, behaviors, and work practices should be prominent in the "new" culture

Step 3 → Talk openly about problems of present culture and how new behaviors will improve performance

Step 4 → Follow with visible, forceful actions—both *substantive* and *symbolic*—to ingrain a new set of behaviors, practices, and cultural norms

case for why the company's new strategic direction and culture-remodeling efforts are in the organization's best interests and why company personnel should wholeheartedly join the effort to do things somewhat differently. This can be done by:

- Citing reasons the current strategy has to be modified and why new strategic initiatives are being undertaken. The case for altering the old strategy usually needs to be predicated on its shortcomings—why sales are growing slowly, why too many customers are opting to go with the products of rivals, why costs are too high, and so on. There may be merit in holding events where managers and other key personnel are forced to listen to dissatisfied customers or the complaints of strategic allies.

- Citing why and how certain behavioral norms and work practices in the current culture pose obstacles to good execution of new strategic initiatives.

- Explaining why new behaviors and work practices have important roles in the new culture and will produce better results.

Management's efforts to make a persuasive case for changing what is deemed to be a problem culture must be *quickly followed* by forceful, high-profile actions across several fronts. The actions to implant the new culture must be both substantive and symbolic.

Substantive Culture-Changing Actions   No culture-change effort can get very far when leaders merely talk about the need for different actions, behaviors, and work practices. Company executives have to give the culture-change effort some teeth by initiating *a series of actions* that company personnel will see as *unmistakable support* for the change program. The strongest signs that management is truly committed to instilling a new culture include:

1. Replacing key executives who stonewall needed organizational and cultural changes.

2. Promoting individuals who have stepped forward to advocate the shift to a different culture and who can serve as role models for the desired cultural behavior.

3. Appointing outsiders with the desired cultural attributes to high-profile positions—bringing in new-breed managers sends an unambiguous message that a new era is dawning.

4. Screening all candidates for new positions carefully, hiring only those who appear to fit in with the new culture.

5. Mandating that all company personnel attend culture-training programs to better understand the culture-related actions and behaviors that are expected.

6. Designing compensation incentives that boost the pay of teams and individuals who display the desired cultural behaviors, while hitting change-resisters in the pocketbook.

7. Revising policies and procedures in ways that will help drive cultural change.

Symbolic Culture-Changing Actions   There is also an important place for symbolic managerial actions to alter a problem culture and tighten the strategy–culture fit. The most important symbolic actions are those that top executives take to *lead by example*. For instance, if the organization's strategy involves a drive to become the industry's low-cost producer, senior managers must display frugality in their own actions and decisions: inexpensive decorations in the executive suite, conservative expense accounts and entertainment allowances, a lean staff in the corporate office, few executive perks, and so on. At Walmart, all the executive offices are simply decorated; executives are habitually frugal in their own actions, and they are zealous in their own efforts to control costs and promote greater efficiency. At Nucor, one of the world's low-cost producers of steel products, executives fly coach class and use taxis at airports rather than limousines. Top executives must be alert to the fact that company personnel will be watching their actions and decisions to see if they are walking the talk.[27]

Another category of symbolic actions includes holding ceremonial events to single out and honor people whose actions and performance exemplify what is called for in the new culture. A point is made of holding events to celebrate each culture-change success. Executives sensitive to their role in promoting the strategy–culture fit make a habit of appearing at ceremonial functions to praise individuals and groups that get with the program. They show up at employee training programs to stress strategic priorities, values, ethical principles, and cultural norms. Every group gathering is seen as an opportunity to repeat and ingrain values, praise good deeds, and cite instances of how the new work practices and operating approaches have led to improved results.

Leading the Strategy Execution Process

 LO10-8   Recognize what constitutes effective managerial leadership in achieving superior strategy execution.

For an enterprise to execute its strategy in truly proficient fashion and approach operating excellence, top executives have to take the lead in the implementation/execution process and personally drive the pace of progress. They have to be out in the field, seeing for themselves how well operations are going, gathering information firsthand, and gauging the progress being made. Proficient strategy execution requires company managers to be diligent and adept in spotting problems, learning what obstacles lie in the path of good execution, and then clearing the way for progress: the goal must be to produce better results speedily and productively.[28] In general, leading the drive for good strategy execution and operating excellence calls for three actions on the part of the manager:

- Staying on top of what is happening and closely monitoring progress
- Putting constructive pressure on the organization to execute the strategy well and achieve operating excellence
- Initiating corrective actions to improve strategy execution and achieve the targeted performance results

Staying on Top of How Well Things Are Going

One of the best ways for executives to stay on top of strategy execution is by regularly visiting the field and talking with many different people at many different levels—a technique often labeled *managing by walking around* (MBWA). Walmart executives have had a long-standing practice of spending two to three days every week visiting stores and talking with store managers and employees. Jeff Bezos, Amazon.com's CEO, is noted for his frequent facilities visits and his insistence that other Amazon managers spend time in the trenches with their people to prevent overly abstract thinking and getting disconnected from the reality of what's happening.[29]

Most managers practice MBWA, attaching great importance to gathering information from people at different organizational levels about how well various aspects of the strategy execution are going. They believe facilities visits and face-to-face contacts give them a good feel for what progress is being made, what problems are being encountered, and whether additional resources or different approaches may be needed. Just as important, MBWA provides opportunities to give encouragement, lift spirits, shift attention from old to new priorities, and create excitement—all of which help mobilize organizational efforts behind strategy execution.

Putting Constructive Pressure on Organizational Units to Achieve Good Results and Operating Excellence

Managers have to be out front in mobilizing the effort for good strategy execution and operating excellence. Part of the leadership requirement here entails fostering a results-oriented work climate in which performance standards are high and a spirit of achievement is pervasive. Successfully leading the effort to foster a results-oriented, high-performance culture generally entails such leadership actions and managerial practices as:

- *Treating employees with dignity and respect.*
- *Encouraging employees to use initiative and creativity in performing their work.*
- *Setting stretch objectives* and clearly communicating an expectation that company personnel are to give their best in achieving performance targets.
- *Focusing attention on continuous improvement.*
- *Using the full range of motivational techniques and compensation incentives to reward high performance.*

- *Celebrating individual, group, and company successes.* Top management should miss no opportunity to express respect for individual employees and show appreciation of extraordinary individual and group effort.[30]

While leadership efforts to instill a spirit of high achievement into the culture usually accentuate the positive, there are negative reinforcers too. Low-performing workers and people who reject the results-oriented cultural emphasis have to be weeded out or at least moved to out-of-the-way positions. Average performers have to be candidly counseled that they have limited career potential unless they show more progress in the form of additional effort, better skills, and improved ability to deliver good results. In addition, managers whose units consistently perform poorly have to be replaced.

Initiating Corrective Actions to Improve Both the Company's Strategy and Its Execution

The leadership challenge of making corrective adjustments is twofold: deciding when adjustments are needed and deciding what adjustments to make. Both decisions are a normal and necessary part of managing the strategic management process, since no scheme for implementing and executing strategy can foresee all the events and problems that will arise.[31] There comes a time at every company when managers have to fine-tune or overhaul the company's strategy or its approaches to strategy execution and push for better results. Clearly, when a company's strategy or its execution efforts are not delivering good results, it is the leader's responsibility to step forward and push corrective actions.

KEY POINTS

Implementing and executing strategy is an operations-driven activity revolving around the management of people and business processes. The managerial emphasis is on converting strategic plans into actions and good results. *Management's handling of the process of implementing and executing the chosen strategy can be considered successful if and when the company achieves the targeted strategic and financial performance and shows good progress in making its strategic vision a reality.*

Like crafting strategy, executing strategy is a job for a company's whole management team, not just a few senior managers. Top-level managers have to rely on the active support and cooperation of middle and lower-level managers to push strategy changes into functional areas and operating units, and to see that the organization actually operates in accordance with the strategy on a daily basis.

Eight managerial tasks crop up repeatedly in company efforts to execute strategy:

1. *Building an organization capable of executing the strategy successfully.* Building an organization capable of good strategy execution entails three types of organization-building actions: *(a) staffing the organization*—assembling a talented, can-do management team, and recruiting and retaining employees with the needed experience, technical skills, and intellectual capital, *(b) acquiring, developing, and strengthening key resources and capabilities* that will enable good strategy execution, and *(c) structuring the organization and work*

effort—organizing value chain activities and business processes and deciding how much decision-making authority to push down to lower-level managers and frontline employees.

2. *Allocating ample resources to strategy-critical activities.* Managers implementing and executing a new or different strategy must identify the resource requirements of each new strategic initiative and then consider whether the current pattern of resource allocation and the budgets of the various subunits are suitable.

3. *Ensuring that policies and procedures facilitate rather than impede effective strategy execution.* Anytime a company alters its strategy, managers should review existing policies and operating procedures, proactively revise or discard those that are out of sync, and formulate new ones to facilitate execution of new strategic initiatives.

4. *Adopting business processes that drive continuous improvement in how strategy execution activities are performed.* Reengineering core business processes and continuous improvement initiatives such as total quality management (TQM) or Six Sigma programs all aim at improved efficiency, lower costs, better product quality, and greater customer satisfaction.

5. *Installing information and operating systems that enable company personnel to perform essential activities.* Well-conceived, state-of-the-art support systems not only facilitate better strategy execution but also strengthen organizational capabilities enough to provide a competitive edge over rivals.

6. *Tying rewards directly to the achievement of performance objectives.* For an incentive compensation system to work well, *(a)* the monetary payoff should be a major piece of the compensation package, *(b)* the use of incentives should extend to all managers and workers, *(c)* the system should be administered with care and fairness, *(d)* the incentives should be linked to performance targets spelled out in the strategic plan, *(e)* each individual's performance targets should involve outcomes the person can personally affect, *(f)* rewards should promptly follow the determination of good performance, and *(g)* monetary rewards should be supplemented with liberal use of nonmonetary rewards.

7. *Fostering a corporate culture that promotes good strategy execution.* The psyche of corporate cultures varies widely. There are five types of unhealthy cultures: *(a)* those that are highly political and characterized by empire-building, *(b)* those that are change resistant, *(c)* those that are insular and inwardly focused, *(d)* those that are ethically unprincipled and are driven by greed, and *(e)* those that possess clashing subcultures that prevent a company from coordinating its strategy execution efforts. High-performance cultures and adaptive cultures both have positive features that are conducive to good strategy execution.

8. *Exerting the internal leadership needed to propel implementation forward.* Leading the drive for good strategy execution and operating excellence calls for three actions on the part of the manager: *(a)* staying on top of what is happening, closely monitoring progress, and learning what obstacles lie in the path of good execution; *(b)* putting constructive pressure on the organization to achieve good results and operating excellence; and *(c)* pushing corrective actions to improve strategy execution and achieve the targeted results.

ASSURANCE OF LEARNING EXERCISES

1. The heart of Zara's strategy in the apparel industry is to outcompete rivals by putting fashionable clothes in stores quickly and maximizing the frequency of customer visits. Concepts & Connections 10.1 discusses the capabilities that the company has developed in the execution of its strategy. How do its capabilities lead to a quick production process and new apparel introductions? How do these capabilities encourage customers to visit its stores every few weeks? Does the execution of the company's site selection capability also contribute to its competitive advantage? Explain.   LO10-1

LO10-2   2.   Implementing and executing a new or different strategy call for new resource allocations. Using your university's library resources, search for recent articles that discuss how a company has revised its pattern of resource allocation and divisional budgets to support new strategic initiatives.

LO10-3   3.   Netflix avoids the use of formal policies and procedures to better empower its employees to maximize innovation and productivity. The company goes to great lengths to hire, reward, and tolerate only what it considers mature, "A" player employees. How does the company's selection process affect its ability to operate without formal travel and expense policies, a fixed number of vacation days for employees, or a formal employee performance evaluation system?

LO10-4   4.   Concepts & Connections 10.2 discusses Charleston Area Medical Center's use of Six Sigma practices. List three tangible benefits provided by the program. Explain why a commitment to quality control is important in the hospital industry. How can the use of a Six Sigma program help medical providers survive and thrive in the challenging industry climate?

LO10-5   5.   Company strategies can't be implemented or executed well without a number of information systems to carry on business operations. Using your university's library resources, search for recent articles that discuss how a company has used real-time information systems and control systems to aid the cause of good strategy execution.

LO10-6   6.   Concepts & Connections 10.3 provides a sampling of motivational tactics employed by several companies (many of which appear on *Fortune*'s list of the "100 Best Companies to Work For" in America). Discuss how rewards at SAS, Salesforce.com, Publix, and Hilcorp aid in the strategy execution of each company.

LO10-7   7.   Concepts & Connections 10.4 discusses Epic's strategy-supportive corporate culture. What are the standout features of Epic's corporate culture? How does Epic's culture contribute to its winning best-in-class awards year after year? Howe does the company's culture make Epic a good place to work?

LO10-8   8.   Leading the strategy execution process involves staying on top of the situation and monitoring progress, putting constructive pressure on the organization to achieve operating excellence, and initiating corrective actions to improve the execution effort. Using your university's library resources, discuss a recent example of how a company's managers have demonstrated the kind of effective internal leadership needed for superior strategy execution.

⊙ EXERCISES FOR SIMULATION PARTICIPANTS

LO10-1   1.   How would you describe the organization of your company's top management team? Is some decision making decentralized and delegated to individual managers? If so, explain how the decentralization works. Or are decisions made more by consensus, with all co-managers having input? What do you see as the advantages and disadvantages of the decision-making approach your company is employing?

LO10-2   2.   Have you and your co-managers allocated ample resources to strategy-critical areas? If so, explain how these investments have contributed to good strategy execution and improved company performance.

LO10-6   3.   Does your company have opportunities to use incentive compensation techniques? If so, explain your company's approach to incentive compensation. Is there any hard evidence you can cite that indicates your company's use of incentive compensation techniques has worked? For example, have your company's compensation incentives actually boosted productivity? Can you cite evidence indicating the productivity gains have resulted in lower labor costs? If the productivity gains have *not* translated into lower labor costs, then is it fair to say that your company's use of incentive compensation is a failure?

4. If you were making a speech to company personnel, what would you tell them about the kind of corporate culture you would like to have at your company? What specific cultural traits would you like your company to exhibit? Explain. **LO10-7**

5. Following each decision round, do you and your co-managers make corrective adjustments in either your company's strategy or how well the strategy is being executed? List at least three such adjustments you made in the most recent decision round. What hard evidence (in the form of results relating to your company's performance in the most recent year) can you cite that indicates the various corrective adjustments you made either succeeded or failed to improve your company's performance? **LO10-8**

⬡ ENDNOTES

1. Christopher A. Bartlett and Sumantra Ghoshal, "Building Competitive Advantage Through People," *MIT Sloan Management Review* 43, no. 2 (Winter 2002).

2. Justin Menkes, "Hiring for Smarts," *Harvard Business Review* 83, no. 11 (November 2005); and Justin Menkes, *Executive Intelligence* (New York: HarperCollins, 2005).

3. Larry Bossidy and Ram Charan, *Execution: The Discipline of Getting Things Done* (New York: Crown Business, 2002).

4. Jim Collins, *Good to Great* (New York: HarperBusiness, 2001).

5. C. Helfat et al., *Dynamic Capabilities: Understanding Strategic Change in Organizations* (Malden, MA: Blackwell, 2007); and R. Grant, *Contemporary Strategy Analysis,* 6th ed. (Malden, MA: Blackwell, 2008).

6. G. Dosi, R. Nelson, and S. Winter, eds., *The Nature and Dynamics of Organizational Capabilities* (Oxford, England: Oxford University Press, 2001).

7. B. Kogut and U. Zander, "Knowledge of the Firm, Combinative Capabilities, and the Replication of Technology," *Organization Science* 3, no. 3 (August 1992), pp. 383–97.

8. S. Karim and W. Mitchell, "Path-Dependent and Path-Breaking Change: Reconfiguring Business Resources Following Business," *Strategic Management Journal* 21, nos. 10–11 (October–November 2000), pp. 1061–82; L. Capron, P. Dussauge, and W. Mitchell, "Resource Redeployment Following Horizontal Acquisitions in Europe and North America, 1988–1992," *Strategic Management Journal* 19, no. 7 (July 1998), pp. 631–62.

9. Alfred Chandler, *Strategy and Structure* (Cambridge, MA: MIT Press, 1962).

10. Stanley E. Fawcett, Gary K. Rhoads, and Phillip Burnah, "People as the Bridge to Competitiveness: Benchmarking the 'ABCs' of an Empowered Workforce," *Benchmarking: An International Journal* 11, no. 4 (2004).

11. Rosabeth Moss Kanter, "Collaborative Advantage: The Art of the Alliance," *Harvard Business Review* 72, no. 4 (July–August 1994), pp. 96–108.

12. Michael Hammer and James Champy, *Reengineering the Corporation* (New York: HarperBusiness, 1993).

13. Charles A. O'Reilly and Michael L. Tushman, "The Ambidextrous Organization," Harvard Business Review 82, no. 4 (April 2004), pp. 74–81.

14. M. Walton, *The Deming Management Method* (New York: Pedigree, 1986); J. Juran, *Juran on Quality by Design* (New York: Free Press, 1992); Philip Crosby, *Quality Is Free: The Act of Making Quality Certain* (New York: McGraw-Hill, 1979); S. George, *The Baldrige Quality System* (New York: John Wiley & Sons, 1992); and Mark J. Zbaracki, "The Rhetoric and Reality of Total Quality Management," *Administrative Science Quarterly* 43, no. 3 (September 1998).

15. Robert T. Amsden, Thomas W. Ferratt, and Davida M. Amsden, "TQM: Core Paradigm Changes," *Business Horizons* 39, no. 6 (November–December 1996).

16. Peter S. Pande and Larry Holpp, *What Is Six Sigma?* (New York: McGraw-Hill, 2002); Jiju Antony, "Some Pros and Cons of Six Sigma: An Academic Perspective," *The TQM Magazine* 16, no. 4 (2004); Peter S. Pande, Robert P. Neuman, and Roland R. Cavanagh, *The Six Sigma Way: How GE, Motorola and Other Top Companies Are Honing Their Performance* (New York: McGraw-Hill, 2000); Joseph Gordon and M. Joseph Gordon, Jr., *Six Sigma Quality for Business and Manufacture* (New York: Elsevier, 2002); Godecke Wessel and Peter Burcher, "Six Sigma for Small and Medium-Sized Enterprises," *The TQM Magazine* 16, no. 4 (2004).

17. Based on information posted at www.sixsigma.com, November 4, 2002.

18. Kennedy Smith, "Six Sigma for the Service Sector," *Quality Digest Magazine,* May 2003, www.qualitydigest.com (accessed September 28, 2003).

19. As quoted in "A Dark Art No More," *The Economist* 385, no. 8550 (October 13, 2007).

20. Charles A. O'Reilly and Michael L. Tushman, "The Ambidextrous Organization," *Harvard Business Review* 82, no. 4 (April 2004).

21. See Steven Kerr, "On the Folly of Rewarding A while Hoping for B," *Academy of Management Executive* 9, no. 1 (February 1995); Steven Kerr, "Risky Business: The New Pay Game," *Fortune,* July 22, 1996; Doran Twer, "Linking Pay to Business Objectives," *Journal of Business Strategy* 15, no. 4 (July–August 1994).

22. Jeffrey Pfeffer and John F. Veiga, "Putting People First for Organizational Success," *Academy of Management Executive* 13, no. 2 (May 1999); Linda K. Stroh and Paula M. Caliguiri, "Increasing Global Competitiveness Through Effective People Management," *Journal of World Business* 33, no. 1 (Spring 1998); and articles in *Fortune* on the 100 best companies to work for (various issues).

23. Joanne Reid and Victoria Hubbell, "Creating a Performance Culture," *Ivey Business Journal* 69, no. 4 (March–April 2005).

24. Jay B. Barney and Delwyn N. Clark, *Resource-Based Theory: Creating and Sustaining Competitive Advantage* (New York: Oxford University Press, 2007).

25. John P. Kotter and James L. Heskett, *Corporate Culture and Performance* (New York: Free Press, 1992).

26. Kurt Eichenwald, *Conspiracy of Fools: A True Story* (New York: Broadway Books, 2005).

27. Judy D. Olian and Sara L. Rynes, "Making Total Quality Work: Aligning Organizational Processes, Performance Measures, and Stakeholders," *Human Resource Management* 30, no. 3 (Fall 1991).

28. Larry Bossidy and Ram Charan, *Confronting Reality: Doing What Matters to Get Things Right* (New York: Crown Business, 2004); Larry Bossidy and Ram Charan, *Execution: The Discipline of Getting Things Done* (New York: Crown Business, 2002); John P. Kotter, "Leading Change: Why Transformation Efforts Fail," *Harvard Business Review* 73, no. 2 (March–April 1995); Thomas M. Hout and John C. Carter, "Getting It Done: New Roles for Senior Executives," *Harvard Business Review* 73, no. 6 (November–December 1995); Sumantra Ghoshal and Christopher A. Bartlett, "Changing the Role of Top Management: Beyond Structure to Processes," *Harvard Business Review* 73, no. 1 (January–February 1995).

29. Fred Vogelstein, "Winning the Amazon Way," *Fortune,* May 26, 2003.

30. Jeffrey Pfeffer, "Producing Sustainable Competitive Advantage Through the Effective Management of People," *Academy of Management Executive* 9, no. 1 (February 1995).

31. Cynthia A. Montgomery, "Putting Leadership Back into Strategy," *Harvard Business Review* 86, no. 1 (January 2008).

APPENDIX

Key Financial Ratios: How to Calculate Them and What They Mean

Ratio	How Calculated	What It Shows
Profitability Ratios		
1. Gross profit margin	$\dfrac{\text{Sales revenues} - \text{Cost of goods sold}}{\text{Sales revenues}}$	Shows the percentage of revenues available to cover operating expenses and yield a profit. Higher is better, and the trend should be upward.
2. Operating profit margin (or return on sales)	$\dfrac{\text{Sales revenues} - \text{Operating expenses}}{\text{Sales revenues}}$ or $\dfrac{\text{Operating income}}{\text{Sales revenues}}$	Shows the profitability of current operations without regard to interest charges and income taxes. Higher is better, and the trend should be upward.
3. Net profit margin (or net return on sales)	$\dfrac{\text{Profits after taxes}}{\text{Sales revenues}}$	Shows after-tax profits per dollar of sales. Higher is better, and the trend should be upward.
4. Total return on assets	$\dfrac{\text{Profits after taxes} + \text{Interest}}{\text{Total assets}}$	A measure of the return on total monetary investment in the enterprise. Interest is added to after-tax profits to form the numerator since total assets are financed by creditors as well as by stockholders. Higher is better, and the trend should be upward.
5. Net return on total assets (ROA)	$\dfrac{\text{Profits after taxes}}{\text{Total assets}}$	A measure of the return earned by stockholders on the firm's total assets. Higher is better, and the trend should be upward.
6. Return on stockholders' equity	$\dfrac{\text{Profits after taxes}}{\text{Total stockholders' equity}}$	Shows the return stockholders are earning on their capital investment in the enterprise. A return in the 12–15% range is "average," and the trend should be upward.
7. Return on invested capital (ROIC) – sometimes referred to as return on capital (ROCE)	$\dfrac{\text{Profits after taxes}}{\text{Long-term debt} + \text{Total stockholders' equity}}$	A measure of the return shareholders are earning on the long-term monetary capital invested in the enterprise. Higher is better, and the trend should be upward.
8. Earnings per share (EPS)	$\dfrac{\text{Profits after taxes}}{\text{Number of shares of common stock outstanding}}$	Shows the earnings for each share of common stock outstanding. The trend should be upward, and the bigger the annual percentage gains, the better.
Liquidity Ratios		
1. Current ratio	$\dfrac{\text{Current assets}}{\text{Current liabilities}}$	Shows a firm's ability to pay current liabilities using assets that can be converted to cash in the near term. Ratio should definitely be higher than 1.0; ratios of 2 or higher are better still.
2. Working capital	$\text{Current assets} - \text{Current liabilities}$	Bigger amounts are better because the company has more internal funds available to (1) pay its current liabilities on a timely basis and (2) finance inventory expansion, additional accounts receivable, and a larger base of operations without resorting to borrowing or raising more equity capital.
Leverage Ratios		
1. Total debt-to-assets ratio	$\dfrac{\text{Total debt}}{\text{Total assets}}$	Measures the extent to which borrowed funds (both short-term loans and long-term debt) have been used to finance the firm's operations. A low fraction or ratio is better—a high fraction indicates overuse of debt and greater risk of bankruptcy.

Ratio	How Calculated	What It Shows
2. Long-term debt-to-capital ratio	$$\frac{\text{Long-term debt}}{\text{Long-term debt} + \text{Total stockholders' equity}}$$	An important measure of creditworthiness and balance sheet strength. It indicates the percentage of capital investment in the enterprise that has been financed by both long-term lenders and stockholders. A ratio below 0.25 is usually preferable since monies invested by stockholders account for 75% or more of the company's total capital. The lower the ratio, the greater the capacity to borrow additional funds. Debt-to-capital ratios above 0.50 and certainly above 0.75 indicate a heavy and perhaps excessive reliance on long-term borrowing, lower creditworthiness, and weak balance sheet strength.
3. Debt-to-equity ratio	$$\frac{\text{Total debt}}{\text{Total stockholders' equity}}$$	Shows the balance between debt (funds borrowed both short-term and long-term) and the amount that stockholders have invested in the enterprise. The farther the ratio is below 1.0, the greater the firm's ability to borrow additional funds. Ratios above 1.0 and definitely above 2.0 put creditors at greater risk, signal weaker balance sheet strength, and often result in lower credit ratings.
4. Long-term debt-to-equity ratio	$$\frac{\text{Long-term debt}}{\text{Total stockholders' equity}}$$	Shows the balance between long-term debt and stockholders' equity in the firm's *long-term* capital structure. Low ratios indicate greater capacity to borrow additional funds if needed.
5. Times-interest-earned (or coverage) ratio	$$\frac{\text{Operating income}}{\text{Interest expenses}}$$	Measures the ability to pay annual interest charges. Lenders usually insist on a minimum ratio of 2.0, but ratios progressively above 3.0 signal progressively better creditworthiness.

Activity Ratios

1. Days of inventory	$$\frac{\text{Inventory}}{\text{Cost of goods sold} \div 365}$$	Measures inventory management efficiency. Fewer days of inventory are usually better.
2. Inventory turnover	$$\frac{\text{Cost of goods sold}}{\text{Inventory}}$$	Measures the number of inventory turns per year. Higher is better.
3. Average collection period	$$\frac{\text{Accounts receivable}}{\text{Total sales} \div 365}$$ or $$\frac{\text{Accounts receivable}}{\text{Average daily sales}}$$	Indicates the average length of time the firm must wait after making a sale to receive cash payment. A shorter collection time is better.

Other Important Measures of Financial Performance

1. Dividend yield on common stock	$$\frac{\text{Annual dividends per share}}{\text{Current market price per share}}$$	A measure of the return that shareholders receive in the form of dividends. A "typical" dividend yield is 2–3%. The dividend yield for fast-growth companies is often below 1% (maybe even 0); the dividend yield for slow-growth companies can run 4–5%.
2. Price-earnings ratio	$$\frac{\text{Current market price per share}}{\text{Earnings per share}}$$	P-E ratios above 20 indicate strong investor confidence in a firm's outlook and earnings growth; firms whose future earnings are at risk or likely to grow slowly typically have ratios below 12.
3. Dividend payout ratio	$$\frac{\text{Annual dividends per share}}{\text{Earnings per share}}$$	Indicates the percentage of after-tax profits paid out as dividends.
4. Internal cash flow	After tax profits + Depreciation	A quick and rough estimate of the cash a company's business is generating after payment of operating expenses, interest, and taxes. Such amounts can be used for dividend payments or funding capital expenditures.
5. Free cash flow	After tax profits + Depreciation − Capital expenditures − Dividends	A quick and rough estimate of the cash a company's business is generating after payment of operating expenses, interest, taxes, dividends, and desirable reinvestments in the business. The larger a company's free cash flow, the greater is its ability to internally fund new strategic initiatives, repay debt, make new acquisitions, repurchase shares of stock, or increase dividend payments.

Airbnb, Inc., in 2017

connect

JOHN D. VARLARO Johnson & Wales University

JOHN E. GAMBLE Texas A&M University–Corpus Christi

"In the future, you will own what [assets] you want responsibility for," commented CEO and founder of Airbnb, Brian Chesky, concerning the sharing economy in an interview with Trevor Noah on *The Daily Show* in March 2016.[1] Airbnb was founded in 2008 when Chesky and a friend decided to rent their apartment to guests for a local convention. To accommodate the guests, they used air mattresses and referred to it as the "Air Bed & Breakfast." It was that weekend when the idea—and the potential viability—of a peer-to-peer room-sharing business model was born. While not yet a publicly traded company in 2017, Airbnb had seen immense growth and success in its nine-year existence. The room-sharing company had expanded to over 190 countries with more than 3 million listed properties, and had an estimated valuation of $30 billion. Airbnb seemed poised to revolutionize the hotel and tourism industry through its business model that allowed hosts to offer spare rooms or entire homes to potential guests, in a peer-reviewed digital marketplace.

This business model's success was leveraging what had become known as the sharing economy. Yet, with its growth and usage of a new business model, Airbnb was now faced with resistance, as city officials, owners and operators of hotels, motels, and bed and breakfasts were all crying foul. While these traditional brick-and-mortar establishments were subject to regulations and taxation, Airbnb hosts were able to circumvent and avoid such liabilities due to participation in Airbnb's digital marketplace. In other instances, Airbnb hosts had encountered legal issues due to city and state ordinances governing hotels and apartment leases. Stories of guests who would not leave and hosts needing to evict them because city regulations deemed the guests apartment leasees were beginning to make headlines.

As local city and government officials across the United States, and in countries like Japan, debated regulations concerning Airbnb, Brian Chesky needed to manage this new business model, which had led to phenomenal success within a new, sharing economy.

Overview of Accommodation Market

Hotels, motels, and bed and breakfasts competed within the larger, tourist accommodation market. All businesses operating within this sector offered lodging, but were differentiated by their amenities. Hotels and motels were defined as larger facilities accommodating guests in single or multiple rooms. Motels specifically offered smaller rooms with direct parking lot access from the unit and amenities such as laundry facilities to travelers who were using their own transportation. Motels might also be located closer to roadways, providing guests quicker and more convenient access to highways. It was also not uncommon for motel guests to segment a longer road trip as they commuted to a vacation destination, thereby potentially staying at several motels during their travel. Hotels, however, invested heavily in additional amenities as

EXHIBIT 1

Hotel, Motel, and Bed and Breakfast Industry Costs as Percentage of Revenue, 2015

Costs	Hotels/Motels	Bed and Breakfasts
Wages	26%	23%
Purchases	27%	21%
Depreciation	10%	9%
Marketing	2%	2%
Rent and Utilities	8%	11%
Other	12%	16%

Source: www.ibisworld.com, rounded to nearest percent.

EXHIBIT 2

Major Market Segments for Hotels/Motels and Bed and Breakfast/Hostels Sectors, 2015

Market Segment	B&Bs	Hotels
Recreation	80%*	70%**
Business	12%	18%
Other, including meetings	8%	12%
Total	100%	100%

*The bed and breakfast market is primarily domestic.

**Includes both domestic and international travelers. Approximately 20 percent is associated with international travelers.

Source: www.ibisworld.com.

they competed for all segments of travelers. Amenities, including on-premise spa facilities and fine dining, were often offered by the hotel. Further, properties offering spectacular views, bolstering a hotel as the vacation destination, may contribute to significant operating costs. In total, wages, property, and utilities, as well as purchases such as food, account for 61 percent of the industry's total costs (see Exhibit 1).[2]

Bed and breakfasts, however, were much smaller, usually where owner-operators offered a couple of rooms within their own home to accommodate guests. The environment of the bed and breakfast—one of a cozy, home-like ambience—was what the guest desired when booking a room. Contrasted with the hotel or motel, a bed and breakfast offered a more personalized, yet quieter atmosphere. Further, many bed and breakfast establishments were in rural areas where the investment to establish a larger hotel may have been cost prohibitive, yet the location itself could be an attraction to tourists. In these areas individuals invested in a home and property, possibly with a historical background, to offer a bed and breakfast with great allure and ambience for the guests' experiences. Thus, the bed and breakfast competed through offering an ambience associated with a more rural, slower pace through which travelers connected with their hosts and the surrounding community. A comparison of the primary market segments of bed and breakfasts and hotels in 2015 is presented in Exhibit 2.

While differing in size and target consumer, all hotels, motels, and bed and breakfasts were subject to city, state, and federal regulations. These regulations covered areas such as the physical property and food safety, access for persons with disabilities, and even alcohol distribution. Owners and operators were subject to paying fees for different licenses to operate. Due to operating as a business, these properties and the associated revenues were also subject to state and federal taxation.

In addition to regulations, the need to construct physical locations prevented hotels and motels from expanding quickly, especially in new international markets. Larger chains tended to expand by purchasing preexisting physical locations, or through mergers and acquisitions, such as Marriott International Inc.'s acquisition of Starwood Hotels and Resorts Worldwide in 2016.

A Business Model for the Sharing Economy

Startup companies have been functioning in a space commonly referred to as the "sharing economy" for several years. According to Chesky, the previous model for the economy was based on ownership.[3] Thus, operating a business first necessitated ownership of the assets required to do business. Any spare capacity the business faced—either within production or service—was a direct result of the purchase of hard assets in the daily activity of conducting business.

EXHIBIT 3

Airbnb Estimated Revenue and Bookings Growth, 2010–2017 (in millions)

Costs	2010	2011	2012	2013	2014	2015	2016	2017
Estimated Revenue	$6	$44	$132	$264	$436	$675	$945	$1,229
Estimated Bookings Growth	273%	666%	200%	100%	65%	55%	40%	30%

Source: Ali Rafat, "Airbnb's Revenues Will Cross Half Billion Mark in 2015," *Analysts Estimate,* March 25, 2015, skift.com/2015/03/25/airbnbs-revenues-will-cross-half-billion-mark-in-2015-analysts-estimate/.

Airbnb and other similar companies, however, operated through offering a technological platform, where individuals with spare capacity could offer their services. By leveraging the ubiquitous usage of smartphones and the continual decrease in technology costs, these companies provided a platform for individuals to instantly share a number of resources. Thus, a homeowner with a spare room could offer it for rent. Or, the car owner with spare time could offer [his or her] services a couple of nights a week as a taxi service. The individual simply signed up through the platform and began to offer the service or resource. The company then charged a small transaction fee as the service between both users was facilitated.

Within its business model, Airbnb received a percentage of what the host received for the room. For Airbnb, its revenues were decoupled from the considerable operating expenses of traditional lodging establishments and provided it with significantly smaller operating costs than hotels, motels, and bed and breakfasts. Rather than expenses related to owning and operating real estate properties, Airbnb's expenses were that of a technology company. Airbnb's business model in 2017, therefore, was based on the revenue-cost-margin structure of an online marketplace, rather than a lodging establishment. With an estimated 11 percent fee per room stay, it was reported that Airbnb achieved profitability for a first time in 2016.[4] The company's revenues expected to increase from an estimated $6 million in 2010 to a projected $1.2 billion by 2017 (see Exhibit 3).

A Change in the Consumer Experience and Rate

Airbnb, however, was not just leveraging technology. It was also leveraging the change in how the current consumer interacted with businesses. In conjunction with this change seemed to be how the consumer had deemphasized ownership. Instead of focusing on ownership, consumers seemed to prefer sharing or renting. Other startup companies have been targeting these segments through subscription-based services and on-demand help. From luxury watches to clothing, experiencing—and not owning—assets seemed to be on the rise. Citing a more experiential-based economy, Chesky believed Airbnb guests desired a community and a closer relationship with the host—and there seemed to be support for this assertion.[5] A recent Goldman Sachs study showed that once someone used Airbnb, their preference for a traditional accommodation was greatly reduced.[6] The appeal of the company's value proposition with customers had allowed it to readily raise capital to support its growth, including an $850 million cash infusion in 2016 that raised its estimated valuation to $30 billion. A comparison of Airbnb's estimated market capitalization to the world's largest hoteliers is presented in Exhibit 4.

EXHIBIT 4

Estimated Market Capitalization Comparison, 2016 (in billion $)

Competitor	Market Capitalization (in billions $)
Marriott International Inc.	$40
Airbnb	30
Hilton Worldwide Holdings	22
Intercontinental Hotels Group	11

Sources: Yahoo Finance (accessed June 20, 2017); "Airbnb Settles Lawsuit with its Hometown, San Francisco," *New York Times,* https://www.nytimes.com/2017/05/01/technology/airbnb-san-francisco-settle-registration-lawsuit.html (accessed June 20, 2017).

Recognizing this shift in consumer preference, traditional brick-and-mortar operators were responding. Hilton was considering offering a hostel-like option to travelers.[7] Other entrepreneurs were constructing urban properties to specifically leverage Airbnb's platform and offer rooms only to Airbnb users, such as in Japan[8] where rent and hotel costs were extremely high.

To govern the community of hosts and guests, Airbnb had instituted a rating system. Popularized by companies such as Amazon, eBay, and Yelp, peer-to-peer ratings helped police quality. Both guests and hosts rated each other in Airbnb. This approach incentivized hosts to provide quality service, while encouraging guests to leave a property as they found it. Further, the peer-to-peer rating system greatly minimized the otherwise significant task and expense of Airbnb employees assessing and rating each individual participant within Airbnb's platform.

Not Playing by the Same Rules

Local and global businesses criticized Airbnb for what they claimed were unfair business practices and lobbied lawmakers to force the company to comply with lodging regulations. These concerns illuminated how due to its business model, Airbnb and its users seemed to not need to abide by these same regulations. This could have been concerning on many levels. For the guest, regulations exist for protection from unsafe accommodations. Fire codes and occupation limits all exist to prevent injury and death. Laws also exist to prevent discrimination, as traditional brick-and-mortar accommodations are barred from not providing lodging to guests based on race and other protected classes. But, there seemed to be evidence that Airbnb guests had faced such discrimination from hosts.[9]

Hosts might also expose themselves to legal and financial problems from accommodating guests. There had been stories of hosts needing to evict guests who would not leave, and due to local ordinances the guests were actually protected as apartment leasees. Other stories highlighted rooms and homes being damaged by huge parties given by Airbnb guests. Hosts might also be exposed to liability issues in the instance of an injury or even a death of a guest.

Finally, there were accusations of businesses using Airbnb's marketplace to own and operate accommodations without obtaining the proper licenses. These locations appeared to be individuals on the surface, but were actually businesses. And, because of Airbnb's platform, these pseudo-businesses could operate and generate revenue without meeting regulations or claiming revenues for taxation.

In 2016, however, Airbnb had acted in response to some of these issues. A report was written and released by Airbnb, detailing both discrimination on its platform and how it would be mitigated. Airbnb also settled its lawsuit with San Francisco. The city was demanding Airbnb enforce a city regulation requiring host registration, or incur significant fines. As part of the settlement, Airbnb agreed to offer more information on its hosts within the city.[10]

"We Wish to Be Regulated; This Would Legitimize Us"

Recognizing that countries and local municipalities were responding to the local business owner and their constituents' concerns, Chesky and Airbnb have focused on mobilizing and advocating for consumers and business owners who utilize the app. Airbnb's website provided support for guests and hosts who wished to advocate for the site. A focal point of the advocacy emphasized how those particularly hit hard at the height of the recession relied on Airbnb to establish a revenue stream, and prevent the inevitable foreclosure and bankruptcy.

Yet, traditional brick-and-mortar establishments subject to taxation and regulations have continued to put pressure on government officials to level the playing field. "We wish to be regulated; this would legitimize us," Chesky remarked to Noah in the same interview on *The Daily Show*.[11] Proceeding forward and possibly preparing for a future public offering, Chesky would need to manage how the progressive business model—while fit for the new, global sharing economy—may not fit older, local regulations.

ENDNOTES

1 Interview with Airbnb founder and CEO Brian Chesky, *The Daily Show with Trevor Noah,* Comedy Central, February 24, 2016.

2 *IBISWorld Industry Report 72111: Hotels & Motels in the US,* www.ibisworld.com.

3 Interview with Airbnb founder and CEO Brian Chesky, *The Daily Show with Trevor Noah, Comedy Central,* February 24, 2016.

4 B. Stone and O. Zaleski, "Airbnb Enters the Land of Profitability," *Bloomberg,* January 26, 2017, https://www.bloomberg.com/news/articles/2017-01-26/airbnb-enters-the-land-of-profitability (accessed June 20, 2017).

5 Interview with Airbnb founder and CEO Brian Chesky, *The Daily Show with Trevor Noah,* Comedy Central, February 24, 2016.

6 J. Verhage, "Goldman Sachs: More and More People Who Use Airbnb Don't Want to Go Back to Hotels," *Bloomberg,* February 26, 2016, www.bloomberg.com/news/articles/2016-02-16/goldman-sachs-more-and-more-people-who-use-airbnb-don-t-want-to-go-back-to-hotels.

7 D. Fahmy, "Millennials Spending Power Has Hilton Weighing a 'Hostel-Like' Brand," March 8, 2016, *Bloomberg Businessweek,* www.bloomberg.com/businessweek.

8 Y. Nakamura and M. Takahashi, "Airbnb Faces Major Threat in Japan, Its Fastest-Growing Market," *Bloomberg,* February 18, 2016, www.bloomberg.com/news/articles/2016-02-18/fastest-growing-airbnb-market-under-threat-as-japan-cracks-down.

9 R. Greenfield, "Study Finds Racial Discrimination by Airbnb Hosts," *Bloomberg,* December 10, 2015, www.bloomberg.com/news/articles/2015-12-10/study-finds-racial-discrimination-by-airbnb-hosts.

10 K. Benner, "Airbnb Adopts Rules to Fight Discrimination by Its Hosts," *New York Times,* (September 8, 2016) http://www.nytimes.com/2016/09/09/technology/airbnb-anti-discrimination-rules.html (accessed June 20, 2017).

11 Interview with Airbnb founder and CEO Brian Chesky, *The Daily Show with Trevor Noah,* Comedy Central, February 24, 2016.

Costco Wholesale in 2017: Mission, Business Model, and Strategy

 connect

ARTHUR A. THOMPSON JR. The University of Alabama

Five years after being appointed as Costco Wholesale's president and chief executive officer (CEO), Craig Jelinek had demonstrated the ability to enhance the company's standing as one of the world's biggest and best consumer goods merchandisers. His predecessor, Jim Sinegal, co-founder and CEO of Costco Wholesale from 1983 until year-end 2011, had been the driving force behind Costco's 29-year evolution from a startup entrepreneurial venture into the third largest retailer in the United States, the seventh largest retailer in the world, and the undisputed leader of the discount warehouse and wholesale club segment of the North American retailing industry. Jelinek was handpicked by Sinegal to be his successor. Since January 2012, Jelinek had presided over Costco's growth from annual revenues of $89 billion and 598 membership warehouses at year-end fiscal 2011 to annual revenues of $119 billion and 715 membership warehouses at year-end fiscal 2016. Going into 2017, Costco ranked as the second largest retailer in both the United States and the world (behind Walmart).

Company Background

The membership warehouse concept was pioneered by discount merchandising sage Sol Price, who opened the first Price Club in a converted airplane hangar on Morena Boulevard in San Diego in 1976. Price Club lost $750,000 in its first year of operation, but by 1979 it had two stores, 900 employees, 200,000 members, and a $1 million profit. Years earlier, Sol Price had experimented with discount retailing at a San Diego store called Fed-Mart. Jim Sinegal got his start in retailing at the age of 18, loading mattresses for $1.25 an hour at Fed-Mart while attending San Diego Community College. When Sol Price sold Fed-Mart, Sinegal left with Price to help him start the San Diego Price Club store; within a few years, Sol Price's Price Club emerged as the unchallenged leader in member warehouse retailing, with stores operating primarily on the West Coast.

Although Price originally conceived Price Club as a place where small local businesses could obtain needed merchandise at economical prices, he soon concluded that his fledgling operation could achieve far greater sales volumes and gain buying clout with suppliers by also granting membership to individuals—a conclusion that launched the deep-discount warehouse club industry on a steep growth curve.

When Sinegal was 26, Sol Price made him the manager of the original San Diego store, which had become unprofitable. Price saw that Sinegal had a special knack for discount retailing and for spotting what a store was doing wrong (usually either not being in the right merchandise categories or not selling items at the right price points)—the very things that Sol Price was good at and that were at the root of Price Club's growing success in the marketplace. Sinegal soon got the San Diego store back into the black. Over the next several years, Sinegal continued to build his prowess and talents for discount merchandising. He mirrored Sol Price's attention to detail and absorbed all the nuances and subtleties of his mentor's style of operating—constantly improving store operations, keeping operating costs and overhead low, stocking items that moved quickly, and charging ultra-low prices that kept customers coming back to shop. Realizing that he had mastered the tricks of running a successful membership warehouse business from Sol Price, Sinegal decided to leave Price Club and form his own warehouse club operation.

Sinegal and Seattle entrepreneur Jeff Brotman (now chairman of Costco's board of directors) founded Costco, and the first Costco store began operations in Seattle in 1983—the same year that Walmart launched its warehouse membership format, Sam's Club. By the end of 1984, there were nine Costco stores in five states serving over 200,000 members. In December 1985, Costco became a public company, selling shares to the public and raising additional capital for expansion. Costco became the first ever U.S. company to reach $1 billion in sales in less than six years. In October 1993, Costco merged with Price Club. Jim Sinegal became CEO of the merged company, presiding over 206 PriceCostco locations, with total annual sales of $16 billion. Jeff Brotman, who had functioned as Costco's chairman since the company's founding, became vice chairman of PriceCostco in 1993 and was elevated to chairman of the company's board of directors in December 1994, a position he continued to hold in 2017.

In January 1997, after the spin-off of most of its non-warehouse assets to Price Enterprises Inc., PriceCostco changed its name to Costco Companies Inc. When the company reincorporated from Delaware to Washington in August 1999, the name was changed to Costco Wholesale Corporation. The company's headquarters was in Issaquah, Washington, not far from Seattle.

Jim Sinegal's Leadership Style

Sinegal was far from the stereotypical CEO. He dressed casually and unpretentiously, often going to the office or touring Costco stores wearing an open-collared cotton shirt that came from a Costco bargain rack and sporting a standard employee name tag that said, simply, "Jim." His informal dress and unimposing appearance made it easy for Costco shoppers to mistake him for a store clerk. He answered his own phone, once telling ABC News reporters, "If a customer's calling and they have a gripe, don't you think they kind of enjoy the fact that I picked up the phone and talked to them?"[1]

Sinegal spent considerable time touring Costco stores, using the company plane to fly from location to location and sometimes visiting 8 to 10 stores daily (the record for a single day was 12). Treated like a celebrity when he appeared at a store (the news "Jim's in the store" spread quickly), Sinegal made a point of greeting store employees. He observed, "The employees know that I want to say hello to them, because I like them. We have said from the very beginning: 'We're going to be a company that's on a first-name basis with everyone.'"[2] Employees genuinely seemed to like Sinegal. He talked quietly, in a commonsensical manner that suggested what he was saying was no big deal.[3] He came across as kind yet stern, but he was prone to display irritation when he disagreed sharply with what people were saying to him.

In touring a Costco store with the local store manager, Sinegal was very much the person-in-charge. He functioned as producer, director, and knowledgeable critic. He cut to the chase quickly, exhibiting intense attention to detail and pricing, wandering through store aisles firing a barrage of questions at store managers about sales volumes and stock levels of particular items, critiquing merchandising displays or the position of certain products in the stores, commenting on any aspect of store operations that caught his eye, and asking managers to do further research and get back to him with more information whenever he found their answers to his questions less than satisfying. Sinegal had tremendous merchandising savvy, demanded much of store managers and employees, and definitely set the tone for how the company operated its discounted retailing business. Knowledgeable observers regarded Jim Sinegal's merchandising expertise as being on a par with Walmart's legendary founder, Sam Walton.

In September 2011, at the age of 75, Jim Sinegal informed Costco's Board of Directors of his intention to step down as CEO of the company effective January 2012. The board elected Craig Jelinek, president and chief operating officer since February 2010, to succeed Sinegal and hold the titles of both president and CEO. Jelinek was a highly experienced retail executive with 37 years in the industry, 28 of them at Costco, where he started as one of the company's first warehouse managers in 1984. He had served in every major role related to Costco's business operations and merchandising activities during his tenure.

When he stepped down as CEO, Sinegal retained his position on the company's Board of Directors and, at the age of 79, was re-elected to another three-year term on Costco's board in December 2015.

Costco Wholesale in 2016

In June 2017, Costco was operating 732 membership warehouses, including 510 in the United States and Puerto Rico, 95 in Canada, 37 in Mexico, 28 in the United Kingdom, 25 in Japan, 13 in South Korea, 13 in Taiwan, eight in Australia, two in Spain, and one in Iceland. Costco also sold merchandise to members at websites in the United States, Canada, the United Kingdom, Mexico, South Korea, and Taiwan. Almost 89 million cardholders were entitled to shop at Costco as of June 2017; in fiscal year 2016,

membership fees generated over $2.6 billion in revenues for the company. Annual sales per store averaged about $162 million ($3.1 million per week) in 2016, some 86 percent higher than the $86.9 million per year and $1.7 million per week averages for Sam's Club, Costco's chief competitor. In 2014, 165 of Costco's warehouses generated sales exceeding $200 million annually, up from 56 in 2010; and 60 warehouses had sales exceeding $250 million, including two that had more than $400 million in sales.[4] Costco was the only national retailer in the history of the United States that could boast of average annual revenue in excess of $160 million *per location.*

Exhibit 1 contains a financial and operating summary for Costco for fiscal years 2000, 2005, 2011, and from 2013 through 2016.

EXHIBIT 1

Selected Financial and Operating Data for Costco Wholesale Corp., Fiscal Years 2000, 2005, 2011, and 2013–2016 ($ in millions, except for per share data)

	Fiscal Years Ending on Sunday Closest to August 31						
Selected Income Statement Data	2016	2015	2014	2013	2011	2005	2000
Net sales	$116,073	$113,666	$110,212	$102,870	$87,048	$51,862	$31,621
Membership fees	2,646	2,533	2,428	2,286	1,867	1,073	544
Total revenue	118,719	116,199	112,640	105,156	88,915	52,935	32,164
Operating expenses							
Merchandise costs	102,901	101,065	98,458	91,948	77,739	46,347	28,322
Selling, general, and administrative	12,068	11,445	10,899	10,104	8,682	5,044	2,755
Preopening expenses	78	65	63	51	46	53	42
Provision for impaired assets and store closing costs	—	—	—	—	9	16	7
Operating income	3,672	3,624	3,220	3,053	2,439	1,474	1,037
Other income (expense)							
Interest expense	(133)	(124)	(113)	(99)	(116)	(34)	(39)
Interest income and other	80	104	90	97	60	109	54
Income before income taxes	3,619	3,604	3,197	3,051	2,383	1,549	1,052
Provision for income taxes	1,243	1,195	1,109	990	841	486	421
Net income	$ 2,350	$ 2,377	$ 2,058	$ 2,039	$ 1,462	$ 1,063	$ 631
Diluted net income per share	$ 5.33	$ 5.37	$ 4.65	$ 4.63	$ 3.30	$ 2.18	$ 1.35
Dividends per share (not including special dividend of $5.00 in 2015 and $7.00 in 2013)	$ 1.70	$ 1.51	$ 1.33	$ 1.17	$ 0.89	$ 0.43	0.00
Millions of shares used in per share calculations	441.3	442.7	442.5	440.5	443.1	492.0	475.7
Balance Sheet Data							
Cash and cash equivalents	$ 3,379	$ 4,801	$ 5,738	$ 4,644	$ 4,009	$ 2,063	$ 525

Selected Income Statement Data	Fiscal Years Ending on Sunday Closest to August 31						
	2016	2015	2014	2013	2011	2005	2000
Merchandise inventories	8,969	8,908	8,456	7,894	6,638	4,015	2,490
Current assets	15,218	17,299	17,588	15,840	13,706	8,238	3,470
Current liabilities	15,575	16,540	14,412	13,257	12,050	6,761	3,404
Net property and equipment	17,043	15,401	14,830	13,881	12,432	7,790	4,834
Total assets	33,163	33,440	33,024	30,283	26,761	16,514	8,634
Long-term debt	4,061	4,864	5,093	4,998	2,153	711	790
Stockholders' equity	12,079	10,843	12,515	11,012	12,573	8,881	4,240
Cash Flow Data							
Net cash provided by operating activities	$3,292	$4,285	$3,984	$3,437	$3,198	$1,773	$1,070
Warehouse Operations							
Warehouses at beginning of year[a]	686	663	634	608	572	417	292
New warehouses opened (including relocations)	33	26	30	26	24	21	25
Existing warehouses closed (including relocations)	(4)	(3)	(1)	0	(4)	(5)	(4)
Warehouses at end of year	715	686	663	634	592	433	313
Net sales per warehouse open at year-end (in millions)[b]	$161.0	$165.7	$164.0	$162.0	$147.1	$119.8	$101.0
Average annual growth at warehouses open more than a year	4%	7%	6%	6%	10%	7%	11%
Members at year-end							
Businesses (000s)	7,300	7,100	6,900	6,600	6,300	5,000	4,200
Gold Star members (000s)	36,800	34,000	31,600	28,900	25,000	16,200	10,500
Add-on cardholders (employees of business members, spouses of Gold Star members)	42,600	40,200	37,900	35,700	32,700	n.a.	n.a.
Total cardholders	86,700	81,300	76,400	71,200	64,000	—	—

[a] Prior to 2011, the company's warehouses—30 of which were opened in 2007 and two others in 2008–2009—were consolidated and reported as part of Costco's total operations at the beginning of fiscal 2011.

[b] Sales for new warehouses opened during the year are annualized.

Note: Some totals may not add due to rounding and the fact that some line items in the company's statement of income were not included in this summary, for reasons of simplicity.

Sources: Company 10-K reports for fiscal years 2000, 2005, 2011, 2013, 2015, and 2016.

Costco's Mission, Business Model, and Strategy

Numerous company documents stated that Costco's mission in the membership warehouse business was: "To continually provide our members with quality goods and services at the lowest possible prices."[5] However, in their "Letter to Shareholders" in the company's 2011 Annual Report, Costco's three top executives—Jeff Brotman, Jim Sinegal, and Craig Jelinek—provided a more expansive view of Costco's mission, stating:

The company will continue to pursue its mission of bringing the highest quality goods and services to market at the lowest possible prices while providing excellent customer service and adhering to a strict code of ethics that includes taking care of our employees and members, respecting our suppliers, rewarding our shareholders, and seeking to be responsible corporate citizens and environmental stewards in our operations around the world."[6]

The centerpiece of Costco's business model entailed generating high sales volumes and rapid inventory turnover by offering fee-paying members attractively low prices on a limited selection of nationally branded and selected private-label products in a wide range of merchandise categories. Rapid inventory turnover—when combined with the low operating costs achieved by volume purchasing, efficient distribution, and reduced handling of merchandise in no-frills, self-service warehouse facilities—enabled Costco to operate profitably at significantly lower gross margins than traditional wholesalers, mass merchandisers, supermarkets, and supercenters. Membership fees were a critical element of Costco's business model because they provided sufficient supplemental revenues to boost the company's overall profitability to acceptable levels. Indeed, it was common for Costco's membership fees to exceed its entire net income, meaning that the rest of Costco's worldwide business operated on a slightly below breakeven basis (see Exhibit 1)—which translated into Costco's prices being exceptionally competitive when compared to the prices that Costco members paid when shopping elsewhere.

A second important business model element was that Costco's high sales volume and rapid inventory turnover generally allowed it to sell and receive cash for inventory before it had to pay many of its merchandise vendors, even when vendor payments were made in time to take advantage of early payment discounts. Thus, Costco was able to finance a big percentage of its merchandise inventory through the payment terms provided by vendors rather than by having to maintain sizable working capital (defined as current assets minus current liabilities) to facilitate timely payment of suppliers.

Costco's Strategy

The key elements of Costco's strategy were ultra-low prices, a limited selection of nationally branded and private-label products, a "treasure hunt" shopping environment, strong emphasis on low operating costs, and ongoing expansion of its geographic network of store locations.

Pricing   Costco's philosophy was to keep customers coming in to shop by wowing them with low prices and thereby generating big sales volumes. Examples of Costco's 2015 sales volumes that contributed to low prices in particular product categories included

156,000 carats of diamonds, meat sales of $6.4 billion, seafood sales of $1.3 billion, television sales of $1.8 billion, fresh produce sales of $5.8 billion (sourced from 44 countries), 83 million rotisserie chickens, 7.9 million tires, 41 million prescriptions, 6 million pairs of glasses, and 128 million hot dog/soda pop combinations. Costco was the world's largest seller of fine wines ($965 million out of total 2015 wine sales of $1.7 billion).

For many years, a key element of Costco's pricing strategy had been to cap its markup on brand-name merchandise at 14 percent (compared to 20- to 50-percent markups at other discounters and many supermarkets). Markups on Costco's private-label Kirkland Signature items were a maximum of 15 percent, but the sometimes fractionally higher markups still resulted in Kirkland Signature items being priced about 20 percent below comparable name-brand items. Kirkland Signature products—which included vitamins, juice, bottled water, coffee, spices, olive oil, canned salmon and tuna, nuts, laundry detergent, baby products, dog food, luggage, cookware, trash bags, batteries, wines and spirits, paper towels and toilet paper, and clothing—were designed to be of *equal or better* quality than national brands.

As a result of these low markups, Costco's prices were just fractionally above breakeven levels, producing net sales revenues (not counting membership fees) that exceeded all operating expenses (merchandise costs + selling, general, and administrative expenses + preopening expenses and store relocation expenses) and contributed only several million dollars to operating profits. As can be verified from Exhibit 1, without the revenues from membership fees, Costco's net income after taxes would be minuscule because of its ultra-low pricing strategy and practice of capping the margins on branded goods at 14 percent and private-label goods at 15 percent.

Jim Sinegal explained the company's approach to pricing:

> We always look to see how much of a gulf we can create between ourselves and the competition. So that the competitors eventually say, "These guys are crazy. We'll compete somewhere else." Some years ago, we were selling a hot brand of

jeans for $29.99. They were $50 in a department store. We got a great deal on them and could have sold them for a higher price but we went down to $29.99. Why? We knew it would create a riot.[7]

At another time, he said:

> We're very good merchants, and we offer value. The traditional retailer will say: "I'm selling this for $10. I wonder whether we can get $10.50 or $11." We say: "We're selling this for $9. How do we get it down to $8?" We understand that our members don't come and shop with us because of the window displays or the Santa Claus or the piano player. They come and shop with us because we offer great values.[8]

Indeed, Costco's markups and prices were so fractionally above the level needed to cover company-wide operating costs and interest expenses that Wall Street analysts had criticized Costco management for going all out to please customers at the expense of increasing profits for shareholders. One retailing analyst said, "They could probably get more money for a lot of the items they sell."[9] During his tenure as CEO, Sinegal had never been impressed with Wall Street calls for Costco to abandon its ultra-low pricing strategy, commenting: "Those people are in the business of making money between now and next Tuesday. We're trying to build an organization that's going to be here 50 years from now."[10] He went on to explain why Costco's approach to pricing would remain unaltered during his tenure:

> When I started, Sears, Roebuck was the Costco of the country, but they allowed someone else to come in under them. We don't want to be one of the casualties. We don't want to turn around and say, "We got so fancy we've raised our prices, and all of a sudden a new competitor comes in and beats our prices."[11]

Product Selection Whereas typical supermarkets stocked about 40,000 items and a Walmart Supercenter or a SuperTarget might have 125,000 to 150,000 items for shoppers to choose from, Costco's merchandising strategy was to provide members with a selection of approximately 3,700 active items that could be priced at bargain levels and thus provide members with significant cost savings. Of these, about 80 percent were quality brand-name products

and 20 percent carried the company's private-label Kirkland Signature brand, which were a growing percentage (over 20 percent) of merchandise sales. The Kirkland Signature label appeared on everything from men's dress shirts to laundry detergent, pet food to toilet paper, canned foods to cookware, olive oil to beer, automotive products to health and beauty aids. According to Craig Jelinek, "The working rule followed by Costco buyers is that all Kirkland Signature products must be equal to or better than the national brands, and must offer a savings to our members." Management believed that there were opportunities to increase the number of Kirkland Signature selections and gradually build sales penetration of Kirkland-branded items to 30 percent of total sales. Costco executives in charge of sourcing Kirkland Signature products constantly looked for ways to make all Kirkland Signature items better than their brand name counterparts and even more attractively priced. Costco members were very much aware that one of the great perks of shopping at Costco was the opportunity to buy top quality Kirkland Signature products at prices substantially lower than name brand products.

Costco's product range covered a broad spectrum—rotisserie chicken, all types of fresh meats, seafood, fresh and canned fruits and vegetables, paper products, cereals, coffee, dairy products, cheeses, frozen foods, flat-screen televisions, iPods, digital cameras, fresh flowers, fine wines, caskets, baby strollers, toys and games, musical instruments, ceiling fans, vacuum cleaners, books, apparel, cleaning supplies, DVDs, light bulbs, batteries, cookware, electric toothbrushes, vitamins, and washers and dryers—but the selection in each product category was deliberately limited to fast-selling models, sizes, and colors. Many consumable products like detergents, canned goods, office supplies, and soft drinks were sold only in big-container, case, carton, or multiple-pack quantities. In a few instances, the selection within a product category was restricted to a single offering. For example, Costco stocked only a 325-count bottle of Advil—a size many shoppers might find too large for their needs. Sinegal explained the reasoning behind limited selections:

> If you had 10 customers come in to buy Advil, how many are not going to buy any because you

EXHIBIT 2

Costco's Sales by Major Product Category, Selected Years 2005–2016

	2016	2015	2010	2005
Food (fresh produce, meats and fish, bakery and deli products, and dry and institutionally packaged foods)	36%	36%	33%	30%
Sundries (candy, snack foods, tobacco, alcoholic and nonalcoholic beverages, and cleaning and institutional supplies)	21%	21%	23%	25%
Hardlines (major appliances, electronics, health and beauty aids, hardware, office supplies, garden and patio, sporting goods, furniture, cameras, and automotive supplies)	16%	16%	18%	20%
Softlines (including apparel, domestics, jewelry, housewares, books, movie DVDs, video games and music, home furnishings, and small appliances)	12%	11%	10%	12%
Ancillary and Other (gasoline, pharmacy, food court, optical, one-hour photo, hearing aids, and travel)	15%	16%	16%	13%

Source: Company 10-K reports, 2005, 2011, and 2016.

just have one size? Maybe one or two. We refer to that as the intelligent loss of sales. We are prepared to give up that one customer. But if we had four or five sizes of Advil, as most grocery stores do, it would make our business more difficult to manage. Our business can only succeed if we are efficient. You can't go on selling at these margins if you are not.[12]

The approximate percentage of net sales accounted for by each major category of items stocked by Costco is shown in Exhibit 2.

Costco had opened ancillary departments within or next to most Costco warehouses to give reasons to shop at Costco more frequently and make Costco more of a one-stop shopping destination. Some locations had more ancillary offerings than others:

	2015	2010	2007
Total number of warehouses	686	540	488
Warehouses having stores with			
Food Court	680	534	482
One-Hour Photo Centers	656	530	480
Optical Dispensing Centers	662	523	472
Pharmacies	606	480	429
Gas Stations	472	343	279
Hearing Aid Centers	581	357	237

Note: The company did not report the number of ancillary offerings for its 715 warehouses at year-end 2016.

Source: Company 10-K reports, 2007, 2011, and 2015.

Costco's pharmacies were highly regarded by members because of the low prices. The company's

practice of selling gasoline at discounted prices at those store locations where there was sufficient space to install gas pumps had boosted the frequency with which nearby members shopped at Costco and made in-store purchases (only members were eligible to buy gasoline at Costco's stations). Almost all new Costco locations in the United States and Canada were opening with gas stations; globally, gas stations were being added at locations where local regulations and space permitted.

Treasure-Hunt Merchandising While Costco's product line consisted of approximately 3,700 active items, some 20 to 25 percent of its product offerings were constantly changing. Costco's merchandise buyers were continuously making one-time purchases of items that would appeal to the company's clientele and likely sell out quickly. A sizable number of these items were high-end or name-brand products that carried big price tags—like $1,000 to $2,500 big-screen HDTVs, $800 espresso machines, expensive jewelry and diamond rings (priced from $50,000 to as high as $250,000), Movado watches, exotic cheeses, Coach bags, cashmere sport coats, $1,500 digital pianos, and Dom Perignon champagne. Dozens of featured specials came and went quickly, sometimes in several days or a week—like Italian-made Hathaway shirts priced at $29.99 and $800 leather sectional sofas. The strategy was to entice shoppers to spend more than they might by offering irresistible deals on big-ticket items or name-brand specials and, further, to keep the mix of featured and treasure-hunt items constantly changing so that bargain-hunting shoppers would go to Costco more frequently than for periodic "stock up" trips.

Costco members quickly learned that they needed to go ahead and buy treasure-hunt specials that interested them because the items would very likely not be available on their next shopping trip. In many cases, Costco did not obtain its upscale treasure-hunt items directly from high-end manufacturers like Calvin Klein or Waterford (who were unlikely to want their merchandise marketed at deep discounts at places like Costco); rather, Costco buyers searched for opportunities to source such items legally on the gray market from other wholesalers or distressed retailers looking to get rid of excess or slow-selling inventory.

Management believed that these practices kept its marketing expenses low relative to those at typical retailers, discounters, and supermarkets.

Low-Cost Emphasis

Keeping operating costs at a bare minimum was a major element of Costco's strategy and a key to its low pricing. As Jim Sinegal explained:

> Costco is able to offer lower prices and better values by eliminating virtually all the frills and costs historically associated with conventional wholesalers and retailers, including salespeople, fancy buildings, delivery, billing, and accounts receivable. We run a tight operation with extremely low overhead which enables us to pass on dramatic savings to our members.[13]

While Costco management made a point of locating warehouses on high-traffic routes in or near upscale suburbs that were easily accessible by small businesses and residents with above-average incomes, it avoided prime real estate sites in order to contain land costs.

Because shoppers were attracted principally by Costco's low prices and merchandise selection, most warehouses were of a metal pre-engineered design, with concrete floors and minimal interior décor. Floor plans were designed for economy and efficiency in use of selling space, the handling of merchandise, and the control of inventory. Merchandise was generally stored on racks above the sales floor and displayed on pallets containing large quantities of each item, thereby reducing labor required for handling and stocking. In-store signage was done mostly on laser printers; there were no shopping bags at the checkout counter—merchandise was put directly into the shopping cart or sometimes loaded into empty boxes. Costco warehouses ranged in size from 73,000 to 205,000 square feet; the average size was about 144,500 square feet. Newer units were usually in the 150,000- to 205,000-square-foot range, but the world's largest Costco warehouse was a 235,000-square-foot store in Salt Lake City that opened in 2015. Images of Costco's warehouses are shown in Exhibit 3.

Warehouses generally operated on a seven-day, 70-hour week, typically being open between 10:00 a.m. and 8:30 p.m. weekdays, with earlier closing hours on the weekend; the gasoline operations outside many stores usually had extended hours. The shorter hours of operation as compared to those of traditional retailers, discount retailers, and supermarkets resulted in lower labor costs relative to the volume of sales.

Growth Strategy

Costco's growth strategy was to increase sales at existing stores by 5 percent or more annually and to open additional warehouses, both domestically and internationally. Average annual growth at stores open at least a year was 10 percent in fiscal 2011, 6 percent in both fiscal 2013 and 2014, 7 percent in fiscal 2015, and 4 percent in 2016. In fiscal 2011, sales at Costco's existing warehouses grew by an average of 10 percent chiefly because members shopped Costco warehouses an average of 4 percent more often and spent about 5 percent more per visit than they did in fiscal 2010 (see Exhibit 1 for recent average annual sales increases at existing stores). Costco expected to open 31 new warehouses in its fiscal year beginning September 1, 2016: 16 in the United States, 8 in Canada, and 1 each in Japan, Australia, Mexico, Taiwan, South Korea, France, and Iceland (the new locations in France and Iceland were its first warehouses in these two countries). As of June 2017, 17 of the 31 planned new warehouses had already been opened.

EXHIBIT 3

Images of Costco's Warehouses

©Jeramey Lende/Shutterstock

©Helen89/Shutterstock

©Cassiohabib/Shutterstock

©Trong Nguyen/Shutterstock

©Cassiohabib/Shutterstock

©Andriy Blokhin/Shutterstock

EXHIBIT 4

Selected Geographic Operating Data, Costco Wholesale Corporation, Fiscal Years 2005, 2010, 2015–2016 ($ in millions)

	United States Operations	Canadian Operations	Other International Operations	Total
Year Ended August 30, 2016				
Total revenue (including membership fees)	$86,579	$17,028	$15,112	$118,719
Operating income	2,326	778	568	3,672
Capital expenditures	1,823	299	527	2,649
Number of warehouses	501	91	123	715
Year Ended August 30, 2015				
Total revenue (including membership fees)	$84,451	$17,341	$14,507	$116,299
Operating income	2,308	771	545	3,624
Capital expenditures	1,574	148	671	2,393
Number of warehouses	487	90	120	697
Year Ended August 29, 2010				
Total revenue (including membership fees)	$59,624	$12,501	$ 6,271	$ 78,396
Operating income	1,310	547	220	2,077
Capital expenditures	804	162	89	1,055
Number of warehouses	416	79	45	540
Year Ended August 28, 2005				
Total revenue (including membership fees)	$43,064	$ 6,732	$ 3,155	$ 52,951
Operating income	1,168	242	65	1,475
Capital expenditures	734	140	122	996
Number of warehouses	338	65	30	433

Note: The dollar numbers shown for "Other" countries represent only Costco's ownership share, since all foreign operations were joint ventures (although Costco was the majority owner of these ventures); the warehouses operated by Costco Mexico in which Costco was a 50-percent joint venture partner were not included in the data for the "Other" countries until Fiscal Year 2011.

Source: Company 10-K reports, 2016, 2015, 2010, and 2007.

Exhibit 4 shows a breakdown of Costco's geographic operations for fiscal years 2005, 2010, 2015, and 2016.

Marketing and Advertising

Costco's low prices and its reputation for making shopping at Costco something of a treasure hunt made it unnecessary to engage in extensive advertising or sales campaigns. Marketing and promotional activities were generally limited to monthly coupon mailers to members, weekly e-mails to members from Costco.com, occasional direct mail to prospective new members, and regular direct marketing programs (such as *The Costco Connection,* a magazine published for members), in-store product sampling, and special campaigns for new warehouse openings.

For new warehouse openings, marketing teams personally contacted businesses in the area that were potential wholesale members; these contacts were supplemented with direct mailings during the period immediately prior to opening. Potential Gold Star (individual) members were contacted by direct mail or by promotions at local employee associations and businesses with large numbers of employees. After a membership base was established in an area, most new memberships came from word of mouth (existing members telling friends and acquaintances about their shopping experiences at Costco), follow-up messages distributed through regular payroll or other organizational communications to employee groups, and ongoing direct solicitations to prospective business and Gold Star members.

Website Sales

Costco operated websites in the United States, Canada, Mexico, the United Kingdom, Taiwan, and South Korea—both to enable members to shop for many in-store products online and to provide members with a means of obtaining a much wider variety of value-priced products and services that were not practical to stock at the company's warehouses. Website sales accounted for 4 percent of net sales in fiscal 2016, versus 3 percent in 2015 and 2014. Examples of items that members could buy online at low Costco prices included sofas, beds, entertainment centers and TV lift cabinets, outdoor furniture, office furniture, kitchen appliances, billiard tables, and hot tubs. Members could also use the company's websites for such services as digital photo processing, prescription fulfillment, travel, the Costco auto program (for purchasing selected new vehicles with discount prices through participating dealerships), and other membership services. In 2015, Costco sold 465,000 vehicles through its 3,000 dealer partners; the big attraction to members of buying a new or used vehicle through Costco's auto program was being able to skip the hassle of bargaining with the dealer over price and, instead, paying an attractively low price pre-arranged by Costco. At Costco's online photo center, customers could upload images and pick up the prints at their local warehouse in little over an hour.

Supply Chain and Distribution

Costco bought the majority of its merchandise directly from manufacturers, routing it either directly to its warehouse stores or to one of the company's cross-docking depots that served as distribution points for nearby stores and for shipping orders to members making online purchases. Depots received container-based shipments from manufacturers, transferred the goods to pallets, and then shipped full-pallet quantities of several types of goods to individual warehouses via rail or semitrailer trucks, generally in less than 24 hours. This maximized freight volume and handling efficiencies. Going into 2016, Costco had 23 cross-docking depots with a combined space of 9.3 million square feet in the United States, Canada, and various other international locations. When merchandise arrived at a warehouse, forklifts moved the full pallets straight to the sales floor and onto racks and shelves (without the need for multiple employees to touch the individual packages/cartons on the pallets)—the first time most items were physically touched at a warehouse was when shoppers reached onto the shelf/rack to pick it out of a carton and put it into their shopping cart. Very little incoming merchandise was stored in locations off the sales floor in order to minimize receiving and handling costs.

Costco had direct buying relationships with many producers of national brand-name merchandise and with manufacturers that supplied its Kirkland Signature products. Costco's merchandise buyers were always alert for opportunities to add products of top quality manufacturers and vendors on a one-time or ongoing basis. No one manufacturer supplied a significant percentage of the merchandise that Costco stocked. Costco had not experienced difficulty in obtaining sufficient quantities of merchandise, and management believed that if one or more of its current sources of supply became unavailable, the company could switch its purchases to alternative manufacturers without experiencing a substantial disruption of its business.

Costco's Membership Base and Member Demographics

Costco attracted the most affluent customers in discount retailing—the average annual income of Costco members was approximately $100,000 (in 2015 Costco management believed the 8.6 million subscribers to the company's monthly *Costco Connection* magazine had an average annual income of $156,000).[14] Many members were affluent urbanites, living in nice neighborhoods not far from Costco warehouses. One loyal Executive member, a criminal defense lawyer, said, "I think I spend over $20,000 to $25,000 a year buying all my products here from food to clothing—except my suits. I have to buy them at the Armani stores."[15] Another Costco loyalist said, "This is the best place in the world. It's like going to church on Sunday. You can't get anything better than this. This is a religious experience."[16]

Costco had two primary types of memberships: Business and Gold Star (individual). Business memberships were limited to businesses, but included individuals with a business license, retail sales license, or other evidence of business existence. A business membership also included a free household card (a significant number of business members shopped at Costco for their personal needs). Business members also had the ability to purchase "add-on" membership cards for up to six partners or associates in the business. Costco's current annual fee for Business and Gold Star memberships was $60 in the United States and Canada and varied by country in its other international operations. Individuals in the United States and Canada who did not qualify for business membership could purchase a Gold Star membership, which included a household card for another family member (additional add-on cards could not be purchased by Gold Star members). Members could shop at any Costco warehouse.

Both Business and Gold Star members in the United States, Canada, Mexico, and the United Kingdom could upgrade to an Executive membership (which included a free household card). In the United States and Canada, the annual fee for Executive members was $120; the fee for Executive membership varied elsewhere. The primary appeal of upgrading to an Executive membership was becoming eligible for 2 percent rebate savings on qualified pre-tax purchases at Costco (rebate certificates were issued annually and could be used toward purchases of most merchandise at the front-end registers of Costco warehouses—rebate awards could not be used to purchase alcohol and tobacco products, gasoline, postage stamps, and food court items). The 2 percent rebate for Executive members was capped at $1,000 for any 12-month period in the United States and Canada (equivalent to annual qualified pre-tax purchases of $50,000); the maximum rebate varied in other countries. Executive members also were eligible for savings and benefits on various business and consumer services offered by Costco, including merchant credit card processing, small-business loans, auto and home insurance, long-distance telephone service, check printing, and real estate and mortgage services; these services were mostly offered by third-party providers and varied by state—Executive members did not receive 2 percent rebate credit on purchases of these ancillary services. In fiscal 2016, Executive members represented 39 percent of Costco's cardholders (including add-ons) and accounted for two-thirds of total company sales (equal to average sales of just over $160,000 per Executive member). Costco's member renewal rate was approximately 90 percent in the United States and Canada, and 88 percent on a worldwide basis in 2016. Recent trends in membership are shown at the bottom of Exhibit 1.

In general, with variations by country, Costco members could pay for their purchases with certain debit and credit cards, co-branded Costco credit cards, cash, or checks; in the United States and Puerto Rico, members could use a co-branded Citi/Costco Visa Anywhere credit card for purchases at Costco and elsewhere, Costco Cash cards, and all Visa cards. Costco accepted merchandise returns when members were dissatisfied with their purchases. Losses associated with dishonored checks were minimal because any member whose check had been dishonored was prevented from paying by check or cashing a check at the point of sale until restitution was made. The membership format facilitated strictly controlling the entrances and exits of warehouses, resulting in limited inventory losses of less than two-tenths of 1 percent of net sales—well below those of typical discount retail operations.

Warehouse Management

Costco warehouse managers were delegated considerable authority over store operations. In effect, warehouse managers functioned as entrepreneurs running their own retail operation. They were responsible for coming up with new ideas about what items would sell in their stores, effectively merchandising the ever-changing lineup of treasure-hunt products, and orchestrating in-store product locations and displays to maximize sales and quick turnover. In experimenting with what items to stock and what in-store merchandising techniques to employ, warehouse managers had to know the clientele who patronized their locations—for instance, big-ticket diamonds sold well at some warehouses but not at others. Costco's best managers kept their finger on the pulse of the members who shopped their warehouse location to stay in sync with what would sell well, and they had a flair for creating a certain element of excitement, hum, and buzz in their warehouses. Such managers spurred above-average sales volumes—sales at Costco's top-volume warehouses ran about $4 million to $7 million a week, with sales exceeding $1 million on many days. Successful managers also thrived on the rat race of running a high-traffic store and solving the inevitable crises of the moment.

Compensation and Workforce Practices

In September 2016, Costco had 126,000 full-time employees and 92,000 part-time employees. Approximately 15,000 hourly employees at locations in California, Maryland, New Jersey, and New York, as well as at one warehouse in Virginia, were represented by the International Brotherhood of Teamsters. All remaining employees were non-union.

Starting wages for entry-level jobs for new Costco employees were raised to $13.00 to $13.50 in March 2016; hourly pay scales for warehouse jobs ranged from $13 to $24, depending on the type of job. The highest paid full-time warehouse employees could earn about $22.50 per hour after four years; compensation for a Costco pharmacist was in the $45 to $50 per hour range. Salaried Costco employees earned anywhere from $30,000 to $125,000 annually.[17] For example, salaries for merchandise and department managers were in the $65,000 to $80,000 range; salaries for supervisors ranged from $45,000 to $75,000; salaries for database, computer systems, and software applications developers/analysts/project managers were in the $85,000 to $125,000 range; and salaries for general managers of warehouses ranged from $90,000 to $145,000. Employees enjoyed the full spectrum of benefits. Salaried employees were eligible for benefits on the first of the second month after the date of hire. Full-time hourly employees were eligible for benefits on the first day of the second month after completing 250 eligible paid hours; part-time hourly employees became benefit-eligible on the first day of the second month after completing 450 eligible paid hours. The benefit package included the following:

- Health care plans for full-time and part-time employees that included coverage for mental illness, substance abuse, and professional counseling for assorted personal and family issues.

- A choice of a core dental plan or a premium dental plan.

- A pharmacy plan that entailed (1) co-payments of $3 for generic drugs and $10 to $50 for brand-name prescriptions filled at a Costco warehouse or online pharmacy and (2) co-payments of $15 to $50 for generic or brand-name prescriptions filled at all other pharmacies.

- A vision program that paid up to $60 for a refraction eye exam (the amount charged at Costco's Optical Centers) and had $175 annual allowances for the purchase of glasses and contact lenses at Costco Optical Centers. Employees located more than 25 miles from a Costco Optical Center could visit any provider of choice for annual eye exams and could purchase eyeglasses from any in-network source and submit claim forms for reimbursement.

- A hearing aid benefit of up to $1,750 every four years (available only to employees and their eligible dependents enrolled in a Costco medical plan, and the hearing aids had to be supplied at a Costco Hearing Aid Center).

- A 401(k) plan open to all employees who have completed 90 days of employment whereby Costco matched hourly employee contributions by 50 cents on the dollar for the first $1,000 annually to a maximum company match of $500 per year. The company's union employees on the West Coast qualified for matching contributions of 50 cents on the dollar to a maximum company match of $250 a year. In addition to the matching contribution, Costco also normally made a discretionary contribution to the accounts of eligible employees based on the number of years of service with the company (or in the case of union employees based on the straight-time hours worked). For other than union employees, this discretionary contribution was a percentage of the employee's compensation that ranged from a low of 3 percent (for employees with 1 to 3 years of service) to a high of 9 percent (for employees with 25 or more years of service). Company contributions to employee 410(k) plans were $436 million in fiscal 2014, $454 million in fiscal 2015, and $489 million in 2016.

- A dependent care reimbursement plan in which Costco employees whose families qualified could pay for day care for children under 13 or adult day care with pretax dollars and realize savings of anywhere from $750 to $2,000 per year.
- Long-term and short-term disability coverage.
- Generous life insurance and accidental death and dismemberment coverage, with benefits based on years of service and whether the employee worked full-time or part-time. Employees could elect to purchase supplemental coverage for themselves, their spouses, or their children.
- An employee stock purchase plan allowing all employees to buy Costco stock via payroll deduction so as to avoid commissions and fees.

Although Costco's longstanding practice of paying good wages and good benefits was contrary to conventional wisdom in discount retailing, cofounder and former CEO Jim Sinegal, who originated the practice, firmly believed that having a well-compensated workforce was very important to executing Costco's strategy successfully. He said, "Imagine that you have 120,000 loyal ambassadors out there who are constantly saying good things about Costco. It has to be a significant advantage for you. . . . Paying good wages and keeping your people working with you is very good business."[18] When a reporter asked him about why Costco treated its workers so well compared to other retailers (particularly Walmart, which paid lower wages and had a skimpier benefits package), Sinegal replied: "Why shouldn't employees have the right to good wages and good careers. . . . It absolutely makes good business sense. Most people agree that we're the lowest-cost producer. Yet we pay the highest wages. So it must mean we get better productivity. Its axiomatic in our business—you get what you pay for."[19]

Good wages and benefits were said to be why employee turnover at Costco typically ran under 6 to 7 percent after the first year of employment. Some Costco employees had been with the company since its founding in 1983. Many others had started working part-time at Costco while in high school or college and opted to make a career at the company. One Costco employee told an ABC *20/20* reporter, "It's

a good place to work; they take good care of us."[20] A Costco vice president and head baker said working for Costco was a family affair: "My whole family works for Costco, my husband does, my daughter does, my new son-in-law does."[21] Another employee, a receiving clerk who made about $40,000 a year, said, "I want to retire here. I love it here."[22] An employee with over two years of service could not be fired without the approval of a senior company officer.

Selecting People for Open Positions Costco's top management wanted employees to feel that they could have a long career at Costco. It was company policy to fill the vast majority of its higher-level openings by promotions from within; at one recent point, the percentage ran close to 98 percent, which meant that the majority of Costco's management team members (including warehouse, merchandise, administrative, membership, front end, and receiving managers) had come up through the ranks. Many of the company's vice presidents had started in entry-level jobs. According to Jim Sinegal, "We have guys who started pushing shopping carts out on the parking lot for us who are now vice presidents of our company."[23] Costco made a point of recruiting at local universities; Sinegal explained why: "These people are smarter than the average person, hard-working, and they haven't made a career choice."[24] On another occasion, he said, "If someone came to us and said he just got a master's in business at Harvard, we would say fine, would you like to start pushing carts?"[25] Those employees who demonstrated smarts and strong people management skills moved up through the ranks.

But without an aptitude for the details of discount retailing, even up-and-coming employees stood no chance of being promoted to a position of warehouse manager. Top Costco executives who oversaw warehouse operations insisted that candidates for warehouse managers be top-flight merchandisers with a gift for the details of making items fly off the shelves. Based on his experience as CEO, Sinegal said, "People who have a feel for it just start to get it. Others, you look at them and it's like staring at a blank canvas. I'm not trying to be unduly harsh, but that's the way it works."[26] Most newly appointed warehouse managers at Costco came from the ranks of assistant warehouse managers who had a track record of being shrewd merchandisers and tuned into what new or different products might sell well given the clientele that patronized their particular warehouse. Just having the requisite skills in people management, crisis management, and cost-effective warehouse operations was not enough.

Executive Compensation

Executives at Costco did not earn the outlandish salaries that had become customary over the past decade at most large corporations. In Jim Sinegal's last two years as Costco's CEO, he received a salary of $350,000 and a bonus of $190,400 in fiscal 2010 and a salary of $350,000 and a bonus of $198,400 in fiscal 2011. Co-founder and Chairman Jeff Brotman's compensation in 2010 and 2011 was the same as Sinegal's. Craig Jelinek's salary as president and CEO in fiscal 2016 was $700,000, and he received a bonus of $81,600; Chairman Jeff Brotman's salary was $650,000 and his bonus was also $81,600. Other high-paid officers at Costco received salaries in the $660,000 to $700,000 range and bonuses of $50,000 to $52,640 in fiscal 2016.

Asked why executive compensation at Costco was only a fraction of the amounts typically paid to top-level executives at other corporations with revenues and operating scale comparable to Costco's, Sinegal replied: "I figured that if I was making something like 12 times more than the typical person working on the floor, that that was a fair salary."[27] To another reporter, he said: "Listen, I'm one of the founders of this business. I've been very well rewarded. I don't require a salary that's 100 times more than the people who work on the sales floor."[28] During his tenure as CEO, Sinegal's employment contract was only a page long and provided that he could be terminated for cause.

However, while executive salaries and bonuses were modest in comparison with those at other companies Costco's size, Costco did close the gap via an equity compensation program that featured awarding restricted stock units (RSUs) to executives based on defined performance criteria. The philosophy at Costco was that equity compensation should be the largest component of compensation for all executive officers and be tied directly to achievement of pre-tax income targets. In fiscal 2016, the Compensation Committee of the Board of Directors granted RSUs to Craig Jelinek and Jeff Brotman (worth about $5.56 million on the date of the grant but subject to time-vesting restrictions) and shares worth about $2.9 million on the date of grant but also subject to various restrictions to three other top-ranking executives. In December 2016, Jim Sinegal was deemed to be the beneficial owner of 1.5 million shares of Costco stock, Jeff Brotman the beneficial owner of almost 464,000 shares, and Craig Jelinek the beneficial owner of 289,000 shares. All directors and officers as a group (24 persons) were the beneficial owners of almost 3.28 million shares in December 2016.

Costco's Business Philosophy, Values, and Code of Ethics

Jim Sinegal, who was the son of a steelworker, had ingrained five simple and down-to-earth business principles into Costco's corporate culture and the manner in which the company operated. The following are excerpts of these principles and operating approaches:

1. **Obey the law**—The law is irrefutable! Absent a moral imperative to challenge a law, we must conduct our business in total compliance with the laws of every community where we do business. We pledge to:

   - Comply with all laws and other legal requirements.
   - Respect all public officials and their positions.
   - Comply with safety and security standards for all products sold.
   - Exceed ecological standards required in every community where we do business.
   - Comply with all applicable wage and hour laws.
   - Comply with all applicable antitrust laws.
   - Conduct business in and with foreign countries in a manner that is legal and proper under United States and foreign laws.
   - Not offer, give, ask for, or receive any form of bribe or kickback to or from any person or pay to expedite government action or otherwise act in violation of the Foreign Corrupt Practices Act or the laws of other countries.

- Promote fair, accurate, timely, and understandable disclosure in reports filed with the Securities and Exchange Commission and in other public communications by the company.

2. **Take care of our members**—Costco membership is open to business owners, as well as individuals. Our members are our reason for being—the key to our success. If we don't keep our members happy, little else that we do will make a difference. There are plenty of shopping alternatives for our members, and if they fail to show up, we cannot survive. Our members have extended a trust to Costco by virtue of paying a fee to shop with us. We will succeed only if we do not violate the trust they have extended to us, and that trust extends to every area of our business. We pledge to:

   - Provide top-quality products at the best prices in the market.
   - Provide high-quality, safe, and wholesome food products by requiring that both vendors and employees be in compliance with the highest food safety standards in the industry.
   - Provide our members with a 100 percent satisfaction guaranteed warranty on every product and service we sell, including their membership fee.
   - Assure our members that every product we sell is authentic in make and in representation of performance.
   - Make our shopping environment a pleasant experience by making our members feel welcome as our guests.
   - Provide products to our members that will be ecologically sensitive.
   - Provide our members with the best customer service in the retail industry.
   - Give back to our communities through employee volunteerism and employee and corporate contributions to United Way and Children's Hospitals.

3. **Take care of our employees**—Our employees are our most important asset. We believe we have the very best employees in the warehouse club industry, and we are committed to providing them with rewarding challenges and ample opportunities for personal and career growth. We pledge to provide our employees with:

   - Competitive wages.
   - Great benefits.
   - A safe and healthy work environment.
   - Challenging and fun work.
   - Career opportunities.
   - An atmosphere free from harassment or discrimination.
   - An Open-Door Policy that allows access to ascending levels of management to resolve issues.
   - Opportunities to give back to their communities through volunteerism and fundraising.

4. **Respect our suppliers**—Our suppliers are our partners in business and for us to prosper as a company, they must prosper with us. To that end, we strive to:

   - Treat all suppliers and their representatives as we would expect to be treated if visiting their places of business.
   - Honor all commitments.
   - Protect all suppliers' property assigned to Costco as though it were our own.
   - Not accept gratuities of any kind from a supplier.
   - If in doubt as to what course of action to take on a business matter that is open to varying ethical interpretations, TAKE THE HIGH ROAD AND DO WHAT IS RIGHT.

   If we do these four things throughout our organization, then we will achieve our ultimate goal, which is to:

5. **Reward our shareholders**—As a company with stock that is traded publicly on the NASDAQ stock exchange, our shareholders are our business partners. We can only be successful so long as we are providing them with a good return on the money they invest in our company . . . . We pledge to operate our company in such a way that our present and future stockholders, as well as our employees, will be rewarded for our efforts.[29]

Environmental Sustainability

In recent years, Costco management had undertaken a series of initiatives to invest in various environmental and energy-saving systems. The stated objective was to ensure that the company's carbon footprint grew at a slower rate than the company's sales growth. Going into 2017, Costco had rooftop solar photovoltaic systems in operation at 91 of its warehouses; some warehouses used solar power to light their parking lots. All new facilities were being designed and constructed to be more energy efficient. Costco's metal warehouse design, which included use of recycled steel, was consistent with the requirements of the Silver Level LEED Standard—the certification standards of the organization Leadership in Energy and Environmental Design (LEED) were nationally accepted as a benchmark green building design and construction. Costco's recently developed non-metal designs for warehouses had resulted in the ability to meet Gold Level LEED Standards.

Energy-efficient lighting and energy-efficient mechanical systems for heating, cooling, and refrigeration were being installed in all new facilities and at growing numbers of older facilities. Internet-based energy management systems had been installed, giving Costco the ability to regulate energy usage on an hourly basis at all of its warehouses in North America and at some international locations. These energy-saving initiatives, along with installation of LED lighting and warehouse skylights, had reduced the lighting loads on Costco's sales floors by over 50 percent from 2001 to 2016. In 2017, nearly 120 warehouses were participating in the company's water efficiency program, with savings ranging from 20 percent to 25 percent. Recycled asphalt was being used for paving most warehouse parking lots.

Other initiatives included working with suppliers to make greater use of sales-floor-ready packaging, changing container shapes from round to square (to enable more units to be stacked on a single pallet on warehouse sales floors and to conserve on trucking freight costs), making greater use of recycled plastic packaging, reusing cardboard packaging (empty store cartons were given to members to carry their purchases home), and expanding the use of non-chemical water treatment systems used in warehouse cooling towers to reduce the amount of chemicals going into

sewer systems. In addition, a bigger portion of the trash that warehouses generated each week, much of which was formerly sent to landfills, was being recycled into usable products or diverted to facilities that used waste as fuel for generating electricity.

Costco was committed to sourcing all of the seafood it sold from responsible and environmentally sustainable sources that were certified by the Marine Stewardship Council; in no instances did Costco sell seafood species that were classified as environmentally endangered and it monitored the aquaculture practices of its suppliers that farmed seafood. The company had long been committed to enhancing the welfare and proper handling of all animals used in food products sold at Costco. According to the company's official statement on animal welfare, "This is not only the right thing to do, it is an important moral and ethical obligation we owe to our members, suppliers, and most of all to the animals we depend on for products that are sold at Costco."[30] As part of the company's commitment, Costco had established an animal welfare audit program that utilized recognized audit standards and programs conducted by trained, certified auditors and that reviewed animal welfare both on the farm and at slaughter.

Costco had been an active member of the Environmental Protection Agency's Energy Star and Climate Protection Partnerships since 2002 and was a major retailer of Energy Star qualified compact florescent lamp (CFL) bulbs and LED light bulbs.

Competition

The wholesale club and warehouse segment of retailing in North America was an estimated $175 billion business in 2016. There were three main competitors—Costco Wholesale, Sam's Club, and BJ's Wholesale Club. In early 2017, there were about 1,460 warehouse locations across the United States and Canada; most every major metropolitan area had one, if not several, warehouse clubs. Costco had about a 59 percent share of warehouse club sales across the United States and Canada, with Sam's Club (a division of Walmart) having roughly a 34 percent share and BJ's Wholesale Club and several small warehouse club competitors close to a 7 percent share.

Competition among the warehouse clubs was based on such factors as price, merchandise quality and selection, location, and member service. However, warehouse clubs also competed with a wide range of other types of retailers, including retail discounters like Walmart and Dollar General, supermarkets, general merchandise chains, specialty chains, gasoline stations, and Internet retailers. Not only did Walmart, the world's largest retailer, compete directly with Costco via its Sam's Club subsidiary, but its Walmart Supercenters sold many of the same types of merchandise at attractively low prices as well. Target, Kohl's, Kroger, and Amazon.com had emerged as significant retail competitors in certain general merchandise categories. Low-cost operators selling a single category or narrow range of merchandise—such as Trader Joe's, Lowe's, Home Depot, Office Depot, Staples, Best Buy, PetSmart, and Barnes & Noble—had significant market shares in their respective product categories. Notwithstanding the competition from other retailers and discounters, the low prices and merchandise selection found at Costco, Sam's Club, and BJ's Wholesale were attractive to small-business owners, individual households (particularly bargain-hunters and those with large families), churches and nonprofit organizations, caterers, and small restaurants. The internationally located warehouses faced similar types of competitors.

Brief profiles of Costco's two primary competitors in North America are presented in the following sections.

Sam's Club

The first Sam's Club opened in 1984, and Walmart management in the ensuing years proceeded to grow the warehouse membership club concept into a significant business and major Walmart division. The concept of the Sam's Club format was to sell merchandise at very low profit margins, resulting in low prices to members. The mission of Sam's Club was "to make savings simple for members by providing them with exciting, quality merchandise and a superior shopping experience, all at a great value."[31]

In early 2017, there were 660 Sam's Club locations in the United States and Puerto Rico, many of which were adjacent to Walmart Supercenters, and about 100 Sam's Club locations in Mexico, Brazil, and China. (Financial and operating data for the Sam's Club locations in Mexico, Brazil, and China were not separately available because Walmart grouped its reporting of all store operations in 27 countries outside the United States into a segment called Walmart International that did not break out different types of stores.) In fiscal year 2017 (ending January 31, 2017), the Sam's Club locations in the United States and Puerto Rico had record revenues of $59 billion (including membership fees), making it the eighth largest retailer in the United States. Sam's Clubs generally ranged between 94,000 and 161,000 square feet, with the average at the end of fiscal 2017 being 133,900 square feet; several newer locations were as large as 190,000 square feet. All Sam's Club warehouses had concrete floors, sparse décor, and goods displayed on pallets, simple wooden shelves, or racks in the case of apparel. In 2009 and 2010, Sam's Club began a long-term warehouse remodeling program for its older locations.

Exhibit 5 provides financial and operating highlights for selected years from 2001 to 2016.

Merchandise Offerings   Sam's Club warehouses stocked about 4,000 items, a big fraction of which were standard and a small fraction of which represented special buys and one-time offerings. The treasure-hunt items at Sam's Club tended to be less upscale and less expensive than those at Costco. The merchandise selection included brand-name merchandise in a variety of categories and a selection of private-label items sold under the "Member's Mark," "Daily Chef," and "Sam's Club" brands. Most club locations had fresh-foods departments that included bakery, meat, produce, floral products, and a Sam's Café. A significant number of clubs had a one-hour photo processing department, a pharmacy that filled prescriptions, hearing aid and optical departments, tire and battery centers, and self-service gasoline pumps. Sam's Club guaranteed it would beat any price for branded prescriptions. Members could shop for a wider assortment of merchandise (about 61,000 items) and services online at www.samsclub.com; the Sam's Club website attracted an average of 18.6 million unique visitors monthly. The percentage

EXHIBIT 5

Selected Financial and Operating Data for Sam's Club, Fiscal Years 2001, 2010, 2015–2017

Sam's Club	2017	2016	2015	2010	2001
Net sales in the United States and Puerto Rico, excluding membership fees[a] (millions of $)	$57,365	$56,828	$58,020	$47,806	$26,798
Operating income in the United States (millions of $)	1,671	1,820	1,976	1,515	942
Assets in the United States and Puerto Rico (millions of $)	14,125	13,998	13,995	12,073	3,843
Number of U.S. and Puerto Rico locations at year-end	660	655	647	605	475
Average sales per year-end U.S. and Puerto Rican location, excluding membership fees (in millions of $)	$ 86.9	$ 86.8	$ 89.6	$ 79.0	$ 56.4
Sales growth at existing U.S. and Puerto Rico warehouses open more than 12 months:					
Including gasoline sales	0.5%	(3.2)%	0.0%	(1.4)%	n.a.
Not including gasoline sales	1.8%	1.4%	2.1%	0.7%	n.a.
Average warehouse size in the United States and Puerto Rico (square feet)	133,900	133,700	134,000	133,000	122,100

[a.] The sales figure includes membership fees and is only for warehouses in the United States and Puerto Rico. For financial reporting purposes, Walmart consolidates the operations of all foreign-based stores into a single "international" segment figure. Thus, separate financial information for only the foreign-based Sam's Club locations in Mexico, China, and Brazil is not separately available.

Source: Walmart's 10-K reports and annual reports, fiscal years 2016, 2010, and 2001.

composition of sales across major merchandise categories was:

Merchandise Categories	Fiscal Years Ending January 31		
	2017	2016	2015
Grocery and consumables (dairy, meat, bakery, deli, produce, dry, chilled or frozen packaged foods, alcoholic and nonalcoholic beverages, floral, snack foods, candy, other grocery items, health and beauty aids, paper goods, laundry and home care, baby care, pet supplies, and other consumable items)	59%	59%	57%
Fuel and other categories (gasoline, tobacco, tools and power equipment, and tire and battery centers)	20%	20%	23%
Technology, office and entertainment (electronics, wireless, software, video games, movies, books, music, toys, office supplies, office furniture, photo processing, and gift cards)	6%	7%	7%
Home and apparel (home improvement, outdoor living, grills, gardening, furniture, apparel, jewelry, housewares, toys, seasonal items, mattresses, and small appliances)	9%	9%	8%
Health and wellness (pharmacy, hearing and optical services, and over-the-counter drugs)	6%	5%	5%

Walmart's Fiscal Year 2016 10-K Report.

Membership and Hours of Operation The annual fee for Sam's Club business members was $45 for the primary membership card, with a spouse card available at no additional cost. Business members could add up to eight business associates for $45 each. Individuals could purchase a "Sam's Savings" membership card for $45. The membership cards for both individuals and businesses had an "Instant Savings" where limited-time promotional discounts were electronically loaded on a member's card and automatically applied at checkout. A Sam's Club Plus premium membership for business and individuals cost $100; in addition to eligibility for Instant Savings, Plus members had early shopping hour privileges, received discounts on select prescription drugs, and earned cash-back rewards of $10 for every $500 they spent in qualifying pretax purchases. Cash-back rewards could be used for purchases, membership fees, or redeemed for cash. About 600,000 small-business members shopped at Sam's Club weekly.

Regular hours of operations were Monday through Friday from 10:00 a.m. to 8:30 p.m., Saturday from 9:00 a.m. to 8:30 p.m., and Sunday from 10:00 a.m. to 6:00 p.m.; Business and Plus cardholders had the ability to shop before the regular operating hours Monday through Saturday beginning at 7 a.m. All club members could use a variety of payment methods, including Visa credit and debit cards, American Express cards, and a co-branded Sam's Club "Cash-Back" Mastercard. The pharmacy and optical departments accepted payments for products and services through members' health benefit plans.

Distribution Approximately 68 percent of the non-fuel merchandise at Sam's Club was shipped from some 25 distribution facilities dedicated to Sam's Club operations that were strategically located across the continental United States, and in the case of perishable items, from nearby Walmart grocery distribution centers; the balance was shipped by suppliers direct to Sam's Club locations. Of these 25 distribution facilities, 6 were owned/leased and operated by Sam's Club and 19 were owned/leased and operated by third parties. Like Costco, Sam's Club distribution centers employed cross-docking techniques whereby incoming shipments were transferred immediately to outgoing trailers destined for Sam's Club locations; shipments typically spent less than 24 hours at a cross-docking facility and in some instances were there only an hour. A combination of company-owned trucks and independent trucking companies were used to transport merchandise from distribution centers to club locations.

Employment In 2017, Sam's Club employed about 100,000 people across all aspects of its operations in the United States. While the people who worked at Sam's Club warehouses were in all stages of life, a sizable fraction had accepted job offers because they had minimal skill levels and were looking for their first job, or needed only a part-time job, or were wanting to start a second career. More than 60 percent of managers of Sam's Club warehouses had begun their careers at Sam's Club as hourly warehouse employees and had moved up through the ranks to their present positions.

BJ's Wholesale Club

BJ's Wholesale Club introduced the member warehouse concept to the northeastern United States in the mid-1980s and, as of June 2017, had a total of 213 warehouses in 15 eastern states extending from Maine to Florida. A large percentage of these facilities were full-sized warehouse clubs that averaged about 114,000 square feet, but there were over 20 smaller format warehouse clubs that averaged approximately 73,000 square feet and were located in markets too small to support a full-sized warehouse. Approximately 85 percent of BJ's full-sized warehouse clubs had at least one Costco or Sam's Club warehouse operating in their trading areas (within a distance of 10 miles or less).

In late June 2011, BJ's Wholesale agreed to a buyout offer from two private equity firms and shortly thereafter became a privately held company. Exhibit 6 shows selected financial and operating data for BJ's for fiscal years 2007 through 2011—the last years its financial and operating data were publicly available.

Product Offerings and Merchandising Like Costco and Sam's Club, BJ's Wholesale sold high-quality, brand-name merchandise at prices that were significantly lower than the prices found at supermarkets, discount retail chains, department stores, drugstores, and specialty retail stores like Best Buy. Its merchandise lineup of about 7,000 items included consumer electronics, prerecorded media, small appliances, tires, jewelry, health and beauty aids, household products, computer software, books, greeting cards, apparel, furniture, toys, seasonal items, frozen foods, fresh meat and dairy products, beverages, dry grocery items, fresh produce, flowers, canned goods, and household products. About 70 percent of BJ's product line could be found in supermarkets. Private-label goods accounted for approximately 10 percent of food and general merchandise sales. Members could purchase additional products at the company's website, www.bjs.com.

BJ's warehouses had a number of specialty services that were designed to enable members to complete more of their shopping at BJ's and to encourage more frequent trips to the clubs. Like Costco and Sam's Club, BJ's sold gasoline at a discounted price as a means of displaying a favorable price image to prospective members and providing added value to existing members; in 2012, there were gas station operations at 107 BJ's locations. Other specialty services included full-service optical and

EXHIBIT 6

Selected Financial and Operating Data, BJ's Wholesale Club, Fiscal Years 2007–2011

Selected Income Statement Data (in millions, except per share data)	Jan. 29 2011	Jan. 30 2010	Jan. 31 2009	Feb. 2 2008	Feb. 3 2007 (53 weeks)
Net sales	$10,633	$9,954	$9,802	$8,792	$8,280
Membership fees	191	182	178	176	162
Other revenues	53	51	48	47	54
Total revenues	10,877	10,187	10,027	9,014	8,497
Cost of sales, including buying and occupancy costs	9,697	9,081	9,004	8,091	7,601
Selling, general and administrative expenses	934	875	799	724	740
Operating income	208	224	221	195	144
Net income	$ 95	$ 132	$ 135	$ 123	$ 72
Diluted earnings per share:	$ 1.77	$ 2.42	$ 2.28	$ 1.90	$ 1.08
Balance Sheet and Cash Flow Data (in millions)					
Cash and cash equivalents	$ 101	$ 59	$ 51	$ 97	$ 56
Current assets	1,292	1,173	1,076	1,145	1,070
Current liabilities	987	1,006	909	946	867
Working capital	305	167	167	199	203
Merchandise inventories	981	930	860	877	851
Total assets	2,322	2,166	2,021	2,047	1,993
Long-term debt	—	1	1	2	2
Stockholders' equity	1,144	1,033	985	980	1,020
Cash flow from operations	229	298	224	305	173
Capital expenditures	188	176	138	90	191
Selected Operating Data					
Clubs open at end of year	189	187	180	177	172
Number of members (in thousands)	9,600	9,400	9,000	8,800	8,700
Average sales per club location (in millions)	$ 56.3	$ 53.2	$ 54.6	$ 49.7	$ 48.1
Sales growth at existing clubs open more than 12 months	4.4%	(1.9)%	9.4%	3.7%	1.2%

Source: Company 10-K reports for 2011, 2010, 2008, and 2007.

hearing centers (more than 150 locations), food courts, a check printing service, vacation and travel packages, DirecTV packages, members-only Geico auto insurance deals, garden and storage shed installations, members-only Verizon deals, patios and sunrooms, a propane tank filling service, an automobile buying program, a car rental service, tire services, and electronics and jewelry protection plans. Most of these services were provided by outside operators in space leased from BJ's. In early 2007, BJ's abandoned prescription filling and closed all of its 46 in-club pharmacies.

Strategy Features That Differentiated BJ's

BJ's had developed a strategy and operating model that management believed differentiated the company from Costco and Sam's Club:

- Offering a wide range of choice—7,000 items versus 3,700 to 4,000 items at Costco and Sam's Club.

- Focusing on the individual consumer via merchandising strategies that emphasized a customer-friendly shopping experience.

- Clustering club locations to achieve the benefit of name recognition and maximize the efficiencies of management support, distribution, and marketing activities.

- Trying to establish and maintain the first or second industry leading position in each major market where it operated.
- Creating an exciting shopping experience for members with a constantly changing mix of food and general merchandise items and carrying a broader product assortment than competitors.
- Supplementing the warehouse format with aisle markers, express checkout lanes, self-checkout lanes, and low-cost video-based sales aids to make shopping more efficient for members.
- Being open longer hours than competitors; typical hours of operation were 9 a.m. to 7 p.m. Monday through Friday and 9 a.m. to 6 p.m. Saturday and Sunday.
- Offering smaller package sizes of many items.
- Accepting manufacturers' coupons.
- Accepting more credit card payment options.

Membership   BJ's Wholesale Club had about 9.6 million members in 2011 (see Exhibit 6). In 2017, individuals could become Inner Circle members for a fee of $50 per year that included a second card for a household member; cards for up to three other family members and friends could be added to an Inner Circle member's account for an additional $30 per card. Business memberships cost $50 annually and provided one Primary Business card and one free supplemental card for a business associate at no additional charge; up to eight additional supplemental cards could be purchased for $50 each. Both individual and business members could upgrade to a BJ's Perks Rewards membership for a fee of $100 per year and earn 2 percent cash back on in-club and online purchases. Perks Card members paying the $100 membership fee could apply for a BJ's Perks Plus™ credit card (MasterCard), which had no annual credit card fee and earned 3 percent cash back on in-club and online purchases, 10 cents off per gallon at BJ's gas stations, and 1 percent cash back on all non-BJ's purchases everywhere else MasterCard was accepted. Individuals and businesses with a BJ's Perks Reward™ membership could also upgrade further by applying for a BJ's Perks Elite™ MasterCard, which

had no annual fee and earned 5 percent cash back on in-club and online purchases, 10 cents off per gallon at BJ's gas stations, and 1 percent cash back on all non-BJ's purchases everywhere MasterCard was accepted. BJ's accepted MasterCard, Visa, Discover, and American Express cards at all locations; members could also pay for purchases by cash, check, or magnetically encoded Electronic Benefit Transfer cards (issued by state welfare departments). Manufacturer's coupons were accepted for merchandise purchased at the register in any club where the product was sold. BJ's accepted returns of most merchandise within 30 days after purchase.

Marketing and Promotion   BJ's increased customer awareness of its clubs primarily through direct mail, public relations efforts, marketing programs for newly opened clubs, and a publication called *BJ's Journal,* which was mailed to members throughout the year.

Warehouse Club Operations   BJ's warehouses were located in both freestanding locations and shopping centers. As of 2011, construction and site development costs for a full-sized BJ's club were in the $6 million to $10 million range; land acquisition costs ranged from $3 million to $10 million but could be significantly higher in some locations. Each warehouse generally had an investment of $3 million to $4 million for fixtures and equipment. Pre-opening expenses at a new club ran $1.0 million to $2.0 million. Including space for parking, a typical full-sized BJ's club required 13 to 14 acres of land; smaller clubs typically required about 8 acres. Prior to being acquired in 2011, BJ's had financed all of its club expansions, as well as all other capital expenditures, with internally generated funds.

Merchandise purchased from manufacturers was routed either to a BJ's cross-docking facility or directly to clubs. Personnel at the cross-docking facilities broke down truckload quantity shipments from manufacturers and reallocated goods for shipment to individual clubs, generally within 24 hours. BJ's worked closely with manufacturers to minimize the amount of handling required once merchandise is received at a club. Merchandise was generally displayed on pallets containing large quantities of each item, thereby reducing labor required for handling, stocking, and restocking. Backup merchandise was generally stored in steel racks above the sales floor. Most merchandise was pre-marked by the manufacturer so it did not require ticketing at the club. Full-sized clubs had approximately $2 million in inventory. Management was able to limit inventory shrinkage to 0.20 percent or less of net sales by strictly controlling the exits of clubs, generally limiting customers to members, and using state-of-the-art electronic article surveillance technology.

ENDNOTES

[1] As quoted in Alan B. Goldberg and Bill Ritter, "Costco CEO Finds Pro-Worker Means Profitability," an ABC News original report on *20/20,* August 2, 2006, http://abcnews.go.com/2020/Business/story?id=1362779 (accessed November 15, 2006).

[2] Ibid.

[3] As described in Nina Shapiro, "Company for the People," *Seattle Weekly,* December 15, 2004, www.seattleweekly.com (accessed November 14, 2006).

[4] "How Much Does a Costco Store Sell Each Year?" *Investopedia,* June 19, 2015, http://www.investopedia.com/stock-analysis/061915/how-much-does-costco-store-sell-each-year-cost.aspx#ixzz3zF8H31dL (accessed February 4, 2016).

[5] See, for example, Costco's "Code of Ethics," posted in the investor relations section of Costco's website under a link entitled "Corporate Governance and Citizenship" (accessed on February 4, 2016).

[6] Costco Wholesale, 2011 Annual Report, for the year ended August 28, 2011, p. 5.

[7] Ibid., pp. 128–29.

[8] Steven Greenhouse, "How Costco Became the Anti-Wal-Mart," *The New York Times,* July 17, 2005, www.wakeupwalmart.com/news (accessed November 28, 2006).

[9] As quoted in Greenhouse, "How Costco Became the Anti-Wal-Mart," *The New York Times,* July 17, 2005, www.wakeupwalmart.com/news (accessed November 28, 2006).

[10] Shapiro, "Company for the People," *Seattle Weekly,* December 15, 2004, www.seattleweekly.com (accessed November 14, 2006).

[11] Greenhouse, "How Costco Became the Anti-Wal-Mart," *The New York Times,* July 17, 2005, www.wakeupwalmart.com/news (accessed November 28, 2006).

[12] Matthew Boyle, "Why Costco Is So Damn Addictive," *Fortune,* October 30, 2006, p. 132.

[13] Costco's 2005 Annual Report.

[14] Jeremy Bowman, "Who Is Costco's Favorite Customer?" *The Motley Fool,* June 17, 2016, www.fool.com (accessed June 5, 2017); J. Max Robins, "Costco's Surprisingly Large-Circulation Magazine," *MediaPost,* March 6, 2015, www.mediapost.com (accessed June 5, 2017).

[15] Goldberg and Ritter, "Costco CEO Finds Pro-Worker Means Profitability," an ABC News original report on *20/20,* August 2, 2006, http://abcnews.go.com/2020/Business/story?id=1362779 (accessed November 15, 2006).

[16] Ibid.

[17] Based on information posted at www.glassdoor.com (accessed February 28, 2012).

[18] Ibid.

[19] Shapiro, "Company for the People," *Seattle Weekly,* December 15, 2004, www.seattleweekly.com (accessed November 14, 2006).

[20] Goldberg and Ritter, "Costco CEO Finds Pro-Worker Means Profitability," an ABC News original report on *20/20,* August 2, 2006, http://abcnews.go.com/2020/Business/story?id=1362779 (accessed November 15, 2006).

[21] Ibid.

[22] Greenhouse, "How Costco Became the Anti-Wal-Mart," *The New York Times,* July 17, 2005, www.wakeupwalmart.com/news (accessed November 28, 2006).

[23] Goldberg and Ritter, "Costco CEO Finds Pro-Worker Means Profitability," an ABC News original report on *20/20,* August 2, 2006, http://abcnews.go.com/2020/Business/story?id=1362779 (accessed November 15, 2006).

[24] Boyle, "Why Costco Is So Damn Addictive," *Fortune,* October 30, 2006, p. 132.

[25] Shapiro, "Company for the People," *Seattle Weekly,* December 15, 2004, www.seattleweekly.com (accessed November 14, 2006).

[26] Ibid.

[27] Goldberg and Ritter, "Costco CEO Finds Pro-Worker Means Profitability," an ABC News original report on *20/20,* August 2, 2006, http://abcnews.go.com/2020/Business/story?id=1362779 (accessed November 15, 2006).

[28] Shapiro, "Company for the People," *Seattle Weekly,* December 15, 2004, www.seattleweekly.com (accessed November 14, 2006).

[29] Costco Code of Ethics, posted in the Investor Relations section of Costco's website www.costco.com (accessed February 8, 2016).

[30] "Mission Statement on Animal Welfare," posted at www.costco.com in the Investor Relations section (accessed February 8, 2016).

[31] Walmart 2010 Annual Report, p. 8.

Competition in the Craft Brewing Industry in 2017

 connect

JOHN D. VARLARO Johnson & Wales University

JOHN E. GAMBLE Texas A&M University–Corpus Christi

Locally produced or regional craft beers caused a seismic shift in the U.S. beer industry during the early 2010s with the gains of the small, regional newcomers coming at the expense of such well-known brands as Budweiser, Miller, Coors, and Bud Light. Craft breweries, which by definition sold fewer than 6 million barrels (bbls) per year, expanded rapidly with the deregulation of intrastate alcohol distribution and retail laws and a change in consumer preferences toward unique and high-quality beers. The growing popularity of craft beers allowed the total beer industry in the United States to increase by 6.7 percent annually between 2011 and 2016 to reach $39.5 billion. The production of U.S. craft breweries more than doubled from 11.5 million bbls per year to about 24.6 million bbls per year during that time. In addition, production by microbreweries and brewpubs accounted for 90 percent of craft brewer growth in 2016.[1]

The industry had begun to show signs of a slowdown going into 2017, with Boston Beer Company, the second largest craft brewery in the United States and known for its Samuel Adams brand, experiencing a 4 percent sales decline in 2016 that erased two years of of growth. The annual revenues of Anheuser-Busch InBev SA, whose portfolio included global brands Budweiser, Corona, and Stella Artois and numerous international and local brands, remained relatively consistent from 2014 to 2016. However, the sales volume of Anheuser-Busch's flagship brands and its newly acquired and international brands such as Corona, Goose Island, Shock Top, Beck's, and St. Pauli Girl allowed it to control 45.8 percent of the U.S. market for beer in 2016.[2]

Industry competition was increasing as grain price fluctuations affected cost structures and growing consolidation within the beer industry—led most notably by AB InBev's acquisition of several craft breweries, Grupo Modelo, and its pending $104 billion acquisition of SABMiller—created a battle for market share. While the market for specialty beer was expected to gradually plateau by 2020, it appeared that the slowing growth had arrived by 2017. Nevertheless, craft breweries and microbreweries were expected to expand in number and in terms of market share as consumers sought out new pale ales, stouts, wheat beers, pilsners, and lagers with regional or local flairs.

The Beer Market

The total economic impact of the beer market was estimated to be 2.0 percent of the total U.S. GDP in 2016 when variables such as jobs within beer production, sales, and distribution were included.[3] Exhibit 1 presents annual beer production statistics for the United States between 2006 and 2016.

Although U.S. production had declined since 2008, consumption was increasing elsewhere in the world, resulting in a forecasted global market of almost $700 billion in sales by 2020.[4] Global growth seemed to be fueled by the introduction of

Barrels of Beer Produced in the United States, 2006–2016 (in millions)

Year	Barrels Produced (in millions)*
2006	198
2007	200
2008	200
2009	197
2010	195
2011	193
2012	196
2013	192
2014	193
2015	191
2016	189

*Rounded to the nearest million.

Source: Alcohol and Tobacco Tax and Trade Bureau website.

Top 10 U.S. Breweries in 2015

Rank	Brewery
1	Anheuser-Busch, Inc.
2	MillerCoors
3	Pabst Brewing Co.
4	D.G. Yuengling and Son, Inc.
5	Boston Beer Co.
6	North American Breweries
7	Sierra Nevada Brewing Co.
8	New Belgium Brewing Co.
9	Craft Brewing Alliance
10	Lagunitas Brewing Co.

Source: Brewers Association.

Top 10 Global Beer Producers by Volume, 2014–2015

Rank	Producer	Volume (millions of barrels)* 2014	Volume (millions of barrels)* 2015
1	AB InBev	351	353
2	SABMiller	249	250
3	Heineken	180	186
4	Carlsberg	110	107
5	Tsingtao (Group)	78	72
6	Molson Coors Brewing Company	54	54
7	Beijing Yanjing	45	41
8	Kirin	36	35
9	Castel BGI	26	26
10	Asahi	26	24

*Not in original report. Computed using 1 hL = .852 barrel for comparison; to nearest million bbl.

Source: AB InBev 20-F SEC Document, 2015 and 2016

differing styles of beer to regions where consumers had not previously had access and the expansion of demographics not normally known for consuming beer. Thus, exported beer to both developed and developing regions helped drive future growth. As an example, China recently saw a number of domestic craft breweries producing beer as well as experimenting with locally and regionally known flavors, enticing the domestic palette with flavors such as green tea.

The Brewers Association, a trade association for brewers, suppliers, and others within the industry, designated a brewery as a craft brewer when output was less than 6 million barrels annually and the ownership was more than 75 percent independent of another non-craft beer producer or entity. The rapid increase in popularity for local beers allowed the number of U.S. brewers to reach almost 5,500 in 2016—nearly double the number in 2012. Of these breweries, 99 percent were identified as craft breweries with distribution ranging from local to national. While large global breweries occupied the top four positions among the largest U.S. breweries, five craft breweries were ranked among the top 10 largest U.S. brewers in 2015—see Exhibit 2.

Exhibit 3 shows the production volume of the 10 largest beer producers worldwide for 2014 and 2015. The number of craft breweries in each U.S. state are presented in Exhibit 4.

EXHIBIT 4

Number of Craft Brewers by State, 2015

State	Brewers	State	Brewers
Alabama	24	Montana	49
Alaska	27	Nebraska	33
Arizona	78	Nevada	34
Arkansas	26	New Hampshire	44
California	518	New Jersey	51
Colorado	284	New Mexico	45
Connecticut	35	New York	208
Delaware	15	North Carolina	161
Florida	151	North Dakota	9
Georgia	45	Ohio	143
Hawaii	13	Oklahoma	14
Idaho	50	Oregon	228
Illinois	157	Pennsylvania	178
Indiana	115	Rhode Island	14
Iowa	58	South Carolina	36
Kansas	26	South Dakota	14
Kentucky	24	Tennessee	52
Louisiana	20	Texas	189
Maine	59	Utah	22
Maryland	60	Vermont	44
Massachusetts	84	Virginia	124
Michigan	205	Washington	305
Minnesota	105	West Virginia	12
Mississippi	8	Wisconsin	121
Missouri	71	Wyoming	23

Source: Brewers Association.

The Beer Production Process

The beer production process involves the fermentation of grains. The cereal grain barley is the most common grain used in the production of beer. Before fermentation, however, barley must be malted and milled. Malting allows the barley to germinate and produce the sugars that would be fermented by the yeast, yielding the sweetness of beer. By soaking the barley in water, the barley germinates, or grows, as it would when planted in the ground. This process is halted through the introduction of hot air and drying after germination began.

After malting, the barley is milled to break open the husk while also cracking the inner seed that has begun to germinate. Once milled, the barley is mashed, or added to hot water. The addition of the hot water produces sugar from the grain. This mixture is then filtered, resulting in the wort. The wort is then boiled, which sterilizes the beer. It is at this stage that hops are added. The taste and aroma of beer depend on the variety of hops and when the hops were added.

After boiling, the wort is cooled and then poured into the fermentor where yeast is added. The sugar created in the previous stages is broken down by the yeast through fermentation. The different styles of beer depend on the type of yeast used, typically either an ale or lager yeast. The time for this process could take a couple of weeks to a couple of months. After fermentation, the yeast is removed. The process is completed after carbon dioxide is added and the product is packaged.

Beer is a varied and differentiated product, with over 70 styles in 15 categories. Each style is dependent on a number of variables. These variables are controlled by the brewer through the process, and could include the origin of raw materials, approach to fermentation, and yeast used. For example, Guinness referenced on its website how barley purchased by the brewer was not only grown locally, but was also toasted specifically after malting, lending to its characteristic taste and color. As another example of differentiation through raw materials, wheat beers, such as German-style *hefeweizen,* are brewed with a minimum of 50 percent wheat instead of barley grain.

Development of Microbreweries and Economies of Scale

Although learning the art of brewing takes time, beer production lends itself to scalability and variety. For example, an amateur—or home brewer—could brew beer for home consumption. There had been a significant increase in the interest in home brewing, with over 1 million people pursuing the hobby in 2016.[5] It was also not uncommon for a home brewer to venture into entrepreneurship and begin brewing for commercial sales. However, beer production was highly labor intensive with much of the work done by hand. A certain level of production volume was necessary to achieve breakeven and make the microbrewery a successful commercial operation.

A small nanobrewery may brew a variety of flavor experiences and compete in niche markets, while the macrobrewery may focus on economies of scale and mass produce one style of beer. Both may attract consumers across segments, and were attributed to the easily scalable yet highly variable process of brewing beer. In contrast, a global producer such as AB InBev could produce beer for millions of consumers worldwide with factory-automated processes.

Legal Environment of Breweries

As beer was an alcoholic beverage, the industry was subject to much regulation. Further, these regulations could vary by state and municipality. One such regulation was regarding sales and distribution.

Distribution could be distinguished through direct sales (or self-distribution), and two-tier and three-tier systems. Regulations permitting direct sales allow the brewery to sell directly to the consumer. Growlers, bottle sales, as well as taprooms were all forms of direct, or retail, sales. There were usually requirements concerning direct sales, including limitations on volume sold to the consumer.

Even where self-distribution was legal, the legal volumes could be very small and limited. Very few brewers were exempt from distributing through wholesalers, referred to as a three-tier distribution system. And often to be operationally viable, brewers need access to this distribution system to generate revenue. In a three-tier system, the brewery must first sell to a wholesaler—the liquor or beer distributor. This distributor then sells to the retailer, who then ultimately sells to the consumer.

This distribution structure, however, had ramifications for the consumer, as much of what was available at retail outlets and restaurants was impacted by the distributor. This was further impacted by whether a brewery bottles or cans its beer, or distributes through kegs. While restaurants and bars could carry kegs, retail shelves at a local liquor store needed to have cans and bottles, as a relatively small number of consumers could accommodate kegs for home use. Thus, there may only be a few liquor stores or restaurants where a consumer may find a locally brewed beer. In states that do not allow self-distribution or on-premise sales, distribution and exposure to consumers could represent a barrier for breweries, especially those that were small or new.

The Alcohol and Tobacco Tax and Trade Bureau (TTB) was the main federal agency for regulating this industry. As another example of regulations, breweries were required to have labels for beers approved by the federal government, ensuring they meet advertising guidelines. In some instances, the TTB may need to approve the formula used for brewing the specific beer prior to the label receiving approval. Given the approval process, and the growth of craft breweries, the length of time this takes could reach several months. For a small microbrewery first starting, the delay in sales could potentially impact cash flow.

Employment law was another area impacting breweries. The Affordable Care Act (ACA) and changes to the Fair Labor Standards Act (FLSA) greatly affected labor cost in the industry. Where the ACA mandated health care coverage by employers, the FLSA changed overtime rules for employees previously classified as exempt or salaried. Finally, many states and municipalities passed or were considering passing increases to minimum wage. These changes in regulations could lead to significant increases in business costs, potentially impacting a brewery's ability to remain viable or competitive.

Lawsuits might also impact breweries' operations. Trademark infringement lawsuits regarding brewery and beer names were common. Further, food-related lawsuits could occur. In 2017, there were potential lawsuits against breweries distributing in California that did not meet the May 2016 requirement of providing an additional sign warning against pregnancy and BPA (Bisphenyl-A) consumption. BPA was commonly found in both cans and bottle caps, and thus breweries were potentially legally exposed, exemplifying the potential legal exposure to any brewery.

Suppliers to Breweries

The main suppliers to the industry were those who supply grain and hops. Growers might sell direct to breweries or distribute through wholesalers. Brewers who wish to produce a grain-specific beer would be required to procure the specific grain. Further, recipes might call for a variety of grains, including rye, wheat, and corn. As previously mentioned, the definition of craft was changed not only to include a higher threshold for annual production, but it also was changed to not exclude producers who used other grains, such as corn, in their production. Finally, origin-specific beers, such as German- or Belgian-styles, might also require specific grains.

The more specialized the grain or hop, the more difficult it was to obtain. Those breweries, then, competing based on specialized brewing were required to identify such suppliers. Conversely, larger, global producers of single-style beers were able to utilize economies of scale and demand lower prices from suppliers. Organically grown grains and hops suppliers would also fall into this category of providing specialized ingredients, and specialty brewers tend to use such ingredients.

Exhibit 5 illustrates the amount of grain products used between 2010 and 2014 in the United States by breweries.

It was estimated that hops acreage within the United States grew more than 70 percent from 2011 to 2016,[6] which seems to follow the growing demand due to the increased number of breweries. Hops were primarily grown in the Pacific Northwest states of Idaho, Washington, and Oregon. Washington's Yakima Valley was probably one of the more recognizable geographic-growing regions. There were numerous varieties of hops, however, and each contributes a different aroma and flavor profile. Hop growers have also trademarked names and varieties of hops. Further, as with grains, some beer styles require specific hops. Farmlands that were formerly known for hops have started to see a rejuvenation of this crop, such as in New England. In other areas, farmers were introducing hops as a new cash crop. Some hops farms were also dual purpose, combining the growing operations with brewing, thus serving as both a supplier of hops to breweries while also producing their own beer for retail. Recent news reports, however, were citing current and future shortages of hops due to the increased number of breweries. Rising temperatures in Europe led to a diminished yield in 2015, further impacting hops supplies. For breweries using recipes that require these specific hops, shortages could be detrimental to production. In some instances, larger beer producers had vertically integrated into hops farming to protect their supply.

Suppliers to the industry also include manufacturers and distributors of brewing equipment, such as fermentation tanks and refrigeration equipment. Purification equipment and testing tools were also necessary, given the brewing process and the need to ensure purity and safety of the product.

Depending on distribution and the distribution channel, breweries might need bottling or canning equipment. Thus breweries might invest heavily in automated bottling capabilities to expand capacity. Recently, however, there had been shortages in 16-ounce aluminum cans.

How Breweries Compete: Innovation and Quality versus Price

The consumer might seek out a specific beer or brewery's name, or purchase the lower-priced globally known brand. For some, beer drinking might also be

---

EXHIBIT 5

Total Grain Usage in the Production of Beer, 2010–2014 (in millions of pounds)					
Grain*	2010	2011	2012	2013	2014
Corn	701	629	681	593	574
Rice	714	749	717	724	604
Barley	88	128	136	158	169
Wheat	22	24	26	30	33
Malt	4,147	4,028	4,117	3,916	3,689

*Includes products derived from the type of grain for brewing process.

Source: Alcohol and Tobacco Tax and Trade Bureau website.

seasonal, as tastes change with the seasons. Lighter beers were consumed in hotter months, while heavier beers were consumed in the colder months. Consumers might associate beer styles with the time of year or season. Oktoberfest and German-style beers were associated with fall, following the German-traditional celebration of Oktoberfest. Finally, any one consumer might enjoy several styles, or choose to be brewery or brand loyal.

The brewing process and the multiple varieties and styles of beer allow for breweries to compete across the strategy spectrum—low price and high volume, or higher price and low volume. Industry competitors, then, might target both price point and differentiation. The home brewer, who decided to invest several thousand dollars in a small space to produce very small quantities of beer and start a nanobrewery, might utilize a niche competitive strategy. The consumer might patronize the brewery on location, or seek it out on tap at a restaurant given the quality and the style of beer brewed. If allowed by law, the brewery might offer tastings or sell onsite to visitors. Further, the nanobrewer was free to explore and experiment with unusual flavors. To drive awareness, the brewer might enter competitions, attend beer festivals, or host tastings and "tap takeovers" at local restaurants. If successful, the brewer might invest in larger facilities and equipment to increase capacity with growing demand.

The larger, more established craft brewers, especially those considered regional breweries, might compete through marketing and distribution, while offering a higher value compared to the mass production of macrobreweries. However, the consumer might at times be sensitive to and desire the craft beer experience through smaller breweries—so much so that even craft breweries who by definition were craft might draw the ire of the consumer due to its size and scope. Boston Beer Company was one such company. Even though James Koch started it as a microbrewery, pioneering the craft beer movement in the 1980s, some craft beer consumers do not view it as authentically craft.

Larger macrobreweries mass produced and competed using economies of scale and established distribution systems. Thus, low cost preserves margins as lower price points drive volume sales. Many of these brands were sold en masse at sporting and entertainment venues, as well as larger restaurant chains, driving volume sales.

Companies like SABMiller and AB InBev possessed brands within their portfolio that were sold under the perception of craft beer, in what Boston Beer Company deems the better beer category—beer with a higher price point, but also of higher quality. For example, Blue Moon—a Belgian-style wheat ale—was produced by MillerCoors. Blue Moon's market share had increased significantly since 2006 following the rise in craft beer popularity, competing against Boston Beer Company's Sam Adams in this better beer segment. AB InBev had also recently acquired the larger better-known craft breweries, including Goose Island, in 2011. With a product portfolio that included both low-price and premium craft beer brands, macrobreweries were competing across the spectrum and putting pressure on breweries within the better and craft beer segments—segments demanding a higher price point due to production.

However, a lawsuit had claimed the marketing of Blue Moon was misleading and its marketing obscured the ownership structure. Although the case was dismissed, it further illustrated consumer sentiment regarding what was perceived as craft beer. It also illustrated the power of marketing and how a macrobrewery might position a brand within these segments.

Consolidations and Acquisitions

In 2015 AB InBev offered to purchase SABMiller for $108 billion, which was approved by the European Union and finalized in 2016. To allow for the acquisition, many of SABMiller's brands were required to be divested. Asahi Group Holdings Ltd. purchased the European brands Peroni and Grolsch from SABMiller. Molson Coors purchased SABMiller's 58 percent ownership in MillerCoors LLC—originally a joint venture between Molson Coors and SABMiller. This transaction provided Molson Coors with 100 percent ownership of MillerCoors. It should be noted that AB InBev and MillerCoors represented over 80 percent of the beer produced in the United States for domestic consumption.

Purchases of craft breweries by larger companies had also increased during the 2010s. AB InBev had purchased 10 craft breweries since 2011, including Goose Island, Blue Point, and Devil's Backbone Brewing. MillerCoors—whose brands already included Killian's Irish Red, Leinenkugel's, and Foster's—acquired Saint Archer Brewing Company. Ballast Point Brewing & Spirits was acquired by Constellations Brands. Finally, Heineken NV purchased a stake in Lagunitas Brewing Company. It would seem that craft beer and breweries had obtained the attention of not only the consumer, but also the larger multinational breweries and corporations.

Profiles of Beer Producers

Anheuser-Busch InBev

As the world's largest producer by volume, AB InBev employed over 150,000 people in 26 different countries. The product portfolio included the production, marketing, and distribution of over 200 beers, malt beverages, as well as soft drinks in 130 countries. These brands included Budweiser, Stella Artois, Leffe, and Hoegaarden.

AB InBev managed its product portfolio through three tiers. Global brands, such as Budweiser, Stella Artois, and Corona, were distributed throughout the world. International brands (Beck's, Hoegaarden, Leffe) were found in multiple countries. Local champions (i.e., local brands) represented regional or domestic brands acquired by AB InBev, such as Goose Island in the United States and Cass in South Korea. While some of the local brands were found in different countries, it was due to geographic proximity and the potential to grow the brand larger.

AB InBev estimated its market share in China as 19 percent, United States 46 percent, Brazil 68 percent, and Mexico 58 percent.[7] Its strength in brand recognition and focused marketing on what it deemed as core categories resulted in AB InBev as the top brewery in the United States, Brazil, and Mexico markets, and number three in China by volume. AB InBev reported that its 2016 volumes declined in Asia Pacific, parts of Latin America,

and Europe, Middle East, and Africa. However, AB InBev's total revenue increased by 3 percent in 2016, led by 6 percent and 14 percent growth attributed to Stella Artois and Corona, respectively.

AB InBev invested heavily in marketing. Budweiser planned to sponsor the 2018 and 2022 FIFA World Cups™, as it had sponsored the 2014 competition. This marketing helped bolster the Budweiser brand, which experienced revenue growth of 3 percent in 2016. Bud Light—which was the best-selling beer in the United States in 2016, is official sponsor of the National Football League through 2022.

AB InBev had also actively acquired other brands and breweries since the 1990s, including Labatt in 1995, Beck's in 2002, Anheuser-Busch in 2008, and Grupo Modelo in 2013. All of these acquisitions preceded the SABMiller purchase. These acquisitions provided AB InBev greater market share and penetration through combining marketing and operations to all brands. The reacquisition of the Oriental Brewery in 2014 was a good example of the potential synergies garnered. Cass was the leading beer in Korea and was produced by Oriental Brewery; however, while Cass represented the local brand for AB InBev in Korea, Hoegaarden was distributed in Korea, along with the global brands of Budweiser, Corona, and Stella Artois.

A summary of AB InBev's financial performance from 2014 to 2016 is presented in Exhibit 6.

Boston Beer Company

Boston Beer Company was the second largest craft brewer by volume in the United States with sales of 4 million barrels in 2016. The company's 2016 sales volume declined by 100,000 barrels in 2016, but it remained the fifth largest overall brewer in the United States—see Exhibit 2. The company history states the recipe for Sam Adams was actually company founder Jim Koch's great-great-grandfather's recipe. The story of Boston Beer Company and Jim Koch's success was referenced at times as the beginning of the craft beer movement, often citing how Koch originally sold his beer to bars with the beer and pitching on the spot.

This beginning seemed to underpin much of Boston Beer Company's strategy as it competed in

EXHIBIT 6

Financial Summary for AB InBev, 2014–2016 (in millions of $)

	2016	2015	2014
Revenue	$45,517	$43,604	$47,063
Cost of sales	(17,803)	(17,137)	(18,756)
Gross profit	27,715	26,467	28,307
Selling, general and administrative expenses	(15,171)	(13,732)	(10,285)
Other operating income/expenses	732	1,032	1,386
Non-recurring items	(394)	136	(197)
Profit from operations (EBIT)	12,882	13,904	15,111
Depreciation, amortization and impairment	3,477	3,153	3,354
EBITDA	$16,360	$17,057	$18,465

Sources: AB InBev Annual Reports, 2015, 2016.

the higher value and higher price-point category it referred to as the *better beer segment*. Focusing on quality and taste, Boston Beer Company marketed Samuel Adams Boston Lager as the original beer Koch first discovered. The company also produced several Sam Adams seasonal beers, such as Sam Adams Summer Ale and Sam Adams October-fest. Other seasonal Sam Adams beers had limited release in seasonal variety packs, including Samuel Adams Harvest Pumpkin and Samuel Adams Holi-day Porter. In addition, there was also a Samuel Adams Brewmaster's Collection, a much smaller, limited release set of beers at much higher points, including the Small Batch Collection and Barrel Room Collection. Utopia—its highest-priced beer—was branded as highly experimental and under very limited release.

In the spirit of craft beer and innovation, several years ago Boston Beer Company launched a craft brew incubator as a subsidiary, which had led to the successful development and sales of beers under the Traveler Beer Company brand. The incubator, Alchemy and Science, also built Concrete Beach Brewery and Coney Island Brewery. Alchemy and Science contributed to 7 percent of the total net sales in 2015 and 4 percent of net sales in 2016.

Boston Beer Company offered three non-beer brands. The Twisted Tea brand was launched in 2001 and the Angry Orchard brand was originated in 2011. Truly Spiked & Sparkling was a 5 percent alcohol

sparkling water launched in 2016. These other brands and products competed in the flavored malt beverage and the hard cider categories, respectively.

A summary of Boston Brewing Company's finan-cial performance from 2014 to 2016 is presented in Exhibit 7.

Craft Brew Alliance

Craft Brew Alliance was the sixth largest craft brew-ing company in the United States, and was ranked ninth for overall brewing by volume in 2016. Founded in 2008, it represents the mergers between Redhook Brewery, Widmer Brothers Brewing, and Kona Brew-ing Company. Each with substantial history, the decision to merge was to help assist with growth and meeting demand. The Craft Brew Alliance also included Omission Brewery, Resignation Brewery, and Square Mile Cider Company. In addition to these brands, Craft Brew Alliance operated Five brewpubs. In total, there were 820 people employed at Craft Brew Alliance, producing just over 1 million barrels in 2016.

Craft Brew Alliance utilized automated brewing equipment and distributed nationally through the Anheuser-Busch wholesaler network alliance, lever-aging many of the logistics and thus cost advan-tages associated. Yet, it remained independent, leveraging both its craft brewery brands and the cost advantage associated with larger distribution

EXHIBIT 7

Financial Summary for Boston Brewing Company, 2014–2015 (in thousands of $)

	2016	2015	2014
Revenue	$968,994	$1,024,040	$966,478
Excise taxes	(62,548)	(64,106)	(63,471)
Cost of goods sold	(446,776)	(458,317)	(437,996)
Gross profit	459,670	501,617	465,011
Advertising, promotional and selling expenses	244,213	273,629	250,696
General and administrative expenses	78,033	71,556	65,971
Impairment of assets	(235)	258	1,777
Operating income	137,659	156,174	146,567
Interest income	56	56	21
Other expense, net	(594)	(1,220)	(994)
Provision for income taxes	49,772	56,596	54,851
Net Income	$ 87,349	$ 98,414	$ 90,743

Source: Boston Beer Company Annual Reports, 2015, 2016.

networks. It was the only independent craft brewer to achieve this relationship and sought to leverage the partnership to distribute its products in international markets.

Craft Brew Alliance engaged in contract brewing—a practice where space capacity in production was utilized to produce beer under contract for sale under a different label or brand. In addition, it had partnerships with retailers like Costco and Buffalo Wild Wings, garnering further consumer exposure as well as sales.

A summary of Craft Brew Alliance's financial performance from 2014 to 2016 is presented in Exhibit 8.

Strategic Issues Confronting Craft Breweries in 2017

The vast majority of the craft breweries might produce only enough beer for the local population in their area. Many of these breweries started the same way as the larger breweries: Home brewers or hobbyists

EXHIBIT 8

Financial Summary for Craft Brew Alliance, 2014–2016 (in thousands of $)

	2016	2015	2014
Revenue	$202,507	$204,168	$200,022
Cost of sales	(142,908)	(141,972)	(141,312)
Gross profit	59,599	62,196	58,710
Selling, general and administrative expenses	59,224	57,932	53,000
Operating income	375	4,264	5,710
Income before provision for income taxes	(306)	3,718	5,099
Provision for income taxes	14	1,500	2,022
Net Income	$ 320	$ 2,218	$ 3,077

Sources: Craft Brew Alliance Annual Reports, 2015 and 2016.

decided to start to brew and sell their own beer. Many obtained startup capital through their own savings or solicited investments from friends and family.

Given their entrepreneurial beginnings, these microbreweries and even smaller nanobreweries were usually located in industrial spaces. They were solely operated by the brewer-turned-entrepreneur, or a small staff of two or three. This staff would help with brewing and production, as well as potentially brewery tours and visits—probably the most common marketing and consumer relations tactic utilized by smaller breweries. While almost all breweries offered tours and tastings, these became ever more critical to the smaller brewery with limited capital for marketing and advertising. If onsite sales were available, the brewer could sell growlers to visitors.

Social media websites also offered significant exposure for free and had become a foundational element of brewery marketing. These websites helped the brewery reach the craft beer consumer, who tended to seek out and follow new and upcoming breweries. There were also mobile phone applications specific to the craft beer industry that could help a startup gain exposure. Participating in craft beer festivals, where local and regional breweries were able to offer samples to attendees, was another opportunity to gain exposure.

Some small microbreweries did not have enough employees for bottling and labeling, and had been known to solicit volunteers through social media.

To gain exposure and boost sales, the brewery might host events at local restaurants, such as tap-takeovers, where several of its beers are featured on draft. If enough consumers were engaged, local restaurants were enticed to purchase more beer from the distributor of the brewery. However, any number of variables—raw material shortages, tight retail competition, price-sensitive consumers—could dramatically impact future viability.

The number of beers available to the consumer throughout all segments and price points had continued to steadily climb since the mid-2000s. While the overall beer industry had seemed to plateau, the significant growth appeard to be in the craft beer, or better beer segments. Further, larger macrobreweries and regional craft breweries were seizing the opportunity to acquire other breweries as a method of obtaining distribution and branding synergies, while also mitigating the amount of direct competition. Complicating the competitive landscape were increasing availability and price fluctuations of raw materials. These sporadic shortages might impact the industry's growth and affect the production stability of breweries, especially those smaller operations that did not have capacity to purchase in bulk or outbid larger competitors. Overall, the growth in the consumers' desire for craft beer was likely to continue to attract more entrants, while encouraging larger breweries to seek additional acquisitions of successful craft beer brands.

ENDNOTES

[1] "Steady Growth for Small and Independent Brewers," *Brewers Association*, March 28, 2017, https://www.brewersassociation.org/press-releases/2016-growth-small-independent-brewers/ (accessed December 17, 2017).

[2] Beer sales are commonly measured by barrels in America and hectoliters in Europe. The conversion is 1 hL = 0.852 barrel [U.S. beer]. AB InBev reported 233.7 million hL and 45.8 percent of the market in the 2016 20-K SEC filing. The Alcohol and Tobacco Tax and Trade Bureau Statistical Report for Beer in December 2015 shows production to be about 190.5 million barrels.

[3] "Beer Serves America: A Study of the U.S. Beer Industry's Economic Contribution in 2016," The Beer Institute and The National Beer Wholesalers Association, May 2017, http://beerservesamerica.org/ (accessed June 18, 2017).

[4] "World Beer Market—Opportunities and Forecasts, 2014–2020," www.alliedmarketresearch.com/beer-market (accessed May 24, 2016).

[5] American Homebrewers Association, Homebrewing Stats, https://www.homebrewersassociation.org/membership/homebrewing-stats/ (accessed December 17, 2017).

[6] Hop Growers of America 2016 Statistical Report, https://www.usahops.org/img/blog_pdf/76.pdf (accessed June 17, 2017) .

[7] AB InBev March 2016 20-F Report. Rounded to nearest percent.

Fitbit, Inc., in 2017: Can It Revive Its Strategy and Reverse Mounting Losses?

case 4

ROCHELLE R. BRUNSON Baylor University

MARLENE M. REED Baylor University

Fitbit revolutionized the personal fitness activity in 2009 with the introduction of its Tracker wearable activity monitor. By 2016 the company was a hit in the marketplace with Fitbit devices becoming nearly ubiquitous with fitness enthusiasts and health-conscious individuals wearing the devices and checking them throughout the day. The company's sales of activity monitors had increased from 5,000 units in 2009 to 21.4 million connected health and fitness devices by year-end 2015. The company executed a successful IPO (initial public offering) in 2015 that boosted liquidity by $4.1 billion and recorded revenues of $1.86 billion by the conclusion of its first year as a public company.

Fitbit's chief managers expected 2016 revenues in the range of $2.4 billion to $2.5 billion. However, on the last day of February 2016 the price of Fitbit stock plunged nearly 20 percent after the company announced that the sales and earnings in the first quarter would fall short of analysts' forecasts. The company's revenues increased by nearly 17 percent from 2016 to 2017 and its number of devices sold increased from 21.4 million in 2015 to 22.3 million in 2016. However, the company's cost of revenue increased from 51.5 percent in 2015 to 61 percent in 2016. The dramatic cost of revenue increases coupled with rapidly increasing operating expenses resulted in a net loss of $102 million in 2016 for Fitbit.

Fitbit's financial troubles accelerated in 2017 with the company reporting revenue for the first quarter of 2017 of $299 million and a net loss of $60.1 million. While the company's financial travail in 2016 was related primarily to increasing costs, the weak first quarter 2017 performance was driven by a decline in the number of devices sold. The company sold only 2,956 devices in the first quarter of 2017 compared to 4,842 during the first quarter of 2016. Correspondingly, Fitbit's revenue declined from $505 million during the first quarter of 2016 to $299 million during the first quarter of 2017. The accelerating collapse of Fitbit's competitive advantage and financial performance created a crisis for founders James Park and Eric Friedman, who were now faced with promptly establishing a new strategic course to save the company.

Background on Fitbit

Fitbit was founded in October 2007 by James Park (CEO) and Eric Friedman (CTO). The two men started the company after noticing the potential for using sensors in small wearable devices to track individuals' physical activities. Before they had a prototype, Park and Friedman took a circuit board in a wooden box around to venture capitalists to raise money. In 2008, Park and Friedman addressed the TechCrunch50 Conference drumming up preorders for their product. Neither man had any manufacturing experience, so they traveled to Asia and sought out suppliers and a company to produce the device for them.

Fitbit put its product named "Tracker" on the market at the end of 2009, and the company shipped approximately 5,000 units at that time. They had additional orders for 2,000 units on the books.

The product Park and Friedman developed was called an "activity monitor" which was a wireless-enabled wearable technology device (see Exhibit 1). The purpose of the Fitbit was to measure personal data such as number of steps walked, heart rate, quality of sleep, and steps climbed. The device could be clipped to one's clothing and worn all the time—even when the wearer was asleep. Included with the Tracker was a wireless base station that could receive data from the Tracker and charge its battery. The base station uploaded data to the Fitbit website when connected to a computer. This feature allowed the consumer to have an overview of physical activity, track goals, keep food logs, and interact with friends. The use of the website was free for the consumer.

Thereafter, the company developed a number of devices utilizing the Tracker technology. These devices are shown in Exhibit 2. Some of the later devices located the sensor technology in a watch that could be worn on the wrist (see Exhibit 3).

On May 17, 2015, Fitbit filed for an IPO with the Securities and Exchange Commission with an NYSE (New York Stock Exchange) listing. The IPO brought in $4.1 billion. The stock was initially priced at $20 but shortly thereafter the shares were trading for $35.

A study in 2015 by Diaz et al., published in the *International Journal of Cardiology,* investigated the Fitbit to see how reliable the device was, and whether it could be used to monitor patients' physical activity between clinic visits. The research indicated that the Fitbit One and Fitbit Flex reliably estimated step counts and energy expenditure during walking and running. These researchers also found that the hip-based Fitbit outperformed the Fitbit watch.[1]

Another study in 2015 by Cadmus-Bertram et al., published in the *American Journal of Preventive Medicine,* had essentially the same outcome as the Diaz study. Their study examined the Fitbit Tracker and website as a low-touch physical activity intervention. They were attempting to evaluate the feasibility of integrating the Fitbit Tracker and website into a physical activity intervention for postmenopausal women. Their conclusions were that the Fitbit was well accepted in their sample of women and was associated with increased physical activity at 16 weeks. In other words, merely wearing the Fitbit seemed to heighten the amount of physical exercise in which the women engaged.[2]

However, another study undertaken by Sasaki et al. in 2015 and reported in the *Journal of Physical Activity and Health* found that the Fitbit wireless activity tracker worn on the hip systematically underestimated the activity energy expended. These researchers suggested that the Fitbit management should consider refining the energy expenditure prediction algorithm to correct this consistent underestimation of activity in order to maximize the physical activity benefits for weight management and other health-related concerns.[3]

Mission of Fitbit

According to Fitbit, "The mission of Fitbit is to empower and inspire you to live a healthier, more active life. We design products and experiences that fit seamlessly into your life so that you can achieve your health and fitness goals, whatever they may be."[4]

The Activity Tracking Industry

There were a number of companies that would be considered competitors of Fitbit in activity tracking—companies such as Garmin (originally producing GPS equipment for cars) and Under Armour (originally

EXHIBIT 1   **Fitbit Ultra**

Source: Denis Kortunov/Fitbit, Inc.

EXHIBIT 2

Activity Tracker Devices Developed by Fitbit

Name of Device	Capabilities and Options	Date First Unit Sold
Fitbit Tracker	Device with a clip to fit on clothing Sensed user movement Measured steps taken, distance walked, calories burned, floors climbed In black and teal only	2008
Fitbit Ultra	Digital clock Stopwatch Altimeter that measured slope of floors "Chatter" messages that occurred when Ultra moved New colors of plum and blue	2011
Fitbit Aria	Wi-Fi smart scale Recognized users wearing Fitbit trackers Measured weight, body mass index, and percentage of body fat	2012
Fitbit One	More vivid digital display Separate clip and charging cable Wireless sync dongle Used Bluetooth 4.0	September 2012
Fitbit Zip	Size of a quarter Tracked steps taken, distance traveled, and calories burned Included a disposable battery Lower price than other Fitbits	September 2012
Fitbit Flex	Worn on the wrist Tracked movement 24 hrs a day including sleep patterns	May 2013
Fitbit Force	LED display showing time and daily activity Tracked activities in real time Vibrating alarm	October 2013
Fitbit Charge	Replacement for Fitbit Force Wristband displayed caller ID	October 2014
Fitbit Surge	Similar to a smart watch Monitored heart rate Tracked pace, distance, and elevation using GPS	October 2014
Fitbit Blaze	Similar to a smart watch Focused on fitness first Colored touchscreen Exchangeable strap and frame	2016
Fitbit Alta HR	PulsePure heart rate tracking; Sleep tracking; 7-day battery life Four colors and three sizes	2017

Source: Fitbit, Inc. website.

producing undergarments for men). There were also companies such as Apple who produce smart watches that perform many of the same tasks as Fitbit's devices.

Another company entering the market late was Jawbone. This company was formed in 1999, and its consumer devices were Bluetooth headphones and speakers initially and later fitness trackers. With the increased competition in the activity tracking industry beginning in 2015, Jawbone dropped to seventh place in the second quarter from fifth place in the first quarter among makers of wearable tracking devices.

Xiaomi, a Chinese company, shipped 15.7 million wearable activity trackers in 2016. That gave the company a 15.4 percent global market share, which was second to Fitbit with Apple, Garmin, and Samsung behind the two leaders. In 2014, Xiaomi had shipped

Source: Tom Emrich/Fitbit, Inc.

1.1 million units and garnered only 4 percent of the world market share.

The presence of Apple in the market had been almost as noteworthy as Xiaomi's. The Apple watch was first marketed in 2015, and in that year its market share went to 14.2 percent. This was despite a much higher price for the Apple product relative to either Fitbit or Xiaomi.

For many years, neuroscientists had only the electroencephalogram, or EEG, to detect signals that carried different stages of sleep or brain power surges brought about by seizures. This was a very cumbersome process. Then, in 2007, Dr. Philip Low in San Diego invented the Sleep Parametric EEG Automated Recognition System (SPEARS) algorithm. This invention allowed physicians the ability to create a cluster map of brain activity with information that was gleaned from one electrode. This advancement caught the attention of Tan Le, CEO of Emotiv (a company that manufactured EEG rigs for consumers). Le believes wearable activity devices may be the appropriate venue for this new medical breakthrough. This would open up far-reaching new uses for wearable activity tracking devices.[5]

Demand for wearable devices continued to increase through 2016 with shipments growing to 33.9 million units in the fourth quarter of 2016 alone and annual shipments growing by 16.9 percent when compared to 2015. The market was segmented between single-function products and smart wearables, many running third-party applications. An activity tracker industry observer noted, "Like any technology market, the wearables market is changing. Basic wearables started out as single-purpose devices tracking footsteps and are morphing into multi-purpose wearable devices, fusing together multiple health and fitness capabilities and smartphone notifications."[6]

New entrants to the industry such as Fossil created new fashion segments within the activity tracking industry and helped generate consumer interest in hybrid watches and other fashion accessories with fitness tracking capabilities. The innovations of another group of new entrants included non-wrist worn trackers such as earpieces and clothing items with activity tracking sensors. Such devices made up only 1 percent of industry sales in 2016 but reflected the continuing growth opportunities in the industry. An analyst for IDC Mobile Device Trackers commented in mid-2017, "With the entrance of multiple new vendors with strengths in different industries, the wearables market is expected to maintain a positive outlook, though much of this growth is coming from vendor push rather than consumer demand."[7] Exhibit 4 presents the shipments and market shares of the top five wearables vendors for 2014 through 2016.

Problems for Fitbit

Antenna

There were early problems with the design of Fitbit. For one thing, the antenna did not work properly. In regard to the antenna problems, CEO James Park said, "In my hotel room I was thinking this is it. We literally took a piece of foam and put it on the circuit board to fix an antenna problem."[8]

Design Flaw

The Fitbit Ultra had a permanently curved shape that allowed it to be clipped onto a piece of clothing. However, the plastic in the unit could not handle the strain at the looped end and would continually break. When this occurred, Fitbit offered the consumer replacement or repair of the unit.

EXHIBIT 4

Top Five Wearables Vendors by Shipments and Market Share, 2014–2016 (units in millions)

Vendor	2014 Unit Shipments	2014 Market Share	2015 Unit Shipments	2015 Market Share	2016 Unit Shipments	2016 Market Share
Fitbit	10.9	37.9%	22.0	26.8%	22.5	22.0%
Xiaomi	1.1	4.0%	12.0	14.7%	15.7	15.4%
Apple	0.0	0.0%	11.6	14.2%	10.7	10.5%
Garmin	2.0	7.1%	5.8	7.0%	6.1	5.9%
Samsung	2.7	9.2%	3.2	3.9%	4.4	4.3%
Others	12.0	41.9%	27.4	33.4%	43.0	42.0%
Total	28.8	100.0%	81.9	100.0%	102.4	100.0%

Source: *IDC Worldwide Quarterly Wearable Device Tracker,* February 23, 2016; March 2, 2017.

Allergic Reactions

From the beginning of the company, Fitbit was plagued by problems. When Fitbit added Fitbit Flex and Fitbit Force to its list of products, the company began receiving complaints that the watchband was irritating the skin of consumers. The irritation was discovered to be caused by allergic reactions to nickel, and the products were recalled in early 2014. As many as 9,000 customers were reportedly affected, and the Force was replaced by a new model named Fitbit Charge, which was believed to be allergen free. Unfortunately, customers continued to complain about allergic reactions to the new device as well.

Too Much Information

One of the greatest strengths of Fitbit from the very beginning was its website. By utilizing Bluetooth technology, information from the Fitbit could be uploaded to the web in order to track energy expended and compare one's performance with other Fitbit users. However, the company discovered in 2011 that users who recorded their sexual activity (time spent, not activity) were sharing their information with the world unknowingly. Therefore, Fitbit realized that sharing all of a customer's information with the world was not a good idea, and the company changed the website so that information posted by the users was private by default.

Privacy Issues

U.S. Senator Chuck Schumer declared in August 2014 that Fitbit was a "privacy nightmare." He further stated that users' movements and health data were being tracked by the company and sold to third parties without their knowledge.[9] Schumer asked that the U.S. Federal Trade Commission undertake the regulation of fitness trackers. In response to this charge, Fitbit suggested that it did not sell data to third parties and would be glad to have the opportunity to work with Senator Schumer on this issue.

Cost of Launching New Products

In Fitbit's Form 8-K filing on February 22, 2016, the company warned that the costs that were related to two new products would negatively affect first quarter earnings in 2016. They further stated that research and development would hurt operating margins in 2016. The two new products that Fitbit suggested it would launch in 2016 were Fitbit Blaze and Fitbit Alpha, and these two products would incur very large manufacturing costs. In addition, Fitbit's full-year research and development budget included the company's Digital Health strategy.[10]

Financial Performance

Going into 2016, Fitbit management expected to record revenues of $2.4 billion to $2.5 billion as a result of new products and expansion into new geographic territories. In addition, the company stated that it expected gross margins to range from 48.5 to 49.0 percent. Fitbit also expected adjusted EBITDA (earnings before interest, taxes, depreciation, and amortization) to range from $400 million to $480 million for the 2016 fiscal year.

The projections were based on Fitbit's stellar 2015 fiscal year when annual revenue increased to $1.86 billion from $745 million in 2014 and net earnings increased to $175.7 million from $131.8 million in 2014. However, 2016 proved to become a much more troubling year than managment expected. The company's 2016 revenues failed to meet expectations, it recorded a loss of $102.8 million, and adjusted EBITDA fell from $389.9 million in 2015 to $30.0 million in 2016. The company's declining financial performance continued during the first quarter of 2017 with its net loss exceeding $60 million for the three-month period ending April 17, 2017. Exhibit 5 presents Fitbit's consolidated statements of operations for 2014 through the first quarter of 2017. The company's condensed consolidated balance sheets for 2015 and 2016 are presented in Exhibit 6.

Analysts' Assessments

Analysts were becoming concerned about Fitbit's long-term viability as early as February 2016 when its share price declined by 20 percent by month-end. An analyst with Global Equities Research, Trip Chowdry,

suggested that he believed the stock could fall another 50 percent and speculated, "Gradually the market for single-purpose devices (fitness tracker) is heading toward zero, and there is nothing FIT can do to reverse the trend."[11] In addition, Chowdry commented that unlike Apple, Inc., Fitbit does not have a group of developers or a way of generating income as Apple does. Even though the Fitbit tracker products were much cheaper than Apple's ($129 as compared to $349 for the cheapest Apple Watch Sport), Apple had an inventory of more products than Fitbit. Activity tracking is just a feature used by Fitbit, and this feature was being used in many other devices by a variety of companies.

Leerink analysts were cautious about projections for sales increases at Fitbit and suggested a target price to buy the stock of $18. The analysts suggested that ongoing sales would likely remain sluggish after initial increases related retailer inventory needs for new products were satisfied.[12]

Fitbit's Strategic Inflection Point

Going into mid-2017, James Park and Eric Friedman were confronted with how best to bolster Fitbit's

EXHIBIT 5

Fitbit, Inc., Consolidated Statements of Operations, 2014–First Quarter 2017 (in thousands)

	First Quarter 2017	2016	2015	2014
Revenue	$298,942	$2,169,461	$1,857,998	$745,433
Cost of revenue	180,643	1,323,557	956,935	387,776
Gross profit	118,299	845,884	901,063	357,657
Operating expenses:				
Research and development	87,785	320,191	150,035	54,167
Sales and marketing	91,174	491,255	332,741	112,005
General and administrative	30,746	146,903	77,793	33,556
Change in contingent consideration			(7,704)	
Total operating expenses	209,678	958,349	552,865	199,728
Operating income	(91,379)	(112,465)	348,198	157,929
Interest income (expense), net	1,096	3,156	(1,019)	(2,222)
Other expense, net	533	14	(59,230)	(15,934)
Income before income taxes	(89,750)	(109,295)	287,949	139,773
Income tax expense	(29,671)	(6,518)	112,272	7,996
Net income	$ (60,079)	$ (102,777)	$ 175,677	$131,777

Source: U.S. Securities and Exchange Commission, Form 8-K, Fitbit, Inc., for fiscal 2015; Form 10-K for 2016; Form 10-Q First Quarter 2017.

EXHIBIT 6

Fitbit, Inc., Condensed Consolidated Balance Sheets, 2015–2016

Assets	December 31, 2016	December 31, 2015
Current assets		
Cash and cash equivalents	$ 301,320	$ 535,846
Marketable securities	404,693	128,632
Accounts receivable, net	477,825	469,200
Inventories	230,387	178,146
Prepaid expenses & other current assets	66,346	43,530
Total current assets	1,480,571	1,355,414
Property and equipment, net	76,553	44,501
Goodwill	51,036	22,157
Intangible assets, net	27,521	12,216
Deferred tax assets	174,097	83,020
Other assets	10,448	1,758
Total assets	$1,820,226	$1,519,066
Liabilities, Redeemable Convertible Preferred Stock and Stockholders' Equity		
Current liabilities		
Accounts payable	$ 313,773	$ 260,842
Accrued liabilities	390,561	200,099
Deferred revenue	49,904	44,448
Income taxes payable	7,694	2,868
Total current liabilities	761,932	508,257
Other liabilities	59,762	29,358
Total liabilities	821,694	537,615
Stockholders' equity		
Common stock & paid-in capital	859,368	737,841
Accumulated other comprehensive income	(978)	691
Retained earnings	140,142	242,919
Total stockholders' equity	998,532	981,451
Total liabilities and stockholders' equity	$1,820,226	$1,519,066

Source: Fitbit, Inc., 2016 10-K.

market standing and turn around the company's rapidly deteriorating financial performance. It was a common comment among analysts that Fitbit needed to be more than a one-product company. Since the activity tracking feature was being used in many other devices by a variety of companies, Fitbit had to think of new uses of the tracker as well as new devices. As one journalist suggested, "Standalone fitness trackers are iPods in a world that's moving to iPhones."[13]

After all, Park had recently commented, "The next big leap will come when we tie into more detailed clinical research and create devices that can make lightweight medical diagnoses. You look at blood glucose meters today, I wouldn't necessarily say that those are the most attractive or consumer-friendly devices. I would say consumer-focused companies, whether it's us or Apple, probably have an inherent advantage in the future."[14] One possibility for the company was to become a platform—rather than just a product.

That would entail moving into niche markets with devices that are designed for very specific and unique purposes. Some of the possibilities would be moving further into health care and corporate health care.[15]

Central to these issues was the soundness of the company's competitive strategy and the degree to which it was matched to current industry conditions. Park and Friedman had developed what appeared to be a flawless strategy that was executed with great proficiency in the six years leading up to its 2015 IPO. However, the market's rapid transition had surprised Fitbit's management team who, as of mid-2017, had yet to adjust its strategy. It was certain that Fitbit management would need to develop a new strategic approach to restore the company's competitiveness and profitability.

ENDNOTES

[1] Keith M. Diaz, David J. Krupka, Melinda J. Chang, James Peacock, Yao Ma, Jeff Goldsmith, Joseph E. Schwartz, and Karina W. Davidson, "Fitbit: An Accurate and Reliable Device for Wireless Physical Activity Tracking," *International Journal of Cardiology,* no. 185 (2015), pp. 138–140.

[2] Lisa A. Cadmus-Bertram, Bess H. Marcus, Ruth E. Patterson, Barbara A. Parker, and Brittany L. Morey, "Randomized Trial of a Fitbit-Based Physical Activity Intervention for Women," *American Journal of Preventive Medicine* 49, no. 3 (2015), pp. 414–418.

[3] Jeffer Eidi Sasaki, Amanda Hickey, Marianna Mavilia, Jacquelynne Tedesco, Denish John, Sarah Kozey Keadle, and Patty S. Freedson, "Validation of the Fitbit Wireless Activity Tracker for Prediction of Energy Expenditure," *Journal of Physical Activity and Health* 12 (2015), pp. 149–154.

[4] Fitbit home page, www.fitbit.com/about (accessed March 3, 2016).

[5] Betsy Isaacson, "A Fitbit for Your Brain Is Around the Corner," *Newsweek.com,* April 13, 2016, www.newsweek.com/human-brain-eeg-technology-neuroscience-443368.

[6] As quoted in "Wearables Aren't Dead, They're Just Shifting Focus as the Market Grows 16.9% in the Fourth Quarter, According to IDC," *Business Wire*, March 2, 2017, http://www.businesswire.com/news/home/20170302005298/en/Wearables-Arent-Dead-Theyre-Shifting-Focus-Market.

[7] Ibid.

[8] Gary Marshall, "The Story of Fitbit: How a Wooden Box Became a $4 Billion Company," December 30, 2015, www.wareable.com/fitbit/youre-fitbit-and-you-know-it-how-a-wooden-box-became-a-dollar-4-billion-company (accessed March 2, 2016).

[9] Ibid., p. 5.

[10] U.S. Securities and Exchange Commission, Form 8-K Filing for fiscal year 2015 for Fitbit, Inc.

[11] Caitlin Huston, "Fitbit's Stock Is Tanking and It May Have More to Drop," *MarketWatch,* February 23, 2016, www.marketwatch.com/story/fitbits-stock-is-tanking-and-it-may-have-more-to-drop/ (accessed March 11, 2016).

[12] Ibid., p. 3.

[13] James Stables, "Fitbit Charge HR Review," *Fitbit Review,* December 15, 2015, www.wareable.com/fitbit/fitbit-charge-hr-review/ (accessed March 1, 2016).

[14] Ibid.

[15] Ibid., p. 7.

lululemon athletica, inc., in 2017: Is the Company on the Path to Becoming a High Performer Once Again?

ARTHUR A. THOMPSON   The University of Alabama

On June 1, 2017, shareholders of lululemon athletica—a designer and retailer of high-tech athletic apparel sold under the lululemon athletica and ivivva athletica brand names—were pleasantly surprised by the company's announcement of a stronger-than-expected 5 percent increase in sales revenues in the first quarter of fiscal 2017 compared to the first quarter of fiscal 2016. But shareholders were still uneasy about the company's prospects.

Two months earlier, on March 29, 2017, lululemon CEO Laurent Potdevin had told Wall Street analysts in a conference call that the company was off to a slow start in 2017, an outcome he attributed mainly to customer disappointment with the heavy emphasis on all-black and all-white assortments of apparel items on store racks and the merchandise displays on the company's e-commerce website. In times past, lululemon's offerings of fitness and workout gear had included many bold-color and patterned selections that were among the company's best-selling items. Potdevin went on to say, "We should have been bolder with the color assortment. You are going to see more color showing up and we've added creative resources to bring visual merchandising to life in a more powerful way."

During the same conference call, lululemon said that it foresaw fiscal 2017 revenues of between $2.55 billion to $2.6 billion and per-share earnings of $2.26 to $2.36, numbers that were below Wall Street's current 2017 estimates of $2.62 billion in revenues

and earnings of $2.56 per share. Investors swiftly responded to the forecasts of lower sales and earnings by punishing lululemon's stock price. In after-hours trading on March 29, lululemon's stock price fell 18 percent below the day's $66.30 closing price. By the close of trading on March 30, 2017, lululemon's stock price had declined to $50.76, some 23.5 percent below the price 24 hours earlier. Over the next 11 weeks, the company's stock price traded between $48 and $54, closing on June 9, 2017, at $50.70, nearly 37 percent below the all-time high price of $81.81 in March 2013 when troubling signs of a falloff in store sales and customer traffic first began to appear at lululemon.

From modest beginnings as a family-owned startup company with 14 stores and sales of $40.7 million in January 2005, lululemon had rocketed to retailing prominence in North America during 2006 to 2012, building a fast-growing chain of over 200 retail stores in Canada and the United States that sold fashionable high-tech yoga and workout apparel at premium prices. Net sales rose 38 percent to almost $1.4 billion in fiscal year 2012 (ending February 3, 2013). But in March 2013, the company's highly regarded brand image took a hit when design and quality problems in its women's black Luon fabric bottoms provoked widespread complaints from customers that the sheer nature of the fabric was too revealing of the garments worn underneath. The design flaw was widely publicized in the media, chiefly because lululemon had become a high-profile, fast-growing company with a popular and somewhat glamorous product offering and because its rapidly rising stock price had attracted considerable investor attention.

Over the next four years, annual sales revenue growth at lululemon stores remained stubbornly stuck far below the 37.9 percent gain in fiscal 2012—revenues grew 16.1 percent in fiscal 2013, 12.9 percent in 2014, 14.6 percent in 2015, and 13.8 percent in 2016. Moreover, average annual sales at lululemon's retail stores open at least 12 months had dropped from a record high of $5.83 million per store in fiscal 2012, to $5.44 million in 2013, to $4.95 million in 2014, to $4.57 million in 2015, to $4.47 million in 2016—a disturbingly large 23.3 percent decline.

Not surprisingly, lululemon executives were doing their best to identify effective ways to rejuvenate the company's sales growth. The issues of what to do seemed to hinge on answering several questions. Were the two disappointing performance metrics of slower revenue growth and eroding sales per retail store only a reflection of lingering damage to the company's brand image stemming from the embarrassing publicity surrounding the revealing nature of the Luon fabric bottoms? Or were other troublesome factors also at work? Was the market signaling that the "fad for lululemon apparel" was over? Had the heretofore "must have" appeal of lululemon's functional and stylish apparel among fitness-conscious women been undercut by mounting competition from rival makers of women's fitness apparel, like The Gap's 55 new Athleta-branded retail stores that specialized in women's fitness apparel?

Had the recent moves of Under Armour, Nike, and adidas to offer much bigger selections of fashionable, high performance athletic and fitness apparel for women drawn sales and market share away from lululemon? Could the slowdown in revenue growth be due to a significant fraction of the company's customers switching to lower-priced brands and/or brands they considered to be more trendy or appealingly designed? Were all of these factors in play and, if so, what market opportunities remained for lululemon management to pursue to pump up the company's performance?

Likewise, the company's shareholders were in a quandary about whether to hold onto their shares in hopes of a big turnaround in the company's future prospects or to sell their shares and shift the proceeds to other investments. Even if top management came up with some promising ways to spur the company's sales and profitability, how long would it be before stockholders could reasonably expect for the company's $51 stock price (as of June 9, 2017) to climb steadily toward $80 per share (where it was trading in March 2013)?

Company Background

A year after selling his eight-store surf, skate, and snowboard-apparel chain called Westbeach Sports, Chip Wilson took the first commercial yoga class offered in Vancouver, British Columbia, and found the result exhilarating. But he found the cotton clothing used for sweaty, stretchy power yoga completely inappropriate. Wilson's passion was form-fitting performance fabrics and in 1998 he opened a design studio for yoga clothing that also served as a yoga studio at night to help pay the rent. He designed a number of yoga apparel items made of moisture-wicking fabrics that were light, form-fitting, and comfortable and asked local yoga instructors to wear the products and provide feedback. Gratified by the positive response, Wilson opened lululemon's first real store in the beach area of Vancouver in November of 2000.

While the store featured yoga clothing designed by Chip Wilson and his wife, Shannon, Chip Wilson's vision was for the store to be a community hub where people could learn and discuss the physical aspects of healthy living—from yoga and diet to running and cycling, plus the yoga-related mental aspects of living a powerful life of possibilities. But the store's clothing proved so popular that dealing with customers crowded out the community-based discussions and training about the merits of living healthy lifestyles. Nonetheless, Chip Wilson and store personnel were firmly committed to healthy, active lifestyles, and Wilson soon came to the conclusion that for the store to provide staff members with the salaries and opportunities to experience fulfilling lives, the one-store company needed to expand into a multi-store enterprise. Wilson believed that the increasing number of women participating in sports—and specifically yoga—provided ample room for expansion, and he saw lululemon athletica's yoga-inspired performance apparel as a way to address a void in the women's athletic apparel market. Wilson also saw the company's mission as one of providing people with the components to live a longer, healthier, and more fun life.

Several new stores were opened in the Vancouver area, with operations conducted through a Canadian operating company, initially named Lululemon Athletica, Inc., and later renamed lululemon canada, inc. In 2002, the company expanded into the United States and formed a sibling operating company, Lululemon Athletica USA Inc. (later renamed as lululemon usa, inc), to conduct its U.S. operations. Both operating companies were wholly owned by affiliates of Chip Wilson. In 2004, the company contracted with a franchisee to open a store in Australia as a means of more quickly disseminating the lululemon athletica brand name, conserving on capital expenditures for store expansion (since the franchisee was responsible for the costs of opening and operating the store), and boosting revenues and profits. The company wound up its fiscal year ending January 31, 2005, with 14 company-owned stores, 1 franchised store, and net revenues of $40.7 million. A second franchised store was opened in Japan later in 2005. Franchisees paid lululemon a one-time franchise fee and an ongoing royalty based on a specified percentage of net revenues; lululemon supplied franchised stores with garments at a discount to the suggested retail price.

Five years after opening the first retail store, it was apparent that lululemon apparel was fast becoming something of a cult phenomenon and a status symbol among yoga fans in areas where lululemon stores had opened. Avid yoga exercisers were not hesitating to purchase $120 color-coordinated lululemon yoga outfits that felt comfortable and made them look good. Mall developers and mall operators quickly learned about lululemon's success and began actively recruiting lululemon to lease space for stores in their malls.

In December 2005, with 27 company-owned stores, 2 franchised stores, and record sales approaching $85 million annually, Chip Wilson sold 48 percent of his interest in the company's capital stock to two private equity investors: Advent International Corporation, which purchased 38.1 percent of the stock, and Highland Capital Partners, which purchased a 9.6 percent ownership interest. In connection with the transaction, the owners formed lululemon athletica inc. to serve as a holding company for all of the company's related entities, including the two operating subsidiaries, lululemon canada inc. and lululemon usa inc. Robert Meers, who had 15 years of experience at Reebok and was Reebok's CEO from 1996 to 1999, joined lululemon as CEO in December 2005. Chip Wilson headed the company's design team and played a central role in developing the company's strategy and nurturing the company's distinctive corporate culture; he was also chairman of the company's Board of Directors, a position he had held since founding the company in 1998. Wilson and Meers assembled a management team with a mix of retail, design, operations, product sourcing, and marketing experience from such leading apparel and retail companies as Abercrombie & Fitch, Limited Brands, Nike, and Reebok.

Brisk expansion ensued. The company ended fiscal 2006 with 41 company-owned stores, 10 franchised stores, net revenues of $149 million, and net income of $7.7 million. In 2007, the company's owners elected to take the company public. The initial public offering took place on August 2, 2007, with the company selling 2,290,909 shares to the public and various stockholders selling 15,909,091 shares of their personal holdings. Shares began trading on the NASDAQ under the symbol LULU and on the Toronto Exchange under the symbol LLL.

In 2007, the company's announced growth strategy had five key elements:

1. ***Grow the company's store base in North America.*** The strategic objective was to add new stores to strengthen the company's presence in locations where it had existing stores and then selectively enter new geographic markets in the United States and Canada. Management believed that the company's strong sales in U.S. stores demonstrated the portability of the lululemon brand and retail concept.

2. ***Increase brand awareness.*** This initiative entailed leveraging the publicity surrounding the opening of new stores with grassroots marketing

programs that included organizing events and partnering with local fitness practitioners.

3. *Introduce new product technologies.* Management intended to continue to focus on developing and offering products that incorporated technology-enhanced fabrics and performance features that differentiated lululemon apparel and helped broaden the company's customer base.

4. *Broaden the appeal of lululemon products.* This initiative entailed (1) adding a number of apparel items for men, (2) expanding product offerings for women and young females in such categories as athletic bags, undergarments, outerwear, and sandals, and (3) adding products suitable for additional sports and athletic activities.

5. *Expand beyond North America.* In the near term, the company planned to expand its presence in Australia and Japan and then, over time, pursue opportunities in other Asian and European markets that offered similar, attractive demographics.

The company grew rapidly. Fitness-conscious women began flocking to the company's stores not only because of the fashionable products but also because of the store ambience and attentive, knowledgeable store personnel. Dozens of new lululemon athletic retail stores were opened annually, and the company pursued a strategy of embellishing its product offerings to create a comprehensive line of apparel and accessories designed for athletic pursuits such as yoga, running training, and general fitness; technical clothing for active female youths; and a selection of fitness and recreational items for men. Revenues topped $1 billion in fiscal 2011 and reached almost $1.6 billion in fiscal 2013.

Headed into fiscal year 2017, the company's products could be bought at its 351 retail stores in the United States and Canada, 27 stores in Australia and New Zealand, and 28 stores in nine other countries, in addition to the company's website www.lululemon.com and assorted other locations. In the company's most recent fiscal year ending January 29, 2017, retail store sales accounted for 72.7 percent of company revenues, website sales accounted for 19.3 percent, and sales in all other channels (showroom sales, sales at outlet centers, sales from temporary locations, licensing revenues, and wholesale sales to premium yoga studios, health clubs, fitness centers, and a few other retailers) accounted for 8.0 percent.

Exhibit 1 presents highlights of the company's performance for fiscal years 2012 to 2016. Exhibit 2 shows lululemon's revenues by business segment and geographic region for the same period.

lululemon's Evolving Senior Leadership Team

In January 2008, Christine M. Day joined the company as executive vice president, Retail Operations. Previously, she had worked at Starbucks, functioning in a variety of capacities and positions, including president, Asia Pacific Group (July 2004 to February 2007); co-president for Starbucks Coffee International (July 2003 to October 2003); senior vice president, North American Finance & Administration; and vice president of Sales and Operations for Business Alliances. In April 2008, Day was appointed as lululemon's president and chief operating officer, and was named chief executive officer (CEO) and member of the Board of Directors in July 2008. During her tenure as CEO, Day expanded and strengthened the company's management team to support its expanding operating activities and geographic scope, favoring the addition of people with relevant backgrounds and experiences at such companies as Nike, Abercrombie & Fitch, The Gap, and Speedo International. She also spent a number of hours each week in the company's stores observing how customers shopped, listening to their comments and complaints, and using the information to tweak product offerings, merchandising, and store operations.

Company founder Chip Wilson stepped down from his executive role as lululemon's chief innovation and branding officer effective January 29, 2012, and moved his family to Australia; however, he continued on in his role of chairman of the company's Board of Directors and focused on becoming a better board chairman, even going so far as to take a four-day course on board governance at Northwestern University.[1] Christine Day promoted Sheree Waterson, who had joined the company in 2008 and had over 25 years of consumer and retail

Financial and Operating Highlights, lululemon athletica, Fiscal Years 2012–2016 (in millions of $)

Selected Income Statement Data	Fiscal Year 2016 (Ending Jan. 29, 2017)	Fiscal Year 2015 (Ending Jan. 31, 2016)	Fiscal Year 2014 (Ending Feb. 1, 2015)	Fiscal Year 2013 (Ending Feb. 2, 2014)	Fiscal Year 2012 (Ending Feb. 3, 2013)
Net revenues	$ 2,344.4	$ 2,060.5	$ 1,797.2	$ 1,591.2	$ 1,370.4
Cost of goods sold	1,144.8	1,063.4	833.0	751.1	607.5
Gross profit	1,199.6	997.2	914.2	840.1	762.8
Selling, general, and administrative expenses	778.5	628.1	538.1	448.7	386.4
Operating profit	421.2	369.1	376.0	391.4	376.4
Net profit (loss)	303.4	266.0	239.0	279.5	271.4
Earnings per share—basic	$2.21	$1.90	$1.66	$1.93	$1.88
Earnings per share—diluted	2.21	1.89	1.66	1.91	1.85
Balance Sheet Data					
Cash and cash equivalents	$ 734.8	$ 501.5	$ 664.5	$ 698.6	$ 590.2
Inventories	298.4	284.0	208.1	188.8	155.2
Total assets	1,657.5	1,314.1	1,296.2	1,252.3	1,051.1
Stockholders' equity	1,360.0	1,027.5	1,089.6	1,096.7	887.3
Cash Flow and Other Data					
Net cash provided by operating activities	$ 385.1	$ 298.7	$ 314.4	$ 278.3	$ 280.1
Capital expenditures	149.5	143.5	119.7	106.4	93.2
Store Data					
Number of corporate-owned stores open at end of period	406	363	302	254	211
Sales per gross square foot at corporate-owned stores open at least one full year	$1,521	$1,541	$1,678	$1,894	$2,058
Average sales at corporate-owned stores open at least one year	$4.47 million	$4.57 million	$4.95 million	$5.44 million	$5.83 million

Source: Company 10-K reports for fiscal years 2012, 2013, 2014, 2015, and 2016.

industry experience, as chief product officer to assume responsibility for product design, product development, and other executive tasks that Wilson had been performing. Shortly after the quality problems with the black Luon bottoms occurred, Sheree Waterson resigned her position and left the company. In October 2013, lululemon announced that Tara Poseley had been appointed to its Senior Leadership Team as chief product officer and would have responsibility for overseeing lululemon's design team, product design activities, merchandising, inventory activities, and strategic planning. Previously, Poseley held the position of interim president at Bebe Stores, Inc; president of Disney Stores North America (The Children's Place); CEO of Design Within Reach (DWR); and a range of senior merchandising and design management positions during her 15-year tenure at Gap Inc.

In the aftermath of the pants recall in March 2013, the working relationship between Christine Day and Chip Wilson deteriorated. Wilson made it clear that he would have handled the product recall

EXHIBIT 2

lululemon athletica's Revenues and Income from Operations, by Business Segment and by Geographical Region, Fiscal Years 2012–2016 (dollars in millions)

	Fiscal Year 2016 (Ending Jan. 29, 2017)	Fiscal Year 2015 (Ending Jan. 31, 2016)	Fiscal Year 2014 (Ending Feb. 1, 2015)	Fiscal Year 2013 (Ending Feb. 2, 2014)	Fiscal Year 2012 (Ending Feb. 3, 2013)
Revenues by Business Segment					
Corporate-owned stores	$1,704.4	$1,516.3	$1,348.2	$1,229.0%	$1,090.2
Direct-to-consumer (e-commerce sales)	453.3	401.5	321.2	263.1	197.3
All other channels*	186.7	142.7	127.8	99.1	82.9
Total	$2,344.4	$2,060.5	$1,797.2	$ 1,591.2	$1,370.4
Percentage Distribution of Revenues by Business Segment					
Corporate owned stores	72.7%	73.6%	75.0%	77.3%	79.6%
Direct-to-consumer (e-commerce sales)	19.3%	19.5%	17.9%	16.5%	14.4%
All other channels*	8.0%	6.9%	7.1%	6.2%	6.0%
Total	100.0%	100.0%	100.0%	100.0%	100.0%
Income from Operations (before general corporate expenses), by Business Segment					
Corporate owned stores	$ 415.6	$ 346.8	$ 356.6	$ 372.3	$ 375.5
Direct-to-consumer (e-commerce sales)	186.2	166.4	132.9	110.0	84.7
All other channels*	22.3	5.8	9.5	14.0	19.9
Total income from operations (before general corporate expenses)	$ 624.1	$ 519.0	$ 499.0	$ 496.3	$ 480.1
Revenues by Geographic Region					
United States	$1,726.1	$1,508.8	$1,257.4	$ 1,052.2	$ 839.9
Canada	447.2	416.5	434.3	454.2	461.6
Outside of North America	171.1	135.2	105.5	84.8	68.9
Total	$2,344.4	$2,060.5	$1,797.2	$ 1,591.2	$1,370.4
Percentage Distribution of Revenues by Geographic Region					
United States	73.6%	73.2%	70.0%	66.1%	61.3%
Canada	19.1%	20.2%	24.2%	28.5%	33.7%
Outside of North America	7.3%	6.6%	5.9%	5.3%	5.0%
Total	100.0%	100.0%	100.0%	99.9%	100.0%

*The "All other channels" category included showroom sales, sales at lululemon outlet stores, sales from temporary store locations, licensing revenues, and whole-sale sales to premium yoga studios, health clubs, fitness centers, and other wholesale accounts.

Source: Company 10-K Reports, Fiscal Years 2012, 2013, 2014, 2015, and 2016.

incident differently and that he did not think there were problems with the design of the product or the quality of the fabric. But the differences between Day and Wilson went beyond the events of March 2013, especially when some consumers began to complain about the quality of the replacement pants. Wilson returned from Australia in May 2013, and weeks

later Christine Day announced she would step down as CEO when her successor was named. A lengthy search for Day's replacement ensued.

In the meantime, Chip Wilson triggered a fire-storm when, in an interview with Bloomberg TV in November 2013, he defended the company's design of the black Luon bottoms saying, "Quite frankly, some women's bodies just actually don't work" with the pants. Although a few days later he publicly apologized for his remarks suggesting that the company's product quality issues back in March 2013 were actually the fault of overweight women, his apology was not well received. In December 2013, Wilson resigned his position as chairman of lululemon's Board of Directors and took on the lesser role of non-executive chairman. A few months later, Wilson announced that he intended to give up his position as non-executive chairman prior to the company's annual stockholders meeting in June 2014 but would continue on as a member of the company's Board of Directors (in 2013 and 2014, Wilson was the company's largest stockholder and controlled 29.2 percent of the company's common stock).

In early December 2013, lululemon announced that its Board of Directors had appointed Laurent Potdevin as the company's chief executive officer and a member of its Board of Directors; Potdevin stepped into his role in January 2014, and to help ensure a smooth transition Christine Day remained with lululemon through the end of the company's fiscal year (February 2, 2014). Potdevin came to lululemon having most recently served as president of TOMS, a company founded on the mission that it would match every pair of shoes purchased with a pair of new shoes given to a child in need. Prior to TOMS, Potdevin held numerous positions at Burton Snowboards for more than 15 years, including president and CEO from 2005 to 2010; Burton Snowboards, headquartered in Burlington, Vermont, was considered to be the world's premier snowboard company, with a product line that included snowboards and accessories (bindings, boots, socks, gloves, mitts, and beanies); men's, women's, and youth snowboarding apparel; and bags and luggage. Burton grew significantly under Potdevin's leadership, expanding across product categories and opening additional retail stores.

Tension between Chip Wilson and lululemon's Board of Directors erupted at the company's annual shareholder's meeting in June 2014 when he voted his entire shares against re-election of the company's chairman and another director. In February 2015, after continuing to disagree with lululemon executives and board members over the company's strategic direction and ongoing dissatisfaction with how certain lululemon activities were being managed, Wilson resigned his position on lululemon's Board of Directors. In August 2014, he sold half of his ownership stake to a private equity firm. In June 2015, lululemon filed documents with the Securities and Exchange Commission enabling Wilson to sell his remaining 20.1 million shares (equal to a 14.6 percent ownership stake worth about $1.3 billion) in the event he wished to do so.

Meanwhile, Wilson, together with his wife and 27-year-old son J.J., formed a new company in 2014–Kit and Ace–that specialized in high-end clothing for men and women made from a machine-washable, high-performance, cashmere fabric. The innovative clothing line was designed for all-day wear and included a range of items suitable for running errands or attending an evening event. J.J. Wilson was in charge of running the business until September 2016 when a new president was brought in, 20 percent of the head-office staff of 280 persons were laid off (in addition to 10 percent laid off earlier in the year), company operations were restructured, and plans were announced to close 15 locations over the next two years. Prior to the layoffs and restructuring, Kit and Ace had 61 retail locations (including short-term lease "pop-up" stores) in the United States, Canada, Australia, Britain, New Zealand, and Japan and a total of 700 employees. Except for the pop-ups, the stores featured onsite tailors and sparkling water, as well as art and design elements from local artists and photographers. In April 2017, Kit and Ace announced it was immediately closing all of its locations in the United States, Australia, and the United Kingdom, some of which were thought to be popular and profitable (although the company as a whole had yet to become profitable). All seven Canadian locations were to remain open; a Facebook posting said customers could continue to purchase at the company's website, www.kitandace.com.

The Yoga Marketplace

According to the "2016 Yoga in America" study conducted by the *Yoga Journal* and *Yoga Alliance,* in 2015, there were 36.7 million people in the United States who had practiced yoga in the last six months in a group or private class setting, up from 20.4 million in

2012 and 15.8 million in 2008.[2] About 72 percent of the people who engaged in group or class yoga exercises were women, and close to 62 percent of all yoga practitioners were in the age range of 18 to 49.[3] About 74 percent of the people who practiced yoga in 2015 had done so for five years or less. The level of yoga expertise varied considerably: 56 percent of yoga practitioners considered themselves as beginners, 42 percent considered themselves as "intermediate," and 2 percent considered themselves to be in the expert/advanced category. Spending on yoga classes, yoga apparel, and related items was an estimated $16.8 billion, up from $10.3 billion in 2012 and $5.7 billion in 2008.[4] Spending was forecasted to grow at a compound annual rate of just over 3 percent through 2020.[5]

The market for sports and fitness apparel was considerably larger, of course, than just the market for yoga apparel. The global market for all types of sportswear, activewear, and athletic apparel, estimated to be about $148 billion in 2015, was forecasted to grow about 4.3 percent annually and reach about $185 billion by 2020.[6] In the United States, sales of activewear and all types of gym and fitness apparel (which included both items made with high-tech performance fabrics that wicked away moisture and items made mostly of cotton, polyester, stretch fabrics, and selected other manmade fibers that lacked moisture-wicking and other high-performance features) was the fastest growing segment of the apparel industry.[7]

lululemon's Strategy and Business in 2017

lululemon athletica viewed its core mission as "creating components for people to live longer, healthier, fun lives."[8] The company's primary target customer was

> a sophisticated and educated woman who understands the importance of an active, healthy lifestyle. She is increasingly tasked with the dual responsibilities of career and family and is constantly challenged to balance her work, life, and health. We believe she pursues exercise to achieve physical fitness and inner peace.[9]

In the company's early years, lululemon's strategy was predicated on management's belief that other athletic apparel companies were not effectively addressing the unique style, fit, and performance needs of women who were embracing yoga and a variety of other fitness and athletic activities. Lululemon sought to address this void in the marketplace by incorporating style, feel-good comfort, and functionality into its yoga-inspired apparel products and by building a network of lululemon retail stores, along with an online store at the company's website, to market its apparel directly to these women. However, while the company was founded to address the unique needs and preferences of women, it did not take long for management to recognize the merits of broadening the company's market target to include fitness apparel for activities other than yoga and apparel for population segments other than adult women.

In 2009, lululemon opened its first ivivva-branded store in Vancouver, British Columbia, to sell high quality, premium-priced dance-inspired apparel to female youth (ivivva was a word that lululemon made up). The Vancouver store was soon profitable, and 11 additional company-owned ivivva stores were opened in Canada and the United States during 2010 to 2013. From 2014 to 2016, the opening of new ivivva stores accelerated, bringing the total to 55 stores at the end of fiscal 2016.

In 2013 and 2014, the company began designing and marketing products for men who appreciated the technical rigor and premium quality of athletic and fitness apparel. Management also believed that participation in athletic and fitness activities was destined to climb as people over 60 years of age became increasingly focused on living longer, healthier, active lives in their retirement years and engaged in regular exercise and recreational activities. Another demand-enhancing factor was that consumer decisions to purchase athletic, fitness, and recreational apparel were being driven not only by an actual need for functional products but also by a desire to create a particular lifestyle perception through the apparel they wore. Consequently, senior executives had transitioned lululemon's strategy from one of focusing exclusively on yoga apparel for women to one aimed at designing and marketing a wider range of healthy lifestyle-inspired apparel and accessories for women and men and dance-inspired apparel for girls.

As lululemon began fiscal year 2017, the company's business strategy had six core components:

- Broaden the lululemon product line to include both more items and items suitable for purposes other than just fitness-related activities.
- Grow lululemon's store base, both in North America and outside of North America.
- Broaden awareness of the lululemon brand and the nature and quality of the company's apparel offerings.
- Incorporate next-generation fabrics and technologies in the company's products to strengthen consumer association of the lululemon and ivivva brands with technically advanced fabrics and innovative features, thereby enabling lululemon to command higher prices for its products compared to the prices of traditional fitness and recreational apparel products made of cotton, rayon, polyester, and/or other manmade fibers lacking the performance features of high-tech fabrics.
- Provide a distinctive in-store shopping experience, complemented with strong ties to fitness instructors and fitness establishments, local athletes and fitness-conscious people, and various community-based athletic and fitness events.
- Grow traffic and sales at the company's websites (www.lululemon.com and www.ivviva.com) to provide a distinctive and satisfying ivivva online shopping experience and to extend the company's reach into geographic markets where it did not have retail stores.

Product Line Strategy

As of June 2017, lululemon offered a diverse and growing selection of premium-priced performance apparel and accessories for women and men that were designed for healthy lifestyle activities such as yoga, swimming, running, cycling, and general fitness. Currently, the company's range of offerings included:

Women		Men
• Sports bras	• Swimwear	• Tops
• Tanks	• Socks and	• Jackets
• Sweaters and	underwear	and hoodies
wraps	• Scarves	• Pants and shorts
• Jackets and	• Gear bags	• Gear bags and
hoodies	• Caps and	backpacks
• Long-sleeve and	headbands	• Caps and gloves
short-sleeve tops	• Sweat cuffs	• Swimwear
and tees	and gloves	• Socks and
• Pants and crops	• Water bottles	underwear
• Shorts	• Yoga mats	• Run accessories
• Skirts and	and props	• Yoga mats, props,
dresses	• Instructional	and instructional
• Outerwear	yoga DVDs	DVDs

Exhibit 3 shows a sampling of lululemon's products for men and women.

As 2017 progressed and more ivivva stores were either closed or converted to lululemon stores, a growing percentage of ivivva revenues were being generated at the ivivva website. The ivivva product line, while featuring dancing apparel, also included apparel for yoga and running. Specific ivivva-branded items included leotards, shorts, dance pants, crop pants, tights, sports bras, tank tops, tees, jackets, hoodies, pullovers, caps, headbands, socks, bags, and other accessories.

lululemon's Strategy of Offering Only a Limited Range of Apparel Sizes   In the months following the product recall of the too-sheer pants in March 2013, lululemon officially revealed in a posting on its Facebook page that it did not offer clothing in plus sizes because focusing on sizes 12 and below was an integral part of its business strategy; according to the company's posting and to the postings of lululemon personnel who responded to comments made by Facebook members who read the lululemon posting:

> Our product and design strategy is built around creating products for our target guest in our size range of 2 to 12. While we know that doesn't work for everyone and recognize fitness and health come in all shapes and sizes, we've built our business, brand, and relationship with our guests on this formula.

EXHIBIT 3

Examples of lululemon Apparel Items

(top left) © Dina Rudick/The Boston Globe via Getty Images; (top right) © Xaume Olleros/Bloomberg via Getty Images; (middle left) © Joe Raedle/Getty Images; (middle right and bottom) © Stuart C. Wilson/Getty Images

We agree that a beautiful healthy life is not measured by the size you wear. We want to be excellent at what we do, so this means that we can't be everything to everybody and need to focus on specific areas. Our current focuses are in innovating our women's design, men's brand, and building our international market.

At this time, we don't have plans to change our current sizing structure which is 2 to 12 for women.[10]

Retail Distribution and Store Expansion Strategy

After several years of experience in establishing and working with franchised stores in the United States, Australia, Japan, and Canada, top management in 2010 decided that having franchised stores was not in lululemon's best long-term strategic interests. A strategic initiative was begun to either acquire the current stores of franchisees and operate them as company stores or convert the franchised stores to a joint venture arrangement where lululemon owned the controlling interest in the store and the former franchisee owned a minority interest. By year-end 2011, all lululemon stores were majority-owned. However, in January 2015, lululemon decided to enter into a license and supply arrangement with a partner in the Middle East which granted the partner the right to operate lululemon branded retail locations in the United Arab Emirates, Kuwait, Qatar, Oman, and Bahrain for an initial term of five years. Lululemon retained the rights to sell lululemon products through its e-commerce websites in these countries. Under this arrangement, lululemon supplied the partner with lululemon products, training, and other support. A similar licensing arrangement was entered into with a partner in Mexico in November 2016, but no licensed stores were operating in Mexico as of January 29, 2017.

As of January 29, 2017, lululemon's retail footprint included:

- 245 company-operated stores in the United States (45 states and the District of Columbia)
- 51 company-operated stores in Canada
- 27 company-operated stores in Australia
- 9 company-operated stores in the United Kingdom
- 5 company-operated stores in New Zealand
- 3 company-operated stores in Singapore, Hong Kong, and China
- 2 company-operated stores in South Korea

In June 2017, some four years later, the largest size appearing in the size guide for women on lululemon's website was 12/XL which was said to be suitable for a 33-inch waist and 43-inch hips.

- 1 company-operated store in Germany, Puerto Rico, and Switzerland
- 3 licensed stores in the United Arab Emirates (not included in statistics relating to company-operated stores)
- 1 licensed store in Qatar (not included in statistics relating to company-operated stores)
- 42 ivivva stores in the United States
- 13 ivivva stores in Canada

In addition, the company operated over 50 small showrooms in various locations in the United States, Canada, Germany, France, Sweden, the Netherlands, Japan, and Malaysia where it was contemplating opening new retail stores in upcoming years. Five new lululemon stores were opened in the first quarter of fiscal 2017.

Management had announced that new store openings would be concentrated in the United States, Asia, and Europe, primarily in those locations where showrooms were already open or would be opening soon. In spite of lululemon's recent declines in sales-per-square-foot performance (see the bottom portion of Exhibit 1), management believed its sales revenues per square foot of retail space were close to the best in the retail apparel sector—for example, the stores of specialty fashion retailers like Old Navy, Banana Republic, The Gap, and Abercrombie & Fitch typically had 2016 annual sales averaging less than $500 per square foot of store space.

However, in June 2017, lululemon unexpectedly announced that it would move sales and promotion of its girls' ivivva dance and activewear apparel to a mostly online format; plans called for closing 40 of the company's 55 ivivva-branded stores, along with all ivivva showrooms and other temporary locations. Approximately half of the remaining 15 ivivva stores, all located in metropolitan locations and having a sizable clientele, were to remain open and continue to retail ivivva apparel; the other seven to eight ivivva stores were scheduled to be converted into lululemon stores. Management indicated the ivivva restructuring would likely be completed by November 1, 2017. In announcing the change in strategy for ivivva, lululemon forecast that the ivivva restructuring would result in a charge of $50 million to $60 million against fiscal 2017 earnings, of which $17.7 million was recognized in the first quarter of fiscal 2017 (which reduced the company's first quarter 2017 diluted earnings per share from $0.32 to $0.23).

lululemon's Retail Stores: Locations, Layout, and Merchandising

The company's retail stores were located primarily on street locations, in upscale strip shopping centers, in lifestyle centers, and in malls. Typically, stores were leased and were 2,500 to 3,000 square feet in size. Most all stores included space for product display and merchandising, checkout, fitting rooms, a restroom, and an office/storage area. While the leased nature of the store spaces meant that each store had its own customized layout and arrangement of fixtures and displays, each store was carefully decorated and laid out in a manner that projected the ambience and feel of a homespun local apparel boutique rather than the more impersonal, cookie-cutter atmosphere of many apparel chain stores.

The company's merchandising strategy was to sell all of the items in its retail stores at full price.[11] Special colors and seasonal items were in stores for only a limited time—such products were on 3-, 6-, or 12-week life cycles so that frequent shoppers could always find something new. Store inventories of short-cycle products were deliberately limited to help foster a sense of scarcity, condition customers to buy when they saw an item rather than wait, and avoid any need to discount unsold items. In one instance, a hot-pink color that launched in December was supposed to have a two-month shelf life, but supplies sold out in the first week. However, ample supplies of core products that did not change much from season to season were inventoried to minimize the risk of lost sales due to items being out of stock. Approximately 95 percent of the merchandise in lululemon stores was sold at full price. [12]

One unique feature of lululemon's retail stores was that the floor space allocated to merchandising displays and customer shopping could be sufficiently cleared to enable the store to hold an in-store yoga class before or after regular shopping hours. Every store hosted a complimentary yoga class each week that was conducted by a professional yoga instructor from the local community who had been recruited to be a "store ambassador"; when the class concluded, the attendees were given a 15 percent-off coupon to use in shopping for products in the store. From time to time, each store's yoga ambassadors demonstrated their moves in the store windows and on the sales floor. Normally, each store displayed pictures of its local yoga ambassadors on its walls. Exhibit 4 shows the exteriors of representative lululemon athletica stores.

lululemon's Showroom Strategy

Over the years, lululemon had opened showrooms in numerous locations both inside and outside North

EXHIBIT 4

Representative Exterior Scenes at lululemon Stores

(left and right): @Stuart C. Wilson/Getty Images

America as a means of introducing the lululemon brand and culture to a community, developing relationships with local fitness instructors and fitness enthusiasts, and hosting community-related fitness events, all in preparation for the grand opening of a new lululemon athletica retail store in weeks ahead. Showroom personnel:

- Hosted get-acquainted parties for fitness instructors and fitness enthusiasts.
- Recruited a few well-regarded fitness instructors in the local area to be "store ambassadors" for lululemon products and periodically conduct in-store yoga classes when the local lululemon retail store opened.
- Advised people visiting the showroom on where to find great yoga or Pilates classes, fitness centers, and health and wellness information and events.
- Solicited a select number of local yoga studios, health clubs, and fitness centers to stock and retail a small assortment of lululemon's products.

Showrooms were only open part of the week so that showroom personnel could be out in the community meeting people, building relationships with yoga and fitness instructors, participating in local yoga and fitness classes and talking with attendees before and after class, promoting attendance at local fitness and wellness events, and stimulating interest in the soon-to-open retail store. Lululemon used showrooms as a means of "pre-seeding" the opening of a lululemon retail store primarily in those locations where no other lululemon retail stores were nearby. Because the showroom strategy had worked so well in getting lululemon stores off to a good start, management quickly adopted the use of showrooms to pre-seed the opening of ivivva stores. As of late June 2017, lululemon had around 15 showrooms for its lululemon brand; all ivivva showrooms were in the process of closing down operations.

Wholesale Sales Strategy

Lululemon marketed its products to select premium yoga studios, health clubs, and fitness centers as a way to gain the implicit endorsement of local fitness personnel for lululemon branded apparel, familiarize

their customers with the lululemon brand, and give them an opportunity to conveniently purchase lululemon apparel. Also, when certain styles, colors, and sizes of apparel items at lululemon retail stores were selling too slowly to clear out the inventories of items ordered from contract manufacturers, lululemon typically shipped the excess inventories to one or more of the 11 lululemon factory outlet stores in North America to be sold at discounted prices and also sold these items on its website accessed at a menu selection labeled "we made too much."

Lululemon management did not want to grow wholesale sales to these types of establishments into a significant revenue contributor. Rather, the strategic objective of selling lululemon apparel to yoga studios, health clubs, and fitness centers was to build brand awareness, especially in new geographic markets both in North America and other international locations where the company intended to open new stores. Wholesale sales to lululemon's outlet stores were made only to dispose of excess inventories and thereby avoid in-store markdowns on slow-selling items.

The company's wholesale sales to all these channels accounted for net revenues of $186.7 million (8.0 percent of total net revenues) in fiscal 2016, some 30.8 percent more than the net revenues of $142.7 million (6.9 percent of total net revenues) from these channels in fiscal 2011. The big increase was primarily the result of sales at three recently opened (2015) outlet stores that were open for the full year in fiscal 2016, increased net revenues at the company's other 11 outlet locations, and an increase in the number of showroom locations.

Direct-to-Consumer Sales Strategy

In 2009, lululemon launched its e-commerce website, www.lululemon.com, to enable customers to make online purchases, supplement its already-functioning phone sales activities, and greatly extend the company's geographic market reach. Management saw online sales as having three strategic benefits: (1) providing added convenience for core customers, (2) securing sales in geographic markets where there were no lululemon stores, and (3) helping build brand awareness, especially in new markets, including those outside of North America. As of early 2017, the company operated country- and region-specific websites in Australia, Europe, the Middle East, and Asia, and brand specific websites for both lululemon and ivivva (www.ivivva.com) products in North America. Lululemon provided free shipping on all lululemon and ivivva orders to customers in North America; a shipping fee was charged to buyers in a number of international destinations.

The merchandise selection that lululemon offered to online buyers differed somewhat from what was available in the company's retail stores. A number of the items available in stores were not sold online; a few online selections were not available in the stores. Styles and colors available for sale online were updated weekly. On occasion, the company marked down the prices of some styles and colors sold online to help clear out the inventories of items soon to be out of season and make way for newly arriving merchandise—online customers could view the discounted merchandise by clicking on a "we made too much" link.

Direct-to-consumer sales at the company's websites had become an increasingly important part of the company's business, with e-commerce sales climbing from $106.3 million in fiscal 2011 (10.6 percent of total net revenues) to $453.3 million in fiscal 2016 (19.3 percent of total revenues)—equal to a compound annual growth rate of 33.7 percent.

In addition to making purchases, website visitors could browse information about what yoga was, what the various types of yoga were, and their benefits; learn about fabrics and technologies used in lululemon's products; read recent posts on lululemon's yoga blog; and stay abreast of lululemon activities in their communities. The company planned to continue to develop and enhance its e-commerce websites in ways that would provide a distinctive online shopping experience and strengthen its brand reputation. In 2016, the company's websites were all redesigned and relaunched to improve their look and functionality.

Product Design and Development Strategy

Lululemon's product design efforts were led by a team of designers based in Vancouver, British Columbia, partnering with various international designers. The design team included athletes and users of the company's products who embraced lululemon's design philosophy and dedication to premium quality. Design team members regularly visited retail stores in a proactive effort to solicit feedback on existing products from store customers and fitness ambassadors and to gather their ideas for product improvements and new products. In addition, the design team used various market intelligence sources to identify and track market trends. On occasion, the team hosted meetings in several geographic markets to discuss the company's products with local athletes, trainers, yogis, and members of the fitness industry. The design team incorporated all of this input to make fabric selections, develop new products, and make adjustments in the fit, style, and function of existing products.

The design team worked closely with its apparel manufacturers to incorporate innovative fabrics that gave lululemon garments such characteristics as stretchability, moisture-wicking capability, color fastness, feel-good comfort, and durability. Fabric quality was evaluated via actual wear tests and by a leading testing facility. Before bringing out new products with new fabrics, lululemon used the services of leading independent inspection, verification, testing, and certification companies to conduct a battery of tests on fabrics for such performance characteristics as pilling, shrinkage, abrasion resistance, and color-fastness. Lastly, lululemon design personnel worked with leading fabric suppliers to identify opportunities to develop fabrics that lululemon could trademark and thereby gain added brand recognition and brand differentiation.

Where appropriate, product designs incorporated convenience features, such as pockets to hold credit cards, keys, digital audio players, and clips for heart rate monitors and long sleeves that covered the hands for cold-weather exercising. Product specifications called for the use of advanced sewing techniques, such as flat seaming, that increased comfort and functionality, reduced chafing and skin irritation, and strengthened important seams. All of these design elements and fabric technologies were factors that management believed enabled lululemon to price its high-quality technical athletic apparel at prices above those of traditional athletic apparel.

Typically, it took 8 to 10 months for lululemon products to move from the design stage to availability in its retail stores; however, the company had the capability to bring select new products to market in as little as two months. Management believed its lead times were shorter than those of most apparel brands due to the company's streamlined design and development process, the real-time input received from customers and ambassadors at its store locations, and the short times it took to receive and approve samples from manufacturing suppliers. Short lead times facilitated quick responses to emerging trends or shifting market conditions.

Lululemon management believed that its design process enhanced the company's capabilities to develop top quality products and was a competitive strength that helped differentiate lululemon apparel from the offerings of rival brands.

Sourcing and Manufacturing

Production was the only value chain activity that lululemon did not perform internally. Lululemon did not own or operate any manufacturing facilities to produce fabrics or make garments. In 2016, fabrics were sourced from a group of approximately 65 fabrics manufacturers. Garments were produced by approximately 35 contract manufacturers, five of which produced approximately 63 percent of the company's products in fiscal 2016. However, the company deliberately refrained from entering into long-term contracts with any of its fabric suppliers or manufacturing sources, preferring instead to transact business on an order-by-order basis and rely on the close working relationships it had developed with its various suppliers over the years. During fiscal 2016, approximately 47 percent of the company's products were produced in Southeast Asia, approximately 28 percent in South Asia, approximately 15 percent in China, approximately 1 percent in North America, and the remainder in other regions. The company's North American manufacturers helped provide lululemon with the capability to speed select products to market and respond quickly to changing trends and unexpectedly high buyer demand for certain products.

Lululemon took great care to ensure that its manufacturing suppliers shared lululemon's commitment to quality and ethical business conduct. All manufacturers were required to adhere to a vendor code of ethics regarding quality of manufacturing, working conditions, environmental responsibility, fair wage practices, and compliance with child labor laws, among others. Lululemon utilized the services of a leading inspection and verification firm to closely monitor each supplier's compliance with applicable law, lululemon's vendor code of ethics, and other business practices that could reflect badly on lululemon's choice of suppliers.

Distribution Facilities

Lululemon shipped products to its stores from five owned or leased distribution facilities in the United States, Canada, and Australia. The company owned a 307,000-square-foot distribution center in Columbus, Ohio, and operated a leased 145,000-square-foot facility in Vancouver, British Columbia, a second 110,000-square-foot facility in Vancouver, and a leased 150,000-square-foot facility in Sumner, Washington, to supply stores in Canada, the United States, and some locations in Europe and Africa. A leased 55,000-square-foot distribution center in Melbourne, Australia, supplied stores in Australia and New Zealand. In some instances, the company utilized third-party logistics providers to warehouse and distribute finished goods from their warehouses in Hong Kong, China, and the Netherlands. Management believed its five internally operated facilities, together with its third-party logistics providers, would be sufficient to accommodate its expected store growth and expanded product offerings over the next several years. Merchandise was typically shipped to retail stores through third-party delivery services multiple times per week, thus providing stores with a steady flow of new inventory.

lululemon's Community-Based Marketing Approach and Brand-Building Strategy

One of lululemon's differentiating characteristics was its community-based approach to building brand awareness and customer loyalty. Local fitness practitioners chosen to be ambassadors introduced their fitness class attendees to the lululemon brand, thereby leading to interest in the brand, store visits, and word-of-mouth marketing. Each yoga-instructor ambassador was also called upon to conduct a complimentary yoga class every four to six weeks at the local lululemon store they were affiliated with. In return for helping drive business to lululemon stores and conducting classes, ambassadors were periodically given bags of free products, and large portraits of each ambassador wearing lululemon products and engaging in physical activity at a local landmark were prominently displayed on the walls of their local lululemon store as a means of helping ambassadors expand their clientele.

Every lululemon store had a dedicated community coordinator who developed a customized plan for organizing, sponsoring, and participating in local athletic, fitness, and philanthropic events. In addition, each store had a community events bulletin board for posting announcements of upcoming activities, providing fitness education information and brochures, and promoting the local yoga studios and fitness centers of ambassadors. There was also a chalkboard in each store's fitting room area where customers could scribble comments about lululemon products or their yoga class experiences or their appreciation of the assistance/service provided by certain store personnel; these comments were relayed to lululemon headquarters every two weeks. Customers could use a lululemon micro website to track their progress regarding fitness or progress toward life goals.

Lululemon made little use of traditional print advertising or television advertisements, preferring instead to rely on its various grassroots, community-based marketing efforts and the use of social media (like Facebook and Twitter) to increase brand awareness, reinforce its premium brand image, and broaden the appeal of its products.

Store Personnel

As part of the company's commitment to providing customers with an inviting and educational store environment, lululemon's store sales associates, who the company referred to as "educators," were coached to personally engage and connect with each guest who entered the store. Educators, many of whom had prior experience as a fitness practitioner or were avid runners or yoga enthusiasts, received approximately 30 hours of in-house training within the first three months of their employment. Training was focused on (1) teaching educators about leading a healthy

and balanced life, exercising self-responsibility, and setting lifestyle goals, (2) preparing them to explain the technical and innovative design aspects of all lululemon products, and (3) providing the information needed for educators to serve as knowledgeable references for customers seeking information on fitness classes, instructors, and events in the community. New hires that lacked knowledge about the intricacies of yoga were given subsidies to attend yoga classes so they could understand the activity and better explain the benefits of lululemon's yoga apparel.

People who shopped at lululemon stores were called "guests," and store personnel were expected to "educate" guests about lululemon apparel, not sell to them. To provide a personalized, welcoming, and relaxed experience, store educators referred to their guests on a first name basis in the fitting and changing area, allowed them to use store restrooms, and offered them complimentary fresh-filtered water. Management believed that such a soft-sell, customer-centric environment encouraged product trial, purchases, and repeat visits.

Core Values and Culture

Consistent with the company's mission of "providing people with the components to live a longer, healthier and more fun life," lululemon executives sought to promote and ingrain a set of core values centered on developing the highest-quality products, operating with integrity, leading a healthy balanced life, and instilling in its employees a sense of self responsibility and the value of goal setting. The company sought to provide employees with a supportive and goal-oriented work environment; all employees were encouraged to set goals aimed at reaching their full professional, health, and personal potential. The company offered personal development workshops and goal-coaching to assist employees in achieving their goals. Many lululemon employees had a written set of professional, health, and personal goals. All employees had access to a "learning library" of personal development books that included Steven Covey's *The Seven Habits of Highly Effective People,* Rhonda Byrne's *The Secret,* and Brian Tracy's *The Psychology of Achievement.*

Chip Wilson had been the principal architect of the company's culture and core values, and the company's work climate through 2013 reflected his business and lifestyle philosophy. Wilson had digested much of his philosophy about personal development and life in general into a set of statements and prescriptions that he called "the lululemon manifesto." In recent years, several portions of Wilson's original manifesto had been dropped, but the latest version was still considered to be a core element of lululemon's culture. The bold thoughts expressed in the manifesto were deliberately intended to provoke individual reflections and thoughtful conversations among people both inside and outside lululemon—sample portions of a recent manifesto are shown in Exhibit 5. Senior executives believed the company's work climate and core values helped it attract passionate and motivated employees who were driven to succeed and who would support the company's vision of "elevating the world from mediocrity to greatness"—a phrase coined by Chip Wilson in the company's early years.

Top management believed that its relationship with company employees was exceptional and a key contributor to the company's success.

Competition

Competition in the market for athletic and fitness apparel was principally centered on product quality, performance features, innovation, fit and style, distribution capabilities, brand image and recognition, and price. Rivalry among competing brands was vigorous, involving both established companies who were expanding their production and marketing of performance products and recent entrants attracted by the growth opportunities.

Lululemon competed with wholesalers and direct sellers of premium performance athletic apparel made of high-tech fabrics, most especially Nike, The adidas Group AG (which marketed athletic and sports apparel under its adidas, Reebok, and Ashworth brands), and Under Armour. Nike had a powerful and well-known global brand name, an extensive and diverse line of athletic and sports apparel, fiscal 2016 apparel sales of $9.1 billion ($4.7 billion in North America), and 2016 total revenues (footwear, apparel, and equipment) of $32.4 billion. Nike was the world's largest seller of athletic footwear and athletic

EXHIBIT 5

A Selection of the Evolving Collection of Bold Thoughts that Comprise the lululemon Manifesto, June 2017

- Creativity is maximized when you are living in the moment.
- A daily hit of athletic-induced endorphins gives you the power to make better decisions, helps you be at peace with yourself, and offsets stress.
- Do one thing a day that scares you.
- Listen, listen, listen, then ask strategic questions.
- Practice yoga so you can remain active in physical sports as you age.
- Your outlook on life is a direct reflection of how much you like yourself.
- That which matters the most should never give way to that which matters the least.
- This is not your practice life. This is all there is.
- Jealousy works the opposite way you want it to.
- Have you woken up two days in a row uninspired? Change your life!
- Don't trust that an old age pension will be sufficient.
- The conscious brain can only hold one thought at a time. Choose a positive thought.
- Children are the orgasm of life. Just like you did not know what an orgasm was before you had one, you won't know how great children are until you have them.
- Nature wants us to be mediocre because we have a greater chance to survive and reproduce. Mediocre is as close to the bottom as it is to the top, and will give you a lousy life.
- The perfect tombstone would read "all used up."
- Friends are more important than money.
- The pursuit of happiness is the source of all unhappiness.

Source: The version of the lululemon Manifesto posted at www.lululemon.com and accessed June 14, 2017.

apparel, with over 44,000 retail accounts worldwide, 1,045 company-owned stores, 52 distribution centers, e-commerce websites in 40 countries, and selling arrangements with independent distributors and licensees in over 190 countries; its retail account base for sports apparel in the United States included a mix of sporting goods stores, athletic specialty stores, department stores, and skate, tennis, and golf shops.

Reebok and adidas were both global brands that generated worldwide sports apparel revenues of approximately $8.2 billion in 2016; their product lines consisted of high-tech performance garments for a wide variety of sports and fitness activities, as well as recreational sportswear. The adidas Group sold products in virtually every country of the world. In 2016, its extensive product offerings were marketed through third-party retailers (sporting goods chains, department stores, independent sporting goods retailer buying groups, lifestyle retailing chains, and Internet retailers), 1,757 company-owned and franchised adidas and Reebok "concept" stores, 902 company-owned adidas and Reebok factory outlet stores, 152 other adidas and Reebok stores with varying formats, and over 50 company websites (including www.adidas.com and www.reebok.com).

Under Armour, an up-and-coming designer and marketer of performance sports apparel, had total sales of $4.8 billion in 2016, of which $3.2 billion was in apparel. Like lululemon, Under Armour's apparel products were made entirely of technically advanced, high-performance fabrics and were designed to be aesthetically appealing, as well as highly functional and comfortable. Under Armour regularly upgraded its products as next-generation fabrics with better performance characteristics became available. Under Armour's product line included apparel for men, women, and children. Management was actively pursuing efforts to grow its sales to $7.5 billion by year-end 2018 and $10 billion by year-end 2020. Under Armour's business was currently concentrated in North America (83 percent of 2016 sales revenues), but it was accelerating efforts to expand globally. Under Armour products were available in over 17,000 retail stores worldwide in 2016, 11,000 of which were in North America. Under Armour also sold its products directly to consumers through 18 company-owned Brand House stores, over 151 Under Armour factory outlet stores, and company websites. Plans called for having some 200 Factory House and Brand House locations in North America and 800 such stores in 40+ countries by year-end 2018.

Nike, The adidas Group, and Under Armour all aggressively marketed and promoted their high performance apparel products and spent heavily to grow consumer awareness of their brands and build brand loyalty. All three sponsored numerous athletic events, provided uniforms and equipment with their logos to collegiate and professional sports teams, and paid millions of dollars annually to numerous high-profile male and female athletes to endorse their products. Like lululemon, they designed their own products but outsourced the production of their garments to contract manufacturers.

The Emergence of a New Formidable Competitor Specializing in Sports and Fitness Apparel for Women

In 2011, fashion retailer Gap, with such brands as Gap, Banana Republic, and Old Navy, launched a new retailing chain named Athleta to compete head-on against lululemon in the market for comfortable, fashionable, high-performance women's apparel for workouts, sports, physically active recreational activities, and leisure wear. Athleta had grown from one retail store in 2011 to over 132 retail stores worldwide (120 in North America) as of June 2017; 15 to 20 new Athleta stores were expected to open in 2017. Athleta's expanding product line included swimwear, tops, bras, jackets, sweaters, pants, tights, shorts, t-shirt dresses, performance footwear, sneakers, sandals, bags, headwear, and gear, plus a newly introduced line of Athleta Girl apparel. Athleta's products were colorful, stylish, and functional. In June 2017, the array of apparel items and color selections at Athleta's website exceeded those at lululemon's website; Athleta apparel items were typically available in sizes XXS, XS, S, M, L, XL, and plus sizes 1X and 2X that accommodated bust sizes of 30 to 50 inches, waist sizes of 23 to 43 inches, and hip sizes of 32.5 to 52.5 inches. Athleta utilized well-known women athletes and local fitness instructors to serve as brand ambassadors by blogging for Athleta's website, teaching classes at local stores, and testing Athleta garments. In 2012, Athleta initiated its first national advertising campaign, "Power to the She," to promote the Athleta brand. In 2016 and 2017, "The Power of She" was the tagline for Athleta's ad campaigns. Athleta products were sold at www.athleta. gap.com and www.athleta.com); in addition, Athleta had a special social media website, www.athleta.net/ chi, that connected women with interests in sports and fitness, nutrition and health, tutorials and training plans, and travel and adventure. In 2017, Gap, Inc., had 3,200 company-operated retail stores and 459 franchised stores worldwide that operated under such brand names as Gap, Old Navy, Banana Republic, Athleta, Piperlime, Weddington Way, and Intermix. The product offerings at the 1,346 Gap-branded stores included a GapFit collection of fitness and athleisure products for women.

Several other national and regional retailers of women's apparel, seeking to capitalize on growing sales of activewear made of high-tech fabrics, were marketing one or more brands of fitness apparel suitable for yoga, running, gym exercise, and leisure activities. A few were selling these items under their own labels. For example, the 1,195 company-owned Victoria's Secret stores in the United States, Canada, and Great Britain, the several hundred franchised Victoria's Secret stores in about 50 other countries, and the company's website, www.VictoriasSecret.com, were marketing a line of Victoria Sport apparel that included tops, sport bras, running shorts, sport shorts, track pants, capri pants, gym pants, sport pants, cardigans, sweatshirts, hoodies, and accessories. Nordstrom, a nationally respected department store retailer, was merchandising its own Zella line of attire for yoga, cross-training, workouts, swimming, and "beyond the workout;" many of the initial products in the Zella collection were designed by a former member of lululemon's design team. Zella-branded products were offered in regular sizes (XXS, XS, S, M, L, XL, and XXL) and plus sizes (1X, 2X, and 3X). Nordstrom was also marketing several other brands of activewear for women, men, and juniors, including Nike, Under Armour, Patagonia, Reebok, and adidas. In 2017, Nordstrom's activewear offerings could be purchased at 123 Nordstrom full-line department stores (typically 140,000 to 250,000 square feet in size) and 216 Nordstrom Rack off-price stores (typically 30,000 to 50,000 square feet in size), at Nordstrom's website (www.nordstrom.com), and at the Nordstrom Rack website (www.nordstromrack.com).

Typically, the items in the GapFit, Athleta, and Zella collections were priced 10 percent to 25 percent below similar kinds of lululemon products. Likewise, Nike, Under Armour, adidas, and Reebok apparel items were usually less expensive than comparable lululemon-branded items.

ENDNOTES

[1] Beth Kowitt and Colleen Leahey, "LULULEMON: In an Uncomfortable Position," *Fortune,* September 16, 2013, p. 118.

[2] "2016 Yoga in America Study," conducted by *Yoga Journal* and *Yoga Alliance,* January 2016, www.yogaalliance.org (accessed April 29, 2016); and "Yoga in America," *Yoga Journal,* press release dated December 5, 2012, www.yogajournal.com (accessed April 7, 2014).

[3] "2016 Yoga in America Study," conducted by *Yoga Journal* and *Yoga Alliance,* January 2016, www.yogaalliance.org (accessed April 29, 2016).

[4] "2016 Yoga in America Study," conducted by *Yoga Journal* and *Yoga Alliance,* January 2016, www.yogaalliance.org (accessed April 29, 2016); and "Yoga in America" *Yoga Journal,* press release dated December 5, 2012, www.yogajournal.com (accessed April 7, 2014).

[5] According to a snapshot summary of a research report conducted by Technavio issued May 2017 and titled *Global Yoga Apparel Market 2017–2021,* www.technavio.com (accessed June 12, 2017).

[6] PR Newswire, "World Sports Apparel Market Is Estimated to Garner $184.6 Billion by 2020—Allied Market Research," October 8, 2015, www.prnewswire.com (accessed May 2, 2016).

[7] Renee Frojo, "Yoga Clothing Retailers Go to the Mat for Market Share," *San Francisco Business Times,* December 28, 2012, www.bizjournals.com/sanfrancisco (accessed April 10, 2014).

[8] As posted on www.lululemon.com, accessed May 2, 2016.

[9] Company 10-K Report for the fiscal year ending January 29, 2017, p. 1.

[10] Kim Basin, "Lululemon Admits Plus-Size Clothing Is Not Part of Its 'Formula'" *Huffington Post,* August 2, 2013, www.huffingtonpost.com (accessed April 7, 2014).

[11] Dana Mattoili, "Lululemon's Secret Sauce," *The Wall Street Journal,* March 22, 2012, pp. B1-B2.

[12] Ibid.

Gap Inc.: Can It Develop a Strategy to Connect with Consumers in 2017?

JOHN D. VARLARO Johnson & Wales University

JOHN E. GAMBLE Texas A&M University–Corpus Christi

"To not be considering Amazon and others would be—in my view—delusional," Art Peck, CEO of Gap Inc., remarked during a conversation with investors in May 2016. Faced with increased competition and a changing demographic amid a shifting shopping landscape, Peck needed to reverse Gap Inc.'s current trajectory and consider alternatives to improve sales and maintain its number two overall ranking.[1] But after two full years into Peck's turnaround strategy, Gap Inc. continued to decline and showed no real signs that it was again resonating with consumers.

Complicating Peck's turnaround strategy was the increase in shopping mall vacancies, as well as the increased competition in retail. While higher-end malls continued to see improvements in foot traffic in 2016, consumers decreased shopping at lower-end malls, where empty storefronts were becoming common. Further, as shoppers became comfortable with online shopping, larger percentages of retail sales were occurring through e-commerce. Yet, companies such as the Indetix Group, known for its Zara brand, continually increased sales and expanded locations regardless of these environmental factors. Peck pondered how Gap could defend against unfavorable external factors and craft a strategy well-matched to the retail environment going into the late-2010s.

Company History and Performance

Gap Inc. operated stores in 70 different countries in 2016 and was positioned as casual attire, with an emphasis on blue jeans and khakis. Offering apparel for the whole family, brands also included GapKids, babyGap, and GapMaternity. Banana Republic, in contrast, offered styles from business casual to formal, where attire could be both work and everyday. The Old Navy brand was positioned to compete at a lower price point in the casual, everyday apparel category.

The company was founded in 1969 by Doris and Don Fisher. The company first began selling Levi-branded jeans due to Don's experience in trying to find his own pair that fit. Initially meant to target a younger demographic, the name was derived from the phrase "generation gap." Gap started offering its own Gap-branded jeans in 1972, and went public in 1973. Gap acquired Banana Republic in the early 1980s, and launched the Old Navy brand in the 1990s. The company acquired the Athleta athletic apparel brand and launched its online fashion marketplace Piperlime in 2008 and acquired boutique retail chain Intermix in 2013. The company closed the Piperlime website and one retail location in 2015.

Gap became a household name in the 1990s through its clever advertising and merchandising strategy that made it largely responsible for making the jeans-and-T-shirt style ubiquitous during that decade. The company's strategy led to large and regular increases in net sales, which increased from $1.9 billion in 1990 to $11.6 billion in 1999.[2] Its net sales by the end of the decade were almost double the $6.6 billion in 1997.

EXHIBIT 1

Financial and Operating Summary for Gap, Inc., Fiscal 2012 - Fiscal 2016 (in millions except per share, store count, and employee data)

	2016	2015	2014	2013	2012
Operating Results ($ in millions)					
Net sales	$ 15,516	$ 15,797	$ 16,435	$ 16,148	$ 15,651
Gross margin	36.3%	36.2%	38.3%	39.0%	39.4%
Operating margin	7.7%	9.6%	12.7%	13.3%	12.4%
Net income	$ 676	$ 920	$ 1,262	$ 1,280	$ 1,135
Cash dividends paid	$ 367	$ 377	$ 383	$ 321	$ 240
Per Share Data (number of shares in millions)					
Basic earnings per share	$1.69	$2.24	$2.90	$.78	$2.35
Diluted earnings per share	$1.69	$2.23	$2.87	$2.74	$2.33
Weighted-average number of shares—basic	399	411	435	461	482
Weighted-average number of shares—diluted	400	413	440	467	488
Cash dividends declared and paid per share	$0.92	$0.92	$0.88	$0.70	$0.50
Balance Sheet Information ($ in millions)					
Merchandise inventory	$ 1,830	$ 1,873	$ 1,889	$ 1,928	$ 1,758
Total assets	$ 7,610	$ 7,473	$ 7,690	$ 7,849	$ 7,470
Working capital	$ 1,862	$ 1,450	$ 2,083	$ 1,985	$ 1,788
Total long-term debt, less current maturities	$ 1,248	$ 1,310	$ 1,332	$ 1,369	$ 1,246
Stockholders' equity	$ 2,904	$ 2,545	$ 983	$ 3,062	$ 2,894
Other Data ($ and square footage in millions)					
Cash used for purchases of property and equipment	$ 524	$ 726	$ 714	$ 670	$ 659
Acquisition of business, net of cash acquired	$ 4	$ —	$ —	$ —	$ 129
Percentage increase (decrease) in comparable sales	(2)%	(4)%	—%	2%	5%
Number of company-operated store locations open at year-end	3,200	3,275	3,280	3,164	3,095
Number of franchise store locations open at year-end	459	446	429	375	312
Number of store locations open at year-end	3,659	3,721	3,709	3,539	3,407
Square footage of company-operated store space at year-end	36.7	37.9	38.1	37.2	36.9
Percentage increase (decrease) in square footage of company-operated store space at year-end	(3.2)%	(0.5)%	2.4%	0.8%	(0.8)%
Number of employees at year-end	135,000	141,000	141,000	137,000	136,000

Source: Gap Inc. 2015 10-K.

The company's sales growth declined dramatically in the 2000s as its merchandise became stale. The decline in sales growth had become a decline in total sales by 2015—see Exhibit 1. Art Peck replaced Gap CEO Glen Murphy in February 2015 and was charged with reversing the company's long-running lackluster performance and recent sales decline. Peck had joined Gap in 2005 and had held various executive positions with the company where he spearheaded the company's franchising initiative, executed its outlet store strategy, and led its digital and e-commerce division.

Comparable store sales declined 3 percent for the company between 2015 and 2016. The greatest declines were with Banana Republic, which had experienced 7 percent and 10 percent declines for 2015 and 2016, respectively. Comparable store sales for Gap stores declined by 2 percent and Old Navy comparable store sales increased 1 percent between 2015 and 2016. Driving the decline in comparable store sales was the decline in the company's sales per square foot, which had fallen from $361 in 2014 to $337 in 2015 and to $334 in 2016.

EXHIBIT 2

Gap Inc.'s Net Sales by Brand and Region, Fiscal 2014–Fiscal 2016

($ in millions) Fiscal 2016	Gap Global	Old Navy Global	Banana Republic Global	Other (2)	Total	Percentage of Net Sales
U.S. (1)	$ 3,113	$6,051	$2,052	$773	$11,989	77%
Canada	368	490	223	3	1,084	7
Europe	630	—	59	—	689	5
Asia	1,215	220	109	—	1,544	10
Other regions	159	53	28	—	210	1
Total	$ 5,455	$6,814	$2,471	$776	$15,516	100%
Sales growth (decline)	(5)%	2%	(7)%	9%	(2)%	

($ in millions) Fiscal 2015	Gap Global	Old Navy Global	Banana Republic Global	Other (2)	Total	Percentage of Net Sales
U.S. (1)	$ 3,303	$5,987	$2,211	$712	$12,213	77%
Canada	348	467	229	3	1,047	7
Europe	726	—	71	—	797	5
Asia	1,215	194	112	—	1,521	10
Other regions	159	27	33	—	219	1
Total	$ 5,751	$6,675	$2,656	$715	$15,797	100%
Sales growth (decline)	(7)%	1%	(9)%	(2)%	(4)%	

($ in millions) Fiscal 2014	Gap Global	Old Navy Global	Banana Republic Global	Other (2)	Total	Percentage of Net Sales
U.S. (1)	$ 3,575	$5,967	$2,405	$725	$12,672	77%
Canada	384	500	249	4	1,137	7
Europe	824	—	93	—	917	6
Asia	1,208	149	145	—	1,502	9
Other regions	174	3	30	—	207	1
Total	$ 6,165	$6,619	$2,922	$729	$16,435	100%
Sales growth (decline)	(3)%	6%	2%	8%	2%	

(1) U.S. includes the United States, Puerto Rico, and Guam.
(2) Includes Piperlime, Athleta, and Intermix.

Source: Gap Inc. 2015 10-K.

The sales decline at Gap was reflected in every major brand except Old Navy, which experienced a 2 percent increase in sales in 2016. Sales per geographic region either declined or were unchanged from 2015 to 2016 except Canada and Asia, which grew by 3.5 percent and 1.5 percent, respectively. When compared to 2011, net sales across brands had only increased from $14.5 billion to $15.5 billion in six years. Exhibit 2 shows Gap Inc. sales by brand and region for 2014 through 2016.

Amid the decline in store performance, leadership at Gap Inc. continued closures of underperforming stores in 2016 to improve operating costs. The closures affected Banana Republic, Gap stores in North America and Europe, and Old Navy stores in Asia—see Exhibit 3. The company's balance sheets for 2015 and 2016 are presented in Exhibit 4.

Overview of the Family Clothing Store Industry

With estimated revenues over $101.9 billion in 2016, competitors within this industry carried clothing lines and apparel for men, women, and children. Annual growth for the industry averaged 1.8 percent between

EXHIBIT 3

Gap Inc. Number of Store Locations, Openings, Closings, and Total Square Footage By Brand and Location, Fiscal 2015 Versus Fiscal 2016

	January 30, 2016	Fiscal 2016		January 28, 2017	
	Number of Store Locations	Number of Stores Opened	Number of Stores Closed	Number of Store Locations	Square Footage (in millions)
Gap North America	866	14	36	844	8.8
Gap Asia	305	27	21	311	3.0
Gap Europe	175	2	13	164	1.4
Old Navy North America	1,030	27	14	1,043	17.4
Old Navy Asia	65	5	57	13	.2
Banana Republic North America	612	9	20	601	5.0
Banana Republic Asia	51	—	3	48	0.2
Banana Republic Europe	10	—	9	1	—
Athleta North America	120	12	—	132	0.6
Piperlime North America*	—	—	—	—	—
Intermix North America	41	3	1	43	0.1
Company-operated stores total	3,275	99	174	3,200	36.7
Franchise	446	56	43	456	N/A
Total	3,721	155	217	3,659	36.7
Increase (decrease) over prior year				(1.7)%	(3.2)%

*The final location was closed in 2015.

Source: Gap Inc. 2015 10-K.

2011 and 2017 and is expected to grow by 1.6 percent annually between 2016 and 2021 to reach $110.4 billion. Key drivers of industry growth included per capita disposable income and demographic trends. Typically sales of clothing to women made up the majority of industry sales. Also, age demographics with gainful employment and disposable income were the largest purchasers of clothing in the United States. The percentage of revenue accounted for by demographic group is presented in Exhibit 5.

Brick-and-Mortar Retailers and E-commerce Sales

The first quarter of 2017 saw almost $106 billion in e-commerce sales in the United States, as compared to $92 billion in the first quarter of 2016.[3] While total retail sales had increased 5 percent from the first quarter of 2016, total e-commerce sales in the United States had increased by 15 percent for the same period in 2016 and accounted for almost 9 percent of total U.S. retail sales during the quarter.[4]

The shift toward increasing consumer confidence in online shopping was evident in the sale of clothing and clothing accessories. Between 2010 and 2015, e-commerce sales of clothing and accessories experienced 185 percent growth, while traditional brick-and-mortar retail channel sales grew by 111 percent. Exhibit 6 compares the U.S. annual sales of clothing and clothing accessories by brick-and-mortar and e-commerce channels for 2011 through 2015 of family clothing industry within Clothing and Clothing Accessories.

The Hyperconnected Consumer and the Decline of Malls

A retailer selling through both brick-and-mortar stores and online marketplaces, while utilizing social media and e-mail for communications with consumers, was referred to as omnichannel. Combining both *omnipresence* (always there) and *distribution channel,* the practice considered that the consumer did not need to be physically present in a store to shop,

EXHIBIT 4

Gap Inc. Consolidated Balance Sheets, Fiscal 2015–Fiscal 2016 ($ and shares in millions except par value)

	January 28, 2017	January 30, 2016	January 31, 2015
ASSETS			
Current assets:			
Cash and cash equivalents	$1,783	$1,370	$1,515
Merchandise inventory	1,830	1,873	1,889
Other current assets	702	742	913
Total current assets	4,315	3,985	4,317
Property and equipment, net	2,616	2,850	2,773
Other long-term assets	679	638	600
Total assets	$7,610	$7,473	$7,690
LIABILITIES AND STOCKHOLDERS' EQUITY			
Current liabilities:			
Current maturities of debt	$ 65	$ 421	$ 21
Accounts payable	1,243	1,112	1,173
Accrued expenses and other current liabilities	1,113	979	1,020
Income taxes payable	32	23	20
Total current liabilities	2,453	2,535	2,234
Long-term liabilities:			
Long-term debt	1,248	1,310	1,332
Lease incentives and other long-term liabilities	1,005	1,083	1,141
Total long-term liabilities	2,253	2,393	2,473
Commitments and contingencies			
Stockholders' equity:			
Common stock $0.05 par value	20		
Authorized 2,300 shares for all periods presented; Issued and Outstanding 397 and 421 shares	81	20	21
Retained earnings	2,749	2,440	2,797
Accumulated other comprehensive income	54	85	165
Total stockholders' equity	2,904	2,545	2,983
Total liabilities and stockholders' equity	$7,610	$7,473	$7,690

Source: Gap Inc., 2015 10-K.

purchase, or even think about shopping. Through a communication channel, such as an e-mail, a shopper could be brought to an online storefront. Browsing and shopping, then, could occur at anytime, anywhere.

The buying habits of the consumer had shifted since the growth of the Internet in the 1990s, as well as with smartphones in the mid-2000s. Most retailers were either online or brick and mortar. Further, in the early years of the online marketplace, there was often disbelief that a consumer would be willing to purchase a product online, either due to not seeing it or the sheer logistics of purchase and delivery.

The tongue-in-cheek question of "Who would buy a 50-pound bag of dog food online?" might help illustrate this point. In other instances, experiments where a person would attempt to shop exclusively through online, and not visit any brick-and-mortar establishments, would make the newscast.

However, as technology and logistics improved, so did the ubiquitous nature of technology and its role in a consumer's life. Logistics and delivery systems improved. Further, the introduction of smartphones made Internet browsing—and shopping—easier. To this degree of adoption, demographics whose experiences with such technology had begun at earlier ages

EXHIBIT 5

Demographic Characteristics of Family Clothing Store Industry Customers, 2016

Percentage of Total Revenue by Segment within Family and Clothing Stores

Segment	Percentage
Women's	60.1%
Men's	32.1%
Children's	7.8%

Percentage of Total Revenue by Generation within Family and Clothing Stores

Market	Percentage
65 years and older	10.0%
Baby Boomers	24.5%
Generation X	35.5%
Generation Y	22.5%
Other	7.5%

Source: www.ibisworld.com.

EXHIBIT 6

Clothing and Clothing Accessories Annual Sales by Channel, 2011–2015*

Channel	2015	2014	2013	2012	2011
Brick & Mortar**	$255,831	$250,775	$246,313	$239,493	$228,438
E-commerce***	52,128	46,833	40,262	33,579	28,309

*Estimated values, in millions of dollars.

**Clothing and clothing accessories, stores NAICS code 448.

***Itemized line "clothing and clothing accessories," under Total Electronic Shopping and Mail-Order Houses NAICS code 45411.

Source: U.S. Census Bureau.

have now become a primary consumer. Thus, they did not experience as wide a divide between online and brick and mortar as previous demographics. The word *hyperconnected* recognized then the consumer's relationship with a brand, and that the single act of purchasing had moved into this omnipresent, hyperconnected relationship through both online and brick and mortar.

These trends had contributed to both the increase in online sales as well as the decline in malls. Global online retail sales increased in 2014 by 20 percent to $840 billion. This figure was attributable to the increased sales by online retailers, but also the increased presence of brick-and-mortar retailers online.[5] Between 2000 and 2015, online purchases for some categories increased from 30 cents to 70 cents per dollar spent.[6]

Second, the mall as destination declined. As the percentage of online sales increased dramatically, foot traffic in shopping malls decreased. While the loss in foot traffic mostly impacted the lower-productive malls, storefronts are now empty, once occupied by brands like Nordstrom and JCPenney. Due to these shifts, retailers are closing the nonperforming anchor stores in lieu of their higher-performing locations. In 2016, Macy's announced over 30 store closings and the restructuring of over 4,000 jobs[7] and Nordstrom announced its plan to restructure approximately 400 jobs.[8] As these anchor store locations were closed, foot traffic continued to fall, trickling down into the non-anchor retailers. For example, American Apparel, Aeropostale, and Pac Sun had all filed for bankruptcy protection, while Bebe, The Limited, and Wet Seal had determined to close all locations.[9]

The mall, as depicted in movies such as the 1990s movie *Mall Rats,* is no longer the place to hang out and be seen, either. Instead, the cultivation of an online presence through social media seems to help substitute. Thus, showing off a new outfit could be accomplished through photo-sharing apps and even video. A haul video—where the purchases from a shopping excursion are uploaded—could be accomplished without the shopping mall. In addition, views and comments could be tracked and quantified in an online environment.

Competition through Fast Fashion

Clothing was traditionally designed, manufactured, and then shipped to the retailer for sale, much of it occurring prior to the beginning of the season. These designs could be from in-house designers, who used current trends, including fashion on display at fashion shows, to anticipate consumers' preferences. Retailers usually purchased inventory in bulk for the season to help improve costs. Buying an inventory of multiple designs for one season could also create a buffer when one style or design is not purchased, or is overpurchased, by the consumer. If a style did not sell in one location, it was usually internally transferred to another location. Or, eventually it was sold through a discount or staged-markdown sale. These markdowns occurred at the end of seasons, and helped facilitate space for incoming stock while minimizing losses associated with designs that did not sell well for a season.

This traditional approach, however, was not only costly but also could lead to missing consumer demands. In addition, it assumed the consumer wished to purchase and maintain the clothing for a longer period of time. Fast fashion was the systematic shortening of the production-to-sales logistics within fashion retail. Fast fashion viewed clothing as a consumable and was moved faster through the retailer process. Pushing these sales was a shortened production-to-retail cycle, where internal designers observed customer preferences and made orders and changes mid-season. Thus, while most traditional retailers placed their large production orders before a season, fast-fashion retailers placed a majority of their orders mid-season, allowing flexibility and overall lower costs and losses due to unsold or markdown apparel. The faster-fashion cycle also pushed the consumer to visit retailers more, as they continually monitored new clothing, while treating clothes as a disposable commodity.

Profiles of Competitors

Inditex Group

No retailer seemed to epitomize the fast-fashion approach more than Inditex Group. The company was able to quickly launch fresh, new apparel lines to meet rapidly evolving consumer preferences through its vertically integrated design and manufacturing strategy. The company's designers closely monitored new fashion and style trends to create new lines as often as every month for its Zara brand stores and other retail brands. The company was able to get its new items in stores quickly by use of a tightly managed global logistics network that included 658 fabric manufacturers and 4,136 factories. The result was a stylish inventory of moderately priced apparel items that create a shopping frenzy in many of its stores across Europe and the rest of the world. In total, the company's supply chain was supported by 1,725 suppliers and 6,298 factories in 2015.

Inditex Group operated over 7,013 locations in 88 countries and 29 online markets in 2016. Its brands included Zara, Pull & Bear, Massimo Dutti, Bershka, Stradivarius, Oysho, Zara Home, and Uterqüe. In 2015, Inditex Group opened 330 new locations in 56 countries. In addition, Inditex Group started distributing its Zara brand through an official storefront on the largest online Chinese sales platform, Tmall.com.[10] The popularity of its Zara concept with consumers was reflected in its financial performance. Zara stores totaled to only 2,002 of the company's 7,000+ stores, but the brand accounted for 65 percent and 67 percent of the company's revenues and earnings before interest and taxes (EBIT), respectively, in 2016. Exhibit 7 presents a financial summary for the Inditex Group for 2013 through 2016.

Abercrombie & Fitch

Abercrombie & Fitch sells casual attire under its brands Abercrombie & Fitch, Hollister, and Gilly Hicks. Besides women's and men's clothing, it also sells children's clothing under its abercrombie kids brand. Abercrombie & Fitch was not a fast-fashion retailer and operated through a traditional logistics channel. It experienced a 13 percent decrease in net sales

EXHIBIT 7

Financial Summary for Inditex Group, 2013–2016 (in millions of dollars*)

	2016	2015	2014	2013
Revenue	$26,341	$23,617	$20,472	$14,800
Cost of merchandise	(11,336)	(9,957)	(8,529)	(6,019)
Gross Profit	15,005	13,661	11,942	8,781
Operating expenses, including other losses/income	(9,239)	(8,353)	(7,297)	(5,307)
Amortization and Depreciation	(1,201)	(1,155)	(1,023)	(757)
Profit from operations (EBIT)	4,543	4,156	3,614	2,702
Net Earnings (after income taxes)	3,571	3,257	2,836	2,108

*Converted from euros with conversation rate of 1 euro = 1.13 U.S. dollars; rounded to nearest million dollar.

Sources: Inditex Group Annual Report, 2013, 2015.

EXHIBIT 8

Abercrombie & Fitch Global Locations by Brand, 2015–2017*

Brand	2017	2016	2015
Abercrombie U.S.	311	340	361
Abercrombie International	44	39	32
Hollister U.S.	398	414	433
Hollister International	145	139	135

*Numbers represent figures at beginning of year.

Source: Abercrombie & Fitch 2016 10-K.

EXHIBIT 9

Financial Summary for Abercrombie & Fitch Co., 2013–2016 (in millions of dollars)

	2016	2015	2014	2013
Revenue	$3,327	$3,519	$3,744	$4,117
Gross Profit	2,029	2,157	2,314	2,575
Operating Income	15	73	114	81
Net Income	4	36	52	55

Source: Abercrombie & Fitch Co. 2016 10-K.

between 2011 and 2015, and another 5 percent decline in 2016. A casualty of the competitive climate and a failing strategy was its Gilly Hicks branded stores, which were discontinued in 2014 and 2015. The company also closed 50 of its other branded stores in the United States in 2016—see Exhibit 8. A summary of financial performance for 2013 through 2016 is presented in Exhibit 9.

In Search of a New Strategy for Gap Inc.

Art Peck and Gap Inc. were faced with stark changes in the retail industry. As the consumer's desire to shop and congregate at the mall decreased, steep declines in foot traffic created ghost malls in some suburban areas, with empty storefronts and missing anchor stores. Yet contradicting this trend was the continual growth in industry retail sales, bolstered by online sales. These online retail sales were not just staggering, but the tremendous success of some online retailers were significant. Most notably, Amazon alone may have accounted for 60 percent of the growth in 2015 online sales.[11]

Exacerbating the dilemma for Gap Inc. was the fast-fashion strategies of Inditex Group and others that had succeeded in meeting the consumer's desire for fresh styles of clothing and were rapidly expanding in North America and other markets quicker than other competitors. Moving forward, Peck and Gap's other key managers needed to identify a strategy to reverse its recent sales decline. However, such a plan would likely fail without a viable approach to reaching the hyperconnected consumer seeking superior customer value.

ENDNOTES

1 As quoted in "Gap Would Consider Using Amazon to Help Fix Its Sales Problems," *Fortune*, May 18, 2016, http://fortune.com/2016/05/18/gap-amazon-sales/ (accessed December 19, 2017).

2 Gap Inc. 1999 10-K.

3 U.S. Census Bureau of the Department of Commerce. Figure reflects seasonality adjustment.

4 Ibid.

5 "Global Retail E-Commerce Keeps On Clicking: The 2015 Global Retail E-Commerce Index," *ATKearney*, April 2015, www.atkearney.com/consumer-products-retail/e-commerce-index/full-report/-/asset_publisher/87xbENNHPZ3D/content/global-retail-e-commerce-keeps-on-clicking/10192 (accessed June 19, 2016).

6 J. Boak and A. D'innocenzio, "As Online Shopping Intensifies, Outlook Dims for Mall Store," Associated Press, May 13, 2016, https://apnews.com/51e799fb6060487c951be8089eb056c4/us-retail-sales-show-solid-gain-despite-woes-store-chains (accessed December 19, 2017).

7 H. Malcolm, "Macy's Announces Layoffs, Lists 36 Store Closures," *USA Today*, January 7, 2016, www.usatoday.com/story/money/2016/01/06/macys-announces-layoffs-restructuring-after-disappointing-2015/78373358/ (accessed May 14, 2016).

8 J. I. Tu, "Nordstrom Profit Plunges as Mall Stores Struggle," *The Seattle Times*, May 12, 2016, www.seattletimes.com/business/retail/nordstrom-comes-up-short-on-profit-joining-apparel-sectors-funk/ (accessed May 14, 2016).

9 "Bebe to Close All Stores, Becoming Latest Retail Casualty," USA Today, (n.d.) Accessed April 21, 2017, from https://www.usatoday.com/story/money/2017/04/21/bebe-stores-liquidation/100736290/

10 Ibid.

11 T. Garcia, "Amazon Accounted for 60% of U.S. Online Sales Growth in 2015," *MarketWatch*, May 3, 2016, www.marketwatch.com/story/amazon-accounted-for-60-of-online-sales-growth-in-2015-2016-05-03.

CASE

GoPro in 2017: Will Its Turnaround Strategy Restore Profitability?

7

DAVID L. TURNIPSEED University of South Alabama

JOHN E. GAMBLE Texas A&M University–Corpus Christi

GoPro had been among the best examples of how a company could create a new market based upon product innovations that customers understood and demanded. However, by late-2015, the action camera product niche appeared saturated. The company had grown from a humble beginning as a homemade camera tether and plastic case vendor in 2004 to an action camera vendor with $350,000 in sales in 2005 (its first full year of operation) to a global seller of consumer electronics with revenue of $1.6 billion in 2015. The company's shares had traded as high as $98 in October 2014, just months after its initial public offering (IPO) in June 2014. In 2014, GoPro was ranked number one most popular brand on YouTube with more than 640 million views, and an average of 845,000 views daily. In 2015, average daily views were up to 1.01 million.

Abruptly, in the third quarter of 2015, GoPro's magic disappeared and, by the fourth quarter of 2015, its revenues dropped by 31 percent from the prior year. In addition, its net income fell by 128 percent to a net loss of $34.5 million. By the end of December 2015, the stock traded at less than $20. The plummet continued, and by the end of December 2016, revenues had dropped another 27 percent to $1.2 billion from $1.6 billion in 2015. In addition, the company recorded a net loss of $419 million in fiscal 2016, helping drive its share price to less than $9.00 in December 2016. A summary of the company's financial performance for 2011 through 2016 is presented in Exhibit 1. The performance of GoPro's shares from June 2014 through July 2017 is presented in Exhibit 2.

The company launched a turnaround plan in early 2017 to reverse its decline, with its first quarter sales in 2017 increasing by 19 percent from the first quarter 2016 and its operating expenses declining by $50 million. Its adjusted EBITDA improved from a $87 million loss in the first quarter of 2016 to a $46 million loss in the first quarter of 2017. The improvement was driven by a trade-up program that provided GoPro owners with $100 off a HERO5 Black or $50 off a HERO5 Session when they traded in a previous generation GoPro camera and growth in international markets. The HERO5 Black was the best-selling digital image camera in the United States in the first quarter of 2017 and GoPro's drone Karma with the HERO5 camera was the number-two selling drone priced over $1,000 in the United States. During first quarter of 2017, 60 percent of the company's revenue was generated outside the United States and between 70 percent and 90 percent of GoPro camera users in international markets used cameras in their local language. In addition, its Quik mobile video editing app had been installed 5.2 million times in the first quarter of 2017 and its active users had increased by 160 percent from the same period in 2016.

Although the first quarter offered promising signs of a turnaround, it was far too early to know if the first quarter 2017 improvement was sustainable. Many investors and industry observers viewed the action camera market as an overly saturated niche. In fact, the first quarter improvement in financial performance

EXHIBIT 1

Financial Summary for GoPro, Inc., 2011–2016 (in thousands, except per share amounts)

Consolidated statements of operations data:	2016	2015	2014	2013	2012	2011
Revenue	$1,185,481	$1,619,971	$1,394,205	$985,737	$526,016	$234,238
Gross profit	461,920	673,214	627,235	361,784	227,486	122,555
Gross margin	39.0%	41.6%	45.0%	36.7%	43.2%	52.3%
Operating income	(372,969)	54,748	187,035	98,703	53,617	38,779
Net income	(419,003)	36,131	128,088	60,578	32,262	24,612
Net income per share:						
Basic	$(3.01)	$0.27	$1.07	$0.54	$0.07	$0.26
Diluted	$(3.01)	$0.25	$0.92	$0.47	$0.07	$0.24

Source: GoPro, Inc., 2016 10-K.

EXHIBIT 2   **GoPro's Stock Performance, June 2014–July 2017**

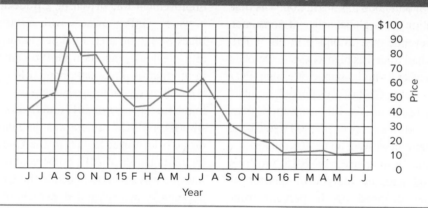

had yet to reverse the company's downward trend in its stock price performance as of mid-2017.

Company History

GoPro began as the result of business failures. GoPro's founder, Nick Woodman, grew up in Silicon Valley, the son of wealthy parents (his father brokered the purchase of Taco Bell by Pepsi). Woodman started an online electronics store, EmpowerAll.com,

which failed, and subsequently started an online gaming service, Funbug, that failed in the dot-com crash of 2001, costing investors $3.9 million. Woodman consoled himself after the failure of Funbug with an extended surfing vacation in Indonesia and Australia. While on vacation, he fashioned a wrist strap from a broken surfboard leash and rubber bands to attach a disposable Kodak camera to his wrist while on the water. Woodman's friend and current GoPro creative director, Brad Schmidt, joined the vacation, worked with the camera strap, and observed that Woodman needed a camera that could withstand the sea.

After his vacation, Woodman returned home and focused on developing a comprehensive camera, casing, and strap package for surfers. Originally incorporated as Woodman Labs, the company began doing business in 2004 as GoPro. Woodman found a 35-mm camera made in China that cost $3.05, and sent his homemade plastic case and $5,000 to an unknown company, Hotax. A few months later, Woodman received his renderings and a 3-D model from the company, and sold his first GoPro camera in September 2004, at an action-sports trade show. Also that year, GoPro hired its first employee, Neil Dana, who was Woodman's college roommate.

The two-man company grossed $350,000 in 2005, the first full year of operation. Woodman wanted to keep the company private as long as possible: he invested $30,000 personally, his mother contributed $35,000, and his father added $200,000. In a fortunate coincidence for GoPro, in fall 2006 Google purchased a then-small company, YouTube, and in spring 2007 the GoPro HERO3 with VGA video was launched. According to Woodman, the competing name-brand cameras available at the time did not have good video quality. The combination of GoPro's HERO3 video quality and the increasing popularity of YouTube caused GoPro's sales to triple in 2007.

In 2007, although the company had revenues in the low seven figures, Woodman began to question his ability to take the firm further. He negotiated a deal to turn the company over to a group of outside investors, but before the deal was finalized (which was at the beginning of the 2008 financial crisis), the investors wanted to lower the valuation of the company. GoPro was profitable, and Woodman did not believe that the company was having any ill effects from the economy. He refused to negotiate the company's value down, and the company's sales were over $8 million that year. The company's growth continued and in 2010, Best Buy began carrying GoPro products, which was a clear indication that the company was accepted in the market.

In May 2011, GoPro received $88 million in investments from five venture capital firms (including Steamboat Ventures—Disney's venture capital company) which enabled Woodman, his family, and some GoPro executives to take cash from the company. Also in 2011, GoPro acquired CineForm, a small company that had developed a proprietary codex that quickly and easily converted digital video files among different formats. CineForm had used this codex in several movies including *Need for Speed* and *Slumdog Millionaire*. As part of GoPro, Cine-Form altered its 3-D footage tool into an editing program that became the company's first desktop application, GoPro Studio.

In December 2012 a Taiwanese manufacturing company, Foxconn (trading as Hone Hai Precision Industry Co.), bought 8.8 percent of GoPro for $200 million, which brought the value of the privately held company to about $2.25 billion, and *Forbes* reported Woodman's personal net worth to be about $1.73 billion. GoPro sold 2.3 million cameras and grossed $531 million in 2012; and in December of that year, GoPro replaced Sony as the highest-selling camera brand at Best Buy.

Sales of GoPro cameras at snow-sports retailers increased by 50 percent for the 2012–2013 ski season. GoPro almost doubled its revenues in each of three consecutive years, from $234.2 million in 2011, to $525 million in 2012, and $985 million in 2013, according to the U.S. Securities and Exchange Commission (SEC). Although revenues increased 87 percent in 2013, in that year the decrease in revenue growth became obvious. According to its IPO filing, as of December 2013 the company had not derived any revenue from the distribution of its content on the GoPro Network; however, it announced plans to pursue new streams of revenue from the distribution of GoPro content. GoPro formed a new software division in 2013. Also in that year, the National Academy of Television Arts and Sciences recognized the company with a Technology and Engineering Emmy Award in the Inexpensive Small Rugged HD Camera category.

In June 2014, GoPro went public at an IPO price of $24.00 which valued the company at $2.7 billion. The IPO included a lockup agreement that prevented the Woodmans from selling any shares of GoPro stock for six months; four months later on October 2, 2014, the Woodmans made a donation of 5.8 million shares of GoPro stock into the Jill and Nick Woodman Foundation. A press release about the foundation stated that details about its mission would be announced at a later date, according to CNN. Share prices dropped 14 percent after the announcement and angered investors. Also, GoPro failed to meet investors' expectations when it released its first earnings report in August 2014.

GoPro increased emphasis on software and video sharing in 2015. In that year, GoPro tied with Apple on the Google Brand Leaderboard, which measures the most popular brands on YouTube. According to Google, more than 4.6 years of content was uploaded to YouTube in 2015 with GoPro in the title, an increase of 22 percent from 2014. Also in 2015, the company launched the GoPro Channel on Amazon Fire TV and Fire TV Stick with a custom-designed streaming channel that was a one-stop destination for delivering on-demand GoPro videos to Amazon customers.

Another 2015 development was the GoPro Channel on the PlayStation Network which allowed PlayStation owners to stream GoPro content on-demand, and browse GoPro cameras and accessories. PlayStation joined GoPro's growing roster of distribution partners including Amazon Fire TV, Roku, Comcast Watchable, Sky, Vessel Entertainment, Xbox, LG, and Virgin America. The GoPro Mobile App was downloaded 2.75 million times in the fourth quarter, totaling almost 24 million cumulative downloads; Q4 installs of GoPro Studio totaled nearly 1.7 million, totaling over 15 million cumulative installs, with average daily video exports of over 49,000 in the fourth quarter.

GoPro purchased Kolor, a French company with experience making software for capturing and displaying virtual reality in 2016, and acquired Replay and Splice, two leading mobile video editing apps. Replay was video editing software that GoPro rebranded as Quik, and Splice was an app that promised desktop-level performance for editing video on an iPhone. The Kolor group assisted in the launch of a virtual reality social media platform that functioned both on the web and as an app. According to *The Verge* (June 2, 2016), Woodman understood that "the hardware-first chapter of GoPro" was coming to the end. He recognized that market saturation had created the problem, explaining it as "content guilt." According to Woodman, "Most people don't even watch their GoPro footage." He blamed the company for creating the problem by solving the capture side but leaving customers hanging in postproduction.

In April 2016, the investment bank Piper Jaffray reported that GoPro was gaining market share in a declining market, and that action camera ownership declined to 28 percent among teenage consumers, down from 31 percent a year previous, and 40 percent in 2013. This trend clearly indicated the need for GoPro to transform into something more than an action camera company. The GoPro brand and reputation had been made as a hardware company, and moving that reputation to a new market (i.e., software) would be difficult. Although GoPro created the market for wearable cameras, it found the content-creation software field crowded. Plus, *The Verge* (June 2, 2016) pointed out that the company had no clear way to monetize its software. According to Woodman, building the software team had been the most time-consuming project the company had undertaken. He believed that the benefits of success would be large because the amount of video being consumed was huge, and the market research company NPD Group reported that more than 80 percent of smartphone users stream video. Woodman also believed in the potential of Karma, GoPro's camera drone, scheduled for release in early 2016.

GoPro's third quarter 2016 performance produced large losses, with Woodman firing 15 percent of his workforce. The company's president, Tony Bates, announced plans to leave the company at year end after little more than two years with the company. The Karma drone, which had been postponed several times, was eventually released in November 2016. Problems quickly became apparent with the drone—it stopped flying and crashed—that required GoPro to issue a recall and discontinue selling the product until February 2017. Shortly after sales resumed, Woodman claimed that the drone was "exceeding our expectations" (*Fortune,* April 27, 2017). However, GoPro CFO, Brian McGee, said that the bulk of Karma's sales had come from being bundled with the HERO5 camera. According to McGee, GoPro made more money from the sale of a camera than from the sale of a drone.

In early 2017, GoPro announced a new 360-degree camera, Fusion, but provided few details. The company planned a pilot release of Fusion in summer 2017, and a launch with a limited release at the end of 2017. According to Woodman, professional users would be the main market for Fusion, which was a much smaller market than the traditional consumers that had bought GoPro's other cameras.

The Action Camera Industry from 2014 to 2017

Sales in the global action camera industry grew 44 percent in 2014, reaching 7.6 million units, and retail value of $3.2 billion. Camera unit sales increased by 38 percent in North America in 2014. However, the largest growth came from the Asia Pacific region, which was up by 114 percent. Sales of action cameras worldwide reached 10.5 million in 2017, up from 8.4 million in 2015. Although the action camera market was expected to enjoy continued sales growth through at least 2019, several factors, including lengthening replacement cycles, were expected to slow the growth rate.

Consumer sales, primarily for extreme sports, had accounted for the largest part of global demand up to mid-2015, but professional sales, primarily driven by TV production, security, and law enforcement, were expected to increase. In 2014, consumers were responsible for 86 percent of action camera sales, with the remainder coming from professional uses. Although GoPro dominated the action camera industry in mid-2015, there was increased competition from other companies, including Garmin, TomTom, Canon, JVC, Ion America, Polaroid, and Sony. Other competitors were focusing on the adjacent market of wearable cameras for security and police officers.

A defining characteristic of the action camera industry in 2015 was the increase in the number of competitors. In early 2015, the market was experiencing rapid growth and attracted many new entrants, which had the expected effect on price (lower), quality (higher), and features (more). A list of producers of action cameras in June 2017 is presented in Exhibit 3.

EXHIBIT 3

Action Camera Producers, June 2017

Key Brands

Drift Innovation	Rollei
Garmin	Sony
GoPro	iON

Other Brands

Contour	Amkov	Polaroid
Braun	Casio	Xiaomi
Sjcam	JVC Kenwood	Kodak
Chilli Technology	Ricoh	Toshiba
Decathlon	Panasonic	Veho
HTC	Ordro	

Source: *Market Publishers Report Database,* June 2017.

Another 2015 industry trend was price polarization. Sales of low-end camera models priced under $200.00 and high-end models (including GoPro's $499.00 HERO4 Black) experienced increasing growth. The action camera industry experienced significant change in early 2015. A Futuresource analyst reported that the 360-degree capture that had recently become available would drive virtual reality applications over the coming months, especially for sports broadcasting. The company envisioned the percentage of 360-degree video action cameras growing from 1 percent in 2015 to 14 percent by 2019. In 2014, 95 percent of action cameras sold could take high-definition video with at least 720p resolution, and approximately 85 percent of action cameras could take HD video in 1080p. About half of cameras sold could record video in ultra-high-definition 2160p, or 4K.

In 2016, the action camera industry experienced adjustments in usage: The demand for action cameras for professional applications had grown exponentially due to the focus on better viewing of sports events. Action cameras were increasingly being used for TV production and to record closer details of sports. The National Hockey League and Fishing League Worldwide had signed major contracts with iON, GoPro, and other vendors, and that professional segment of the industry was expected to have a high growth rate. Also, Global Market Insights pointed out increasing popularity of action cameras among all age groups and advanced product features as other factors providing massive growth potential.

The security industry was also finding increasing usage for action cameras in 2016, which added more fuel to the industry growth. Action cameras and especially drone-mounted action cameras were expected to be used increasingly in security applications globally. A leading vendor in the action camera–drones, Lifeline Response, had developed a smartphone app that could fly a drone to a needed location in emergencies. According to Technavio Research, professional use of action cameras would exceed casual usage by 2020.

In addition to increased demand for action cameras for professional applications, the industry was expanding also due to demand from developing countries, with the largest growth in the Asia Pacific region. Increasing disposable income, an increase in social networking, and rapid growth in adventure sport tourism were factors increasing sales in emerging countries. Several action camera vendors sponsored extreme sporting events in various emerging economies to promote their camera brands. Although European growth was predicted to be stable from 2016 to 2023, the global action camera market was projected to grow at an annual rate of 14.6 percent between 2017 and 2021.

The revenue growth rate in the action camera industry was expected to be lower than the growth rate in unit sales, due to a general price decline. The average action camera price is expected to decline to $226.00 by 2020, depressed primarily by a global increase in supply. In the first quarter 2016, Technavio forecast that the value, by revenue, of the global action camera industry, which was $2.35 billion in 2015, was expected to reach about $6 billion by 2020. However, young consumers were increasingly choosing smartphone cameras over traditional, which meant they were less likely to purchase an action camera.

The popularity of social networking sites was a major driver of the action camera industry in 2017 and price polarization continued as a crucial trend. Vendors began "bundling" their products (cameras and numerous accessories) to increase demand for cameras and accessories. Bundle packaging increased demand by offering cost-effectiveness to customers because the bundling reduced or eliminated the need to purchase additional equipment. Other industry trends in 2017 were increasing numbers of new entrants, which reduced prices, and increasing significance of the smartphone with enhanced quality and features which depressed demand. The saturation of the action camera market niche and the declining prices contributed to the June 2017 bankruptcy filing of iON Worldwide, a major competitor in the industry.

The Drone Industry in 2017

According to Gartner, the personal and commercial drone industry as measured by revenue increased by 35.6 percent between 2015 and 2016 to reach $4.5 billion. Gartner projected industry revenue to increase an additional 34.3 percent between 2016 and 2017. Unit shipments in the industry increased by 60.3 percent in 2016 when compared to 2015 shipments and was projected to increase by 39.0 percent between 2016 and 2017. The industry was expected to grow to $11 billion in revenues by 2021.

The majority of personal drones were purchased for video and photography, while commercial drones tended to be used for geographic information system (GIS) mapping or delivery. The civilian drone fleet was expected to grow from approximately one million in 2016 to more than 3.5 million by 2011, while the commercial drone fleet to increase from about 40,000 units in 2016 to 420,000 in 2021.

FAA regulations in 2017 limited commercial drones to a select few industries and uses such as aerial surveying in the agriculture, mining, and oil and gas sectors. However, emerging technologies such as collision avoidance and geo-fencing would make drone flying safer, and make regulators feel more comfortable with larger numbers of drones taking to the skies. The military sector was expected to continue to lead all other sectors in drone spending through 2024, due to the high cost of military drones and the increasing number of countries seeking to acquire them.

While holiday sales of drones priced $50 to $100 helped drive unit sales, drones priced over $300 accounted for 84 percent of industry revenues and 40 percent of unit volume sales between 2016 and early 2017. Drones with premium features such as autopilot capabilities sold nearly five times more quickly than basic feature drones. Among the most popular drone features was autopilot functionality that allowed the drone to follow the user, with sales of such devices selling 19 times more quickly than entry-level drones. The average sales price for a drone was more than $550 in April, which gave them one of the highest average retail prices of all technology categories.

Several of the prominent early drone manufacturers were emerging from outside the U.S. market. Among the foreign manufacturers were the Canadian firm Aeryon, Switzerland-based senseFly (owned by France-based Parrot), publicly traded Swedish firm CybAero, Shenzhen, China-based DJI, and Korea-based Gryphon. DJI had become the number-one selling drone brand through its commitment to innovation and partnerships with Sony for camera components and Apple for distribution in Apple Stores. Parrot abandoned drone manufacturing in mid-2017 to focus on drone software. Exhibit 4 presents the drone industry's leading brands in units sold in April 2017.

EXHIBIT 4

Top-Selling Drone Brands Ranked by Percentage of Shipments, April 2017

Rank	Brand Name	Market Share
1	DJI	36%
2	3D Robotics	19%
3	Parrot	7%
4	Yuneec	7%
	Others	31%
	Total	100%

Source: The NPD Group/Retail Tracking Service, 12 months ending April 2017.

GoPro's Business Model and Strategy

The action camera industry was a relatively young and evolving industry, and GoPro evolved within the industry. Although the company began as an action camera company, it had rapidly evolved into a diversified lifestyle company. The company's business focus, as set out in its 2015 annual report, was to develop product solutions that enabled consumers to capture, manage, share, and enjoy some of the most important moments in their lives. In addition to selling action cameras to capture live events, the company developed GoPro Entertainment, and planned to diversify into a number of related businesses, including software and drones.

Reflecting awareness of the problems facing the company and opportunities on the horizon, GoPro set out its business strategy in its 2016 Annual Report. The core of the business was helping consumers capture and share experiences, and it was committed to developing solutions that created an easy experience for consumers to capture, create, and enjoy personal content. The company believed that when consumers used GoPro products and services, they enabled authentic content that increased awareness for the company, and drove a self-reinforcing demand for its products. Revenue growth was expected to be driven by the introduction of new cameras, drones, accessories, and software applications.

Key components of GoPro's growth strategy for 2017 and beyond included the following:

1. Drive profitability through improved efficiency, lower costs, and better execution. The company pointed out that it had incurred material operating losses in 2016 and future success depended in part upon its ability to manage operating expenses effectively.

2. Make the smartphone central to the GoPro experience. The company sought to eliminate the pain point of managing content, and make it a near automatic process for its users to stay engaged in an activity without having to pause to document their experience.

3. Market the improved GoPro experience to their extended community. The company believed that the global market for enabling people to self-capture compelling photo and video content of their everyday life was large.

4. Grow the business internationally. GoPro believed that international markets represented a significant growth opportunity.

5. Expand the GoPro experience for advanced users. The company intended to continue pursuing its goal of developing the world's most versatile cameras, drones, and stabilization products.

GoPro also increased its focus on solutions designed to simplify organizing, editing, and sharing content, and planned release of a content management platform for 2017—the GoPro for Desktop—which would facilitate offloading, accessing, and editing content. The company focused on product leadership and innovation in its cameras, and also in mounts, accessories, and batteries.

GoPro's management envisioned the company as an entertainment brand. The distribution of content originally produced by GoPro was referred to as GoPro Entertainment, and the company attempted to leverage the sale of its cameras through GoPro Entertainment. The company continued to invest in GoPro Entertainment by developing, distributing, and promoting GoPro Entertainment programming on its own and partner platforms.

New products for 2017 included the company's next-generation capture device, the HERO5, the GoPro drone Karma, and devices to enable virtual reality content capture. In April 2017, NPD Group reported that the Karma was the second best-selling drone over $1,000 in the United States based upon unit sales.

Sales Channels

At the end of 2016, GoPro products were sold through direct sales channels in over 100 countries and over 40,000 retail outlets. The company also sold indirectly through its distribution channel. The direct sales channel had gained slightly in 2016, providing 55 percent of revenue, compared to 52 percent in 2015. GoPro distributors accounted for the difference, with indirect sales decreasing from 48 percent in 2015 to 45 percent in 2016. A small number of distributors and retailers accounted for a large portion of GoPro's revenue: the 10 largest customers (by revenue) contributed 50, 52, and 52 percent of revenues in fiscal 2016, 2015, and 2014, respectively.

Direct Sales   GoPro sold directly to large and small retailers in the United States, Europe, the Middle East, and Africa, and directly to consumers throughout the world through its e-commerce channels. The company believed that diverse direct sales channels were a key differentiator for the company and it segregated its products among those channels. GoPro used independent specialty retailers who generally carried higher-end products, and targeted its customers who were believed to be the early adopters of new technology. Big-box retailers with a national presence such as Amazon, Walmart, Target, and Best Buy were a second component of the direct sales channel. These retailers carried a variety of GoPro products and targeted its particular end user. GoPro felt that this allowed the company to maintain in-store product differentiation between its sales channels and protected its brand image in the specialty retail markets. Amazon accounted for 11 percent and 12 percent of GoPro's total revenues in 2016 and 2015, respectively, compared to Best Buy with 17 percent and 14 percent of GoPro's sales in 2016 and 2015, respectively.

Mid-market retailers with a large regional or national presence were also part of GoPro's direct sales channel. Retailers focusing on sporting goods, consumer electronics, hunting, fishing, and motor sports carried a small subset of GoPro products targeted toward its end users. The full line of GoPro products were sold directly to consumers through the company's online store, gopro.com. The company marketed its e-commerce channel through online and offline advertising. GoPro felt that its e-commerce sales provided insight into its customers' shopping behavior and provided a platform from which the company could inform and educate its customers on the GoPro brand, products, and services.

Indirect Sales/Distributors   GoPro sold to over 50 distributors who resold its products to retailers in international markets and to some mid-market vertical retailers in the United States. The company provided a sales support staff to help the distributors with planning product mix, marketing, in-store merchandising, development of marketing materials, order assistance, and education about the GoPro products. During 2015, GoPro converted part of its distributor sales into direct sales.

Merchandising, Marketing, and Advertising

GoPro's merchandising strategy focused on point-of-purchase displays that were provided to retailers at no cost. The POP displays showed GoPro content on a large video monitor, with GoPro's cameras and accessories arranged around the video monitor screen. At the end of 2016, the company had over 29,000 displays in retail outlets. The company's marketing and advertising efforts were focused on consumer engagement by exposing them to GoPro content, believing that this approach enhanced the brand while demonstrating the performance, versatility, and durability of its products. GoPro's marketing and advertising programs spanned a wide range of consumer interests and attempted to leverage traditional consumer and lifestyle marketing.

Social media were the core of GoPro's consumer marketing. The company's customers captured and shared personal GoPro content on social media platforms such as YouTube, Twitter, Facebook, Pinterest, and Instagram. User-generated content and GoPro originally produced content were integrated into advertising campaigns across billboards, print, television commercials, online, and other home advertising, and at consumer and trade shows. The company estimated that social media views of GoPro content reached approximately 238 million, up over 40 percent year-over-year, driven by an estimated 160 percent year-over-year increase in Facebook views. In 2016, GoPro gained almost 6 million new followers to its social accounts, an estimated 30 percent increase over 2015, and a total of approximately 25.5 million followers.

GoPro's lifestyle marketing emphasized expansion of its brand awareness by engaging consumers through relationships with influential athletes, entertainers, brands, and celebrities who used GoPro products to create and share content with their consumers and fans. The company worked directly with its lifestyle partners to create content that was leveraged to their mutual benefit across the GoPro Network.

GoPro's Financial Performance

GoPro's 2016 revenues of $1.19 billion represented a 27 percent decrease from 2015 revenues of $1.62 billion, largely due to a 28 percent decrease in units shipped. GoPro's average inventory selling prices in 2016 were about the same as in 2015. The company reported that it did not experience any notable pricing pressure during 2016 in the average selling price of its individual cameras shopped during the year. The company reported a gross margin of about 39 percent for 2016, down from 42 percent in 2015.

GoPro's operating expenses were up by $216.4 million to $835 million in 2016 (70 percent of net revenue) compared to $618 million (38 percent of net revenue) in 2015. The company attributed the increased operating expenses primarily to higher advertising and promotion costs, restructuring costs, and increased labor costs due to a 25 percent growth in employees in 2016. The company undertook cost cutting in the first and fourth quarters of 2016 by reducing the global workforce as well as other restructuring activities to reduce operation expenses.

GoPro's Consolidated Statements of Operations for 2014 to 2016 are presented in Exhibit 5. Its balance sheets for 2015 and 2016 are shown in Exhibit 6.

GoPro's sales were predominately from the Americas, with Europe, the Middle East, and Africa a distance second—see Exhibit 7. Revenue from outside the United States was 53 percent, 52 percent, and 43 percent of the company's revenues for fiscal 2016, 2015, and 2014, respectively; and GoPro expected this portion to continue to be a significant part of revenues. Although there were no clear trends in the composition of sales revenue in the Americas, Europe, the Middle East, and Africa, there was an upward trend of revenue from outside the United States and from the Asia Pacific region. GoPro's supply chain partners had operations in Singapore, China, Czech Republic, the Netherlands, and Brazil. The company intended to expand operations in these, and perhaps other, countries as it increased its international presence.

EXHIBIT 5

GoPro, Inc., Consolidated Statements of Operations, 2014–2016 (in thousands, except per share data)

	Year Ended December 31,		
	2016	2015	2014
Revenue	$1,185,481	$1,619,971	$1,394,205
Cost of revenue	723,561	946,757	766,970
Gross profit	461,920	673,214	627,235
Operating expenses:			
Research and development	358,902	241,694	151,852
Sales and marketing	368,620	268,939	194,377
General and administrative	107,367	107,833	93,971
Total operating expenses	834,889	618,466	440,200
Operating income (loss)	(372,969)	54,748	187,035
Other expense, net	(2,205)	(2,163)	(6,060)
Income (loss) before income taxes	(375,174)	52,585	180,975
Income tax expense	43,829	16,454	52,887
Net income (loss)	$ (419,003)	$ 36,131	$ 128,088

Source: GoPro, Inc. 2015 10-K.

EXHIBIT 6

GoPro, Inc., Consolidated Balance Sheets, 2015–2016 (in thousands, except par values)

	December 31, 2016	December 31, 2015
Assets		
Current assets:		
Cash and cash equivalents	$192,114	$ 279,672
Marketable securities	25,839	194,386
Accounts receivable, net	164,553	145,692
Inventory	167,192	188,232
Prepaid expenses and other current assets	38,115	25,261
Total current assets	587,813	833,243
Property and equipment, net	76,509	70,050
Intangible assets, net	33,530	31,027
Goodwill	146,459	57,095
Other long-term assets	78,329	111,561
Total assets	$922,640	$1,102,976
Liabilities and Stockholders' Equity		
Current liabilities:		
Accounts payable	$205,028	$ 89,989
Accrued liabilities	211,323	192,446
Deferred revenue	14,388	12,742
Total current liabilities	430,739	295,177
Long-term taxes payable	26,386	21,770
Other long-term liabilities	18,570	13,996
Total liabilities	475,695	330,943

(Continued)

	December 31, 2016	December 31, 2015
Stockholders' equity:		
Preferred stock, $0.0001 par value, 5,000 shares authorized; none issued	—	—
Common stock and additional paid-in capital, $0.0001 par value, 500,000 Class A shares authorized,104,647 and 100,596 shares issued and outstanding, respectively; 150,000 Class B shares authorized, 36,712 and 36,005 shares issued and outstanding, respectively	757,226	663,311
Treasury stock, at cost, 1,545 and 1,545 shares, respectively	(35,613)	(35,613)
Retained earnings (accumulated deficit)	(274,668)	144,335
Total stockholders' equity	446,945	772,033
Total liabilities and stockholders' equity	$922,640	$1,102,976

Source: GoPro, Inc., 2016 10-K.

Source: GoPro, Inc., 2015 10-K.

EXHIBIT 7

GoPro, Inc., Revenues by Geographic Region, 2014–2016

(in thousands)	Year ended December 31,			2016 vs. 2015	2015 vs. 2014
	2016	2015	2014	% Change	% Change
Units shipped	4,762	6,584	5,180	(28)%	27%
Americas	$ 619,784	$ 868,772	$ 890,352	(29)%	2%
Percentage of revenue	52.3%	53.6%	63.9%		
Europe, Middle East, & Africa	366,352	535,262	371,197	(32)%	44%
Percentage of revenue	30.9%	33.0%	26.6%		
Asia Pacific region	199,345	215,939	132,656	(8)%	63%
Percentage of revenue	16.8%	13.4%	9.5%		
Total revenue	$1,185,481	$1,619,971	$1,394,205	(27)%	16%

Source: GoPro, Inc. 2016 10-K.

According to NPD market research, in 2015, on a dollar sales basis, GoPro held 6 of the top 10 products, including the number-one spot, in the digital camera/camcorder category, and was number one in accessory unit sales with 6 of the top 10 selling accessories. In the fourth quarter 2015, on a unit sales basis, GoPro had 6 of the top 10 action cameras in Europe, including all of the top five spots in December. Global sales were more than 50 percent of fiscal 2015 revenue, and combined Asian and European revenue increased 49 percent from 2014. China remained a top 10 market for GoPro in the fourth quarter.

Despite GoPro's struggles, its camera managed to hold on to the top four spots in *PC Mag's* 2017 best action camera list. Also, GoPro reported in April 2017 that NPD data indicated that the HERO line of cameras occupied the top three of the top five spots, on a unit basis, in the digital image industry in the United States in the first quarter of 2017. Non-U.S. markets generated 60 percent of GoPro's first quarter revenue. Between 70 and 90 percent of the HERO5 camera users in China, Germany, Spain, Italy, France, and Japan were using their cameras in their local language.

GoPro Product Offerings in 2017

In 2017, GoPro's action camera offerings comprised three models: HERO Session, HERO5 Session, and

HERO5 Black. The HERO Session had one-button controls, was waterproof to 10 meters without a separate housing, and would automatically capture video and photos right-side-up even if mounted upside down. The HERO Session was small, the lightest of all GoPro cameras, and could record up to two hours on a charged battery. The Session was ranked as the fourth (of the 10 ranked) best action camera by *PC Magazine* in 2017 and sold for $149.99 in mid-2017.

The HERO5 Session was a very small camera that could be operated with simple voice commands. It could record in 4K video, with 10MP photos in single, burst, or time-lapse modes. The HERO5 Session was waterproof to 10 meters, featured advanced video stabilization, and had one-button control. Owners could purchase a GoPro Plus subscription and upload their photos and videos directly to the cloud and review, edit, and share their content on the go. The HERO5 Session placed third on *PC Magazine's* 2017 list and sold for $299.99 in mid-2017.

GoPro's HERO5 Black was the company's most advanced camera. The HERO5 Black had advanced video stabilization, was waterproof to 10 meters, had time-lapse capability, built-in Wi-Fi and Bluetooth, a smart remote that allowed multiple camera control up to 600 feet, enhanced low-light capability, and could capture high-fidelity sound. The HERO5 Black sold for $399.99.

The Karma drone went on sale in October 2016 after numerous delays. Purchasers immediately noticed that the drone experienced battery overheating and flight failure. Two and a half weeks after GoPro began selling the Karma, the company halted sales and announced a recall of the drone. Purchasers were given full refunds, plus, as an apology, GoPro provided purchasers a HERO5 Black camera. According to Nick Woodman, a defective battery was not secured in its hanger. The problem was corrected and Karma was released again in February 2017. In mid-2017, the Karma was priced at $799.99 or $1,099.99 with a HERO5 included.

GoPro's Omni was a virtual reality system, operated with six cameras. Video footage from the cameras could be put together to create a 360-degree video. The Omni was priced at $4,999.00 (which included 6 HERO4 Black cameras), or $1,199.99 for purchasers who already owned the cameras.

Other products in the GoPro line in 2017 included:

- **GoPro Plus:** a cloud-based storage solution that enabled subscribers to access, edit, and share content. HERO5 cameras could automatically upload new photos and videos to subscribers' GoPro cloud accounts.
- **Quik:** GoPro's primary mobile editing app that simplified smartphone edits.
- **Capture:** a mobile app that allowed users to preview and play back shots, control their GoPro cameras and share content using smartphones.
- **Karma Grip:** a handheld or body-mountable camera stabilizer that helped achieve zero-shake video.
- **Accessories:** GoPro offered a large line of mountable, wearable, and voice-activated accessories.

Profiles of Select Rivals in the Action Camera Industry in 2017

Sony

Sony competed in the action camera market with a lineup of nine cameras ranging in price from $199.99 to $599.99. The Sony X1000VR was the company's top of the line and was a 4K camera with a 170 wide-angle lens and professional quality output. The camera recorded at a high rate to give better resolution and better low-light pictures. Sony's AS20 and AS50 were the company's entry-level products and produced high-definition video and still images, and included SteadyShot stabilization, low-light capabilities, and a panoramic lens. Other models included built-in stereo microphones, high-speed data transfer to capture fast action, HDMI output for sharing video on TVs, and wireless uploading to smartphones or tablets.

Nikon

Camera giant Nikon announced in January 2016 that it was entering the action camera market. The company's first in its line of action cameras was the KeyMission 360, which recorded 360-degree video in 4K ultra-high-definition. The camera was dust, shock, and temperature resistant, waterproof to 100 feet, and included electronic vibration reduction to help produce sharp video. *Technowize* reported that the KeyMission 360 had the best audio quality of any action camera on the market. The KeyMission 360 was the "parent" camera in Nikon's family of action cameras. The KeyMission 360 captured the 10th position on *PC Magazine's* Best Action Cameras of 2017 and was priced at $499.95. Nikon also offered the KeyMission 80 at $279.95 and the KeyMission 170 at 399.95 in mid-2017.

Garmin International

Garmin International was far better known as a global leader in GPS navigation than for its action cameras; however, in 2013 the company released its first action camera, the VIRB. The VIRB had a color display and was manufactured in a waterproof housing so an extra protective case was unnecessary. The success of the VIRB led to two new Garmin action cameras in 2015—the VIRB X and the VIRB XE, the VIRB Ultra 30 in 2016, and the VIRB 360 in 2017. All models had GPS, Wi-Fi, and full sensor support. The new models had support for Bluetooth data streams that allowed the use of a microphone to narrate action in real time, plus a Garmin app that enabled transfer of video and photos from the camera to a smartphone and then to social media. Gauges such as altitude and speed could be applied to the video. The VIRB X was priced at $299.99, the VIRB XE and Ultra 30 were priced at $399.99, and the VIRB 360 was priced at 799.99.

Kodak

Kodak's PixPro SP1, priced at $199.00, was ranked number five in *PC Magazine's* Best Action Cameras of 2017 rankings. The PixPro had a waterproof case, produced high-quality video, could withstand drops from six feet, had an integrated display for framing shots, stereo microphones, image stabilization, a zoom lens, built-in Wi-Fi, and could be paired with iOS and Android smartphones.

Kodak extended its line to include three 360-degree models and waterproof and shockproof SPZ1. The SPZ1 was Kodak's lowest priced action camera at

$129.99. The company's 360-degree 1080p action camera was priced at $259.99 and its 360-degree 4K cameras ranged from $449.99 to $499.99.

Polaroid

Polaroid entered the action camera market in 2012 with a line of three low-priced cameras manufactured by C&A Marketing (a Polaroid license), but sold under the Polaroid name. The first Polaroid action cameras were the XS7, priced at $69.00; the XS20, priced at $99.00; and the XS100, priced at $199.00. The Polaroid CUBE was added to the Polaroid action camera line in 2014. The CUBE recorded up to 90 minutes of video in HD 1080p quality.

In 2015, Polaroid upgraded the CUBE to the CUBE+ which included Wi-Fi, image stabilization, HD 1440p video, and an 8 megapixel still capture feature. The CUBE+ was splash-resistant, shockproof, and included a microphone; numerous mountings were available for applications ranging from bikes to helmets to dogs. The CUBE+ could stream footage in real time and was compatible with both iOS and Android. A Wi-Fi enabled CUBE+ could pair with a smartphone for real-time view controls and shot framing. There was one control on the CUBE+ for on/off and to switch from video to still. The CUBE+ was priced at $129.99 in mid-2017.

GoPro's Declining Financial Performance in 2015 and 2016

GoPro's expected sales for the fourth quarter of 2015 were $511 million. However, actual sales were $436 million, representing a 31 percent drop year-over-year. Fourth quarter sales were negatively affected by the poor market acceptance of the HERO4 camera. Retailers cut prices on the HERO4 and the company announced the end of the entry-level HERO. The results of the product realignment were charges of about $57 million to revenue, and the company expected sales revenue to drop by over 50 percent in the first quarter of 2016.

Compounding the company's financial problems was its increasing costs. Even though fourth quarter 2015 sales were down 31 percent from the same period the prior year, costs of revenue decreased only 7 percent. Consequently, gross profit dropped by 58 percent from the fourth quarter 2015, resulting in a fourth quarter 2015 operating loss of $41.3 million. Net loss for the fourth quarter of 2015 was $34.5 million. After the fourth quarter results were released, after-hours trading in GoPro stock was halted. When trading resumed, share prices fell by more than 20 percent. The stock price decline left GoPro's shares worth about 10 percent of their peak value of $98.47, which was reached in October 2014.

GoPro faced further problems in 2015 as the manufacturer of Polaroid's CUBE action camera, C&A Marketing, sued GoPro for patent violation. The suit alleges that GoPro infringed on C&A Marketing's patent for its Polaroid CUBE, which was almost two years old when GoPro released its HERO4 Session. C&A Marketing asked for a halt on all GoPro HERO4 Session cameras, plus monetary damages, and all of GoPro's profit on the camera.

GoPro's management provided warning guidance for investors for the first quarter and full year of 2016,

which indicated the seriousness of the sales and earnings downturn. The company's managers failed to reverse the downturn with fiscal 2016 revenues going on to decline 27 percent to $1.2 billion from $1.6 billion in 2015. The company also recorded a net loss of $419 million in fiscal 2016 and saw its share price decline to less than $9.00 in December 2016.

GoPro's Performance in Mid-2017

GoPro's operations produced mixed results in early 2017. While first quarter 2017 gross revenue was up by 19.1 percent year-over-year, gross margin dropped to 31.4 percent from 32.5 percent in the same period in 2016. Operating income was down by 27 percent and net income decreased by 3.4 percent from the same period in 2016. The first quarter earnings release did not provide encouragement to investors with GoPro's shares closing down 8 percent to its seventh-lowest close of $8.25. Exhibit 8 presents GoPro's quarterly Statements of Operations for the first quarter of 2016 and the first quarter of 2017.

EXHIBIT 8

GoPro, Inc., Statement of Operations, First Quarter 2017 Versus First Quarter 2016 (in thousands, except per share amounts)

| | Three Months Ended March 31, | | |
	2017	2016	% Change
Revenue	$ 218,614	$ 183,536	(19.1)%
Gross margin			
GAAP	31.4%	32.5%	(110) bps
Non-GAAP	32.3%	33.0%	(70) bps
Operating loss			
GAAP	$ (88,215)	(121,435)	(27.4)%
Non-GAAP	$ (60,287)	$ (96,798)	(37.7)%
Net loss			
GAAP	$ (111,150)	$ (107,459)	3.4%
Non-GAAP	$ (62,783)	$ (86,740)	(27.6)%
Diluted net loss per share			
GAAP	$ (0.78)	(0.78)	—%
Non-GAAP	$ (0.44)	(0.63)	(30.2)%
Adjusted EBITDA	$ (45,669)	$ (86,771)	(47.4)%

Source: GoPro 10-Q, April 28, 2017.

The NPD Group's Retail Tracking Service reported that in the United States, in the first quarter 2017, GoPro had three of the top five—including the top three spots—on a unit basis in the digital image category. The HERO5 Black was the top-selling digital image camera in the United States in the first quarter on both a unit and dollar basis. According to NPD, in March 2017, the Karma drone with a HERO5 camera, was the second best-selling drone over $1,000 in the United States on a unit basis.

Although the Karma drone was achieving early market success in mid-2017, analysts were cautious about what contribution its sales would make to GoPro's overall financial situation. Although the hobby market for drones was large, Chinese DJI had a commanding lead in the industry and was known to aggressively cut its prices to defend its market position. Such price cutting would make it difficult for GoPro to compete given its cost structure and poor financial condition.

GoPro offered guidance for the second quarter of 2017, which included revenue of $270 million, +/- $10 million and gross margins of 33.5 percent, +/- 1 percent. The company intended to continue to focus on expense reduction, and forecast second quarter operating expenses at $122 million to $126 million. The adjusted EBITDA was forecast to range from a -$15 million to -$5 million. Despite the financial weaknesses, GoPro remained the leader in the action camera industry in mid-2017. The ability of its top management to craft and execute strategies to sustain its market leadership in action cameras, gain market share in drone applications, and develop future innovations would determine the success of its turnaround.

Ricoh Canada

JONATHAN FAST Queen's University

PRESCOTT C. ENSIGN Wilfrid Laurier University

In January 2016, Glenn Laverty, president and CEO of Ricoh Canada Inc., was going to meet with his executive management team to develop the company's strategy for the next three years (see Exhibit 1). Ricoh Canada Inc. (RCI), a wholly owned subsidiary of Ricoh Americas Corporation, had its head office in Toronto, Ontario, and employed over 2,100 people in Canada. Its parent, Ricoh Company Ltd., headquartered in Japan, was an international leader in the digital imaging and document management industry. It operated in more than 200 countries and regions, and employed 108,000 people worldwide. Ricoh Company Ltd. had worldwide sales of $20 billion in 2015.

RCI was facing saturation in the market segment that was its primary source of revenue—delivery and maintenance of printing/copying devices to customers. Canon and Xerox were both strong competitors in this segment, and Laverty was concerned: "We will see an increasingly rapid shrinkage in our traditional market during the next five years." Areas of opportunity included document management systems and IT services. RCI defined services as a combination of onsite and offsite resources that supported business operations infrastructure. These resources included cloud computing, remote monitoring, and other innovations. RCI could have used this technology to make customer information more secure, mobile, and personal.

Laverty openly admitted his dilemma with services by saying, "What services to develop further and how aggressively to market them is still an unknown." He knew providing more services would require additional investment, but the questions of how much and to what area were the real issues. Given RCI's current financial position, how realistic was it for RCI to transition to a services company?

Company Background

Ricoh Canada Inc. adopted its current name in 1997, but had been operating in Canada under various names since 1924. RCI was a sales organization that used a lease and service model with its office imaging equipment. All the equipment was manufactured in Ricoh's high-quality and efficient facilities in Japan. A transfer pricing system was used when product was shipped from the parent corporation to its subsidiaries. To summarize, RCI's focus was on using its direct channel and dealer network to sell and service the inventory coming from Japan. RCI moved into digital printing in the 1990s and became a dominant player in the Canadian market. It accounted for 20 percent of Canadian market sales in the high-end multifunction product segment in 2015.

In August 2008, the parent company, Ricoh Company Ltd., acquired IKON Office Solutions (IKON) for $1.6 billion. IKON was the world's largest independent provider of document management systems and services. It used copiers, printers, and multifunction printer technologies from leading manufacturers, and document management software and systems from companies like Captaris Inc., Kofax

Note: The quotes in this case were based on interviews. We thank the executives at Ricoh Canada Inc. for graciously meeting with us.

Quotes and other material used by permission of Thunderbird School of Global Management.

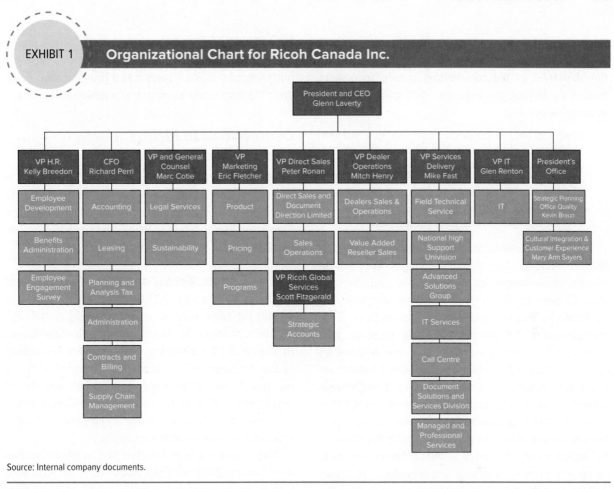

EXHIBIT 1 Organizational Chart for Ricoh Canada Inc.

Source: Internal company documents.

Ltd., and Electronics for Imaging Inc. The acquisition strengthened Ricoh's North American direct sales network and gave it control of the dealer network on which its largest competitor, Canon Inc., relied heavily. Following the acquisition, workforce integration did not take place as rapidly as Ricoh Company Ltd. management had anticipated.

State of the Market

In 2015, Laverty had asked his management team to look at the state of the services market. The way he saw it, three trends were pushing RCI toward services: shifts in technology, user behavior, and corporate behavior. The advent of digital storage and document management technologies meant that customers were printing fewer documents. Using digital documents allowed for faster and more effective

workflows as well as greater accessibility. Digital documents were available to anyone over the Internet. Laverty mentioned, "Modern businesses were striving to become paperless offices, which is a very scary thing for anyone at Ricoh to say out loud."

The team found that the Canadian services market was worth $24 billion in 2015. By comparison, the size of the hardware/break and fix market—RCI's primary revenue source—was $4.5 billion $5 billion to with growth in 2015 of 2 percent. It was clear that technological advancements in tablet and mobile device networks were disrupting RCI's legacy business. By 2019, the printer/copier market was estimated to shrink by 3 percent annually, and this downward trend would accelerate after that point. Laverty pointed out, "It has never been easier not to print something, and that means trouble for everyone in the industry. We have to adapt or face extinction."

Early signs of this were already present; mergers and acquisitions activity had been rampant in the traditional market as big competitors sought to protect profits by buying competitors. As Laverty told his management team:

> If we stay only in the printer business, RCI will be squeezed at both ends. We will see a decline in sales and a decline in the subsequent stream of income from maintenance. Where the market will stabilize once it begins to contract is unknown. So we have to move beyond this segment. Planning for negative growth is not acceptable.

When the services market was broken down further, it became clear that big changes were taking place with medium-sized businesses. It could be seen that 42 percent of services spending was going to be made by medium-sized businesses in 2016. This represented a 7.4 percent spending increase year over year. The cost of services had come down to an inclusive price point where medium-sized businesses could take advantage of what was offered and, consequently, usage was increasing. After seeing this, VP of Services Mike Fast commented, "What we are seeing here is the good kind of deflation which is produced by increases in efficiency allowing better products to be sold cheaper and to a wider market." RCI had a 2 percent market share in the services market for medium-sized businesses or, in RCI terms, firms that fit into RCI's geographic/key named accounts classifications. Another major trend was small to medium-sized businesses shifting toward cloud services where IT infrastructure was handled for them. As volume on the cloud increased, cloud services were able to achieve economies of scale and flexibility. From a consumer perspective, using the cloud was much more cost-effective than upgrading an in-house server network and corresponding support resources. Finally, companies were demanding software to better share information across an organization whether it be document management, process management, or communication management.

Consumer studies of the services market indicated that consumers considered a long list of factors when assessing a provider. These included cost-effectiveness; environmental sustainability; information security and compliance; business process streamlining; change management; worker productivity; information optimization; and strategic infrastructure. VP of Marketing Eric Fletcher advised Laverty that all of his team's research had been pointing to one factor: "The primary interest of consumers was a provider who could unify services in the company at a reasonable cost."

Competition in Ricoh Canada Inc.'s Market

The segments that RCI traditionally competed in were extremely competitive (see Exhibits 2 and 3). Competitors could be broken down into two groups: Tier 1 and Tier 2. The following describes RCI's competitors' recent strategic moves.

Tier 1—Canon, Xerox, and HP
Canon Canada Inc. had relied heavily on IKON for both unit sales and service infrastructure, so it was focusing on rebuilding this channel after IKON was acquired by Ricoh. In March 2010, Canon Inc. acquired Océ NV (based in the Netherlands) to increase its market share in the digital space as well as to expand its research and development. Canon Inc. was positioned as a leader in managed print and content services according to Gartner Inc.'s proprietary research.

Xerox Corporation entered the services market in February 2010 with the acquisition of Affiliated Computer Services Inc. (ACS), an IT services firm based in Dallas, Texas. In Canada, Xerox was maintaining traditional core unit sales while encouraging its sales force to sell services. Its cash flow from the traditional product lines was expected to fund the expansion into services. Xerox Canada had performed well with its major accounts in health care and government. Recently, Xerox had launched cloud services.

Hewlett-Packard Company (HP), in Canada and worldwide, had a very strong brand and customer network for its IT hardware. It was using this reputation to move into services. HP acquired EDS (Electronic Data Systems) on August 28, 2008, to give it the ability to combine hardware and services to create holistic offerings to customers. The integration of services with hardware was ongoing.

Tier 2—Konica Minolta and Others
Konica Minolta Business Solutions Canada Ltd. was strong in the A3 (standard European format) printer segment. Its pricing on a cost per page basis was low,

EXHIBIT 2

Laser Printer Market Share for A4, A3, Dealer, and Direct Segments, 2012–2015

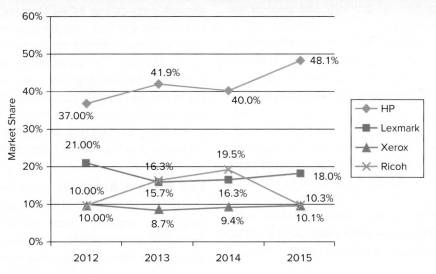

Source: Internal company documents.

EXHIBIT 3

Market Share for Multifunction Products (Printer, Scanner, Fax) over $1,000, 2012–2015

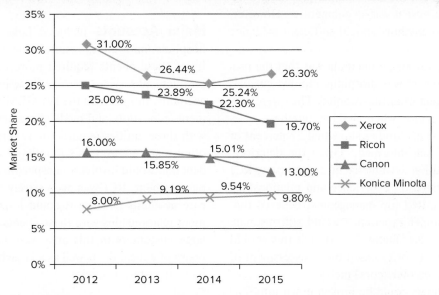

Source: Internal company documents.

almost to the point of disrupting the market. Also, it was introducing a new A3 color lineup, making it hard for others to compete within the A3 color segment. Konica Minolta products had good image quality and performance.

Lexmark had left the inkjet printing business and turned its attention to improving its A4 (standard North American format) laser printer lineup. Lexmark was on an acquisition spree, year after year gobbling up software companies to support its growth objectives. Samsung Electronics Canada Inc. was expanding its A3 product lineup. Other competitors were also retooling print offerings but were not moving into services as aggressively as those in Tier 1.

Other Within the services landscape there were several large competitors—specifically, Google, IBM, and Amazon with highly developed cloud services.

Ricoh Canada Inc.'s Customer Base

RCI had sold business-to-business (B2B) with 89 percent of sales made directly to business customers, and the remaining 11 percent of sales made by independent dealers. RCI did not have a business-to-consumer (B2C) line, although most of RCI's primary competitors (Canon, Xerox, and HP) did. Laverty did not see the B2C market providing long-term growth because it was so competitive. However, he was open to anything should sufficient evidence be presented.

Part of RCI's strategic dilemma was that the profile of its customers was morphing rapidly; customers were changing what they wanted. They were also discriminating more when making purchase decisions. Laverty said, "Studies show that 57 percent of customers are well informed." Given the deterioration of information asymmetry in the industry, RCI was trying to build on experience and relationships with customers. RCI top management believed that a positive customer experience would still resonate more than any other factor. Laverty felt this should continue to be a priority based on an assessment of the NPS (net promoter score) metric.

RCI's customers could be broken down into four classes based on the size of the client. These were geographic accounts, key named accounts, major accounts, and strategic accounts.

Geographic Accounts were RCI's smallest customers and typically had only one location. New customers in this segment were generally targeted through cold calling by RCI's sales force. The way this worked was that a salesperson was given a postal code and then pitched products to all small businesses within it. The estimated success rate of cold calling was 1 in 10. Most new business based on client count was generated in this manner. These customers offered the highest margins because the transactions were usually isolated, rather than drawn-out business deals where RCI would be fighting on price.

Key Named Accounts were small to medium-sized enterprises that had five or six locations. Like geographic accounts, these entities were also targeted through cold calling. The sales representatives attached to these accounts had more tenure, giving them a higher probability of developing and nurturing a relationship. Existing accounts in this segment were prime targets for off-cycle selling. That is, once under contract they were asked to buy more from RCI. According to VP of Sales Peter Ronan, "Marketing services would fit very well between hardware cycles because it would allow us to increase our share of a customer's wallet through a business relationship that is already established."

Major Accounts included large customers like hospitals and colleges/universities. The complexity of these clients required more customization in product and service offerings. Together with strategic accounts, this defined the key GEM market (government, education, and medical market). Transactions with these entities required more internal resources, often requiring up to six months or more to close a deal that would involve a salesperson as well as upper management. RCI was aggressively targeting health care accounts because it could leverage its government relationships with these clients. Some of RCI's large customers in this area were Canada's largest board of education as well as a large health care company in eastern Canada.

Strategic Accounts were RCI's largest customers and included banks and substantial government units. They were also the hardest deals to close.

These customers generally sent a request for proposal (RFP) to major competitors in the industry and based their decisions on bids, causing the formality of this segment to be considerably higher than the others. These clients required a lot of attention, and it generally took six months or more before a deal was finalized. RCI had not yet determined if the RFP process was an advantage or disadvantage. RCI's track record in this realm was mixed, but it had managed to win contracts with a large life insurance company, two of Canada's big five banks, and Canada's largest food retailer. Government units were an area where RCI would have liked to have focused more resources because they offered exposure into the broader public sector. For example, under Canada's government-run health care system, hospitals could buy products using the same prices set in government contracts without having to send out a separate tender. See Exhibit 4 for a review of projected growth in spending for major and strategic accounts.

Service Offerings in 2016

RCI's services could be broken into three segments: Technical Services (traditional break and fix), Professional Services, and Managed Services. Technical Services was the largest in terms of revenue, producing $193 million, or 39 percent of revenue in 2015, but the growth potential was limited (see Exhibit 5). RCI's total revenue from Professional Services and Managed Services was $52 million in 2015. With regard to Professional Services and Managed Services, Laverty stated, "Currently, we don't have a lot of volume in these areas, but we have some cool technology. We are just not completely sure how to use all of it. Also, given our relative inexperience in the services market, we need to figure out where RCI should operate relative to competitors."

Technical Services was based on the legacy business and involved servicing machines in the field. From the standpoint of a service-level agreement, customers had become more demanding, and RCI had been able to grow its market share in this area by meeting or exceeding customer expectations. The field technical team was the backbone of the service agreements. RCI had a very strong ERP system (Baan) and 550 well-trained personnel. VP of Services Mike Fast said, "These guys aren't your traditional copier technicians; they are highly trained, and have competencies, like networking skills, that extend beyond the machine."

EXHIBIT 4

Projected Spending Growth for Major Accounts and Strategic Accounts, 2015–2019						
Who	2015	2016	2017	2018	2019	Trends
Health care	7%	6%	7%	6%	6%	• Paper intensive to electronically automated • Cloud-based storage and sharing • Mobile workflow
Legal	4%	4%	4%	5%	5%	• Huge growth in electronically stored information • Legal process outsourcing • Working remotely and information security
Government	−1%	−1%	2%	2%	3%	• Shared cloud hubs in 65% of provinces by 2015 • Need for more cross-government collaboration
College/university	3%	3%	3%	4%	4%	• More e-learning on smaller budgets • Looking for cost reductions and ongoing support
Public school K–12	0%	2%	3%	4%	3%	• More e-learning on smaller budgets • Looking for cost reductions and ongoing support
Private school K–12	5%	4%	4%	4%	4%	• More e-learning on smaller budgets • Looking for cost reductions and ongoing support

Source: Internal company documents.

EXHIBIT 5

Revenue, Market Share, and Margin for Ricoh Canada Services, 2015

Services Revenue Breakdown	2015	Percentage of Total Revenue	Market Share	Margin	Annual Market Growth
Break/Fix—Hardware maintenance and support	$ 193M	39%	23%	36%	2%
Total Technical	**$193M**				
Managed Document Services (MDS)—Business process consulting	$ 4M	<1%	1%	21%	3%
Legal Document Services (LDS)— Litigation support services	$ 5M	$<1%	30%	60%	2%
Ricoh Document Management (RDM)—Print, fulfillment, and imaging	$ 5M	1%	1%	20%	−5%
Ricoh Management Services (RMS)—Onsite/offsite resources	$ 25M	5%	25%	13%	1%
Total Managed Services	**$ 40M**				
IT/Professional Services—Solution consulting, IT hardware, remote monitoring, deployment services	$ 12M	2%	0%	46%	Consulting—18% IT Services —5% ($900B global market)
Cloud—Software as a service (SaaS), backup as a service (BaaS)					SaaS—17.9% ($14.5B global market) BaaS— 40%
	$ 0	0%	0%	N.A.	($5.6B global market)
Total Professional Services	**$ 12M**				

Note: N.A. = Not applicable.

Source: Author created.

Professional Services helped customers streamline and better integrate their workflow processes. The solutions currently offered included: Managed Document Services (MDS), IT hardware, and remote monitoring and deployment services. MDS was designed to increase the efficiency of information transfer within an organization. For example, the software could read scanned images and automatically route documents to those who approved and/or used them. This concept could extend point-to-point across an organization using programmed rules that fit the business's structure. MDS helped a small or large company increase its workflow efficiency, manage its network, enhance its security, and troubleshoot when problems arose. Revenue for MDS was reported under Managed Services due to corporate restructuring, but was controlled as a part of Professional Services.

Professional Services helped a prospective company build the IT components, including both hardware and software, necessary to run company workflows. Although not yet released, IT services included cloud services and disaster recovery support. RCI's cloud services were intended to be a gateway to critical information. Corporate planning was underway in Japan and margins for this segment of the business were expected to be 56 percent at launch in the first quarter of 2016. The profile of Professional Services as RCI described it is found in Exhibit 6.

Managed Services encompassed three areas: (1) imaging print and fulfillment (Ricoh Document Management or RDM); (2) onsite managed services (Ricoh Management Services or RMS); and (3) litigation support services (Legal Document Services or LDS). Image print and fulfillment was just as the name suggests. RCI had two centers: one located in Aurora, Ontario, and the other in Vancouver, British Columbia. The items (e.g., books or posters) were printed for customers and then held in inventory.

Profile of Ricoh Canada Inc.'s IT and Professional Services (IT/PS)

RCI's IT and Professional Services division is dedicated to creating a tailored suite of IT Services and software solutions designed to assist clients in meeting their business objectives. The IT/PS team delivers expert technical and business solution expertise to support any size organization, in any industry in a consistent, reliable, and cost-effective manner.

RCI's IT/PS department is well equipped to address customer business challenges such as helping maintain competitive advantage while mitigating risk, fulfilling compliance & industry governance measures, ensuring predictable cost and operating expense support & accountability—all standardized around customer business needs. RCI's role is to assist customers in meeting their organizational objectives & goals while maximizing business potential and minimizing infrastructure support costs and security exposure.

RCI's services team works directly with industry leading IT vendors to deliver world-class end-to-end technology solutions to customers that result in reduced IT project costs and greater ROI on technology investments. RCI offers a single source for business solutions designed to deliver tangible business outcomes for customers that are services-centric, technology-enabled, and people-driven.

Source: Internal company documents.

Onsite managed services were customer-specific services such as conference management, internal print room management, and reception services. Legal Document Services was a niche service to support law firms during litigation through a process called electronic document discovery. RCI scanned legal documents and recorded them digitally so that law firms could search and retrieve them.

Services support teams (consultants and solution engineers) operated as an overlay structure to the sales channel, with sales owning the customer relationship. Support teams educated the sales channel and identified opportunities within the market. The sales team engaged the support team as subject matter experts when pursuing opportunities with potential customers. Furthermore, support teams also engaged in more traditional consulting activities focused on enterprise software and hardware needs. Teams from this group went into businesses, studied operations, and then made recommendations. This gave RCI the ability to design the most efficient workflow for the business, providing comprehensive solutions. In general, the consulting service was free for customers who subsequently bought RCI products. Independent dealers were able to use these support teams to supplement operations, improve knowledge, and integrate with RCI.

RCI Sales Team

RCI's direct sales force of 380 people was focused on maintaining existing customer relationships while hunting for *net* new opportunities. For a breakdown of the sales force by customer segment, see Exhibit 7. The difference between a new customer and a net new customer was that a net new customer had never purchased an RCI product before. For the sales force, the time spent on repeat business versus new business was approximately at a 4 to 1 ratio. Over half of new business in any given year, based on the number of clients, came from geographic accounts that were acquired through cold calling. Senior salespeople managed major and strategic accounts, while new hires targeted geographic customers primarily through cold calling. Overall, RCI had a reputation for treating its salespeople well.

Ricoh Canada's Sales Force Breakdown by Customer Segment, 2015

Dealer Operations	2
Sales—Corporate	21
Sales—Major Accounts	84
Sales—Geographic/Key Named Accounts	175
Sales—Strategic Accounts	23
Sales—DDLP (Document Direction Limited Partnership)	51
Selling Dealer	15
Selling Software	9
Total	380

Source: Author created.

RCI's sales force would need additional training if RCI was to continue to expand its services offerings. The current estimate was $6,095 per person (this included rep costs, instructor costs, material, training sessions, a technology show, and revenue lost from not selling during training). Kevin Braun, director of quality and strategic planning, believed this cost might even be too low, saying:

> My belief is that we do not spend enough on training our sales team. This is a new area for most of them and we are heavily relying on support staff to assist them in these early stages. This issue is of high priority for the EMT [executive management team], but it is my personal opinion this number should be close to doubled. Finally, the recruitment process for salespeople also needs to change—to candidates that have more content/specific knowledge in services.

RCI's independent dealer network would have to undergo significant change to address a large-scale shift to services. First, salespersons at the dealers would have to learn about services and how to sell them. In the past, they had only sold hardware. Second, dealers would have to be interested in selling services. At many dealers, salespeople were vested in their positions or near retirement so were not motivated. Glenn Laverty and Peter Ronan recognized the problem: "We must find a way to encourage the sale of our services or find new dealers that specialize in selling our services. Although hardware is still a very important part of RCI's business, we must figure out a way to balance the legacy business while creating growth in services."

The Financial Quagmire

RCI's investment capital came from income generated by its legacy business. The current CFO, Richard Perri, said, "The issue RCI presently faces from a financial perspective is how to allocate these funds to generate the best returns." Laverty and Perri wondered how realistic it was for RCI to invest in services growth given RCI's current financial position. Laverty said, "We have to make sure we have the internal resources to make a dent in the services market. A lot of these things take scale, and at the very least we need to know how much growth to plan for."

See Exhibit 8 for a summary of revenue, expenses, and total gross profit for 2015, and Exhibit 9 for the 2015 balance sheet.

RCI's revenue was affected by exchange rate fluctuations because the products it sold were manufactured in Japan and inventoried in the United States on their way to Canada. CFO Richard Perri told Laverty, "We need to consider hedging these currencies to provide stability in business planning. The greenback, in particular, has been the subject of much speculation given proposed interest rate increases."

Management

In the prior five years, RCI had experienced 110 percent turnover in its executive management team; some had left voluntarily, while others had been forced out. This turnover reflected the need for creative thinking in the executive suite. The replacements were tech savvy, had fresh ideas, and could think outside the box, but the high turnover had created a leadership crisis. According to Laverty, "Recruiting new people and getting them up to speed as a team has not been as fast as we had hoped. It takes time for everyone to settle in. This makes it even more crucial for us to have a strategy for RCI that we can unify around."

Performance Management

Because RCI was part of a Japanese corporation, it followed the practices of its parent. RCI was heavily involved in planning, assessing past performance, and revising goals. Every month, each member of the RCI executive management team had a one-on-one meeting with the head of Ricoh Americas Corporation in Caldwell, New Jersey. At that meeting, they reviewed past performance and future initiatives. RCI executives also traveled to Japan biannually for weeklong meetings with their counterparts from other regions to discuss the future of the company on a global scale. Laverty often told his management team, "As an organization, we must always be actively looking for criticism from our customers that will help us refine and improve our operations." To this end, everyone took the concept of *kaizen* (continuous improvement) seriously.

EXHIBIT 8

Financial Summary for Ricoh Canada, 2013–2015

Income Statement	2013	2014	2015
Revenue			
Sales (Hardware)	$ 82,370	$192,116	$192,790
Key (incl. DDLP)	84,771	89,232	91,701
Major Accounts	65,085	69,239	68,338
Strategic Accounts	14,628	14,202	14,551
Dealer Sales	17,887	19,442	18,200
Rental & Other	6,307	7,008	10,059
Affiliate	1,201	1,452	2,824
Parts, Supplies, & Paper	43,111	44,512	45,728
Service	185,475	187,013	192,546
IT/PS Services	6,622	8,209	12,402
IT Services	478	784	1,477
Cloud	0	0	0
Professional Services	6,144	7,425	10,925
Managed Services	36,411	37,004	40,667
Total Revenue	461,497	477,313	497,016
Total Gross Profit	154,538	158,386	159,467
Sales GP%	33.24%	33.99%	29.10%
Key (incl. DDLP) GP%	41.44%	42.34%	36.10%
Major Accounts GP%	29.75%	29.86%	26.80%
Strategic Accounts GP%	11.93%	13.06%	8.10%
Dealer Sales GP%	24.55%	25.19%	19.20%
Expenses			
Sales	53,541	54,634	56,094
IT/PS Services	3,242	3,308	3,647
Managed Services	2,966	3,026	3,303
Dealer	2,739	2,795	2,780
Marketing	8,642	8,818	9,226
Operations	29,261	29,858	30,348
G&A	23,843	24,330	23,283
Amortization	2,431	2,481	2,739
Total Expenses	126,665	129,250	131,420
Operating Profit	$ 27,873	$ 29,136	$ 28,047

Source: Internal company documents.

RCI placed emphasis on what it called a Net Promoter Score (NPS). This score was based on customers' responses to the question: "Would you recommend RCI to another company?" RCI's NPS scores were consistently high (see the Customer Satisfaction Survey 2009-2015 in Exhibit 10), while scores from other companies that utilized an NPS assessment were often negative, indicating that more customers would not recommend that company than who would. This metric measured the emotional connection a customer felt during interactions with RCI; it was particularly valuable for providing input on a customer's satisfaction with an employee (e.g., when a machine was being fixed or when dealing with a local sales representative). RCI was dedicated to the success of its customers, which gave it a reputation as one of the most trusted brands in the market.

EXHIBIT 9

Ricoh Canada's Balance Sheet, 2013–2015

Balance Sheet	2013	2014	2015
Assets			
Current Assets			
Cash and cash equivalents	$ 26,363	$ 33,358	$ 59,228
Trade Accounts receivable, net	97,631	102,786	97,565
Inventories	38,056	42,562	34,070
Other Current Assets	10,255	9,941	10,786
	172,305	188,647	201,649
Lease receivable	5,427	8,102	5,957
Property, plant and equipment, net	6,063	11,620	12,039
Goodwill	20,306	44,863	44,863
Intangibles, net	15,618	15,601	15,601
Other Assets	10,388	5,705	9,119
	57,802	85,892	87,579
Total Assets	$230,107	$274,539	$289,228
Liabilities			
Current Liabilities			
Accounts payable and accrued liabilities	$ 40,986	$ 48,900	$ 56,217
Due to affiliates	20,609	24,588	28,657
Current portion of Lease payable	3,610	4,307	4,406
Other Current Liabilities	6,446	7,691	8,075
	71,650	85,485	97,356
Lease payable	4,720	5,631	5,722
Promissory note	11,916	14,217	13,146
Other long-term liabilities	1,324	1,580	1,800
	17,960	21,428	20,668
Shareholders' Equity			
Share Capital	72,634	86,659	74,868
Contributed Surplus	11,615	13,857	15,670
Retained Earnings	56,248	67,108	80,666
	140,496	167,625	171,204
Total Liabilities & Shareholders' Equity	$230,107	$274,539	$289,228

Source: Internal company documents.

RCI's focus on NPS began because of its lease and service business model—where interactions with the customer were frequent, particularly for machine maintenance. RCI believed that a positive social experience helped promote a long-term relationship, and with 80 percent of RCI's sales effort focused on repeat customers, it was easy to see why a long-term focus on customers was important. Employees were trained in interpersonal skills so that they handled interactions positively. Laverty often reminded everyone, "It is amazing just how far a smile can go."

Services Growth Strategies

RCI's management team was considering a number of growth strategies for Professional Services and Managed Services. These included growth by acquisitions, partnerships, alliances, and/or organic growth.

Any domestic acquisition would have to be funded by RCI. Even in terms of global acquisitions, such as in the case of IKON, RCI was responsible for financing the Canadian arm of that business. But, were partnerships and alliances more critical for the transition to services than outright acquisitions? Could

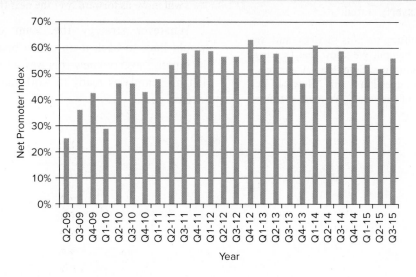

EXHIBIT 10 | **Results for Ricoh Canada Customer Satisfaction Survey, 2009–2015**

Source: Internal company documents.

a partnership or alliance be used for knowledge transfer to Ricoh? How feasible was it to think that another company could provide a foundation for how RCI would compete in the services market?

Could Ricoh Canada Inc. rely solely on organic growth? If history were a guide, RCI would have to rely on the head office in Japan to develop innovations in services. By itself, RCI did not have the engineering personnel to develop products because almost all research and development efforts were done in Japan and the United States. In this situation, RCI would have focused on cost-cutting initiatives in the legacy business and sales of existing services technology, while waiting for Japan to introduce new offerings. In addition, because services developed in Japan or the United States were designed for launch on a global scale, RCI was limited in its ability to tailor products to the Canadian marketplace. But as Laverty told his team, "Perhaps this isn't impossible. How different can the services in Canada be from those of businesses globally?"

The Final Decision

As president and CEO, Laverty wrote to his management team:

> With a corporate shift to Managed and Professional Services, RCI will have to ensure that the

Ricoh brand does not erode. We will have to get past the hurdle of being known as the printer guys if we intend to become more than that. Customers will need to be assured that RCI is a serious player in the Managed Services and Professional Services industries, especially when continued support in key functionalities such as cloud services is a priority for a prospective customer. RCI must also figure out a way to handle failures when delivering new services. Any failures could give a signal to the market that we are not competent in those services or are not ready to handle large-scale projects. Since this is new territory for RCI, there is no doubt that unexpected challenges will occur. We must work closely with Eric Fletcher, VP of Marketing, who may be the deciding vote on when the process will occur. With all the competition in the services area, we must move ahead and make our strategic decisions in the very near future.

Given Ricoh Canada Inc.'s focus on planning, the management team had its work cut out for it. Having just a generic strategy of growth was not enough. They would need to create SMART goals (Specific, Measurable, Attainable, Relevant, and Time-bound) as they moved forward. In his communication to the management team, Laverty reminded them, "Our goals must be specific enough so we can measure progress and adjust. Without specific goals, we will lose sight of what is important and end up stuck between two markets."

In concluding, Laverty stated:

> The market is shifting towards services, and we must not be left behind. We know that figuring this out raises more questions than it answers. But the important question is still: "How can we grow in the area of services?" We must examine our strengths and come up with a sustainable growth strategy, one that we can put in place that will move us forward over the next three years.

Whatever strategy the team chose, Laverty would have to back it up to the board of directors in Japan. Laverty knew this was a tall order, but he felt his team was ready to work hard to reach this stretch goal.

Mondelēz International's Diversification Strategy in 2017: Has Corporate Restructuring Benefited Shareholders?

JOHN E. GAMBLE Texas A&M University–Corpus Christi

Mondelēz International was among the world's largest snack foods makers with seven billion-dollar brands including Cadbury, LU, Milka, Cadbury Dairy Milk, Trident, Nabisco, and Oreo. The company's brand portfolio in 2017 included another 44 well-known brands such as Triscuit, Toblerone, Wheat Thins, Ritz, Philadelphia, Nilla, BelVita, Chips Ahoy!, and Tang. Even though some of its brands had histories dating over 100 years, the company had come into existence only in 2012 after a corporate restructuring at Kraft Foods. Kraft Foods Inc. was the world's second-largest processed foods company in 2012 with annual revenues of more than $54 billion in 2011. The company's global lineup of brands included Maxwell House, Oreo, Cadbury, Chips Ahoy!, Honey Maid, Dentyne, Velveeta, Cheez Whiz, Oscar Mayer, and Kraft. In all, the company had 12 brands with annual revenues exceeding $1 billion each and approximately 80 brands that generated annual revenues of more than $100 million each. The majority of Kraft Foods's brands held number-one market shares in their product categories, which created strong business units in North America, Europe, and developing markets.

Even though Kraft Foods's business units produced strong profits, slow growth in the processed foods industry in North America and parts of Europe had restricted the company's ability to deliver increases in shareholder value. In fact, the trading range of the company's shares in 2011 was relatively unchanged from that in 2007 when it became an independent company after a spin-off by the Altria Group (formerly Philip Morris). Some of the lackluster growth in its share price could be attributed to the economic slowdown that began in 2007, but the company's upper management and its board believed the underlying cause of its poor market performance was a corporate strategy that was not sufficiently focused on growth.

The company implemented a corporate restructuring in 2012 to create a high-growth global snacks business and a high-margin North American grocery business. The new snacks-oriented company would include all of Kraft Foods's business units and brands in Europe and developing markets, plus its U.S. snacks business and would be named Mondelēz International. *Mondelēz* (pronounced mohn-dah-Leez) was a newly coined word that drew on "mundus," the Latin root for the word *world,* and "delez," which was meant to express "delicious." The creators of the name added "International" to capture the global nature of the business. The remainder of the company's Kraft Foods North American business unit would become known as Kraft Foods Group upon completion of the spin-off.

By 2017, Mondelēz International had successfully achieved its internationalization goals, with 76 percent of its revenues generated outside the United States in 2016. But the United States remained the company's largest market, making up 18 percent, 21 percent, and 24 percent of its sales in 2014, 2015, and 2016, respectively. No other country accounted for 10 percent of Mondelēz's sales.

However, the overall effectiveness of the corporate restructuring was questionable with the company's stock performance largely tracking the S&P 500 and its revenues in decline. The company's income from continuing operations grew from 2014 to 2015, but only because of a $6.8 billion pretax gain from the spin-off of its coffee business in France. Absent a large asset sale in 2016, the company's operating income fell from $8.8 billion in 2015 to $2.6 billion in 2016. The company's total net revenues had declined from $34.2 billion in 2014 to $29.6 billion in 2015 and to $25.9 billion in 2016.

Drawing focus on the need for improved performance, activist investor William Ackman took a $5.5 billion stake in the company in July 2015. Ackman believed that management should dramatically improve the company's performance or that the company should be a candidate for acquisition by a better-performing industry rival. Ackman increased his stake in the company in January 2017 to 6.4 percent of outstanding shares. A summary of Mondelēz International's financial performance from 2012 to 2016 is presented in Exhibit 1. The performance of the company's stock performance between July 2012 and July 2017 is presented in Exhibit 2.

Company History

Mondelēz International's marquee brands all had rich histories that began with the efforts of entrepreneurs who were inspired to launch new businesses

---

EXHIBIT 1

Financial Summary for Mondelēz International, Inc., 2012–2016 (in millions, except per share amounts)

	2016	2015	2014	2013	2012
Continuing Operations					
Net revenues	$25,923	$29,636	$34,244	$35,299	$35,015
Earnings from continuing operations, net of taxes	1,659	7,291	2,201	2,332	1,606
Net earnings attributable to Mondelēz International:					
Per share, basic	1.07	4.49	1.29	1.30	0.90
Per share, diluted	1.05	4.44	1.28	1.29	0.88
Cash Flow and Financial Position					
Net cash provided by operating activities	2,838	3,728	3,562	6,410	3,923
Capital expenditures	1,224	1,514	1,642	1,622	1,610
Property, plant and equipment, net	8,229	8,362	9,827	10,247	10,010
Total assets	$61,538	$62,843	$66,771	$72,464	$75,421
Long-term debt	13,217	14,557	13,821	14,431	15,519
Total Mondelēz International shareholders' equity	25,161	28,012	27,750	32,373	32,276
Shares outstanding at year end	1,528	1,580	1,664	1,705	1,778
Per Share and Other Data					
Book value per shares outstanding	$ 16.47	$ 17.73	$ 16.68	$ 18.99	$ 18.15
Dividends declared per share	0.72	0.64	0.58	0.54	1.00
Common stock closing price at year end	44.33	44.84	36.33	35.30	25.45
Number of employees	90,000	99,000	104,000	107,000	110,000

Source: Mondelēz International, Inc., 2016 10-K.

EXHIBIT 2

Performance of Mondelēz International, Inc., Common Shares, July 2012–July 2017

(a) Trend in Mondelēz International's Common Stock Price

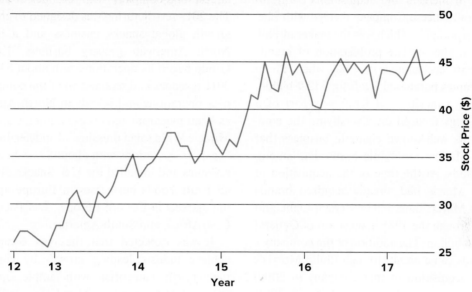

(b) Performance of Mondelēz International's Stock Price versus the S&P 500 Index

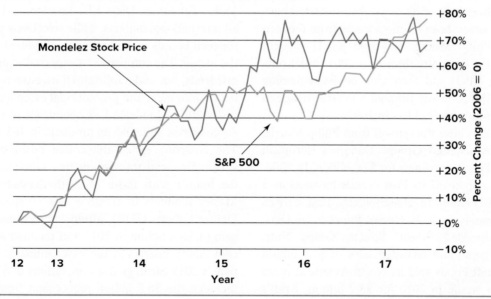

that could provide consumers with value and support for their families. But Mondelēz International, as a corporate entity, resulted from the 2012 spin-off of Kraft Foods's North American grocery business to shareholders. Under the terms of the proposal, each Kraft Foods Inc. shareholder received one share of the newly created Kraft Foods Group for every three shares of Kraft Foods Inc. owned by the shareholder. At the conclusion of the spin-off, Kraft Foods Inc. changed its name to Mondelēz International, Inc. and its ticker symbol became MDLZ. The KFT ticker symbol was retired after the transaction. Shares of the newly formed Kraft Foods Group would trade under the ticker symbol KRFT.

Kraft Foods's broad portfolio of brands resulted from a series of mergers and acquisitions dating to 1928 when Kraft Cheese Company merged with Phenix Cheese Corporation, which was the maker of Philadelphia cream cheese. The proliferation of brands owned by Kraft accelerated in 1988 when Philip Morris Companies purchased Kraft for $12.9 billion. Philip Morris's acquisition of Kraft was part of a corporate strategy focused on diversifying the company beyond its well-known cigarette business that included the Marlboro, Virginia Slims, Parliament, and Basic brands. At the time of the acquisition of Kraft, Philip Morris had already acquired brands such as Oscar Mayer, Tang, Jell-O, Crystal Light, and Post cereals through the 1985 acquisition of General Foods for $5.6 billion. The addition of the company's Nabisco brands came about through Philip Morris's $18.9 billion acquisition of that company in 2000. Kraft Foods's return to independence began in 2001, when Philip Morris (renamed Altria Group in 2003) began the divestiture of its non–tobacco-related businesses to protect those business assets from tobacco litigation. Philip Morris first sold an 11 percent interest in the company through a 2001 initial public offering (IPO) and then spun off its remaining interest in the company through a tax-free dividend to Altria Group shareholders in 2007.

Immediately after the spin-off from Philip Morris, Kraft Foods acquired Groupe Danone's European cracker and cookie business for $7.6 billion. In 2008, Kraft Foods spun off its Post cereals business as a tax-free distribution to shareholders. Post cereals included brands such as Honey Bunches of Oats, Pebbles, Shredded Wheat, Selects, Grape Nuts, and Honeycomb and recorded sales of $1.1 billion in 2007. Kraft Foods sold its North American pizza business to Nestlé in 2010 for $3.7 billion. Kraft's frozen pizza brands included the DiGiorno, Tombstone, and Jack's brands in the United States and the Delissio brand in Canada. The company's divested pizza business also produced and distributed California Pizza Kitchen branded frozen pizzas under license. Also in 2010, Kraft Foods spent $18.5 billion to acquire United Kingdom–based Cadbury, which was the maker of Cadbury chocolates, Halls cough drops, Clorets breath-freshening gum, and Trident, Dentyne, and Stride chewing gum.

By 2011, Kraft Foods remained the world's second-largest food company, with revenues of $54.4 billion. The 2012 restructuring was designed to create a high-growth global snacks business and a high-margin North American grocery business. Kraft Foods Group began its operations with about $19 billion in 2011 revenues and retained all of the company's business operations and brands in North America such as Kraft macaroni and cheese dinner, Capri Sun, and Miracle Whip salad dressing. Mondelēz International began its operations with about $35.8 billion in 2011 revenues and included the U.S. Snacks divisions and all Kraft Foods businesses in Europe and developing markets in Eastern Europe, Asia/Pacific, Middle East/Africa, and South America.

It was expected that the new company could achieve industry-leading growth by competing in high-growth categories with ample opportunities for product innovation. Mondelēz would focus on its powerful, iconic global brands such as Cadbury, Milka, Toblerone, Oreo, LU, Tassimo, and Jacobs in all international markets, while selectively promoting regional brands with strong growth potential outside the region. The company was expected to pay modest dividends, but make substantial investments in product development and promotional campaigns.

By 2017, Mondelēz had operations in more than 80 countries and sold its products in 165 countries. The company exited the coffee business in 2015 with a financial transaction that combined its coffee brands with those of Netherlands-based D.E. Master Blenders to create a new company, Jacobs Douwe Egberts (JDE). Mondelēz recorded a pretax gain of $6.8 billion in 2015 and retained a 43.5 percent equity interest in the new company. The company's 2015 earnings from operations of $7.3 billion included the $6.8 billion pretax gain from the July 2015 spin-off of its Maxwell House, Jacobs, Gevalia, Carte Noire, Tassimo, and other coffee and hot beverage brands. The company's 43.5 percent interest in JDE was valued at $4.5 billion in 2015. The company announced near year-end 2015 that it would exchange a portion of its equity ownership in JDE for an ownership position in coffee producer and brewing equipment maker, Keurig Green Mountain Inc.

The Keurig transaction was completed in March 2016 and reduced Mondelēz's ownership position in JDE to 26.5 percent in return for a 24.2 percent ownership stake in Keurig.

The company also made small acquisitions and divestitures in 2015 and 2016 that included the acquisition of U.S. snack foods company Enjoy Life Foods for $81 million and the divestiture of its 50 percent interest in a Japanese coffee joint venture for $225 million and the sale of local Finnish biscuit brands for $16 million. Also in 2016, Mondelēz International attempted to acquire Hershey to create the world's largest candy company. The nonprofit trust that controlled Hershey was ultimately able to block the buyout attempt.

Mondelēz International's Corporate Strategy and Business Segment Performance in 2017

Mondelēz International's strategy was directed at exploiting its powerful brands of snack foods across the 165 country markets where its products were sold. Brands such as Oreo, Milka, Cadbury, Nabisco, Honey Maid, Trident, and Tang were popular in almost all markets where the company competed and provided for a range of products that cut across most all consumer snacking desires. For example, the company's product line included biscuits or cookies, chocolate, candy, gum, and beverages. The company's acquisitions were directed at expanding its brand portfolio into rapidly growing snack categories. The company's 2015 acquisition of Enjoy Life Foods added allergen-free and gluten-free chips and nut-free chocolate and seed and fruit products to its lineup of snacks.

The company's strategy sought to expand margins through programs to boost cost-efficiency in its manufacturing and supply chain activities. However, the company was committed to providing additional resources needed to expand marketing and sales capabilities in key markets, especially in emerging markets. The company announced its Sustainability 2020 goals in 2015 for reducing carbon emissions, reducing deforestation within its agricultural supply chain, focusing on water reduction efforts, and reducing packaging and manufacturing waste. The promotion of moderation in snacking was also an important element of the company's social responsibility and sustainability strategy.

The company was organized into four reportable segments based on geographic markets: North America; Latin America; Europe; and Asia, Middle East, and Africa (AMEA). Within each geographic reporting division were five product categories—biscuits (including cookies, crackers, and salted snacks), chocolate, gum and candy, beverages, and cheese and grocery. Exhibit 3 presents a financial summary for its geographic segments for 2014 through 2016. The revenue contributions of each product category in each geographic region are presented in Exhibit 4.

EXHIBIT 3

Financial Summary for Mondelēz International's Geographic Segments, 2014–2016 (in millions)

Net revenues

	2016	2015	2014
Latin America	$ 3,392	$ 4,988	$ 5,153
AMEA	5,816	6,002	6,367
Europe	9,755	11,672	15,788
North America	6,960	6,974	6,936
Net revenues	$25,923	$29,636	$34,244

(Continued)

(Continued)

Earnings from continuing operations before income taxes	2016	2015	2014
Operating income:			
Latin America	$ 271	$ 485	$ 475
AMEA	506	389	530
Europe	1,267	1,350	1,952
North America	1,078	1,105	922
Unrealized gains/(losses) on hedging activities	(94)	96	(112)
General corporate expenses	(291)	(383)	(317)
Amortization of intangibles	(176)	(181)	(206)
Gains on coffee business transactions and divestitures	9	6,822	—
Loss on deconsolidation of Venezuela	—	(778)	—
Acquisition-related costs	(1)	(8)	(2)
Operating income	2,569	8,897	3,242
Interest and other expense, net	(1,115)	(1,013)	(688)
Earnings from continuing operations before income taxes	$ 1,454	$ 7,884	$ 2,554

Total assets	2016	2015	2014
Latin America	$ 5,156	$ 4,673	6,470
AMEA	10,031	10,460	10,549
Europe	19,934	21,026	27,240
North America	20,694	21,175	21,287
Equity method investments	5,585	5,387	662
Unallocated assets	138	122	563
Total assets	$61,538	$62,843	$66,771

Depreciation expense	2016	2015	2014
Latin America	$ 92	$ 94	$ 118
AMEA	161	155	154
Europe	253	299	407
North America	141	165	174
Total depreciation expense	$ 647	$ 713	$ 853

Capital expenditures	2016	2015	2014
Latin America	$ 321	$ 354	$ 460
AMEA	349	381	451
Europe	294	517	553
North America	260	262	178
Total capital expenditures	$ 1,224	$ 1,514	$ 1,642

Source: Mondelēz International, Inc., 2016 10-K.

All of the five business segments competed in product markets that were characterized by strong competitive rivalry that required strong distribution and marketing skills to attract consumer demand and ensure product availability in supermarkets, discount clubs, mass merchandisers, convenience stores, drug

EXHIBIT 4

Mondelēz International's Net Revenues by Product Category and Geographic Region, 2014–2016 (in millions)

For the Year Ended December 31, 2016

	Latin America	AMEA	Europe	North America	Total
Biscuits	$ 734	$1,588	$ 2,703	$5,565	$10,590
Chocolate	743	1,901	4,840	255	7,739
Gum & Candy	938	953	916	1,140	3,947
Beverages	657	611	177	—	1,445
Cheese & Grocery	320	763	1,119	—	2,202
Total net revenues	$3,392	$5,816	$ 9,755	$6,960	$25,923

For the Year Ended December 31, 2015

	Latin America	AMEA	Europe	North America	Total
Biscuits	$1,605	$1,539	$ 2,680	$5,569	$11,393
Chocolate	840	1,928	5,050	256	8,074
Gum & Candy	1,091	1,003	1,015	1,149	4,258
Beverages	767	730	1,763	—	3,260
Cheese & Grocery	685	802	1,164	—	2,651
Total net revenues	$4,988	$6,002	$11,672	$6,974	$29,636

For the Year Ended December 31, 2014

	Latin America	AMEA	Europe	North America	Total
Biscuits	$1,322	$1,442	$ 3,259	$5,486	$11,509
Chocolate	1,054	2,073	5,997	296	9,420
Gum & Candy	1,176	1,098	1,232	1,154	4,660
Beverages	940	836	3,902	—	5,678
Cheese & Grocery	661	918	1,398	—	2,977
Total net revenues	$5,153	$6,367	$15,788	$6,936	$34,244

Source: Mondelēz International, Inc. 2016 10-K.

stores, and retail food locations serviced by its food distribution operations. Brand building, consumer health and wellness, and advertising and promotions were all critical to success in the industry. In fact, Mondelēz's ability to compete against lower-priced branded and store-brand products was a function of its ability to successfully differentiate its products from lower-priced alternatives. Also, differentiation was essential to retaining shelf space as the retail grocery industry consolidated and provided retailers with greater leverage in negotiations with food manufacturers. The company's successful differentiation of its products had also allowed it to achieve organic revenue growth of 1.3 percent in 2016 and 1.4 percent in 2015 through net price increases.

The company's processed foods divisions had experienced cost increases as inflationary forces had led to higher prices for commodities used in the manufacture of its products such as coffee, cocoa, oils, nuts, and sugar. However, Mondelēz utilized commodity hedging to protect against spikes in ingredient costs. In addition, price increases made possible by its strong product differentiation had more than offset the increased cost of commodity inputs in 2015. Also, the production of Mondelēz International's products was regulated by the U.S.

Food and Drug Administration in the United States, and similar organizations in the 165 countries where its products were sold. The company's packaging practices were also regulated by governmental agencies in the United States and the European Union.

Latin America

In 2016, Modelēz International's Latin American division experienced a 32.0 percent decline in revenue because of the deconsolidation of its Venezuelan operations, unfavorable exchange rates and declining sales. The strong U.S. dollar relative to the Brazilian real, Mexican peso, Venezuelan bolivar, and Argentinean peso accounted for the majority of exchange rate losses. The sales decline was brought about by the elimination of selected low-margin products from its product mix and consumer resistance to price increases. The spin-off of the company's coffee brands also affected sales in Latin America in 2015. Modelēz's operating income decreased by 44.1 percent in 2016 as a result of higher raw material costs in addition to the factors that also contributed to the division's decline in revenue.

Asia, Middle East, Africa (AMEA)

Modelēz International's revenues in AMEA declined by $186 million during 2016–primarily for the same reasons that caused the decline in net revenues in Latin America. Exchange rate losses related to the value of the U.S. dollar relative to the Australian dollar, Chinese yuan, Indian rupee, South African rand, Egyptian pound, Nigerian naira, and Philippine peso; consumer resistance to price increases; the elimination of low-margin products; and spin-off of coffee brands all contributed to the decline. Operating income for the segment increased by 30.1 percent between 2015 and 2016 because of lower manufacturing costs, higher net pricing, and the elimination of costs associated with its former coffee business. However, the cost reductions were partially offset by the division's higher raw material costs, decline in unit sales volume limiting scale economies, and unfavorable exchange rates.

Europe

Segment revenues declined by 16.4 percent in Europe between 2015 and 2016 after the spin-off of the company's coffee brands and the effect of exchange rate adjustments, sales volume declines, and lower net pricing associated with price discounting. The segment's operating income declined by 6.1 percent in 2016 because of coffee deconsolidation costs and higher ingredient costs. Earlier in the decade, the segment had been among the company's most successful divisions, with traditionally strong revenue and operating income growth. The company held a number-one position in the snack foods industry in Europe, which was growing 1.4 times faster than the overall European processed foods industry. While growth in the snack foods industry in Europe was attractive, developing markets in Latin America and Asia offered the most attractive growth opportunities for Modelēz, Nestlé, and other food companies in 2017.

North America

Net revenues decreased by $14 million or 0.2 percent between 2015 and 2016 because of an accounting calendar change, price discounts on biscuits, and declining sales volumes. The cost of price discounts on biscuits was partially offset by price increases on chocolate, gum, and candy. Operating income in North America decreased by 2.4 percent between 2015 and 2016 because of higher advertising and promotional costs, the year-over-year impact of the prior-year calendar change, higher ingredient costs, and lower net pricing. The division was able to limit its decrease in operating income through lower manufacturing costs, lower selling, general and administrative expenses, and the sale of an intangible asset.

Modelēz International's Performance in Mid-2017

Modelēz International's results since its spin-off from Kraft Foods had been underwhelming with no sustained growth in revenues or profit measures when excluding the effects of one-time extraordinary items. Both revenues and net earnings before divestiture gains had been in decline since 2013—see Exhibits 1 and 5. While trends in its revenues and operating income had been mostly negative, its stock had performed relatively well since the divestiture of its coffee brands. The divestiture and subsequent

EXHIBIT 5

Mondelēz International, Inc. Consolidated Statements of Earnings, 2014–2016 (in millions, except per share amounts)

	2016	2015	2014
Net revenues	$25,923	$29,636	$34,244
Cost of sales	15,795	18,124	21,647
Gross profit	10,128	11,512	12,597
Selling, general and administrative expenses	6,540	7,577	8,457
Asset impairment and exit costs	852	901	692
Gains on divestitures	(9)	(6,822)	—
Loss on deconsolidation of Venezuela	—	778	—
Amortization of intangibles	176	181	206
Operating income	2,569	8,897	3,242
Interest and other expense, net	1,115	1,013	688
Earnings before income taxes	1,454	7,884	2,554
Provision for income taxes	(129)	593	353
Gain on equity method investment exchange	43	—	—
Equity method investment net earnings	301	—	—
Net earnings	1,669	7,291	2,201
Noncontrolling interest earnings	(10)	(24)	(17)
Net earnings attributable to Mondelēz International	$ 1,659	$ 7,267	$ 2,184
Per share data:			
Basic earnings per share attributable to Mondelēz International	$1.07	$4.49	$1.29
Diluted earnings per share attributable to Mondelēz International	$1.05	$4.44	$1.28

Source: Mondelēz International, Inc., 2016 10-K.

equity interest in the coffee business had resulted in some changes to its balance sheets. The company's balance sheets for 2015 and 2016 are presented in Exhibit 6.

The company's results for the first quarter of 2017 showed signs of stabilization with revenues for the first three months of the year declining by 0.6 percent and its operating profit for the first quarter of 2017 improving from $722 million to $840 million. Net earnings for the quarter ending March 31, 2017, of $633 million were 13.6 percent higher than net earnings of $554 in the same quarter the year prior. Mondelēz 's improvements in operating income and net income were primarily the result of lower restructuring costs and the benefit of a settlement of a Cadbury tax dispute.

Mondelēz International Chairwoman and CEO Irene Rosenfeld was bullish on the company's results for

the first quarter of 2017. "We had a solid start to the year despite challenging market conditions. We delivered both top-line organic growth and strong margin expansion in the quarter, while also making critical investments for our future. We remain confident in and committed to our balanced strategy for both top- and bottom-line growth, continuing to focus on what we can control to deliver long-term value creation for our shareholders."[1]

Although Mondelēz International's senior management believed the company's strategy was on track to deliver long-term value to shareholders, investors such as William Ackman were less convinced. In fact, some degree of its relatively strong stock performance since 2016 was a result of takeover rumors involving the company. In August 2016, Mondelēz shares rose when news that its attempt to acquire Hershey had failed, with investors seeing the

EXHIBIT 6

Mondelēz International, Inc., Consolidated Balance Sheets, 2015–2016 (in millions)

	2016	2015
ASSETS		
Cash and cash equivalents	$ 1,741	$ 1,870
Trade receivables (net of allowances of $58 at December 31, 2016, and $54 at December 31, 2015)	2,611	2,634
Other receivables (net of allowances of $93 at December 31, 2016, and $109 at December 31, 2015)	859	1,212
Inventories, net	2,469	2,609
Other current assets	800	633
Total current assets	8,480	8,958
Property, plant and equipment, net	8,229	8,362
Goodwill	20,276	20,664
Intangible assets, net	18,101	18,768
Prepaid pension assets	159	69
Deferred income taxes	358	277
Equity method investments	5,585	5,387
Other assets	350	358
TOTAL ASSETS	$61,538	$62,843
LIABILITIES		
Short-term borrowings	$ 2,531	$ 236
Current portion of long-term debt	1,451	605
Accounts payable	5,318	4,890
Accrued marketing	1,745	1,634
Accrued employment costs	736	844
Other current liabilities	2,636	2,713
Total current liabilities	14,417	10,922
Long-term debt	13,217	14,557
Deferred income taxes	4,721	4,750
Accrued pension costs	2,014	2,183
Accrued postretirement health care costs	382	499
Other liabilities	1,572	1,832
TOTAL LIABILITIES	36,323	34,743
Commitments and Contingencies		
EQUITY		
Common Stock, no par value (5,000,000,000 shares authorized and 1,996,537,778 shares issued at December 31, 2016, and December 31, 2015)	—	—
Additional paid-in capital	31,847	31,760
Retained earnings	21,149	20,700
Accumulated other comprehensive losses	(11,122)	(9,986)
Treasury stock, at cost (468,172,237 shares at December 31, 2016, and 416,504,624 shares at December 31, 2015)	(16,713)	(14,462)
Total Mondelēz International Shareholders' Equity	25,161	28,012
Noncontrolling interest	54	88
TOTAL EQUITY	25,215	28,100
TOTAL LIABILITIES AND EQUITY	$61,538	$62,843

Source: Mondelēz International, Inc., 2016 10-K.

failure as an opening for a takeover of Mondelēz by a larger food company.

In December 2016, the company's share spiked by 12 percent after a rumor emerged that Kraft-Heinz was planning to acquire Mondelēz. Kraft-Heinz was the world's fifth largest food company at the time and had resulted from the 2015 merger between Kraft Foods Group and H. J. Heinz Company. Mondelēz International shares surged an additional 5 percent in February 2017 after the collapse of a planned merger between Kraft-Heinz and Unilever. The failure of the merger of Kraft-Heinz and Unilever gave investors stronger confidence that Kraft-Heinz would purchase the company and drove Mondelēz shares to an all-time high by May 2017. Going into the last half of 2017, Mondelēz management was confident in its corporate strategy and projected that the company would achieve at least 1 percent organic revenue growth and a 16 percent operating income margin to deliver double-digit growth in EPS by year-end.

ENDNOTE

[1] As quoted in "Mondelez International Reports Q1 Results," *Globe Newswire,* May 2, 2017.

Robin Hood

■ connect*   JOSEPH LAMPEL Alliance Manchester Business School

It was in the spring of the second year of his insurrection against the High Sheriff of Nottingham that Robin Hood took a walk in Sherwood Forest. As he walked, he pondered the progress of the campaign, the disposition of his forces, the Sheriff's recent moves, and the options that confronted him.

The revolt against the Sheriff had begun as a personal crusade. It erupted out of Robin's conflict with the Sheriff and his administration. However, alone Robin Hood could do little. He therefore sought allies, men with grievances and a deep sense of justice. Later he welcomed all who came, asking few questions and demanding only a willingness to serve. Strength, he believed, lay in numbers.

He spent the first year forging the group into a disciplined band, united in enmity against the Sheriff and willing to live outside the law. The band's organization was simple. Robin ruled supreme, making all important decisions. He delegated specific tasks to his lieutenants. Will Scarlett was in charge of intelligence and scouting. His main job was to shadow the Sheriff and his men, always alert to their next move. He also collected information on the travel plans of rich merchants and tax collectors. Little John kept discipline among the men and saw to it that their archery was at the high peak that their profession demanded. Scarlett took care of the finances, converting loot to cash, paying shares of the take, and finding suitable hiding places for the surplus. Finally, Much the Miller's son had the difficult task of provisioning the ever-increasing band of Merry Men.

The increasing size of the band was a source of satisfaction for Robin, but also a source of concern. The fame of his Merry Men was spreading, and new recruits were pouring in from every corner of England. As the band grew larger, their small bivouac became a major encampment. Between raids the men milled about, talking and playing games. Vigilance was in decline, and discipline was becoming harder to enforce. "Why," Robin reflected, "I don't know half the men I run into these days."

The growing band was also beginning to exceed the food capacity of the forest. Game was becoming scarce, and supplies had to be obtained from outlying villages. The cost of buying food was beginning to drain the band's financial reserves at the very moment when revenues were in decline. Travelers, especially those with the most to lose, were now giving the forest a wide berth. This was costly and inconvenient to them, but it was preferable to having all their goods confiscated.

Robin believed that the time had come for the Merry Men to change their policy of outright confiscation of goods to one of a fixed transit tax. His lieutenants strongly resisted this idea. They were proud of the Merry Men's famous motto: "Rob the rich and give to the poor." "The farmers and the townspeople," they argued, "are our most important allies. How can we tax them, and still hope for their help in our fight against the Sheriff?"

Robin wondered how long the Merry Men could keep to the ways and methods of their early days. The Sheriff was growing stronger and becoming better organized. He now had the money and the men and was beginning to harass the band, probing for its weaknesses. The tide of events was beginning to turn against the Merry Men. Robin felt that the campaign must be decisively concluded before the Sheriff had a chance to deliver a mortal blow. "But how," he wondered, "could this be done?"

Robin had often entertained the possibility of killing the Sheriff, but the chances for this seemed increasingly remote. Besides, killing the Sheriff might satisfy his personal thirst for revenge, but it would not improve the situation. Robin had hoped that the perpetual state of unrest and the Sheriff's failure to collect taxes would lead to his removal from office. Instead, the Sheriff used his political connections to obtain reinforcement. He had powerful friends at court and was well regarded by the regent, Prince John.

Prince John was vicious and volatile. He was consumed by his unpopularity among the people, who wanted the imprisoned King Richard back. He also lived in constant fear of the barons, who had first given him the regency but were now beginning to dispute his claim to the throne. Several of these barons had set out to collect the ransom that would release King Richard the Lionheart from his jail in Austria. Robin was invited to join the conspiracy in return for future amnesty. It was a dangerous proposition. Provincial banditry was one thing, court intrigue another. Prince John had spies everywhere, and he was known for his vindictiveness. If the conspirators' plan failed, the pursuit would be relentless and retributions swift.

The sound of the supper horn startled Robin from his thoughts. There was the smell of roasting venison in the air. Nothing was resolved or settled. Robin headed for camp promising himself that he would give these problems his utmost attention after tomorrow's raid.

Rosen Hotels & Resorts

connect

RANDALL D. HARRIS Texas A&M University–Corpus Christi

"That's really what it's all about, isn't it?" said Harris Rosen, president of Rosen Hotels & Resorts. "Exemplary service. What we've discovered, and I'm sure that others have identified as well, is that there is a distinct relationship between enthusiastic, happy associates and the company that they work for." Rosen, 76, was the founder, president, and chief operating officer of Rosen Hotels & Resorts. Founded in 1974 in Orlando, Florida, Rosen began with the purchase of one hotel in June of 1974 during the 1970's OPEC oil embargo and a slumping tourist market. In 2016, he presided over a chain of seven hotels and two wholly owned subsidiaries in the greater Orlando, Florida, metropolis.

A special attitude and an infectious warmth seemed to exude from all of the Rosen Hotels & Resorts associates. "We have excellent leadership," said Sarah Sherwin, conference center sales manager at Rosen Shingle Creek, one of the seven hotels in the Rosen Hotels portfolio. "Having Mr. Rosen locally, he's just someone who's great to look up to. He takes care of his associates and he gives back to the community. It's nice to know I'm working for an organization such as ours," she said. Exhibit 1 presents an overview of Rosen Hotels & Resorts. Exhibit 2 presents a photo of Rosen Shingle Creek, the company's premier 1,501-guest room conference facility.

The Golden Rule really described the culture of the Rosen Hotels organization, according to Jonni Kimberly, director of human resources. "It's one thing for a manager in an organization to put their hand on your shoulder and say 'I understand what you're going through,' but it's another thing to say 'I understand what you're going through and we're going to help you go through

it,'" said Kimberly. This level of caring was reflected in real services for Rosen associates. There was an onsite health care clinic that associates could visit while on the clock and an outreach center to assist associates and their dependents with real-life situations, like the loss of a family member or a medical emergency.

Guests at Rosen Hotels & Resorts said they enjoyed a tremendous hotel experience. "I had the experience of my life at this hotel," one guest said, talking about Rosen Shingle Creek. "The staff were really friendly and professional. The hotel was very clean, beautiful, and peaceful. I love it!" Customers often spoke about the friendly staff, competitive room rates, and the spacious, clean, and comfortable rooms. Many Rosen Hotels guests were long-time repeat customers. Some, in fact, had been returning for 25 to 30 years.

The Rosen ethos was also reflected in the company's commitment to corporate social responsibility. In 1993, as it became clear that financial success for the Rosen organization was ensured, Harris Rosen had an epiphany and began to give back. The Tangelo Park Program, which was created out of that decision, ensured that every child living in the Tangelo Park neighborhood would have not only a free preschool education, but that each of them would be able to go to college, technical school, or a Florida public university, free of charge. This made Rosen Hotels & Resorts not only a terrific place to visit but also an active and caring member of the greater Orlando, Florida, community.

EXHIBIT 1

Rosen Hotels & Resorts—Locations and Subsidiaries

Hotel/ Subsidiary Name	Address	Target Market/ Subsidiary Focus	Website
Rosen Inn	6327 International Drive Orlando, FL 32819	Leisure Traveler	www.roseninn6327.com/
Rosen Inn International	7600 International Drive Orlando, FL 32819	Leisure Traveler	roseninn7600.com/
Rosen Inn Pointe Orlando	9000 International Drive Orlando, FL 32819	Leisure Traveler	www.roseninn9000.com/
Rosen Plaza Hotel	9700 International Drive Orlando, FL 32819	Convention Traveler	www.rosenplaza.com/
Rosen Centre Hotel	9840 International Drive Orlando, FL 32819	Convention Traveler	www.rosencentre.com/
Rosen Shingle Creek	9939 Universal Blvd. Orlando, FL 32819	Convention Traveler	www.rosenshinglecreek.com/
Clarion Inn Lake Buena Vista	8442 Palm Parkway Lake Buena Vista, FL 32836	Leisure Traveler	www.clarionlbv.com/
ProvInsure	9700 International Drive Orlando, FL 32819-8114	Health Care, Risk Management, Benefits	www.provinsure.com/
Millennium Technology Group	7657 Golf Channel Drive Orlando FL, 32819	Information Technology	mtg-fl.com/

Source: Rosen Hotels & Resorts.

EXHIBIT 2

Rosen Shingle Creek

© RosalreneBetancourt 11/Alamy Stock Photo

U.S. Hotel and Motel Industry

Companies in the U.S. hotel and motel industry provided short-term accommodations in hotels, motels, motor hotels, and resort hotels and motels. Many establishments also offered other services such as food and beverages, recreation, conference facilities, laundry, and onsite parking. The industry was highly concentrated, with the top five companies earning approximately 42 percent of industry revenue. Exhibit 3 shows selected financial and operating statistics for the top five lodging chains in 2015.

Recent Performance

Following the global financial crisis of 2007–2008, growth recovered in the U.S. hotel and motel industry and had been strong from 2011 to 2015. Overall, the hotel industry had outperformed the broader U.S. economy and was driven by robust demand growth from both leisure and business travelers, as well as international business and leisure travelers visiting the United States. Over the five years to 2015, the industry was expected to grow at an annualized rate of 3.7 percent to reach $166.5 billion in revenues.

EXHIBIT 3

Selected Financial and Operating Statistics for the Five Major U.S. Hotel Chains, 2015

Company Name	U.S. Market Share	Number of Properties	Number of Employees, 2015	Revenues, 2015	Net Income, 2015	Key Brands
Hilton Worldwide Holdings Inc.	13.7%	4,000	157,000	$22.9 billion	$748 million	Hilton, Hilton Garden Inn, Doubletree, Embassy Suites, Hampton, Homewood Suites
Marriott International, Inc.	13.5%	4,175	127,500	$22.5 billion	$859 million	Marriott, Ritz-Carlton, SpringHill Suites, Fairfield Inn, Residence Inn, Courtyard, Townplace Suites
Intercontinental Hotels Group PLC	7.5%	4,900	7,797	$12.5 billion	$391 million	Intercontinental, Crowne Plaza, Holiday Inn, Holiday Inn Express, Staybridge Suites, Candlewood Suites
Starwood Hotels & Resorts Worldwide Inc.	3.7%	1,207	188,000	$5.8 billion	$489 million	Sheraton, Westin, W, Four Points by Sheraton, St. Regis, Le Meridien, Element
Wyndham Worldwide Corporation	3.7%	5,700	37,700	$5.5 billion	$612 million	Ramada, Super 8 Motels, Travelodge, Days Inn, Howard Johnson, Amerihost Inn, Knights Inn, Villager, Wingate Inns

Sources: IBISWorld; Mergent Online.

Approximately 50 percent of industry revenue came from domestic leisure travelers. According to the U.S. Travel Association, about three out of every four trips were taken for leisure purposes. Business travelers accounted for about 30.5 percent of industry revenue. In the business segment, general business travel accounted for about 18.2 percent of industry revenue while meetings, conferences, and events accounted for 12.3 percent of industry spending. In general, business travelers spent more than leisure travelers, making them an attractive segment of the market for hotel and motel chains to pursue. International visitors to the United States accounted for about 19.5 percent of industry revenue. Major countries of origin for international visitors included Canada, Mexico, the United Kingdom, Japan, and Germany.

Hotel development had been sluggish following the global economic recession. Development of new hotels hit a low in 2011. As the economy began to accelerate from 2011 to 2015, demand for hotel rooms began to move ahead of room inventory, causing room rates to rise. In the hotel industry, the metric used to track this was called RevPAR, or revenue per available room. RevPAR was typically calculated as the average daily room rate times the occupancy rate. In 2015, industry RevPAR had continued to rise, and hotel chains were planning for increased hotel expansions and new hotel and motel openings.

Online Hotel Reservations

The widespread adoption and increasing usage of the Internet had greatly benefited the U.S. hotel and motel industry. Hotel operators were increasingly using the Internet to gather information about prospective and future clients, target and focus their marketing campaigns, manage customer reservations, and purchase supplies for their properties, all while lowering costs. Guest rewards programs frequently used targeted e-mails to communicate with their members to drive repeat hotel business, particularly for frequent travelers.

Travelers were also increasingly using the Internet to connect to lodging providers. In 2015, the number-one channel by which hotel guests booked their reservation was the websites of the major hotel/motel chains. Fully 27.9 percent of all bookings in 2014 were via the hotel website. Hotel website bookings were up 6.9 percent in fiscal 2014, almost double the growth rate of the industry. Online travel agents, such as Expedia and Priceline.com, were 14.9 percent of all hotel/motel bookings. Increasingly, hotel operators were selling a portion of their unsold rooms via these online travel agents, thereby increasingly their revenues and occupancy rates. Exhibit 4 presents the channels for hotel room reservations in 2014.

The platform by which customers were purchasing online was also beginning to be increasingly conducted via mobile applications. Mobile technologies, including smartphones, tablets, and wearable devices, were an increasingly important technological gateway for room bookings. Adara Global estimated that two in three hotel guests had a smartphone, with 78 percent smartphone ownership for frequent travelers between the ages of 18 to 48. Hotel chain La Quinta Inn & Suites estimated that mobile devices drove 23 percent of its digital traffic in 2012. HotelMarketing.com was forecasting that mobile was poised to become the dominant method for online booking in the very near future, particularly for last-minute hotel reservations.

Orlando, Florida: The Number-One Tourist Destination

The number-one tourist destination in the United States was Orlando, Florida. In 2015, the greater Orlando metropolitan area hosted 66 million visitors, according to Visit Orlando. Many visitors to Orlando, particular from outside the United States, arrived via the Orlando International Airport (Airport Code: MCO). Orlando International Airport handled 35 million passengers in 2014, up almost 3 percent for the year, according to the Orlando Economic Development Commission. The primary driver for hotel occupancy in Orlando was tourist attractions: Orlando boasted four major theme parks (including Walt Disney World, Universal Studios, and SeaWorld Orlando), as well as two water parks. Travel to Orlando was also heavily driven by trade shows and conventions hosted at the Orange County Convention Center. In 2014, the convention center hosted 1.1 million attendees, an all-time high.

The 2015 demand in the Orlando market for hotel and motel rooms was very strong. Tracking national trends, hotel operators had been slow to expand or build new hotels following the 2007–2008 recession. As a result, room inventory in Orlando increased only 1.7 percent in the first half of 2015, while demand for rooms increased 5.7 percent. As a result, room occupancy rates, average daily rates, and revenue per available room (RevPAR) had all shown strong growth in 2015. Exhibit 5 shows metro Orlando hospitality statistics for 2012 to 2014.

Orlando Tourism and Lodging Patterns

The Orlando hotel market was divided into seven submarkets. Two of these markets, the Lake Buena

EXHIBIT 4

Share of Hotel and Motel Reservations by Booking Method, 2014

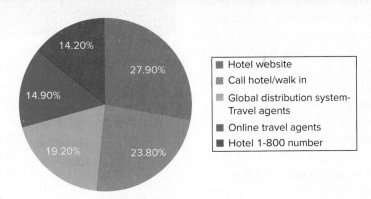

- Hotel website — 27.90%
- Call hotel/walk in — 23.80%
- Global distribution system-Travel agents — 19.20%
- Online travel agents — 14.90%
- Hotel 1-800 number — 14.20%

Sources: TravelClick; IBISWorld.

EXHIBIT 5

Metro Orlando Hospitality Statistics, 2012–2014

Average Daily Room Rate ($)

Rank	Submarket	2012	2013	2014
1	Lake Buena Vista	$103.65	$114.98	$120.62
2	International Drive	$109.03	$111.84	$119.02
3	Orlando South	$ 98.00	$ 99.13	$104.76
4	Orlando Central	$ 76.00	$ 77.50	$ 84.43
5	Kissimmee East	$ 74.96	$ 77.29	$ 82.06
6	Orlando North	$ 70.72	$ 71.76	$ 76.01
7	Kissimmee West	$ 65.44	$ 62.25	$ 62.97

Hotel Occupancy Rate (%)

Rank	Submarket	2012	2013	2014
1	Lake Buena Vista	76.1%	77.1%	81.3%
2	Orlando South	70.0%	73.4%	76.2%
3	International Drive	70.6%	71.5%	74.5%
4	Orlando Central	63.0%	66.5%	70.1%
5	Kissimmee East	62.0%	62.9%	64.3%
6	Orlando North	57.3%	61.9%	63.9%
7	Kissimmee West	54.2%	55.0%	59.4%

Source: HVS Miami.

Vista district and the International Drive district, accounted for approximately 64 percent of total hotel inventory. The Lake Buena Vista district represented hotels and motels that were adjacent or nearby to the Walt Disney World Resort, located to the southwest of Orlando along the Interstate 4 corridor. The International Drive district, located in the central or west central part of Orlando, was the area closest to the Universal Studios theme parks, Sea World, and the Orange County Convention Center. International Drive ran north–south along Interstate 4, north of the Disney complex. Hotel development and demand growth had been particularly heavy in both of these areas. In addition, International Drive was increasingly becoming a tourist destination of its own accord, with restaurants, nightclubs, and a brand-new 400-foot observation wheel. Exhibit 6 presents Metro Orlando Inventory Distribution in 2015.

Orlando was the second-largest hotel market in the United States, with 489 properties and 127,420 rooms. The largest hotel owner and operator in the market, with 19 properties and 24,432 rooms, was the Walt Disney World Resort. Disney alone accounted for approximately 20 percent of the Orlando hotel market. Most of the Disney properties were located in the Lake Buena Vista district near the Walt Disney World Resort. All of the major hotel and motel chains had a presence in the Orlando market. Rosen Hotels &

EXHIBIT 6

Metro Orlando Hotel Inventory Distribution, 2015

Legend:
- International Drive
- Lake Buena Vista
- Kissimmee East
- Orlando South
- Orlando Central
- Orlando North
- Kissimmee West

Source: HVS Miami.

Resorts, with seven properties and approximately 6,300 rooms, held about 5 percent of the Orlando market. The majority of the Rosen properties were located on International Drive, near Universal Studios and the Orange County Convention Center, with one property in the Lake Buena Vista district near Walt Disney World.

Company History

"He came from a very humble family on the lower East Side of New York City," said Dr. Abraham Pizam, dean of the Rosen College of Hospitality at the University of Central Florida. "Whatever he achieved throughout the years, he achieved by his own sweat, tears, and brains." Harris Rosen traveled a long road to reach the current success of Rosen Hotels & Resorts. Rosen recalled when he did all of the gardening, and many of the other roles, by himself at his first hotel. "One has to sacrifice, I think," Rosen said, "Although living where you work for 16 years is a bit crazy. But it required that kind of attention." Exhibit 7 presents a timeline of key events in the Rosen Hotels & Resorts history.

At the age of 10, Harris Rosen worked weekends for his dad at the Waldorf Astoria hotel in New York City. His father was a security engineer and poster painter and earned extra money creating place cards for the hotel's fancy banquets. Harris's job (for which he was paid one penny per card) was to erase any pencil marks on the card and place them in a shoebox in alphabetical sequence. Then Harris and his dad would take the cards to the Waldorf ballroom. There they would meet with the banquet manager, who would have the cards placed around the appropriate table. To get to the ballroom, Harris and his dad would often have to take an elevator. One day as they were entering the elevator, Harris noticed a beautiful young blonde woman standing next to a tall, distinguished gentleman. Harris quietly asked his dad to introduce him to the young lady. His dad said, "First I will introduce you to the gentleman." Harris met Ambassador Joseph Kennedy (U.S. ambassador to Great Britain), who then introduced Harris to the young lady— Marilyn Monroe. Meeting Marilyn Monroe helped determined Harris's destiny because he thought if he could meet someone like Marilyn Monroe in the elevator of a hotel, then the hotel industry was really a business that he wanted to consider.

EXHIBIT 7

Key Milestones in the Rosen Hotels & Resorts History

1974: Harris Rosen purchases a Quality Inn, now known as the *Rosen Inn International.*

1975: Rosen purchases the International Inn, now known as the *Rosen Inn.*

1984: The Quality Inn Plaza, now known as *Rosen Inn at Pointe Orlando,* opens after construction is completed.

1987: Comfort Inn Lake Buena Vista, now known as *Clarion Inn Lake Buena Vista,* opens.

1989: GRSC Insurance Agency, now named *ProvInsure,* is incorporated and opens.

1991: Clarion Plaza, now known as *Rosen Plaza,* opens for convention guests.

1991: The first Rosen Medical Center opens adjacent to the Rosen Inn International.

1993: The Tangelo Park Pilot Program is launched, guaranteeing children an education.

1995: Rosen's second full-service convention property, Omni Rosen, opens. Now known as the *Rosen Centre Hotel.*

1997: *Millennium Technology Group* opens for business.

2004: The University of Central Florida Rosen College of Hospitality Management opens.

2006: *Rosen Shingle Creek* opens for convention business with 1,501 guest rooms and 462,000 square feet of meeting space.

2012: Brand-new 12,000-square-foot Rosen Medical Center opens.

Source: Rosen Hotels & Resorts.

Upon completing high school, Harris was admitted to Cornell University's School of Hotel Administration, where he majored in hotel management. A member of the ROTC program, he graduated from Cornell after four years and immediately went into the military. After basic training at Fort Bragg, North Carolina, he served as a first lieutenant for three years, including overseas assignments in Asia and Europe. Harris still returns to Fort Bragg, home of the 82nd Airborne, to do an annual 15,000-foot jump with the Golden Knights. After Rosen was discharged from the military he returned to New York City and went to work at the Waldorf Astoria.

The only job available at the Waldorf at the time was a file clerk in the Personnel department. In a relatively short time, Rosen worked his way up to sales manager in the Convention Sales department and then was promoted to the Hilton Hotels Management Training Program. During the next several years, Harris worked in six Hilton Hotels throughout the United States. In Dallas, Texas, he was hired by an insurance company owner who had just acquired a hotel in Acapulco, Mexico. Harris moved to Acapulco to manage the hotel. After about a year there, the presidency in Mexico changed. The new government passed a law that prevented non-Mexican citizens from owning more than 49 percent of any real estate property. As a result, Harris's boss sold 51 percent of his equity in the Acapulco hotel. A Mexican group took over the hotel, and Harris was terminated.

Disheartened, he drove to California and quickly learned that the Walt Disney Company was planning a huge new development, Walt Disney World, in Orlando, Florida. Rosen applied for a job and was hired as an administrator of hotel planning for Walt Disney World. He spent about a year in California and then moved to Orlando, working as a planning and hotel management supervisor for several years. Walt Disney World opened in October 1971. In 1973, he was called in for a meeting with his boss. Harris hoped that the meeting was about a promotion and a raise. Instead, he was told that even though he did a great job for the company, he was not a good fit for the Disney organization. Harris was again terminated.

In October 1973, the Organization of the Petroleum Exporting Countries (OPEC) had declared an oil embargo. In the United States, gas prices spiked and supplies were being rationed. As a result, in Orlando, the tourism industry was in complete disarray. Many hotels were in serious financial trouble; some had declared bankruptcy and others were being foreclosed. Despite these circumstances, Harris believed that he could succeed. He started looking for a hotel to purchase. After months of searching, he found a small motel in Orlando on International Drive with frontage onto Interstate 4. He approached the owner of the hotel about a meeting.

The owner, desperate to get out of the hotel business, hugged Rosen tightly after hearing of Rosen's interest in buying the hotel. "He actually cracked one of my ribs," said Rosen. The financial condition of the hotel was stressed as well. The property was operating at 15 percent occupancy and was hemorrhaging

cash. The owner also told Rosen that he had not had a chance to spend any time with his wife and three children and was a mess both psychologically and physically. The owner regarded Rosen as a lifesaver.

After a series of meetings, Harris Rosen found himself in a room with the hotel owner and a representative from the hotel's mortgage company. The banker asked Rosen, "Harris, how much money do you have in the bank?" Rosen paused for a moment and then said, "Sir, I have about $20,000 in the bank." The banker extended his hand and said, "We have a deal. $20,000 down, and you assume the $2.5 million mortgage."

The deal was struck right then and there on June 24, 1974. "Wow," thought Rosen, "I just purchased a hotel running at 15 percent occupancy. I must be crazy!" He walked into his office, sat down behind his desk, and cried. He thought that he had just done the dumbest thing in the world. However, Harris Rosen also had a plan. He began to aggressively market his property to the many motor coach companies along the East Coast, traveling (often hitchhiking) to court their business, and offering them dramatically discounted room rates to secure their business. "Motor coaches were still able to get gas," said Rosen. Eventually, the OPEC oil embargo ended and business began to slowly pick up. Rosen bought a second hotel a year later, and from there his business began to grow. "And that," said Rosen, "was just the beginning."

Organization and Leadership

In 2016, Rosen Hotels & Resorts consisted of seven hotels: Rosen Inn International, Rosen Inn, Rosen Inn Pointe Orlando, Rosen Plaza, Rosen Centre, Rosen Shingle Creek, and the Clarion Inn Lake Buena Vista. Each hotel had its own management team and staff. There were also two subsidiaries, the ProvInsure Insurance Company and the Millennium Technology Group. ProvInsure handled health care, onsite clinics, benefits, risk management and consulting both for Rosen Hotels and for outside clients. The Millennium Technology Group was involved with technology solutions including network security, technology compliance issues, IT staffing, videoconferencing, phone systems, and technology consulting.

In addition to the leadership of the seven hotels and the two subsidiaries, there were a number of centralized functions. Human resources was centralized, as well as health services, reservations, and convention marketing. Harris Rosen's office was onsite at the Rosen Inn International, where he had been for 42 years. "We are not a stereotypical company," said Rosen, "For example, we have never had an organization chart. I don't like them. I don't believe they serve any real purpose and instead they can inhibit a free flow of ideas and suggestions crucial to the success of any company."

Sarah Sherwin at Rosen Shingle Creek agreed. "Everyone shares ideas with each other. It's a true open door policy. We do follow some form of organizational structure, I report to my director, associate director, and so forth, but if I do have an idea, I can go straight to Mr. Rosen, I can go straight to whomever the respective department head is, it's no problem at all. It's welcomed." Jonni Kimberly thought that this open approach to communication was a big part of what made Rosen Hotels not only an excellent place to visit, but a great place to work. "So, you can have an idea," she said, "and you can share the idea and see your idea implemented, and you can see all of that happen pretty quickly."

The company promoted heavily from within, and turnover was arguably the lowest in the hospitality industry. "We only recruit externally if we have to," said Kimberly, "When we opened what is now Rosen Plaza, it was our first convention facility and we recruited externally because we had to. That was 26 years ago and a lot of those folks are still with us."

Summarizing his leadership philosophy, Rosen said, "To be a leader, you must always set an example. Leading from the front is essential."

Strategy

The hotels within Rosen Hotels & Resorts competed in two sectors of the Orlando hotel market: leisure and convention. Rosen Inn, Rosen Inn International, Rosen Inn Pointe Orlando, and Clarion Inn Lake Buena Vista all competed in the leisure segment, with the location of three of these hotels on International Drive, putting them in close proximity to Universal Studios. International Drive had also become a destination itself, with dozens of restaurants, tourist sites, and attractions all along International Drive as well. The Clarion Inn Lake Buena Vista, the remaining leisure

hotel, competed with hotels near Walt Disney World. The International Drive hotels competed mostly in the economy price range, while the Clarion Inn hotel competed at a slightly higher rate.

In addition, Rosen had three convention hotels: Rosen Plaza, Rosen Centre, and the Rosen Shingle Creek. Both the Rosen Plaza and the Rosen Centre were located next to the Orange County Convention Center, and competed in the meeting convention and trade show markets. Rosen Shingle Creek, in addition to catering to the convention market, was a convention and meeting facility in its own right, with close to 500,000 square feet of meeting space. The Shingle Creek facility featured the second-largest column-free ballroom in America, with over 95,000 square feet of space. The convention hotels competed in the upper midscale to upscale price range.

The Rosen Hotels competed in the leisure and convention markets on a number of competitive factors, including location, facilities, amenities, food and beverages, price, and customer service. "The hospitality industry," said Rosen, "is an industry driven primarily by just one thing, great service!!!"

Yield Management and Pricing Strategy

Harris Rosen was generally credited with being a pioneer in yield management. "Most of us think that the airlines invented the process of yield management, but he was one of the first to adopt it officially in his hotels, more than 40 years ago," said Abraham Pizam, dean of the Rosen College of Hospitality. Simply put, yield management was hotel room pricing that reflected supply and demand, and that kept the hotel as full as possible. When times got tough, Rosen hotels would drop their prices. "You cannot generate revenue from an empty room," said Rosen. "We call it heads in beds," said Sarah Sherwin. "You know, as long as you have heads in beds, you're creating jobs for everyone; it's important to make sure that our hotels are occupied, so that our housekeepers have jobs, and they can feed their families." Other hotels, including Disney, had also begun to practice some type of yield management. However, very few hotels could compete with Rosen Hotels on price because recently constructed hotels had been paid for in cash, leaving Rosen Hotels completely debt free.

Employee Benefits

"The benefits package, featuring our own onsite medical clinic, is probably among the best in the industry," said Harris Rosen. Rosen Hotels was self-insured, meaning that much of the company's health care was actually funded and run by the Rosen organization. And—it was affordable. "It's very affordable," said Sarah Sherwin, "Very affordable monthly and our co-pay at the clinic is $5. Annual physicals are complimentary, bloodwork is free, co-pays for offsite visits are $35, and hospital visits do not exceed $750 per hospital visit for a maximum of two visits per year. After the second hospital stay, there is no charge. Hospital visits won't break the bank," she said, "We're really well taken care of." "Our health care plan 'RosenCare' has been analyzed by health care experts who have determined if America replicated the

Rosen Healthcare program as a nation we could save a minimum of $1 trillion a year," said Rosen. Other associate benefits included generic prescription coverage provided by Walmart. "About 93 percent of our associates do not pay anything for their prescriptions," said Rosen.

Rosen Hotels also assisted with retirement planning, and had a family outreach center. "Our outreach center has a social worker and a psychologist, where we deal with helping people through the loss of a family member, emergency situations, housing, and child care," said Jonni Kimberly, "Whatever a person needs, there's a place at work for them to go to get help." Another notable benefit for associates was education scholarships. Dependents of Rosen associates were eligible for free tuition scholarships after the associate had been with the company for three years of service. Rosen associates received free tuition scholarships for themselves to attend college after five years of service. Exhibit 8 presents highlights of the Rosen Hotels benefits package. "If your associates

EXHIBIT 8

Rosen Hotels & Resorts—Associate Benefits

Medical Coverage and Insurance
Rosen Hotels & Resorts provides accessible and affordable health care for Rosen associates and their dependents. Primary care physicians are located in the Rosen Medical Center, located steps away from most Rosen properties. Associates can visit the Medical Center "on the clock." The Medical Center includes a fitness facility and an onsite physical therapy wing.

Prescription Coverage
Prescription coverage is included as part of associate medical benefits. Co-pays are inexpensive and in some cases free of charge.

Family Outreach Center
The mission of the Family Outreach Center is to help people help themselves. The center provides social service information, referrals and emergency support to Rosen associates and their dependents.

Day Care Supplement
The Rosen organization provides a supplement to day care costs for dependent children of associates under the age of four.

Retirement Planning
Rosen associates are encouraged to begin retirement savings by deferring a portion of their income to a 401K retirement account. Rosen Hotels & Resorts matches a portion of weekly retirement deferrals.

Career Training and Advancement
All new employees receive a full-day orientation session. Ongoing training includes certification courses, language classes, and professional development workshops.

Education
After five years of employment, associates receive a scholarship to attend a public or private college or attend a vocational school of their choice. Dependents of Rosen associates are eligible for educational scholarships after the associate has reached three years of employment.

Source: Rosen Hotels & Resorts.

are happy, and if they really love working for you, they will treat guests with the kindness and benevolence you've never, ever imagined," said Rosen.

Rosen Goes Green

Rosen Hotels & Resorts prided themselves on their green initiatives. "As a company, we've always been dedicated to environmentally sound practices and keenly focused on evaluating and improving green standards wherever possible," said DeeDee Baggitt, Rosen Hotel's director of engineering and facilities. Six of the Rosen Hotels carried the Two Palm Green Lodge designation under the Florida Department of Environmental Protection's Green Lodging Program. Rosen Shingle Creek carried a Three Palm designation, and engaged in a number of leading green initiatives, including converting used cooking oil from the hotel into biofuel to operate their golf course equipment. All three of the Rosen convention hotels also carried an APEX designation for meeting or exceeding sustainable meeting standards. The Rosen Medical Center, built in 2012, was a LEED Certified building. "We don't claim to be experts, but we can say that we have been practicing conservation efforts for many years and continue to look for ways to reduce, reuse, and recycle wherever possible," said Rosen.

Corporate Social Responsibility

In 1993, Harris Rosen was sitting in his office. "It was kind of like an epiphany," said Rosen. "I stopped what I was doing, and I heard my inner voice say it was time to say 'Thank you, God.'" Out of that moment was born Rosen Hotels's commitment to corporate social responsibility. Rosen explained,

> Within a very short period of time we put together a program for the Tangelo Park Program (an underserved community), providing every 2, 3, and 4 year old in the Tangelo Park neighborhood with a free preschool education. After high school every youngster who is accepted to a community college, four-year public college, or technical school will have everything paid for—room, board, tuition, books, etc. In the 23 years we have been engaged with the Tangelo Park program we have sent 350 youngsters to college from

a neighborhood that was graduating 55 percent from high school. During the past 8 years our high school graduation rate has soared to 100 percent and about 70 percent of our kids go on to college; and 77 percent of them graduate either from the two-year program or the four-year program. Everything, of course, is paid for.

"This has been so good for the children of Tangelo Park," said Diondra Newton, principal at Tangelo Park Elementary. "You see a huge difference between kids who did the program and those who come from elsewhere." One of Tangelo Park's recent high school graduates, going on to college, agreed. "He has taken the burden off me and my entire family," said Arian Plaza. Exhibit 9 shows a picture of Harris Rosen. He was currently replicating the Tangelo Park program in an even more challenging downtown Orlando neighborhood, the Parramore district, which was five times the size of Tangelo Park.

For the past 20 years the Harris Rosen Foundation had been involved in relief efforts in Haiti, providing school supplies, health care supplies, and more than 250 water filtration systems capable of providing clean drinking water for approximately 200,000 people. A school was also under construction near Port Au Prince.

Approximately 15 years ago, Rosen had donated the land and funds for what was now the largest hospitality college in the nation. The Rosen College of Hospitality at the University of Central Florida had

EXHIBIT 9

Harris Rosen

© Gary W. Green/Orlando Sentinel/McClatchy-Tribune/Tribune Content Agency LLC/Alamy Stock Photo

more than 3,500 students and was ranked the fifth best hospitality college in the world. Harris Rosen had created a $5 million scholarship endowment at the college that provided more than 160 scholarships annually. The Harris Rosen Foundation had also recently assisted in the completion of a new auditorium at the Jack & Lee Rosen Southwest Orlando Jewish Community Center. The preschool at the center was considered among the very best in Central Florida.

"I realize that some people are a bit leery when I talk to them about my concept of 'responsible capitalism' but I absolutely believe that we have an obligation to offer a helping hand to those in need," said Rosen. "For me, an individual who has been blessed beyond anything I could ever have imagined, it is essential to demonstrate my gratitude."

Financial Performance

Rosen Hotels & Resorts was a private company. It considered itself a rather unusual private-sector company because the company was completely debt free. "If we are planning any refurbishing, renovation, or other capital initiatives or perhaps considering constructing new properties, we do not start until we have sufficient funds in the bank," said Rosen. "Recently, we had a rather extensive refurbishing program that lasted over five years and we spent close to $200 million. We believe it is a significant advantage to be a debt-free company."

Rosen Shingle Creek was Rosen Hotels & Resorts's signature property. Rosen, discussing this property, provided insights on the financial management of the company:

> In 2006, on my birthday, September 9, we completed the construction of Rosen Shingle Creek—a 1,501-room property with a beautiful golf course and about a half million square feet of meeting space. The construction was completed in about 18 months at a cost of approximately $200,000 per room or $300 million. We believe our cost was significantly less than what major hotels might spend per room primarily because we are so intimately involved with planning the architectural work, and of course the construction, enabling us to save a tremendous amount of money.

Another recent event offered a look at financial decision making. The company has recently opened Zayde's kosher catering at the Rosen Plaza Hotel, offering kosher catering at both onsite and off-site venues. "One of our catering managers came to me and demonstrated rather clearly that he believed there was a great market for kosher foods," said Rosen. "We studied it, asked lots of questions, and without much fanfare made the decision to proceed. The cost? About $3.5 million. The return on that investment if we are fortunate could be less than five years."

STR Analytics published comparative financial results for the hotel industry. Comparative hotel financial results for independent Orlando hotels in the economy class are presented in Exhibit 10. These financial results were comparable to the leisure hotels in the Rosen Hotel chain, such as Rosen Inn (which was Rosen's property closest to Universal Studios), Rosen Inn International, and Rosen Inn Pointe Orlando.

Future Outlook

"So here we are," said Harris Rosen, "42 years later, debt free, approximately 6,300 rooms, about 4,500 associates who work with us. Close to 6,000 covered lives, including dependents." Rosen believed that his hotel group would continue to grow. "I suspect that before I leave we'll add perhaps another 1,000 rooms," he said. Several hotels had recently gone through renovations, and plans were under way to add rooms at the three convention properties. "But we don't do any refurbishing or construction until we have enough money in the bank," said Rosen, "That in many instances is hundreds of millions of dollars."

Analysts are generally positive on growth in the hotel industry through 2020. Orlando also continues to lead the United States in tourism and in growth, particularly in leisure travel. Rosen, however, sounded a cautionary note. "Generally speaking, there is a lot of uncertainty in the world today," he said, "That is impacting every aspect of our business." Rosen was concerned about a number of markets that Orlando had relied on for many years, including Brazil and Puerto Rico. Rosen said that the strategy was to keep the hotels in top shape. "There's always something to do," he said. "If we're not building something, we are renovating or refurbishing, which we believe are critical for our success."

EXHIBIT 10

Orlando Comparative Hotel Financial Results for Independent Hotels—Economy Class, 2013–2014

	2013	2013	2014	2014
	Amount per Available Room	Amount per Occupied Room Night	Amount per Available Room	Amount per Occupied Room Night
REVENUE				
Rooms	$10,926	$52.60	$12,862	$54.04
Food	1,316	6.34	1,615	6.79
Beverage	347	1.67	488	2.05
Other Food & Bev	10	0.05	23	0.10
Other Operated Departments	1,440	6.93	1,420	5.97
Miscellaneous Income	407	2.00	1,110	4.70
TOTAL REVENUE	14,446	69.59	17,518	73.65
DEPARTMENTAL EXPENSES				
Rooms	4,159	20.02	5,114	21.49
Food & Beverage	1,528	7.35	1,759	7.39
Other	617	2.97	644	2.70
TOTAL DEPARTMENTAL EXPENSES	6,304	30.35	7,517	31.58
TOTAL DEPARTMENTAL PROFITS	8,142	39.20	10,002	42.02
OPERATING EXPENSES	5,058	24.35	5,750	24.16
GROSS OPERATING PROFIT	$ 3,084	$14.85	$ 4,252	$17.87
EBITDA	$ 1,949	$ 9.38	$ 2,931	$12.31

Source: STR Analytics.

Guests at Rosen Hotels & Resorts continued to be amazed at the quality, customer service, and value at the company's Orlando hotels. "I would definitely stay here again," said one satisfied customer, "We felt safe, and there was lots to see and enjoy." When asked about what made the Rosen organization unique, Rosen replied, "I think we care just a little bit more. We are driven to always try to do the right thing."

TOMS Shoes in 2016: An Ongoing Dedication to Social Responsibility

MARGARET A. PETERAF Tuck School of Business at Dartmouth

SEAN ZHANG AND MEGHAN L. COONEY Research Assistants, Dartmouth College

While traveling in Argentina in 2006, Blake Mycoskie witnessed the hardships that children without shoes experienced and became committed to making a difference. Rather than focusing on charity work, Mycoskie sought to build an organization capable of sustainable, repeated giving, where children would be guaranteed shoes throughout their childhood. He established Shoes for a Better Tomorrow, better known as TOMS, as a for-profit company based on the premise of the "One for One" Pledge. For every pair of shoes TOMS sold, TOMS would donate a pair to a child in need. By mid-2016, TOMS had given way over 50 million pairs of shoes in over 70 different countries.[1]

As a relatively new and privately held company, TOMS experienced consistent and rapid growth despite the global recession that began in 2009. By 2015, TOMS had matured into an organization with nearly 500 employees and almost $400 million in revenues. TOMS shoes could be found in several major retail stores such as Nordstrom, Bloomingdale's, and Urban Outfitters. In addition to providing shoes for underprivileged children, TOMS also expanded its mission to include restoring vision to those with curable sight-related illnesses by developing a new line of eyewear products. For an overview of how quickly TOMS expanded in its first seven years of business, see Exhibit 1.[2]

Company Background

While attending Southern Methodist University, Blake Mycoskie founded the first of his six startups, a laundry service company that encompassed seven colleges and staffed over 40 employees. Four startups and a short stint on *The Amazing Race* later, Mycoskie found himself vacationing in Argentina where he not only learned about the alpargata shoe originally used by local peasants in the 14th century, but also witnessed the extreme poverty in rural Argentina.

Determined to make a difference, Mycoskie believed that providing shoes could more directly impact the children in these rural communities than

---

EXHIBIT 1

TOMS' Growth in Employees and Sales, 2006–2015

	2015	2014	2013	2012	2011	2010	2009	2008	2007	2006
Total Employees	470	450	400	320	250	72	46	33	19	4
Thousands of Pairs of Shoes Sold	25,000	10,000	7,250	2,700	1,300	1,000	230	110	50	10

Source: PrivCo, Private Company Financial Report, "TOMS Shoes, Inc.," created April 18, 2016.

delivering medicine or food. Aside from protecting children's feet from infections, parasites, and diseases, shoes were often required for a complete school uniform. In addition, research had shown that shoes were found to significantly increase children's self-confidence, help them develop into more active community members, and lead them to stay in school. Thus, by ensuring access to shoes, Mycoskie could effectively increase children's access to education and foster community activism, raising the overall standard of living for people living in poor Argentinian rural areas.

Dedicated to his mission, Mycoskie purchased 250 pairs of alpargatas and returned home to Los Angeles, where he subsequently founded TOMS Shoes. He built the company on the promise of "One for One," donating a pair of shoes for every pair sold. With an initial investment of $300,000, Mycoskie's business concept of social entrepreneurship was simple: sell both the shoe and the story behind it. Building on a simple slogan that effectively communicated his goal, Mycoskie championed his personal experiences passionately and established deep and lasting relationships with customers.

Operating from his apartment with three interns he found on Craigslist, Mycoskie quickly sold out his initial inventory and expanded considerably, selling 10,000 pairs of shoes by the end of his first year. With family and friends, Mycoskie ventured back to Argentina, where they hand-delivered 10,000 pairs of shoes to children in need. Because he followed through on his mission statement, Mycoskie was able to subsequently attract investors to support his unique business model and expand his venture significantly.

When TOMS was founded, TOMS operated as the for-profit financial arm while a separate entity titled "Friends of TOMS" focused on charity work and giving. After 2011, operations at Friends of TOMS were absorbed into TOMS's own operations as TOMS itself matured. In Friends of TOMS's latest accessible 2011 501(c)(3) filing, assets were reported at less than $130,000.[3] Moreover, as of May 2013, the Friends of TOMS website was discontinued while TOMS also ceased advertising its partnership with Friends of TOMS in marketing campaigns and on its corporate website. The developments suggested that Friends of TOMS became a defunct entity as TOMS incorporated all of its operations under the overarching TOMS brand.

Industry Background

Even though Mycoskie's vision for his company was a unique one, vying for a position in global footwear manufacturing was a risky and difficult venture. The industry was both stable and mature—one in which large and small companies competed on the basis of price, quality, and service. Competitive pressures came from foreign as well as domestic companies and new entrants needed to fight for access to downstream retailers.

Further, the cost of supplies was forecast to increase between 2013 and 2020. Materials and wages constituted over 70 percent of industry costs—clearly a sizable concern for competitors. Supply purchases included leather, rubber, plastic compounds, foam, nylon, canvas, laces, and so on. While the price of leather rose steadily each year, the price of rubber also began to climb at an average annual rate of 7.6 percent. Wages were expected to increase at a rate of 5.8 percent over a five-year period due to growing awareness of how manufacturers took advantage of cheap, outsourced labor.[4]

In order to thrive in the footwear manufacturing industry, firms needed to differentiate their products in a meaningful way. Selling good-quality products at a reasonable price was rarely enough; they needed to target a niche market that desired a certain image. Product innovation and advertising campaigns therefore became the most successful competitive weapons. For example, Clarks adopted a sophisticated design, appealing to a wealthier, more mature customer base. Nike, adidas, and Skechers developed athletic footwear and aggressively marketed their brands to reflect that image. Achieving economies of scale, increasing technical efficiency, and developing a cost-effective distribution system were also essential elements for success.

Despite the presence of established incumbents, global footwear manufacturing was an attractive industry to potential entrants based on the prediction of increased demand and therefore sales revenue. Moreover, the industry offered incumbents one of the highest profit margins in the fashion industry. But because competitors were likely to open new locations and expand their brands in order to discourage competition, new companies' only option was to attempt to undercut them on cost. Acquiring capital equipment and machinery to manufacture footwear on a large scale was expensive. Moreover, potential entrants also needed to launch costly large-scale marketing campaigns to promote brand awareness. Thus, successful incumbents were traditionally able to maintain an overwhelming portion of the market.

Building the TOMS Brand

Due to its humble beginnings, TOMS struggled to gain a foothold in the footwear industry. While companies like Nike had utilized high-profile athletes like Michael Jordan and Tiger Woods to establish brand recognition, TOMS had relatively limited financial resources and tried to appeal to a more socially conscious consumer. Luckily, potential buyers enjoyed a rise in disposable income over time as the economy recovered from the recession. As a result, demand for high-quality footwear increased for affluent shoppers, accompanied by a desire to act (and be *seen* acting) charitably and responsibly.

While walking through the airport one day, Mycoskie encountered a girl wearing TOMS shoes. Mycoskie recounts:

> I asked her about her shoes, and she went on to tell me this amazing story about TOMS and the model that it uses and my personal story. I realized the importance of having a story today is what really separates companies. People don't just wear our shoes, they tell our story. That's one of my favorite lessons that I learned early on.

Moving forward, TOMS focused more on selling the story behind the shoe rather than product features or celebrity endorsements. Moreover, rather than relying primarily on mainstream advertising, TOMS emphasized a grassroots approach using social media and word of mouth. With over 3.5 million Facebook "likes" and over 2 million Twitter "followers" in 2016, TOMS's social media presence eclipsed that of its much larger rivals, Skechers and Clarks. Based on 2016 data, TOMS had fewer "followers" than Nike, and fewer "likes" than both Nike and adidas. However, TOMS had more "followers" and "likes" per dollar of revenue. So when taking company size into account, TOMS also had a greater media presence than the industry's leading competitors (see Exhibit 2 for more information).

TOMS's success with social media advertising can be attributed to the story crafted and championed by Mycoskie. Industry incumbents generally dedicated a substantial portion of revenue and effort to advertising since they were simply selling a product. TOMS, on the other hand, used its mission to ask customers to buy into a *cause,* limiting their need to devote resources to brand-building. TOMS lets its charitable work and social media presence generate interest for the company organically. This strategy also increased the likelihood that consumers would place repeat purchases and share the story behind their purchases with family and friends. TOMS's customers took pride in supporting a grassroots cause instead of a luxury footwear supplier and encouraged others to share in the rewarding act.

EXHIBIT 2

TOMS Use of Social Media Compared to Selected Footwear Competitors

	2015 Revenue (Mil. of $)	Facebook "Likes"	"Likes" per Mil. of $ in Revenue	Twitter "Followers"	"Followers" per Mil. of $ in Revenue
TOMS	$ 390	3,522,891	9,033	2,170,000	5,564
Clarks	2,123	1,634,803	770	42,300	20
Skechers	3,150	1,921,582	610	32,700	10
Adidas	16,920	23,362,006	1,380	2,650,000	157
Nike	30,700	24,020,024	782	4,070,000	133

Source: Author data from Facebook and Twitter, April 11, 2016; revenue numbers obtained from MarketWatch.

A Business Model Dedicated to Socially Responsible Behavior

Traditionally, the content of advertisements for many large apparel companies focused on the attractive aspects of the featured products. TOMS's advertising, on the other hand, showcased its charitable contributions and the story of its founder Blake Mycoskie. While the CEOs of Nike, adidas, and Clarks rarely appeared in their companies' advertisements, TOMS ran as many ads with its founder as it did without him, emphasizing the inseparability of the TOMS's product from Mycoskie's story. In all of his appearances, Mycoskie was dressed in casual and friendly attire so that customers could easily relate to him and his mission. This advertising method conveyed a small-company feel and encouraged consumers to connect personally with the TOMS brand. It also worked to increase buyer patronage through differentiating the TOMS product from others. Consumers were convinced that every time they purchased a pair of TOMS, they became instruments of the company's charitable work. Representative advertisements for TOMS Shoes are presented in Exhibit 3.

As a result (although statistical measures of repeating-buying and total product satisfaction among TOMS's customers were not publicly available), the volume of repeat purchases and buyer enthusiasm likely fueled TOMS's success in a critical way. One reviewer commented, "This is my third pair of TOMS and I absolutely love them! . . . I can't wait to buy more"[5] Another wrote, "Just got my 25th pair! Love the color! They . . . are my all-time favorite shoe for comfort, looks & durability. AND they are for a great cause!! Gotta go pick out my next pair."[6]

Virtually all consumer reports on TOMS shoes shared similar themes. Though not cheap, TOMS footwear was priced lower than rivals' products, and customers overwhelmingly agreed that the value was worth the cost. Reviewers described TOMS as comfortable, true to size, lightweight, and versatile ("go with everything"). The shoes had "cute shapes and patterns" and were made of canvas and rubber that molded to customers' feet with wear. Because TOMS products were appealing and trendy yet also basic and comfortable, they were immune to changing fashion trends and consistently attracted a variety of consumers.

Representative Advertisements for TOMS Shoes Company

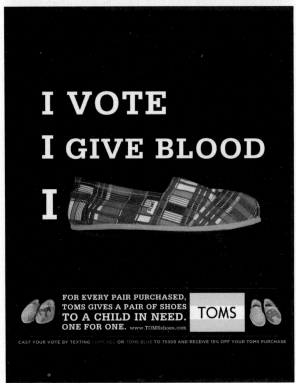

Instead of appealing to consumers desire for stylish footwear, TOMS advertisement instead addresses the consumer's sense of social consciousness by encouraging people to not only provide shoes to a child in need, but to also vote.

Source: TOMS.

In addition to offering a high-quality product that people valued, TOMS was able to establish a positive repertoire with its customers through efficient distribution. Maintaining an online shop helped TOMS save money on retail locations but also allowed it to serve a wide geographic range. Further, the company negotiated with well-known retailers like Nordstrom and Neiman Marcus to assist in distribution. Through thoughtful planning and structured coordination, TOMS limited operation costs and provided prompt service for its customers.

Giving Partners

As it continued to grow, TOMS sought to improve its operational efficiency by teaming up with "Giving

Partners," nonprofit organizations that helped distribute the shoes that TOMS donated. By teaming up with Giving Partners, TOMS streamlined its charity operations by shifting many of its distributional responsibilities to organizations that were often larger, more resourceful, and able to distribute TOMS shoes more efficiently. Moreover, these organizations possessed more familiarity and experience dealing with the communities that TOMS was interested in helping and could therefore better allocate shoes that suited the needs of children in the area. Giving Partners also provided feedback to help TOMS improve on its giving and distributional efforts.

Each Giving Partner also magnified the impact of TOMS shoes by bundling its distribution with other charity work that the organization specialized in. For example, Partners in Health, a nonprofit organization that spent almost $100 million in 2012 on providing health care for the poor (more than TOMS's total revenue that year), dispersed thousands of shoes to schoolchildren in Rwanda and Malawi while also screening them for malnutrition. Cooperative giving further strengthened the TOMS brand by association with well-known and highly regarded Giving Partners. Complementary services expanded the scope of TOMS's mission, enhanced the impact that each pair of TOMS had on a child's life, and increased the number of goodwill and business opportunities available to TOMS.

In order to ensure quality of service and adherence to its fundamental mission, TOMS maintained five criteria for Giving Partners:[7]

- Repeat Giving: Giving partners must be able to work with the same communities in multiyear commitments, regularly providing shoes to the same children as they grow.

- High Impact: Shoes must aid Giving Partners with their existing goals in the areas of health and education, providing children with opportunities they would not have otherwise.

- Considerate of Local Economy: Providing shoes cannot have negative socioeconomic effects on the communities where shoes are given.

- Large Volume Shipments: Giving Partners must be able to accept large shipments of giving pairs.

- Health/Education Focused: Giving Partners must give shoes only in conjunction with health and education efforts.

As of 2016, TOMS had built relationships with over 100 Giving Partners including Save the Children, U.S. Fund for UNICEF, and IMA World Health. In order to remain accountable to its mission in these joint ventures, TOMS also performed unannounced audit reports that ensured shoes were distributed according to the One for One® model.

Building a Relationship with Giving Partners

Having Giving Partners offered TOMS the valuable opportunity to shift some of its philanthropic costs onto other parties. However, TOMS also proactively maintained strong relationships with its Giving Partners. Kelly Gibson, the program director of National Relief Charities (NRC), a Giving Partner and nonprofit organization dedicated to improving the lives of Native Americans, highlighted the respect with which TOMS treated its Giving Partners:

> TOMS treats their Giving Partners (like us) and the recipients of their giveaway shoes (the Native kids in this case) like customers. We had a terrific service experience with TOMS. They were meticulous about getting our shoe order just right. They also insist that the children who receive shoes have a customer-type experience at distributions.

From customizing Giving Partner orders to helping pick up the tab for transportation and distribution, TOMS treated its Giving Partners as valuable customers and generated a sense of goodwill that extended beyond its immediate One for One® mission. By ensuring that its Giving Partners and recipients of shoes were treated respectfully, TOMS developed a unique ability to sustain business relationships that other for-profit organizations more concerned with the financial bottom line did not.

Maintaining a Dedication to Corporate Social Responsibility

Although TOMS manufactured its products in Argentina, China, and Ethiopia (countries that have all been cited as areas with a high degree of child and forced labor by the Bureau of International Labor Affairs), regular third-party factory audits and a Supplier Code of Conduct helped ensure compliance with fair labor standards.[8] Audits were conducted on both an announced and unannounced basis while the Supplier Code of Conduct was publicly posted in the local language of every work site. The Supplier Code of Conduct enforced standards such as minimum work age, requirement of voluntary employment, non-discrimination, maximum workweek hours, and right to unionize. It also protected workers from physical, sexual, verbal, or psychological harassment in accordance with a country's legally mandated standards. Workers were encouraged to report violations directly to TOMS, and suppliers found in violation of TOMS's Supplier Code of Conduct faced termination.

In addition to ensuring that suppliers met TOMS's ethical standards, TOMS also emphasized its own dedication to ethical behavior in a number of ways. TOMS was a member of the American Apparel and Footwear Association (AAFA) and was registered with the Fair Labor Association (FLA). Internally, TOMS educated its own employees on human trafficking and slavery prevention and partnered with several organizations dedicated to raising awareness about such issues, including Hand of Hope.[9]

Giving Trips

Aside from material shoe contributions, TOMS also held a series of "Giving Trips" that supported the broader notion of community service. Giving Trips were firsthand opportunities for employees of TOMS and selected TOMS customers to partake in the delivery of TOMS shoes. These trips increased the transparency of TOMS's philanthropic efforts, further engaging customers and employees. They generated greater social awareness as well, since participants on these trips often became more engaged in local community service efforts at home.

From a business standpoint, Giving Trips also represented a marketing success. First, a large number of participants were customers and journalists unassociated with TOMS who circulated their stories online through social media upon their return. Second, TOMS was able to motivate participants and

candidates to become more involved in their mission by increasing public awareness. In 2013, instead of internally selecting customers to participate on the Giving Trips, TOMS opted to hold an open voting process that encouraged candidates to reach out to their known contacts and ask them to vote for their inclusion. This contest drew thousands of contestants and likely hundreds of thousands of voters, although the final vote tallies were not publicly released.

Environmental Sustainability

Dedicated to minimizing its environmental impact, TOMS pursued a number of sustainable practices that included offering vegan shoes, incorporating recycled bottles into its products, and printing with soy ink. TOMS also used a blend of organic canvas and postconsumer, recycled plastics to create shoes that were both comfortable and durable. By utilizing natural hemp and organic cotton, TOMS eliminated pesticide and insecticide use that adversely affected the environment.

In addition, TOMS supported several environmental organizations like Surfers Against Sewage, a movement that raised awareness about excess sewage discharge in the UK. Formally, TOMS was a member of the Textile Exchange, an organization dedicated to textile sustainability and protecting the environment. The company also participated actively in the AAFA's Environmental Responsibility Committee.

Creating the TOMS Workforce

When asked what makes a great employee, Mycoskie blogged,

> As TOMS has grown, we've continued to look for these same traits in the interns and employees that we hire. Are you passionate? Can you creatively solve problems? Can you be resourceful without resources? Do you have the compassion to serve others? You can teach a new hire just about any skill . . . but you absolutely cannot inspire creativity and passion in someone that doesn't have it.[10]

The company's emphasis on creativity and passion was part of the reason why TOMS relied so heavily on interns and new hires rather than experienced workers. By hiring younger, more inexperienced employees,

TOMS was able to be more cost-effective in terms of personnel. The company could also recruit young and energetic individuals who were more likely to think innovatively and outside the box. These employees were placed in specialized teams under the leadership of strong, experienced managerial talent. This human intellectual capital generated a competitive advantage for the TOMS brand.

Together with these passionate individuals, Mycoskie strove to create a family-like work atmosphere where openness and collaboration were celebrated. With his cubicle located in one of the most highly trafficked areas of the office (right next to customer service), Mycoskie made a point to interact with his employees on a daily basis, in all-staff meetings, and through weekly personal e-mails while traveling. Regarding his e-mails, Mycoskie reflected,

> I'm a very open person, so I really tell the staff what I'm struggling with and what I'm happy about. I tell them what I think the future of TOMS is. I want them to understand what I'm thinking. It's like I'm writing to a best friend.[11]

This notion of "family" was further solidified through company dinners, ski trips, and book clubs where TOMS employees were encouraged to socialize in informal settings. These casual opportunities to interact with colleagues created a "balanced" work atmosphere where employees celebrated not only their own successes, but also the successes of their co-workers.

Diversity and inclusion were also emphasized at TOMS. For example, cultural traditions like the Chinese Lunar New Year were celebrated publicly on the TOMS's company blog. Moreover, as TOMS began expanding and distributing globally, the company increasingly sought to recruit a more diverse workforce by hiring multilingual individuals who were familiar with TOMS's diverse customer base and could communicate with its giving communities.[12]

The emphasis that Mycoskie placed on each individual employee was one of the key reasons why employees at TOMS often felt "lucky" to be part of the movement.[13] Coupled with the fact that TOMS employees knew their efforts fostered social justice, these "Agents of Change," as they referred to themselves, were generally quite satisfied with their work, making TOMS *Forbes*'s 4th Most Inspiring Company in 2014. Overall, the culture allowed TOMS to recruit and retain high-quality employees invested in achieving its social mission.

Financial Success at TOMS

With a compound annual growth rate (CAGR) of 4.8 percent from 2010 to 2014, global footwear

EXHIBIT 4

Revenue Comparison for TOMS Shoes and the Footwear Industry, 2006–2015

	2015	2014	2013	2012	2011	2010	2009	2008	2007	2006
TOMS (in Mils. of $)										
Revenue	$ 390	$370.9	$ 285	$101.8	$ 46.9	$ 25.1	$ 8.4	$ 3.1	$ 1.2	$0.2
Growth (%)	5.1%	30.1%	180%	117%	86.9%	199%	171%	158.3%	500%	—
Industry (in Bils. of $)										
Revenue	$191.6	$189.3	$175.3	$164.4	$169.4	$152.1	$148.6	$155.6	$131.3	N.A.
Growth (%)	1.2%	8.0%	6.6%	−3.0%	11.4%	2.4%	−4.5%	18.5%	19.9%	—

Note: N.A., Not available.

Source: "Global Footwear Manufacturing," *IBISWorld*, April 18, 2016, http://clients1.ibisworld.com/reports/gl/industry/currentperformance.aspx?entid=500.

manufacturing developed into an industry worth over $289.7 billion.[14] While TOMS remained a privately held company with limited financial data, the estimated growth rate of TOMS's revenue was astounding. In the seven years after his company's inception, Mycoskie was able to turn his initial $300,000 investment into a company with over $200 million in yearly revenues. As shown in Exhibit 4, the average growth rate of TOMS on a yearly basis was 145 percent, even excluding its first major spike of 457 percent. During the same period, Nike experienced a growth rate of roughly 8.5 percent, with a *decline* in revenues from 2009 to 2010.

The fact that TOMS was able to experience consistent growth despite financial turmoil post-2008 illustrates the strength of the One for One movement to survive times of recession. Mycoskie attributed his success during the recession to two factors: (1) As consumers became more conscious of their spending during recessions, products like TOMS that gave to others actually became *more* appealing (according to Mycoskie); (2) the giving model that TOMS employed is not "priced in." Rather than commit a percentage of profits or revenues to charity, Mycoskie noted that TOMS simply gave away a pair for every pair it sold. This way, socially conscious consumers knew exactly where their money was going without having to worry that TOMS would cut back on its charity efforts in order to turn a profit.[15]

Production at TOMS

Although TOMS manufactured shoes in Argentina, Ethiopia, and China, only shoes made in China were brought to the retail market. Shoes made in Argentina and Ethiopia were strictly used for donation purposes. TOMS retailed its basic alpargata shoes in the $50 price range, even though the cost of producing each pair was estimated at around $9.[16] Estimates for the costs of producing TOMS's more expensive lines of shoes were unknown, but they retailed for upwards of $150.

In comparison, manufacturing the average pair of Nike shoes in Indonesia cost around $20, and they were priced at around $70.[17] Factoring in the giving aspect, TOMS seemed to have a slightly smaller markup than companies like Nike, yet it still maintained considerable profit margins. More detailed information on trends in TOMS's production costs and practices is limited due to the private nature of the company.

The Future

Because demand and revenues were predicted to increase in the global footwear manufacturing industry, incumbents like TOMS needed to find ways to defend their position in the market. One method was to continue to differentiate products based on quality, image, or price. Another strategy was to focus on research and development (R&D) and craft new brands and product lines that appealed to different audiences. It was also recommended that companies investigate how to mitigate the threat posed by an increase in supply costs.

In an effort to broaden its mission and product offerings, TOMS began to expand both its consumer base and charitable-giving product lines. For its customers, TOMS started offering stylish wedges, ballet flats, and even wedding apparel in an effort to reach more customers and satisfy the special needs of current ones. For the children it sought to help, TOMS expanded past its basic black canvas shoe offerings to winter boots to help keep children's feet dry and warm during the winter months in cold climate countries.

On another front, TOMS entered the eyewear market in hopes of restoring vision to the 285 million blind or visually impaired individuals around the world. For every pair of TOMS glasses sold, TOMS restored vision to one individual either through donating prescription glasses or offering medical treatment for those suffering from cataracts and eye infections. TOMS recently focused its vision-related efforts in Nepal, but also hoped to expand globally as the TOMS eyewear brand grew. As of 2016, TOMS had teamed up with 15 Giving Partners to help restore sight to 360,000 individuals in 13 countries.

ENDNOTES

[1] TOMS website, April 4, 2016, www.toms.com/what-we-give-shoes.

[2] Blake Mycoskie, web log post, *The Huffington Post,* May 26, 2013, www.huffingtonpost.com/blake-mycoskie/.

[3] *501c3Lookup,* June 2, 2013, 501c3lookup.org/FRIENDS_OF_TOMS/.

[4] "Global Footwear Manufacturing," *IBISWorld,* March 2014, clients1.ibisworld.com/reports/gl/industry/keystatistics.aspx?entid=500.

[5] Post by "Alexandria," TOMS website, June 2, 2013, www.toms.com/red-canvas-classics-shoes-1.

[6] Post by "Donna Brock," TOMS website, January 13, 2014, www.toms.com/women/bright-blue-womens-canvas-classics.

[7] TOMS website, June 2, 2013, www.toms.com/our-movement-giving-partners.

[8] Trafficking Victims Protection Reauthorization Act, United States Department of Labor, June 2, 2013, www.dol.gov/ilab/programs/ocft/tvpra.htm; TOMS website, June 2, 2013, www.toms.com/corporate-responsibility.

[9] Hand of Hope, "Teaming Up with TOMS Shoes," *Joyce Meyer Ministries,* June 2, 2013, www.studygs.net/citation/mla.htm.

[10] Blake Mycoskie, "Blake Mycoskie's Blog," *Blogspot,* June 2, 2013, blakemycoskie.blogspot.com/.

[11] Tamara Schweitzer, "The Way I Work: Blake Mycoskie of TOMS Shoes," *Inc.,* June 2, 2013, www.inc.com/magazine/20100601/the-way-i-work-blake-mycoskie-of-toms-shoes.html.

[12] TOMS Jobs website, June 2, 2013, www.toms.com/jobs/l.

[13] Daniela, "Together We Travel," TOMS Company Blog, June 3, 2013, blog.toms.com/post/36075725601/together-we-travel.

[14] "Global—Footwear," *Marketline: Advantage,* April 18, 2016.

[15] Mike Zimmerman, "The Business of Giving: TOMS Shoes," *Success,* June 2, 2013, www.success.com/articles/852-the-business-of-giving-toms-shoes.

[16] Brittney Fortune, "TOMS Shoes: Popular Model with Drawbacks," *The Falcon,* June 2, 2013, www.thefalcononline.com/article.php?id=159.

[17] *Behind the Swoosh* [Film]. Dir. Jim Keady, 1995.

GLOSSARY

B

backward integration   **Backward integration** involves performing industry value chain activities previously performed by suppliers or other enterprises engaged in earlier stages of the industry value chain.

balanced scorecard   The **balanced scorecard** is a widely used method for combining the use of both strategic and financial objectives, tracking their achievement, and giving management a more complete and balanced view of how well an organization is performing.

benchmarking   **Benchmarking** is a potent tool for learning which companies are best at performing particular activities and then using their techniques (or "best practices") to improve the cost and effectiveness of a company's own internal activities.

best-cost provider strategies   **Best-cost provider strategies** are a *hybrid* of low-cost provider and differentiation strategies that aim at satisfying buyer expectations on key quality/features/performance/service attributes and beating customer expectations on price.

best practice   A **best practice** is a method of performing an activity that consistently delivers superior results compared to other approaches.

blue ocean strategies   **Blue ocean strategies** offer growth in revenues and profits by discovering or inventing new industry segments that create altogether new demand.

broad differentiation strategy   The essence of a **broad differentiation strategy** is to offer unique product or service attributes that a wide range of buyers find appealing and worth paying for.

business ethics   **Business ethics** involves the application of general ethical principles to the actions and decisions of businesses and the conduct of their personnel.

business model   A company's **business model** sets forth how its strategy and operating approaches will create value for customers, while at the same time generating ample revenues to cover costs and realizing a profit. The two elements of a company's business model are its (1) customer value proposition and (2) its profit formula.

business strategy   **Business strategy** is primarily concerned with strengthening the company's market position and building competitive advantage in a single business company or a single business unit of a diversified multibusiness corporation.

C

capability   A **capability** is the capacity of a company to competently perform some internal activity. Capabilities are developed and enabled through the deployment of a company's resources.

cash cow   A **cash cow** generates operating cash flows over and above its internal requirements, thereby providing financial resources that may be used to invest in cash hogs, finance new acquisitions, fund share buyback programs, or pay dividends.

cash hog   A **cash hog** generates operating cash flows that are too small to fully fund its operations and growth; a cash hog must receive cash infusions from outside sources to cover its working capital and investment requirements.

competitive strategy   A **competitive strategy** concerns the specifics of management's game plan for competing successfully and securing a competitive advantage over rivals in the marketplace.

corporate culture   **Corporate culture** is a company's internal work climate and is shaped by its core values, beliefs, and business principles. A company's culture is important because it influences its traditions, work practices, and style of operating

corporate restructuring   **Corporate restructuring** involves radically altering the business lineup by divesting businesses that lack strategic fit or are poor performers and acquiring new businesses that offer better promise for enhancing shareholder value.

corporate social responsibility (CSR)   **Corporate social responsibility (CSR)** refers to a company's *duty* to operate in an honorable manner, provide good working conditions for employees, encourage workforce diversity, be a good steward of the environment, and actively work to better the quality of life in the local communities in which it operates and in society at large.

corporate social responsibility strategy   A company's **corporate social responsibility strategy** is defined by the specific combination of socially beneficial activities it opts to support with its contributions of time, money, and other resources.

corporate strategy Corporate strategy establishes an overall game plan for managing a *set of businesses* in a diversified, multibusiness company.

cost driver A cost driver is a factor having a strong effect on the cost of a company's value chain activities and cost structure.

D

driving forces Driving forces are the major underlying causes of change in industry and competitive conditions.

dynamic capability A dynamic capability is the ability to modify, deepen, or reconfigure the company's existing resources and capabilities in response to its changing environment or market opportunities.

E

economic risks Economic risks stem from the stability of a country's monetary system, economic and regulatory policies, and the lack of property rights protections.

economies of scope Economies of scope are cost reductions stemming from strategic fit along the value chains of related businesses (thereby, a larger scope of operations), whereas *economies of scale* accrue from a larger operation.

environmental sustainability Environmental sustainability involves deliberate actions to protect the environment, provide for the longevity of natural resources, maintain ecological support systems for future generations, and guard against the ultimate endangerment of the planet.

ethical relativism According to the school of **ethical relativism,** different societal cultures and customs create divergent standards of right and wrong; thus, what is ethical or unethical must be judged in the light of local customs and social mores, and can vary from one culture or nation to another.

ethical universalism According to the school of **ethical universalism,** the same standards of what is ethical and what is unethical resonate with peoples of most societies, regardless of local traditions and cultural norms; hence, common ethical standards can be used to judge employee conduct in a variety of country markets and cultural circumstances.

F

financial objectives Financial objectives relate to the financial performance targets management has established for the organization to achieve.

first-mover advantages and disadvantages Because of **first-mover advantages and disadvantages**, competitive advantage can spring from *when* a move is made as well as from *what* move is made.

forward integration Forward integration involves performing industry value chain activities closer to the end user.

G

global strategies Global strategies employ the same basic competitive approach in all countries where a company operates and are best suited to industries that are globally standardized in terms of customer preferences, buyer purchasing habits, distribution channels, or marketing methods. This is the **think global, act global** strategic theme.

H

horizontal scope Horizontal scope is the range of product and service segments that a firm serves within its focal market.

I

integrative social contracts theory According to **integrative social contracts theory,** universal ethical principles based on collective views of multiple cultures combine to form a "social contract" that all employees in all country markets have a duty to observe. Within the boundaries of this social contract, there is room for host-country cultures to exert *some* influence in setting their own moral and ethical standards. However, *"first-order"* universal ethical norms always take precedence over *"second-order"* local ethical norms in circumstances in which local ethical norms are more permissive.

internal capital market A strong **internal capital market** allows a diversified company to add value by shifting capital from business units generating *free cash flow* to those needing additional capital to expand and realize their growth potential.

international strategy A company's **international strategy** is its strategy for competing in two or more countries simultaneously.

J

joint venture A **joint venture** is a type of strategic alliance that involves the establishment of an independent corporate entity that is jointly owned and controlled by the two partners.

K

key success factors Key success factors are the strategy elements, product attributes, competitive capabilities, or intangible assets with the greatest impact on future success in the marketplace.

L

low-cost leader A **low-cost leader**'s basis for competitive advantage is lower overall costs than competitors'. Success in achieving a low-cost edge over rivals comes from eliminating and/or curbing "nonessential" activities and/or outmanaging rivals in performing essential activities.

M

macro-environment   The **macro-environment** encompasses the broad environmental context in which a company is situated and is comprised of six principal components: political factors, economic conditions, sociocultural forces, technological factors, environmental factors, and legal/regulatory conditions.

mission statement   A well-conceived **mission statement** conveys a company's purpose in language specific enough to give the company its own identity.

multidomestic strategy   A **multidomestic strategy** calls for varying a company's product offering and competitive approach from country to country in an effort to be responsive to significant cross-country differences in customer preferences, buyer purchasing habits, distribution channels, or marketing methods. **Think local, act local** strategy-making approaches are also essential when host-government regulations or trade policies preclude a uniform, coordinated worldwide market approach.

N

network structure   A **network structure** is the arrangement linking a number of independent organizations involved in some common undertaking.

O

objectives   **Objectives** are an organization's performance targets—the results management wants to achieve.

outsourcing   **Outsourcing** involves contracting out certain value chain activities to outside specialists and strategic allies.

P

PESTEL analysis   **PESTEL analysis** can be used to assess the strategic relevance of the six principal components of the macro-environment: political, economic, sociocultural, technological, environmental, and legal forces.

political risks   **Political risks** stem from instability or weakness in national governments and hostility to foreign business; **economic risks** stem from the stability of a country's monetary system, economic and regulatory policies, and the lack of property rights protections.

R

realized strategy   A company's **realized strategy** is a combination of *deliberate planned elements* and *unplanned emergent elements*. Some components of a company's deliberate strategy will fail in the marketplace and become *abandoned strategy elements*.

related businesses   **Related businesses** possess competitively valuable cross-business value chain and resource matchups; **unrelated businesses** have dissimilar value chains and resources requirements, with no competitively important cross-business value chain relationships.

resource   A **resource** is a competitive asset that is owned or controlled by a company.

resource bundles   Companies that lack a standalone resource that is competitively powerful may nonetheless develop a competitive advantage through **resource bundles** that enable the superior performance of important cross-functional capabilities.

resource fit   A diversified company exhibits **resource fit** when its businesses add to a company's overall mix of resources and capabilities and when the parent company has sufficient resources to support its entire group of businesses without spreading itself too thin.

S

scope of the firm   The **scope of the firm** refers to the range of activities the firm performs internally, the breadth of its product and service offerings, the extent of its geographic market presence, and its mix of businesses.

social complexity   **Social complexity** and **causal ambiguity** are two factors that inhibit the ability of rivals to imitate a firm's most valuable resources and capabilities. Causal ambiguity makes it very hard to figure out how a complex resource contributes to competitive advantage and therefore exactly what to imitate.

spin-off   A **spin-off** is an independent company created when a corporate parent divests a business either by selling shares to the public via an initial public offering or by distributing shares in the new company to shareholders of the corporate parent.

strategic alliance   A **strategic alliance** is a formal agreement between two or more companies to work cooperatively toward some common objective.

strategic fit   **Strategic fit** exists when value chains of different businesses present opportunities for cross-business skills transfer, cost sharing, or brand sharing.

strategic group   A **strategic group** is a cluster of industry rivals that have similar competitive approaches and market positions.

strategic group mapping   **Strategic group mapping** is a technique for displaying the different market or competitive positions that rival firms occupy in the industry.

strategic intent   A company exhibits **strategic intent** when it relentlessly pursues an ambitious strategic objective, concentrating the full force of its resources and competitive actions on achieving that objective.

strategic objectives   **Strategic objectives** relate to target outcomes that indicate a company is strengthening its market standing, competitive vitality, and future business prospects.

strategic vision   A **strategic vision** describes "where we are going"—the course and direction management has charted and the company's future product-customer-market-technology focus.

strategy   A company's **strategy** is the set of actions that its managers take to outperform the company's competitors and achieve superior profitability.

stretch objectives   **Stretch objectives** set performance targets high enough to stretch an organization to perform at its full potential and deliver the best possible results.

sustainable business practices   **Sustainable business practices** are those that meet the needs of the present without compromising the ability to meet the needs of the future.

sustainable competitive advantage   A company achieves **sustainable competitive advantage** when an attractively large number of buyers develop a durable preference for its products or services over the offerings of competitors, despite the efforts of competitors to overcome or erode its advantage.

SWOT analysis   **SWOT analysis** is a simple but powerful tool for sizing up a company's internal strengths and competitive deficiencies, its market opportunities, and the external threats to its future well-being.

T

think local, act local   **Think local, act local** strategy-making approaches are also essential when host-government regulations or trade policies preclude a uniform, coordinated worldwide market approach.

transnational strategy   A **transnational strategy** is a **think global, act local** approach to strategy making that involves employing essentially the same strategic theme (low-cost, differentiation, focused, best-cost) in all country markets, while allowing some country-to-country customization to fit local market conditions.

U

uniqueness driver   A **uniqueness driver** is a value chain activity or factor that can have a strong effect on customer value and creating differentiation.

unrelated businesses   **Unrelated businesses** have dissimilar value chains and resources requirements, with no competitively important cross-business value chain relationships.

V

value chain   A company's **value chain** identifies the primary activities that create customer value and related support activities.

values   A company's **values** are the beliefs, traits, and behavioral norms that company personnel are expected to display in conducting the company's business and pursuing its strategic vision and mission.

vertical scope   **Vertical scope** is the extent to which a firm's internal activities encompass one, some, many, or all of the activities that make up an industry's entire value chain system, ranging from raw-material production to final sales and service activities.

vertically integrated   A **vertically integrated** firm is one that performs value chain activities along more than one stage of an industry's overall value chain

VRIN tests for sustainable competitive advantage   The **VRIN tests for sustainable competitive advantage** ask if a resource or capability is *valuable, rare, inimitable,* and *nonsubstitutable.*

INDEXES

Organization